DREADNOUGHT TO DARING

Dreadnought to Daring

100 Years of Comment, Controversy and Debate in The Naval Review

Edited by

CAPTAIN PETER HORE, RN

Seaforth

PUBLISHING

Copyright © The Naval Review 2012

First published in Great Britain in 2012 by
Seaforth Publishing,
Pen & Sword Books Ltd,
47 Church Street,
Barnsley S70 2AS

www.seaforthpublishing.com

British Library Cataloguing in Publication Data
A catalogue record for this book is available from the British Library

ISBN 978 1 84832 148 9

Typeset and designed by MATS Typesetting, Leigh-on-Sea, Essex

Printed and bound by CPI Group (UK) Ltd, Croydon, CR0 4YY

Contents

DONORS TO *THE NAVAL REVIEW* CENTENARY APPEAL

Up to £20,000

Anonymous
The Gosling Foundation Limited
The MacRobert Trust *

Up to £10,000

The B G S Cayzer Charitable Trust *
Edinburgh Trust No 2 Account *
The Shauna Gosling Trust *
The Headley Trust *
The Guy Hudson Memorial Trust * *
Iliffe Family Charitable Trust *
The Honourable Company of Master Mariners
The Mountbatten Memorial Trust *
John Murray *
Portland Port Limited *
Clive Richards Charity * * *
R J D Technology * * * *
Ultra Electronics plc * * * * *
Commander A J W Wilson RN

Up to £500

Admiral Sir Peter Abbott GBE KCB, Captain H J Abraham RN, Lieutenant Commander A M J Ainsley RN, Lieutenant Commander J F Allan RNZNVR, Captain C G Allen OBE RN, W S Anderson Esq, Professor D Andrews, Rear Admiral J H A J Armstrong CBE, Admiral Sir Jonathan Band GCB, Reverend D G Banham BD, Commodore A J Bannister CBE RN, Captain A D Barlow RN, M E Barrett Esq, Captain M K Barritt RN, Captain M E Barrow CVO DSO RN, Rear Admiral P E Bass CB, Admiral of the Fleet Sir Benjamin Bathurst GCB, Captain J F T Bayliss RN, Vice Admiral Sir Lancelot Bell Davies KBE, Dr T J Benbow, Commodore P M Bennett OBE RN, Commander R B Berry RN, Captain M Bickley RN, Captain P W Binks RN, Commander J M Bird RN, Vice Admiral Sir Jeremy Blackham KCB, Lieutenant Commander C C Blakey OBE RD JP RNR, Commodore D J Brice RN, Lieutenant Commander R D Bridge RD RNR, Commodore R A Y Bridges RN, Captain G P Brocklebank RN, Commodore B P S Brooks RN, Admiral Sir Brian Brown KCB CBE, C Brown Esq, Commodore M P Bullock MBE RN, Captain P Burrell RN, Captain G V Buxton CBE RN, Captain J R J Carew OBE RFA, Captain R F Channon RN, Lieutenant Commander P R Chant RN, Captain L W L Chelton RN, Rear Admiral T C Chittenden, Rear Admiral R A G Clare CBE, Commodore A I H Clark RN, Commander M T Clark RN, Professor R R Clements MBE, Rear Admiral R F Cobbold CB, Lieutenant Commander W J K Cody RNR, Captain D Conley RN, Captain J G F Cooke OBE RN, Vice Admiral R G Cooling, Lieutenant Commander R N Corfield RN, Sub Lieutenant S J D Corsan RNVR, Captain G T Costello RN, Captain J K Coulthard RN, Captain I W Craig RN, Rear Admiral F W Crickard RCN, Commodore H J Critchley RN, Vice Admiral Sir Geoffrey Dalton KCB, Lieutenant Commander R I Day RN, Captain F E A de Almeida Brazilian Navy, Rear Admiral Sir Jeremy de Halpert KCVO CB, Dr H W Dickinson, Rear Admiral P G V Dingemans CBE DSO, Vice Admiral Sir David Dobson KBE, Commodore P T Docherty OBE RN, Commodore J Drent RCN, Rear Admiral Allan du Toit AM RAN, Vice Admiral Sir Anthony Dymock KBE CB, Captain G A Eades CBE RN, Admiral Sir James Eberle GCB, Commodore C V Ellison RN, Captain M J D Farrow OBE RN, Captain D J Fifield RN, Commodore R D Finlayson RN, Admiral Sir Ian Forbes KCB CBE, Vice Admiral Sir John Forbes KCB, Rear Admiral P M Franklyn CB MVO, Lieutenant Commander N A Franks RN, P J Freeman Esq, Vice Admiral Sir Toby Frere KCB, Lieutenant General Sir Robert Fulton KBE, Rear Admiral Sir John Garnier KCVO CBE, Captain R L Garnon-Williams RN, Rear Admiral J R S Gerard-Pearse CB, Captain P H R Glennie RN, Captain W E B Godsal RN, Rear Admiral J V P Goldrick AM CSC RAN, Commander A C Grattan-Cooper RN, Captain J S Grenfell RN, Lieutenant Commander R M Griffiths RNR, Sir John Guinness CB, Captain R L Guy LVO RN, Lieutenant Commander D J P Hadler RN, Professor S W Haines, Captain P Hames RN, Professor Richard Harding, Commodore N J G Harland RN, Rear Admiral M G T Harris JP, Captain D Hart Dyke CBE LVO RN, Professor J B Hattendorf, Captain M J Hawthorne RN, Captain R J P Heath CBE RN, Captain G M Heathcote RN, Lieutenant P D Henshaw RN, Captain A A Hensher MBE RN, Commodore P W Herington RN, Rear Admiral J B Hervey CB OBE, Vice Admiral Sir Robert Hill KBE, Rear Admiral J R Hill, J D Hilton Esq,

* Support for individual chapters, as follows: The BGS Cayzer Charitable Trust, Chapter 2;
John Murray, Chapter 4; The Mountbatten Memorial Trust, Chapter 7; The Headley Trust,
Chapter 8; The MacRobert Trust, Chapters 9 and 10; The Shauna Gosling Trust, Chapter 18;
Iliffe Family Charitable Trust, Chapter 19; Portland Port Limited, Chapter 22;
Edinburgh Trust No 2 Account, Chapter 27

** Support for the Alan Villiers Memorial Lecture at Oxford

***Sponsor of the Clive Richards Prize for the best published article in *The Naval Review*
by a Lieutenant or below

**** Sponsor of the R J D Technology Maritime Technology Prize at Kingston University

***** Sponsor of *The Naval Review* Centenary Fellowship

The advent of steam power had a dramatic effect on the design and construction of both merchant and war ships. With the parallel development of weapons, it also introduced a radical new element to the discussion of naval strategy and tactics. The publication of The Naval Review was the response of a group of far-seeing naval officers, who recognised the need for new directions in professional and strategic thought.

After a hiatus during the First World War, the Review was revived, and ever since it has made a vital contribution to the debate about how to make the best use of the new designs for ships and armaments as they came into service. As the rate of technological development continues as fast as ever, the need for The Naval Review is as great as ever.

All the editors and contributors to the Review deserve to be congratulated on its achievements over its first hundred years. I wish it continued success in a world where the need for deep thought and considered reflection is unlikely to diminish in the foreseeable future.

Introduction

THE Royal Navy has played a prominent role at almost every level of British and international culture, strategy, discovery, and technology, and has amassed a rich legacy. It has built a heritage in which other navies are proud to participate and to which many more aspire. Under the White Ensign, large parts of the globe were colonised by English-speaking people, free trade developed, the United States' Monroe doctrine flourished, slave traffic was stopped, and the oceans were charted and the knowledge gained was made readily available for the benefit of all. The world wars of the eighteenth, nineteenth and twentieth centuries were won through the exercise by the Royal Navy of a maritime strategy, often without any allies, and in breadth of achievement the Royal Navy has been compared in its impact and successes to the legions of Rome and the grand armies of France. On these grounds alone any examination of such an influential organisation must be deemed worthy of study.

And since for most of the last hundred years some of the most erudite and literary of the Royal Navy's officers have written for *The Naval Review*, no such study could be undertaken without an examination of a journal intended for private circulation amongst its officers, a journal which may be said to be the Royal Navy at prayer.

The Naval Review was part of a revolution in naval affairs at the beginning of the twentieth century. It was first published in 1913 by the Naval Society as the principal organ of a corresponding society whose aim was to encourage thought and discussion on topics affecting the fighting efficiency of the Royal Navy. It was very nearly strangled in childhood by the first of many attempts by senior naval officers to suppress it or to censor its contents, and indeed it was suspended, in October 1915, after less than a dozen quarterly issues. However, the Editor, Admiral Sir William Henderson, continued to collect material until after the end of the First World War when, in the autumn of 1919, he could announce that members of the Naval Society could send their contributions direct to him and 'to encourage free discussion and criticism it is thought best that all articles should be anonymous.'

In a hierarchic and uniformed society, newly emerged from the deferential Victorian age, this is an unexpected and even counterintuitive pronouncement, and it is a principle which finds few parallels in other disciplined services or professions. Nevertheless, many officers, junior and senior, took advantage of this rule including, I have detected, at least four future Admirals of the Fleet.

However, the founders were dispersed by the war and Henderson, in his words, 'ran the show myself', even writing a large part of *The Naval Review* himself: for example, he, Herbert Richmond and Reginald Plunkett wrote half of all the articles in the first edition. Post-war, Henderson hoped for more contributors and, as he made clear later, he was more interested in the process of exchanging of ideas than in literary excellence.

There were opponents to *The Naval Review* like Admiral Jellicoe whose objections, on the specious grounds of security, were dismissed by Henderson and the founders as 'puerile'. There is little evidence that others, as some have claimed, saw *The Naval Review* merely as a safety valve which would give a voice to young officers and divert them from writing to the press. Rather, as can be shown, suspension of *The Naval Review* freed Henderson and others of the Young Turks from any inhibition about writing to the press or enlisting their powerful friends and relations in aspects of the naval revolution.

However, the Young Turks of the Naval Society wanted nothing less than reform. They were mindful that the leadership of the Navy, however brave and intelligent they were, like the First Sea Lord, Arthur Wilson, VC, had shown themselves unable to make a proper case for the Navy.[1] The Young Turks wanted all the 'Old Gang' removed and, though not directly as a result of their efforts, between 1910 and 1919 there were an astonishing seven First Sea Lords. But while there is no doubt that the pages of *The Naval Review* record the inner workings of the Royal Navy and the context in which the naval revolution took place, it is more difficult to assess what direct or indirect influence the *Review* has had on the Navy's development.

This centenary volume, aptly called *From Dreadnought to Daring*, attempts to answer that question. Contributors were specifically asked to make some judgement about how far *The Naval Review* has predicted policy in its pages or influenced the outcome of debate. The extent to which some have been able to address the question directly, and others only by implication, while others have avoided the issue, is itself a measure of how far *The Naval Review* has anticipated or reflected the Royal Navy's development. Certainly, examination of the authors' names reveals just how many officers who reached senior rank were contributors to *The Naval Review* and it is notable that nearly every First Sea Lord of recent years has, as a junior officer, written for the *Review*.

In this volume the origins of *The Naval Review* are explored through the character of its founders and their inspiration, as are the modern sea-kings – only a few score men – who have gained the distinction of an obituary in *The Naval Review*. Uniquely, one civilian, Sir Julian Corbett, is honoured with a chapter to himself for the contribution which he made to maritime strategy and for his influence over the founders.

The Naval Review was founded on the eve of the First World War and whatever high-minded ideals the founders had were immediately overshadowed by the tactical and strategic problems which faced the Royal Navy. Here some of those problems are examined, including how best to use that newfangled device, the submarine; the reintroduction of the convoy; the Dardanelles campaign on which so much had been staked; and the dependency upon a fleet train of the new, oil-powered Navy.

Many external commentators have written, usually flatteringly, about the quality of the Navy's people, and it is not surprising that people and personnel issues have featured widely in *The Naval Review*. Many of the personnel issues have, by their nature, been transient, unlike some of the contributors, some of whom have seemed like permanent features on the pages of the *Review*. However, included here is a perceptive essay on shipboard life and organisation, and an analysis of officer structure and training. The problem of teaching and learning from history, which has echoed down the century, is also fully addressed, as is the law of the sea, another subject which the founders thought should be taught and learned by naval officers.

One of the subjects which taxed the founders and the early readers of *The Naval Review* was the concept of an Empire Navy in which the Dominions would build, man and train their own fleets after British models and these fleets would serve in wartime under a single operational command. The idea foundered not least because the Admiralty in London showed little willingness to turn the British Navy into an Imperial Navy and give the Dominions a share in its control and administration. Nevertheless, such were the commonality of equipment and customs throughout the navies of the British Empire and later the Commonwealth that, if aggregated, a large, global Navy would be recognisably British in origin and character. The story of this 'White Ensign Navy' is told in three contributions from Australia, Canada and India, and two on the Simon's Town and Singapore naval bases.

Henderson, when he was able to resume publication in 1919, made clear what he expected of the Naval Society by publishing as the lead article a description of the United States Navy Institute as 'a club at once social and professional, which is not restricted to any club-house on any avenue in any

city, but which spreads over all the oceans to all of our ships and stations
... the embodiment of the thought of the Navy ... the unofficial custodian
of the Navy's professional hopes and fears [which] looks ahead into the
future, and back into the past, and keeps track of the happenings of the
present.' The Naval Society never developed like the Naval Institute, and
in 1929 even the name was quietly dropped from the title page of *The
Naval Review*. The Royal Navy's often dichotomous relation with the
United States Navy merits two essays in contrast and comparison

A debate in the pages of *The Naval Review* which has characterised the
development of the Royal Navy itself is the struggle for naval air: a story
of rapid advance to the point where, in 1918, the Royal Naval Air Service
was one of the largest air forces in the world, an air force which had
pioneered anti-submarine warfare, close-air-support and long-range
strategic bombardment; it invented some of the greatest technological ideas
like the offset island, the steam catapult, the angled flight deck and the ski-
jump; and for fifty years through the Pacific War, the Korean War and the
Falklands War would be Britain's only successful air force. Yet they were
years of continuous struggle to maintain the Fleet Air Arm. This story, as
told in the pages of *The Naval Review* and now in this centenary volume,
epitomises the rise and fall of British naval sea power over the last century.
Read one after the other they present a depressing litany of continuous and
naive political underperformance by the Navy.

By contrast, the debate about submarines has been less controversial and
more subdued, not least because many aspects of submarine operations,
especially during the Cold War, are still wrapped in secrecy. Nevertheless,
the early tactical development of the submarine is featured here, as is the
debate about the operational uses and deployment of the submarine, and
the impact upon the Navy of its assuming the responsibility for the nuclear
deterrent.

The Naval Review also contains a wealth of important historical
information and 'The Empire Strikes Back' contains a comparison of the
fighting in the Falklands and its reporting in 1914 and 1982. However,
space has not permitted any further examination of the wealth of
operational histories and reminiscences from the fine grain of history in
The Naval Review, nor of the often self-deprecating humour which has
increasingly featured in the *Review*.

Other issues are reflected in the centenary volume. These include the
design of ships, the balance of big ships versus small ships, and the short
fat frigate, and 'A View from Bath' contains a warning that national
disregard of engineering expertise and, in particular, the Navy's loss of the
Royal Corps of Naval Constructors has been both an augury and a
symptom of decline.

From Dreadnought to Daring closes with essays which illustrate how the Royal Navy has come to terms with its reduced status, two more on the Reserves and on the Royal Marines which maybe contain seeds of the future, and the current Editor's concluding remarks which form the prologue to the next century of *The Naval Review*.

One hundred years ago Britain had a choice whether to become involved in a continental war or to keep to the maritime strategy which had served it so well for so many long years and, on what I regard as the blackest day in British and Royal Navy history, made the wrong choice. I have no doubt that the founders of *The Naval Review* would be astounded that a hundred years later Britain is embroiled in a continental war in Afghanistan at the expense of more essential, long-term maritime aspects of our national security.[2] The difference between then and now, perhaps, is that the then leaders of naval thought were all naval officers, Henderson, Richmond, Plunkett, the Dewar brothers and the Hughes-Halletts, and their contemporaries. With the exception of the civilian Julian Corbett, who was the godfather of *The Naval Review*, the academic community's focus was on the Navy Records Society and the Society for Nautical Research. Then also the founders were well-connected in Parliament and the press and some of the early contributors to the *Review* went on to be correspondents of *The Times* and the *Daily Telegraph*. Today (*pace* the present members of *The Naval Review*) there are very few naval officers of influence in Parliament or able to access the press in order to make the naval case. Today the naval case seems to have been abandoned to the academics, and naval officers have been silenced – except in the pages of *The Naval Review*.

As yet, very few commentators have had access to the mine of information which is available in the pages of *The Naval Review*, or the papers of its founders and editors which lie scattered between Portsmouth, London and Cambridge.[3] It is the hope that *From Dreadnought to Daring* will draw attention to the wealth of material available and this will lead to a more informed and better-articulated case for the Royal Navy and for a maritime strategy.

II

Since its foundation *The Naval Review* has championed the principle of anonymous publication. Over time, usage has changed and contributors have increasingly used pseudonyms or initials, and nowadays contributors are more likely to use their proper names, or their own initials. This usage has given rise to much speculation as to the identity of authors and for this centenary volume the Trustees and Committee of *The Naval Review* have decided that, subject to conditions, the identities of authors of articles more than thirty years old should be revealed.

The Editor remains the sole person to whom the identities of all the contributors are known: however, the Editor's records are not complete. As Rear Admiral James Goldrick, RAN has pointed out, Admiral Sir William Henderson's copies of *The Naval Review* covering the years up to Volume XVII in 1930 are on the shelves of the Royal United Services Institute in Whitehall and these are annotated by the Editor with the identities of authors. Commander Alastair Wilson has pointed out that the Secretary-Treasurer also has some knowledge of the identities of the writers of articles, because he has to pay them their expenses, but he does not necessarily know the identities of the writers of letters to the Editor or of reviews. It is, of course, sometimes possible to identify writers who used their initials by consulting a contemporary list of members, or the Navy Lists, though with caution, because some writers did not use their own initials. Further, the names of some contributors are inscribed in the record volumes of *The Naval Review* (currently held in the library of the University of Salford). Nevertheless there are intermittent gaps in the record and in 1924–5, 1941–61 and parts of the 1980s and 1990s the record is silent.

Meanwhile, the copyright of articles in *The Naval Review* remains with the authors and, if researchers enquire as to their identity, this may be given by the Editor at his discretion.

So, the convention adopted in this centenary volume is that: 'unsigned' means just that, and 'signed' is followed by the initials or pseudonym which the author used: in either case this followed by 'by' if the author's name is known and it was more than thirty years ago.

The numbering of the volumes of *The Naval Review* and their binding, especially of the earlier volumes, varies slightly and gives rise to some difficulty. Here the convention adopted is that references are given relative to the electronic copy of the *Review* – because that is how I believe most readers will in future access the *Review* – and I have given the year, the number and the page, sufficient, I think, for most readers to find the original article.

III

The centenary of *The Naval Review* has been marked by a number of events, including the publication of *From Dreadnought to Daring*, and these events and the generous support of individuals and of companies is acknowledged elsewhere in these covers. My part in this has been the privilege to have been asked by the Trustees to edit this work, and I thank them for the confidence which they have placed in me.

Lady [Candy] Blackham took charge of the fundraising and also advised upon the content of this book, for which she deserves special thanks.

For their help in accomplishing this work, I should like to thank the contributors, who have so willingly undertaken the task of reading nearly a hundred years' worth of *The Naval Review*, for their thoughts and judgement, and for entering into a dialogue with me over what is important or is not.

I should like to thank Admiral Sir Julian Oswald for his friendship and advice in undertaking this project and for his role in the task of refereeing, only a few weeks before his death, some of the contributions by senior officers to this centenary volume. Other nameless referees have also helped and without the confidence which they gave me it would have been impossible to complete this volume.

I should also like to thank the editorial board, Admiral Sir Ian Forbes, Vice Admiral Sir Jeremy Blackham, Rear Admiral Rodney Lees, Roger Welby-Everard, Esq, and Commodore Paul Herington, for their advice, comment and guidance, as well as unnamed members of *The Naval Review* for their opinion.

I am fortunate in owning a complete run of *The Naval Review*, which belonged to the naval officers-come-authors Commander Charles Hardinge Drage (the years 1913–35), John Winton (aka Lieutenant Commander John Pratt) (the years 1936–75), and since 1976 to myself, but without the help of Roger Welby-Everard's digitised copy of the *Review*, it would have been near-impossible to consult and reference some half a million pages of the *Review*, and for this and much else I thank him.

I am extraordinarily grateful too for the help and advice of Robert Gardiner and Julian Mannering of Seaforth Publishing, who share a passion for ships and the sea and have between them more than fifty years of commissioning the very best in maritime literature, and I should also like to thank warmly Stephanie Rudgard-Redsell who so skilfully copy-edited this volume.

For the content of this work, for the balance of the essays, and for any errors of omission or commission or mistakes in references or quotation, I alone am responsible.

Nevertheless, confident that what a world-class institution like the Royal Navy has been thinking for the last one hundred years would be of interest to the contemporary world and to future researchers, the editor respectfully offers *From Dreadnought to Daring*.

PGH
Iping, OCTOBER 2012

1 The Founders

Rear Admiral James Goldrick, RAN

O N 27 October 1912 at 55 Bury Road, Alverstoke, six Royal Navy and one Royal Marine Artillery were gathered at the behest of Captain Herbert Richmond to discuss the formation of a Correspondence Society for the Propagation of Sea-Military Knowledge.[1] Richmond's lieutenant was Commander Kenneth Dewar in a scheme which became first the Naval Society and then *The Naval Review*.[2]

The selection of attendees was opportunistic but deliberate. Imbued with the desire to reform the Royal Navy, Richmond and Dewar had the idea that the critical period for educating officers was between the ages of twenty and thirty-five.[3] The members of the newly established War Staff Course, of which Dewar was on the directing staff, would be ideal for a society for the advancement of ideas within the naval profession. Of the fourteen officers on course, four were at Bury Road – Commander Reginald Plunkett, Lieutenant Roger Bellairs, Lieutenant Thomas Fisher, and Lieutenant Henry Thursfield.[4] The Marine, Captain Edward Harding, was a gunnery instructor. The selection was Dewar's, and Richmond could not even remember Bellairs and Harding when he wrote up his diary.[5] Nevertheless, they were an impressive group. Richmond and Plunkett would both serve as commanders-in-chief. Dewar, Bellairs and Thursfield would reach flag rank on the retired list, the latter two achieving much more in later years.[6] Fisher would die early, but with a knighthood to recognise extraordinary war service. Harding had already played a key role in the development of naval fire control and was to retire as a colonel.

The officers at the meeting, however haphazard their selection, were therefore both representative of the loose coterie of reformist feeling sometimes nicknamed the 'Young Turks' and of the new generation of talented and better educated – even if sometimes self-educated – officers starting to achieve higher rank within the Navy. Whether the undoubted improvement in the quality of the officer corps owed more to the

1

introduction of competitive examinations for entry in 1881 or to the enthusiasm for the Service that came with the Navy's expansion after 1889 is difficult to say.[7] What must, however, be clear about what would become *The Naval Review* (*NR*)and the 'Young Turks' was that not all the Young Turks would write for the *NR*, nor would all that was written in the *NR* be by the Young Turks – or even their fellow travellers.

To those who attended the meeting must be added another founder, retired Admiral William Henderson, first editor and more than any other responsible for placing the *NR* on firm foundations and developing its ethos. He was not the first choice (that was the far more difficult Admiral Sir Reginald Custance) but he proved an inspired one, the result of Dewar's approach to Henderson's nephew, Lieutenant (later Admiral Sir) Reginald Henderson.[8]

It is notable that many of the founders and their friends were associated with the academic, literary and artistic establishments of the United Kingdom to a greater degree than has been the case for the Royal Navy since. Richmond was the son and grandson of highly successful artists, Thursfield's father a distinguished Oxford don who became naval correspondent of *The Times*. Drax was the younger son of one of the oldest Irish peerages and his brother an adventurer and author of some repute. Bellairs' elder brother, formerly a naval officer, was a Member of Parliament (MP). There were others associated with the group who were equally well connected, notably Commander W W (later Admiral Sir William) Fisher, whose brothers included a future cabinet minister and a future chairman of Barclays Bank and whose sisters married distinguished academics and musicians, including the composer Ralph Vaughan Williams. Amongst his cousins were Virginia Woolf and Vanessa Bell.[9] Commander (later Admiral Sir) William 'Bubbles' James's grandfather was the Pre-Raphaelite artist John Everett Millais and his other grandfather a Lord of Appeal in Ordinary.[10]

The challenges which the *NR* faced in the First World War and its aftermath have been analysed elsewhere.[11] While the attempt to censor or suppress the *NR* was a significant issue in itself, the founders' involvement in the Great War is more deserving of mention here.[12] Richmond and Dewar have received most attention, perhaps as much because of their later writing as the actual significance of their service and their attempts to change the direction of the naval war in 1917.[13] While Henderson worked incessantly behind the scenes to influence affairs, several of the others were influentially placed within the Navy at war. Plunkett was Beatty's War Staff Officer in the battlecruisers from 1913 until after Jutland, while Bellairs was firstly Torpedo Officer on

Jellicoe's staff from 1914 and 1916 and then the C-in-C Grand Fleet's War Staff Officer until 1919. Thursfield was the War Staff Officer to Vice Admiral Sir William Pakenham, commanding the battlecruisers, from 1917 until the end of the war.

Admiral Sir William Henderson (1845–1931)

Henderson, nicknamed 'Busy William', had been associated with an earlier effort to create a professional forum in the shape of the short-lived Junior Naval Professional Association of 1872 and was well aware of the potential pitfalls in creating a Naval Society.[14] Henderson enjoyed a long career, including operations ashore in East Africa in 1890, before spending four years as Admiral Superintendent of Devonport Dockyard and retiring in 1908. He had his share of travails, particularly in command of the armoured cruiser *Edgar* (1894–96), when he was criticised for deficiencies in the ship's organisation in the wake of the foundering of a ship's pinnace and the death of forty-eight onboard, but Henderson's reports commented very favourably on his zeal and energy.[15] Throughout his service, Henderson devoted much effort to reform and naval education. He was an early correspondent and friend of Alfred Thayer Mahan, a correspondence initiated as early as 1888 by Mahan after reading a commentary by Henderson on an article (by Philip Colomb) on the naval defence of the United Kingdom.[16]

Henderson took a more ambitious approach to the Naval Society than Richmond or Dewar and immediately wrote to other flag officers and to influential political figures to enlist their support.[17] He was only partly successful, as the travails of the *NR* in the coming conflict were to demonstrate, but he succeeded in creating a much larger membership than Richmond or Dewar had expected. Significantly, it was Henderson who suggested extending membership to the new Dominion Navies.[18] It was an even shrewder touch to formally include as eligible for membership not only 'the First Lord and Civil Members of the Admiralty' but also 'the Minister of Defence for Australia and the Minister in charge of the Naval Service of Canada'. By the end of 1913, 519 members had enlisted.[19]

Henderson was indefatigable in developing the *NR* and the impression gained from his work as editor is one of collegiality and encouragement of the young, the first contribution by a midshipman being in 1915.[20] He largely avoided the pitfalls of commenting from retirement on the current state of the Service unless (as with officer education and training) it was in continuation of long-held concerns. Rather, his method was to raise issues and to describe practices as they had applied in his time and to put questions much more often than he provided answers. This approach is most clearly seen in 'Thoughts on the Service: An Older Point of View' in which Henderson makes thoughtful comparisons with other navies and the civilian world, while continuing to press his ideas of officer training.[21] Obituary tributes by Richmond and Henderson's successor as editor, Admiral Sir Richard Webb, were forthright in their acknowledgement of Henderson's achievement. It was only appropriate that the influence of the Young Turks (Bellairs was probably instrumental in the nomination) had achieved a knighthood for Henderson in 1924, remarkable recognition for an officer who at the age of seventy-eight, after sixteen years on the retired list, was still in harness.

Admiral Sir Herbert Richmond (1871–1946)

Herbert Richmond is the most well-known of the founders, not only due to his own work on naval history and strategy, but through the biography written by Professor Arthur Marder, *Portrait of an Admiral*. Published in 1952 and including extracts from his dairies between 1909 and 1920, the book did not serve Richmond well, conveying the impression of a prickly, over-zealous and intolerant personality whose failure to get to the top could be explained by his intemperate commentary. As Captain Stephen Roskill noted, even if it were accepted that Richmond would have gone further had he been more moderate, the portrait conveyed was 'by no means wholly true.' What he had intended as a safety valve had become a permanent record of his views.[22] Together with Dewar's polemic autobiography of 1939, *The Navy from Within*, it also coloured historical understanding of the development of Admiralty policy, particularly with regard to the naval staff to a degree only now being corrected by scholarship.[23] Drax himself suggested this to Marder in assessing the first volume of *From the Dreadnought to Scapa Flow*.[24] It is also likely that the publication of Richmond's diaries brought about a permanent gap in the historical record when Drax destroyed large parts of his own correspondence with Richmond and Bellairs before depositing his papers at Churchill College.[25] *Portrait of an Admiral* certainly roused indignation amongst Jellicoe supporters such as Admiral Sir Frederic Dreyer as it made clear the extent of Richmond's intrigue against Jellicoe as First Sea Lord in 1917.[26] It also required colleagues to spring to the defence of Richmond's memory.[27]

What was he actually like? Richmond was clearly a talented officer, achieving four first-class certificates in his examinations for lieutenant. He had considerable charm, great energy, a strong creative streak and some artistic skills, in addition to being an efficient seaman. He was well read and spoke both French and Italian. Yet, although consistently well reported upon, without aspersions as to any defects of character, Richmond was not assessed as professionally exceptional until he assisted with reforms to navigation training and with the introduction of the new programme of officer education known as the Selborne scheme.[28] A torpedo specialist following a period surveying, despite his relative youth at thirty-two, he was in the middle of his term amongst those promoted to commander, indicative of the speed with which the Royal Navy was expanding and the competition he faced. Richmond had a successful commission as executive officer of the cruiser *Crescent* on the South Atlantic station from 1904 to 1906, which in extra-curricular terms he put to good use through the study of naval history and correspondence with Julian Corbett. Three years of 'special service' at the Admiralty disillusioned him as to the coherency of Admiral Fisher's policies as First Sea Lord, but the Second Sea Lord, Sir William May, was sufficiently impressed to ask the newly promoted Captain Richmond to join his staff when he took command of the Home Fleet in March 1909, and then to serve as his flag captain in *Dreadnought* until May hauled down his flag in March 1911. It was a signal compliment, although a flag captain was usually junior in seniority. That Richmond's next commands were second-class cruisers supporting the training schools was no indication of lack of success in the big ship, but recognition of his place on the captains' list, and probably, despite his complaints as to professional inactivity, more congenial than a unit on an overseas station.[29]

Richmond's reports continued to indicate a particularly capable officer, most notably in seagoing appointments, a judgement consistent from *Dreadnought* to *Erin* in 1919. As Vice Admiral Sir Henry Oliver commented at the end of that year, Richmond was 'an excellent [and] able officer who should do well in the higher ranks.'[30] There are other indicators of Richmond's fundamental good sense, such as the aftermath of the '*Dreadnought* hoax', the 1910 affair in which members of the Bloomsbury group dressed up as the Emperor of Abyssinia and his suite and conducted a formal visit to the flagship. As captain of the *Dreadnought*, Richmond showed the party around. Since he knew at least one of the perpetrators, Adrian Stephen, and W W Fisher (the Flag Commander and also present) was cousin not only to Stephen but to another of the party, his sister Virginia, it is remarkable that the disguises were not penetrated, and possible that they were by at least one present. When the story reached the press, *Dreadnought* and her admiral became a laughing stock. Richmond's reaction on meeting Stephen in London was at first to pretend 'to be horrified ...

After a second or two, though, he began to laugh and, in fact, took the whole affair in the best of good humours.' This was not the case for W W Fisher, at whom the hoax seems to have been aimed.[31]

Richmond had a frustrating war. He did not enjoy his service as Assistant Director of the Operations Division and translation to the Mediterranean in early 1915 for liaison duties with the unenterprising Italian fleet proved no better. He returned to the United Kingdom later in the year but had to content himself with command of the pre-Dreadnought *Commonwealth* until April 1917 when he finally joined the Grand Fleet proper in command of the battleship *Conqueror*. In April 1918 Richmond returned to the Admiralty as Director of the Training and Staff Duties Division, a move clearly intended to allow him a part in planning for the post-war Navy. It was not a success. Richmond's dislike of the early entry of cadets and his views on training were opposed to the majority of Service feeling (particularly its leadership) and he himself was frustrated at not being involved in operational planning. His major contribution, before he returned to sea in the battleship *Erin* at the beginning of 1919, was to urge the preservation of the newly created Plans Division, arguing successfully that its removal from routine and daily operations was vital in allowing proper planning and attention to the future.[32]

Richmond's post-war career reflected an understandable but limited judgement as to his potential for employment. Commanding the Naval War Course as a rear admiral and inaugurating the Imperial Defence College as a vice admiral meant that his educational and academic skills were employed to good effect. If he was intensely frustrated by the number of his War College students who fell under the 'Geddes' Axe', any list of the directing staff and students of the first courses of the IDC would demonstrate that Richmond had had the opportunity to shape the future leadership of the British Empire's military forces in the Second World War.[33] Even if Brigadier (later Field Marshal) John Dill had to persuade him to abandon scholastic purity in favour of practicality (and the limited time available) in devising the initial syllabus, Richmond's approach to the preparation of officers for high command and high policy positions has stood the test of time.[34]

Nevertheless, there is truth to Barry Hunt's comment that Richmond's IDC appointment provided a 'congenial puddle for an intellectual frog'.[35] The nation might have been even better served had he been employed elsewhere, as his time at the Naval War Course and as C-in-C East Indies between 1923 and 1925 demonstrated. While at Greenwich, Richmond wrote and lectured extensively on naval operations and the principles by which maritime forces should operate in conflict. The *Naval War Manuals* of 1921 and of 1925 show his influence and his eagerness to develop an offensive spirit in battle.[36] They also indicate a sophisticated understanding of the need for the future fleet to adopt an 'all arms' approach. As he wrote in his diary in November 1920, 'Tactics will take a wholly different form. Smaller formations of great ships will make the torpedo attack a wholly different matter. Torpedo planes will play a part we have hardly thought of, submarines will have a more difficult role, formations will be looser, co-operation of all arms even more important than today.'[37]

As C-in-C, Richmond's analysis of the limitations of British Far East strategy and his work to develop a more effective framework in planning for conflict against Japan demonstrated his grasp of national strategic requirements.[38] Furthermore, he achieved good relations with other authorities during his command, particularly General Lord Rawlinson, whose premature death robbed Britain of an influential advocate of a more balanced approach to the Far Eastern question.[39] Unfortunately, Richmond was neither fully within the inner circle of the senior Grand Fleet and Battle Cruiser Fleet veterans who dominated the Admiralty, nor was he regarded, perhaps on the basis of his naval staff service in 1914–15 and 1918, as a comfortable colleague in the staff environment. Bringing him to Whitehall as an Assistant or as Deputy Chief of Naval Staff was never likely.

His absence from the centre of things contributed to one of Richmond's most significant failings in his mature work. Service within the Admiralty would have provided additional context to his thinking and forced him to focus more upon the present and the future. Largely isolated from material issues, Richmond did not properly understand the changing effects on maritime warfare of technology and became increasingly blind to the fact that some developments were so significant that he needed to rethink the way in which he regarded naval strategy. For example, in an *NR* article in 1943 entitled 'The Modern Conception of Sea Power', Richmond provided an excellent analysis of the constituents of sea power and emphasised that it did not depend simply upon naval strength alone. His arguments as to the need for the co-ordinated direction of all the units involved in achieving control of the sea are compelling. However, although his grasp of general principles was acute, Richmond did not recognise the extent to which the air arm had replaced the heavy gun as the arbiter, noting of the Battles of the Coral Sea and Midway that they 'got no further than affairs of outposts in which the advanced guards of aircraft only got into action.'[40] The fact that the air attacks launched by each side represented the main striking power of the opposed fleets had passed him by, even, as at Midway, when decisive results were achieved. There can be little excuse for this in 1943, however far removed Richmond was from the front line. Mahan once pointed out that principles were constant but that precedents changed, largely because of the evolution of technology and thus of specific naval capabilities.[41] Richmond was prone to maintain precedents when there had been critical changes.

Richmond's lack of senior policy experience and technological understanding also contributed to some inconsistency of judgement in his campaigns, including those on the size of the fighting ship for which he employed the pages of the *NR*.[42] It is arguable that Richmond did neither himself nor the Navy any service by his calls for moderate dimensions as a mechanism for arms control, particularly as he became preoccupied with specific and rigid limits. While his theses made a great deal of sense, particularly when they were combined with his call for limitations based on strategic need, not artificial tonnage totals, his target was the wrong one and he served only to undermine the Admiralty's efforts to get the best out of the several interwar naval treaties. It was when Richmond focused more directly on the overall erosion of British naval strength that he was on much firmer ground. His work on belligerent rights also provided an important counterpoint to efforts to achieve 'freedom of the seas' at the expense of Britain's exercise of its historical advantages.[43] The Admiralty welcomed Richmond's interventions when they supported current policy, but there was bitter resentment when they did not. Admiral Chatfield in particular was profoundly alienated by Richmond, describing him after the war as an 'able but irresponsible' analyst.[44] Chatfield commented elsewhere that Richmond eventually 'descended from his position of advantage amongst the clouds of Mount Olympus where he used to declaim against such vulgar matters as *materiel* and *weapons* and ... explain at great length how unimportant they are.'[45] Chatfield had a point, but the tragedy is that the naval staff did not bring Richmond into their counsels, which might have allowed him to align his views much more closely with the Admiralty, while clarifying some of the staff's own thinking.

Knighted in 1926 and promoted admiral in 1929, Richmond eventually retired at his own request in 1931. He had hoped for a home port as C-in-C but his public statements on disarmament probably sealed any hope of further employment. Richmond had enough pride to refuse in 1930 to serve as chairman of the International Conference on Load Lines for Merchant Ships.[46] However, he was delighted to be appointed Vere Harmsworth Professor of Imperial and Naval History at Cambridge in 1934. Retiring again after two years, Richmond was immediately appointed Master of Downing College, where he remained until his death. It was a safe and highly congenial harbour. Nevertheless, however happy Richmond may have been in this new environment, it is probably fair to say that any contentment he possessed came not just from his continuing academic work.[47] Richmond was to the end a sailor-scholar and it is impossible to consider him as a historian without recognising that he was a very capable seagoing officer and commander and that these aspects were just as integral to his identity.

Although Richmond's use of the *NR* as a vehicle for testing ideas rapidly diminished after his retirement, he remained actively involved in the journal until his death. His articles tended to relate to the questions of naval education, imperial defence and belligerent rights, while he was a prolific book reviewer. After 1939, when Richmond was devoting much of his limited remaining energy to commentary in other journals such as the *Fortnightly Review*, the rate of articles dropped further. But it is significant that his last two substantial contributions should be in 1943 with 'The Modern Conception of Sea Power' and in 1944, when he wrote approvingly of the re-establishment of the Royal Canadian Naval College on educational lines and with an entry age which reflected his own proposals over many years.[48]

Vice Admiral Kenneth G B Dewar (1879–1964)

Dewar is in many ways the most tragic figure amongst the founders. He failed to achieve high rank on the active list and retired a disappointed man, embittered by the events which saw him removed from command of the battleship *Royal Oak* and court-martialled after he and his executive officer had fallen out with their embarked flag officer. As an anonymous naval near-contemporary commented, he 'was, without any doubt, a clear and original thinker. He also had the defects of these qualities, amongst others a contemptuous attitude towards anything with which he disagreed, a certain exudation of omniscience in argument, and a growing intolerance.'[49] It was a fair criticism of this austere Scot and one reflected in Dewar's later confidential reports, which acknowledged his intellect but repeatedly cast doubts on his leadership and human sympathy.[50]

A specialist gunnery officer, Dewar was in the vanguard of the gunnery revolution and his ships achieved consistently outstanding results. This brought him in 1910 to the battleship *Dreadnought* as first and gunnery lieutenant and into contact with Herbert Richmond, a type of naval officer Dewar 'had never met before.'[51] Richmond had a profound influence upon Dewar, but the latter never came near to matching the quality and insight of Richmond's best work, although he laboured hard on naval history in later years.

Dewar did good work during the First World War, but his outlook was not improved by his experience of the Dardanelles, or of monitor command (the unreliable *Marshal Ney* and the *Raglan*) or service in the Operations Division from 1917. Promoted captain in June 1918, as Assistant Director of Plans he was deeply involved in the negotiations culminating in the Treaty of Versailles, for which work he was created CBE in 1920. Doubts as to his judgement began with the conflict caused by production of the staff history of the Battle of Jutland, known as the *Staff Appreciation*. Written with his older brother, A C Dewar, this was deeply critical of Jellicoe and too extreme in its judgements to sit easily with any fair-minded analysis. It pleased Beatty, but was rapidly discredited and the Admiralty was forced to withdraw the volume even from internal circulation.[52]

The *Royal Oak* affair was fundamentally the result of incompatible personalities rubbing on each other in an enclosed environment in which there was too little to occupy them. Dewar needed to complete three years sea time as a captain to qualify for flag rank, even on the retired list, so was appointed to the *Royal Oak* in 1927, as flag captain to Rear Admiral Bernard Collard. The Admiralty, for the best of motives, tried to provide all officers with the opportunity to achieve the required service. With a bloated post list and a diminishing number of major units, this had the effect of reducing tenures in command and placing senior captains in flagships with junior rear admirals. Part of the sensitivity to the problems in the *Royal Oak* when they emerged was that there had already been at least one clash of personalities in the First Battle Squadron.[53] Collard's choleric behaviour caused *Royal Oak*'s executive officer, H M Daniel, to complain formally to Dewar and the latter forwarded the submission with his own remarks to the First Battle Squadron's commander, Vice Admiral J D Kelly who wasted no time informing the C-in-C, Sir Roger Keyes.[54] The submissions were considered improper and both officers immediately relieved (as was Collard). Their courts martial followed. Dewar was dismissed his ship and, although re-employed to complete his sea time, retired on promotion to rear admiral in 1929.

Dewar later stood for parliament as a Labour candidate in Portsmouth but was soundly defeated. He published his autobiography, *The Navy from Within*, in early 1939, but it made only a passing impression. Dewar's reply (his first appearance in the *NR* since the 1920s) to the gentle criticisms expressed by Captain B H Smith in his book review indicated that the scars of the *Royal Oak* were unhealed, although, perhaps as ever, amongst the recriminations were some sensible suggestions on other naval questions.[55] The war found him in the Admiralty where he was installed in the Historical Section, remaining until April 1948.[56] A historical focus marked Dewar's contributions when he returned to the *NR* after a long hiatus in 1951. Ranging from studies of naval administration to a lengthy series on the major naval events of the First World War, most notably the Dardanelles and Jutland, their value is more in the light that they cast on Dewar and the axes that he continued to grind than for their historical merit.

Rear Admiral Roger Bellairs (1884–1959)

Although he was to serve after the Second World War as head of the Naval Historical Section, Roger Bellairs' appearances in the *NR* were few. One, 'The Training of Officers: A Criticism', in 1921 is significant in that he not only endorsed the recent confirmation of the division between executive and engineering officers and a much reduced emphasis on engineering in the training of the former, but also espoused a relatively limited approach to higher education. Bellairs' view was that lengthy education in strategy and tactics should be confined to those who 'have special aptitude' and that it would be wasted on the majority.[57]

There is an air of the mandarin in Bellairs' commentary and perhaps good reason for this. Bellairs was writing from the position of Naval Assistant to the First Sea Lord. He had moved from War Staff Officer to the C-in-C Grand Fleet to the battleship *Resolution* as executive officer in July 1919, but remained in that post less than four months before Beatty, newly installed as First Sea Lord, ordered him to Whitehall. It is a tribute to Bellairs' skills as a staff officer that he should have been able to support (and impress) both Jellicoe and Beatty. Unlike several of the other founders, Bellairs' only contribution to the *NR* after 1928 was an obituary notice for Admiral Jellicoe in 1936. It is likely that the discretion of the inner office became habitual. It also had other effects.

Bellairs remained Naval Assistant until 1925, giving him an almost unbroken and practically unprecedented period of eleven years in staff appointments.[58] He then served as captain of the cruiser *Effingham* in the East Indies, but also as flag captain and chief of staff to the C-in-C, before returning to the Admiralty in 1928 as Director of Plans. Not until December 1930 did Bellairs assume command of a private ship and it was the premier command in the Navy, the battleship *Rodney* in the Atlantic Fleet, where he relieved the formidable Andrew

Cunningham, whose career to that point had been the converse of Bellairs (and who thought that the *NR* was 'subversive').[59]

The Invergordon mutiny of 1931, in which the *Rodney*'s ship's company were deeply involved, did not result from particular defects in the organisation of the ship and Bellairs displayed more tact than some. As Roskill has noted, 'one feels that few if any other Post Captains who found themselves in the position of those commanding the worst ships would have done any better.'[60] Nevertheless, the evidence of one of his junior officers, Sub Lieutenant (later Captain) Reginald Whinney, is that Bellairs was not well attuned to his ship's company and relied too much upon his commander. In speaking to his sailors on one key occasion, what Bellairs 'said came over with no force – but worse, once again he tended to talk over the heads of his audience.'[61] Whitehall had not been the best preparation for such a command.

Bellairs' talents were sufficiently admired for him to be given a second chance and he was watched closely by the new C-in-C, Admiral Sir John 'Joe' Kelly. The latter's final report, however, was decisive. It also reflected closely Whinney's comments, particularly as to Bellairs' over-reliance on his personally selected executive officer. Kelly acknowledged Bellairs' gifts, but confirmed that his talents lay in staff appointments, not at sea.[62]

Bellairs retired on promotion to rear admiral, but his skills could not be wasted and in 1932 he was appointed as British Naval Representative on the League of Nations Permanent Advisory Commission, where he remained until the outbreak of war. He spent the conflict as a special staff officer in the Admiralty, deeply involved in a wide range of sensitive issues, such as the development of working relations with the United States Navy, and later the planning for D-Day. In May 1948 Bellairs became head of the Naval Historical Section, where he remained until August 1956. In that year he received a CBE, perhaps not the full due for his long backroom services, but some recognition to add to his long held CB and CMG.

Admiral Sir Reginald Plunkett-Ernle-Erle-Drax (1880–1967)

Reginald Plunkett is perhaps the most attractive personality amongst the younger founders. He has not been well served by the portmanteau surname of Plunkett-Ernle-Erle-Drax which he adopted in order to inherit substantial estates and which was the subject of considerable international ribaldry at the time of his mission to Moscow in 1939. Yet Drax's personality and talents could not have been further removed from the world of P G Wodehouse and he himself probably believed that Paris (or, in this case, Charborough Park) was worth a mass.[63]

Drax did not usually work on the same theoretical plane as Richmond, although his contributions to the *NR*, particularly in the early years, reveal an incisive intellect and an ability to match Richmond in argument.[64] His closing comments from an exchange over home defence gently recommended 'a little more of kindly toleration' in a way that Drax was to repeat over the years when faced by the more trenchant efforts of other contributors. He certainly had a greater sympathy with technology than Richmond and his last published work, in 1962, was on solar heating.[65] Equally notable, at the age of twenty-four, Drax published, albeit anonymously, his first book *The Modern Officer of the Watch*. This highly practical work, which includes some commentary still relevant today, was repeatedly reprinted and revised. Drax revealed his identity and acknowledged his own 'temerity' in the preface to the second, 1907 edition.[66]

Drax enjoyed the most successful career of all the founders. After Jutland and promotion to captain, he commanded the light cruiser *Blanche* and received the DSO for service in that ship. He was Director of the Staff College from 1919 to 1922 and later President of the Allied Naval Control Commission in Germany. Promoted rear admiral in 1928, he served as Rear Admiral First Battle Squadron in 1929–30, Director of Manning from 1930 to 1932 and then C-in-C North America and West Indies as a vice admiral until 1934. Created KCB, he served as C-in-C Plymouth from 1935 to 1938, being promoted admiral in 1936. These later flag appointments were the better of the second tier and Drax might have expected to retire after Plymouth. He was, however, soon re-employed to assess the Admiralty's war plans. His earlier efforts to influence strategic planning had won few friends on the naval staff and clearly irritated Chatfield through criticism of a lack of offensive spirit.[67] However, the new First Sea Lord, Roger Backhouse, had different views and in 1939 utilised Drax to help assess the implications of over-stretch and recast the Navy's strategy to focus on the threats of Germany and Italy.[68] He was then despatched as leader for abortive negotiations with the Soviet Union just before the outbreak of the Second World War. While Drax's own account shows his good sense, it must remain doubtful just how serious the Chamberlain government was in sending only military officers to settle what was fundamentally a political matter.[69] By way of reward, he received, unusually, a second home port appointment as C-in-C Nore, where he remained until 1941. Service in the Home Guard and then as Commodore of Convoys followed until 1945.

Over fifty years, his last being in 1963, Drax's interventions in the *NR* were consistently forward-looking. In 1930, before the Invergordon mutiny, he published 'Quo Vadis', an appeal to members to answer the question within the pages of the *NR* as to 'In what way (or ways) can we produce the greatest increase in the fighting efficiency of the Royal Navy?'[70] In later years, in addition to commentaries on national and naval strategy, he provided advice to younger officers which, if occasionally too like Shakespeare's Polonius, nevertheless demonstrated his abiding concern and sympathy.[71] But, above all, as he reminded K G B Dewar in 1960 after the latter's articles on Jutland, the future counted for the *NR*, not the past. In Drax's view the real task was not to rail about the failures of the Navy but to 'tell us how our officers and men can be trained to ensure that the errors of the past will not be repeated?'[72]

Rear Admiral Henry Thursfield (1882–1963)

Thursfield presents as a highly competent officer, admiring of Richmond in particular, but not himself a revolutionary. He made his name as the commissioning Torpedo Officer of the battlecruiser *Invincible* which had been fitted with electrically powered main armament, a disastrous experiment which required heroic efforts from Thursfield and his team to make work at all. In 1911, the inspecting admiral noted that 'I consider it entirely due to [the T staff's] zeal and exertion that the ship has been able to carry out her firings.'[73] Thursfield's later career included service as executive officer of the *Dreadnought* before he joined Sir William Pakenham as War Staff Officer in 1917. After the war, he was asked by Drax to be his deputy at the Naval Staff College – significantly, instead of Dewar – before command of the cruiser *Comus*. He later served on a naval mission to Greece and as Director of the Tactical Division. His final appointment was as captain of the *Royal Oak* but, to his bitter disappointment, he was retired on promotion to rear admiral.[74] He had been watched closely by a succession of flag officers and it is clear that doubts as to his energy and strength of personality grew. His final report by Vice Admiral Sir William Fisher was decisive: the *Royal Oak* had been a good ship, but in Fisher's view she would have been better with a harder driving Captain. He commented that had Thursfield 'chosen any profession not demanding extended influence over others, I feel sure he would have got to the absolute top.'[75]

Thursfield did not write for the *NR* until 1932, the time of his retirement, and his articles tended to be in support of Richmond's approach to officer training or reviews of recent works, rather than original contributions. Nevertheless, they displayed good sense, as well as a certain literary skill. It was thus not surprising that in 1936 he was appointed naval correspondent to *The Times* (a post long held by his father) and then editor of *Brassey's Naval Annual*. This dual role made Thursfield one of the leading naval commentators in the United Kingdom and he fulfilled the role well, being generally judicious and balanced in his analysis, emphasising the need for inter-service co-ordination and co-operation, as well as keeping up with technological change, even into the 1950s and 1960s.[76] From the time of his movement to full-time journalism, Thursfield's contributions to the *NR* diminished, although in 1957 he provided a perceptive review of the second volume of Arthur Marder's collected correspondence of Jack Fisher.[77] However, he remained closely connected with the *NR* for the rest of his life, serving as a trustee and making a last contribution in a short retrospective for the Golden Jubilee in 1963. In this, Thursfield made it clear that he thought the *NR* was aimed at younger officers and that its contributions should primarily be from the young and junior, 'the category of those for whom it was designed.'[78] He died in October the same year.

Commander Sir Thomas Fisher (1883–1925)

Thomas Fisher is the least known of the founders, but potentially one of the most interesting. He made only one contribution (a translation of an article 'Modern Naval Education' in 1913 from the French *Revue Maritime)* and died untimely, but his achievements suggest great talent, as did his confidential reports, which repeatedly described him as 'brilliant'. Not only did he play a significant role in the Naval Trade Division for much of the First World War, for which he was appointed CBE, but he went on, as an acting captain, to represent both the Admiralty and the Ministry of Shipping with the United States Shipping Board in 1918–19. That he must have been extremely successful was demonstrated by his retention in Washington at the request of the Ambassador and his knighthood in 1920, an honour unprecedented for a thirty-seven-year-old executive branch commander.[79] Lloyd George's 'dreadful knights' notwithstanding and even in a more generous era of honours, knighthood at that age and that rank was remarkable. Fisher followed this by appointment after voluntary retirement in 1920 as general manager of Canadian Pacific Steamships. The record of the company, including significant expansion, suggests that Fisher succeeded making the transition into commerce.[80] He died of a stroke at the age of only forty-two.

Colonel Edward Harding (?–1934)

A Royal Marines contemporary of Maurice (later Lord) Hankey, Edward Harding was deeply involved in the efforts to improve Royal

Navy gunnery in the first decade of the century. He had written several influential articles on gunnery fire control in the *United Services Magazine* and then, under a pseudonym (Rapidan), in 1902 in *Engineering*. Those from the latter journal were collected and published as a book under the original title *The Tactical Employment of Naval Artillery* and they created considerable interest. Appointed to the Ordnance Department in 1903, Harding was soon employed as an assistant to the director, John Jellicoe, and became embroiled in the controversy over the fire control systems developed by the inventor, Arthur Pollen. Harding did not remain the responsible assistant after Jellicoe was relieved as Director of Naval Ordnance by Reginald Bacon (his role was assumed by Frederic Dreyer in a severe conflict of interest), but he remained a steadfast supporter of Pollen and testified on his behalf to the Royal Commission on Awards to Inventors in 1925.[81] During this period, Harding certainly made himself into one of the Navy's gunnery experts and his contributions in the Naval Ordnance Department included the internal analysis of the gunnery lessons of the Russo-Japanese War.[82]

Harding's seagoing gunnery expertise makes it unsurprising that his first contributions to the *NR* should be a three-part series in 1913, 'Studies in the Theory of Naval Tactics'. They are an impressive collection, Harding attempting to fuse both moral and material issues in analysing the challenges of modern naval warfare. His understanding of gunnery and the importance of achieving the concentration of fire and 'the employment of movement with respect to its effect on weapon technique' confirms his technical sophistication, but his arguments to assert the paramouncy of the human factor, the subject of his leading article, indicate both extensive reading (notably of Clausewitz) and some imagination.[83] His third article is a plea for divisional tactics, rather than the 'cumbrous' line of twenty to thirty ships. In all, Harding proved an accurate prophet.

Ironically, Harding's war was largely on land, initially with the Royal Naval Division. It was not a good one. Sent to the Mediterranean in charge of a Marine battery, he spent eighteen months as a camp commandant in Egypt, with the additional duty in 1916 as commander of Alexandria's coast defences. His health suffered, perhaps permanently, and he was invalided home in 1917. Harding's service had earned the waspish comment by a senior officer that he had 'little knowledge of the methods applicable to staff duties and is not inclined to put extra energy into his work to rectify this.'[84] The strong impression is that Harding was misemployed and that his notion of staff duties was not that of the land element. Fit for sea later in 1917, he was appointed to the battleship *Emperor of India* for a year before again being invalided. Once recovered, Harding was posted at the start of 1919 to the Training and Staff Duties Division, perhaps at Richmond's behest, but too late to work with him. Harding's career was not considered over by the Royal Marines and he returned to the Corps to command a battalion during the coal strike. He was finally promoted Lieutenant Colonel in February 1921 but retired at his own request in July 1922, with the honorary rank of Colonel. His health was probably permanently damaged, for he died at the age of fifty-seven. Harding's contributions to the *NR* after the Great War were limited, but significant. His perceptive review of Sir Percy Scott's autobiography opens a window on the challenges facing those attempting to improve naval gunnery.[85]

Retrospective

It would be easy to conclude this collective biography of the founders with the injunction to seek their monument within the pages of *The Naval Review* and the electronic reality of its website. But this would confuse what they had intended as a means for the end itself, the insurance that 'the errors of the past will not be repeated.' The legacy of the founders lies not within our journal but in the operational record of the Navy from 1939 onwards. Richmond and his contemporaries found much to content themselves in the achievements of their Service from the outset of the Second World War and with good reason. The Battle of the River Plate, the *Altmark* incident, and the first and second Battles of Narvik were only the start of a record of calculated aggression, and a sustained demonstration that strategic defence requires tactical offensiveness to be truly effective, and which warmed the hearts of the most discontented from the previous conflict. It is significant that Richmond's primary concerns in 1939–45 were not with the Royal Navy itself but with the way in which the Government was managing, or mismanaging its strategic priorities, particularly with regard to the protection of shipping and the over-emphasis on the flawed bombing campaign.

Nevertheless, the uncertain position of the Royal Navy within the United Kingdom's national understanding in the early years of the twenty-first century does raise one question. If the founders were to assemble at the centenary, would they be moved to form a 'Society for the Propagation of Sea-Military Knowledge' *within* the Service – or *outside* it?

2 The Sea-Kings of Britain 1913–2013

Commander Alastair Wilson

'Let us now praise famous men' –
Men of little showing –
For their work continueth,
And their work continueth,
Broad and deep continueth,
Greater than their knowing!

TWO generations of naval officers were given their basic knowledge of naval history from a text book, *The Sea Kings of Britain*, by Geoffrey Callender (1875–1946), which remained in use at Dartmouth until 1949. It has since been denigrated by academics as being poor history, but the admirals whose lives and actions formed the core of Callender's book inspired the young officers who fought the First World War, and who became the admirals of the Second World War.

The Naval Review has been very sparing of obituaries of distinguished officers, leaving them to the newspapers, or to the *Dictionary of National Biography*. However, in its hundred years, *The Naval Review* has published thirty-two such memoirs. These naval officers' naval officers comprise:

Admiral of the Fleet Sir Arthur Wilson
Admiral Sir William Henderson
Vice Admiral Sir William Creswell
Admiral Sir Reginald Custance
Admiral of the Fleet Viscount Jellicoe
Admiral of the Fleet Earl Beatty
Admiral Sir William Fisher
Admiral of the Fleet Sir Dudley Pound
Admiral Sir Bertram Ramsay
Admiral Sir Herbert Richmond
Admiral Sir Richard Webb
Admiral Ronald Hopwood

Admiral Sir Max Horton
Admiral of the Fleet Lord Cunningham
Admiral of the Fleet Earl Mountbatten
Admiral Sir Richard Onslow
Admiral of the Fleet Lord Tovey
Admiral of the Fleet Lord Fraser
Admiral Sir Geoffrey Oliver
Captain Stephen Roskill
Admiral Sir Caspar John
Vice Admiral Sir Charles Hughes-Hallett
Vice Admiral Sir Aubrey Mansergh
Admiral Sir Peter Stanford
Admiral of the Fleet Lord Fieldhouse
Vice Admiral Sir Peter Gretton
Admiral of the Fleet Sir William Staveley
Admiral of the Fleet Lord Lewin
Vice Admiral Sir Roderick Macdonald
Rear Admiral John Nunn
Vice Admiral Sir Louis Le Bailly
Admiral of the Fleet Sir Henry Leach

To these may be added a memoir of Sir Julian Corbett, whose studies of naval history and strategy were of great influence in the early days of *The Naval Review*.

The quotation above from Kipling, based on Ecclesiasticus 44, would not be a bad epitaph, for one of the abiding strengths of the Royal Navy has been its continuity, each generation taking its example from its forebears. Twelve of them reached that pinnacle of a naval officer's career, to be First Sea Lord. Another five may be described as fighting admirals, men who had the opportunity to prove themselves in battle, as many of the First Sea Lords had also done. And another four might be described as thinking officers whose written words influenced their generation and later, and it is worth remarking that two of these were engineer officers.

One name is missing, that of Admiral of the Fleet Lord Fisher, 'Jacky' Fisher, who dragged the Royal Navy into the twentieth century and left his mark not just on the materiel of the fleet, but on the personnel, both the officer corps and ratings. He died in 1920, and one might have expected some notice of his death. The editor might well have considered that Fisher's passing had been sufficiently covered in the newspapers, but one can suggest several reasons why the *NR* did not comment. The first is that the *NR* was still finding its feet; it was still merely the journal of the Naval Society, discussing current problems of interest to naval officers, and there was no editorial in which to mark significant naval events. It was still on probation as far as the Admiralty was concerned, and there were many senior officers who were no great friends of Fisher, not merely for the Fisher-Beresford spat of 1908–9, but also because of his apparent desertion of his post in 1915. However, in 1930 the NR published a review of Admiral Bacon's biography of Fisher, and the editor invited comments which amounted to a memoir of Fisher.[1]

There are two other Great War leaders whose names do not appear: Sir Roger Keyes (1872–1945), and Sir Philip Vian (1894–1968). We cannot now say why the editors chose not to seek appreciations of Keyes and Vian. Historians may suggest that both were incomplete, if not flawed, characters. Keyes was an impetuous and inspiring war leader but, when Beatty retired, was passed over for the post of First Sea Lord, as being something of a political liability; and the reputation of Vian, whose sea commands in Home waters, the Mediterranean, at D-Day, and in the Pacific must ensure his place in history, was that of a prickly character who inspired respect rather than affection.

Space does not permit us to examine in detail the memoirs of all those named, so we have made an arbitrary selection from the different categories.

Admiral Sir William Henderson, KBE (1845–1931)

Admiral Sir William Henderson was the NR's first editor, steering what was then officially the Naval Society and its periodical through the difficult days of the First World War to what was, in effect, a restart in 1919, then to a gradual expansion in the 1920s, thence to a formally-established charity, with a constitution which still guides us today. So it was entirely appropriate that it should have been one of our founding fathers, Admiral Richmond, who wrote the appreciation.[2]

Vice Admiral Sir William Creswell, KCMG, KBE (1852–1933)

The next modern sea-king was the founding father of the Royal Australian Navy, Vice Admiral Sir William Creswell. He was the subject of a long article by Admiral B M Chambers, which was more a blow-by-blow description of the formation of the RAN than an appreciation of the qualities of the man who, 'should be held in remembrance by coming generations of naval officers, for his career was unique and one which can never be duplicated, for the conditions which led to the creation of the present Australian Navy can hardly ever arise again'.[3]

Admiral Sir Reginald Custance, GCB, KCMG, CVO (1847–1935)

A gunnery officer, Custance's name is not well known to many naval officers at the start of the twenty-first century, but he was one of the earliest of our modern, thinking admirals, who later wrote two books on the theory and practice of maritime warfare. Vice Admiral H W W Hope wrote a memoir, reminding readers of Custance's fire-control experiments carried out in Custance's flagship, the pre-Dreadnought *Venerable*, in the Mediterranean 1903–4.[4] After describing the situation of the fleet's gunnery in 1902, and the non-existent gunnery control arrangements in *Venerable*, Hope described the nature of the trials, and the conclusion: the need for a single elevated control position and electrical transmission of data. After the initial trials to determine the need for instrumentation, the equipment was fitted in Malta and the ship completed the practical firing trials. Hope wrote, 'It is not an exaggeration to say that the present day fleet owes a great debt of gratitude to Sir Reginald for the thorough, painstaking and able way in which he met and overcame the initial difficulties and created a method of long range firing by which the gunnery efficiency of the fleet has been raised from firing at ranges of 2,000 yards to firing at ranges of 20,000 yards.'

Hope eulogised Custance's personal and mental qualities: 'He was very fond of entertaining junior officers and trying to get their views on current affairs. He never aired his own views; I don't think he was ever heard to lay down the law on any subject … a great student of naval history and an authority on naval strategy … Sir Reginald was far above our heads.' These characteristics made Custance an untypical Victorian naval officer, and Hope ended by describing him as 'a fine seaman, a great Admiral, and a gentleman in the best sense of the word.'

Admiral of the Fleet Earl Jellicoe, GCB, GCVO, OM (1859–1935)

Hardly surprisingly, the death of Jellicoe, described by Churchill as 'the only man who could lose the war in an afternoon', was marked by a number of memoirs, not merely by his contemporaries (Admirals Sir Richard Phillimore and Sir Herbert Heath) but also by a more junior officer, Paymaster Captain H W E Manisty, who had served with him in the battleships *Ramillies* and *Centurion* when a young clerk, and later in the Admiralty. The *NR*'s tributes to him opened with the King's message published in the court circular.[5] It continued with the tribute paid in the House of Commons by the Prime Minister, Stanley Baldwin. The latter put Jellicoe's achievement in a nutshell: 'He obtained and maintained the undisputed command of the sea before, during and after the Battle of Jutland. His was the controlling and directing mind of the greatest assembly of naval power the world has ever seen, and very possibly ever will see. The trust reposed in him was a tremendous trust. The responsibility was perhaps the greatest single responsibility on any man in the war. All of us who were at home at that time were sheltered behind the Grand Fleet.'

The memoirs written by his naval colleagues were more personal, and recorded, among other things, his reputation for encyclopaedic knowledge. Heath summed up Jellicoe's attributes: 'In my service experience I never met another whose influence was so much felt by all who came in contact with him, and that influence of the best for the individual and the Service generally.'

It is clear that he was admired and respected throughout the fleet from his days as a young gunnery officer. Captain Manisty expressed it when he described his last meeting with the Admiral about a year before his death: 'We had met near Blackfriars Underground Station where he had to collect a bag from the left luggage room. He would not let me carry it for him: we were both going westward; the train was full; and we "strap-hung" for our journey. He was returning from Victoria station to the Isle of Wight that evening. Simple and self-contained – as always. I wish he had let me carry that bag.'

Admiral of the Fleet Earl Beatty, GCB, GCVO, DSO, OM (1871–1936)

Beatty and Jellicoe died within four months of each other, and it is probably fair to say that Beatty's earlier death (he was sixty-five, Jellicoe was seventy-six) was in some measure due to the difference in their temperaments and in the lives they led. Both had carried heavy burdens in war and both continued in public service afterwards, but Beatty's years as First Sea Lord were much more taxing than Jellicoe's governor-generalship of New Zealand. Jellicoe's home life was, like his temperament, calm and relaxing, whereas Beatty's was mercurial and unrestful.

Two of the four memoirs to Beatty were contributed by officers of a similar temperament, the fire-eating Admiral Sir Walter Cowan and Admiral of the Fleet Lord Keyes. Both Beatty and Jellicoe had state funerals, and were honoured by having their likenesses in bronze displayed, appropriately, in Trafalgar Square.

The *NR* reprinted the tribute of the Archbishop of Canterbury, who spoke of Beatty's 'ardent and forceful personality', and who quoted a naval comrade of Beatty's as saying that he was 'the very embodiment of the fighting spirit of the Navy.' The *NR* also reproduced the tribute by Admiral of the Fleet Lord Chatfield, who had been Beatty's flag captain throughout the war, and who referred to Beatty's seven and a half years as First Sea Lord which

> proved that he was not only a great seaman, but possessed the highest ability as an administrator. It was his wise and undaunted action in those difficult post-war years that saved the Navy from an even worse fate than befell it ... It has been stated that Lord Beatty was not a 'thinker'; that he lacked foresight and was a man who mainly acted on the spur of the moment. This by no means does justice to him ... He always most carefully planned for the future ... He inspired all under him and seemed able to impart to them a measure of that self-confidence that he himself possessed in such an outstanding degree.[6]

The final memoir was by Admiral Sir Reginald Plunkett-Ernle-Erle-Drax, who had been Beatty's staff officer operations. Among other things, he remarked (no doubt with his tongue jammed firmly in his cheek) that 'Many people have speculated on whether he might have added still further to his laurels by taking up some occupation such as that of a governor abroad or perhaps Master of the Quorn.' He concluded by citing the opinion of Admiral Hugh Rodman, USN (who had commanded the US Battle Squadron attached to the Grand Fleet): 'He was one of the finest and most inspiring leaders I have ever known. Too much praise cannot be awarded to him. He was one of the world's greatest naval commanders.'

Admiral Sir William Fisher, GCB, GCVO (1875–1937)

Sir William Fisher's memoir did not conform to the remainder of our sea-kings, in that it was not written by his peers or subordinates – but a former First Lord of the Admiralty, Leopold Amery, First Lord (1922–24). The NR's heading for the memoir was 'The Undefeated Spirit'.[7] His whole family were intellectually gifted (Fisher himself, while C-in-C Mediterranean, maintained a correspondence in Latin with a Croatian professor he had met in Split) and Amery wrote, 'This universality of his interest, coupled with his unquestioned grasp of his profession and technical duties was one of the secrets of his success. It enabled him to see every problem in the round, and not merely from the professional angle, and in its proper setting and background.'

One of Fisher's greatest achievements was his tenure as Director of the Anti-Submarine Division of the Admiralty, under Rear Admiral Duff, which he took up in May 1917, at the height of the crisis. Amery wrote that:

profoundly conscious of the immense responsibility of his task, and of the gravity of the situation, he remained cool and unflustered, full of resource, with his mind darting everywhere for fresh expedients and fresh talent to enlist. Undefeated in spirit, he mastered and wore down the enemy with almost uncanny success as month after month saw the greatest of all menaces to the Allied cause gradually reduced to a minor inconvenience.

'Few men,' Amery wrote, 'did more to win the war.' 'The best description of his personality,' Amery concluded, 'I have seen is in a letter from an old colleague who described him as "large in mind and body and entirely straight in both". My own first impression, years ago, was of the unusual combination of sheer size with exuberant vitality, mental and physical.'

Admiral of the Fleet Sir Dudley Pound, GCB, GCVO (1877–1943)

Sir Dudley Pound became First Sea Lord in June 1939. He was then halfway through an extra year as C-in-C Mediterranean, and had expected to retire to enjoy country living and sports, but the unexpected death of Sir Roger Backhouse pitched Pound into office at a crucial moment. His death came four years into the war, after he had very literally worn himself out in the service of the Navy and his country. The editor compiled 'a short personal appreciation from contributions made by his friends and those officers who had served with him at close quarters', one of which said 'Dudley Pound started from scratch with nothing but his determination, ability and fine physique to aid him. From first to last he was full out all the time, and drove his human machine so hard that in the end it could stand no more. But by that time the work was done.'[8]

The memoir spoke of the 'extreme simplicity of his character' which 'may also have made him somewhat reserved.' In consequence he had few close friends, but for those 'even when almost over-whelmed with problems of great difficulty he always found time to think of and enquire about one's little doings and those of his family. His patience was wonderful.' He avoided snap decisions – 'if he had one hour in which to decide, he might take 59 minutes and 59 seconds, but if he had one second, he took three-quarters of it ... the result was that he produced the most considered answer that could be made in the time available.'

Admiral Sir Bertram Ramsay, KCB, KBE, MVO (1883–1945)

Sir Bertram Ramsay, who was killed on duty in an air crash in 1945, can justifiably be described as the architect of the Allies' defeat of Nazi

Germany, 1943–45. He was involved in the planning and execution of the North African and Sicily landings in 1942–3, and became the Allied Naval Commander-in-Chief for Operation Neptune in 1944, responsible for the planning and oversight of the execution of the D-Day landings, in which no soldier was lost to enemy action in the cross-channel phase. Had he lived, he would have been as worthy of a peerage as any other of the great Second World War commanders.

His memoir combined a note from the editor, and from Captain Lionel Dawson, a contemporary and long-time friend, and another from Captain George Creasy, who had been his Chief of Staff in the planning for Operation Neptune.[9]

Dawson explained his abilities thus: 'A man, I think, most avidly conscious of the importance of detail in everything and with a surprising aptitude for ensuring that those who served with him implemented his views on any question ... Ruthless in the enforcement of his wishes ... it was quite incredible how ... the question of their correctness almost inevitably turned out to be as he had designed.'

Creasy wrote: 'He was also a good man to work with. His eager mind was always quick to grasp the essentials of a problem, however complicated, and his decisions were lucid and clearly expressed. Almost invariably he had very definite views of his own, but he was equally invariably ready to hear and consider any counter arguments. Once convinced that another view was well-founded he would generously acknowledge it and, once adopted, he would support it wholeheartedly.'

Admiral Sir Herbert Richmond, KCB (1871–1946)

Captain A C Dewar described Admiral Richmond, whose name appears at the head of the list of founding fathers in the front of every edition of the NR, thus: 'In the long list of British flag officers he fills a niche of his own. Distinguished as a historian and naval writer, he flew his flag as a Commander-in-Chief, held a Chair of Naval History, and died as Master of a Cambridge College.'[10]

Admiral Ronald Hopwood, CB (1868–1949)

Hopwood did not make his mark on operational history of the Royal Navy, but was a 'yellow admiral' who reached flag rank at the end of the First World War and was immediately retired. His memoir highlighted 'his simple faith [which] never wavered: his faith in his God, his King, his Country, and the Service he loved so well.'[11] However, his verses decorate naval homes, whether in the Meon Valley or the South Hams.

Admiral Sir Max Horton, GCB, DSO** (1883–1951)

Admiral Horton was one of the earliest submariners, receiving his first command, HM Submarine *A1* in 1905. In the First World War he proved himself courageous and bold – hence the three DSOs, gained in the North Sea and the Baltic. In due course he reached flag rank, but his last post before the Second World War was the seeming backwater of the Reserve Fleet where, realising that war was coming, he bent his considerable energy to preparing for war.

In 1942, he was sent to command the Western Approaches, based in Liverpool, where, despite having no fleet to command, he won the Battle of the Atlantic, arguably the most important sea battle of the war. The importance of his contribution was recognised by a state funeral.

His memoir was written by one of his staff officers, Commander Richard Phillimore.[12] He wrote:

> Well do I remember the thrill of my first interview with him and being told that as far as possible he solved his own problems at Western Approaches without constant recourse to the Admiralty and that he wanted his staff to do the same. He was that *rara avis* among admirals, a technician who had completely mastered the scientific discoveries and devices brought in to aid the ships and aircraft engaged in the battle against the U-boats, an ever-changing battle of tactics and weapons and science.

Admiral of the Fleet Viscount Cunningham, Bt, KT, GCB, OM, DSO** (1883–1963)

There will be little argument that Andrew Cunningham was our greatest naval leader during the Second World War. He was, successively, C-in-C Mediterranean for three years, Commander of the Allied Naval Forces for the invasion of North Africa, then, after a brief interlude in Washington, First Sea Lord for the remainder of the war.

His memoir had three contributors, 'DML' (Rear Admiral D M Lees), Admiral of the Fleet Sir Philip Vian, and Vice Admiral J A G Troup, and was short compared to those for his equivalents in the First World War, Jellicoe and Beatty.[13]

Lees and Vian wrote from personal experience of his outstanding qualities of leadership. Lees wrote of 'his superb gift of understanding and leadership', and Vian, who had been a subordinate flag officer under Cunningham, wrote of 'what made Andrew Cunningham such a superlative leader and induced those who served under him to give a little better than their best ...

Unbounded courage and compassion joined
Tempering each other in the victor's mind
Alternately proclaim him good and great
And make the hero and the man complete.'[14]

Troup wrote as a contemporary and personal friend, citing the obituary notice in the *Scotsman,* which spoke of 'his wide understanding, tact and shining honesty in thought and purpose ... earned for him the trust, admiration and esteem of all who knew him ... The least swithering neutrality with truth was anathema to him.'[15]

Admiral Sir Richard Onslow, KCB, DSO*** (1904–1975)

This memoir was contributed by Captain R D Franks, who combined a survey of Onslow's career with quotes from officers and ratings who had served with him from lieutenant to admiral: he remarked that in all those letters 'one dominant theme was "What fun it was."' He summarised Onslow's command of HMS *Ashanti* 'in which he was to win three DSOs, promotion to Captain, and to be worshipped by his ship's company.' He recounted the passage of convoy PQ16 in the words of *Ashanti*'s then First Lieutenant:

Dicky's personality pervaded the whole force, merchant ships and all. He spoke with his usual *élan* at the convoy conference beforehand; daily he steamed up and down the lines of merchant ships chatting them up on the loud hailer, and often being cheered in return ... His Yeoman of Signals [and Yeomen see all that there is of a Captain's character] wrote '... He was a very fine man and much loved by all on board, and I would say that his skill and seamanship saved us from many a peril.'

Franks gave two other quotations which revealed the man: 'He was one of those people who had the ability to project his personality over the water, and being at sea with him was a delight. When he made a signal it was always to the point and often funny and you felt as if you had been spoken to direct. I've always said he was the finest admiral I met in thirty-eight years in the Navy.' And finally, from a commander on his staff, 'Yes, I just loved that man. A hundred per cent joy and inspiration to serve him. It wasn't just his ability to lead, it was the breezy way he did it all. And even the biggest tick-off would almost invariably finish with one of those quips which had everyone rocking with merriment.'[16]

Admiral of the Fleet Earl Mountbatten, KG, PC, GCB, GCVO, DSO, etc (1900–1979)

There were three separate contributors to Earl Mountbatten's memoir: Roskill, who wrote of Mountbatten the leader; Vice Admiral Sir Peter Gretton whose subject was Mountbatten the professional; and Major General J L Moulton, who wrote of Mountbatten the tri-service chief.[17]

Roskill remarked that he had become aware of 'his extraordinary charisma, and of the respect and affection with which he was regarded in the ships in which he served', and he quoted Len Wincott, who as an able seaman had been one of the leaders of the Invergordon Mutiny, and later went to live in Russia. He had served with Mountbatten in *Revenge* in 1923–4, and had never forgotten the send-off the ship's company gave him when he left: 'If there had been more officers like him, there would have been no mutiny.'

Vice Admiral Gretton concluded his more detailed remarks by saying that the editor had invited him to comment on Mountbatten's policy and practice, and this could be summarised as 'Mountbatten's policy was to use the latest scientific advice in, and for, the Navy, and his practice was to use the results with flair, drive and imagination.'

The final section covered Mountbatten's time as Chief of Combined Operations (1942–3), as Supreme Allied Commander Southeast Asia (1943–45), and as Chief of the Defence Staff (1959–65). Moulton wrote 'Mountbatten brought to the task an open mind, tireless energy and enthusiasm, a natural gift for the rapid assimilation of technical information ... and, more important than any of these ... the ability to talk as persuasively to a handful of officers senior to himself as to a mass of ranks and ratings.' And he remarked that much the same qualities enabled him to achieve success in Southeast Asia, without the resources he had originally been promised. As regards Mountbatten's tenure of the post of Chief of Defence Staff, Moulton felt that it was too early to assess his success in integrating the top management of the three Services – but that it was unlikely that anyone else could have done better.

Admiral of the Fleet Lord Tovey, GCB, KBE, DSO (1885–1971)

He was 'Jack' Tovey when as a young destroyer captain in *Onslow* at Jutland he won an exceptionally well-earned DSO, but Sir John when he commanded the Home Fleet in 1941 and hunted down the battleship *Bismarck*. His memoir was written by RWP (possibly Rear Admiral R W Paffard), and emphasised Tovey's tenacity:

> He had immense determination and his pursuit of any objective was relentless. He wasn't ambitious, but he took immense pains to

master every aspect of his profession; he was a fine seaman and shiphandler and a great student of strategy and tactics. He constantly schooled himself to foresee every conceivable situation that might arise and to work out in detail the best way of dealing with it; in consequence he met any crisis with calmness and assurance and acquired the reputation of being an extraordinarily quick thinker in emergency. He always did what he knew to be right and fought against what he believed to be wrong with absolutely no consideration of possible prejudice to his career.

The same characteristic was shown in the story he used to tell against himself, quoting a paragraph from Joe Kelly's confidential report: 'Captain Tovey shares one characteristic with me. In myself I call it tenacity of purpose; in Captain Tovey I can only describe it as sheer bloody obstinacy.'

The memoir conveys well the stress of the hunt for the *Bismarck*, and how Tovey consistently made the right decisions, some requiring considerable moral fortitude, and how, when Churchill was critical of Admiral Wake-Walker's actions during the chase, threatening court martial, Tovey informed the Admiralty that, in that case, he would relinquish his appointment to act as accused's friend.

Admiral Sir Geoffrey Oliver, GBE, KCB, DSO** (1898–1980)

Sir Geoffrey Oliver was a gunnery officer's gunnery officer: as well as the long course, he did the advanced course, 'which he later told me he considered to have been a great waste of time.' He won the Goodenough Medal and the Commander Egerton Prize and he served four appointments at Whale Island, two as a staff officer in the Experimental Department, then as Commander XP, and finally as the Commander of the Island. In between, he managed to sort out the gunnery problems of the battleship *Rodney* which were very considerable, and to earn Their Lordships' approval plus £150 from the Herbert Lott fund.

His memoir was written by his friend and fellow gunnery officer, Stephen Roskill, who wrote 'his company was a constant joy to me – for his interests were very wide and, despite his never-failing modesty, I soon discovered what a vast wealth of knowledge in many fields and subjects he possessed. I also learnt to admire the great strength of character and complete integrity which underlay a quiet and perhaps rather reserved personality.'[18]

He commanded HMS *Hermione* from her commissioning until she was sunk, earning two DSOs, taking part in the hunt for the *Bismarck*, the seizure of Madagascar, and several Malta convoys. From 1942 onwards, he was involved in amphibious operations, training the landing craft crews, and then commanding the naval forces at the Salerno landing, where he stiffened the American resolve when things looked sticky ashore. Admiral Cunningham found him, at this time of considerable crisis:

> on the crest of the wave – calm, imperturbable and completely optimistic of the outcome ... It is as certain that he contributed vitally to the avoidance of a major disaster as it is that the tide was chiefly turned by the naval bombarding ships. For his part in the Salerno assault 'GN' [as he was known] was gazetted Companion of the Bath and also received a higher grade (Commander) of the American Legion of Merit.

His home life was marred by the loss of two of his three children in tragic circumstances, but Roskill concluded: 'His strength of character, and above all his strong though never paraded Christian faith enabled him to surmount those tragedies with the same dauntless determination which characterised his war service.'

Admiral of the Fleet Lord Fraser, GCB, KBE (1888–1981)

Bruce Fraser, yet another gunnery officer in this list, was C-in-C Home Fleet in 1943 when he led the fleet in the action which destroyed the *Scharnhorst*, the last active Nazi capital ship. Later, he was C-in-C British Pacific Fleet (1944–5), and First Sea Lord (1948–50). His memoir reproduced the address made by Sir Henry Leach in Westminster Abbey.[19] Leach said:

> His was also an acutely inquisitive mind, taking nothing for granted but fascinated by technicalities, the essentials of which he quickly grasped. Yet he never boasted of his achievements in technical innovation and the closest he ever came to admitting personal involvement was to give that gentle chuckle, which those close to him came to know so well, and quietly remark 'We tried it and it worked.' Indeed he never boasted of anything and it would be hard to find a man of his talents and position so totally devoid of pretension or pomposity, so unconscious of rank or position, and so very human and endowed with the common touch. He never sought publicity but when it came his way he would use it to promote the Navy, not himself ... The Navy was his whole life. He was a true professional whose particular brand of leadership was by example. He set himself standards of loyalty and integrity which can seldom have been surpassed and I doubt have often been equalled. This was

infectious and an inspiration to all; you knew he would never let you down.

Captain Stephen Roskill, CBE, DSC, DLITT, FBA (1903–1982)

Captain Stephen Roskill was a gunnery officer, whose naval career was effectively terminated by gun-deafness when he reached the upper echelons of the captains' list. Fortunately, he was invited to write *The War at Sea*, and from there his career as an historian progressed triumphantly.[20] His memoir was in two parts; Captain Sainsbury wrote: 'Stephen had a humility which endeared him to those to whom he could reveal it. He may have fallen out with everyone sooner or later: with most he made it up, and not necessarily on his own terms. He was an inspired but also a methodical man: some historians would be better at their craft if they emulated his approach.'[21]

The other part was written by the then Lieutenant James Goldrick, RAN, who described their first meeting:

> He asked me to come and see him for half an hour. I ended up staying until after dusk, and caught a late train from Cambridge after refusing supper. During that day of steady talk, Stephen Roskill revealed much of himself in his desire to pass on something of his enthusiasm for the Navy and naval history to a young officer who had swum into his ken … It was this desire to urge on the young which I think was typical of Stephen Roskill. One cannot open many works of naval history published in the last twenty years which do not contain some acknowledgement to his kindness and good advice.

Admiral of the Fleet Sir Caspar John, GCB (1903–1984)

Sir Caspar John's background was out of the ordinary for his father was the artist, Augustus John, OM, and his aunt was the celebrated painter Gwen John (he also had an uncle who spent his life prospecting unsuccessfully for gold). But he became a pilot after he met 'Jacky' Fisher, who advised him to look forward, not backward, and in due course was the first aviator to become First Sea Lord. His memoir was contributed by another aviator, Vice Admiral Sir Donald Gibson who wrote, 'His major contribution to the Royal Navy stemmed from his formidable intellect, which, combined with a strong but gentle personality and a noble presence, caused him to leave behind a lasting influence.'[22] Gibson added, 'Caspar had a strong bohemian side himself which he kept rather private. Its occasional manifestation much endeared him to the Fleet Air Arm, who loved a figurehead who could share their joys.' As First Sea Lord, John won the battle for the Navy's carrier arm in 1962–3, but had the mortification of seeing it overturned three years later, after he had retired. But

> the spirit of the Service was such after he left that the Fleet Air Arm was able to recover from the blow and play its part in subsequent events ... Though a stickler for high standards in a Service environment, once free, Caspar was fond of dressing informally. He loved pubs and was famous for years for his transport, which was an old London taxi. Once, when he was no longer on the active list, I accused him of keeping us up all night ... 'I always thought it was you people who were keeping me up all night,' he replied ... John's portrait hangs in the wardroom at Yeovilton, a memorial of him to the young aircrew who he inspired. These young men have been recruited, like the RNVR officers of the war years, from a wide social spectrum. Caspar always applauded their efforts, and in his own gentle, rather remote way encouraged them, and he lived to see them on the Flag List, on the Admiralty Board, and as Captains of Carriers.

Admiral of the Fleet Lord Fieldhouse, GCB (1928–1992)

The award of a peerage for naval services in peacetime is a rare event: so John Fieldhouse, as one of only eight such officers in the twentieth century, was clearly exceptional. His memoir was contributed by our then editor, who had known him since his entry to Dartmouth in 1941.[23]

It was as he reached the peak of his career as C-in-C Fleet, that Fieldhouse's moment came:

> It was here that the great responsibility of the conduct of the South Atlantic campaign fell upon him in 1982: a test and an opportunity willingly accepted, the result superbly achieved. The mixture of well-practised procedures and hectic improvisation that were characteristic of the campaign were, in the light of history, nothing new for the Royal Navy; John Fieldhouse emerged as one of their principal exponents and most successful exploiters.

The memoir concluded,

> Finally, he had extraordinarily good judgement. Consistently accurate judgement is a rare quality even in top people, and those who do not have it ought to look on in awe. John knew much better than most what would run and what would not. There is a story that in the first briefing at Northwood in early April 1982, there was a terse final exchange. Prime Minister: 'Can you win?' C-in-C: 'If you give me all the support I ask for, yes.' It was enough: just enough, and I am sure he knew how close it was going to be.

Vice Admiral Sir Peter Gretton, KCB, DSO**, OBE, DSC
(1912–1992)

Peter Gretton was one of the great sea captains of the Second World War. In eighteen months in 1943–4, his escort group played a major part in the defeat of the U-boat threat, fighting three of the four major convoy actions, HX231, ONS5 and SC130 in the months of March, April and May 1943 which caused Dönitz to withdraw the U-boats from the North Atlantic. The distinguished submariner Sir Ian McGeoch wrote:

> It is widely held that the main protagonists at the height of the Battle of the Atlantic were Dönitz and Horton, the great admirals; Gretton, though, after studying all the records, concluded that 'in fact the two chief protagonists were Dönitz and Rodger Winn' (NB Winn was the genius in charge of the Submarine Tracking Room in the Admiralty). In my view it was Admiral Dönitz against each in turn of the 'admirals' (of commander's, or at best captain's, rank), who fought a convoy through, disposing and deploying his ships, with his maritime aircraft in close support, utilising to the best advantage the latest weapons and equipment (without benefit of staff officers) while all the time training his Group as well as his own ship, then bringing the whole force successfully into action when the chance came. Indeed, Dönitz ... acknowledged this when he wrote, concerning the passage of ONS5: 'Such high losses could not be borne ... I regarded this convoy battle as a defeat.'[24]

His memoir also recorded his intellectual side: 'Lord Chesterfield, writing to his son, said "Pliny gave mankind this only alternative – of doing what deserves to be written, or writing what deserves to be read." Peter Gretton achieved both.'

Admiral of the Fleet Lord Lewin, KG, GCB, LVO, DSC (1920–1999)[25]

That Terry Lewin was the most influential Royal Navy officer of the second half of the twentieth century is a statement that is unlikely to be challenged. And of all the memoirs on which we have commented, it is suggested that this is the one, above all others, which is worthy of being read in its entirety both for the quality of the writing, and for the quality of the man revealed. The author was Sir 'Roddy' Macdonald:

> Modest and a good mixer, he was never a 'Know all'; nor did he put down those not in the same league, like me. As Midshipmen we would often argue about different subjects, even Naval History, a subject not covered in formal instruction – 'no time' the excuse. His

hero was James Cook, and we shared admiration of Duncan and Cochrane – no coincidence that all three were ahead of their time in care of people. How lucky the National Maritime Museum was later to be! Formidable knowledge, common sense, enquiring mind, humour, charm, self control, all combined with fine athletic physique and striking ability to get on with every level, marked Terry out early as a quite remarkable personality. A reliable friend, never making demands, he was good fun on a run ashore. Such a paragon presents a challenge to find the flaw. If there were any, I did not come across them either then or in later life.

Admired and respected by all three services; also internationally, Terry Lewin was (unlike Nelson) politically astute. But what was so special about Terry was that he always had time for everyone. He never took sides and seldom criticised people. He gave credit when it was due, never pretending that someone else's idea was his own. He was equally at home with the Queen and the humble sailor. He was a master of his brief and never lost his cool in discussion. I never heard anyone speak ill of him. He was a giant of a man whose love of the Navy and care for its people was inspiring. His leadership, tenacity and downright common sense made him the finest Admiral I knew in my 40 years in the Navy and that says a lot. His country should be grateful. They don't come often.

Vice Admiral Sir Roderick Macdonald, KBE (1921–2001)

When in his turn Macdonald's memoir was written by the then editor, it was brief and to the point, somewhat different from those written seventy to eighty years earlier:[26]

Roddy Macdonald joined the Navy in the same Special Entry as Terence Lewin, in January 1939 ... Roddy's career was more turbulent than Terry's – he once said he had been more 'toad under harrow' and it was a fair judgement – but it took off after a wise appointer made him Commander (Sea Training) in the Portland work-up organisation. Few who were there in 1959 and 1960 will forget his presence ... His service in flag rank included ... the post of (the last) British Commander of NATO Forces in the Mediterranean. But he was much more than a simple sailor. Piper, clan chieftain, writer and above all artist: his paintings, full of elemental energy and love of wild scenery and the sea, had a deserved retrospective exhibition in November 2000 to which, though already unwell, he was happily able to come. Artistry showed too in his way with words. Significantly, one of his articles for the NR was called 'The Gift of the Gab': in discussing the Gift in others, his own shone. And no one who was there will forget his eulogy of Lord Lewin ... once engaging and dignified, always deeply human. *The Naval Review* does not Do Obituaries except on rare occasions. Roddy was a rare person. Enough said.

Vice Admiral Sir Louis Le Bailly, KBE, CB (1915–2011)

Lou Le Bailly was one of only two engineers in our list, and by the time of his death was in a fair way to being a 'national treasure' for his trenchant commonsense opinions, frequently expressed in the national press. The editor wrote:

> There are three related characteristics ... taking his professional skills for granted. These are his passionate love of his country and its Navy, his loyal and committed affection for his family and friends, and his personal and intellectual honesty and courage – enough to lift anyone to greatness as a human being. He was absolutely convinced of the virtues of Great Britain, saw the Royal Navy as critical to its safety and security and took every possible opportunity to support both ... For his many friends he was a tower of strength ... and he went on adding people to this group throughout his life.[27]

Admiral of the Fleet Sir Henry Leach, GCB (1923–2011)

Sir Henry Leach was First Sea Lord when the Falklands crisis of 1982 broke out. The Chief of the Defence Staff was absent in New Zealand, and it was Leach who stiffened the politicians' backbone with these trenchant words: 'Because if we do not [re-take the islands], or if we pussyfoot in our actions and do not achieve complete success, in another few months we shall be living in a different country whose word counts for little.' He then set in motion the preparation of the Task Force which re-took the islands in a short but effective campaign.
Rear Admiral Richard Hill wrote that

> ahead of several other distinguished contenders, he was nominated to become First Sea Lord in 1979. This led to three years of dogged fighting in defence of the service he represented and so much loved, crowned by success that only the furthest-fetched readings of the lessons of history might have predicted, yet which always could have lurked in the shadows of the Unforeseen ... From the start it was clear to the Naval Staff and its chief that the Navy was embattled ... this was, it must be remembered, a decade before the fall of the Berlin wall and the break-up of the Warsaw Pact, and the Soviet threat was regarded as real and growing – and the 'contribution to NATO' that the Navy could make was not so clear or quantifiable ... Finally, the possibility of operations outside the NATO sea area

... though acknowledged by the government, commanded no specific allocation of resources ... Henry Leach thus had many fronts on which to fight, and he fought doughtily on all ... But when Cmnd 8288 emerged in 1981, it looked as though all the struggle had been for little.[28]

However,

Throughout the South Atlantic campaign Henry Leach's firmness of purpose and staunch support of the maritime services ... were apparent everywhere. It was in effect the culmination of all he had stood for ... It was not necessarily what had been expected, but it was what naval forces did and what no other forces could do ... and the service he headed and had so much helped to frame did it supremely well.[29]

Considerations of space have been the sole criterion for the omission of some names from this brief examination of the rare memoirs in *The Naval Review*. Those omitted are in date order:[30]

Admiral of the Fleet Sir Arthur Wilson, VC, GCB, OM, GCVO (1842–1921)
Vice Admiral Sir Tom Troubridge, KCB, DSO* (1895–1949)
Admiral Sir Richard Webb, KCMG, CB (1870–1950)
Vice Admiral Sir Charles Hughes-Hallett, KCB, CBE (1898–1985)
Vice Admiral Sir Aubrey Mansergh, KBE, CB, DSC (1898–1990)
Admiral Sir Peter Stanford, GCB, LVO (1929–1991)
Admiral of the Fleet Sir William Staveley, GCB (1928–1997)
Rear Admiral John Nunn, CB (1925–2009)

Thirty-two naval officers' naval officers. Is there a thread running through these names? All displayed determination, professionalism, humility – in their personal lives, though perhaps not often on the quarterdeck – and the qualities which are still associated with being a gentleman. Their honours were truly deserved. With the exception of Sir Arthur Wilson's memoir which criticised his unwillingness to use a staff and to make plans in advance, there is scarcely a comment which might be construed as adverse. Too good to be true? Possibly – but these were exceptional men.

3 Sir Julian Corbett and the Naval War Course

Professor Andrew Lambert

T*HE Naval Review* was set up and run by naval officers for their peers, with an emphasis on the intellectual component of the profession, and the presence of civilians has been tolerated, in a supporting role. Yet one civilian was granted the accolade of an obituary, a modest tribute to a pivotal figure in the emergence of the *NR*. Herbert Richmond composed a moving notice of his friend and mentor Sir Julian Stafford Corbett (1854–1922), by some margin the most important civilian intellectual to work for the Royal Navy.[1] His impact on the founders was obvious: they were all involved with the War Course and Staff Course, as were a large proportion of the original members. Richmond, Fisher and Dewar all taught on the courses, while Plunkett had been the best lieutenant on the 1908–9 course. They all knew Corbett, and they understood his role in delivering the education that developed their aptitude for war and for peace. While the founders chose a suitably philosophical quotation from Lord Haldane, the only student of Schopenhauer in Herbert Asquith's cabinet, Corbett had taught them the value of studying another German philosopher, Carl von Clausewitz:

> Venturing into the realm of philosophy provides another analytical tool. According to Aristotle intellectual activity falls into one of three categories: scientific, if it aims at the ascertainment of truth; aesthetic, if it has as its goal poetical creation; or practical, if it is directed towards action.[2]

Strategy is a practical subject: it produces results that have a practical utility. It also fits into the category of social science, an attempt to develop theories of human behaviour from the evidence, but the distinction between history and strategy is a matter not of evidence but

37

of intention. If we try to understand what happened in a particular war or campaign we operate as historians. If we want to know how those events might inform future choices we act as strategists. The evidence is the same, the questions are different and the ultimate aim is quite distinct. Yet as Aristotle doubtless understood, intellectual activity cannot always be confined within specific intellectual categories.

While history is concerned with the past it only exists in the present, and is dominated by the age and context in which it has been written. History is a critical intellectual tool, it helps us to organise and render coherent what would otherwise be a mass of undigested experience. Useable strategy can only be devised from reliable evidence of all contributory factors, not least history, and if the evidence is flawed the strategy is vitiated.

Naval History

While naval history had been written in Britain for many centuries, it remained amateurish and inconsistent until the late nineteenth century, when English history became professional. The new historical profession found a self-educated naval historian already applying scholarly methods to the subject. Long-serving naval educator John Knox Laughton recognised that history contained the evidence required to sustain an advanced naval education system.[3] Laughton laid the foundations of modern naval history as a branch of academic enquiry, applying the professional standards of the historian to generate materials primarily intended for the education and information of naval professionals. While he addressed leadership, tactics, doctrine and administration, Laughton did not make a significant contribution to the study of strategy. He was content to leave this subject to his friend Captain Alfred T Mahan, USN. Although he realised that Mahan was no historian, and his conclusions were often derived from unreliable evidence, he could do little more than indicate the problems. Laughton's work was taken to the next level by Corbett, the pre-eminent naval educator of the Edwardian age, a member of Lord Fisher's reform movement, and an adviser to Government throughout the First World War.[4]

Corbett developed a coherent and identifiably British strategic system from history because, after a century of almost unbroken peace and revolutionary technological change, the Navy had lost contact with past experience, and in the process lost faith in the wisdom of their precursors. However, Corbett never considered the use of history to develop strategy as a closed process, he constantly revised and refined his strategic thought through the prism of historical research, and filtered by his practitioner students. Like Clausewitz he recognised the essentially impermanent nature of strategic thought, always hoping to revise his key text.

While Corbett's deceptively elegant 1911 text, *Some Principles of Maritime Strategy*, may summarise his contribution to the education of the Royal Navy, and by extension the emergence of the *NR*, both book and author need to be understood in a broader context. Corbett developed his text through extensive historical research, a long term role in senior level naval education, and a critical contribution to the savage in-service and intra-service debates over strategy and policy that marked the Fisher era. Although written at the behest of Jacky Fisher, to enshrine his strategic legacy, *Some Principles* was intended to serve the educational needs of the mid-career and senior officers whom Corbett had been teaching for the previous eight years. However, the nature and significance of that teaching has been consistently underestimated.[5] The Naval War Course, *Some Principles* and *The Naval Review* all contributed to a process that transformed the intellectual landscape of the Edwardian Royal Navy.

Corbett, an Edwardian gentleman, had obtained a good degree and qualified for the Bar, but spent his days travelling, fishing, and writing novels before pure chance introduced him to naval history. Initially influenced by Laughton and the new Navy Records Society of 1893, Corbett quickly developed an original approach that placed naval history in the broad context of national policy. The ability to balance scholarly rigour with the more didactic demands of a naval audience would be his greatest asset. Forensic legal skills helped to create strategic synthesis from fragmentary evidence. Corbett was too good a historian to use the past as the inevitable precursor of the present; he understood the free play of contingency. *Drake and the Tudor Navy* (1898) traced the first steps toward a national strategy, one that secured England by keeping Europe in balance. He also argued that sea power was not a decisive instrument, especially in the days of Queen Elizabeth I. He stressed how often English aims had been thwarted by the lack of a professional army and the failure of combined operations, emphasising that British strategy was maritime, rather than naval. He repeated the point in *The Successors of Drake* (1900), studying 'the limitation of maritime power', because the 'real importance of maritime power' was its 'influence on military operations'. While he used history to trace the evolution of an English/British strategy Corbett did not have an audience, or the critical advantage of student feedback.

The War Course

In 1900 Corbett began writing for the new *Monthly Review*, edited by his friend Henry Newbolt (author of *Drake's Drum*). In 1902 he produced three articles on naval education, helped by naval friends including Richmond.[6] Corbett supported Fisher's new scheme and curriculum at Dartmouth. His impressive advocacy helped secure public acceptance of radical reform, and secured him a long term role in naval education. From 1903 to 1914 Corbett lectured on the biannual Naval War Course, providing between ten and twelve lectures a session, lectures often repeated at other home ports. As he never held a university post, and rarely spoke to civilian audiences, every book Corbett wrote after 1903 was addressed to a specific audience – naval officers and policymakers.

The Naval War Course began in 1900 combining education, practical staff work and the production of analytical papers for the Admiralty. After running an initial course with a random collection of long-forgotten naval historians, course director Captain Henry May invited Corbett to join him,[7] and like most military educators he wanted something up to date: 'Within reason I would prefer that you should choose your subject. It ought however to be so far modern that some lessons applicable to present day warfare should be deducible from it ... it might be desirable to treat either the tactics or strategy of the period as apart from other considerations.' May did not know Corbett, or his work.[8] It is likely he had been recommended by mutual friend Admiral Sir Reginald Custance, a proponent of history as the key to the underlying principles of naval warfare.[9] When Corbett agreed, May refined his approach, seeking to 'remind naval officers that expediency and strategy are not always in accordance.'[10] May's brief to address 'the deflection of strategy by politics' dominated Corbett's work for the next decade.[11]

Corbett's research-based histories taught him the absolute primacy of accurate scholarship, and context, in contrast to the standard texts of the day by Mahan and Admiral Philip Colomb.[12] Mahan's *The Influence of Sea Power upon History, 1660–1783* (1890) and Colomb's *Naval Warfare: Its Ruling Principles and Practice Historically Treated* (1891) employed examples drawn from existing texts to demonstrate strategic ideas. Both men lectured at institutions of advanced naval education. Both gave didactic purpose priority over historical accuracy. Colomb confessed his inability to conduct original research. Mahan did not see the need. They were political scientists, not historians, and their works were, in part, vitiated by errors of fact and inadequate treatment of evidence. Corbett had the advantage of starting work when the vital role of evidence had been acknowledged, and the system-building synthesis of Mahan had persuaded the Royal Navy that strategy could be taught through historical case studies.

Corbett was soon involved in the development of strategy and policy, and one of Jacky Fisher's inner circle. The War Course took an increasing turn towards staff and planning functions, as the Director of Naval Intelligence was overworked with routine business, and Fisher preferred to run an informal strategic planning unit. When he advised Fisher that the strategic teaching on the War Course was 'amateur rubbish', Corbett was commissioned to provide more lectures.[13] These did not deal with strategic theory directly: they were historical case studies. Captain Edmond Slade lectured on strategy, and helped Corbett produce a guide to the strategic terms used in history lectures.[14] The resulting *Green Pamphlet* became the basis for Corbett's major strategic study of 1911.

The new appointment increased Corbett's role in the War Course, and it came at a pivotal moment in his own intellectual development. A growing mastery of British naval history provided a rich collection of source material from which to develop strategic lessons while his recent introduction to the strategic ideas of Clausewitz provided the theoretical tools and structural framework needed to organise his material into a coherent system. Recognising the anti-intellectual and anti-theoretical tendency of the naval mind, Corbett and Slade opened the *Green Pamphlet* with an argument for theory. Then Corbett discussed Clausewitz's system, focusing on limited and unlimited war.[15] Having established the main lines of his strategic thought he continued his work as the history lecturer to the War Course, before delivering the book-length treatment *Some Principles of Maritime Strategy,* developed through teaching experience, historical study and a significant role in the development of naval policy. Constant audience feedback refined his delivery, while the labour of preparing two major books and several lectures enabled him to test some of the key issues raised by the strategic problem of Great Britain in historical terms. This originality was vital: old research reflects old circumstances, and old questions; only a fresh examination of the evidence can hope to produce contemporary insight.[16]

The object was to generate a national strategic model, and in 1905 Corbett began also to lecture at the Army Staff Course, Camberley.[17] The Commandant, Colonel Henry Rawlinson, proposed Corbett's lectures should examine 'the Function of the Army in relation to gaining command of the sea, and in bringing war with a Continental Power to a successful conclusion.' The November 1905 course examined 'how we can confine enemy's strategy if we are acting with an ally as in 7 Years War.'[18] Corbett's approach was influenced by Colonel G F R Henderson's posthumously published essays.[19] Corbett lectured on combined operations at Camberley and Aldershot in 1905, 1906 and 1907, quoting Henderson on the primary importance of naval objectives in British combined operations. However, the Army soon lost interest in maritime strategy.

The 1905 lectures, delivered to both naval and military courses, were published in 1907 under the telling title *England in the Seven Years' War: A Study of Combined Strategy*. Corbett provided a Clausewitzian overview of Britain's most successful maritime conflict. No British author had previously attempted 'to write history on the large scale with military principles guiding the selection method', harmonising political, diplomatic, naval and military action.[20] Fisher loved the book, emphasising that he and Corbett were on the same wavelength.

Corbett used his Clausewitzian history as the template for the development of contemporary strategy. The construction of his narrative reflected this fact, bending history to serve the didactic purpose, while Clausewitzian theory forced 'events into a posthumously conceived historical pattern.'[21] He did this with such skill that few historians have ever noticed.[22] The exercise proved successful: the students quickly adopted his ideas, using them in course exercises – and he observed 'we are fast becoming something like a General Staff.'[23] This was no accident. Fisher opposed the establishment of a formal naval staff; he wanted a quasi-official body, under his control to deal with the politico-strategic problems thrown up by his bitter rivalries with the staff-led Army and Admiral Sir Charles Beresford.

Corbett achieved a striking success in generating a historically based advanced education system for the Royal Navy, in which the principles of strategy were taught as case studies, and through the study of a Clausewitzian framework. His teaching influenced the men who mattered. Rear Admiral David Beatty attended the spring 1911 Naval War Course at Portsmouth. It proved highly significant, both as an opportunity to learn strategy and an intellectual stimulus. Beatty also met Alfred Chatfield, the brightest of the captains on the course.[24] Chatfield would be his flag captain for the rest of his seagoing service. In July 1911, fresh from the War Course, Beatty turned down the post of second-in-command of the Atlantic Fleet as useless to the preparation for war. Beatty was anything but an unthinking fire-eater – a type with which the pre-war Navy was amply provided. He was an educated, reflective officer, widely read and suitably instructed. He took a serious interest in naval history, while his comprehension of Clausewitz reflected both Corbett's tuition on the War Course and his own experience of combat.[25] Similarly, his definition of the attributes of a good cruiser captain was pure Corbett, drawn almost verbatim from the pages of Corbett's *The Campaign of Trafalgar* of 1910.[26]

In *Trafalgar* Corbett stressed the overriding importance of viewing Nelson's achievement at the strategic level, as a master class in the conduct of naval operations and strategic direction from the centre and the periphery, held together by a clear and effective doctrine to which all the key commanders subscribed, despite the very obvious fact that it was wholly unwritten, and was not shared by every officer in the service. As had been the case since 1900, Corbett had directed his book squarely at the War Course audience – 'he consciously chose his material and shaped his chapters to achieve the effect he required.'[27] The brilliance of the great battle was seen in the grandest context, enhancing the significance of the event, and insuring that the countervailing impact of Austerlitz is given full play. Pitt the Younger's alliance strategy to isolate and crush France was undone by Napoleon's decisive stroke. Only when Britain had allies with enough military power to defeat the French on land would the job be done. Sea power alone was not enough, conclusions in stark contrast to those Mahan had propounded only a decade before, but altogether more soundly based, and more durable. Similarly, Corbett took issue with Mahan on the question of concentration of force. Mahan deprecated any division of the battle fleet, and criticised Admiral Cornwallis's decision to divide his fleet in August 1805. Corbett disagreed, and rightly, stressing the offensive aims that Cornwallis was serving, the critical role his decision played in defeating Napoleon's strategy and bringing about the final battle.[28] *Trafalgar* addressed the conduct of a great campaign, at every level of war from grand strategy to minor tactics, and spoke to statesmen, sailors and soldiers. It is none the less clear that it was intended particularly to show naval officers how intensive historical research could reveal the significance of their day to day life afloat in wartime. It demonstrated the direct connection between the commander's cabin of a detached frigate, and the Prime Minister and his decision makers in London. Corbett hoped naval officers would read his book as they would 'a report on manoeuvres today.'[29]

War Plans

Fisher employed Corbett to write an introduction to the 1906 Ballard Committee War Plans. While older accounts dismiss these plans as a smokescreen, the Ballard plans, largely devised by the War Course and attached experts, were a serious attempt to think through the nature of a major war in the light of the latest experience, especially that obtained in the Russo-Japanese war. It was no accident that at the very same time the Admiralty had two officers working on a naval operational history of that conflict. Fisher wanted Corbett's introduction to the war plans to concentrate on the general strategic principles, which would 'add most materially" to their 'educational value' as 'the Bible of the War Course.'[30] This does not sound much like a smokescreen. Corbett's *Some Principles*, finished in April 1907 met Fisher's specification. It made a significant contribution to the development of the ultimate 'Bible of the War Course', his strategic study of 1911.

Strategy is a practical art: works of strategic theory must always be cross-examined to discover when and why they were written. Corbett wrote his 1907 strategic primer alongside an essay defending Fisher's reforms against 'Recent Attacks on the Admiralty'.[31] Fisher considered this his greatest propaganda piece. In March he defended his Dreadnought policy at the Royal United Services Institution, publicly taking on the anti-Fisher so-called syndicate of discontent in a military forum. It was a bold move, one that taxed his legal mind to develop an argument that would both defeat the obscurantists and avoid giving offence to thin-skinned admirals. He was careful to stress the importance of the correct use of historical evidence. His target was Custance, the leading intellect of the syndicate, a Mahanian thinker with a predilection for seizing odd pieces of evidence and making them fit his schemes.[32] He was also a personal friend of Corbett's and a fellow student of naval tactics.[33] Three months later Corbett published another Fisherite essay, 'The Capture of Private Property at Sea', supporting the Admiralty's position in advance of the Hague Peace Conference.[34]

In 1908 Corbett wrote a Cabinet paper defending Fisher's construction policy. He also supplied Fisher with historical evidence to assert the superior authority of the Admiralty over admirals afloat at the time of the Invasion sub-committee of the Committee of Imperial Defence. That paper closed a period of two years of frenetic activity supporting Fisher's Admiralty regime.[35] Corbett resisted Fisher's call for more propaganda pieces, because he considered his real work lay in service education, and he was conscious that no one else was ready to carry on the work he was doing. His grasp of strategy and policy was unique. Furthermore he understood the dangers of becoming the hired pen of any school of thought within the service, because the need for an advanced education system based on history and strategy would endure long after Fisher left office.

Both Corbett and his friend Captain Slade, now Director of Naval Intelligence, were addressing the long-term need for better education, a

Naval Staff, closer contact with the Army, and planning for combined operations in a maritime strategic context. Fisher knew that any such hopes were doomed in the short term by the ongoing political battles with Lord Charles Beresford. For Fisher the creation of a staff would have been a concession to the Beresford/Custance syndicate, for whom it was a rallying cry, while the Army General Staff simply refused to consider any strategic option other than a continental military role. In such circumstances Fisher needed to keep control of naval planning, keeping the central threads of policy locked up in his own head. While Corbett shared his strategic views, and delivered them with immense ability, he was not an uncritical admirer.

Corbett was wise to pursue long-term issues rather than current political battles: history rarely emerges from such work with honour or dignity, and over time Fisher came to appreciate the value of intellectual honesty.

Strategic Theory

The origins of Corbett's brilliant exposition of national strategic doctrine, *Some Principles of Maritime Strategy* of 1911, lay in the *Green Pamphlet*, the Ballard committee's introduction, and his work for the Invasion Enquiry of 1907–8.[36] His carefully calculated exposition of strategic concepts had three objects: to demolish the premature and inappropriate naval strategy promulgated by Mahan; to combat the Army General Staff and their continental school of thought; and to stress the critical role of economic blockade in wartime. Corbett used Clausewitz, and other German military thinkers, to provide a strong conceptual framework within which to develop the naval case, and to demonstrate that the Army's 'German' intellectual base would equally well support a 'British' strategy. The job was quickly done, without waiting for a contract. Significantly, Corbett adopted a different style of writing in the final version. In the strategy pamphlet and an early draft of the book he employed the full power of his legal mind, irrefutable logic and withering scorn to demolish the fallacies of the unreflective. In the book he used less direct language, and relied far more on historical evidence.[37]

The book retained the Clausewitzian form and structure of the original strategic terms pamphlet, suitably expanded by a broad range of historical examples – many of them from research conducted in the intervening years. Corbett continued his original argument, using the opening chapter to make it clear that strategic theory was not 'a substitute for judgement and experience.' Instead, it was an educational tool that helped commanders to reach their own decisions, equipping them with commonly held ideas and concepts, or doctrine, that improved their ability to convey their intentions to subordinates and army colleagues. That he had to open his book with a justification for using theory suggests his target audience was not predisposed to receive, or necessarily equipped to understand. Unlike Mahan he did not claim that theory could produce absolute rules, only that it would be of great benefit.

Corbett's handling of Clausewitz was sophisticated and nuanced, using his theoretical framework to create a British strategy, informed by his own mastery of naval history. He demonstrated that decisive battle could only be secured under favourable conditions by forcing the enemy to fight; choosing the example of cutting the enemy's vital trade routes. Fisher had long known that Germany's only vital sea trade was the supply of iron ore from Sweden across the Baltic; any threat to this trade would oblige Germany to give battle. Without a sound offensive strategy it would be unrealistic to expect an inferior fleet to give battle. Like Clausewitz: 'Corbett wrote this strategy book as a result of rather than as a key to historical study.'[38] He reduced naval history to order, rendered the strategic issues clear for his students, and pointed up the critical fact that without serious historical research the work of strategists was inevitably flawed. While *Some Principles* was developed from the lecture texts of the Naval War Course, it owed its public appearance to Fisher's anxiety to sustain his legacy. By 1914 Corbett's work was the basis of British strategy. In 1916 the balance of British effort shifted from sea to land, from limited to unlimited – but the framework was pure Corbett.

The commission to write an official history of the Russo-Japanese War enabled Corbett to carry his historical studies into the pre-Dreadnought era. The book demonstrated that the principles of naval warfare involving island nations were largely unaffected by technology, and that maritime warfare was different from continental models. He wrote the book from the Japanese perspective, which was closer to the British standpoint: inconsistent Russian decision-making and a lack of coherent policy failures pointed up the need for a staff. The Japanese did have a staff. He also developed the concept of a limited war, which featured so strongly in *Some Principles*. This remarkable exposition of the strategic direction of war, written to educate the Royal Navy, arrived too late. A few copies were printed in 1914. It was not reprinted until 1994.

The most important consumer of the Russo-Japanese war study was the Secretary of the Committee of Imperial Defence (CID), Colonel Maurice Hankey.[39] Hankey had been a member of the Ballard Committee. In November 1913, with the Russo-Japanese War text complete, the two men discussed future official histories.[40] On 3 March 1914 Churchill, as First Lord of the Admiralty,

> said that the Admiralty were strongly in favour ... The Navy was very ill-provided with histories. There were many memoirs and popular works, but with the exception of two books by Mr Julian Corbett 'England in the Seven Years' War' and 'The Campaign of Trafalgar' – there were no reliable and accurate works on past naval operations, based on a critical examination of original documents, which could be of value to naval officers.

Churchill concluded: 'The Navy was far less well provided with professional literature than the Army. The special subject which was now suggested for investigation by the Historical Section was the British plans for defence in 1793–1805, about which a mass of valuable but undigested information existed.'[41]

The endorsement would have pleased Corbett. While the Treasury representative complained that 'a large amount of work had to be discarded and done again', missing Churchill's point, the CID agreed that historical research was needed. Within a year Corbett was at work on the *Official History of Naval Operations,* another War Course teaching text.

When war broke out, Corbett's life's work, to educate the Royal Navy in the need for sound strategic thought, inter-service co-operation, and recognising the primacy of controlling communications over decisive battle, was incomplete. He served in the Admiralty as an adviser and historian throughout the conflict, notably drafting Jellicoe's war orders in 1914. However, his carefully crafted case for a limited maritime strategy was overridden by the Army: one million British soldiers died.

The Naval Review

Although Corbett may be considered the godfather of *The Naval Review* he scrupulously avoided taking an active part. His only contribution in his lifetime to the *NR* was a three-page essay of 1920 entitled 'Methods of Discussion'.[42] It is significant that Corbett took the time to provide a brief tutorial for students of all ranks at a time when he was heavily committed, deeply engaged in the compilation, drafting and delivery of the Official History, running the Admiralty's Naval Historical Section, and in poor health. It is probable that his old friend Richmond, now director of the Senior Officers' War Course at Greenwich prompted him. He had an opportunity in March 1920 when the War Course reopened. Richmond's strategy lectures were followed by Corbett's three part series 'Imperial Concentration', between 8–11 March.[43] Corbett lectured from the *Official History*, always intended to be the basis for post-war education.[44]

As if to excuse the intervention of a civilian, albeit unsigned, in a restricted naval journal, Corbett opened by stressing that while the *Review* existed to promote discussion, the discussants needed to agree on elementary principles to achieve any useful results. The clarity of thought and rigorous application of method that marked his legal mind were essential for discussions of strategy and doctrine. He knew that without a logical and consistent methodology the fruits of debate would be diffuse, incompatible, and effectively useless. While the lesson was addressed to naval officers, it is likely Corbett was reflecting on the experience of working inside the Admiralty during the war, where examples of muddled thinking and ill-considered argument were not unfamiliar. Corbett explained the difference between inductive and deductive reasoning, the first working from the particular to the general, through the assembly of evidence to develop an argument of general application, while the latter began with general principles and then applied them to specific cases. The deductive method, he warned, was more difficult, and likely to lead the unwary to fallacious conclusions. He took aim at a paper published in the May 1920 issue, 'War from the Aspect of the Weaker Power', which argued that battle could suit the interests of the aforesaid weaker power, as opposed to commerce destroying; although the target was the German naval strategy, any paper that wrapped up by declaring that: 'there is no support in the theory of war or in history, as far as can be seen, for a policy of avoiding battle and aiming at some lesser form of destruction' was sure to rouse Corbett's ire.[45]

He opened his counterpoint by noting the author had begun with an incorrect general point about the functions of government, drawn from Henry Spenser Wilkinson, prominent defence writer and Chichele Professor of Military History at Oxford.[46] In truth, Corbett's real target was Wilkinson, long-term advocate of a German-style naval staff, German methods of military thought and closely associated with the Army General Staff's continental school that had done so much, as Corbett saw it, to pervert the course of British strategy in the Great War. To make matters worse Wilkinson had published an ill-informed, unintelligent carping review of *Some Principles* in the *Morning Post*.[47] At no point did Corbett name Wilkinson: he did not need to. Instead, he carefully noted the failure to understand Clausewitz, and some striking examples of twisting words out of their meaning. Confusing means and ends was a classic problem among naval officers of Corbett's day, predictable enough in the service that trained men to do before it encouraged them to think. Limited objects did not mean limited means; limited war is a political choice, not an operational decision. In 1904–5 Japan had used its entire strength to seize a limited belt of territory from Russia. To dismiss as a fallacy Clausewitz's analysis, that it was not always necessary to destroy an enemy's armed forces, was hardly going to impress someone with Corbett's engagement with the text and the ability to develop its meaning for a British setting. He was infuriated by the old chestnut that battle was a means to an end, the very opposite of the point he had been stressing throughout his naval career. Once again the point was not to lambast the Lieutenant, but to administer a lesson at a higher level, to those who criticised his pre-war writing and his influence on the conduct of the First World War as advocating the avoidance of battle.[48]

What really annoyed Corbett was that a false premise and lax methodology led to the bizarre notion that the object of war was always the destruction of the enemy's armed forces, and that this was a prerequisite for peace. One or two recent examples sufficed to annihilate such nonsense: the Russo-Japanese War and the First World War. The essay had then reversed course, abandoning the dogmatic position it had adopted, and grasped at the alternative, the Corbettian way, of attacking the economic vitals as an alternative to the defeat of the enemy's armed force. As Corbett stressed, states must accept defeat if they find their 'sources of strength for carrying on the war are getting exhausted, and this is the cause, so long experience tells us, why most wars come to an end. Hence it is unnecessary to destroy armed force if you can more easily, more quickly, or with greater certainty destroy the power of sustaining it.' He accepted there were good reasons to prefer a direct attack on the enemy's armed forces, and regretted these had not been developed. Failing to develop the logic of these alternatives risked practitioners missing opportunities to secure a decision by indirect means that were equally rapid, and less costly.

Clearly, Corbett was using his critique of intellectual methodology to emphasise the difference between British maritime and Continental military strategies, and stress that a British officer could arrive at the conclusion that German total war doctrine of mass mobilisation and decisive battle was appropriate to British strategic interests by starting from unsound propositions, and using 'inconsequential inference' to build a doctrine 'which breaks down the moment it is tested by past experiences.' In sum, German strategic writing offered a suitable model for German strategy and doctrine: it could not be simply translated into English and held up as a 'one size fits all' answer to the security needs of a very different state.[49]

Evidently the rejoinder to Wilkinson, and the planned revision of *Some Principles* were at the front of Corbett's mind as he lectured to the revived War Course, the locus of his life's work, and the intellectual home of the *Review*. The evolution of Corbett's strategic thinking over the last eleven years of his life, years filled with striking new examples, the hard lessons of war, and the discipline of official writing, would have been profound. *The Naval Review* note suggests he was preparing to round on his critics, Wilkinson, Custance, and even his old friend Lord Sydenham. All three had publicly blamed him for the failure at Jutland; Sydenham did so in the House of Lords.[50] While Corbett protested in private, he did not have the opportunity to provide a full rebuttal at the time, leaving that task for the *Official History* and the long mooted new edition of *Some Principles*. Instead, he spent his last two years battling an Admiralty Board composed of War Course graduates who had forgotten the key points of his lectures, the educational role of the past, the need for a national, not a universal approach to strategy, and the primacy of an accurate and widely disseminated understanding of history in the evolution of useful doctrine. For Corbett, history provided the ultimate test of any theory or deduction, but it was essential that the history used should be accurate, carefully considered and consistent. The unfortunate Lieutenant had bundled up a lot of Elizabethan history in a package that was profoundly unhistorical, in order to support false deductions. In concluding he advised naval officers to avoid the deductive method: 'Far better to stick to the inductive method. Collect and study the ascertained facts of war history, and patiently build up your doctrine on the solid foundations they afford. It is a practical method far better suited than the other to a naval officer's training and habit of thought.'[51]

He might have added, had he not made the point so well elsewhere, that this was his method, it was also that of Clausewitz, and it stood in contrast to the system-building political science methodologies espoused by lesser strategists. This was the assessment of a gifted teacher, a sound strategist and above all man who had given his life to the service of an organisation he loved. Corbett died suddenly on 22 September 1922, leaving the official history and the education of the Navy tragically incomplete.

Conclusion

History remains the only sure source of understanding for those who do not have experience. The better we understand our history, and the more closely we study the unique, chaotic process of war, where fear, fog and friction defeat the best-laid plans, the less likely it is that we will be surprised next time. History does not give us answers; it helps us by providing the evidence from which we develop our own ideas. Strategy, by imposing system and order on that evidence, speeds up the process of absorption: it allows the many to access the experience and understanding of a truly unique mind. The process is dialectic, history informs strategic questions, which in turn can direct historical research, and ensure the strategist has a more secure foundation in fact as they proceed. The constant dialogue between history and strategy that deployed to such great effect is difficult to sustain, but vital. Or as Friedrich Nietzsche put it: 'You can explain the past only by what is most powerful in the present'.[52]

Corbett's ideas live because they were securely founded on the experience of the past. Strategy made without history may promise shock and awe, but historians have known the danger of applying simple military solutions to complex political problems since Thucydides. Corbett realised, as Karl Marx observed, that those who do not own their history are condemned to repeat it, first as tragedy, then as farce. However, never trust pure strategy – history tells us that nothing is pure, or simple, and elegant systems flatter to deceive. Clausewitz's greatest contribution to practical strategy was the concept of friction, which explains why nothing ever works as it was intended. Corbett not only saw this, but made a point of stressing it, over and over again.

Corbett used history to teach and develop a unique national strategy; he did so with uncommon skill, enormous dedication, and unrivalled impact. While he worked closely with some of the key figures of Edwardian England, and acted inside the official machine throughout the First World War, it was as a man of ideas that he had his greatest impact. He distilled the raw material of the past into a coherent form that outlasted his own lifetime. Corbett found in the past a British strategy that was unique, specific and appropriate. It blended naval and military action, political direction, and economic interests into an almost seamless whole. On the War Course Corbett harmonised history and strategy as the twin pillars of higher-level naval education, and developed the first coherent national strategy in the process. His ideas inspired the founders of the *Review,* and they survived the bloodbath of 1916–18, dominating the strategic thinking of another great historian strategist, Winston Churchill, in another world war. They inspired the post-atomic theory of limited war, keeping alive Clausewitz's critical idea that war was a political act, not just the ultimate expression of nihilism. One way or another his ideas survived the ill-informed attacks of Cold War historians who failed to see the temporary and anomalous nature of the major British military commitment in peacetime being an Army and Air Force on the Rhine. When the Cold War ended, Corbett's work was still the only intellectually coherent explanation of why Britain requires a unique, distinctive maritime strategy. British Maritime Doctrine, published as BR 1806 in 1996, and the Strategic Defence Review of 1999 were Corbettian documents.

4 The Problems of Convoys 1914–1917

Captain Richard Woodman, Elder Brother Trinity House

*T*HE *Naval Review* was first published when the tonnage and global activity of the British merchant marine was at its height. On the eve of the First World War the British-registered fleet numbered about 9,500 vessels, with a further 1,500 registered in the Dominions, chiefly Canada, whose merchant fleet was the world's fourth largest. British steamships grossed about 11,540,000 tons, with the Dominions and colonies possessing another 900,000 tons. This tonnage represented some 48 per cent of the world's total merchant shipping, was four times larger than its closest rival, the German merchant fleet, and it carried a touch under half of the world's entire trade. Such a large number of ships, which included a significant number of sailing vessels, were spread out across the world, with passenger and cargo liners running along their well-advertised, scheduled and traditional routes carrying general cargoes of manufactured goods, frozen meat and other essential foodstuffs. Meanwhile tramps, both steam and sail, awaited the seasonal cargoes such as the Ukrainian grain harvest and the Australian wool clip, making ballast passages to catch these, or carrying imported homogenous cargoes such as ores, grain or full loads of such things as exported railway lines. Many also carried coal intended for foreign markets or the bunker ports used by British merchantmen and, of course, the Royal Navy. That new fuel, oil, was increasingly filling the newfangled oil tanker from either the Persian Gulf or the Gulf of Mexico. From this thumbnail sketch both the economic importance and the strategic vulnerability of the national merchant fleet is immediately obvious, so obvious in fact that a reference in the *NR* to the Germans engaging in a *guerre de course* is supplemented in an article entitled 'Strategical Principles and the Forth-Clyde Canal', 'AX' remarked that 'our trade must be protected.'[1]

That the Royal Navy failed in this *sine qua non* between 1914 and the spring of 1917, thereby causing Their Lordships to admit to the Cabinet that they were losing the war at sea, arose from complex arguments largely opposing the introduction of convoy in the face of aggressive submarine warfare. It is interesting to observe the intellectual processes accompanying this significant failure on the Navy's part, particularly if it is recalled that among contemporary naval officers it was very largely the younger element whose thinking eventually swung in favour of convoy – which rapidly reversed fortunes – even though the duty was unpopular and would, if it were to be introduced, fall largely upon them.

At the outbreak of the First World War the submarine was an unknown and uncertain weapon. Few could have predicted its impact on that vast fleet of merchantmen, so large that Their Lordships considered that the enemy's commerce-raiders might peck at it, but could not destroy it.

This is not the scenario envisioned in the *NR* on the eve of war. In a three-part article, 'The Influence of the Submarine on Naval Policy', the author accurately predicted the impossibility of a submarine operating according to the Prize Laws, or of distinguishing with any great accuracy between an enemy and a neutral vessel, a viewpoint shared with Jacky Fisher.[2] At the same time the author pointed out the very considerable menace such a weapon would be to national survival, accurately and indeed presciently identifying the extreme vulnerability of merchant shipping in the Mediterranean in particular. 'Considering the capabilities of submarines of 1,500 to 2,000 tons displacement,' he remarked, 'it must be conceded that there is great possibility of their appearance in the English Channel or on the great trade routes.' This was followed by the itemising of a number of countermeasures, all of which hard-won experience later introduced, though with the significant exception of the construction of a tunnel between Dover and Calais. Curiously, however, the author did not mention convoy – why? Did he in fact expect its immediate introduction since it had proved a war-winning stratagem in the Great War with France a century earlier? Or had the orthodoxy of the day dispensed with any consideration of convoy?

This question was left hanging; the author in his third part focusing attention on the pertinent query arising from the arrival of the submarine in the naval arsenal, emphasising that: 'modern science and ingenuity have produced an entirely new type of fighting machine which is not governed by the laws of strategy and tactics as we know them, and for the behaviour of which in war, or for the effects they are likely to produce on the course of a war, the teachings of history are valueless, as no precedent exists.'[3] Moreover, the hope that an antidote to the submarine may be found 'is now regarded to be almost impossible.' This was depressing stuff, although one correspondent accurately considered the submarine's nemesis would be the aeroplane, a fact well-known by the end of the war. Significantly, however, the preoccupation was the effect of the submarine in the hands of the enemy on the British battle fleet, not upon trade.

The influence of commerce in war was addressed in the next issue in a gold medal winning essay in which Germany is imagined, perhaps unsurprisingly at that time of rising tension, as the enemy. Here, among the Navy's several tasks was included the protection of trade, a vague, all-encompassing reference which avoided the specific.[4] There was an apparent assumption that trade would be protected and the necessary consequent arrangements in civilian logistics and financial institutions will 'adjust themselves.' The writer summarised the enemy's war against British trade thus: 'a *guerre de course* might be executed by small squadrons and armed merchantmen, with occasional raids against the east coast' where, of course, a steady trade then ran. This is thoughtful enough, if not remarkable, but the absence of the submarine from the equation was, in the light of events, of some significance. Whether or not the author felt some unease it is impossible to guess, but the essay ended with an interesting footnote: 'The bitter criticism levelled against the Navy during the Napoleonic wars, for its failure to check the enemy's fast frigates and privateers will be mild to that which may be expected under similar circumstances in the future.' Therein lay the Royal Navy's dilemma and the cogent prophecy for its near-defeat over the defence of trade by the Kaiser's U-boats.

The author went on to mention the insufficient number of cruisers necessary to carry out the Admiralty's plan for protecting trade, namely, the patrolling of trade routes. Instead of insisting on convoy, the author advocated a self-help scheme, citing the obligation of shipping companies which had received a mail subsidy and its concomitant responsibility to undertake some state service in wartime. These selected ships were 'to be available instantly, they must carry in their holds the same guns as the enemy's ships, and their engine-room and deck complements must have agreed to serve in war ... the guns crews being recruited from a special class of the fleet reserve.'

This smacked of pie-in-the-sky and is an overly rosy assumption of the shipowner's willingness to surrender valuable revenue-earning capacity to the humping around of war stores. Apart from demonstrating a remarkable lack of insight into the regard an owner had for his ships, best summed up by Alfred Holt's famous statement that 'These are my ships!', it entirely ignored the problems that would be associated with the over-stowing of the artillery. Such revelations expose the unfamiliarity of the average naval officer with the management of merchantmen, a matter much written about by articulate masters at the time, among them Captain David Bone of the Anchor Line. There is, nevertheless, a timely warning: 'These ships should not be withdrawn from the carrying trade, as the number of merchant ships requisitioned for purely naval purposes should be kept as low as possible.' In the event, the exigencies of war would require some 5,000 vessels and 50,000 men from the merchant service and fishing fleets to be called to the colours by November 1918, some as reservists, but most under the special arrangements known as the T124 Agreement.

In view of what was to follow, the fourth issue of *The Naval Review* of 1914 is of interest, containing as it does an article entitled 'The Protection of Trade in Past Wars'.[5] The objections to convoy in the age of sail – demurrage, delays and increased costs – were said to be relatively minor, partly inevitable from the highly seasonal nature of many trades and, with the co-operation of shipowners and Lloyd's, a remarkable efficient convoys system had been organised. Although it brought forth the 'cry "more frigates" from every Admiral from Norris to Nelson', this was particularly true of the post-Trafalgar years of the Napoleonic War, that period when French privateering was at its height.

Nevertheless, the author continued: 'The tendency of the Admiralty was always to encourage the convoy system in preference to the cruising system, on several occasions they [*sic*] insisted on compulsory convoy. The reason is obvious. The convoy is economical of force'. Indeed, the Admiralty view was reinforced by the Convoy Act of 1798 and masters could be imprisoned for breaking it by running ahead of a convoy, always a temptation in a fast ship to catch a market. Their Lordships were equally hard on defaulting naval officers, as the case of Captain John Moutray demonstrated in 1779,[6] but a suggestion that one of the Lords Commissioners should have a mercantile background was rejected.[7] Whether or not this was a mistake, the contributor does not say, but he made the remarks that: 'It is a tendency to forget how large a part of the Navy's *duty* [this author's emphasis] in war is concerned with a thorough knowledge of shipping matters … A more thorough appreciation of the strategic side of the protection of trade might have been kept constantly in view', remarked the writer, concluding with a strong argument in favour of convoy, notwithstanding the changes at sea since 1815.

Unfortunately, in 1872, long before the outbreak of war in 1914, the Compulsory Convoy Act had been repealed and Admiralty experience had been forgotten. As John Terraine has pointed out, 'without being too clearly aware of the fact, the Navy underwent a major change in its war strategy.'[8]

Given the date of the issue of the *NR* in which these remarks were made, they are of considerable interest, for convoy was not introduced and would not be for some years, by which time the hard-pressed mercantile marine had 'had to resist an enemy of over-whelming strength alone and unaided, in the outer wastes of the sea, for the most part out of sight of the King's ships.'[9] This summary by the official historian Archibald Hurd was made in 1928, long after the damage had been done. The material appearing in the last issue of the *NR* of that fateful year had, of course, been submitted before the outbreak of war and it was not until the first issue of the following year that we can obtain any insight as to how matters were falling out.

After five months of fighting the mood was chipper: although SMS *Emden* had inflicted an estimated £2,000,000 worth of damage on trade, at the time of writing there were 'only two German cruisers at large.'[10] This statement was followed by a graph showing a steady decline and then levelling off of shipping losses. In the opinion of the writer 'when plotted as a curve they give a very striking forecast of the increasing security of our trade and shipping. To coin an impossible phrase, one might almost call it a "Command of the Sea"', an analysis which would prove all too temporary.

The article contained a good deal more self-congratulation but drew conclusions, particularly as to the economic strangulation of the central powers by the Royal Navy, that would prove entirely accurate. Thereafter the preoccupation was that speculative issue common to the wardrooms on both sides of the North Sea: the timing and location of the great encounter between the Grand and the High Seas Fleets on *Der Tag*.

This early issue of 1915 concluded with the first part of an article examining 'The Influence of Oversea Trade on British Naval Strategy in the Past and Present', which opened with the quotation from Mahan that 'Navies exist for the protection of commerce.'[11] This at least indicated an emerging concern that the lessons of the past might hold something of value for the present conflict, and it would be interesting to know whether any inklings of anxiety as to the safety of trade were then being felt. Insofar as this examination referred to the war then in progress, it contained the then well-rehearsed objections to convoy, namely the increase in demurrage, port congestion and, consequent upon the simultaneous arrival of many bottoms, the flooding of markets, the depression of commodity prices, and the general devaluation of trade, to which was added the old argument that the speed of a convoy is limited to that of its slowest member. To these traditional handicaps, the contemporary anxieties about smoke in great quantities revealing the presence of a convoy was added, while a further technological twist augmented the old argument about comparative speed: 'The great difference in speed of modern vessels renders convoy peculiarly unfitted to modern conditions.'

This rather vague and encompassing presumption was buttressed by the shipowners' resistance to state interference with their private affairs, articulated by enquiry in 1907 when they had informed the Admiralty that it was 'better to pay insurance and risk capture than to wait for convoy.'[12] Hidden beneath this lofty disposal of the fate of their employees was the cogent argument that insurance was generous and, in many though not all cases, the wage bill terminated the moment a ship was destroyed. To all this there were also those mis-givings in the Admiralty that the disparity of performance between merchant ships would preclude them from acting in sufficient concert to manoeuvre satisfactorily in company, to which the entirely erroneous notion that a convoy was a vulnerably large target, may as well be added for good measure.

The commerce protection being advocated was, as already noted, cruiser patrols by armed merchant cruisers which, it was confidently assumed, would be a match for the enemy's own commerce raiders. Apprehension as to the effect of submarines was largely confined to their threat to the battle fleet and the need to maintain squadrons of scouts ahead of major fleet movements. Although it is admitted that time is not on the side of the Germans, 'the more time Germany has the more submarines she can build, and the more crews she can train,' this cautionary note was abandoned a few pages later (p238) by the odd assertion that Germany's 'piratical exploits against us are merely intended to inspire in our people a desire for peace – otherwise they have no military significance.'[13] This misreading of the runes is surprising because in the first three months of 1915 over 140,000 tons of British merchant shipping had been lost to enemy action, over 90,000 of it to submarines.

After the outbreak of war the opening articles in the NR had been entitled 'With the Grand Fleet', and in July 1915 acknowledged, 'There has been the sinking of the *Lusitania* and the torpedoing of American and other neutral vessels without warning ... The enemy's depre-dations with submarines still continue.'[14] The writer went on to reveal something of the state of mind that was to cause others to think the Royal Navy's participation in the war, for all its strategic weight, to have been partial: 'No doubt the end is perhaps deferred, but the final result [of the war] is as certain as it always was. The Grand Fleet, at all events, still goes serenely on its way: The officers of the Fleet are as optimistic as they always were.' At the very least this demonstrated the isolation of the Grand Fleet in its northern base, an opinion reinforced by the author's subsequent comment: 'Reviewing the past it is quite easy to see how the enemy's successes were almost impossible to prevent. The only wonder is that they were not greater than they were.' And even now the alarm was not yet raised, despite the later comment that: 'Probably the murderous activity of their submarines against our merchant shipping is chiefly designed to frighten us.' This was shortly followed by the tonnage figures for sinkings in April, May and June, which amounted to 198,860 tons, a figure described as 'formidable' and which did not show 'any tendency to decrease', but from which that of the *Lusitania* is omitted, 'as her case was a distinctly abnormal one'.

Although the author recognised a danger, this is lightly dismissed with a false analogy:

> Obviously drastic measures are needed, and they must be offensive not merely defensive, but there is every reason to suppose this will be done. All the losses in this war are formidable, every blow struck is a heavy blow, but this is a war in which it does not matter to be nearly beaten – the British Army was nearly beaten on the morning of Waterloo – to win it we must have one side ruinously defeated, while the other, however heavily it may be battered, will be amply rewarded once the victory is won.

A century later the tone of this is chilling.

The caveat that the drastic measures that are mysteriously unspecified but whose introduction is implicit must be 'not merely defensive', suggests dismissal of convoy as a non-starter. The notion of convoy as a purely defensive measure seemed to have taken a peculiar root in the naval thinking of the day. Despite the lessons of history, the idea that a convoy acts as a lure so that, at the moment of attack, the defenders can go over to the offensive, which was what finally achieved victory in the North Atlantic in 1943–45, seems entirely absent.

That the potential of the submarine for use against trade was unrealised is revealed in the next issue of the *NR* for the year 1915, which opened with the admission that the British had not foreseen the employment of German submarines against 'unarmed merchantmen and defenceless trawlers.' This statement was contained in a reprinted letter of 31 July from Mr Arthur Balfour, the First Lord of the

Admiralty, to the editor of the *New York World* in response to a published statement by Count Reventlow.[15] These attacks, Balfour assured the world, have had no economic impact upon his country which, if widely believed, may well explain the complacency emanating from Scapa Flow. The First Lord went even further; in enumerating the 'seven and only seven' tasks of a fleet he listed first and second '[1st] It may drive the enemy's commerce off the sea [and 2nd] It may protect its own commerce,' but then concluded that 'Allied commerce is more secure from attack, legitimate and illegitimate, than it was after Trafalgar.' The extent to which this was true is highly debateable but what was clear is that, in Balfour's mind and therefore in the minds of the Sea Lords, those measures then in place to protect trade were adequate. The only credible explanation for this is that in July 1915, shipping lost to German submarines had gone down to 48,844 tons from 84,025 in May, and 76,497 tons in June, though it was to reach 135,153 tons in August.

Meanwhile *The Naval Review*'s correspondent in Scapa Flow was still swinging round his mooring buoy in early October, content that:

> The Grand Fleet, in its usual quiet way, has 'maintained and consolidated its positions' in all those waters where it sees fit to roam. Our moral ascendancy over the German Navy has never been higher than it is to-day. (Place on this rather intangible fact whatever value you like, it is any way one that cannot be ignored.)
>
> The direct and indirect results of our Navy's work continue to be, on, the whole, eminently satisfactory. These have been so ably summed up in Mr Balfour's brilliant reply to Count Reventlow (reproduced in the Press on August 2nd) that any further comment is superfluous.
>
> Certainly we have lost a large transport in the Mediterranean, and our merchant shipping continues to incur loss from mines and submarines, but these losses may honestly be called more or less inevitable. The great point is that they have no influence whatever on the main course of the war or its final termination.
>
> It has been by no means uncommon among civilians to speak of the tremendous menace of the German submarine and the possibility that, in some future war, these vessels may cut off our food supply. Facts and historical research entirely fail to bear out this idea. Shipowners are prosperous and show no desire whatever to lay their ships up. Insurance is paid regularly and rates are moderate. Freights are high but the increased cost of necessities is sufficiently balanced by increase of wages to the working classes.'[16]

There was a good deal more in this vein culminating in a small note of anxiety: 'the protection of our shipping routes is still our chief naval problem.' Thereafter reassurance is eagerly grasped by acknowledging Balfour's broadcast figures for predicted mercantile shipbuilding, which far exceeded the losses experienced thus far. This was added to his declaration that the tonnage on the British register was, in that autumn of 1915, larger than that of the previous year, by which facts many were sadly misled. Compared to the post-Trafalgar period, the difference was that although losses to corsairs had been high, the number of captures to replace this were higher still; in the next phase of the war at sea in 1915–16, matters were about to get a good deal worse, entirely eroding this sense of confidence.

The first indication that the impact of German submarines on British commerce was causing real concern to the members of the *NR* occurs later in this last issue for 1915. Struck by what he calls 'A Curious Analogy', a destroyer officer endeavours to apply lessons learned in the Boer War, fought largely on the high veldt which, it is claimed, has similarities to the open sea, to the predicament of British shipping. The hit-and-run aspects of submarine warfare are compared to those of the Boer farmers and a not altogether satisfactory comparison was drawn from the measures taken against the latter with which to inform those to be used against the former. The author's arguments were, in the light of events, naive, but evidence of the growing realisation that the only answer lay in an overwhelming superiority of appropriate assets being concentrated against the enemy. Interestingly, the author pointed out that already, in late 1915, a large number of small craft were deployed on or near the home coasts to combat the enemy's submarine presence, and that these were largely naval auxiliaries of one sort or another. Such craft mimicked the vast numbers of mounted infantry and imperial yeomanry (somewhat similarly extemporised) that overwhelmed the veldt, while booms and nets were seen as analogous to the barbed wire and blockhouses that limited the Boers' freedom of action, finally containing them. If this approach was slightly fanciful, failing to grasp the essential virtue of convoy, one has to admire the thinking that led that destroyer officer beyond the comfortable zone of complacency exhibited elsewhere.[17]

This was the last word heard on the subject for some time. There were only two issues of *The Naval Review* nominally for 1916 (but not published until post-war) and from which the correspondent with the Grand Fleet was excluded. Meanwhile the conflict at sea had entered its most threatening and dangerous phase. By the time the 1917 *NR* was available, the crisis of the war at sea had passed. The British Grand

Fleet and the German High Seas Fleets had met on *Der Tag* which had at least left the Grand Fleet dominating the North Sea as our correspondent at Scapa had confidently predicted.

As for that wider conflict, the enemy's war on British trade, that too had come to its culmination when, in the spring of 1917, the losses of British merchantmen to German submarines had reached an appalling peak. In January 109,954 gross registered tons of shipping had gone to the bottom; it was followed in February by 256,394 tons; in March by 283,647 tons; and in April 516,394 tons. With the Germans finally legitimising what had become fact some months earlier with their declaration of a state of unrestricted submarine warfare against Great Britain, a new ferocity engulfed the hapless merchantman. Unannounced torpedoing, rather than an attack on the surface by gunfire, became the norm, removing the last defence the merchantman had had, and which many had exploited with some degree of success, that of a firefight.

With soaring losses and a consequent leaching of confidence and morale among merchant seafarers, Their Lordships were forced to admit to the Cabinet that they were losing the war at sea. Lloyd George's government forced convoy on all parties and, although it took some time for losses to subside to an acceptable level, they nevertheless fell off dramatically. In May they had were down to 320,572 tons and by September had dropped further to 173,437 tons, roughly half the August total. Although this figure would peak sporadically, and never fall below 135,000 tons until October 1918, sinkings of ships in convoy were negligible and merchantmen acquitted themselves sufficiently efficiently to maintain station and convoy cohesion.

This volte-face was articulated in the pages of the *NR* for that year in an article entitled 'The System of Convoys for Merchant Shipping in 1917 and 1918'. This paper was produced by the Ministry of Shipping, which had been set up for the purpose of better controlling the national asset now increasingly recognised as the Merchant Navy. The writer's tone was uncompromising, at sharp variance with the correspondent from Scapa who now, in the light of events, might have been reflecting on his complacency.[18]

> The calculation was that Great Britain would be reduced to submission within six months. This was a scientific forecast, founded on an accurate knowledge of our ocean-going shipping and the demands we had to meet. Had no improvements been made in the Admiralty's system of defence, it would certainly have been fulfilled, though probably the period would have been extended by two or three months.

The article's author castigated the Admiralty for its lack of proper understanding: 'their intelligence with regard to merchant shipping was, to say the least of it, incomplete, or at any rate not tabulated in a comprehensive form which would bring home to the governing bodies the appalling danger which was imminent.' The article then went on to criticise the methodology of the compilation of statistics which:

> Was to magnify the deep-sea trade seven times or, in other words, it was thought that as many ships arrived in a day as really arrived in a week, which, expressed in terms of imports, would have meant some 200 million tons per annum, or about four times the imports of the year before the war.
>
> The protection of merchant shipping by some form of convoy was loosely discussed in January, 1917, but did not develop owing to the objections raised in the paper issued that month giving the naval staff's opinion. The main objections being that the convoy provided a larger target than the single ship and that the delay in assembling the vessels would seriously impair their efficiency. With the existence of this opinion, backed by the false impressions with regard to the numbers requiring protection, it is hardly surprising that the proposal of any convoy system was considered impracticable. The eradication of these notions was an obstacle that had to be overcome ...[19]

Thus the influence of a faulty analytical process had led directly to the loss of men, ships and cargoes. The article went on to discuss the Admiralty's flawed method of attempting to combat the submarine menace, in particular its consequential establishment of killing grounds, particularly in the southwest approaches, which led to 'murmurs against the Admiralty', and widespread concern among seamen and, at last, shipowners. The only successes of the patrol craft the Navy deployed were in the saving of crews but, even so, many were condemned to make exposed boat passages. Indeed, the very patrol system was a menace, the very presence of patrolling auxiliaries indicating to a submarine that a merchantman could not be far away, while their failure to rendezvous with incoming vessels containing war materials or other cargoes of especial value often led to anxious masters, forbidden to approach further, exposing their position by sending wireless messages in the mercantile code, which had itself been compromised and therefore acted as a beacon to the enemy.

In the event, the ability of colliers supplying the Western Front to act in concert, combined with the conduct of troop-ships sailing in company had begun to erode the Admiralty's suspicions of the mercantile marine's ability to act in its own self-defence by maintaining station. The theory of the large target was offset by the consideration that the enemy would, at best, be reduced to a one-shot option, after which he had lost the initiative and would be hunted – howsoever inefficiently, but at least with a degree of intimidation. The takeover of the Admiralty's Transport Division by the Ministry of Shipping along with the appointment of liaison staff began to unravel the misconceptions. In May 1917 an experimental convoy was run from Newport News under a Commodore RNR and escorted by HM Cruiser *Roxburgh*, Captain Whitehead, RN. Another, escorted by two Q-ships, *Rule* and *Mavis*, left Gibraltar under a Captain RN as convoy commodore in the *Clan Gordon*. Both proved satisfactory to all parties.

> Station-keeping, the point on which the Admiralty were very dubious and which was essential to the success of the whole system, was quite good and the captains who were interviewed stated that they had enjoyed more sleep than they had had for months.
>
> Had the convoy system then been put in force immediately on all the routes, as was strongly urged, before the enemy had any inkling of it, there is every ground for saying, from the subsequent success attending convoys, that the losses of the next two months would only have been a fraction of the ships which were sunk before the system was started on the grand scale ...

Thereafter, however, the system was developed with remarkable speed. Ocean escort was provided by a cruiser which 'handed over to a flotilla of small craft which was known as the destroyer escort' once the convoy reached the operating zone of the German submarines. Shipmasters were provided with instructions and appropriate equipment, such as extra signalling flags, fog-buoys, etc, while a commodore and a small signalling staff were sent to 'one of the better ships' in each convoy. The Ministry of Shipping and the Admiralty devised a routeing and coding system to embrace the great variety of British trade. Convoy assembly anchorages were selected and shore staff appointed to liaise with shipmasters and while anti-submarine weaponry was to take some time to develop, by 1918 even some merchantmen were bearing howitzers capable of throwing primitive depth-charges.

Not that the system did not have its problems. As the article revealed there was a chronic shortage of escorts. While armed liners could be commissioned 'under the command of a retired admiral' and act as 'commissioned escort steamers' to act in the place of cruisers, the problem of suitable small escort flotillas was less easy to solve. Nevertheless:

> The success of these convoys was phenomenal. Fourteen convoys comprising 242 steamers were brought in without the loss of a vessel, although the convoys were sometimes attacked and a tanker the *Wabasha* in the fourth convoy from Hampton Roads was hit by a browning shot. With the assistance of the escort on the spot she was brought in with only the loss of part of her cargo, and the offensive side of the system was demonstrated by a heavy attack on the submarine with depth charges. Had she been a solitary ship, even if guarded by several destroyers, it is probable she would have been torpedoed several times until she sank, as indeed happened subsequently on more than one occasion of which the *Bulysses* [a 6,000-ton steamer sunk 145 miles WNW of the Butt of Lewis] is perhaps the most noticeable instance. She got three torpedoes, though surrounded by five Grand Fleet destroyers, which had not the training in escort work possessed by the convoy destroyers.[20]

The article is a most comprehensive review of convoy operations in all its aspects and, following the prevarications, misconceptions and sheer self-delusion that had previously featured in the *NR*, rapidly moved convoy operations into the forefront of the Royal Navy's psyche. There was, as Nelson himself had remarked, no more important duty than the protection of trade. The awful war of attrition waged against solitary merchantmen 'in the outer wastes of the sea', was over and would not be repeated in 1939. For all the difficulties in overcoming the German submarine in the Second World War, the Merchant Navy would no longer be out of sight of the King's ships.

After the war the first issue of the *NR* for 1919 includes on page 95 an article on 'The Navy and the Merchant Service', in which the debt owed by the country to the latter was acknowledged.[21] The extent to which foreign nationals made up the complements of most British merchant ships in the war is emphasised, as is the stalwart service these men had lately rendered Great Britain. In depending upon such men the author suggested that an unjustifiable risk had been taken and that the country had been lucky. He went on to develop a plan for the better encouragement of young Britons into the merchant service which, he pointed out, was an integral part of the nation's sea power. The list of the marine training establishments then extant is surprising, yet the actual intake into either of the sea services was disappointing; in short the attraction of seafaring then was not as popular as today we might perhaps imagine.

It is possible to date our decline as a maritime power, as expressed by both our naval and our mercantile fleets, from around this period, so that on the evidence provided by this post-war edition of *The Naval Review*, one can assume that an anxiety was awakened in at least one contributor. One is compelled to ask, albeit ruefully, what he might have thought about the state of affairs a century later?

5 Blue Oceans, Blue Ensign: The Royal Fleet Auxiliary

Roger Plumtree

AT the beginning of the twentieth century, with major dockyards at Gibraltar, Malta, Simon's Town, Halifax and Bermuda and facilities at Bombay, Singapore, Hong Kong, Sydney, Aden and Alexandria, plus twenty-four coaling stations across the globe, the Royal Navy was well served for support facilities, linked by auxiliaries providing a coal bunkering and global freighting service to and from the various bases. Then on 3 August 1905 the Admiralty directed Commanders-in-Chief that auxiliary vessels were to be known as Royal Fleet Auxiliaries (RFA). Their identification was to be a blue ensign with horizontal anchor (replaced on 16 June 1969 by a vertical gold anchor on the fly).[1] An Order in Council of 1911 stipulated that auxiliaries were to be registered and compliant with the Merchant Shipping Acts and be classified at Lloyd's Registry. By 1914 the RFA comprised ten ships: seven oilers, a collier, a store carrier and a hospital ship. The Grand Fleet at Scapa Flow was supported by oilers, store and armament support ships anchored in Hoy Sound, with their replenishment undertaken by further auxiliaries.

Seventy oilers joined the RFA during the First World War as oil replaced coal, and each pumped fuel alongside the customer in harbour. Admiralty fuel depots were replenished by contracted tankers. Fifteen *War*-class oilers entered service between 1918 and 1920. Each carried approximately 7,000 tons of oil plus naval stores but none had at-sea replenishment capability. Post-war retrenchment saw hulls being discarded or placed in reserve. No new RFA was obtained until 1933 when a merchantman was bought and converted into a naval and victualling stores issue ship, RFA *Reliant*.[2]

Already in 1876, a Captain Scott, RN, had expressed, at the Institute of Naval Architects, the need for underway replenishment. In 1902 the

67

pre-Dreadnought HMS *Trafalgar* carried out trials with the collier *Murial* to demonstrate the viability of transferring coal at sea. In February 1906 experiments were undertaken by HM Ships *Hindustan, Victorious, Dominion* and *Commonwealth*. Each, in turn, towed the oiler *Petroleum* with water being pumped via a 5in copper flexible hose suspended from stirrups.[3] Frequent breakages marred the process and it was discontinued. Later trials resulted in the earlier stirrup method being reintroduced. By the late 1930s the oiler and the receiving ship steamed side by side secured by tended lines, twenty to thirty feet apart, with seamanship the only means of controlling the gap. The hose, passed by derrick, supported a single trough containing one or two copper hoses. Admiral Dudley Pound as chief of staff to the C-in-C Mediterranean in 1935 is credited with the development of fuelling at sea, his obituarist noting:

> He developed fuelling at sea and practised it continually. It has been of the greatest value during the present war. Back in 1930, he ordered the destroyer *Watchman* to oil from the *Renown* (his flagship) during Combined Exercises in the Atlantic. It was blowing half a gale with a heavy ocean swell. However, he did not hesitate to order the operation to be carried through, although the *Watchman* was almost lifted on to the *Renown*. In order to get a good view, he sat in the stern sheets of his barge on the booms, smoking his pipe.[4]

Buoyant rubber hose eventually replaced the copper hose; rubber hoses having been found on a captured German supply ship, the *Gedania*, they were trialled in the *Empire Salvage* in October 1941 followed by further trials in March 1942 by RFA *Eaglesdale* before being accepted for Royal Navy use.[5]

Also, between 1937 and 1942 eighteen *Dale*-class oilers were obtained from the trade while twenty *Wave*-class oilers entered service from 1943 onwards. During the war some fifty oilers were equipped with the latest rigs while the six smaller *Ranger*-class oilers built between 1940–41 were capable of fuelling three ships simultaneously.

The British Pacific Fleet

A Combined Chiefs of Staff Report dated 16 September 1944 stated: 'We have agreed that the British Fleet should participate in the main operations against Japan in the Pacific, with the understanding that this Fleet will be balanced and self-supporting.'[6] Accepting the need for a fleet train and obtaining one were two entirely different matters. The Admiralty requisitioned for forty-seven issuing ships and fourteen store carriers from Canadian shipyards in late 1944.[7] They were denied, as the Ministry of War Transport's shipping priority was to deliver imports into Britain and to supply our armies overseas. The Admiralty were forced to accept a miscellany of ships from a variety of sources and nationalities in lieu.

The fleet train's objective was the rapid provision of the facilities necessary for the sustained operation of the fleet in an area far removed from established bases. The challenge was immense. No British fleet had ever to rely upon at-sea support at such a distance from a traditional dockyard.

Manus in the Admiralty Islands was the support base, to be replenished from Australian ports. From there, the fleet and its train proceeded to Ulithi Atoll (where it refuelled from American oilers) before deploying for operations off Okinawa. Their initial deployment lasted thirty-two days. The fleet spent twenty-six days off the enemy coastline and delivered twelve days of air assault against Japanese airfields besides defending itself against strong air attacks. Oilers replenished the force on seven occasions. The fleet returned to the Philippines for resupply.[8] After an eight-day stay the fleet departed for a further thirty-two days at sea, conducting a further eleven days of air strikes against enemy targets and continual defence against Japanese suicide attacks. Oilers undertook a further eighteen sorties and refuelled the fleet on five occasions. Subsequent operations against the Japanese home islands demonstrated the insufficiency of our oilers and American tankers assisted the British fleet in the final days of operations.

An impediment to British operations was the low speed of the oilers, their limited capacity and their slow pumping timescales. The US oiler *Sabine* replenished the battleship *King George V*, pumping over 820 tons an hour at twice the capability of any British tanker on station. Replenishment was undertaken by a Logistic Support Group that usually comprised three oilers, supported by an escort carrier itself carrying replacement aircraft and air stores for the carriers, with sloops as escorts. In the replenishment area a further escort carrier provided air cover. Besides their fuel, each oiler also carried some five tons of fresh provisions, Petrol, Oil and Lubricants (POL), depth charges and anti-aircraft ammunition, and high priority naval stores demanded by the force. On completion, the oilers departed to Eniwetok to refill. Only twelve oilers were engaged on forward operations, so four groups of three hulls attempted to maintain supplies to the fleet while the remaining ten undertook freighting loads forward to nominated anchorages.

On VJ day 1945 the fleet train numbered 125 ships (712,000 tons of shipping) and was manned by 26,200 men. The RFA component was twelve oilers out of twenty-two. A further thirty-one merchantmen utilised as store carriers or issuing ships had Admiralty Stores Department working parties embarked.

Admiral Sir Bruce Fraser, Commander-in-Chief of the British Pacific Fleet, from his base on the west coast of Australia reminded the Admiralty and Churchill that in attacking the Japanese mainland, 'the distances involved are similar to those of a fleet based in Alexandria, and with advanced anchorages at Gibraltar and the Azores, attacking the North American coast between Labrador and Nova Scotia.' Insufficient, inadequately equipped, and slow ships with inexperienced crews managed via perspiration, innovation and inspiration to keep the fleet at sea. When judged against the US Navy performance, there was much to learn and standards to emulate.[9] Indeed, 'CCHH' who reviewed John Winton's book *The Forgotten Fleet* claimed no American force would have been prepared to operate with such skeleton logistics.[10] He did, however, recognise that 'the habit of replenishment at sea is probably the only lasting memorial to the British Pacific Fleet.'

The Okinawa campaign demonstrated that afloat support in all its ramifications could now become an integral element of maritime operations. One limiting factor was that the 'Royal Navy finished the war with its [steam propulsion] machinery 15 years behind the US Navy, as instanced by the difference in endurance of the two fleets.'[11] Sixteen RFA and twenty-nine requisitioned tankers were lost in the Second World War, as were three store carriers, one victualling ship, one water ship and an armament store carrier.[12]

The Korean War

When hostilities in Korea broke out on 25 June 1950, Commander-in-Chief Far East Fleet had fortuitously deployed his ships to Japanese waters as an alternative to the heat of Hong Kong or Singapore, and this enabled him to liaise with American naval authorities. On 28 June, the Admiralty directed the C-in-C to place the Royal Navy – already in Japanese waters – at the disposal of the United States Naval Commander for Korean Operation in support of the Security Council resolutions, and on station were just two RFAs *Green Ranger* and *Fort Charlotte*.

When an armistice was signed ending 1,128 days of hostilities, thirty-two ships of the Royal Navy had served in the area as had sixteen RFAs, thirteen oilers and three stores/victualling ships plus two merchant-marine manned hulls. Operations had included mine counter-measures, anti-submarine patrols, blockade duties, and shore bombardments and carrier air strikes. *Fort Rosalie*, loaded with the force munitions war reserve plus replacement stock, arrived on station three months after hostilities commenced, while the hired ship *Choysang* freighted ammunition from Hong Kong and Singapore on a periodic basis.

In addition, 'Observer' recorded,

> Behind this force has been a fine collection of auxiliaries, manned by the RFA tankers such as the *Wave Laird, Wave Knight, Wave Chief* and *Wave Premier,* who deliver their replenishments to the ships under way inside the Yellow Sea, as have on occasions the tankers *Green Ranger* and *Brown Ranger.* The supply ship *Fort Charlotte,* the ammunition ship *Fort Rosalie,* the hospital ship *Maine,* not to mention the chartered ammunition carrying ship SS *Choysang.*[13]

Underway replenishment techniques experiments had been trialled throughout 1947–49 in HMS *Bulawayo* which led to the development of improved handling rigs. Light jackstays capable of lifting five hundredweight of stores and heavy jackstays capable of moving two-ton loads were introduced while a special rig capable of a four-ton load was provided for armament support ships.[14] In 1951 *Fort Duquesne* became the first RFA to have a helicopter platform and trials demonstrated the efficacy of vertical replenishment (vertrep). In 1955 the *Tide*-class of fleet oiler entered service with automatic jackstay tensioning winches to facilitate refuelling in bad weather. *Reliant* entered service in 1959 as the Royal Navy's first air stores issuing ship for service in the Far East and by 1962 the RFA force consisted of twenty-one hulls.[15] Two improved *Tides* accepted in 1963 had six RAS derrick rigs and an astern refuelling capability plus the capacity to accommodate three helicopters. The *Fort Duquesne* became the first RFA to have a unified stores organisation in place of the former three departmental divisions.[16] *Regent* and *Resource* became the first RFAs to have an embarked helicopter for vertical replenishment.

By 1975, RFA capability in individual ship terms equalled United States Navy standards. The *Ness*-class store ships were equipped with helicopter decks, better designed temperature-controlled stowage areas and lifts to facilitate store movements.[17] Powered roller conveyors were fitted at each replenishment position capable of moving one-ton pallets. Specially designed forklift trucks lifted stores to the marshalling clearway. Procedures, later enhanced by IT programs, facilitated improved identification of a 'load' tailored specifically to the service or services being supported, with the *Ness*-class outfit eventually comprising some 60,000 different items of naval stores plus sufficient victualling stock to feed 15,000 men for a month, plus clothing and NAAFI ranges.

Total strength was thirty-seven hulls comprising eight fleet oilers, five small oilers, three stores support ships, an air store support ship, two fleet replenishment ships and two armament support ships. Bulk oil shipments were undertaken by four *Leaf*-class and two *Dale*-class oilers.[18] Two store carriers, *Hebe* and *Bacchus*, supported naval, army and RAF bases east of Suez. Six *Sir*-class Landing Ship Logistic (LSL) provided a freighting service to Army authorities, as did the *Empire Gull*, the last Landing Ship Tank (LST) in RFA service. *Eddyforth* distributed aviation fuel (AVCAT) and undertook coastal freighting while *Engadine* provided helicopter support. Manning the service was a mix of British and Commonwealth personnel. Two ships were Maltese manned, two were Seychellois, and twelve by Hong Kong Chinese. Mauritian and Singapore Chinese also provided crews in lesser numbers.[19]

United Nations resolutions in 1965 resulted in the Royal Navy undertaking blockade action to prevent oil entering Rhodesia. Seven RFAs supported the task force at various times. *Tidepool* steamed some 18,000 miles, spent eighty days at sea and undertook seventy-eight RASs, pumping a total of 38,239 tons of oil. *Tidespring* spent ninety days on station, steamed 33,000 miles, but fuelled fewer ships.[20] The irony of the situation was not lost on some. Before the Second World War, the Bulawayo Cup, presented by the people of that Southern Rhodesian town, was awarded annually to the Mediterranean Fleet RFA deemed to have shown outstanding efficiency during RASs.

The Falklands 1982

In the Falklands War, fifteen RFAs were prepared, stored and made available within fourteen days of the alert. RFAs *Resource* and *Olmeda* sailed with the initial force on 5 April 1982. *Fort Austin* sailed from Gibraltar to rendezvous with HMS *Endurance* while *Tidespring* and *Appleleaf* steamed towards Ascension to undertake forward fuel support. *Tidepool* at Curaçao sailed for Ascension to provide further fuel support. The four LSLs, stored to capacity with troops, stores, vehicles, helicopters and artillery, set sail on 7 April and joined with *Stromness* for the journey south.[21] *Brambleleaf* sailed from the Gulf of Oman and proceeded directly to South Georgia to provide forward fuel support to the ships undertaking the island's recapture.

By 15 May, twenty-two RFAs, four-fifths of the service, were involved in the war: *Fort Austin, Regent, Resource, Olmeda, Appleleaf* and *Pearleaf* were providing close support to the Main Battle Group; while *Tidespring, Tidepool, Stromness* and *Plumleaf* had left Ascension and were sailing south with the main amphibious force, which also included all five LSLs; *Blue Rover* was at South Georgia undertaking support duties while *Fort Grange, Olna* and *Bayleaf* were accompanying Cunard liner *QE2* from the UK; and with *Engadine* proceeding south to provide forward helicopter support.

On 20 May a fifty-ship force lay off the Falklands. *Stromness* and *Fort Austin* accompanied the initial assault group into San Carlos followed later by the five LSLs and their troops. RFA personnel were drafted to assist ships taken up from trade (STUFT), with 90 per cent of the RFA communications personnel at sea.

In a few weeks the RFAs experienced ten years of normal flying operations, and *Sir Percival* gave the pilot of the thousandth helicopter to land a liquid award. A flight of 824 Squadron participated in *Olmeda*'s vertrep programme 185 times between April and June. *Resource*'s embarked flight assisted the move of 4,000 pallets, while two Wessex from 848 Squadron on *Regent* lifted 2,562 pallets. *Fort Austin* embarked four Sea Kings and undertook ASW support. *Engadine* experienced 1,606 deck landings and a further 450 deck fuellings.[22] *Stromness*, without an embarked flight, off-loaded some 750 troops by helicopter and issued some 2,900 pallets via vertical replenishment. The five LSLs, not provided with an air flight, had aircraft on deck moving stores, passengers or refuelling.[23] The exploits and sad loss of *Sir Galahad* was detailed in *The Naval Review*.[24] The bravery of RFA personnel during the conflict was awe-inspiring.[25]

Admiral Sir John Fieldhouse, Commander-in-Chief Fleet commended the RFA:

> From the very beginning of the operation, with the ships detached from Exercise SPRINGTRAIN, to Ascension Island, South Georgia and the heat of the battle for the Falkland Islands, the Royal Fleet Auxiliaries have been in the thick of things. They have supported the Task Force with supreme efficiency and flexibility, have never flinched in the face of danger and have fought with great courage. We have grieved at their losses, which were not in vain, and have rejoiced at their triumphs. The land, sea and air elements of the Task Force could not have been operated without the Royal Fleet Auxiliary and we salute them.'[26]

Indeed, the conflict had, in the words of the official historian, demonstrated the crucial importance of naval air power and the presence of forward afloat support: 'The sealift was if anything [even] more remarkable.'[27]

Indeed: the RFA tanker supply chain had delivered 400,000 tons of fuel to the South Atlantic and without this afloat support operations there would have been impossible. This achievement and the force levels of the RFA throughout the remaining 1980s and the 1990s made it possible for the 1998 Strategic Defence Review to say: 'In the post Cold War world, we must be prepared to go to the crisis rather than have the crisis come to us.'[28]

The Gulf Wars

The 1991 Gulf War was totally dependent upon the prompt delivery of equipment and stores before operations could commence.[29] Over 90 per cent of British and American logistic needs were delivered from the sea while in-theatre afloat logistics was equally effective:

> Resupply over nearly 300 miles of ocean was still being effected by a roulement of LSL and Sea King, with the combination of the everwilling 845 Squadron and *Sir Percival* prominent. There were, by this time, three groupings of British ships abreast of Kuwait, allowing me to rotate key units within the area north of the Dhorra Field. *Exeter*, *Brilliant* and *Brave* alternated as CTUs and close escorts. Every conceivable level of afloat support was now available to me, precisely where it was needed – within 50 miles of the very front line. Clear examples of their utility included diving teams from *Diligence* assisting the stricken [USS] *Tripoli*; surgical support to injured crewmen from [USS] *Princeton* being provided onboard *Argus*; *Olna* fuelling USN escorts as a delivery boy just south of their frontline screening stations; and *Fort Grange* pulsing loads into all escorts by vertrep over ideally short transit distances. If one must go to war, then such efficient and timely reassurance as this is always to be coveted – and it was, by many.[30]

Notably, the replacement *Sir Galahad* (in service 1988, sold to Brazil 2007) was the first ship to enter Umn Qasr with humanitarian aid, and, later, *Sir Bedivere* became the training ship for the UK-led Iraqi Navy Training Team. Discussing Desert Shield and Desert Storm, the RFA was described as 'surely one of the most important developments we have made since WWII.'[31]

The RFA and Logistics

Despite these achievements the words Royal Fleet Auxiliary and its acronym are conspicuous by their absence in all volumes of *The Naval Review* prior to 1943. This omission was perhaps understandable when the RFA was a freighting service, but the omission of any perspective of the criticality of fleet oilers when writing on strategic propositions suggests that *NR* contributors did not envisage any lessening of reliance upon traditional dockyards for support. Even in the interwar years when writing on the possibility of war against Japan in the Pacific, the question of support was never adequately addressed in *The Naval Review*.

The term Royal Fleet Auxiliary was first cited in an appreciation of the former First Sea Lord Admiral of the Fleet Sir Dudley Pound (quoted above), whose interest did not stop at the ships and men of the Royal Navy. He had made a point of visiting all the Royal Fleet Auxiliaries, oilers, store ships and armament supply ships. The pleasure and surprise which these visits caused was reflected in the faces of their captains receiving him on his arrival at the gangway and the group of men who were gathered at the rail when he left. The inclusion of this event in his obituary suggests that such visits had not been undertaken by previous C-in-Cs. This seems to validate the 1946 comment:

> Logistics – the science of supply of armed forces in the field – was not a subject about which naval officers thought a great deal before the war. You needed fuel, ammunition and provisions when you came into harbour and there were some organizations in all British naval ports which arranged these things. Most naval officers got as far as knowing that these organizations were staffed by civilians; and they dismissed them, over an evening glass of gin, with the semi-contemptuous comment that it was no good ringing them up on Saturdays because they had started their weekend by then. The only seagoing officers who had anything like direct contact with these organizations were certain officers on the staffs of the commanders-in-chief and flag officers afloat who dealt with supply and administration.[32]

Those of a gentle disposition should not attempt to read the composition of the British Pacific Fleet and its Fleet Train (note the capital letters) which 'Valor' listed in 1946. According to Valor, 'an account of this struggle [to establish the Fleet Train] would make sorry reading: the Ministry of War Transport's reluctance to allocate ships, the hesitation in certain quarters of the Admiralty as to whether they were really required or not, and the vacillations of the Americans over the allocation of ships that they originally said they would provide.' The ships were described as 'this motley collection was made up of White, Blue and Red Ensign ships (some of the latter actually being Norwegians and Dutch) under the command of a rear-admiral.' Roskill however reminded the reader that these 'tankers and store ships needed to supply the Fleet were often unsuitable in performance or equipment.'[33]

Valor went on to describe how the Pacific Fleet on deployment was replenished at sea near its operating area, every four or five days, by a group controlled by the Commander Logistic Support Group, with the evolution lasting up to two days. The replenishment force usually consisted of three or four oilers, two or three escort carriers, a victualling store issuing ship and an armament store issuing ship escorted by frigates, sloops and destroyers. The Commander Logistic Support Group was accommodated in one of the sloops and always remained in area. The amalgamated Task Force and Support Group escorts manoeuvred into one large circular screen. Battleships and carriers usually fuelled from astern by two buoyant hoses and at the same time the latter took aviation spirit by a third smaller hose also from the stern. Cruisers fuelled alongside or astern according to the availability of oilers: destroyers nearly always alongside. Pumping speed was 300 tons an hour with some refuelling taking ten hours. Store replenishment was via block and jackstay with ammunition by whip and inhaul – including the transfer of bombs via that method, enabling the fleet during the Okinawa operation to fly 4,852 sorties, drop 875 tons of bombs and rocket projectiles, destroy 100 enemy aircraft and damage seventy others.[34]

The continuous sea time, its novel support process and the usage of naval aviation as the principal offensive weapon, made the RN's brief participation in the Pacific War a revolution in naval affairs. 'Avis' writing in 1950 called it a magnificent service that was rendered but considered that the whole arrangement was illogical and suggested – for the first time – that the RFA should be placed under the naval staff:

> We used and expanded our existing RFA and added merchant fleet auxiliaries to cope with the new requirements; and whilst not wishing to belittle the magnificent service which they rendered in the Pacific as elsewhere, it cannot be denied that the whole arrangement was illogical and there were from time to time alarming creaks … The RFA should be placed under the direct control of the Naval Staff on the same footing as other HM ships.[35]

In Peace and War

Writing in 1952 'X' continued the theme that naval officers in general paid insufficient interest in logistics, and provided an exposition of the Admiralty Supply Directorates of the time, the expansion in inventories, the general mechanics of supply, and the importance of the RFA in supporting the Fleet.[36] He quoted one example of the expansion and cost of onboard spares. Radio and radar spares for a fleet carrier in 1939 were valued at £15,000; in 1951 the value amounted to

£330,000, and that was the cost for a destroyer in the First World War. He continued:

> Much of our pre-war storage, particularly in naval ports, was destroyed by enemy action, and much of that which was not destroyed is old and uneconomic. We are starting to rationalize our depots, at the same time avoiding key areas, or at least dispersing essential types of stores so that they are not all in one key area. Our long-term policy is to have the main depots outside the main ports and towns. Thus storage at Exeter serves the Devonport area. The construction of a big victualling depot at Botley for the Portsmouth area is well under way. Air stores are duplicated between Perth in Scotland and Llangennech in Wales. Radio and radar stores are kept at a disused ammunition factory at Risley, near Warrington. In the north we have several storages, such as Carfin and Wishaw in the vicinity but clear of the Clyde, and others near the Forth. There are large naval armament depots in Wales, the west Midlands, north-west England and western Scotland.[37]

X recognised the value of at-sea support: the issuing ships employed in peace form the nucleus of the fleet train:

> During the last war, when the British Pacific Fleet was operating some five to six thousand miles away from their advanced base at Sydney, a vast fleet train was necessary to replenish it. This consisted of tankers, various types of store issuing ships and store carriers, hospital ships, repair ships, aircraft repair and supply ships, depot ships, tugs, distilling ships, and so on. Even a floating brewery was planned and came into use. This novel fleet train proved itself indispensable in ocean warfare and the threat from nuclear weapons made it more and more important to keep the Fleet and its supplies on the move in the wide oceans.[38]

The lesson, the reader might think, had been learned, and in 2004 'St Emilion' reinforced this:

> The role of underway replenishment of fuel, food, stores, and ammunition is as important as ever and possibly even more critical in the era of expeditionary operations. I do not see this changing in the future, not least because it is one of the earliest, most widespread and most effective demonstrations of military co-operation and interoperability; ships of the RN have been supplying ships of other nations, and vice versa, since the Second World War. Moreover, it demonstrates one of the most important principles of inter-operability, namely that it is agreement on common procedures,

common communications and key common components that make for interoperability rather than the purchasing of the same platforms from the same manufacturer. This is of fundamental importance if we are to deal with the tough industrial, economic, social and political issues which will increasingly affect defence equipment decision making.[39]

To Be or Not To Be

Meanwhile, in October 1979 M W F Day took considerable exception to a book review written by a very distinguished submariner in which he believed the latter had placed the RFA service in a condescending light by criticising their utilising a third of the space in the publication *Warships of the Royal Navy*. The writer then proceeded to detail the benefits to the fleet of a modern RFA service, in particular the number of helicopters (twenty-eight) operated from RFAs. He finished with a big gun salvo:

> It may upset those who remember the old navy with nostalgic pride, and I often wish I could, but the inherent bias shown against the RFA must be replaced. There should be awareness that, though the ships are not commissioned, though they are different, the Royal Fleet Auxiliary is a necessary and professional service, and we are on the same side. Indeed, the Royal Navy sails ... courtesy RFA.[40]

'Spider' provided a gentle rebuke but believed that the inherent bias was 'an old navy attitude certainly not prevalent today.' He continued that his command of a small group of ships had been a total delight because of the total RN/RFA integration that had been displayed during the Far East deployment.[41]

However, the pages of *The Naval Review* have been filled with various proposals for the RFA to be navalised. Many proposals lapse when evaluated against Doctor Johnson's alleged advice, 'before we honour this man's pretensions, let us enquire into his justifications', as many merely stated the proposition and failed to produce any justification. However, some did.

In 1955 in 'Sea Time for the Asking', 'JWC' repeated the case for navalisation of the RFA because

> Dispersal and mobility are now the keynotes of defence planning, and greater importance than ever before must be attached to afloat support for the fleet. It follows that the transfer of the Royal Fleet Auxiliary Service to the White Ensign – a measure which will ensure that fleet train units are manned by disciplined and mobile personnel instilled with common doctrine and traditions.[42]

Submarines Passing the Dreadnought
W L Wyllie

arly editions of *The Naval Review* were illustrated with coloured, fold-out plans, and reproductions ke this one, an engraving by W L Wyllie originally captioned 'New Factors in the naval scene'.

The first of the 'daughter' navies: HMCS *Rainbow*, an Apollo-class cruiser who served in the RN under the same name, enters the Royal Canadian Navy's Pacific base at Esquimalt for the first time on 7 November 1910. (Canadian War Museum)

On the eve of war, 4 October 1913, the Australian fleet unit, led by HMAS *Australia* arrives in Sydney. (Sea Power Centre, Australia)

Royal Naval Division

France 1916

Up Anchor!

The operations of the Royal Naval Division, which suffered 40 per cent of the Royal Navy's casualties in the First World War, and which was largely manned by RNVR and RM officers and men, were well-reported on in *The Naval Review* in words, pictures and maps. Humour was never far from the pages of *The Naval Review* or life in the Navy, as shown here in a Christmas card from the Royal Naval Division on the Western Front in 1916.

Admiral Sir William Henderson, KBE (1845–1931), from a large naval family in which his two brothers and a nephew all became admirals, was first editor of *The Naval Review* 1913 to 1931.

Admiral Sir Reginald Plunkett-Ernle-Erle-Drax (1880–1967), seen here as captain, was one of the founders, contributed to *The Naval Review* for half a century, and was briefly the acting editor in Henderson's absence abroad.

In 1937 *The Naval Review* carried a nostalgic montage of ships in which Royal princes had served in or commanded included the battleship HMS *Collingwood* in which HM King George VI had, as HRH Prince Albert, served at the Battle of Jutland.

y comparison with the usual pictures of pristine ships, this rare picture shows the armoured cruiser MS *Kent* under self-maintenance after her hunt for the German cruiser SMS *Dresden* after the Battle f the Falklands, 1914. (Martin Reed)

ent's officers: a close inspection of the stripes on their sleeves shows how quickly the RNVR had een integrated in to the regular Navy. (Martin Reed)

Je donne ma parole d'honneur au capitaine
Arthur Snagge que pendant mon voyage, tant
que je serai sous sa garde, je m'abstiendrai de
toute tentative de regagner ma liberté.
   En faisant cette promesse au capitaine
Arthur Snagge, je me considère comme
engagé vis-à-vis de lui, personnellement, et
pour toute la durée de ce voyage

                                    Charles,

Glowworm
1 novembre 1921.   Empereur d'Autriche.
                    Roi de Hongrie

A consequence to the First World War which many may not think of: the surrender
of the Austrian Emperor onboard the monitor HMS *Glowworm*, flagship of the
Senior Naval Officer, Danube Flotilla, on 1 November 1921; many rulers have given their parole
onboard HM Ships, but Charles of Austria was only the third emperor to do so.

A picture which would have been typical of any part of the Royal Navy or its clones
in the interwar years: here, HMAS *Canberra* and an 'S'-class destroyer at the
Hobart Regatta in 1932, with a seaplane from the carrier HMAS *Albatross* overhead.
(Sea Power Centre, Australia)

His Majesty's Armed Dhow *Jedel el Karim*.

12-pdr gun showing improvised caterpillar wheel tread.

Illaloes (tribal mercenaries employed by the Royal Navy).

wo articles in 1921, 'Smashing the Mullah' about an attempt to eradicate lawlessness in Somalia, ould with a change of technology and vocabulary have been written eighty years later about anti-iracy operations. Both articles were illustrated with maps and pictures in *The Naval Review*.

HMS *Diomede* at Moorea, Society Islands.

HMS *Diomede* in George Sound, South Island, NZ.

Napier earthquake, searching for bodies.

Napier earthquake, clearing streets of debris.

Royal Marines in the bush: operations in Western Samoa, 1930.

Naval base at Devonport, Auckland, NZ.

The New Zealand Division of the Royal Navy (as it was known until 1941) in the 1930s: humanitarian relief after natural disasters was a typical role of the Royal Navy, across the world from the Pacific to the Mediterranean. Reproduced above is an original montage from *The Naval Review*.

JWC also envisaged no change of complement, asserting that RFA personnel costs exceeded that of a roughly equivalent number of officers and men; that the current serious lack of sea experience within the RN would be resolved while the avenue of employment thus opened would provide officers and men with an extended career under attractive conditions and thereby stimulate recruiting. He believed that opposition from the vested interests would be overcome by permitting 'adequate safeguards', ie, granting RFA personnel the opportunity of transfer to the White Ensign. Watchkeepers would be obtained from passed-over lieutenant commanders and lieutenants and from sub lieutenants from the Branch List. Selected engine room artificers would be given a new officer appointment when time-expired while chief engineers and supply officers would be individuals no longer required in the active fleet. Ratings completing regular engagements were believed likely to volunteer for a continued seagoing career, better living conditions and the more settled life prevailing in merchant-type vessels. Objections from Admiralty Supply Departments were to be disregarded. The article ended by suggesting if a complete transfer was impracticable, that 'Fleet Attendance' vessels (in immediate support of the fleet) should be transferred, leaving mere 'Freighting' vessels (associated with the procurement and distribution of stores) under the Blue Ensign.

'DHT' replied.[43] He accepted that many naval officers shared such views but considered that the disadvantages outweighed the advantages, and had never been presented. He doubted the probability of time-expired men volunteering: men are leaving the naval service now because there is plenty of lucrative employment ashore while the naval manned ships could not necessarily be those on harbour service. He totally dismissed any likelihood of any merchant seaman accepting naval service when each had the liberty of signing on for one voyage and then staying ashore for as long as each liked. He doubted the value to young ratings: cargo handling, humping oil hoses or watchkeeping as lookouts or helmsmen at sea. His crucial point was that elements of the tanker fleet unused in peacetime on fleet replenishment duties were employed in freighting oil for both naval and commercial customers at market freight rates. He believed a White Ensign-managed fleet would cost more and not pay their way. He considered a naval complement would be double while naval leave entitlements would cost each tanker forty days lost revenue a year and thus accrue a financial loss. Cross-transfer between freighting and fleet attendance hulls for refit purposes would pose problems especially if the hulls changed from Merchant Navy manning standards to RN standards 'very considerable and costly alterations would be necessary.' His closing sentence was straightforward: 'I do not think there would be any opposition from the Admiralty to the naval manning of auxiliaries if it were considered to be practicable, economical or worthwhile from the training aspect but I hope I have been able to show that it is none of these things.'

The correspondence column provided a riposte from 'OBS'.[44] He ridiculed the likelihood of complement equivalence, asserting that the naval complement would need to be at least twice the RFA total to keep the ship to naval standards, citing the naval duty watch in harbour which was matched on an RFA by two quartermasters. (The naval complement of the *Bulawayo* was three times that of the equivalent *Olna*.)[45] Such an expanded complement thus eliminated any likelihood of comfortable accommodation. It would be better, OBS wrote, to have 'our Auxiliary run by first rate Merchant Navy officers' rather than passed-over naval officers. Ouch! He concluded, 'the RFA does a very good job, and does it better than we are likely to be able to do it. Let us keep our hands off and let them get on with it.'

Twenty-six years later, 'A' suggested that a new class of RFA, termed the Auxiliary Oiler Replacement or AOR, merited a naval party approaching 180 people to operate the communication, operations and weapons departments supported by a supply and secretariat cell and intimated that with that complement allied to the hull's limited self-defence and ASW capabilities, it was illogical to have a mix of RFA and RN people, when many tasks could be rationalised.[46] He believed dual working conditions and disciplinary procedures in such a personnel mix would produce bad morale, indiscipline leading to a lowering of efficiency and standards, while the RFA's higher standard of living conditions would exacerbate matters. His solution was full RFA integration into the RN with officer induction via Dartmouth followed later by a sub-specialisation course of RFA allied to options to obtain Merchant Service qualifications. Merchant seamen already in the RFA would be given an option to belong to the RFA sub specialisation.

In a strong riposte 'MD' demolished A's proposition.[47] Questions about operational capability were answered in depth as was the history of whether or not to arm the AOR or fit her with Chaff and eventually 20mm weapons.[48] MD argued that gunnery courses and multi-skilling by the RFA crew was an accepted requirement, while technology fits would enhance action information options via standardisation between the RFA and the fleet.[49] Personnel competences identified by Watchkeeping Certificates produced the surprising information that the RFA standard was higher than that of the Royal Navy and that the latter's Watchkeeping Certificate was not recognised by the RFA because the syllabus was deemed insufficient: officers of the watch in

RFAs had far more responsibility than their naval equivalents. Proposals for RFA personnel to accept RN-style accommodation standards (of that time) was rejected outright on the basis that 'in our lifetime in the service we will spend nearly three times as much sea time at sea on ships as our naval counterparts.' The Merchant Service Act and its Code of Conduct were stated as capable of achieving anything that the Naval Discipline Act (NDA) obtained, although during the Falklands War the RFA did, in fact, operate under the NDA.

It appeared that the only similarity between the RN and the RFA was the grey paint on their hulls, and their *amour propre*. Like Doctor Johnson's assertion 'that he did not think ill of a man but that he believed him to be an attorney', MD traded insults by suggesting that A must be a pusser![50] 'Gentlemen,' MD asked,

> The professional RFA is aware of the needs for the future. It is also aware of the worries and concerns of our colleagues in the Royal Navy, who exercise our 'charter'. I am sure you will find we are going ahead, perhaps not always at 'flank speed' (for fools rush in where angels fear to tread), and we are preparing ourselves to provide you with the support service you will require in the 1990s and the next century. There is a requirement for more exchanges of experience, but that will only be possible with a change of attitudes, and you must be the innovators on that account. Where the Royal Navy leads, the RFA will follow and support.

There were however many more things to admire about service in the RFA including its sea:shore ratio. 'Blackbess' posited what he called the RFA solution as the medicine to cure the Navy's ills:

> Perhaps the RFA have got the balance right with seagoing opportunities, including command, right up until retirement age, accompanied by sensible leave arrangements and relatively few staff assignments ashore. RFA deck officers also spend much longer learning and practising the fundamentals of their profession: seamanship and navigation. By pruning the shore-based structure, adopting similar leave arrangements to the RFA and 'stretching' seagoing commitments across a full career, the RN could allow its officers to 'grow' naturally and make more effective use of their training and experience. Essential staff posts ashore could then be filled by officers with current, and an expectation of ongoing, operational experience. With more officers serving at sea for longer, recruitment targets, training throughput and overall numbers could be reduced considerably.[51]

The Future

The absence of any British naval supply depot east, south or west of Gibraltar only serves to magnify the importance of the service undertaken by the RFA to the Fleet.

The RN/RFA bond has been forged in peace and augmented by blood in war. It has become a relationship that has spanned the globe. It is likely in this century of as yet unknown unknowns that in whatever sea the White Ensign is flown the Blue Ensign will be in company. As Vice Admiral Blackham puts it: 'The Royal Fleet Auxiliary plays a vital role in keeping our prime assets in the right place suitably prepared. The RFA in particular offers more than that. It shows on a daily basis how effective we can be at projecting, and sustaining indefinitely, influence and capability with an effective sea-based logistic train.'[52]

6 The Long Shadow of the Dardanelles on Amphibious Warfare in the Royal Navy

Professor Richard Harding

THERE are few occasions upon which sea power can be expected to exert decisive military or diplomatic pressure with the éclat common in dramatic land battles. In 1805 Trafalgar did not have the impact of Austerlitz. The Battle of the Atlantic did not provide a publicly understood turning point comparable to Operation Cobra in Normandy in July 1944 or the Rhine crossings in March 1945.[1] Sea power, for the most part, relies on a constant pressure, largely invisible to the public, which makes decisive events on shore possible. During the First World War this was clearly the case. Naval blockade exerted continuous pressure on the central powers and preserved the worldwide lines of communication along which the entente powers received the essential supplies to exert overwhelming force on the Western Front in the summer of 1918.

There was one occasion when this vital enabling role might have been exchanged for a dramatic diplomatic *coup de théâtre* – at the Dardanelles in the early months of 1915. The story is well known. The entry of Turkey into the war in October 1914 put pressure upon the Russians, who requested that Britain and France make some demonstration against the Turks to distract them from attacking Russia in the Caucasus. The Russians had suffered serious reverses on the Eastern Front during the opening weeks of the war and Turkish hostility also closed off the possibility of maintaining supplies to the Russians through the Black Sea. Turkey therefore posed a significant problem. However, the prevailing view in London, and other allied capitals, was that, after their poor performance in the Balkan Wars (1912–13), Turkish forces were unlikely to put up much resistance to a first-class European force and they believed that the unpopular government in Constantinople would crumble at the loss of any further prestige. The appearance of an Allied fleet off Constantinople would be that blow to prestige. Turkey would exit the war, the supply lines to Russia would be open and the neutral nations in the Balkans would flock to the Allied cause.

The diplomatic impact was tantalising and the critical operational requirement was for a fleet to advance through the Dardanelles to threaten Constantinople. As the first official report of the Dardanelles Committee concluded, enthusiasm for the potential advantage rather outweighed attention to the planning and preparation necessary to make it happen.[2] Once the First Lord of the Admiralty, Winston Churchill, had got a positive response from the Vice Admiral Commanding in the Eastern Mediterranean, Sir Sackville Carden, that the Dardanelles could be forced by a methodical advance, he vigorously championed the campaign, overcoming or incorporating objections to the scheme. As a result, Carden was urged into action and the plan was expanded and developed even while the opening moves were being undertaken. Troops were allocated for an attack upon, and occupation of, the Gallipoli Peninsula at the same time as naval forces were being assembled to force a passage through the Dardanelles.

Apart from the topographical features of the Dardanelles, with its strong westerly current from the Sea of Marmara, flowing between the broken, hilly country of the peninsula, and a flatter Asiatic coastline, the defences of the Dardanelles consisted principally of forts, mobile howitzer batteries and minefields. Carden's first attack on 19 February 1915 was designed to destroy the outer fortifications to allow minesweeping up towards the Narrows from where his battleships could bombard the two forts of Kilidulbahir and Canakkale. Minesweeping was carried out by converted trawlers, manned by civilian crews. Slowed by the currents and the cumbersome sweeps, and harassed by indirect fire from mobile howitzers out of sight of the warships, the task was dangerous and unnerving. The day was not a success. From the warships, it soon became evident that seeing the individual enemy guns was vital to be able to engage or silence them. A renewed attack on the 25 February was more successful. The outer forts were silenced and the minesweeping proceeded about six miles towards the Narrows. Landings managed to complete the destruction of the forts, but as the days passed resistance on land increased. A reorganisation of the minesweeping by manning the trawlers with volunteers and naval ratings was a move to make this critical function more reliable.[3]

On 18 March, Carden's successor, Rear Admiral John de Robeck, mounted the famous naval attack on the Narrows. The French battleship *Bouvet*, and the British *Irresistible* and *Ocean* were lost to mines, and HMS *Inflexible* badly damaged. The French ships *Gaulois* and *Suffren* retired seriously damaged by gunfire. De Robeck and Rear Admiral Sir Rosslyn Wemyss agreed that a further naval assault was impracticable and, from henceforth, the Navy would support the Middle East Expeditionary Force attack upon the Gallipoli peninsula in the hope that this operation would drive the Turks from their Dardanelles defences and open the way to Constantinople.

During the Gallipoli campaign, which lasted from the landings on 25 April 1915 until the final re-embarkation in the early hours of 9 January 1916, the Royal Navy played a traditional role in supporting the expeditionary army. It landed or embarked troops, animals, equipment and stores. It protected the anchorages and the lines of communication. It provided bombardment support and aerial reconnaissance. Aside from a late plan by Wemyss to break through the Narrows to avert an evacuation of the peninsula, the Navy saw itself as supporting a military operation.[4]

This was the only strategically significant amphibious operation of the First World War. It was a defeat, and the shadow it cast over the British thinking about war in the following years was long and dark. The Dardanelles plan went to the heart of traditional British strategy, adumbrated only a few years before the war by Sir Julian Corbett.[5] This was to exploit the symbiotic relationship between sea power, land forces and economic strength. This 'Easterner' strategy of containing the enemy by sea power, weakening him by eccentric attack, and finally forcing him to terms, had stumbled at the first hurdle and never recovered. On the other hand, the 'Westerner' strategy of a 'Continental Commitment' had engaged Britain in an unprecedented slaughter on the Western Front, but it had, ultimately, been decisive in the defeat of the central powers.

The Royal Navy emerged from the war with its position in British defence assumptions secure.[6] It had not won another Trafalgar, but blockade, commerce protection, and maritime military transportation had proved the importance of sea power. The war had been won on the Western Front, but the British public were disinclined to put their faith in another continental commitment in place of the bulwark of the sea. On the other hand it was not clear how Corbett's eccentric operations and amphibious warfare would fit into the Royal Navy's new world. When war broke out again in 1939, to many observers, Britain did not seem to have advanced in theory or practice.[7] As late as 1943, it seemed that the Dardanelles cast such a shadow that the Navy was timid in the face of such operations. Some historians of the Sicily campaign (July–August 1943) have pointed to experience of the Dardanelles as a reason for Admiral of the Fleet Sir Andrew Cunningham's failure to advance to the heavily defended Straits of Messina to cut the retreat of the Axis forces to the mainland.[8]

Tracing the impact of particular historical events upon subsequent operations is extremely difficult. Experiences may be absorbed and never consciously impinge upon decisions, but exert an influence none the less. Equally, experiences cannot simply be inferred to have an influence. The purpose of this paper is to explore how the experience of the Dardanelles was absorbed into the service through the pages of *The Naval Review* and, more broadly, how amphibious operations were perceived and presented.

The Naval Review was never intended as a vehicle for the extended analyses of operations to be fed into the development of doctrine. It reflected the contemporary professional interests and concerns of naval officers. The Dardanelles would only be reflected in the *NR* in so far as it captured the attention of naval officers as authors and readers over the years. The contributions appear in three distinct forms. The first is the narrative of experience by those who served there, recording their own stories, and setting out the demands placed upon them as future guides for colleagues. Second, were the analyses of, or comments upon, the strategy behind the operation. Initially, these were generalised reports of current proceedings and information. Later, they occurred more commonly in the book reviews which began to appear in 1921. Third, there were the essays on the future of amphibious warfare and the Navy's role in it.

The personal narratives began to appear at the end of 1915. Reports from warships, such as *Prince George, Prince of Wales, Lord Nelson, Amethyst* and *Agamemnon* gave impressions of the routine on board in theatre, cruising, coaling, supporting trawlers, bombarding, covering the landings, and receiving the wounded.[9] The landings at ANZAC and the boat work required to sustain the forces at that point were reported more fully than operations off Cape Helles.[10]

The bombardment of the Narrows and later fire support for the army was a particular interest. The results of the early bombardments of the entrance to the Narrows in February and early March were mixed. Some reported a high degree of accuracy firing directly on observed targets, but the ambitious attempt by *Queen Elizabeth*, firing off Gaba Tepe across the peninsula to the forts at the Narrows, proved futile. The Turkish batteries were also accurate, making life on board the battleships uncomfortable and forcing *Queen Elizabeth* to move station. For those on the destroyers and small ships, working up the Straits, the Turkish fire from the peninsula and Asiatic side was exhilarating. The number of Turkish batteries seemed to be growing daily and on 13 March, *Amethyst* was hit nine times by 6in shells; none was high explosive and some did not explode. Nevertheless, both the increase in batteries and the accuracy of their fire were disconcerting and there was clear sympathy for the civilian-manned minesweeping trawlers who pulled in their sweeps and fled.[11]

Reports or reminiscences of the bombardment appeared periodically until the late 1930s. Both before and after the landing of the Army, it was an aspect that troubled some officers. Authors identified plenty of reasons to explain its lack of success. Aerial reconnaissance and spotting had been inadequate. The ammunition was limited. The guns were worn and not accurate enough to permit close support of the troops. Not enough training had been carried out in bombardment technique.[12] Just as bad was the timing of bombardment activity. The early bombardments warned the Turks of their weak points, which they had time to fortify before the full weight of naval firepower could be gathered together.[13] Very little new was added to information or analysis during the interwar period. The need to score direct hits on shore-based artillery or follow up the suppressing fire by landing Marines who could destroy the batteries seemed to reinforce the old adage that ships could not destroy shore fortifications.[14]

That the campaign was a tragic failure was beyond contentions, but the broader reflections by participants and contemporaries were varied. On the crucial matter of the strategic practicality of a naval break-through, opinion gradually split. At the end of the war the dominant view was in line with the Cromer Report and the Dardanelles Committee, that it was misconceived. Sir Reginald Custance contributed a long series of articles, 'A Study of War', between 1922 and 1925.[15] In his view, whatever the result of the attack on the Narrows, while the Turkish Army held the Gallipoli peninsula the fleet could not be secure in its operations through to the Sea of Marmara.[16] That the naval command, from Fisher to Carden and de Robeck, had been pressured into an extremely doubtful campaign by the First Lord of the Admiralty, Winston Churchill, was an uncomfortable truth. To service chiefs participating in the debates about a single Ministry of Defence after 1918, the Dardanelles campaign was a powerful warning that they were ill-equipped to counter the politician's rhetorical skills and ill-informed enthusiasm in Whitehall committees.[17] A repetition had to be avoided, but the dilution of the service heads' advice in a single ministry seemed to make a repeat more probable.[18] The publication of Winston Churchill's second volume of *The World Crisis* in 1923 revived this anxiety. Churchill's extensive apologia was savaged in a long article by Captain Alfred Dewar in 1924.[19] At the heart of Dewar's argument was the lack of effective staff planning which would have exposed the weakness of the proposed campaign, but Dewar did not spare Churchill, whom he damned:

> His strength lay not in strategy, but in the application of new discoveries to naval use. With a mind powerful, but, in the sphere of strategy, crude and uncritical, he was too easily carried away by the idea of anything new or big – big plans, big guns, big ships, bigger guns and still bigger ships. Churchill in his vehemence, self-confidence, and restless energy had something in common with him, but lacked the rugged strength of the old Admiral [Fisher].'

The lack of fundamental planning was reinforced shortly afterwards in a review, entitled, 'The Mediterranean Muddle', of Wemyss' book *The Navy in the Dardanelles Campaign*, which emphasised the chaos that attended the operation.[20] By the mid 1930s a different view was emerging. In 1934 Sir Roger Keyes, Chief of Staff to de Robeck, and a strong advocate of the naval campaign to force the Narrows, published his memoirs, strongly asserting both the practicality of the plan and its potential strategic impact on Turkey. The review of this work was almost completely uncritical.[21] Keyes had retired from the service in 1931, but remained an influential figure in Parliament and had taken an active interest in the work of the Army's historian, Cecil Aspinall-Oglander, while he was writing the official history of the Gallipoli campaign. The lack of reaction to either the memoirs or the review may be indicative of a changing view within naval circles. The review of Oglander's second volume of official history, published in 1932, had noted Keyes' pressure for a renewed attack on the Narrows as an alternative to evacuation and regretted that this had not been taken up.[22] By 1936, when John North's critical volume, *The Fading Vision*, was reviewed, it was accepted by the reviewer that 'No one who had any share in the naval operations in the Dardanelles or off Gallipoli can be satisfied with the part we played; most of us feel that the work could and ought to have been done better, not only as regards the larger issues but in the details.'[23]

Although the evidence is extremely slim this may be representative of a changing view. In 1921, it was asserted that the Dardanelles had been 'initiated more or less over the heads' of the Naval Staff and further that 'it is absurd to suppose that landing operations and bombardments fill up the whole picture of naval war. It is not too much to say that they do not fill up one-tenth of it.'[24] The significance of the failure both of the Dardanelles operation and Gallipoli campaign, therefore, could be dismissed as tangential to the real role of the Royal Navy. However, during the 1930s a different view predominated. Although the politicians had posed the Navy with a serious problem, combined operations were an essential part of imperial defence and bolder operational command may have overcome the apparently insuperable difficulties.[25] Before the war, the difficultly of running ships through defended channels in the face of modern forts, mobile batteries, torpedoes and mines had raised concerns, but success was not discounted.[26] The attack on the Narrows called that into question and immediately afterwards there was a feeling that the old relationship between forts and ships had not altered and thus, naval bombardment alone was 'foredoomed to failure' and amphibious operations remained the most naturally difficult of all operations.[27] Gradually, this view changed. The reasons for this require far deeper inspection than is possible here, but the willingness to accept that weapons, training and motivation were all inadequate, together with the influence that Churchill and Keyes continued to exert into the late 1930s almost certainly played their parts.

During the interwar years the evolving issue of amphibious operations in imperial defence and, consequently, the role of the Royal Navy, also played into attitudes towards the Dardanelles campaign. Although the experience powerfully suggested that purely naval operations against shore positions were ineffective, the Gallipoli campaign as a whole seemed to point to a combined Army–Navy strategy as being the only practicable way of projecting sea power ashore. The success of the Japanese in their war with Russia 1904–5 had already demonstrated this and technological changes suggested that this co-operation might be easier and more effective in the future. Surprise in attack, which was thought to be fundamental to any success, could become more practicable. In 1922 no less than the military expert and historian Colonel J F C Fuller predicted that within the next ten years amphibious tanks would be developed to land from submarines and have a 300-mile radius on land.[28] Aircraft, which had played a small role in 1915, would be vital in future.[29]

These speculations were never realised and from the perspective of the 1940s, progress since 1919 looked appeared shockingly weak. Nevertheless, the development of amphibious and coastal capability did not atrophy completely. *The Manual of Combined Operations* was updated at intervals as a result of limited exercises. Equipment was

developed and tested.[30] However, during the 1930s the implications of
these technological developments for amphibious operations were not
all positive. Admiral Sir Herbert Richmond noted in his volume *Sea
Power in the Modern World* (1934) that, because of the mobility and
striking power provided by the submarine, modern aircraft and the
mechanised movement of armies, 'An invasion by sea of a great
modern military state may be dismissed as impracticable'.[31] Successful
operations against isolated possessions, or as diversions, might still
take place, but Richmond questioned whether the benefits this
conveyed any longer justified the cost of developing and maintaining
amphibious forces.

Throughout the 1930s the jury was out regarding the practicality of
strategically significant amphibious operations. By 1938, it seemed that
future operations like the Dardanelles would need airfields nearby to
provide supporting air cover and reconnaissance.[32] However, events
were forcing minds to focus on the possibilities. By the late 1930s, the
potential threat from Japan to Hong Kong and Singapore was explicit
and the experience of the Spanish Civil War, in which the Nationalists'
inability to conduct amphibious operations was seen as an important
factor in prolonging that conflict.[33] Events seemed to be highlighting
the potential importance of coastal and amphibious operations. The
balance of significance lay with latter rather than the former. According
to 'OL' in 1934, the Dardanelles had shown that

> Had the correct reading of the maxim been followed, not that forts
> cannot be mastered by ships, but that forts can only be mastered by
> ships working in conjunction with land forces, and had the
> operation been a joint one from the commencement, the attack on
> the peninsula would have approached a 'walk-over', with the fleet,
> in effect, providing a creeping barrage to be followed up closely by
> the troops occupying each position in turn.[34]

Such a judgement was intended to provide encouragement for the future
rather than provide a reasoned assessment of what was possible
in 1915.

When the Second World War broke out in September 1939, opinions
of the Dardanelles campaign, as reflected in the *NR*, had evolved some
way. The initial response that naval operations alone against shore
defences were ineffective remained largely untouched, but the
acceptance that more could have been done by the Navy in 1915 and
in future, with evolving technology, that combined operations with land
and air forces were practicable in many circumstances, had emerged
during the intervening years.[35]

The early war years did not shift this dominant viewpoint. Almost no comment or reflection appeared on the operations at Norway, Dakar or Madagascar. The Dieppe operation of 18 August 1942 received some attention, but none of it particularly enlightening. A note on a subsequent lecture tour by one participant provided little for an informed audience and bemoaned the fact that 'I was rather depressed … by one audience of about a thousand girls who quite obviously had never heard of Dieppe, and didn't seem to care. I might as well have talked to a field of cows; but that was the only really heavy audience I had.'[36] In the same issue there was some reflection on whether it was a success or failure, concluding that it was good experience for a future second front, but accepting that the loss of surprise as a result of running into a night-time convoy should have been anticipated.[37] Given that naval bombardment, and the assumed vulnerability of warships to shore batteries, was so important, it is curious that comparisons with the experience of 1915 were not made.

Operation Husky, the invasion of Sicily, 10 July 1943, provided the first significant reference back to 1915.[38] Here was a direct comparison to Gallipoli and it seemed so much had changed that a comparison was no longer valid. In 1915 two divisions had landed on a total frontage of thirteen miles. In 1943, two armies had landed on a frontage of about 100 miles. Three hundred ships had been involved in the landings at Gallipoli, while 3,000 had been used for the landings on Sicily. Air cover had been essential and effective. Landing craft had provided a new flexibility and mobility. 'Submarines at Gallipoli which seemed to give a death-blow to amphibious operations,' 'at Sicily their menace ha[d] proved to be so trivial as to be negligible.' Naval gunnery had proved extraordinarily effective. US destroyers had broken up a German armoured counter-attack on 13 July. Most of all, it was the meticulous planning that distinguished Husky from Gallipoli and the Dardanelles. It was this factor in the early 1920s that was seen as the most important in leading to the failure in 1915 and seemed to be vindicated by the success in 1943.[39]

As that campaign developed, the failure to outflank the German defences before Catania by amphibious landing was noted. There was a clear contrast here between the US Navy which carried out three landings on the north coast of the island and the failure of the British to carry out any after 10 July until it was too late. Here, the Dardanelles experience did resonate with the author. The coastal batteries on the Italian mainland at Reggio were powerful. Enemy small craft and aircraft posed a real threat. Unlike de Robeck in 1915, Cunningham could not afford to sacrifice capital ships. To this was added the coastal topography which would have prevented an effective exploitation of any landing.[40]

As the war drew to a conclusion, the Dardanelles faded rapidly from the horizon. The shift in the scale and technologies of projecting power ashore, which had been apparent in Husky, were repeated in Operations Neptune and Overlord and the Korean War. Reference to the Dardanelles now only really occurred in book reviews, with little or no contemporary application outside its historical context. The same is true of other operations, particularly Dieppe.[41] However, one important aspect seems to have been taken forward from the accumulated contributions on the subject in the *NR* – planning. Almost from the beginning, the lack of planning and the questions about leadership haunted reflections upon the Dardanelles. Whether the operation to force the Narrows was practicable or likely to produce the diplomatic results that Churchill had confidently predicted was disputed from the early 1920s, and remains in the realm of counter-factual history. Whether the planning was adequate, the weapons good enough, the training effective and the leadership determined were matters upon which more substantial conclusions could be drawn, and by the late 1930s the consensus in the pages of the *NR* was that they were not. The Dardanelles disappeared as a reference point for operational comparison in the 1940s and from live experience in the 1960s. In 1945 the Dardanelles remained a useful general reference point concerning the need for 'clear thinking' for any book reviewer examining works on amphibious warfare in the Napoleonic War.[42] The Falklands campaign of 1982 threw into relief the issues related to the rapid construction of a balanced, modern amphibious expedition, but by then the Dardanelles and Gallipoli had ceased to exert any explicit instructional value. Similarly, Operations Granby and Telic (the Gulf Wars of 1991 and 2003) brought forth no comparison with the Dardanelles.

With the end of the Cold War in 1990 came a refocusing of British maritime strategy to meet the dangers inherent in a more volatile and less predictable world order. A modernised amphibious force structure became a priority as operations in regional conflicts became more common.[43] Implicit in this shift of focus was that Britain would not be attempting a strategically decisive operation against a major world power. Despite the current technological sophistication and operational reach of these actions there is no direct comparison with the ambition of the Dardanelles campaign. The more limited strategic objectives and the expected margin of superiority in the battle space, particularly in association with US maritime assets, makes any direct association with the operational issues remembered from the Dardanelles superficially difficult to apply. The most enduring lesson of the Dardanelles is hubris and the greater the anticipated margin of superiority the greater will be the danger of underestimating the opposition. Amphibious warfare takes place in an extremely dynamic environment and it is quite possible that in future, as at the Dardanelles, amphibious operations will come up against an unexpected hard and painful reality. Recent concerns on both sides of the Atlantic about the growing capability of defensive weaponry suggest that the balance of advantage is still changing and that any given level of investment in doctrinal development, training and material will only produce a temporary advantage.

If there was a long shadow of the Dardanelles evident in the pages of the NR, it was not one forewarning that coastal or amphibious operations were no longer practicable. The wisdom of the specific operation against the Narrows was disputed, but not the importance of applying sea power to the enemy littoral. There was a growing feeling among contributors in the 1930s that the Royal Navy could have done more and been more effective in what it did – but that this required weapons, training, planning and leadership that were more effective. There was also recognition that there was a tension in such operations. They are among the most difficult that a navy can be asked to carry out and investment in specialised equipment and training are vital. However, such operations will only ever be a small part of the total demands and excessive specialisation could lead to a force structure that was unbalanced and incapable of all it needs to do.[44] Contributors were aware of it, but in the aftermath of the First World War, the Royal Navy was not required to resolve this tension.[45] In the post-1945 world this tension has seldom been far from naval planning, and it remains present in, although never dominating, the pages of the NR.[46]

The Gallipoli campaign remains one of the most iconic operations of the twentieth century. While revisionist history has largely rehabilitated the commanders who conducted the war on the Western Front, Gallipoli remains a byword for futility.[47] The Dardanelles operation was a precursor to the main act and almost from the beginning the question of whether the Navy could have achieved more exercised servicemen and historians. However this divided opinion, the recognition that the Navy had to do better in coastal and amphibious operations in the future was understood by those who contributed to the NR. In those pages there were calls for planning, training, effective vehicles and weapons. There was not, however, a sustained analysis of what or how this would be provided, nor a consistent championing of what was needed. It was too small – 'an unusual job' to quote one officer assigned to a Landing Ship Tank in 1945.[48] Nevertheless, the *NR* contributed to a positive background mood for taking up and developing amphibious and offensive coastal capability between 1939 and 1945. In this respect the pages of *The Naval Review* suggest that the experience of the Dardanelles was not the overwhelming negative force in naval thinking that the dominant popular image of the campaign still maintains.

7 The Submarine as Commerce Raider

Peter Padfield

THE potential for submarines to revolutionise naval warfare was recognised before the foundation of *The Naval Review*. It was masked in large measure by the drama of the dreadnought-building competition between Britain and Germany; nonetheless, the first issue of *The Naval Review* in 1913 carried three pieces on the changes wrought by submarines.

A general survey of 'Sea Power in 1913' laid stress on the submarine's ability to render close blockade of enemy ports impossible. Together with a fundamental change in prize law established by the Declaration of Paris 1856, denying belligerents the right to seize enemy goods from neutral ships – unless contraband of war – this appeared to rule out Britain's traditional strategy of sapping her enemies' strength by throttling their commerce: 'the enemy will be able to obtain in neutral ships, supplies that he could not hope to get in his own ships ... His population will therefore obtain a measure of relief, which will reduce the pressure upon them, and tend to prolong the war.'[1]

An altogether wider strategic transformation was envisaged in two articles on 'The Influence of the Submarine on Naval Policy'. The author started from the premise that surface warships would be forced by the invisible threat from submarines to abandon narrow waters such as the North Sea, the English Channel and the Mediterranean; consequently it would be impossible for any belligerent to obtain command of these seas in the accepted sense of the term. He deplored the lack of any consideration of the submarine menace in recent Admiralty statements on naval policy, and quoted from Colonel Repington, military correspondent of *The Times*, who had raised the issue in 1910: 'It is a perfectly hateful idea to senior officers of the Navy that a submarine should dominate waters in which a Dreadnought proudly sails.'[2]

However that may be, it was the author's contention that no naval power would in future be able to dominate narrow seas. This drew him to the prescient conclusion in his second article that if enemies could not gain command of the North Sea or Channel, invasion of the British Isles became impossible and an enemy would have to resort to other means to bring pressure to bear. What other means were there but attacks on British trade? This led him to consider the submarine as a commerce raider.

Obviously it was not the ideal weapon for a traditional *guerre de course*: by surfacing to stop and search a merchantman a submarine rendered herself vulnerable, and manifestly she could not carry a large enough crew to spare men to navigate the prize to port.

> Suppose, for instance, a hostile submarine meets an English merchant ship off the Scillies evidently bound for an English port, what will be the conduct of the commanding officer of the submarine? He cannot deal with the vessel in accordance with International Law, will he then allow her to pass, will he sink or disable her? Even though the vessel is flying a neutral flag, what will he do?

One has to attempt to revisit the comfortably chivalrous mental world of the pre-First World War naval officer to appreciate the boldness of the author's further examination: 'It seems certain that the sinking or molesting of unarmed merchantmen can never be sanctioned by law, but is the law likely to be obeyed?'

A third part of his article came out in 1914[3] but added little to the argument. By this date a public debate on submarines versus dreadnoughts had been ignited by the celebrated pioneer of gunnery accuracy, Admiral Sir Percy Scott, now retired. In a letter to *The Times*, he first pointed out that the chief purpose of the Navy was to protect the food supply, a novel idea to many brought up on the canon of British naval victories, and went on: 'The introduction of vessels that swim under water has, in my opinion, entirely done away with the utility of the ships that swim on top of the water.'[4] He was answered by a fusillade of letters in defence of great ships, and after some weeks felt obliged to write another letter to the paper to meet the several arguments raised against him. Most interesting in the light of what was to come was his rebuttal of the view of Admiral Sir Reginald Bacon – who had built up the submarine service from practically nothing – that 'the idea of attacking commerce by submarine is barbarous.' Scott wrote:

All war is, of course, barbarous, but in war the purpose of the enemy is to crush his foe; to arrive at this, he will attack where his foe is most vulnerable. Our most vulnerable point is our food and oil supply. The submarine has introduced a new method of attacking these supplies. Will feelings of humanity restrain our enemies from using it?[5]

A contributor to *The Naval Review* for that year, 1914, while not mentioning *The Times* correspondence, or Scott or Bacon by name, was firmly in the Bacon camp. In 'The Submarine and the Surface Vessel', he, Richmond, accepted the prime importance of commerce war, but could not see, 'unless the ordinarily accepted rules of warfare are radically altered', how the attack on trade could be carried out by submarines. Richmond pointed to the difficulties and dangers for a submarine of stopping and boarding a merchantman, the subsequent difficulty of supplying a prize crew to navigate her to a home port, and raised the possibility that the ship might be carrying passengers: 'Is it even within the bounds of probability that any officer would deliberately torpedo a ship and sink her in such circumstances? The attitude which would be taken by neutrals, apart from all questions of humanity, would forbid it.'[6]

Two other contributions in 1914 were devoted to trade protection: K G B Dewar's 'The Influence of Commerce in War' was remarkable for anticipating the strategy adopted by the Admiralty in the war which broke out that year: a distant blockade of the North Sea by the main fleet guarding the northern exits, the Dover Strait closed by flotillas and submarines with a battle squadron in support; and the focal and terminal areas of British trade controlled by cruisers and armed merchantmen. Dewar assumed that a systematic *guerre de course* against British trade would be carried out by 'small squadrons, single cruisers and armed merchantmen', but did not mention submarine raiders.[7]

In the second article, 'Protection of Trade in Past Wars', Richmond surveyed the two systems of trade protection used in conjunction by the Admiralty over the centuries, namely convoy and cruising off enemy bases and at shipping focal points. The scholarship was impeccable, the conclusions persuasive:

The tendency of the Admiralty was always to encourage the convoy system in preference to the cruising system ... The reason is obvious. The convoy is the most economical use of force ... If ships are sailing individually every Strait and every landfall requires a cruising force in considerable numbers.[8]

Richmond pointed to the great quantity of ships required under either system, suggesting that this was something usually forgotten in years of peace so that at the beginning of a war the number of cruisers was hopelessly inadequate. The article was entirely historical; there was no mention of submarines.

Another historical survey of trade protection written before the outbreak of war appeared in 1915. While acknowledging the advantage of convoy as 'essentially a concentration of force', Danckwerts held that the many objections to the system had grown more serious in recent years with the profusion of routes and the varying speeds of modern vessels. He considered that the other system of sending out cruisers to search for enemy cruisers and privateers had met a fair measure of success, but far better, in his view, was the destruction of the enemy raiders' bases. He expected most German raiders would be armed merchant cruisers and discounted submarines completely in this role: 'they could sink a limited number of merchant ships or make one follow into port, but they could take possession of none, and they are slow with a small supply of fuel.' Finally, he came down heavily against the convoy system to protect trade, regarding it as 'impossible under modern conditions.'[9]

Taking the six contributions on trade protection before the outbreak of war, the majority, four of the six, ruled out the possibility of the submarine being used for trade war; another was entirely historical, consequently omitted submarines altogether; only one argued for the possibility of enemy submarines flouting existing laws and norms in an effort to cut Britain's supply lines. It is particularly striking that of the four contributions based on a deep study of naval history, none held the submarine as a likely or even possible commerce raider. In the light of what was to come this might give historians of all persuasions cause to ponder. For these authors knew whereof they wrote; there was no failure of historical erudition, quite the reverse, nor of logic – they only failed to break out from the past.

On the other hand, Percy Scott and the great Jacky Fisher, who shared Scott's views on the use of submarines as commerce raiders, had not studied naval history. Whether the equally prescient author of the one series of articles questioning whether the enemy would feel bound by International Law had studied naval history is not known; his contributions do not suggest it.

Now that the names of the anonymous authors can be disclosed, it is not surprising to learn that two of the four historical pieces were written by the founding father of the Naval Society, soon to become the pre-eminent naval historian of his generation, Captain Herbert Richmond, even less surprising, perhaps, that the author who questioned whether submarine commanders would obey International Law was Captain S S Hall, formerly Inspecting Captain of Submarines, who in 1913 collaborated with Lord Fisher on a memorandum prophesying that Germany would use her submarines to attack commerce. Both the First Lord, Winston Churchill, and the First Sea Lord, Prince Louis of Battenberg, declared the paper 'marred by this suggestion.'[10]

The Adoption of the Convoy System in 1917

No discussion of trade protection in the context of submarine attack appeared in *The Naval Review* during the war which broke out in 1914, the 1917 issue which treated the subject at length not appearing until 1919. There can be no doubt, however, that the band of historically minded young officers in the Naval Society played a crucial role in the adoption of the convoy system which eventually defeated the German submarine campaign; indeed Commander R G H Henderson, nephew of Admiral W H Henderson, the first editor of *The Naval Review*, was singled out by Lloyd George in his memoirs as the officer who had penetrated the statistical errors bedevilling the Admiralty attitude to convoy.[11]

The course of the German submarine campaign against merchant shipping was set out by Richmond in 'Considerations of the War at Sea' in the 1917 issue.[12] Of the historically proven measures of trade protection, neither convoy nor cruising was instituted on the outbreak. Richmond ascribed this to underestimation by many people of the part commerce protection had always played – a reproach which we have seen did not apply to members of *The Naval Review*. He went on to suggest that this was partly due to the way in which naval history had been written, concentrating on the operations of the principal fleets and battles.

Richmond outlined the Admiralty response as German submarines began taking a toll of merchant shipping: first, the establishment of patrolling and hunting groups of small craft, many of them yachts, trawlers and drifters – although it was many months before these flotillas were co-ordinated with the trade they were to protect, and without means of locating submerged submarines or attacking with underwater charges they were practically ineffective. 'A pack cannot hunt without scent.' Next, armed ships had been disguised as merchantmen, as in the old wars against privateers, to lure the enemy alongside, when the ensign was hoisted and the guns cleared to deliver a broadside. In the author's view this Q-ship ruse had not been developed on a comprehensive scale for some time, and surprise had been lost.

The crucial phase of the commerce war had been heralded in 1915 by a German Naval Staff paper concluding that an intensified submarine campaign using torpedoes to sink merchantmen indiscriminately without warning would reduce supplies reaching Britain to such an extent she would be forced to sue for peace within six months. The unrestricted campaign then begun was soon discontinued. The author suspected, correctly, that the attitude of America may have been the dominating influence.

By 1917, as is now known, the hopeless position of the German High Seas Fleet vis-à-vis the British Grand Fleet and desperate food shortages within Germany brought about largely by the Allied commercial blockade induced the effective rulers of Germany, the Army leaders, Field Marshal Paul von Hindenburg and General Erich Ludendorff, to relaunch the unrestricted submarine campaign. It was to come perilously close to success.

In the event, convoys for oceanic shipping were introduced just in time to save Britain from disaster. Precisely how this happened is detailed in the 1917 issue in an important article on the convoy system from the viewpoint of the Ministry of Shipping.[13] The author was Sir Norman Leslie, the Ministry of Shipping official acting as liaison with the Admiralty, to whom Commander Henderson applied for figures of arrivals and departures at British ports. Leslie recalled much later: 'When I found out what this extraordinary young man had in mind I caught fire with enthusiasm at once and worked out my side of it eagerly. We spent all day in each other's company.'[14]

Before Henderson's initiative the Naval Staff had lacked the data necessary to evaluate the feasibility of convoy. Leslie explained in his article that they had relied on weekly returns of the huge number of ships which entered and left British ports. These were published for propaganda effect together with the number of ships lost. Leslie doubted whether the Germans had been deceived, but was clear that 'these tabulated returns did mislead those [at the Admiralty] whose energies were being devoted to meet this [submarine] offensive.' For the return of entries and departures included cross-Channel and coasting vessels which might have made several ports in a day, and the figures were not broken down in any way. This had 'resulted in a most erroneous impression being formed as to the number of arrivals from overseas', causing them to be overestimated by a factor of seven; 'or in other words, it was thought that as many [overseas] ships arrived in a day as really arrived in a week.'

The introduction of some form of convoy, he continued, was 'loosely discussed' at the Admiralty in January 1917, the month before the unrestricted campaign was to begin, but a Naval Staff paper raised objections, principally on the grounds that a convoy presented a larger target than a single ship and that delays in assembling convoys would seriously impair the flow of goods. With this opinion paper and the grossly inflated idea of the number of ships requiring protection, it was hardly surprising that a convoy system was considered impracticable.

Instead, the Admiralty adopted a scheme of directing ships according to their route and destination into one of four 'approach areas' patrolled by sloops, Q-ships, trawlers and an occasional destroyer. Each area was some 10,000 square miles in extent; there were too few patrol craft, and as a previous contributor had noted, they were insufficiently equipped either for detecting or destroying submarines. Their position served rather to give German submarine commanders an indication of the traffic routes, and individual merchantmen were picked off almost at will. The area off the southwest of Ireland especially became a graveyard for shipping.

As it became obvious the system was failing, the question of convoys was again raised. It was at this point that Henderson, having failed to obtain figures of the volume of oceangoing ships and their points of origin from any Admiralty department, applied to Norman Leslie at the Ministry of Shipping. The Ministry's card indexes revealed that on average twenty oceangoing ships arrived in British waters every day, of which fifteen came to the United Kingdom, thus showing that in terms of numbers requiring protection convoys were possible. During April 1917 shipping losses averaged ten a day and the Ministry of Shipping brought strong pressure on the Admiralty to introduce a convoy system.

What Leslie omitted here is that Henderson was urging the necessity of convoy directly on the Prime Minister, Lloyd George, behind the back of his own chief, Rear Admiral Alexander Duff, whom the recently appointed First Sea Lord, Admiral Sir John Jellicoe, had appointed to lead the fight against submarines.[15] Henderson's behaviour, which is contrary to every principle of Service or departmental loyalty and to the habit of subservience whereby officers did not disagree with their seniors – and the very causes that his father and Richmond and others had founded the Naval Society for the free expression of differing views – has been judged by Professor Arthur Marder as fully justified by the desperate circumstances of the time. Other officers, including Richmond, supported Henderson, but Marder has called him 'the chief architect of the convoy system.'[16]

To pick up the story as told by Leslie, meetings were convened between the Admiralty and the War Cabinet and representative shipowners, and the War Cabinet decided that convoys should be tried.

Two were organised in May, one from the United States, which had been provoked by the unrestricted submarine campaign into declaring war on Germany in April, the other from Gibraltar. Both reached home waters without loss. Leslie commented in his article: 'Had the convoy system then been put into force immediately on all routes, as was strongly urged ... there is every ground for saying ... that the losses of the next two months would only have been a fraction of the ships which were sunk before the system was started on the grand scale.'[17]

The Admiralty did appoint a committee of four naval officers and a representative of the Ministry of Shipping to draw up a complete system of convoy on 17 May, before the experimental convoys had reached Britain. The Committee's scheme was approved by the Board on 14 June, but by Leslie's account 'in the letter rather than in the spirit, as the indispensable forces were not made available.' It was not until the Shipping Controller again brought urgent pressure to bear that the Board of Admiralty at last provided convoy escorts in the shape of destroyers, sloops, P-boats and trawlers from the patrol areas, after which the convoy system was extended to most overseas shipping. By the end of October, ninety-nine homeward convoys had been brought in with the loss of only 0.66 per cent of the ships in company, seventy-seven convoys escorted outwards with only a 0.57 per cent loss.[18] The haemorrhage of merchant tonnage was stemmed, and with additional American shipping and shipbuilding resources the statistical basis of the German plan was invalidated.

Leslie concluded the article by observing that, unlike the system of patrolling and hunting, when an enemy submarine only had to lie in wait for its unprotected target, the convoy system forced the submarine commander to seek his target, and brought him in contact with the escorts.

Interwar arms limitation

British naval policy in the 1920s and 1930s was framed in the shadow of the mighty financial and industrial power of the United States, and skewed internally by budgetary constraints arising as much from profound anti-war and internationalist sentiment aroused by the horrors of the trenches, as from war debt and trade depression. In consequence British governments bound themselves in successive naval limitation treaties.

During negotiations leading to the treaties British delegations pressed hard not simply to limit but to abolish submarines altogether. It was an impractical, Anglocentric bid and the lesser naval powers, led by France, had little difficulty in rejecting it. Readers of the November

1922 issue of *The Naval Review* were treated to a magnificently Gallic account by the French Rear Admiral Degouy of British discomfiture at the Washington Naval Conference. The British had gone to Washington, in Degouy's view, intent on the reduction, 'if not the complete disappearance of the French Navy, firstly by strictly limiting the tonnage of capital ships, secondly by insisting on the suppression of submarines', resorting to 'sentimental facts' such as the sinking of the *Lusitania* to stir up American public opinion. Yet:

> Is it possible to abolish, with the stroke of a pen, one particular item from the list of engines of war? Notice that the submarine is not a novelty, it has already existed for forty years … Its advantages and disadvantages are common knowledge and every sailor knows well that it is objected to, not so much for its barbarity, but because of the efficacy that it adds to the type of warfare most feared by England.[19]

This was, no doubt, the nub of the matter. The best the British could achieve in the later Treaty of London was a limitation on the size of individual submarines to 2,000 tons and an article stipulating that when attacking merchant ships submarines were to obey International Law, particularly in respect of ensuring the safety of passengers and crew.

Contributors to *The Naval Review* were more realistic about the submarine's right to exist. In 1920 John Creswell asserted that, although the German submarine campaign had been marked 'by a barbarity which we need not expect from any other nation', the submarine commerce destroyer had come to stay.[20] Also in 1920 R G Studd called for changes in naval construction, assuming that submarine attack on trade was almost certain to be a feature, 'and very likely the opening phase' of the next war.[21] And in 1927 a contributor wrote:

> The submarine is the most valueless vessel ever conceived for the purpose of closing down trade unless it is set a task that would have shamed the most abandoned pirates in days gone by. It cannot capture a ship. It cannot carry prize crews or take vessels into port. It can only sink them with all hands without trace … In anticipating another submarine menace we have to admit, therefore, that we expect other great nations to commit the same crimes and follies that our late enemies were guilty of.[22]

All contributors recognised convoy as the answer to future attack on trade; several called for the construction of specialised convoy escort vessels, and Studd proposed a new type of cruiser of modest speed for ocean convoy escort, to be fitted with guns, anti-submarine weapons, kite balloons and aircraft, the design to be as simple as possible 'so that these ships could be turned out in large numbers if the situation demanded.' He concluded:

> Though it is true that indirectly and ultimately the whole structure of naval power rests on the battle fleets, it is equally true that very directly and to an increasing extent in the future, the protection of our overseas trade from submarine attack will rest on the special units for convoy work.[23]

In the final stages of the last war, too late to be of use, Admiralty scientists had developed an active submarine detection system transmitting sound waves under water, named Asdic, now, of course, sonar. The Admiralty continued to focus on the development of Asdic and by the 1930s the Royal Navy believed it had an effective submarine detector and locator. Less concern was shown for anti-submarine weapons such as depth charge throwers, depth bombs for aircraft or, until it was almost too late, specialised escort craft which could be built quickly and cheaply. This was, no doubt, due to the absence of an obvious enemy: Germany did not start building submarines again until 1935. It was not for lack of warnings or suggestions for anti-submarine weapons and escort craft in *The Naval Review*.

The toxic effect of the naval treaties on the Royal Navy's ability to protect the trade routes was brought to notice in 1933 by Herbert Richmond, by now retired from service, and devoting himself to the study of naval history. In a paper he read to the British Commonwealth Peace Federation – one of many manifestations of a 'revival of the cults of pacifism, internationalism and "advanced" thinking', as it was put by one contributor that year[24] – he tried to disabuse members of the idea that British world trade could be secured by the doctrine of Freedom of the Seas, or no right to capture private property at sea, currently enjoying favour in internationalist circles. He did not believe that legal immunity to capture at sea could secure British trade. Yet the Navy's ability to protect trade by force had been undermined by the recent London Treaty limiting Britain to fifty cruisers:

> Before that unhappy and ill-considered treaty the Admiralty had expressed the view that the minimum with which it would be possible to perform the duties required was 70. Before the war we had 120. Some years previously one of our most distinguished naval officers, Admiral Sir Geoffrey Phipps Hornby, had calculated our needs at 186 ... we ended the war with just over 190.[25]

He returned to the charge the following year in an article for *The Naval Review* on Lloyd George's memoirs, a book chiefly remarkable for a scathing attack on the Admiralty's tardy response to the unrestricted submarine campaign of 1917. Richmond had, of course, been intellectual leader of the group of young officers who had been equally critical of the Admiralty under Jellicoe and instrumental in making the case for the convoy system.[26] He nevertheless wrote a balanced review, using the extravagance of Lloyd George's language against him: 'the fear-dimmed eyes of our Mall Admirals', their 'blind obstinacy' and 'stubborn hostility to convoys' were, he suggested, phrases foreign to naval officers' experience, and offensive without being arguments. 'What we have is, in fact, the speech of prosecuting counsel' in a case where witnesses for the defence had not yet been heard. When it was learned what the difficulties were which prevented convoys being brought in earlier, they would be in position to form some sort of judgement. Some things, however, were clear:

> Shipping was our heel of Achilles – and why? Because, primarily, we did not possess sufficient cruisers and flotilla craft to give it the defence it needed. One lesson of the war stands out in unmistakable terms. If we are to survive another war, we shall need a powerful means of dealing with the forces which attack shipping.

Yet, he continued, they had not heard Mr Lloyd George protest against the strategically unscientific compositions with foreign powers which had reduced the Navy's cruiser and flotilla forces to numbers 'far below those which were insufficient to preserve us during the war.' He could not, he ended, deny that there was justice in some of the book:

> But we might expect that one who has seen the effects of weakness at sea might have made some stand when the temporary rulers of the country were engaged in committing the nation and the Empire to quantities of naval strength whose insufficiency is clearly demonstrated by the impressive evidence of his own experience.[27]

Jellicoe's own defence of his stewardship at the Admiralty, *The Submarine Peril*, was published the same year, and reviewed in the same issue of *The Naval Review*. In essence it consisted of a record of the extraordinary exertions made by the team of officers he had brought with him from the Grand Fleet in procuring materiel to fight submarines: seaplanes, aeroplanes, airships, hydrophones, shore hydrophone stations, Otter gear, Q-ships, depth charge throwers, high speed motor-boats and effective mines, which were ordered in huge quantities. Shortage of escort craft, in particular destroyers, had prevented the adoption of convoy before the United States entered the war, which, he asserted, had been the turning point; it had allowed the use of US ports for assembling merchantmen. To have introduced convoy before adequate escort forces were available 'might have been disastrous.'[28]

A further plea for the defence appeared in *The Naval Review* the following year, 1935, written by Captain Bertram Smith, first chief of the Naval War Staff course, and during the war a member of the Trade and Mercantile Division of the Admiralty War Staff. He pointed out that Commander Henderson, whom Lloyd George had praised for discovering the true figures of overseas shipping, so making convoy feasible, had been personal assistant to Admiral Duff, whom Jellicoe had placed in charge of the anti-submarine effort. He did not mention that Henderson had worked behind his chief's back, and he rather spoiled his argument by suggesting that the failure of the patrol area system over which Jellicoe presided had 'forced the enemy to the fateful course of adopting unrestricted submarine warfare with its inevitable result of bringing the United States into the war on our side.' This, he asserted, echoing Jellicoe, had made convoy possible.[29]

A fair verdict on the 1917 Admiralty had been given some years before in *The Naval Review* by Admiral Sir Reginald Custance, a naval historian and controversialist of erratic views who, on this occasion, hit the nail on the head: 'the delay in introducing the convoy system was largely due to the failure to understand the theory behind it, which is that … the escort is placed alongside the convoy as the most likely place to meet and destroy the enemy.'[30]

This was, of course, what Sir Norman Leslie had concluded earlier. Custance went on to assert that the large shipping losses in the war had not been due to inherent defects in the Navy, 'but to its improper use on trade routes and focal centres instead of as escorts to convoys.'

Towards the Second World War

Readers of *The Naval Review* had received warning of Germany's aggressive intent in Admiral Degouy's 1922 article on the Washington Naval Treaty, cited earlier. He had characterised Germany, post Versailles, as a country that had only outwardly disarmed, who took no pains to hide her hatred of France or her passion for revenge, and wished 'to re-establish an Imperial government and place it in the hands of that aggressive dynasty, the Hohenzollerns.'[31]

Instead, it was, of course, the Nazis under Adolf Hitler who eventually took power in 1933. Before that, two further indications of German bellicosity appeared in *The Naval Review*, first, in 1928, the translation of an article by Vice Admiral H Meurer. Readers would have been surprised by Meurer's repeated assertions that Germany had emerged from the late war undefeated at sea or on land. She had succumbed only to economic compulsion: '[whose] foundation in international law is the barbaric right of prize and the further right arising therefrom to cut off millions of non-combatants from the world traffic by means of a commerce blockade, which thus becomes a starvation blockade.'[32]

The German leadership had failed to anticipate the 'ruthless infringement of international rights' by the British government in the form of its 'well thought-out, but illegal remote blockade of all the northern neutrals.' Meurer's conclusion revealed how efficiently the Germany military and academic brigade had rewritten history:

> Had the German people in general and their political leaders in particular been more abundantly gifted with a better understanding of the sea – as aptly expressed by Grand Admiral von Tirpitz in his *Memoirs*, things might have turned out differently for us in the great struggle which was forced upon us!

The following year extracts from a translation of *Der U-boot Krieg 1914–1918* by Vice Admiral Andreas Michelson also characterised the British commercial blockade as 'a monstrous violation of the rights of neutrals' employed in accordance with a 'general plan for starving Germany', while Germany's unrestricted submarine campaign 'was not only necessary, but was the correct method.'[33]

In 1934 reviews of three more German books appeared in *The Naval Review*, including *Germany Prepares for War* by Professor Ewald Banse, the overall theme of which was Germany's future dominance of the world for the world's own good.[34]

Notwithstanding these clues, the difficulty of foreseeing even major changes in political constellations in the near term is exemplified in two *Naval Review* articles the following year, 1935. J Hughes-Hallett writing as 'Alpha' predicted 'with a measure of confidence' that war in western Europe was improbable, 'while in eastern Europe it is almost certain to break out when Germany feels strong enough.'[35] Writing as 'Agna', Hughes-Hallett also saw the Anglo-German Naval Agreement as first and foremost a foundation for Anglo-German friendship, 'which is the cornerstone of Herr Hitler's policy.'[36] Indeed it was at the time. It was also Hitler's policy to split Britain from France, as Agna recognised. In retrospect the significance of the Naval Agreement was the licence it gave Germany to build submarines, thus bilaterally lifting the ban imposed by the Versailles Treaty. As Agna noted, Germany was granted the contingent right to parity with Great Britain in submarines. (This appears to be a rare occasion when an author appeared in the same edition of *The Naval Review* under different pseudonyms.)

The contributors' views mirrored official complacency. In the debate on the Naval Estimates, reported in *The Naval Review* that year,[37] the Parliamentary Secretary to the Admiralty assured the Commons that in the event of war convoy would not be introduced at once since it had great disadvantages 'and would not be welcomed by the trading community until conditions had become so intolerable that they were prepared to make the necessary sacrifices' – an unfortunate choice of words. As for the construction of specialised sloops as convoy escorts, he asked the House to remember two things:

> First, that our anti-submarine defences and devices for finding out exactly where submarines are are so very much better than they were during the war that we should want fewer protection vessels in the convoy. Secondly, that as convoys will not be needed immediately on the outbreak of war it will give us time to improvise protection by destroyers and trawlers whilst orders are given to build the sloops which we shall eventually require.

It is clear that Admiralty confidence was based largely on the capabilities of Asdic – which was nowhere mentioned in *The Naval Review*, possibly because it belonged to the 'material aspects of the profession', possibly for reasons of secrecy. More remarkably the Admiralty appeared to place reliance on International Law:

> We should never assume or anticipate that the indiscriminate attacks on merchant ships from which we suffered during the last war are in the future inevitable or indeed likely. After all the very strongest rules and injunctions are laid down against them by all the canons of international law.

Realism set in over the next few years. Reporting the 1938 estimates debate in *The Naval Review*, 'Teeoh' noted the significant change: the Admiralty now recognised that convoy might be necessary as early as the outbreak of war. While welcoming this conversion, he pointed out the deficiency in the number of destroyers which would be required for escort duties – as Winston Churchill had done during the debate – and concluded that the good news about the new strategy was to be found more in future intentions than present actualities.[38]

The Admiralty's transition to a strategy of convoying from the first day of war inspired another article by Vice Admiral Meurer, extracts of which were published in the May 1939 issue of *The Naval Review*.[39] First questioning whether the prohibition on submarines sinking without warning would really be respected in a future war, Meurer went on to suggest that the less one had to reckon on the clash of large battlefleets as at Jutland 'the more trade warfare is going to become the main operative task of the strategy of naval war.' 'R' appended his own conclusions:

> In the reference at the outset to submarine 'sinking without warning', one may take it for granted that there is no intention to observe any restrictions upon the employment of submarines. To imagine otherwise is to live in a fool's paradise … neither the submarine restrictions nor the Anglo-German naval treaties are of the slightest value. Both will be set aside when it suits Germany.

Readers of *The Naval Review* should have entered the Second World War without illusion.

The Second World War – and Beyond

The November 1939 issue of *The Naval Review* carried a generally optimistic article on the outlook for merchant shipping. Although German operations since the outbreak of war had been almost confined to submarine attacks on seaborne trade, 'The general provision of defensive armament and the rapid organisation of the convoy system with effective escort has made submarine attack a very hazardous business.'[40] Continuing optimism about the effectiveness of convoy defence against submarine attack was again expressed in the February 1940 issue: 'nearly 6,000 ships have been convoyed with the loss of only twelve through enemy action.'[41]

The first note of alarm was sounded by 'Fauteuil' – revealed after the war as Captain Bertram Smith – in the November 1940 issue: 'The shipping losses for the week ended 20 October are a shock and spoil the hope that the bad week in September might have been an abnormal one … The loss is not dangerous by itself, though it is serious.' Smith, who as Fauteuil was to contribute 'Notes on the War at Sea' throughout the war, attributed the losses to 'an exceptional concentration of submarines in one area' through which 'there presumably must have been a corresponding exceptional concentration of convoys.'[42] If he knew that U-boat wolf-pack attacks made possible by radio communication had become the enemy's preferred tactic, or that the submarine successes of the autumn had been due largely to pack attacks on the surface by night, he did not reveal it. In the next issue, February 1941, he referred to 'higher skill and improved appliances' enabling the submarines to 'combine better and attack from a greater distance; perhaps from outside effective Asdic range', but made no mention of night attack or of Asdic's vastly impaired performance against surfaced submarines. In short, readers of *The Naval Review* learned no more of the specifics behind increasing shipping losses than members of the public. He did, however, represent the dangerous situation for the country since the fall of France and the establishment of enemy submarine bases in western France closer to their quarry in the Atlantic.

He compared the current rate of shipping loss of up to 300,000 tons per month with the average loss of 195,000 tons per month between September 1917 and September 1918 when the convoy system had been in full operation and had reduced the previously ruinous rate of 700,000 to 900,000 tons a month, but pointed out that the present rate was rising; then it had been falling. He concluded that much of the present shortage of protection against submarines could be attributed to 'the false security of the inter-war official statements that the submarine danger no longer existed.'[43]

The next issue, May 1941, carried a report of a sombre speech by Winston Churchill on the submarine war on trade, now termed the Battle of the Atlantic. On the result of this battle, Churchill had said, everything turned. So far since the beginning of the war nearly four million tons of British shipping had been lost; most of the loss had been made good by new construction and foreign tonnage coming under British control:

> But what is to happen in future if these losses continue at the present rate? When all is said and done, the only way we can get through the year 1942 without a very sensible contraction of our war effort is by another gigantic building of merchant ships in the United States similar to that prodigy of output accomplished by the Americans in 1918 ... Here then, is the assurance upon which we may count for the staying power without which it will not be possible to save the world from the criminals who assail its future.[44]

It did not sound as if the convoy escorts were winning the battle. In his 'Notes on the War at Sea' in the same issue, Smith could give no reassurance. While those in responsible circles might have information on the factors necessary to judge the course of the battle in the Atlantic, he wrote, this was not available to others; and without the essential data it was not possible to judge 'whether we can last out or, what is equally important, grow in strength to a winning surplus to allow of full military effort.'[45]

He could only repeat this message in subsequent issues: in August 1941, still lacking data, he suggested one ought to be a member of the Crime Club to address the subject; but judging by figures of shipping losses, there was only one word to describe the situation: 'Bad'.[46] In February 1942 he noted that the stupendous shipbuilding programme announced by the President of the United States – which had by this date been forced into active participation in the war against Germany – put the ultimate tonnage situation beyond concern; 'but one wonders where the personnel is coming from.'[47] In May 1942 he wrote that information on trade protection was now 'so sparse and vague that any attempt to deduce results would be a waste effort.'[48]

It is now clear that the Battle of the Atlantic was won in May 1943 when German submarine groups in mid-ocean suffered unsustainable losses from Allied escort groups. Indications of this appeared in Smith's 'Notes on the War at Sea' in the August issue:

> the main transatlantic convoys were practically unmolested in June as a result of our successes against submarines in May ... The outstanding feature of this quarter has been the swing-over from the destruction of our ships to the destruction of the enemy's submarines ... The fact that the number of U-boats encountered in June was markedly less than in May is significant in this connection.'

While his conclusions remained speculative, he was able to provide causes for the turning tide of battle:

> Far more surface escorts ... Faster escorts ... Far more air escorts, enabling U-boats to be found and either destroyed, handed on to surface craft or forced down before they can make contact with the convoy. Better escort team-work from experience and better training. Improved weapons and more of them per ship. Closing of the Atlantic air gap by aircraft of the escort carriers and also by V L R [Very Long Range] aircraft of the Coastal Command.[49]

The other contributory factor, Bletchley Park's success in decoding enemy submarine radio traffic, was, of course, the most closely guarded secret of the war.

Shortly after the end of the war the Admiralty issued a statistical analysis of the Battle of the Atlantic, which was printed in the August 1945 issue of *The Naval Review*;[50] and the following February members were provided with details of the scientific anti-submarine devices and weapons developed during the campaign.[51] Perhaps *The Naval Review*'s major achievement in reportage of the Atlantic battle was the publication in May 1946 of the 'Convoy Diary' of Gerald S Graham, an instructor in naval history at the Canadian Naval College, who was allowed to spend summers at sea. He later gained great distinction as a naval historian. The diary he kept after joining the destroyer, HMS *Harvester*, in August 1942 deserves to rank with any description of the struggle against U-boats – and the Atlantic.[52]

In a 'Postscript', he described how in March 1943 the *Harvester* rammed and sank a U-boat, but suffered such damage she fell easy prey to another. She summoned a corvette to give assistance, and her smoke was visible when the first torpedo struck; hardly a minute later a second hit:

> *Harvester* reared up for a moment, and then split in half, the forecastle and the stern slowly settling. On the surface five Carley rafts, a few float nets, and sundry pieces of wreckage rocked on the swell. Doc ... swam slowly to a raft already filled with survivors ... He grasped a lifeline beside the sub-lieutenant. Of the captain and No 1 there was no sign; the chief engineer was safe but wounded. 'Guns' had reached another raft some one hundred yards away.
>
> They saw the corvette race in and destroy the U-boat which had risen to the surface to survey its handiwork. If death had to come, this was a fitting curtain to the months and months of cruel, painfully exacting, and sometimes unbearably monotonous toil on the North Atlantic. The sub-lieutenant's fingers slipped from the lifeline; Doc followed. A few minutes before the triumphant corvette bore down to the rescue 'Guns' died too.

An article in November 1946 on 'Radio versus the U-boats' filled out the previous account of the scientific contribution to the defeat of the submarine campaign by detailing the development of ship-borne radio detection sets – 'Huff Duff' or high-frequency direction-finding – enabling escorts to locate and take bearings of transmitting U-boats; and the strides made in increasing the effective range and definition of radar. The crucial advance was the invention of the magnetron, making centimetric wave lengths possible. German scientists never made this step. Towards the end of the war they copied a captured British magnetron, but by then it was too late. The lesson to be drawn, the article concluded, was that 'the Navy must always have at its disposal a body of scientists and technicians of the highest calibre.' The recent establishment of the Royal Naval Scientific Service served that goal.[53]

Meanwhile the Navy prepared for the Cold War against the Soviet Union. During the 1950 Navy Estimates debate in the House of Lords, reported in the August issue of *The Naval Review*,[54] the First Lord stated that a prototype anti-submarine frigate embodying all lessons learned during and since the war was being ordered; a frigate capable of rapid and cheap construction in large numbers was being developed; the highest priority was being given to the development of anti-submarine weapons ...

Plus ça change.

8 The Naval Aviation Controversy 1919–1939

Professor Eric Grove

O N 1 April 1918 the Naval Wing of the Royal Flying Corps, or as it had been unilaterally redefined by the Admiralty four years before, the Royal Naval Air Service (RNAS), was reunited with the Military Wing under a single, new Air Ministry. Attempts to produce a more co-ordinated air policy to deal with the inter-service wrangling of the earlier war years had failed. In the context of the apparent weaknesses of Britain's air capabilities dramatically shown up by the major Gotha raid on London on 13 June 1917, drastic action had seemed to be required.[1] The problem was that a new set of inter-service problems had been created. Somewhat belatedly, and perhaps primarily to justify its case to retain the RNAS, the Admiralty had acceded to the cries from the Fleet to provide it with an air arm for direct air support, but it was too late. When the decision was taken to set up the new service, few RNAS airmen were operating in a primarily naval environment and it was hard for the Admiralty to make a strong counter-argument. Ironically, the Grand Fleet got its best air support after the creation of the RAF rather than before it.[2] The stage was set for a major inter-service controversy that would run until in 1939, when the Admiralty obtained full control of the Fleet Air Arm of the Royal Air Force which had been set up as an uneasy compromise in 1924.

The end of the war immediately put the new system under strain, with demobilisation seeing units which had carried out naval functions reduced to a barely operational state. This was pointed out in the *NR* of August 1919 by Oliver Swann, one of the pioneers of naval aviation in Britain and now, like almost all of them, serving in the RAF. He was in fact Deputy Chief of the Air Staff with the rank of brigadier (the RAF having temporarily adopted Military Wing titles). Swann was clearly anxious that the Navy clearly define what air functions it needed;

113

otherwise the needs of the Navy would be neglected.[3] He argued that the value of aircraft to naval operations had been proven during the war and that this had been noted by the Americans and Japanese. Presciently he argued 'if the British navy is to maintain its leading position, it must keep to the fore in the steady development of naval aircraft.'

Swann listed the naval functions of aircraft as: anti-submarine patrol, escort of convoys, searching for mines, fleet reconnaissance, gunnery spotting against targets both ashore and afloat, bombing enemy naval bases, torpedo attack on enemy ships and operations against enemy aircraft. It was the decline of the units specially equipped for these functions that worried Swann. The peacetime Fleet would use harbours and bases and exercise in areas where the RAF would find it difficult to provide the necessary aircraft. Yet it was 'most important that air forces should participate' in naval activities 'on all possible occasions. Naval officers cannot be expected to regard aircraft as a link in their war organisation if the aircraft rarely take part in exercises.'

He recommended the creation of seaplane units at coastal bases at home and in the Empire for anti-submarine, mine searching, long-range fleet reconnaissance and fleet communications. Seaplanes were recommended, as aeroplanes were still too unreliable for safe peacetime operation over the sea. Fleet reconnaissance and gunnery spotting would in future be carried out by aeroplanes concentrated in aircraft carriers. The practice of launching aircraft from ships and alighting on the water was not sustainable in peacetime. Until sufficient carriers were available, small seaplanes would have to be deployed to be used for these duties from shore bases or those carriers still not fitted for landing on. In order to develop the still immature but vital technique of deck landing the small number of available carriers should be attached to RAF shore stations which would become advanced schools for naval work. Swann called for the break-up of the 'Flying Squadron' formed with the creation of an Admiral Commanding Aircraft for the Grand Fleet at the beginning of 1918, and the distribution of its carriers and aircraft amongst the Atlantic, Home, and Mediterranean Fleets, and some RAF shore bases. This was a most necessary step in order to obtain the widest possible employment of, and experience with, aircraft by the Navy. He also advocated the use of the long-range aircraft already used for anti-submarine warfare to reconnoitre for the fleet and the continued use of kite balloons for spotting.

Swann argued that bombing naval bases did not require specialist forces but torpedo bombing certainly did with fast aircraft in ships and larger seaplanes based ashore. He foresaw fleets made up of ships carrying torpedo aircraft and fighters. He called for one carrier and two shore bases to be devoted to torpedo warfare. Fighters were the primary means of anti-air warfare but here, he argued, perhaps controversially, specialisation was less necessary, and a common RAF fighter force would suffice.

Swann concluded his analysis of naval air roles by looking at other possible future 'oversea uses' of aviation. These included naval roles such as shadowing a fleet at night, transporting naval communications and inspecting officers (which would save the destroyers currently used for the purpose) and more general roles such as long distance attack by carrier-based aircraft 'conveyed to near the hostile country by means of aircraft carriers placed at the disposal of the RAF.' He concluded his study of roles thus: 'These various duties need to be borne in mind, and provision made for them, in order that we shall not fall behind other nations. It is hardly feasible at present to make any suggestion as to what aircraft, ships, and forces generally are required for this purpose, though in the matter of aircraft carriers it is only too apparent that a great scarcity exists.' Swann then went on to discuss organisation and administration. He argued that there were arguments both for the current RAF organisation and for a naval air service. As a compromise, to obtain personnel with the necessary experience, a maritime or 'supermarine' branch of the RAF should be formed.

Swann rehearsed the arguments against the current organisation, the lack of training of a large proportion of RAF personnel working on naval operations, and the lack of former RNAS personnel in the upper echelons of the RAF. Swann argued there were strong arguments against allocating a 'Maritime Air Branch' to the Navy. These reflected the gripes of the RNAS airmen in the period 1915–18 after the Admiralty had tried to curb the autonomy conceded by Churchill as First Sea Lord. Much of the time of naval air units would be spent ashore and while 'naval ways and customs may be suitable for use on board ship … they are not entirely convenient for permanent adoption on shore.' Few RN senior naval officers had air experience (RNAS officers had almost all gone to the RAF) and given the naval tendency for centralisation 'naval officers find it very difficult to grant Air Force officers the free hand to conduct their air operations as they should have.' Swann also argued that a naval air arm would require its own procurement and supply organisations. The RAF could not be expected to supply the right aircraft if it was isolated from the Navy, but the Navy would not, Swann asserted, find it easy to develop expertise in the required specialist areas.

Swann concluded that the best solution in current circumstances was the formation of a specialist Maritime Air Branch of the RAF and 'to insist on the latter taking adequate steps to train and support that branch to the satisfaction of naval requirements.' Officers with naval priorities should be thoroughly represented at the top of the RAF, this being achieved in the short term by equal representation of former RNAS officers. However, the Admiralty's current reluctance to discuss naval air operations with the RAF prevented 'the senior officers of the RAF from directing training design or supply into the right channels, and is obviously fatal to the success of the Air Force.'

Swann's Maritime Air Branch, he proposed, should be formed on similar lines to the Royal Marines. 'Air Marines' would serve in ships and coastal stations and, like Royal Marines, would be sufficiently experienced in naval ways to be employed in ships on ship's duties such as harbour watchkeeping.

Swann's views as one of the most experienced naval airmen in the world at the time are worthy of serious consideration. They might have been the basis for a serious inter-service compromise. Sadly, neither his colleagues at the Air Ministry nor the Admiralty were interested, and the obstinate Trenchard insisted on the 'unity of the air'.

In the next issue of the NR, three articles argued for restoration of the Admiralty's air arm. The first, and most idiosyncratic, was by another former RNAS officer, Lt Colonel F L M Boothby, RAF. He wrote: 'Most of us are agreed that it is essential to have one controlling authority of the fighting forces in the air', but that 'the RAF should be taken over by the Admiralty, and run as a separate department, similar to the Royal Marines.' Just what Commodore Sueter was aiming at in Churchill's day. Boothby argued that the proposed peacetime RAF would be the same size as the wartime RNAS, but 'as air power will largely supersede sea power' the best way to make this transition would 'be for the Admiralty to take charge now, so that all the establishments and staffs are available for gradual change, instead of rival establishments and staffs coming into being at great expense, and finally a struggle for existence taking place between the two departments in which, I believe the Admiralty would eventually be defeated, leaving their centuries old sea bases unoccupied and wasted.'[4]

The other two articles, from RN officers, took a rather more conventional naval view. In one, Captain Briggs, who may well have been a former senior RNAS officer who had not transferred to the RAF, defended the original creation of the RAF on the grounds of the inability of the Army and Navy, with all the other wartime demands on them, to give sufficient attention to air requirements. He was also critical of the airmen who sometime hindered this process: 'young and ambitious pioneers who, having absorbed aviation, rightly wished to keep the control of the new force in their own hands.'

Briggs saw aviation becoming ever more important in the operations of both Army and Navy and the third service being a source of continued friction. In straitened financial circumstances the Air Ministry would concentrate on fulfilling its own demands including 'high wages and expensive establishments' leaving little for the aviation progress of the older services.[5] Briggs saw aviation as a vital part of each service for co-operation in operations commanded by officers who knew the value of their supporting air units.

On the subject of personnel Briggs gave a most valuable insider's view of the wartime problems of the RNAS and how its contemporary airmen regarded it and the RFC's Military Wing as a single air force:

> Up to the outbreak of war the personnel for the Air Force had been provided without any difficulty by Navy and Army officers, who, having been well trained in their respective combatant duties, were lent to the Air Force. In many cases they were rich in the knowledge of what was required of them when in the air, and possessed with full and advanced ideas as to the lines on which aircraft were to be developed to meet Navy and Army requirements. Unfortunately, war broke out before these officers had been able to develop the Air Force, and the air was looked upon with very great suspicion by the whole of the Royal Navy, rightly so in many ways, because they had not had a chance of proving their worth, and even when this became apparent to such leaders as Lord Jellicoe and Lord Fisher, as shown in their recent writings, nothing could be done in the way of providing trained personnel, as this was required to man the ships, excepting only a very few officers for administrative and airship duties; the failure to supply an efficient personnel did more to cramp the progress of the force than anything else.[6]

The wartime air service, Briggs argued, had been dominated by those who just knew how to fly but this was but a fifth of a pilot's education. Intimate knowledge of the Navy, only obtained by working with the Navy for a long period was essential to be a naval aviator. Given the need for specialist knowledge, Briggs argued the Air Ministry should be abolished and its various parts absorbed into the War Office, Admiralty and (for civil aviation) Ministry of Transport. This would prevent conflict over naval air requirements between the two ministries. An air committee would act like the long established ordnance committee to sort out problems of logistics and procurement. Future officers of the Army and Navy would be thoroughly conversant with the potential of aviation once the other two services had 'reclaimed their own'. This view was supported by Commander W P Gandell in his short 'A Plea for a Naval Air Service' that argued the case for partition on the grounds that air operations were almost always 'an accessory to land or sea operations.'[7]

The only contribution on the air question in 1920 was by Lt G W Hooper. His view was the Air Ministry should be left only in charge of central supply and strategic air warfare, while supplying equipment to a renewed RNAS and RFC.[8] This was taken forward the following year by Captain G C Dickens who stated roundly that the current air situation was 'inherently wrong', with the Navy not obtaining sufficient quality and quantity of personnel for its needs.[9] The aircrew seconded by the RAF were insufficient in numbers and needed '"sea sense" as well as "air sense".' The fleet had too few aircraft at home, and abroad virtually none. The Army 'usually has some minor war on hand' but the needs of the fleet, which were more important to overall imperial security, were thus neglected. Command of the sea required command of the air over it. Dickens agreed with Hooper that the best solution was Naval and Army Wings and a Central Air Force looking after strategic operations.

Hooper returned to the charge in the next issue.[10] He pointed out the handicaps of the then current system in developing the Fleet's air capabilities in a war of the future. The Naval Air Section of the Naval Staff consisted of only two officers, a Commander and a Paymaster Commander.[11] The Admiralty could also call on Coastal Area RAF Headquarters also located in London. The staff there 'were responsible for Coastal Air Stations and Aircraft Carriers, and are available to the Admiralty for giving advice. They are, however wholly responsible to and organised by the Air Ministry, and though many of their personnel have sea experience, none are now naval officers.' About 30 per cent of battleships and cruisers carried a junior RAF officer for the embarked aircraft but he was in no position to advise the command on air questions, and only two out of forty naval commands had an air officer to advise. Hooper called for a massive education programme on naval aviation within the RN in all the major training establishments, for 'a shore recruited and shore trained Air Force will fail in naval warfare.' Whoever was in charge, 'there *must* be some altogether naval personnel considering the use of the Naval weapon – Naval aircraft.'

Whether or not influenced by the debate in the *NR*, in 1920 the Admiralty did get the RAF to train naval officers to spot for the Fleet's guns. A branch of naval observers was created and by 1922 twelve had qualified.[12] A concerted attempt was made that year by the Admiralty and War Office to abolish the RAF as an economy measure.

The main *NR* aviation article in 1922 was a substantial piece by Captain R A R Plunkett-Ernle-Erle-Drax. In 'The Influence in the Future of Aircraft on Imperial Defence', Plunkett accepted the need for a third service but insisted that aviation was an essential component of land and sea operations.[13] He insisted that 'no fleet will develop its maximum efficiency, either strategically or tactically unless a liberal supply of aircraft can be placed at its disposal.' He ended with a plea for the RAF 'to meet in council with the other forces and determine how they can achieve the closest possible co-operation and mutual help.'

In 1923 Lieutenant C L Howe produced an extensive analysis of the roles of aircraft with the fleet as they stood and looked likely to develop.[14] The immature state of naval aviation was clear with no real fleet carriers yet available. Organisational improvement was, however, on the way. Also in 1923 a sub committee of the Salisbury committee on inter-service co-operation defined the basic parameters of a compromise solution. Though 'It had been decided that it would not be in the best interests of the country and the Empire for the Navy to have absolute control of its own Air Wing', nevertheless the Admiralty was, however, to have much more control over the air personnel working for it. The Navy observer branch would add reconnaissance to its spotting duties, replacing RAF personnel in this role, and 'As regards the RAF personnel, those chosen to form what will now be called the Fleet Air Arm will work continuously with the Navy, so that those everlasting changes in the personnel working with the fleet, which were amongst the principal evils in the old system, will be avoided.'[15]

It was hoped that 'eventually the FAA would become a unit or corps similar to the Royal Marines.' The new scheme was 'undoubtedly far from satisfactory and we must not relax our efforts to obtain absolute control of the Fleet Air Arm' but the new system must be given time 'to get working properly ... then we shall probably find ourselves later on in a stronger position to enforce our demands for still greater control. At least we shall be able to say that we have given the scheme a fair trial.' This would require tact and understanding on both sides and a real attempt by naval officers to understand the FAA as a vital component of naval warfare. The Navy in the past had been too narrow minded in its attitude to the RNAS and this was 'the seed of all the present trouble.' Knowledge of naval operations would strengthen naval arguments 'to obtain that complete control which is so essential.'

In fact, the creation of the Fleet Air Arm of the Royal Air Force only took place the following year after direct inter-service negotiation and the Trenchard-Keyes Agreement. Pilots would have RAF rank, although up to 70 per cent of them would be naval officers with dual rank (shades of the old RNAS). Other aircrew, observers and telegraphist air gunners, would be entirely RN. FAA aircraft would be paid for by the Navy and procured by the Air Ministry to Admiralty requirements. Coastal Area retained full control of land-based maritime aircraft.

The only comment on air policy that year was a short piece pointing out the need for more aircraft than the projected strength of the FAA.[16] In 1925 Lord Sydenham, a member of Curzon's Air Board in 1916, published an article in the NR on the lack of an air policy in the Admiralty and negative Admiralty attitudes that had contributed to the creation of the RAF. He was, however, doubtful that the current compromise would meet fleet requirements.[17] At the end of the year an article from Proceedings by Lt Cdr Ralph Wood, opposing the creation of a US Air Force and defending the record of the US Navy's developments, was reprinted to make a similar point.[18]

The year 1926 saw interesting discussion over the advantages or otherwise of service in the Fleet Air Arm. A short, rather tongue-in-cheek piece by Lt H St J Fancourt elicited responses from Commander I B B Tower, Lt G M B Langley and Lt Cdr C L Howe.[19] Among other issues were the limit on RN pilots to Pilot Officer rank in the RAF, control by two departments leading to contradictory and overlapping instructions, and different service cultures, especially given the short service of RAF officers. The RAF seems to have been trying to improve the quality of personnel sent to the FAA. Langley put it rather well: 'A sense of humour in the Fleet Air Arm takes one far; and if one manages to adopt a philosophical attitude, the very difficulty in getting anything done in the face of the present dual and oscillatory control, brings all the more joy in accomplishing it.' Observers like Langley and Howe seemed happier than pilots. They also insisted that it was proper that they should command the aircraft in which they flew.

Howe produced some 'Fleet Air Arm Notes' that explained how observer training at RAF Lee-on-Solent had improved, despite the difference in philosophy between the services, where the RAF pilot did the observing and the second man was his wireless operator or gunner. 'In the Fleet Air Arm the observer is collector of information, and has the entire direction of affairs in his hands, being responsible for the course steered, for the reports made and for spotting. The pilot is employed in taking the observer where he wants to go, in putting him in the best position and assisting him to collect the required information.'[20] Readers were assured that the 'Our Fleet Air Arm is small, but it is gaining in efficiency day by day.' The system, despite its defects, seemed to be working and providing a basis for expansion when required.

In 1931 Lt Cdr C G Thompson confirmed this but the current organisation of the FAA, he argued was 'but a makeshift'. It had only worked because of the excellent relations between the services in the aircraft carriers, mutual determination to make the system work and the FAA largely being left alone by the higher authorities. The main problems were that few senior officers in carriers or shore bases had FAA experience. Captains RN were fast becoming more experienced in air work but it was hard for RAF wing commanders to obtain the same position with maritime operations. The carriers only carried a single squadron leader, largely for administrative duties, the aircraft being grouped under him in flights, each commanded by a flight lieutenant, to which rank naval pilots could now be promoted. The solution was to create more squadron leaders and to allow naval pilots to be promoted to still higher RAF ranks. The conditions of service for aircrew were not such as to attract the best personnel. Pilots were uncertain of their future prospects and, unless promoted to flight commander, tended to stagnate, as the operational side was the observer's business and, until becoming a flight lieutenant, there was little opportunity to exercise command.[21]

Even the observers had their problems; always doing the same duties, little opportunity to exercise leadership and command, and limited promotion paths, to only four senior observer posts in the four largest carriers. There was no central school for the FAA as for the other branches and this had unfortunate results.

> The atmosphere at Fleet Air Arm bases and stations is not as efficient as it should be. This is possibly due to the inevitable tendency on the part of the naval officer to relax his sea standards when coming ashore if not given enough to do, to coming under a new commanding officer who naturally does not wish to interfere more than necessary with the Fleet Air Arm flights, and to a lack of guidance and upbringing in how things are best run ashore.

The divided structure also led to curious anomalies, especially in the relationship of naval observers and the RAF/RN pilots. At sea the observers were in command for spotter-reconnaissance missions but ashore, although senior observers made out orders for exercises, these were the senior RAF officer's responsibility to execute. The development of new two-seat torpedo bombers and fighter reconnaissance aircraft observers also meant that the man in the second seat would have to be more closely integrated and put under the flight commander's authority.

To solve these problems Thompson called for the creation of an air establishment like HMS *Excellent* or HMS *Vernon*, the combination of pilot and observer, and the formation of FAA squadrons.

Lt P Bethell responded, generally supporting Thompson's article.[22] His article was an informative piece with some useful history and the information that in December 1931 there were fifty-one RAF and ninety-seven RN pilots in the FAA. He described how the conditions of service for naval pilots had been changed in 1927 to attract more volunteers. The original 1924 scheme had been for four years' flying duties with a year's general service and then half going on for another four years' flying. This did not attract enough personnel and, to save the concept of naval pilots, continuous flying service had been introduced in 1927. Advancement was also a problem. Eleven of the twenty-six flights were commanded by RAF officers so the chances of promotion of the about 160 naval pilots was rather slim. By 1932, Bethell reported, the FAA consisted of eight fleet fighter flights, eleven fleet spotter-reconnaissance flights, and seven fleet torpedo-bomber squadrons. A problem was that these tended to be moved around six to eight times a year. This was 'irksome' and 'demoralising in the extreme.' Also there was the problem of pilots having too little responsibility 'and very little work, and one who would rejoice at being so situated is unlikely to make a good officer.'

The next issue contained comments on Bethell's piece by Lt J C Richards.[23] He said that the 'not entirely satisfactory' system depended too much on personal goodwill. Netheravon (where the first pilots' courses had been held) had been better than Leuchars, the station now used. He thought that the problems of combined pilots and observers were insuperable. The jobs required different talents. He was also dubious about squadrons. He concluded with some interesting points comparing the 'pilot only' role of the junior RAF officer with the responsibility of command of even the most junior naval officer. Quoting the case of flights led by RAF officers attacking battleships rather than battlecruisers as ordered, he argued that all flight commanders and above should be RN. Pilots should also be given administrative responsibilities to broaden their officer abilities.

A second commentary was by Lt Cdr F S Slattery.[24] He disagreed that the observer should inevitably be the captain of the aircraft: it should be the senior officer in the aircraft. He also had tactical reservations about the squadron idea but saw its administrative advantages. The discussion was concluded by three pieces in the August issue.[25] Lt C G Thompson defended the combination of pilot and observer; Richards, an experienced carrier pilot, defended pilots who 'are not the busiest of naval officers, but ... they generally have a fair amount of work to do and sometimes work very hard.' Efficiency depended on the closest co-operation and mutual respect of pilot and observer. The main need of the FAA was the promotion of both pilots and observers 'both to stripes and dignity'. Finally, Lt W T Couchman came out against the combination of observers and pilots, before the editor drew the discussion to a close.

As if reflecting the debate in the *NR*, the following year, 1933, FAA squadrons were indeed formed, allowing naval pilots to progress to squadron leader rank. There were ten squadrons, three fighter (800–803), three torpedo bombers (810–812) and four spotter-reconnaissance (820–824). Six additional naval squadron leaders were also appointed to make sixteen in all. Pilots and observers remained separate and no central FAA establishment was set up.

Time was running out, however, on the makeshift of dual control. With Chatfield as First Sea Lord the Admiralty had its eye firmly on rearmament, which meant a larger FAA under full naval control. In the final issue of 1934 and the first of 1935 Commander G A French presented a comprehensive account of the naval air story so far. He concluded: 'The air arm has established itself as another and most potent factor in the make-up of a modern well-balanced fleet, and as such it must be a naval commitment under naval control.'[26]

At the beginning of 1936 Cdr J Hughes-Hallett produced another contribution in which he stressed the important roles of aircraft with the fleet, first reconnaissance, and then gunnery spotting and attack competing for second place. Hughes-Hallett thought attack was more important. Nevertheless, the foundations for effective air defence via guns had been laid, echoes of the Admiralty views rehearsed that year in the Vulnerability of Capital Ships Committee. He also paid attention to the uses of shore-based aircraft, flying boats especially, over which the Admiralty had no direct control. The editor asked for comments, which were printed in the August issue. Ex-RNAS airship pilot Wing Commander (later Air Chief Marshal) Ralph Cochrane, RAF, stressed the importance of land planes in trade defence. Lt Commander V E Kennedy, RAN, made the case for a greatly strengthened Fleet Air Arm, drawing attention to the USN's 1,000 aircraft compared to the Empire's 250.

The third and most important of these pieces was by Lt Cdr W T Couchman who wanted to encourage further thought in the context of the appointment of Sir Thomas Inskip as Minister for the Co-ordination of Defence and Inskip's announcement that the naval air question was to be reviewed.[27] The problem with the current system, Couchman argued, was unsatisfactory design and supply of equipment, with long delays in equipment the mainstream RAF did not require, very unsatisfactory training, and the absence of co-operation with shore-based aircraft in trade and coastal defence. There were, however, advantages: the RAF supplying the mechanics to service the FAA's aircraft; the theoretical availability of many RAF pilots built up by the short service system, and prevention of an excess of officers at junior ranks. Couchman argued that the Navy should accept centralised procurement but under a Supply Board under Inskip. There should be an FAA School at Portsmouth including Lee-on-Solent and Gosport used exclusively by the FAA. Flying boats should be included in the FAA. The personnel question could be partly solved by naval rating aircrew, both as pilots and observers. This last named point was a key component in the Royal Navy's campaign to obtain full naval control as the RAF refused to accept it.[28]

In his reply to these comments, Hughes-Hallett cast doubts on Cochrane's claims for land-based aircraft and was strangely hostile to Kennedy's numerical comparisons.[29] He was also worried that the Navy might be overstating its case and alienating Prime Minister Baldwin. As a kind of postscript, 'Osprey' added a plea for a Fleet Air Arm Reserve, as he doubted the availability of RAF personnel.[30] He suggested the use of RNVR and RAF reserve personnel who would like to serve in the FAA as pilots and RNR/RNVR personnel and civilians with air navigation and wireless telegraphy licences.

As the naval aviation controversy came to a peak in Whitehall, with Chatfield hinting at resignation if the present situation continued, the editor of the NR, Richard Webb, published another 'The Navy and the Air' article, this time by retired Captain B H Smith as the lead in the first issue of 1937.[31] The author had intended this to be an examination of the Vulnerability of Capital Ships Committee's White Paper but it had become clear that the FAA question was more important. This was a reflection of the quite bitter public debate that had been taking place on the matter. Lord Trenchard in particular had been prominent in arguing for the unity of all platforms that operated in the air, Admiral Richmond in arguing for the need of close integration of air and surface forces to attain the end of protecting maritime communications. Smith came down strongly on the side of the latter: 'The nature of an operation in which any unit is engaged or in which any weapon is used is ... determined by the purpose for which the operation is being carried out and not by the nature of the unit or weapon, nor by the element.' Presciently, Smith argued that land-based maritime aircraft would have to come under naval operational control in wartime and for the creation of a wider 'Naval Air Arm' with land- as well as carrier-based aircraft rather than just a ship-based FAA. Countering accusations from that staunch parliamentary critic of the Admiralty, Lord Strabolgi, that the Admiralty was out to partition the RAF, Smith made it clear that he accepted the importance of the third Service in its own sphere of defending the homeland. Nevertheless, the principle of naval control of forces with a wholly naval purpose ought to be accepted. As long as it was, Smith thought the Admiralty should concede continued Air Ministry control of land-based maritime aircraft, at least for the time being. Interestingly, at almost precisely the same time, the First Lord, Sir Samuel Hoare, advised the Sea Lords not to ask for too much.

The second part of the Smith article appeared in May, the month Baldwin was replaced by Chamberlain, a process that held up a final decision.[32] Smith quoted Inskip's public statements that he was conducting an enquiry and then went through the problems of the existing system: its failure to achieve systematic training of the FAA personnel when disembarked; insufficient exercising with RAF coastal units; the difficulty of maintaining strength with the current 'fantastical' conditions of service; the failure to understand that RAF officers needed sufficient time in the FAA; the lack of a dependable reserve; and the restriction on the utilisation of ratings as aircrew and mechanics.

Smith argued that the RAF already recognised the need for specialisation by allocating officers with sea experience, such as those with RNAS backgrounds, to FAA work. This, however, had the effect of sidetracking the officers in question and was therefore unpopular. Such officers were also a wasting asset. Some movement had occurred on use of ratings, with some petty officers being trained as observers, and a proportion of ERAs being put 'through an aero-engineering course, and draft[ing] one as part complement to every ship which carries a plane. But as the responsibility for the upkeep of the machines is wholly RAF they are unable to exercise their knowledge in peace time.'

Making all personnel naval, Smith argued, would in no way reduce the RAF. It would, however, remove shortages caused by unpopular conditions of service, eliminate waste in training RAF pilots for the FAA, tap naval personnel as a reserve, extend aviation knowledge in the fleet, allow the RAF to concentrate on air defence, and improve inter-service relations. Smith got himself into something of a tangle trying to sort out the supply and command and control of the personnel of a land-based maritime air arm under naval control but he was on stronger ground in advocating better shore training of FAA aircrew. He argued for modifications in the procurement system but recognised the need for some continued unification in this area if the problems of the First World War were not to recur.

Smith used the example of the USA and its superior air arm to argue that the possession of a powerful naval air arm was a separate issue from the creation of an air defence force. He also argued strongly that the RAF was now strong and well established enough not to need the Fleet Air Arm any more. He made a point that still has salience today:

> It is very probable that the refusal of the air exponents to acknowledge the necessity of a change is due to an unconscious persistence of the instinct for self-preservation which was forced upon the RAF at its inception, when it was struggling for its right to exist as an independent force. It is therefore important that naval protagonists should emphasize that in their opinion the Navy and the RAF, the sea and the air, are both of such vital importance that neither can be neglected.[33]

Smith found that the case for a naval takeover of maritime aviation 'completely and overwhelmingly convincing.' Under serious Admiralty pressure Inskip agreed, but only up to a point. On 21 July 1937 he presented his report to the Prime Minister. The FAA would be placed under full Admiralty control and be manned and maintained by sailors. The Air Ministry would retain control of procurement and land-based maritime aircraft. The cabinet agreed that the FAA was no longer a necessary part of the rearming RAF. This was announced by the Prime Minister at the end of July. The transition could not be sudden and it is often forgotten that it took until May 1939 for it to be put into effect.

Chamberlain in his announcement on the complete navalisation of the FAA had called for an end to open controversy and even the *NR* seems to have complied. In the last issue of 1937 all Commander Cresswell did was make a plea for the adequate training of what was now Coastal Command.[34] Still, in January 1938 Smith made clear that he still differed with the decision on land-based maritime air but 'even though the decision may have been taken on what we believe to be a wrong principle, it may still be the correct one and the only practicable one. Any other policy would probably have had to be ruled out by the Admiralty on grounds of expediency; for example, the unwieldy growth of yet another specialism' that would be 'incapable of reabsorption into the higher ranks.'[35] Manning and providing for such a force would have been impossible for the Admiralty which might even have had to try to get the RAF to take it back. Smith said that his purpose in writing was 'not to reopen the controversy but in the hope that it is important even from a selfish naval point of view that it should be closed. A continuation of the controversy, if it did nothing worse, could only create an atmosphere which must hamper the Admiralty in their efforts to ensure that the results of co-operation took the right line.' Critical interactions between the services, while necessary, ought to be kept discreet. In the month in which the FAA passed formally to Royal Navy control the last pre-war article on naval aviation also appeared. It was 'Command of Aircraft Units', and was on the question of whether pilots or observers would do so.[36] Observers would indeed soon command squadrons in the newly naval FAA.

Throughout the interwar period of strife over naval aviation the *NR* had benefited from a steady stream of articles which provide an interesting historical perspective on current issues, especially in a period of financial stringency. The 2010 Defence Review with its dynamic of rapid financial cuts rather than strategic logic showed that the old problems still fester as strongly as ever. The RAF, paranoid about its independence, succeeded in cutting the aircraft that were intended primarily to work with the other Services and retain its most independent assets. Out went maritime patrol aircraft and carrier-based fixed wing. The creation of joint organisations for Sea Harriers and transport helicopters has given the junior Service its chance to enforce Trenchard's unity of the air, and not content with the progressive subversion of Joint Force Harrier the RAF seems, at the time of writing, determined to take over ship-based commando helicopters.

The interwar debate, however, clearly demonstrates that the service balance in maritime air operations must be carefully maintained if efficiency is not to suffer. Policymakers ignore at their peril the words that pioneer aviator Swann who wrote in 1919 that it is 'most necessary that the personnel who operate aircraft overseas, who operate aircraft carriers, who embark in aircraft carriers and other ships, who handle aircraft at coastal bases, and who carry out operations for the Navy, be personnel who are thoroughly acquainted with the sea, in fact seamen and who understand naval ways and methods.' Let us hope that this advice will be heeded, when a century later, proper maritime aviation is being reborn.

9 The Post-1945 Struggle for Naval Aviation

Dr Tim Benbow

NONE of the many controversies in post-1945 British defence policy was more bitter or long drawn out than that surrounding naval aviation. Assumptions about the nature of future war and the hyperbolic claims of air enthusiasts combined to raise questions about the value of the Royal Navy in general and the Fleet Air Arm in particular. These attacks were taken up by individuals in Whitehall and Westminster who sought to cut the defence budget and were persuaded that carriers could provide the savings, being old-fashioned in an age of nuclear weapons and jet aircraft. The Navy had to determine the roles and priority within the fleet of naval aviation while simultaneously fighting for its survival.[1]

These debates were reflected in the pages of *The Naval Review*, although what is perhaps surprising is the relatively small number of articles on this important subject. This perception was shared by some of the *NR*'s members, one of whom commented that he had 'been disturbed for some time that so few of the pages of the *Naval Review* are taken up with naval aviation matters. This has been commented on before, but I detect no signs of improvement.'[2]

Interestingly, in November 1947 the editor included 'the role of naval aviation in a future war' in a list of key questions that he encouraged members to address.[3] If the quantity of pieces about naval aviation was smaller than might be expected, however, their quality and in particular the range of viewpoints they represented is more impressive.

The most fundamental questions about the role of naval aviation were given a full airing, including sceptical viewpoints. By 1945 the general view was that the carrier had now taken the place formerly occupied by the battleship.[4] Yet others questioned its importance. 'Blondin', for example, believed that the Navy should focus on numerous, small escorts and saw little role for sea-based air: 'All air functions except close support of ocean convoys will be carried out by land-based aircraft.'[5] The balance of the fleet between carriers and escorts would prove a recurring topic, as would the respective merits of land bases versus carriers. An exchange between two members explored the latter issue in more detail. 'Mate' accepted the importance of air power at sea but did not believe that it should be carrier-based, arguing that the increasing speed and weight of aircraft were exceeding the ability of carriers to accommodate them. He concluded that well-placed bases around the world would allow aircraft to respond rapidly to any situation:

> the fighter appears to be left as the only aircraft of real value to the fleet: for defence against ship or shore attacks, or for interceptions of the main raids on the primary objective – supposing it was fortuitously placed to do so ... The implications of supersonic speed and atomic war appear to affect the future of seaborne air power to a radical extent, in that they eliminate the value of strike aircraft because they are:
>
> (a) inefficient against shore targets when measured in terms of effective weight of attacking power vis-à-vis their land-based counterparts;
> (b) unlikely to survive an attack against the highly organized and concentrated defensive air and surface equipment available to a modern fleet;
> (c) unable to lift the major weapon of war, the atom bomb;
> (d) prevented from keeping pace with the technical developments of shore aircraft because of the physical limitations of the carrier; and, finally,
> (e) handicapped by being borne in a slow-moving medium in an increasingly fast moving world.[6]

In the following issue, 'Tite-Barnacle' replied, questioning whether aircraft were truly becoming too large and fast for carriers:

> The carrier *may* be reaching her zenith, but remembering how often this has been said about the battleship, one is shy of even a short-term prophecy. When the displacement of the battleship was 14,000 tons there were people who proclaimed she was too big and that if to accomplish her function a greater displacement was needed, then she had better disappear. She is now over 50,000 tons. She may at last be moribund, but one still hesitates to commit oneself on that point. New weapons are being evolved and these may give her a new lease of life. Similar remarks apply to the carrier. If, of course, it be

found that all her functions can be better carried out by other means, well, let her go; but if not, and if to be effective, her displacement must be, let us say, 100,000 tons, then 100,000 tons she must be.

This prediction that carriers would continue to evolve proved prescient. He also questioned the superiority of land-based aircraft, pointing out that air bases could not meet all Britain's needs, because of uncertainty over where they would be needed: 'And even had we possessed the seer-like qualities to foretell where in the vast oceans our battles would be fought, could we, even then, have found and equipped the nice big airfields which Mate so confidently asserts the shore can always provide?' There were limits to the number of air bases that could be expected, he added, while during the war many air bases were lost to the enemy; unlike carriers, those that remained could not be regrouped. Moreover, aircraft from a distant shore base would not necessarily reach the scene of action before those from a carrier.[7] Mate came back, replying that his critic had not taken account of his two key assumptions, namely the effect of atomic weapons and of supersonic speed:

> Putting a 600-knot, long-range, OFFENSIVE aircraft in a ship with a fraction of that speed is rather like carting your prospective Derby winner most of the way round the Epsom course in a horsebox. In the time it takes a fleet to weigh and proceed quite a large bomber force of the future could reach a target several hundreds of miles away. ... Airfields is the next point ... He misleadingly stresses their cost, which is less than that of a carrier, let alone a carrier group or a naval base. And of course they can be built incomparably quicker.

He accepted that carriers with strike aircraft would, 'still be indispensable to any force – if the next war is to continue from the point at which the last one ended ... By its nature, the atomic weapon is likely to limit the duration of war to a matter of weeks, possibly days.'[8]

Such exchanges were an accurate reflection of the struggles underway in official circles. The 1950s saw the Admiralty fighting to preserve naval aviation against the concerted attacks of an unholy alliance of the Air Ministry (largely ministers and officials, with the help of some but not all Chiefs of the Air Staff), the Treasury and some other Cabinet ministers, including people who should have known better, such as the ailing Prime Minister Winston Churchill.[9] As these issues were debated in government, a parallel offensive was waged by retired air marshals in parliament and their supporters in the press. *NR* members perceived – with some justice, it must be admitted – an orchestrated campaign with a clear objective: 'In high Royal Air Force circles it is, of course, desired to lay hands on the proportion of the naval finances now spent on the Fleet Air Arm in order to swell the Royal Air Force vote; hence the present all-out attack on the Fleet Air Arm in press and Parliament.'[10] Another article referred to this campaign as 'Propaganda – Belittlement of the Navy by the advocates of air power' and criticised it directly:

> the RAF does not share the Navy's reputation for taciturnity. The utterances of the official, and still more of the unofficial, advocates of air power have frequently gone far beyond what the facts have warranted. Before the war it was stated and restated that bombers had made battleships obsolete ... It is now assumed that everyone is convinced that the battleship is hopelessly obsolete, and the attack has been turned on every type of naval ship from destroyers upwards, and particularly against the aircraft carrier. The standard propaganda techniques are all used. There is not the slightest attempt to present an unbiased picture, and there is a great deal of competent work put into making the resultant tissue of distortions palatable to the public ... public opinion is continually turned against the fleet, for while we have our protagonists in parliament we do not seem to have any in the press. Journalism may be a murky game, but we cannot afford to treat it with contempt. There is a great need for able, cheerful, and scurrilous propaganda of our own.[11]

The case for the Navy was initially argued on the unfavourable grounds of its contribution to a future war which, policy assumed, would be fought from the outset with nuclear weapons. The argument that naval forces would be essential in the 'broken-backed warfare' that would follow an initial nuclear spasm gained little traction. One argument that surfaced occasionally was that hoary old chestnut of the air power case, the alleged vulnerability of carriers. It was, however, entirely possible that the balance of advantage actually favoured carriers:

> This question of 'vulnerability' seems always to be poking up its head. We are repeatedly told that aircraft carriers are highly vulnerable. Maybe they are. But are not all instruments of war bound, by definition, to be vulnerable? Ships do sink, aircraft do blow up, tanks catch fire, and so on. If ships are vulnerable to air attack, are not shore airfields, aircraft factories and parked aircraft also extremely vulnerable? Certainly we took much trouble to attack the enemy's air bases in the last war, and the losses we caused him (and which he sometimes caused us) appear to indicate that a high degree of vulnerability is not peculiar to aircraft carriers. ... before

the Air condemns the aircraft carrier as peculiarly vulnerable to air attack, might it not be wise to look up what happened to them in the last war? Certainly we lost several carriers, but as far as I know not one of our 58 [carriers] was sunk by shore-based aircraft; and of the 111 American ships of that class precisely 4 seem to have been destroyed by that means (3 by 'Kamikaze' bombing). A careful analysis of the effects of the loss to the enemy of shore air bases and of the numbers of aircraft destroyed on the ground during the recent struggle has yet to be made. It might produce some interesting facts about 'vulnerability'.[12]

The principal difficulty for the Admiralty lay not in the vulnerability argument but in the equally fundamental issue of whether there was a viable role for naval aviation in nuclear war, with critics arguing that resources should instead be devoted to the strategic air offensive or, for the less sea-blind who did not conceive the struggle in such a narrow fashion, to escorts for anti-submarine warfare. Some were attracted to the US approach, by which carriers provided mobile offensive bases to attack enemy territory:

the chances of such a floating base being put out of action in the same sense that an airfield in the United Kingdom might be put out of action are much reduced (if only for the reason that the Task Force has got to be located); the period of time it can be operated from is virtually unlimited, despite what critics are apt to claim; and, what transcends all else in importance, it can come into being at will in any seas where ships can operate. This last attribute means that defensive areas or barriers which can be set up across the routes of attacking shorebased aircraft can be outflanked; the enemy will never know where the source of the next attack will be, nor from which direction the attack will come: hence he will have to tie up a disproportionately larger amount of his resources in defensive measures.[13]

The enormous contribution of naval aviation in the Korean War suggested a valuable role even in total war:

An aircraft carrier near the trouble spot can often accomplish, with a few aircraft, that which the entire air force cannot attempt from distant shore bases ... One of the carrier's principal merits, seen in Korea, is its ability to provide short-range air support where this cannot be done from shore bases ... Combining mobility with economy of force, the aircraft carrier will be in greater demand than ever in an unlimited war.[14]

The naval case became somewhat easier to make as the emphasis of policy shifted from fighting to deterring war, but any suggestion that conventional forces, including a balanced Navy, were themselves an essential part of the deterrent threatened to erode the financial savings promised by the mirage of reliance on nuclear weapons alone. The Air Ministry's theological obsession with the indivisibility of air power led it to treat the fleet carriers and especially the strike capability of the Fleet Air Arm as a dangerous rival as well as a source of additional funds for the V-bombers, which it insisted should have absolute priority in defence spending. The Admiralty fought hard to establish the role of naval aviation in nuclear war and succeeded, albeit barely, in retaining the fleet carriers and a balanced Fleet Air Arm. However, a more plausible rationale for the Navy and naval aviation began to emerge.

Although defence policy still prioritised nuclear war, the advance of Soviet nuclear capabilities fostered doubts over the likelihood of such a conflict. Perhaps defence policy could not be reduced to nuclear weapons alone and conventional forces would have a vital role:

> the present policy of seriously reducing the effectiveness of the British Navy while devoting our major efforts to designing forces based on the use of the hydrogen and atomic bombs will not achieve our aim for the maintenance of peace. The Navy has become the 'Cinderella' of the forces and may be incapable of properly representing our still great and powerful country. First and foremost the Navy must be able to contribute aircraft carriers, the most highly mobile form of air force (for ground-based air forces are only mobile within the range of their aircraft and to the extent that large and extensive bases are ready for them to operate from throughout the world) which can provide defence, offensive action and co-operation with land forces. Particularly important will be their ability to support the new kind of warfare developed in Malaya with helicopters. The alternative to these mobile, ship-borne forces is a much more extravagant and expensive organisation of land forces and air bases scattered throughout the world with the obvious provocation to Russia that such encirclement engenders.[15]

As realisation spread that nuclear weapons could result in stalemate between the West and the Soviet bloc, the issue of Britain's wider international interests became increasingly significant. When the march of decolonisation reduced the availability of garrisons and air bases overseas, attention focused on the ability of maritime task forces centred on naval aviation and amphibious shipping to prevent crises emerging, to nip them in the bud if they should break out or to fight limited war. The Admiralty gradually took up the argument that the Navy and its air power might find their most plausible use in cases other than nuclear war. *The Naval Review* reproduced a speech given at Aberdeen University by Admiral of the Fleet Sir Rhoderick McGrigor, as he came to the end of his tenure as First Sea Lord in early 1955:

> In this new era, such a mutually suicidal war must surely be improbable provided NATO retains its unity, its strength and its readiness. What is probable is a continuation of this uneasy peace with the likelihood of outbreaks of bouts of shooting war, such as occurred recently in Korea and Indo-China. It is the task of the Navies of the Commonwealth to help those in distress, and to prevent trouble or deal with it if it does become active. That duty is world-wide. The arrival of a warship has so often calmed an ugly situation, restored confidence and allowed wiser councils to prevail. When, nevertheless, major trouble does occur we may remember as an example how quickly ships of the Royal Navy arrived off Korea, and brought naval guns and air power to the assistance of the hard pressed soldiers and marines ashore ... The lesson of the Pacific and other campaigns in the last war was borne out, that in outlying parts of the world, where air bases are scarce, it is on the Navy that the Army must chiefly depend, not only for the safe arrival of its troops, but also for their support both by gunfire and air power. That is a lesson which still holds good and is one of the factors which requires that in the foreseeable future we should have aircraft carriers as the core of the Fleet both in peace and war. ... Air power at sea is all-important and its place is as the instrument of the Navy in the application of Sea Power.[16]

The experience of the Korean War suggested the marked advantages of mobility and flexibility inherent in naval air power, and the experience of the Suez crisis in 1956 forced the lesson home even more clearly; despite the limitations of the aircraft of the Fleet Air Arm – the result of the priority given to the RAF – the conflict demonstrated that naval aviation enjoyed significant advantages in limited war over its land-based counterparts:

> The Fleet Air Arm proved to be well equipped for the work it had to do over Egypt. Its aircraft are obsolescent, they could not have met *MIGs* handled with ordinary ability in air-to-air combat, but they made a most effective ground attack force. ... The value of aircraft carriers has been the subject of much debate in recent years. This operation has demonstrated that they are a key element in what

The Economist calls the 'Little Deterrent', especially in a world in which land-based air forces have fewer and fewer airfields from which tactical aircraft can reach trouble spots. It was in fact the existence of our carrier force which made this operation possible, for the RAF high level bombers were inaccurate and ineffective, whilst their fighter-bombers were working at the limits of their range and endurance. The Americans have extensive experience of the employment of carrier-based aircraft in the close support of ground forces. We have had much less experience but at Port Said the Aircraft Carrier Squadron provided a Tactical Air Force of the highest quality. This undoubtably made a profound impression on the soldiers. They now know our worth and this will influence their thinking profoundly. Plainly we must study together the possibilities of an airborne 'fire brigade' with carrierborne support; sustained by helicopter carriers such a force would appear to be the most effective answer to many cold war emergencies.[17]

While the Navy still insisted that carriers would play a vital role in total war, it proved tactically expedient to place the main emphasis on more limited conventional operations. This concept was enshrined in the pivotal Sandys Defence White Paper of 1957 which grudgingly acknowledged a role for the Navy in deterring or fighting a war with the Soviet Union but made peacekeeping and limited intervention east of Suez its principal role.[18] The editor of the *NR* was understandably pleased with the 1957 Explanatory Statement on the Navy Estimates: 'From it there appears to emerge a picture of a Navy facing a period full of uncertainties without dismay and without any doubts as to its future usefulness.' He quoted from the speech introducing it by the Parliamentary Secretary:

It is surely not in dispute that we need to be able to deploy air power in many different parts of the world. This can be accomplished either from long strips of concrete on land or from aircraft carriers. Both have their advantages and disadvantages. Hitherto we have thought in terms of the main punch of our air power being land-based and being supplemented where necessary by carrier-borne aircraft. But in proportion as our bases in foreign lands diminish in numbers, either for economic or for political reasons, the more apparent becomes the value of the mobile carrier-based aircraft. ... One of the military lessons we have surely learned from those limited wars in which we have been involved in the last decade is the great importance of being able to deploy air power from a mobile carrier, which can be first into action and can be placed where you want it.

He continued, quoting from the Estimates:

> a number of Task Forces, each consisting of one carrier, armed with
> the most modern weapons and aircraft that we can afford, a cruiser
> and a number of destroyers and frigates for protection both from
> the air and from the sea; to be deployed in the most advantageous
> manner round the world but capable of concentrating at any given
> point should the need arise ... The Carrier Task Group may be in
> the Persian Gulf one day, could be in Aden the next week,
> somewhere far down the East African coast the week after and in
> Singapore twelve days later. No other military organisation can be
> so self-sufficient, so mobile and so versatile, and there is an added
> merit to this mobility – the Navy does not need to remain
> permanently poised in any potential trouble centre, an ever-present
> irritant to local sensibilities. There are many territories where our
> military power would be welcomed in time of trouble but which do
> not wish to have billeted upon them permanent, static forces. They
> like us to call, but not to stay, and that is what the Navy does.[19]

In the years immediately following the 1957 Defence Review, the picture
looked favourable for the Royal Navy and its organic aviation. Both
now had an accepted role in British strategy while their ability to
perform this role was enhanced by long overdue material improvements.
British naval aircraft had lagged far behind modern developments – not
due to any inherent limitations in naval aviation but rather because of
policy decisions to prioritise the RAF during the early years of the Cold
War. There had been awareness in the *NR* of these inadequacies. For
example, in 1953 'VVV' complained that 'the provision of a British
Naval Fighter of the highest performance should have been accorded
super priority a long time ago in the same way, and at the same time as
it was accorded to the RAF Fighter. Failure to do this can but mean that
the Navy must wait a long and indefinite period before this vital weapon
and all that goes with it becomes available for the defence of our sea
communications.'[20] Fighters were undoubtedly a problem but the
shortcomings of British strike aircraft were equally evident:

> Scientific developments have, until the advent of the guided missile,
> left [the Navy] with only one truly offensive weapon capable of
> carrying the war into the enemy's country, namely the carrier
> aircraft. Yet look at the picture presented by Naval Aviation today.
> We have not in squadron service a strike aircraft more modern than
> the Wyvern. Its inadequacy under modern conditions hardly needs
> commenting on. The aircraft carrier may be called the battleship of

the modern fleet, but at present it must be compared to a battleship armed with muzzle-loading cannons, not 14' guns.[21]

By the late 1950s, however, the picture was improving with new fighters such as the Scimitar and Sea Vixen. The *NR* was also able to hail the NA39 strike aircraft (later named the Buccaneer), which survived repeated attempts by the Navy's opponents to have it cancelled. It would:

> give the Navy its first aircraft to be specially designed for a naval role, and one which in every respect has no equal in its particular class. 'This aircraft will be capable of performing a strike role against targets at sea and on land and of providing air support for land operations', said the Ministry of Defence announcement, 'and in the low level strike role the NA39 is ahead of any other aircraft in the world'... Its importance to the Navy is emphasised by the statement of the First Sea Lord last March when he described it as 'the world's first specially designed low level high speed strike aircraft'.[22]

These new aircraft were heavier and faster than early generations but still within the capacity of the wartime carriers when suitably modernised; 1958 also saw the completion of the modernisation of HMS *Victorious* – another project which had been bitterly opposed by the anti-carrier lobby:

> After seven years in dockyard hands, HMS *Victorious*, veteran aircraft carrier of wartime Russian convoys, air actions against the *Bismarck* and *Tirpitz*, and the war against Japan, has been recommissioned and is at present engaged on extensive sea trials. She has been modernised and fitted with all the British-developed aids for the operation of high performance aircraft afloat, and she makes her reappearance in the fleet with a fully angled flight deck, steam catapults, mirror landing aids and other new devices – the world's most up-to-date aircraft carrier.[23]

Such advances in capability came at an opportunity cost and the balance of the fleet was questioned again. 'RAC' considered that too much of the Navy's budget was being devoted to naval aviation at the expense of capabilities required to win a war at sea against submarines (for which he argued carriers have 'very limited' potential) and fast jet aircraft (against which carriers are vulnerable because they can only operate small numbers of advanced fighters). He conceded that carriers were 'invaluable in providing tactical air support for the Army in those increasingly widespread theatres where the RAF cannot operate' but this role should not come at the expense of the Navy's ability to win the naval battle against submarine and air attacks:

> I suggest that current naval policy does not meet our needs in conception, let alone size ... The H-bomb has changed nothing in this respect. We need a large anti-submarine force of all kinds which can meet an almost unlimited submarine threat in any part of the world. We need missiles for air defence. This must be the basis upon which the rest of the Navy stands and we cannot have it until the conception of the 'balanced fleet', which really means a prestige fleet too weak everywhere to decide the issue in war, is dropped.[24]

Other voices, however, supported the emphasis on mobile task forces – including 'one normal carrier, one Commando carrier' plus amphibious landing ships and escorts – for roles other than war with the Soviet Union:

> If, therefore, limited war is recognised as the most likely problem with which the Navy will have to deal in the foreseeable future, then surely it would seem more prudent to build up a well balanced fleet, with adequate proportions of all types required for this, rather than expend the bulk of our limited resources on antisubmarine types solely to meet the Russian submarine threat ...[25]

Despite this debate over what might now be termed 'the war' versus 'a war', the naval leadership was clear that naval aviation would remain essential. One major problem that had been put off, however, now became increasingly pressing: the fight in the early 1950s had been to preserve and modernise the existing carriers. This struggle had been difficult enough but as the ships became older and less capable of operating modern aircraft, the question of a new carrier became unavoidable. At the press conference on the 1960–61 Navy Estimates, Admiral Sir Charles Lambe, the First Sea Lord, 'scotched the rumour that the *Hermes* is the last aircraft carrier we are ever going to build. So long as it is necessary to deploy air power around the world to any point where military force is needed and one cannot operate military forces without having air power in support – so long we are going to need aircraft carriers. "I think it is clear", the First Sea Lord continued, "that unless we find some entirely new strategy or there is disarmament, or something of that sort, we shall go on needing aircraft carriers, and that will mean eventual replacements".'[26]

Such a programme was bound to be costly and as one correspondent noted, the time was not necessarily propitious: 'We must face the fact that a new generation of carriers, with their new aircraft, will be immensely expensive and so perhaps it was more than the Chancellor of the Exchequer could stomach at this time of financial difficulty to commit himself to such large expenditure for many years ahead.'[27] The opposition would not simply come from the Treasury but also from the RAF which, facing the imminent loss of the nuclear deterrent due to the vulnerability of manned aircraft (there's irony), began to fight with growing desperation for the role of tactical air power in support of intervention overseas, which it had hitherto been content to leave to the Navy. The Air Ministry opposed the new carrier project with its own island base scheme with which, it proclaimed, overseas operations could be more effectively and economically supported. As the debate raged, one impressive article systematically demolished the anti-carrier arguments one by one:

(a) *'No overseas commitments in the 1970s'*
    Although this particular school of thought represents the most fundamental objections to the idea of new carriers, they are probably not the most dangerous. Governments of whatever political persuasion in this country are more likely to favour holding the Commonwealth together, and making a due contribution to the containment of Communism. They could not contemplate arriving at the end of this decade with a generation of worn-out weapons and equipment, and nothing to replace them – though opinions may well differ about the reasonable minimum of military preparedness that will serve our purposes.

(b) *'We can't afford it'*
    So long as the economisers will admit that this country ought to have a sensible world-wide strategy for exercising a cold war presence and if necessary exerting a limited war force where our overseas interests are threatened, they may rest assured that such a strategy cannot be achieved by the United Kingdom without the use of aircraft carriers. This is what this country's carriers are for – not as a part of the strategic nuclear deterrent. Moreover, the aircraft carrier will increasingly represent the most economical way for us to deploy aircraft world-wide. ... The economical answer for exerting a world-wide military presence is the flexible deployment of a relatively small number of aircraft by taking them on board mobile airfields to whatever part of the world our interests require.

(c) *'Do it by air'*
    ...The weaknesses in the arguments of those who favour maximum emphasis on the air medium are perhaps these:-

(i)   All the indications are that we are likely to have less air bases abroad, less staging rights and less overflying permissions in the 1970s and onwards than we have today; it is therefore becoming more important than ever to replace our carriers. No scheme for building up a new chain of air bases ashore is likely to prove politically realistic.

(ii) In this connection we must not be misled by talk of 'air strips' to imagine that setting up air bases ashore is a simple matter. Modern aircraft with their requirement for testing and servicing (not to mention defence of the airfield) call for far more than an airstrip.

(iii) Even if the necessary bases could still be guaranteed, professional advice is unanimous that carriers of some kind are indispensable to this strategy, for defence of the seaborne component of the force and for close support of the Army in the early stages of an operation. ... Since we must have carriers, it would be military folly and throwing away money to have second-rate ones.

(iv) The 'do it by air' strategy calls for very large shore-based aircraft and fixed bases ashore, with all their defensive and logistic paraphernalia, in such numbers that it would pretty certainly be prohibitively expensive even if it were politically and militarily feasible.

(d) *'Aircraft carriers are vulnerable'*

...The short answer to these objectors is that all experience has shown the aircraft carrier in a properly constituted task force to be an extremely difficult target to disable ... Quite probably carriers are less vulnerable than airfields ashore. It cannot, however, be denied that carriers, like any other kind of military installation that has yet been invented, are vulnerable to some extent to attack. There is no means of eliminating all risk from military operations and no one would deny that ships must be exposed to certain risks. The final dilemma for members of this school of thought is that since carriers of one kind or another are indispensable to our oversea strategy, they must either decide to accept a certain risk or to go without an effective strategy ...[28]

Such arguments, reflecting closely those presented by the Navy, demolished the case for the island base scheme and in 1963, the decision went in favour of naval aviation. The government announced the acquisition of a new carrier, CVA-01, which was welcomed by *The Naval Review* in an editorial demonstrating an accurate understanding of the policy debate:

The Government's decision to lay down a new aircraft carrier is of the greatest importance to Britain's defence and a vital one for the Royal Navy. Indeed there must have been an almost audible breath of relief in every warship and naval establishment when the news came through. It was fully realised that if the decision had gone against the building of a carrier it would have meant the end of the Royal Navy as we have known it – a balanced force of all arms capable of operating with effective offensive and defensive power anywhere in the world. So the question of approval to build a replacement for the carrier *Victorious*, which will end her useful life about 1970, has been the Admiralty's major pre-occupation for a considerable time ...[29] The arguments against the carrier were that we could get effective defence without large and extremely expensive ships. It was argued that with vertical-take-off aircraft much smaller vessels could provide air cover for convoys. As regards operations in distant parts of the world, it was argued that this could be done by land-based planes owing to modern techniques of flight re-fuelling, vertical-take-off and with mobile aircraft control and warning equipment. Finally, it was argued that the big carrier was far too vulnerable to carry so big a proportion of Britain's defences. The answers to these arguments, and ones that have carried the day, are first the large size of the carrier is due to the large number of aircraft that must be carried for effective striking power, reconnaissance, defence of convoys and self-defence; it would be much more costly to provide several smaller ships for the same purpose. As regards vulnerability, the defences of a carrier-task-force are extremely formidable and in this missile age, the carrier, being mobile, has an immense advantage as an air base over a fixed base on land. As regards overseas operations, there are many situations in which only a carrier could provide the initial and vital air cover and air support for an opposed landing.[30]

The planned acquisition of CVA-01, which was to be called HMS *Queen Elizabeth*,[31] was a stunning victory in the post-1945 battle for naval aviation. The Air Ministry was not ready to accept defeat, however, while the Treasury continued to prove a receptive audience for any claim to offer a cheaper alternative. Before construction could begin, a change of government brought about a reassessment of Britain's military ambitions and how they should be pursued. In retrospect, a 1965 press conference suggested that Denis Healey, the new defence secretary, had already made up his mind:

First of all, of course, we are looking to see whether it is possible to save any more money by spending less on equipment without changing commitments. I believe it may be possible to make further savings on aircraft numbers, even within existing commitments, particularly if we can get more inter-operability between RAF and Naval aircraft and if we can get a more cost effective mix of land- and sea-based air power ... But I do not believe it will be possible to go the whole way towards closing the remaining £200 million gap by further savings on equipment. And the only way to close the gap finally and with any certainty will be to look at the whole range of our commitments as well, and see whether we can revise those so as to give our forces less to do, reduce stretch, and also enable us to work with a smaller total of forces than we have at the present time ... commitments cannot be the sole factor in deciding the shape of your forces, we also have to think about what general capability our forces ought to have in order to support our foreign policy in the very different politico-strategic context which the world will be in the seventies. We have to ask ourselves questions like, 'Is it necessary for us in the seventies, for example, to have the capability to carry out the sort of operation which we tried to carry out in 1956 at Suez, the capability alone to land British forces against moderately sophisticated opposition very, very far from their home bases?' Indeed must we plan to fight a limited war alone anywhere in the world, and if not, what sort of capability should we contribute where to what sort of Allied Forces composed of what Allies? ... By the end of this year I think we shall probably know the limit of the further savings we can make on equipment within the context of existing commitments. Moreover, by the end of this year we shall have to know enough about the new commitments we plan to carry in the seventies to decide, first of all, whether we want to take up the option on the F-111A, and secondly whether we want to go on contract on the first of the new carriers CVA-01.[32]

The writing was on the wall for the new carrier, despite the underlying plausibility of the case that they were an economic and flexible way to protect British interests that remained important – and worldwide.

The struggle for naval aviation in the twenty years following the end of the Second World War was prolonged and for high stakes; the existence of Britain's naval air arm was genuinely at stake. While the nagging feeling remains that *The Naval Review* perhaps did not fully do justice to the naval aviation issue, it did cover the debate from a commendably wide range of perspectives. There was a good balance between coverage of policy announcements and broader discussion of the issues involved. The analysis it provided was well informed and often stood the test of time rather better than some of the arguments levelled against naval aviation by its critics.

sight which must have startled some in 1933: a sailing model of HMS *Victory* commanded by
ymaster Captain J J Batchelor, RN, and manned by officers of HMS *Nelson*.

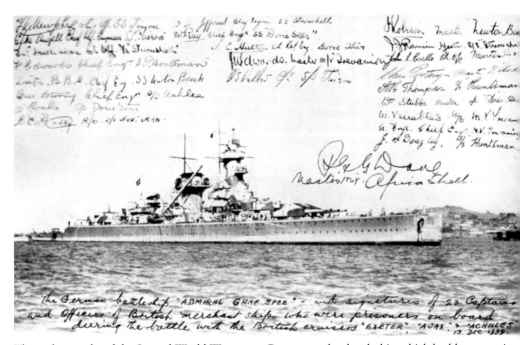

The early months of the Second World War saw a German pocket battleship which had been preying on British merchant ships brought to bay by three British cruisers, HM Ships *Exeter*, *Ajax* and the New Zealand-manned *Achilles*. This photograph, published in *The Naval Review* just a few weeks after the Battle of the River Plate, was signed by the masters and officers of captured British merchant ships who were held prisoner onboard the German *Graf Spee*.

Sketches and maps were all part of the skills of the average naval officer, and used in *The Naval Review*: here, a drawing of Ankenes, Norway, after bombardment on 27/28 May, 1940 to drive out the invading Germans, drawn by an officer in the bombarding cruiser.

OUR FATHERS

To the Memory of the nameless Killed and Wounded.

by Captain Ronald A. Hopwood. R.N.

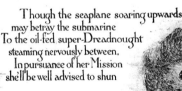

Though the seaplane soaring upwards
may betray the submarine
To the oil-fed super-Dreadnought
steaming nervously between,
In pursuance of her Mission
she'll be well advised to shun

Any interfering cruiser
with the latest seaplane gun.

Thus does Science rule the revels
that our Fathers used to know
While the sea, that bred our Fathers, marks the fashions come and go,
Humours each, but sometimes wonders if the Truth were better sought
In the latest works of Science, or the deeds our Fathers wrought

Quaint and crude our Fathers methods, and their ships and guns the same
Watch them "warping out of Plimouth" when the Great Armada came

Hear them "give the Duke defiance", all their shot and powder spent
Men in truth, but manning makeshifts, still the Duke Medina went

Went in shame and hopeless ruin, with the fear alone in mind
Of our Fathers, spent and weary, hanging grimly on behind
Scant of food, in rags and tatters, "What you have will have to do"
I.   Lacking everything they needed, but the heart that pulled them through.

W L Wyllie

ne 'Sea-King' (see chapter 2), Admiral Ronald Hopwood, wrote stirring verses about the late-
ctorian and Edwardian Navy. This is the first part of a poem, which first appeared in 1913 when it
as used to raise money for wounded seamen, and reprinted in *The Naval Review* in 1941 to raise
orale. The illustrations are by W L Wyllie.

Packing parachutes.

Wrens afloat.

Wren Radio Mechanic (test flight).

Qualified Ordnance Wrens.

Wren Fitters at work.

The Women's Royal Naval Service was not much mentioned in *The Naval Review* until recently, but they were not forgotten, as shown in this montage from a wartime edition of *The Naval Review*.

HMS *King George V.*

Operations off Madagascar.

In the Mediterranean.

In the winter.

In a home port.

Another facsimile page from the wartime *Naval Review* which was allowed to print a varied selection of contemporary scenes of naval operations and life.

Captain 'Johnny' Walker, CB, DSO*** (1896–1944), on the bridge of HMS *Starling*, the Royal Navy's most successful anti-U-boat hunter during the Battle of the Atlantic. In December 1941, while escorting convoy HG-76, Walker's antisubmarine escort group sank four U-boats in what was considered to be the first real convoy escort victory of the Second World War. Groups under Walker's command would go on to sink more U-boats during the Battle of the Atlantic than under any other commander, and he was a key figure in the Allied victory in the Battle of the Atlantic, the most important campaign of the war. The offensive hunting group under Walker's leadership proved to be decisive: he would play 'A Hunting We Will Go' over the ship's Tannoy on return to port.

(Below) Night bombardment. The cruiser HMS *Mauritius* supporting the Fifth Army in Italy in 1943. Support of the army by the navy, and particular by naval gunfire, in battles as far apart as Norway, North Africa, and Normandy, became a regular feature of naval operations in the Second World War.

HMS *Taurus* shows off her Jolly Roger on return to England after eighteen months abroad during which time she had sunk a Japanese submarine. (M R G Wingfield)

The Fairey Swordfish, designed in the late 1930s, remained in front-line service throughout the Second World War: nicknamed the Stringbag, it achieved spectacular success including the attack on the Italian fleet at Taranto on 11 November 1940, the crippling of the German battleship Bismarck in May 1941, and the destruction of some fourteen U-boats. (P G Hore)

As in the previous world war, in 1939 armed merchant cruisers were manned by RNR and RNVR officers and men, and used to help enforce the blockade of Germany and to escort convoys. This fine picture by W L Wyllie appeared in *The Naval Review*.

10 Full Circle: *Queen Elizabeth* to *Invincible* and Back Again

Captain Jeremy Stocker, RNR

ON 14 February 1966 the Cabinet agreed to Defence Secretary Denis Healey's proposal to cancel the first of a new generation of large aircraft carriers, designated CVA-01. The decision was made public a week later in a Defence White Paper

> The present carrier force will continue well into the 1970s; but we shall not build a new carrier (CVA-01). This ship could not come into service before 1973. By then, our remaining commitments will not require her ...
>
> Experience and study have shown that only one type of operation exists for which carriers and carrier-borne aircraft would be indispensable: that is the landing, or withdrawal, of troops against sophisticated opposition outside the range of land-based air cover. It is only realistic to recognise that we, unaided by our allies, could not expect to undertake operations of this character in the 1970s – even if we could afford a larger carrier force.
>
> But the best carrier force we could manage to have in future would be very small. The force of five carriers, which we inherited from the previous government, will reduce to three in a few years' time. Even if CVA-01 were built, the force would be limited to three ships through the 1970s. The total cost of such a force would be some £1,400m over a ten-year period. For this price, we should be able to have only one carrier permanently stationed in the Far East with another normally available at up to 15 days' notice. We do not believe that this could give a sufficient operational return for our expenditure ...
>
> In order to give time to reshape the Navy and to reprovide the necessary parts of the carriers' capability, we attach great importance to continuing the existing carrier force as far as possible into the

1970s. The purchase of Phantom aircraft for the Navy will, therefore, go ahead, though on a reduced scale. The Buccaneer Mk 2 will continue to enter service.

HMS *Ark Royal* will now be given a major refit in Devonport, starting later this year, to enable her to operate both these aircraft until 1974–75. The gradual rundown of the Fleet Air Arm will be carefully arranged in order to safeguard the careers of officers and ratings who are serving the nation so well.'[1]

Grove wrote twenty years later that 'The decision to abandon CVA-01 was perhaps the most traumatic shock to the Royal Navy of the entire postwar period.'[2] Even today, the mid-1960s carrier controversy remains the defining episode in determining the shape of the Fleet over the succeeding half-century.

The cancelled ship was to have been named *Queen Elizabeth*, though this was not at the time public knowledge. Had it been, the government's decision might have proved more politically awkward. Over forty years later, on 3 July 2008 another Labour government signed a contract for production of two new carriers (CVFs), even larger than the aborted CVA-01. The first is to be named *Queen Elizabeth*, and this time the name was well-publicised in advance.

In the intervening years the RN kept alive the ability to operate fixed-wing aircraft at sea by means of the much smaller *Invincible*-class carriers. It was a story of political manoeuvring, innovative design, and operational adaptation which featured episodically in the pages of the *NR*.

The initial reaction to the loss of CVA-01 was mixed. Some viewed it with dismay, were critical of government policy and sceptical about proposed alternatives such as the RAF's island base strategy for continuing an East of Suez presence. They could not see a future without carriers. Captain Archdale wrote that 'The case for carriers is so important to the security of our country that certain misconceptions on this subject … cannot go unchallenged', and concluded 'Fixed wing manned aircraft, and carriers as we know them, remain an essential component of sea power. Without them our shipping, and therefore the security and influence of our country, is at risk: without them it is certain that much of our Army and RAF strengths cannot be safely deployed. The Royal Navy must continue to press for their provision.'[3]

Others, including the *NR*'s then editor, regretted the decision but saw the need to remodel the Fleet for the future:

We can all welcome the fact that some attempt has at last been made to face up to our chronic national dilemma of 'world power' commitments unmatched by 'world power' resources to sustain them ... As regards the main 'talking point', the decision not to build a new generation, or even one, new carrier – CVA01 – it can be argued that this may indeed have been a wise decision for two broad reasons. The first is that the experts have proved to their own satisfaction that the modern, sophisticated carrier must be very big to enable her to carry a worthwhile load of today's aircraft; she also has to carry an enormous amount of complicated and expensive equipment to enable her to deal adequately with such aircraft. This adds up to an appallingly expensive ship which can be held to represent too high a percentage of the country's naval stock-in-trade to put on one keel. It follows from these 'size and cost' con- siderations that we could never have enough modern, sophisticated carriers and that these ships have, in fact, *priced themselves out of our reach*. [Italics in the original.][4]

'Matelot' also saw the need to move on. 'The Carrier decision is a fact of life. Where do we do go from here?' He added 'Unless there is some dramatic and almost unimaginable change in the economic situation and in government policy, we must plan for a Fleet without Carriers.'[5]

A Future Fleet Working Party was established to advise on what it would look like, though its classified deliberations went unreported in the *NR*. Although carriers were off the agenda the working party did move forward an idea that been gestating since about 1960. A new type of escort carrier could operate a number of ASW helicopters (possibly freeing up deck space in the fleet carriers).[6] That a through-deck was the most efficient way to operate more than a couple of aircraft at a time was soon evident. Equally apparent was that such a ship might be able to carry a number of vertical take-off and landing (VTOL) jets. The experimental P1127 had already undertaken trials at sea, and might not even have to wait for new platforms: 'Let our existing Carriers be equipped with VTOL aircraft and helicopters – both British built – and used primarily in the peacekeeping role, with a secondary total war role of convoy protection and air strikes on the high seas.'[7]

The *Tiger*-class cruisers were being modified to take ASW helicopters, so new ships could be presented as replacements for them, rather than the now taboo carriers. Absent the latter, the cruisers became the new capital ships. That there was still a need to get some form of fixed-wing aircraft to sea was evident to most naval officers:

The obvious solution is a new generation of Tactical Aircraft capable of operating either from sea or shore. It has been said that we tried to get this and failed. But, nevertheless this still represents the only circumstance under which we are likely to see aircraft at sea in the late 1970s. And the second point which must be made is that, it is the aircraft, as much the most expensive item, which will determine the type of carrier required.[8]

But this was not the way to move forward. The Navy would try to get a 'through-deck command cruiser' (TDCC) to operate helicopters for ASW and possibly amphibious roles and then try to exploit the design to take a few Harriers to sea. That this would be a carrier in all but name soon became apparent to Lieutenant Commander Croker and others: 'In addition to A/S helicopters, an escort carrier can conveniently operate S/VTOL fighters for reconnaissance, air defence and surface strike against enemy missile ships which may seek to attack the convoy.'[9] 'PRCJ' reminded the readership 'certainly the through-deck ships are capable of carrying out three roles relatively well – as anti-submarine helicopter bases, VTOL operating ships and of course as troop-carrying or landing ships … if we are to retain a limited world-wide capability then they do become useful.'[10]

The lesson of CVA-01 had been learned and the Navy Board was at pains to avoid arousing the opposition of the Air Force, even suggesting that the Harriers might be flown by RAF pilots.[11] 'Cecil' succinctly and accurately predicted the Navy's future requirements:

the Royal Navy needs an absolute minimum of four distinct types of VTOL aircraft, ie:
1. A large ASW helicopter (Antisubmarine warfare).
2. A large transport helicopter.
3. A VTOL light strike aircraft. (Vertical take-off and landing).
4. An AEW/ECM helicopter. (Airborne Early Warning/ Electronic Counter Measures).[12]

While what was to become HMS *Invincible* was still in development the old carriers remained, though in reducing numbers. The 1966 White Paper had intended the existing force to run well into the 1970s while the Fleet acquired compensating capabilities like surface-to-surface missiles and more SSNs, as well shore-based air cover provided by the RAF.

As a result of this transitional plan *Ark Royal* received a major refit between 1967 and 1970, extending her life and allowing her to operate some of the Phantoms that were originally intended for CVA-01. But the stay of execution was short-lived. As the economic situation continued to worsen and a sterling crisis emerged, pressure to reduce the defence budget further intensified. In May 1967 the Cabinet decided to withdraw from East of Suez by the mid 1970s. The early retirement of *Victorious* followed and *Hermes* was converted to a helicopter-only commando carrier starting in 1970. *Ark Royal*, despite her refit, was to go in 1972 and *Eagle* would not now be equipped to take the Phantom. She would also decommission in 1972. The substance of these changes was more immediate than even the 1966 decision, but went largely unnoticed in the *NR*, perhaps because the Navy was already reconciled to the loss of the carriers.

The return of a Conservative government in June 1970 raised hopes of a reprieve and the prospect of at least a two-carrier force for the 1970s. *Ark Royal* did indeed remain until 1978 though *Eagle* still went in 1972, despite Lt Cdr Croker's entreaties, and recruitment of fixed-wing aircrew was not resumed.[13] A future *NR* editor spelled out requirements: 'VSTOL aircraft operating from cruisers, plus a fully developed RAF maritime strike force within the NATO area, with surface-to-surface missiles in a high proportion of surface ships, and Fleet Submarines', and suggested that 'this doesn't look too bad.'[14]

In 1973 the long hoped-for TDCC order finally materialised. The editor, under the heading 'HMS *Invincible* – Cruiser or Carrier?' noted that: 'The Government ordered, on April 17th, "the first of a new class of through-deck cruisers for the Royal Navy." … The outcome appears to be a warship of large "cruiser size" and hull shape equipped for the following functions: tactical command and control; area defence against aircraft and missiles; embarkation, operation and support of large A/S helicopters and (not yet confirmed by Government announcement) V/STOL aircraft.'[15]

The compromises inherent in the ship's 'cruiser' origins were apparent, and the ever-alert Croker questioned whether the ship should carry guided missiles as well as aircraft, and her projected £60m cost (the same in cash terms as CVA-01).[16] Otherwise the *NR* was sur-prisingly muted, despite BBC journalist Nick Childs's 2009 assertion that *Invincible* 'defined the modern Royal Navy.' Perhaps that the ship had been so long in gestation was not news.

Within Whitehall the Navy was still pressing, gently but persistently, for fixed-wing aircraft for the new ship. It had even secured RAF consent for the principle. The operational requirement was a limited one – to 'hack the shad', Soviet reconnaissance aircraft such as the *Bear* D which might shadow the Fleet. By 1974 Labour was back in power and was persuaded and gave approval for the Sea Harrier to go ahead.

By 1978 *Invincible* was in the water and in December the old *Ark Royal* was decommissioned. This momentous change from the old carriers to the new (the word carrier was permissible once again, and the *Invincibles* were finally classified as CVSs, anti-submarine carriers) went unnoticed in the *NR* until it was belatedly, but astutely, marked by D P Norman, 'So ended an era – but so began another.'[17] The first Sea Harrier squadron went to sea, not in *Invincible*, but the old *Hermes*. But no sooner were both ships operational with their new aircraft than another financially-driven defence review threatened to reverse course once again. The sale of *Invincible* to Australia was mooted and the Defence Secretary John Nott made plain his lack of enthusiasm for even a modest carrier capability, though it could prove useful out of area (ie, East of Suez!).[18] The *NR* had little time to respond before a carrier task force was despatched to the South Atlantic.

The conduct of the Falklands campaign, in which the carriers and their aircraft played such a pivotal role, need not be repeated here. Much of the *NR*'s subsequent commentary was based on first-hand accounts. It was left to Lieutenant Commander (later Vice Admiral) Charles Style to summarise the key lessons from Operation Corporate, some five years later. By then *Hermes* had finally gone (to India as *Viraat*) and *Invincible, Illustrious* and the new *Ark Royal* were all in service, though just two operational at any one time. There was little more to be said about the carriers during the final years of the Cold War as they went about NATO business in the North Atlantic and periodically ventured further afield.

Ark Royal was denied a prominent role in the 1991 Gulf War, some thought because the government was keen not to be presented with a prima facie case for carriers in the future.[19] The ship did deploy to the Adriatic two years later in support of operations in Bosnia, a presence which the RN's carriers maintained for the next two and a half years and which culminated with attacks on shore targets in August and September 1995. By now *Invincible* was carrying the new FA2 version of the Sea Harrier, and the following year began to operate RAF Harrier GR7s as well in an embryonic strike carrier role. Operational deployments to the Persian Gulf soon followed. The 1966 assumptions clearly no longer held true, if indeed they ever had.

The *Invincible*-class carriers and their aircraft had proved their worth but both were ageing. The limitations imposed by their humble origins were obvious, despite their successes. A future First Sea Lord set out the case for a future fixed-wing capability at sea:

> A CVS is the only unit which provides for its Task Group a platform capable of the two essential ingredients of military effectiveness. First, it has the broad spectrum of capabilities within one ship, ranging from organic air defence and land attack, through surface

warfare to a highly potent ASW ability, which allows it to carry out the Composite Warfare Commander's duties. Second, it has the C3 facilities on which a Joint Force, Amphibious or Operational Commander wholly depends. Naval aircraft have the mobility, flexibility and versatility which exemplify contemporary defence strategy. The CVS with its CAG can move on the high seas to almost anywhere in the world, where it can poise in international waters without either commitment or the need for host nation support. Naval aircraft may well be first on the scene in a particular operation, a factor which grants the politician and military commander alike a number of options, at immediate notice, not otherwise available. These options include early reconnaissance, special forces insertion and land attack from the air. Naval aircraft come with their own control, fuel, maintenance, logistic support, intelligence and briefing facilities. Recent events in the Adriatic provide vivid evidence of the CVS's worth.

He concluded: 'The force structure needed by the Royal Navy to fulfil its role in the post-Cold War strategic environment is one based on a shift of emphasis from previous plans. It centres on three principal platform types (CVS and CAGs, SSNs and specialist amphibious shipping with the amphibious landing force).'[20]

A future editor of the *Naval Review* gave his conclusion:

The replacement of these hulls when necessary and more importantly the Sea Harrier when it finally becomes obsolete, are key priorities for the Navy Board and there are important moves afoot to turn these aims into reality. I suggest that no one who accepts ... Britain's role in the new century's environment can seriously consider that the Royal Navy could do without aircraft carriers and advanced aircraft if it is to fulfil its national responsibilities.[21]

The need to keep the RAF onboard was understood and the inter-service politics, if not all of the rhetoric, seemed to have changed profoundly. But 'Nonius' made a prophetic remark 'both the light blue and dark blue will need to remember that the only winners in the 1960s internecine strife over CVA-01 and TSR2 [a strike aircraft for the RAF] were our friends in the Treasury. If ever there was an area where a jointly articulated case will be important, it is this.'[22]

Labour returned to power in 1997 committed to a strategic defence review (SDR) and the Navy, newly confident in light of an overtly expeditionary strategy, reopened the carrier debate. The outcome of the SDR, so different to 1966, appeared in part in the October 1998 *NR*:

As the result of a historic proposal from the First Sea Lord and the Chief of the Air Staff, the Royal Navy and Royal Air Force will build on the success of recent operations in the Gulf and co-operate to develop a new Joint Force 2000. The RAF and RN Harrier jets of this force will be able to operate equally effectively from aircraft carriers or land bases ...

In the post Cold War world, we must be prepared to go to the crisis, rather than have the crisis come to us. So we plan to buy two new larger aircraft carriers to project power more flexibly around the world ...

Aircraft carriers will have a wide utility, including for deterrence and coercion. Our current *Invincible* class carriers will be given a wider power projection role by ... combining RN and RAF Harrier aircraft. To meet our longer term needs, we plan to replace our current carriers from around 2012 by two larger, more versatile carriers capable of carrying a more powerful force, including a future carrier borne aircraft to replace the Harrier.[23]

The First Sea Lord added his own commentary: 'The outcome of the biggest single debate in the Review is that we intend to replace our current CVSs with two larger aircraft carriers. They will be capable of operating fixed wing aircraft from the Royal Navy and the Royal Air Force, and helicopters from all three Services. Such a capability is particularly relevant to the demands of the next century, and this decision is of the greatest significance for the Royal Navy.'[24]

The SDR initiated what was to prove a very protracted procurement process, on which a flood of *NR* contributions made comment. Commander James opined:

Realising the full benefits of a joint, tailored air group, of modern ship design and construction and of innovative support and manning concepts poses considerable challenge over the next decade but the prize is deployable UK air power, wherever and whenever required by political and diplomatic pressures. In the uncertain future, no other platform or weapon system will be as relevant to projecting UK influence around the world as will an aircraft carrier, providing it is a truly, *'joint defence asset'*. [Italics in the original.][25]

The weight of correspondence far exceeded that on the demise of CVA-01 and the rise of the CVS. The *NR* had almost as much to say about the former now as it did at the time, as lessons for CVF were identified.[26] A sign of how much times had changed since the bitter controversies between the Royal Navy and the RAF in the 1960s was the appointment of Flag Officer Maritime Aviation (FOMA) as also Air

Officer Commanding No 3 Group RAF, though this amicable arrangement did not last long.[27] Other setbacks followed. *Invincible* paid off for the last time in August 2005 reducing the RN to a single operational carrier. The FA2 went in March 2006 and FAA pilots now flew the RAF's GR7/9 aircraft. With these Harriers heavily committed in Afghanistan, *Illustrious* had to maintain her deck skills courtesy of the US Marine Corps.[28]

The choice of aircraft for the new ships was widely criticised, not least in the *NR*; 'GoCo' summed things up:

> CVF ... is the perfect tool for messing around with other peoples' countries – but only if you really *really* mean it. To be a credible carrier power, one has to be serious about it, which for my money means having the thing pretty much permanently deployed with a fully trained and integrated air group and a single carrier (CV – not VSTOL) variant of the F35,[29] so that every single aircraft in the entire joint force could embark. The wretched crabs simply will not allow that and will continue to do everything in their power to wreck the project.[30]

As the financial squeeze on defence intensified, inter-service tensions re-emerged and the RN had growing cause to question just how committed to a joint air group operating at sea the junior Service really was.

Lieutenant Commander South neatly summed up the proposed programme just as orders were finally announced.

> The procurement programme has been running for nine years and despite this CVF remains an artist's impression on a drawing board. The initial hull design (design DELTA) was identified in 2003 and only now, in August 2007, has an order been announced with desired delivery dates of 2014 and 2016, two years later than originally planned. The ships, *Queen Elizabeth* and *Prince of Wales*, will be configured to operate the STOVL variant of the JCA. The F35B of the United States led Joint Strike Fighter project (JSF) has been selected as the aircraft of choice. Current estimates are that the ships will be 65,000t, be 280 metres long, have a maximum speed of 25 knots and be powered by conventional gas turbines combined with an Integrated Full Electric Propulsion System (IFEP).

In summary he wrote:

> The UK remains firmly committed to the carrier strike programme and sees this as the central hub of its maritime capability for the future. However, as a result of funding limitations imposed by the Government the operational capabilities ... have been constrained

and thus prevented from achieving their full potential. The impact is that the UK, unless it reviews its CVF and aircraft requirement, will procure a carrier strike capability that does not meet the stated needs within the 1998 SDR and that will have similar endurance, reach and force projection ability currently offered by smaller and less expensive ships available on the market today... To ensure the CVF's safety in operational theatres the UK needs a fleet able to deploy with the carrier and CAG to protect and provide logistical support, thus remaining free of the need to utilise land-based assets. The current state of today's Fleet and support infrastructure will prevent the RN achieving this as the fleet replacement programme will result in a further reduction in ship numbers.[31]

Shortly after work actually commenced on the new CVF the rate of construction was slowed yet further to ease an immediate cash crisis but at the expense of a £674m overall *increase* in cost.[32]

The hollow fanfare that followed a prolonged period of prostituting itself to secure two Future Aircraft Carrier (CVF) carrier platforms, spluttered its last gasp of creditability with October's [2010] disclosure of Whitehall's worst kept secret. The British Treasury can't and won't pay for two carriers and their expensive JSF air group. News that the second carrier will be brought into service primarily as a Landing Platform Helicopter (LPH) replacement for HMS *Ocean* is folly and hubris of the highest order.[33]

This was a portent of things to come. The 2010 SDSR, set against a dire financial position, spelled yet further pain for an already fragile Navy. There was one piece of apparently good news; the conventional take-off F35C variant of the JSF would be bought instead of the less capable but more expensive vertical take-off STOVL F35B. But it would be just a single squadron (twelve aircraft, instead of the planned thirty) operating from a 65,000-ton carrier and only the second to be built, *Prince of Wales*, fitted with catapults and arrester gear. The first, *Queen Elizabeth*, would go to sea without fixed-wing aircraft and her future was in doubt. In the meantime, *Ark Royal* paid off early and the Harriers were put into storage. Future RN F35 pilots were taken out of flying training. The RN will therefore have no organic fixed-wing capability for almost a decade (the gap in the late 1970s was less than two years).

Freeman in the *NR* described this as one of 'the most bizarre planning decisions in recent times.'[34] He went on to outline the baleful background: 'This has, unfortunately, been an accident waiting to happen. Ever since the demise of the Sea Harrier under separate RN control, the future of the joint force Harrier, even with a new engine, has looked doubtful ... In reality, the Navy's fixed wing capability has in recent years been much less than it appeared to be and the SDSR decision completes the process of attenuation.'

May 2012 brought yet another, and possibly not the final, twist. Having determined that fitting 'cats and traps' to the second carrier would take longer and be more expensive than originally thought, the government reverted to the original plan to acquire the STOVL F35B. These will go to sea in *Queen Elizabeth* in 2018.

The Royal Navy has waited long and paid a heavy price for its carrier aspirations, only to see them largely dashed at the last moment. Via the *Invincibles* and the Sea Harrier, the Royal Navy has come almost full circle.

11 From the Honourable East India Company's Marine to Indian Navy

Commodore Ranjit B Rai, IN

IT is not generally appreciated even in India, let alone abroad, that India was a leading maritime nation in the very early days of history. The Indian Ocean was the scene of tremendous maritime activity at a time when Europe was emerging from the Stone Age. It is now generally accepted that the Arabs, the Persians and the Indians were among the first to master the art of navigation and deep-sea sailing ... two thousand years ago Indian navigators sailed from ports in India to places as far as Cambodia and Bali, where flourishing Indian colonies existed. An indication of the advanced state that maritime affairs reached in India can be gained from the fact that an authoritative work on administration, written in the 4th century BC, lays down the functions of the Board of Shipping which was one of the six great departments of the Maurya Emperors. At the head of it was a Minister assisted by a staff of Port Commissioners and Harbour Masters. Some records of the first century AD show that ships on arrival at Broach (at the mouth of the Narbada) were met by Government pilot boats and berthed in regular basins.

So wrote 'VAK' in 1953, reflecting the tone of several articles over the years in *The Naval Review*.[1]

Not only *NR* authors outlined India's ancient legacy of maritime activity: the religious treatise, Rig Veda (*véda* meaning 'knowledge' in Sanskrit), articulated around 2000 BC, credits Varuna, Lord of Oceans, with knowledge of the navigable routes used by ships, and describes naval expeditions which used hundred-oared ships to spread India's influence in other kingdoms; and Atharva Veda, codified in 500 BC, mentions that the boats were strongly constructed, and recognises the oceans as the repository of treasures, the most valuable being Amrit, the nectar of immortality. There are references to India in Greek literature, which records a flourishing trade with the Romans via Mesopotamia, and the Roman writer Pliny writes about Indian traders carrying away large quantities of gold from Rome, in payment for the much-sought-after Indian products like precious stones, silks, spices, sandalwood, perfumes and indigo. Between the fifth and tenth centuries AD, the kingdoms of Vijayanagaram (the present day State of Andhra Pradesh) and Kalinga (Orissa) had established their rule over present-day Malaysia, Sumatra and Western Java.

Significantly, the modern Indian Navy is conscious of and takes pride in its ancient antecedents, and, for example, the launch of each new ship is marked by the breaking of a coconut on the bows and chanting of Sanskrit verses to bless the ship and all who sail in her.

From the eleventh century the Persian Mahamud of Ghazni (971–1030) repeatedly plundered northwest India, and the Mamluks, Khaljis, Tughlaks, Sayyids, Lodis and finally the mighty Mongol invasions from Central Asia imposed Muslim rule on India. Descended from Genghis Khan and Tamerlane, it was Babur (1483–1531) who in 1526 established the rule of his dynasty which lasted three hundred years. His grandson Emperor Akbar consolidated the hold of the Mughal Empire in India, and established a Meer Bahri, with a naval headquarters or admiralty, and a Mughal Navy in the Bay of Bengal to ward off pirate attacks in the east by the Muggs and the Arkanese. But the Mughals failed to appreciate the importance of sea power, and in the west, where Vasco da Gama landed in 1498, in three naval battles, Cochin in 1503, Chaul in 1508, and Diu in 1509, the Portuguese wrested control for the next hundred years until 1612 when a Captain Thomas Best, in his Deptford-built flagship *Red Dragon*, defeated the Portuguese in the first Battle of Suvali (anglicised to Swally) off Surat on the Gujarati coast, northwest India.

The several incarnations of the Indian Navy since, the years of British inspiration and then rule are charted by articles in the *NR*: the Honourable East India Company's Marine (1613–86), the Bombay Marine (1686–1830), the Indian Navy (1830–63), reversion to the Bombay Marine (1863–77), Her Majesty's Indian Marine (1877–92), the Royal Indian Marine (1892–1934) and the Royal Indian Navy (1934–45).

One of the earliest of these articles called in 1924 for India to develop its own Navy:

At present, Navy is, as it were, imported at the expense of the Indian Government for policing Indian waters. Let the Royal Indian Marine (RIM) be given back their fighting powers for this purpose, and the local seawork [sic] would be carried out more conveniently and more economically. At the same time the prestige of the RIM would return and increase; and, further, they would be still more fitted for service in conjunction with the Royal Navy in wartime.[2]

This is a proposition which will be tested at the end of this chapter.

The articles include two by one of the *NR*'s founders, Herbert Richmond, who while Commander-in-Chief, East Indies Squadron, 1923–25 had used his leisure hours to study the naval strategy in the Indian Ocean and complete a first draft of *The Navy in India 1763–1783*, published in 1931.[3]

However, the Battle of Swally led directly to the English East India Company establishing a small navy, the Honourable East India Company's Marine, with a base at Surat responsible for the protection of trade in the Gulf of Cambay. This force would play an important role in surveying the Arabian, Persian and Indian coastlines, and is the ancestor of the Survey Branch of the present Indian Navy which has now surveyed most areas of the Indian Ocean.

In 1667 the Honourable East India Company (HEIC) shifted its base to Bombay. There was a hiccup: the capture of Mughal ships trading between Surat and Bombay in December 1688 led to the seizure of the English factory at Surat and an attack on Bombay. The HEIC was forced to sue for peace and the Mughal Emperor Aurangzeb only agreed peace on condition that the English Governor, Sir John Child, be banished from India. Subsequently the island of Bombay and Bombay Castle, site of the present-day Indian Navy barracks were let to the HEIC at a peppercorn rent, and ships of the Bombay Marine began to employ local Indian seamen, mainly Muslim seafarers. Interestingly Charles II referred to Bombay as 'Our Manor of East Greenwich'.[4]

As Captain R H Garstin told his audience at the RN War College, Greenwich in 1927, the period 1689–97 was a critical one for the newly named Bombay Marine. A French fleet of six sail was operating in the Indian Ocean, but a particular problem was European pirates, sailing sometimes out of New York, who:

> made their appearance, amongst whom were the redoubtable Captains Kidd, Avery and Chivers. The Marine was numerically inadequate to deal with the situation, consequently the Company suffered heavy losses amongst their trade vessels. The pirates were particularly annoying, for they committed depredations on Mogul ships, and as they flew English colours, the natives were unable to differentiate between the pirates and the Company's ships, the result being that the Company's ships were blamed for the misdeeds of the pirates, and this led to trouble with the Mogul which seriously imperilled trade. When the peace treaty was signed in 1697 the situation became easier, and the Company was able to provide ships to convoy the vessels of the Mogul, which were employed in taking pilgrims to Mecca.

During the eighteenth century the Bombay Marine was engaged in defending the Company's factories on the Indian coast, whose safety was threatened by native powers: operations included the destruction of Maratha strongholds at Colaba (at the entrance to Bombay), Savaranadrug and Vijayadrug. More organised piracy had also spread from the Caribbean and the marauders settled in Madagascar and Mauritius, from where they made life difficult for East Indiamen. The Bombay Marine grew in response and by the mid century British naval forces in the Indian Ocean consisted of some six naval warships and seventeen vessels of the East India Company.[5] During the French wars it was customary for the vessels of the Bombay Marine to co-operate with the Royal Navy squadrons; for example, squadrons served under Admiral Boscawen in 1748, Admiral Watson in 1754–57, Admiral Cornish at the capture of Pondicherry in 1761, and as a result learned emulation and efficiency. The core of the Bombay Marine consisted of the locally built 44-gun frigates *Protector* and *Bombay*, the 28-gun *Guardian* and *Revenge* and many minor ships. The officers were Europeans but the ship's companies were three-fourths Indian.

A Marine battalion, with English officers and Sepoy marines was formed in 1777. They fought as the 1st (Marine) Battalion, 11th Regiment of Bombay Native Infantry against Haider Ali and his son Tipu Sultan, known as the Tiger of Mysore, a man of exceptional valour. However, Tipu lacked a navy to provide a sea-frontier against the English who kept attacking the Malabar Coast where he was weak. Tipu sought unity with Indian rulers but no one was prepared to help him in his efforts against the English. Tipu even employed French mercenaries and wrote to Napoleon and the Ottoman Caliph, but they too were of no help. At the end of the century, after fighting the English to the bitter end, the Tiger of Mysore fell, sword in hand. What became the 10th (Marine) Battalion, 2nd Bombay Pioneers was one of the oldest regiments in India, and saw, until disbanded in 1932, more foreign service than any other.

In 1798 marine regulations were revised and the duties of the Service were clearly defined as the protection of trade, suppression of piracy and general duty as vessels of war, convoying transports and carrying of troops, and maritime survey. Improvements were also made in the internal economy of the Service and more fine new vessels were built locally. Eventually the master shipbuilders of the famous Wadia family of Parsees would build more than two hundred teak-built warships and merchant sailing ships.

Amongst other achievements the Bombay Marine helped wrest Trincomalee from the Dutch in 1799, took part in the capture of

Mauritius and the conquest of Java in 1810–14, and suppressed piracy in the Persian Gulf 1814–24. The paddle-steamer, *Diana*, built at Kyd's Dock, Kidderpore in 1823 was the first of its kind east of the Cape of Good Hope and gave a good account of herself in the First Burmese War in 1824,[6] and a packet service, using the Bombay-built 411-ton steamship *Hugh Lindsay*, was established with the Red Sea in 1829. However, London never appreciated the Service's prowess in service of the British Crown, and the pay of the Bombay Marine was inferior to that in the Indian Army. Resentment led to the resignation of Captain Maxwell in 1827 and the directors of the East India Company heard him out in London. This led to permission to wear the Union Jack and fly a red pennant, and a Captain RN was appointed as the Superintendent of the Bombay Marine Corps. On 1 May 1830 this became the Indian Navy.

Meanwhile piracy was again rife, this time off the Arabian coast; they were a tough and cruel lot who attempted to place a stranglehold on trade and it was the cruisers of the Bombay Marine operating in the Persian Gulf in 1797 to 1820 who defeated the Joasrni pirates of what would become the Trucial Coast.[7]

Briefly, Lord William Bentinck, Governor General of India 1833–35, tried to get the Royal Navy to replace the Indian Navy. However, the Indian Navy captured Aden in 1839, its gunboats operated in the Sindh campaign helping to secure what is now Baluchistan, operated on the Euphrates, took part in the New Zealand Wars, the Anglo-Sikh Wars, and the second Burmese War (1852–3). A Bengal Marine was established at Calcutta and lasted until the late nineteenth century, though the division of the Indian Navy into eastern and western fleets survives into modern times.

During the Siege of Multan in 1848 a force of six officers and 100 gunners with two 8in howitzers and four 18-pounder guns had been dispatched by steamship up the Indus river, and during the great Mutiny of 1857 both the Indian Navy and Bengal Marine remained loyal to the British. Their ships transported the East India Company's treasury from Calcutta to Bombay, and a naval brigade of eighty British officers and 1,800 men reinforced the Army while the guns of the Indian Navy played on the gates of Delhi.

But it was clear that the East India Company itself had outlived its time. In 1858 Queen Victoria assumed direct rule of the Indian Empire, the Army took priority, and prize appointments passed to the military, the naval arm was reduced and in 1863 the Indian Navy was disbanded, leaving only a rump of the Bombay and Bengal Marines.

The last flagship of the old Indian Navy was to have been a 50-gun screw frigate, *Dalhousie*, built of Malabar teak in Bombay dockyard, with engines shipped out by Robert Napier from Glasgow.[8] What remained of the Bombay Marine was devoted to transport, cable-laying and hydrographic surveying with four steam transport ships, capable, nevertheless, of laying a submarine cable from Suez to Bombay in 1869.

When Victoria assumed the title of Empress of India, Her Majesty's Indian Marine was created with one division each, with dockyards and ships at Calcutta and Bombay. In 1877, the Indian Marine Act placed its officers on similar footing to officers of the Royal Navy. Its duties were to transport troops and government stores; maintain forces at Aden, the Andamans, Burma, and the Persian Gulf; to perform police, lighthouse-keeping and other duties; and maintain local government launches and vessels, and those used for military purposes; and marine survey.

Anticipating the Admiralty's early twentieth-century ideas of an Empire Navy, Marine Acts of 1884 and 1887 provided for ships of the Indian Marine to be taken over in emergency. Meanwhile, the Indian Marine was successfully deployed in Egypt and Burma, and in 1892 the Empress Victoria conferred the title of Royal Indian Marine. The RIM saw service as far afield as Egypt, the Northwest Frontier (where parties of seamen helped to bridge rivers) and China.

In fact, in the First World War four troopships, six ambulance, two survey ships, and five steamers operated in Burma and the Persian Gulf. Two further hospital ships were loaned to the Royal Navy, and C-in-C East Indies took command of an expanded Indian fleet of 105 executive officers and eighty-five engineers. Hundreds of thousands of Indian troops were transported to Egypt, Iraq and Africa, and Indian ships patrolled the Suez and took part in landings along the Tigris and Euphrates. Wheat and grain was transported in Indian ships to Europe and the Alexandra Docks were built at Bombay. However, there was resentment in the RIM ranks as they felt it was neither Royal nor Indian: three Indians were commissioned on a temporary, wartime basis, but junior British officers were still being inducted into it (sometimes as a consolation prize for not getting into the Royal Navy).

Post-war, 'VAK' took up the history of the Indian Navy (in all its broadest meaning): 'After the Armistice in 1918 the RIM went back to its pre-war task. Fortunately for the Service, the Government soon afterwards decided to set up a Committee under General Lord Rawlinson, the then Commander-in-Chief in India, to submit recommendations for the reorganisation of the Service as a combatant force.' The Imperial Conference of 1926 recognised that 'the defence of India already throws upon the Government of India responsibilities of a specially onerous character, and takes note of their decision to create a Royal Indian Navy.'[9] Back to VAK: 'The White Ensign was hoisted on board all RIM ships in 1928 and the Service was organised on combatant lines. It was not, however, until September, 1934, that the Service formally became the Royal Indian Navy.'

By 1922, when India was paying £100,000 per annum to the Admiralty, the demands for greater indigenisation were growing, not least among the Anglo-Indian community, led by Rear Admiral H L Mawbey and Sir Henry Gidney. A disappointed Mawbey resigned but this led to T S Shankar Iyer taking over as Controller of Marine Accounts. A signal school was established at Carnac Bunder at Bombay where Indian warrant officers and signalmen Lascars were trained and from where classes were sent to England.

A committee made fresh recommendations for the RIM to be reduced, but this time Rawlinson intervened. He set up a committee with C-in-C East Indies, Admiral Sir Herbert Richmond, and the Director of the RIM, Captain Sir Edward Headlam.[10] Two Indian officers, D N Mukherji, a Hindu, and H M S Choudri, a Muslim, were sent to England for training and in 1934 the Royal Indian Navy was inaugurated at Mumbai under Rear Admiral Humphrey Walwyn as Flag Officer Commanding Royal Indian Navy (FOCRIN). The RIN also became the senior service in India, and Lord Willingdon, the Viceroy (1931–36), congratulated the service and hoped the RIN would take a worthy place among the Navies of the Empire.[11]

As Headlam outlined in the NR, first Flag Officers were lent by the Admiralty, and:

> experiment is to be made of introducing Indianisation into the officer rank and of seeing if young Indian gentlemen trained at public schools in England and India will take to a naval career; this new entry will be limited to one out of every three of new entries. With regard to the warrant officers, petty officers and ratings, these will remain Indians ... Our Indian ratings who are Mahomedans are all recruited from the Ratnagiri district south of Bombay.

Earlier a Captain Munro had cited the difficulties in employing Indian seamen as those of religion, food, climate, discipline, and language. Headlam dismissed these, 'I am glad to be able to say after 33 years in the RIM with its consequent intimate association with Indian seamen, that I have never experienced any difficulties whatever on these points.'

Lt H M S Choudri (who would later command the Pakistani Navy) commanded a guard at the coronation of King George VI and was a divisional officer in HMIS Indus at Spithead naval review in 1937. By

1938 worries about the security of the British Empire led to rapid expansion of the RIN.

On 1 October 1939 the RIN was composed of 114 officers and 1,732 ratings: the fleet consisted of five sloops, one survey ship and one patrol craft and the largest guns were 4in 12-pounders. Five sloops of the RIN were placed under the C-in-C East Indies for service in the Red Sea, Gulf of Aden and the Persian Gulf, forming part of the Arabian Bengal Ceylon Escort Force (ABCEF) which soon played an important part in operations against Italian East Africa and in the brief campaign in Iran. HMIS *Ratnagiri* under Lt S G Karmarkar, RINR (later the first Indian officer to command British officers in HMIS *Cauvery*), took part in landings at Mersa Taclai, Eritrea in February 1941. HMI Ships *Hiravati* and *Prabhavati* began sweeping mines in the North Massawa Channel in October. In 1943 a Women's Royal Indian Naval Service was formed.

The Royal Indian Navy distinguished itself in the war. First, in November 1942 when the minesweeper *Bengal* and the Dutch motor tanker she was escorting, each armed with one 4in gun, chased off the Japanese raiders *Kikoku Maru* and *Kamikawn Maru*, each mounting six 5.5in guns: 'The *Bengal* has opened a fine tradition for the Royal Indian Navy, and the two ships as consorts proved themselves fit descendants of their ancestors who were such worthy foes when naval traditions were in the making.'[12] Again at the end of the war was the sinking of the German *U-198* after one of the longest chases in the history of anti-submarine warfare. Four days after the hunt began, HMIS *Godavari* directed HMS *Findhorn* in a textbook action to destroy the U-boat.[13]

But at the end of the war a swift demobilisation led to a naval mutiny of 1946: the men felt unsure of their future and looked to independence as a solution, and were inspired by the stories of the Indian National Army and by Mahatma Gandhi's actions. Comments on the Indian mutiny are strangely absent from the *NR*. The mutiny started as a strike by ratings at the training establishment HMIS *Talwar*. The strike spread to other ships and cities, and was joined by the men of the air force and local police. Indian naval officers and men began calling themselves the Indian National Navy, offered left-handed salutes to white officers and defied their orders. Rioting spread and ships in mutiny hoisted the flags of the Congress, the Muslim League and the red flag of the Communist Party of India. Cdr S G Karmarkar was rushed down to Bombay to take command of the situation from British officers in *Talwar* who had taken shelter in the wardroom. 'SG' pacified the men, protected the white officers' dignity, and tactfully quelled the mutiny.

Indian independence began at the midnight hour on 14 August 1947: in Prime Minister Pandit Nehru's words, 'Long years ago we made a tryst with destiny, and now the time comes when we shall redeem our pledge, not wholly or in full measure, but very substantially. At the stroke of the midnight hour, when the world sleeps, India will awake to life and freedom.' At independence the RIN consisted of thirty-two ageing vessels with 11,000 officers and men, but Viceroy Rear Admiral Lord Louis Mountbatten helped script a long-term plan which included supply of second-hand and new warships, aircraft and an aircraft carrier from the British, to reduce war debts to India. The senior leadership was still drawn from the Royal Navy, with Rear Admiral John Hall as the first C-in-C, Royal Indian Navy.

In 1948 the cruiser, HMS *Achilles*, of River Plate fame, became HMIS *Delhi*, changing in 1950 to INS *Delhi* when India became a republic and dropped all royal prefixes. Meanwhile Admiral Sir Stephen Carlill, the last British Chief of Naval Staff (India), 'propounded the concept of a "blue water" Navy and convinced the government of India to strengthen the Naval air arm and to acquire an aircraft carrier to provide effective control over the sea and air, in spite of opposition from various quarters within the country.'[14]

Between 1957 and 1960 a leap took place with the arrival of cruiser INS *Mysore* (ex-HMS *Nigeria*) and nine new frigates from Britain, the hydrographic service was expanded, and training schools revamped to accommodate expansion.

On 22 April 1958 Vice Admiral Ram Dass Katari became the first Indian Chief of Naval Staff, though some Royal Navy officers remained in key positions, and on 28 March that year, standing on the quarterdeck of *Mysore*, Prime Minister Jawaharlal Nehru said:

From this ship I look at India and think of our country and its geographic situation – on three sides there is the sea and on the fourth high mountains – in a sense our country maybe said to be in the very lap of an ocean. In these circumstances I ponder over our close links with the sea and how the sea has brought us together. From time immemorial the people of India have had very intimate connections with the sea. They had trade with other countries and they had also built ships. Later on the country became weak. Now that we are free, we have once again reiterated the importance of the sea. We cannot afford to be weak at sea ... history has shown that whatever power controls the Indian Ocean has, in the first instance, India's seaborne trade at her mercy, and in the second, India's very independence itself.[15]

Nevertheless, since 1947 Nehru had been taking advice from Professor P M S Blackett, a renowned British physicist who had pioneered naval operational research in the British Navy during the Second World War, as to what the India Navy needed rather than what the British wanted it to have.[16] In 1961 India's first aircraft carrier, INS *Vikrant* (ex-HMS *Hercules*), arrived at Bombay after a very successful and accident-free work-up off Malta, where she embarked her British Sea Hawk fighters, and some French Breguet Alize anti-submarine aircraft.[17] However, after India's humiliation in its border war with China in 1962, the Army was given priority for funding, and the Navy's share of the defence budget shrank.

Reflecting on events Lord Mountbatten claimed:

> I have a specially soft spot in my heart for the Indian Navy, having done so very much for it from the time I was the Supreme Allied Commander and had most of the Navy serving under me from 1943 to 1946 until I was Viceroy and then Governor General, when I took a great personal part in the division and reconstitution of the Navy ... Ever since then I have been instrumental in getting almost all of the requirements of the Indian Navy met by the British Government, including the two cruisers, the aircraft carrier, the destroyers, the organisations for building the frigates at Bombay, etc.

He added, 'I had even managed to get more favourable terms for the construction of a British submarine but alas it all took so long that this particular transaction fell through.'[18]

The submarine project collapsed for financial and political reasons in 1965, marking the beginning of the Indian Navy's turn to the Soviet Union for its needs: the Soviets were willing to provide large long-term loans.

In September 1965, in a seventeen-day war with Pakistan over Kashmir, the Indian Navy was ordered not to operate above 22° North, and only to retaliate if attacked.[19] The Indian Navy was humiliated: it was clear the government in Delhi had no experience of using a navy in war. Shaken, the Indian Navy turned more to the Soviet Union for ships, submarines and aircraft as well as training. Many officers and sailors would spend long desultory spells over the next decade, without families, in ports like Vladivostok, Poti and Leningrad in the bitter cold to bring back ten *Petya*-class frigates, Iluyshin aircraft, the submarine tender *Amba*, eight Foxtrot-class submarines and sixteen *Osa*-class missile boats armed with Styx missiles. With this fleet, the employment and the results of the Indian Navy in the 1971 Indo-Pakistan War was very different.[20]

Towards the end of the twentieth century indigenisation of the Indian
Navy referred not to its people but to its material:

> A large number of imported equipments [sic] have been inducted into
> the Indian Navy ... The subsequent maintenance/replacement has
> posed a formidable task mainly due to lack of foreign back up support
> by way of logistics, documentation and sometimes, even expertise by
> way of personnel. With a view to curb this trend a general policy was
> evolved to gradually replace these imported equipments covering main
> propulsion package and associated auxiliaries along with other
> domestic auxiliaries by indigenous equipments. Thus a new era of
> pursuing a policy of 'Self-reliance through indigenisation' came into
> being ... has now borne rich dividends.[21]

2001 would be declared the 'year of Indigenisation.'

In preparation to switch from being a buyer's navy to a builder's navy,
the Mazagon Dock in Mumbai (formerly Bombay) was rejuvenated by
the build locally of British-designed 2,800-ton *Leander*-class frigates. By
1977 Indian constructors had designed and were preparing to build
three 6,700-ton *Delhi*-class destroyers capable of carrying two Sea King
helicopters. The *NR* noted:

> A fine example of indigenous capability is the 'Godavari' Class
> Guided Missile Frigates, incorporating a modified design of the
> British Leander Class Frigate, Soviet and Italian Weapon Systems
> and electronic packages from diverse western sources. This
> interfacing of systems of different origins and the operating of two
> Sea King Helicopters from a vessel of this size has been inter-
> nationally recognised and lauded.[22]

Legendary Soviet Admiral of the Fleet Sergei Gorshkov became such a
fond figure to the Indians that familiar stories about him began to
circulate.[23] Gorshkov visited India four times and many claim him to be
the 'founder benefactor' of today's Indian Navy. He certainly applauded
the ingenuity of the Indian Navy, which in the 1980s received eight
Tupolev maritime patrol aircraft and five powerful Kashin-class
destroyers. The IN also leased a Charlie-class nuclear submarine, INS
Chakra, between 1987–91, a development which was closely watched
by the *NR*.[24]

The *NR* noted that the miscellaneous flotilla which comprised the
RIN in 1947 had:

> emerged a mammoth three dimensional, quick response, missile-
> armed navy with over a hundred ships [which had] graduated from

slow speed reciprocating engines to high speed gas turbines – the basic guiding principle being that only new technology can win a war ... the present watchword for the design of warships [is] the philosophy of 'design for continuity' as against the previously held concepts of 'design for cost' and 'design for change'. The 'design for continuity' now lies in nuclear propulsion. The early introduction of nuclear power for marine propulsion will perhaps change the balance of power in southeast Asia, making the Indian Navy a force to reckon with.[25]

The Soviets also helped build the sprawling dockyard facilities at Vishakapatnam and a new naval base south of Vishakapatnam, similar to one already built at Karwar near Goa – which has a 12,000-ton Rolls Royce-supported ship lift and berthing and repair facilities for the 44,000-ton aircraft carriers INS *Vikramaditya* (ex-*Gorshkov*) and an indigenous-designed aircraft carrier known as the Air Defence Ship (in imitation of the Royal Navy's ruse in obtaining a carrier by calling it a Through Deck Cruiser).[26]

The successfully built-under-licence line of West German Type 1500 submarines, known as the Shishumar class in India, and the ten Kilo-class Soviet submarines, which arrived in India between 1986 and 2000, are all now ageing and another six new locally-built submarines are being planned. India's first home-built nuclear submarine, the 6,500-ton INS *Arihant*, is likely to join the fleet in 2013, and two more will follow. An 8,500-ton nuclear *Akula*-type boat will join from Russia in early 2012 on lease and officers and crew are training in Vladivostok. Again, the *NR* noted, 'In the acquisition of submarines, India has picked up the best of both worlds, getting the SSK type from West Germany and the Kilo-class from the USSR.'[27]

In an article entitled 'Naval Power in South East Asia', Mohan Singh strongly urged that the rightful place for maritime reconnaissance is with the Navy, noting that so far in India, as in Britain, maritime reconnaissance had been provided by the Indian Air Force since its inception over forty years ago.[28] When controversy arose the Indian government did not dither but took the decision in 1975 to transfer maritime reconnaissance to the Indian Navy.[29] The writer could probably hear the applause of Royal Navy members of the *NR*.

The naval air arm was upgraded in the 1980s and the IN purchased two squadrons of the vertical and short take-off and landing Sea Harriers from British Aerospace to replace an earlier generation of Sea Hawks, and aircraft carrier INS *Viraat* (ex-HMS *Hermes*) arrived in 1987. The 44,500 ton INS *Vikramaditya* (ex-*Gorshkov*) is planned to arrive in 2013 from Russia after modernisation and will operate Russian aircraft, while India's home-built nuclear-powered submarine INS *Arihant*, fitted out with eight 700km-range nuclear-tipped missiles is expected to be operational around the same time, which could change the balance of power in the Indian Ocean forever.

Nor has the Indian Navy ever been lacking in intellectual and strategic thought. There was always a small but active core of Indian naval officers who followed the tenets of *The Naval Review*, 'Think Wisely. Plan Boldly. Act Swiftly.', and Indian membership actually grew in the year after independence and the declaration of a republic.[30]

In 1969 the *NR* carried what appears to be the first review of a book by an Indian Navy officer, in which Captain P S Bindra, a former student at the RN Staff College and the US Naval War College, analysed the impact of the closure of the Suez Canal.[31] In the same year a Dr Geoffrey Williams offered the possibility of the 'appearance in the Indian Ocean of the South African Navy, the Indian Navy, the Indonesian Navy, and the Chinese Navy – and even the Japanese Navy, in a naval free-for-all.'[32] And on cue the next edition of the *NR* carried a prophetic article about China's interest in African mineral resources and noted that 'Chinese naval forces have been sighted patrolling the Indian Ocean by a squadron of the Indian Navy cruising off the Andaman Islands.'[33]

Reviewing this Captain Khanna concluded:

> It is inevitable that for historic, geographic, economic and geo-political reasons, India has to implement a maritime strategy that safeguards its security, economic as well as military. While there are many facets to a viable maritime strategy, the strengthening of the navy will be a central feature of this strategy. Considering the Indian Navy's vast responsibilities, it has further to build up its capabilities to fulfil all its roles. Lastly, the Indian Navy has to deter any further conflict keeping in view the country's interest and ensuring peace in the region. India, being non-aligned, has no expansionist designs for having a foothold beyond its shores. Its only aims are to ensure peace in this region of Indian Ocean for economic growth in a tranquil environment.[34]

Following the 1971 war between India and Pakistan, Mohan Singh had surmised that

> the importance of the Indian Ocean has been highlighted all the more ... India is keen to keep the Indian Ocean free of big power politics, but it is going to be a tough job ... the strategic importance

of the Indian Ocean has been well driven home to India, and the Indian Navy, in order to play its role, will have to be boosted and expanded ... The high-ups in the Navy have to do some judicious thinking to work out a sound, comprehensive plan for the Navy's present and future requirements.[35]

The 'high-up' in the Indian Navy who rose to the challenge of putting a cerebral cloak on the Indian Navy's material requirements was (then) Commodore Raja Menon, in a two-part article, 'The Growth of Navies', lending as the editor called it, 'a lot of stick to the logic of naval force structures in history and up to the present day.'[36] Captain Khanna's view was less theoretical and more nationalistic:

India occupies an important geo-strategic position in the Indian Ocean ... With so many littoral states around her with whom she has old trading and cultural links ... India has a very important role to play ... By all means there is need to raise the living standards of all people and to provide them with food, shelter and clean drinking water. But this will only be possible if India retains its freedom which means that it should have a strong navy capable of meeting any challenge.[37]

However, Menon's ideas crystallised in 1989 with his landmark publication *Maritime Strategy and Continental Wars*; Menon's argument was Corbettian: technology would give fleets new means of waging war effectively against the land and that superiority in the littoral or 'brown waters' would be key to waging joint warfare successfully.[38] Meanwhile, Commodore Banger, another regular Indian contributor to *The Naval Review*, made a proposal which may yet receive more attention, acknowledging the debt which the Indian Navy owed to the Royal Navy, and, regretting the 'visible decline in the interaction (if not relationship) between the two navies'. He suggested that 'there is a lot to be mutually gained from one another's experiences. Let the wealth of information separately held by the two navies be shared as true members of the Commonwealth. It is not too late to make a beginning for the mutual benefit of the two Navies and further, for the Commonwealth Navy as a whole.'[39] And most recently the present writer has highlighted the potential clash at sea between India and China in 'China's String of Pearls vs India's Iron Curtain in the Indian Ocean: it is a C3IC Issue'.[40]

From the pages of the *NR* it is clear the Indian Navy traces its recent pedigree back to the Royal Navy, it took birth when the RN was at its zenith, and has drunk the milk of RN traditions, customs, organisation and operational practices. Strategically, it owes a debt to the RN officers and men who shaped and trained it, including Mountbatten and others who scripted a long term naval plan before even India achieved independence. These plans are now being realised. The child came of age in the 1971 Indo-Pakistan War, and today it is maturing from 'buyer's navy' to a 'builder's navy'.

The earliest of the articles in *The Naval Review* called for India to develop its own navy, and today a plan called Maritime Agenda Vision 2020 envisages the introduction of nuclear submarines and an investment of US$50bn to build around fifty warships and submarines, including two aircraft carriers, and includes the INS *Vikramaditya* (former *Admiral Gorshkov*) slated for commissioning on the Indian Navy's Navy Day on 4 December 2012 in Russia. The IN also plans to acquire 120 aircraft and helicopters by 2020, as well as new naval bases and infrastructure, and there are high hopes that India's robust economy will be capable of delivering that investment. In addition India's coastguard is planned to have seventy-five ships and forty-three aircraft and helicopters, which like the old Bengal Marine, will protect the Bay of Bengal, now under threat not from pirates but terrorists. Separately, the legacy of a strong survey branch has enabled the Indian Navy to become a hydrographical force with over a dozen ships which have conducted surveys throughout the Indian Ocean basin.

What is clear also is that Indian naval writers contributed significantly to *The Naval Review* and have gained much from the free and frank ideas expressed therein.

Today India is aware of its ancient role at sea: we say 'Shan Noh Varunah', the modern Indian Navy's motto adapted from the Rig Veda which invokes Lord Varuna, the Lord of the Oceans, to bless the nation's Navy in its endeavours.

12 A Distance Beyond Geography: The Royal Canadian Navy

Michael Whitby

T HE relationship between *The Naval Review* and the Canadian Navy over the first century of each organisation's existence was distant at best. It was not, however, the broad reaches of the North Atlantic that formed the only divide. The journal gave coverage to various aspects of Canada's Navy and maritime defence over the years, but it was almost always expressed by British officers from a British point of view. Except for infrequent instances, Canadians only engaged intermittently on the issues brought forward. There was, for example, no steady stream of 'Letters from Canada' as there was from Australia. Moreover, Canadian membership was never high – there were just four members in the mid 1930s – so they were not just a passive audience but an almost non-existent one. This was not to say that the Canadian content of the *NR* was uninformed or uninteresting; it is just evident that the journal had minimal influence on the development of Canada's Navy and on its naval thinking in general. As a British journal intended for a British readership that should not really surprise.

First Steps

The Royal Canadian Navy (RCN) first entered the pages of the *NR* from the second volume, when 'BX', Lieutenant Commander W S Chalmers, contributed an article titled 'Canada and the Navy'.[1] Following the establishment of the RCN on 4 May 1910, 'a department for the control of naval affairs was constituted at Ottawa under the direction of a Rear Admiral, and represented in Parliament by a Minister of Marine.[2] A naval college[3] was established at Halifax, the [cruisers] *Niobe* and *Rainbow* were purchased for training purposes, and the administration of the dockyards at Halifax and Esquimalt was taken over by the Naval Department.' Recruitment was a problem from

169

the start, and the author attributed this to the character of the typical Canadian. 'The social position of individuals in Canada is, as a rule based on their worldly wealth', he observed, 'and the chief ambition of the average citizen is to make money quickly and to place himself in a position to enjoy the blessings of the land to the full.' Consequently, even when parents sent their boys to the Royal Military College of Canada at Kingston, they were chiefly doing so 'in order that discipline may develop their characters, so that they may be more successful in business and the more lucrative walks of life.'[4] The goal was not military or naval service, but to prepare youth for prosperity.

National character and circumstance also had an impact upon the lower deck. Desertion rates were high, which Chalmers noted was officially attributed to the fact that 'the majority of recruits are drawn from towns remote from the sea, and that the surroundings of a ship do not come up to expectations.' Not helping was the fact that *Niobe* and *Rainbow* seldom left the lee of the Canadian coast, so that 'vista of distant lands which is so cherished by the average youth is still left to their imagination.' Pay was also an issue, with naval rates at about one-sixth of what a young man could expect to earn ashore. All this left Chalmers to conclude:

> The Canadian boy is a good youth and, in the opinion of the writer, is of superior physique to the same class of English boy. He is obliging, willing, amenable to discipline, and takes great interest in his work. But where the spirit of ambition exists, there is generally the thirst for the dollar, whilst the fact of the ships lying idle is sufficient to deter any youth with a seafaring spirit from joining.

The view that the average Canadian was engrossed with economic opportunity lingered. In 1914, Lieutenant D Rahill, writing anonymously on the Royal Australian Navy, noted BX's point that, in Canada, 'The principal topic is money, and public spirit seems lacking.' 'Just so,' Rahill agreed: 'There is no doubt that in Canada there is lack of that feeling of personal responsibility which is essential to the provision of ships and money, and what is worse, an absence of national spirit which provides men and keeps a navy alive.'[5] Unfortunately, there was no challenge to this point of view from the Canadian side of the Atlantic.

In terms of Canada and the RCN, imperial defence was the main issue that absorbed the attention of the NR. This subject had been at the heart of debate around the establishment of Canada's naval service. As Chalmers noted, Sir Wilfred Laurier's Liberal government wanted to create a local force capable of defending Canadian concerns, which in case of an emergency, could be placed 'at the disposal of His Majesty for general service in the Royal Navy.' In contrast, the Conservative party, under Sir Robert Borden, wanted to focus on the general defence of the Empire and called for a gift to British coffers to finance the construction of three super-dreadnoughts. For the first and only time in Canadian history, naval policy was at the forefront of debate in a general election. Chalmers observed 'Party politics run riot, and it is not often that the voter is able to form an opinion of the true interests of the Empire, without having his ideas distorted by some politician or the daily paper.' Clearly unimpressed with the quality of debate, Chalmers sought compromise, but only in a limited sense. 'The taxpayers of Canada', he argued, 'should realise the futility of allowing the development of a local navy to take precedence over the reinforcement of the main fleet, the destruction of which would at once render their country open to attack.' Canada should indeed 'provide herself with a small local navy, manned by Canadians, consisting of submarines and torpedo craft to defend her coastal waters, and a few small cruisers to protect her ends of the trade routes', but only after she had made financial and personnel contributions 'to the main fighting fleet of the Empire.'

Writing in the same issue as BX, Admiral Henderson criticised the concept of dominions providing financial gifts to cover the cost of dreadnoughts. The sheer amount of money required would raise suspicions about whether or not it was spent and distributed correctly. Moreover, 'when a people are taxed for expenditure on armaments they rightly or wrongly console themselves with the notion that the greater part of the resulting revenue is re-spent within the community.' This would not apply under the 'gift to Britain' scenario. Also, if ships were built in the Dominions, although costs could run as much as 40 per cent higher, 'the Dominions would cheerfully accept the additional cost, for the sake of feeling that their navies are their own.'[6] Like BX, Henderson deplored the highly partisan nature of the naval debate in Canada but argued 'that even if a donation of three super-dreadnoughts is forced through the Canadian Parliament, it will be against the opinion of a very large section of the people, who are in favour of a navy of their own, and in view of the arguments advanced in the foregoing, it cannot be doubted they are in the right.' As it was, Borden's gift stalled in Parliament and Canada was forced to make do with the few antiquated ships that became widely known as the 'Tin-Pot navy'.[7]

Debate over Canada's role in imperial naval defence would endure for decades, but the outbreak of the Great War brought a degree of realism to discussion about the RCN. In 1915, amidst detailed articles on the progress of the war at sea, Lieutenant Commander H B Pilcher, writing anonymously, speculated on 'The Future of the Royal Canadian Navy'. Basing his argument on the RCN's experience to that point of the war, and assuming that the RN would be available to help with local defence – a false assumption as it turned out – the author thought the RCN should join with the Australian and New Zealand Navies to form a joint squadron to defend imperial interests in the Pacific into the future. Although the author gave a tip of the hat to fiscal realities that might follow the war, he nonetheless thought the Canadian contribution would be prodigious: 'If Canada decides to develop a unit of her own, the future unit would probably consist of one battle cruiser, some light cruisers, six destroyers, six submarines, one depot ship, mine-layers and sweepers, and seaplanes.'[8] Unlike many naval analysts, Pilcher looked past the actual warships to personnel and training considerations, and provided a detailed description of a force comprising a limited permanent force supported by a comprehensive naval reserve. Although the composition of the various reserve components outlined would differ from what eventuated, the author accurately foresaw the importance of the reserves to the future RCN.[9]

Pilcher emphasised that the loan of RN personnel would be key to the development of an effective training system, and here again he was on the mark. He also foresaw problems that might occur if the wrong type of individual was sent to Canada:

> There is a delicate subject connected with the selection of officers from the Royal Navy which should, however, not be ignored. The democracy of Canada and the other self-governing Dominions is undoubtedly far in advance of the democracy of Great Britain in some ways, and many officers who are first-class officers in the Royal Navy will fail in the navies of the self-governing Dominions through their inability to adapt themselves to their new surroundings. It really means that the officers should, in addition to having the necessary tact, be men with the gift of understanding and working with a people of a nationality slightly different from their own. ... Nearly all the mistakes, made by ministers and officers of Great Britain dealing with her Empire in past history, were due to the fact that they forgot or failed to realise that they were often dealing with men of a different nationality of their own.

Pilcher was an astute observer indeed. However, despite his warning, for years sparks flew as a result of the perceived arrogance of some British officers towards their Canadian counterparts – who, it must be accepted, were sometimes overly sensitive to any slight, real or imagined. The situation lasted for decades, and, of course, also surfaced in relations between the RN and other Dominion navies. Such is the baggage of Empire.

In closing his analysis, Pilcher expressed concern that Canada would forget the lessons of the war after victory was won. 'The great danger, as far as the future of the Canadian Naval Service is concerned is over reaction ... It is the business of those in authority to see that the reaction is not too great and strike now while the iron is hot, and not wait until forgetfulness and returning material prosperity have resumed his sway.' That did not occur, and Pilcher's hope that the foundations of 'a great Canadian fleet' would be laid came to nought. In 1922, the government gutted the fleet to just two destroyers, closed the naval college and limited the RCN to a small number of personnel.

The Great War

The *NR* devoted copious pages to First World War naval operations, but it should not surprise that the experiences of the RCN do not appear in these accounts. At the outbreak of war the RCN consisted of just the obsolete cruisers *Niobe* and *Rainbow*. RN cruisers based on Halifax protected the vast North Atlantic shipping network upon which the Allied war effort would become increasingly dependent, and the RCN cruisers operated as part of the British squadrons. The only Canadian operations under Canadian control were local patrols carried out by minor war vessels taken up from civilian departments. Neither Ottawa nor London saw any need to change this situation. Prime Minister Robert Borden did not want to stir up the still contentious naval question alluded to earlier, and was happy to comply with British advice that Canada's war effort should focus on the provision of soldiers for the Western Front. British leaders, moreover, promised that if enemy warships did operate in Canadian waters, they would immediately dispatch additional forces to deal with the threat. That proved illusory. When German U-cruisers launched attacks on the Canadian Atlantic coast late in the war, the British were in no position to fulfil their promise. Canada was on its own, and quickly patched together a force of anti-submarine trawlers to patrol the coast. In the only encounter with a German submarine, the trawler *Hochelaga* chose to seek assistance rather than engage the enemy, thus allowing the submarine to escape. Although the RCN helped run the convoy organisation from ashore, the service fired no shot in anger and derived no fighting heritage from the Great War.

None of this was discussed in the *NR*. A remarkable 1917 article on the Allied shipping organisation included a valuable description of

Canadian aspects of the North Atlantic convoy system.[10] However, although it included mention of German U-cruisers operating off the Canadian and American coasts, it made no reference to the role of the RCN or its personnel who so effectively managed the convoys out of Canadian ports like Halifax and Sydney. In 1920, Rear Admiral Bertram Mordaunt Chambers, Port Convoy Officer at Halifax,[11] provided the only personal account of the Canadian naval experience in the war with his recollections of the devastating Halifax explosion of December 1917:

> At 9 o'clock that morning I had just finished breakfast. It was not unpleasant after three years of the North Sea and Scapa to find oneself in a well-appointed dining room, and to know that one could enjoy the good things there set forth without any qualms induced by thoughts of food shortage. It was, however, well that I resisted any temptation to linger. At 9.10am I was accustomed to leave my house for the office, and therefore at 9 o'clock exactly I left the dining room where I had been seated, facing a large plate-glass window. Six minutes later those windows were swept in spines and splinters across the room, clearing the table, in their passage, and were skipping or cutting deep gashes in the wall and sideboard on the opposite side of the room. Had I been five minutes late that morning, death or loss of sight to myself and my little son would have resulted.[12]

Chambers's narrative of the days following the explosion, which caused some two thousand casualties and devastated a large part of the port and the naval base, provided an invaluable first-person account of naval activities during the aftermath of the calamity.[13]

The Canadian Navy in the Interwar Years

Throughout the interwar period, the lingering debate over Canada's role in imperial defence was the one subject that consistently arose in the NR. Most of these articles were, of course, written from the British perspective, but some authors clearly recognised that the First World War experience had had a profound impact on Canada, especially in terms of its foreign policy. Although the country retained its strong attachment to Britain, it would no longer automatically become involved in imperial entanglements – the government's refusal to provide forces during the 1922 Chanak incident provided an example of this.[14] In 1934, Commander S D Spicer, writing as 'SDS', observed Canada's detachment with evident bitterness: 'it is difficult to find much ground for hope that Canada will make any serious contribution to the naval defence of the Empire and its seaborne trade. She would rewrite the Whale Island motto *"Nisi vis bellum, para pacem"*, and make this the guiding principle of her foreign policy.'[15]

Three years later, a Canadian officer offered a more reassuring appreciation. Fresh off the Royal Navy Staff Course, where he no doubt had plenty of opportunity to debate Canada's position, Commander Cuthbert Taylor, RCN, observed that despite the numerous influences that caused Canada to follow a more independent foreign policy, 'It is impossible to visualise any Dominion, and certainly not Canada, holding back in a war in which the Empire was involved. Public opinion in Canada would not allow it.'[16] In that, of course, he was completely accurate. Nonetheless, Taylor was uncertain of the role the RCN would play in any future conflict. In a comment that could be made at any time in Canadian history, he noted 'Canada is not sea-minded today. This may seem remarkable, observing that she is one of the leading exporting countries in the world, but Canadian eyes are not on the sea but on her undeveloped interior.' Taylor was confident the 'inland Canadian (that is the majority)' realised 'in war some form of naval defence is necessary', however, 'What the future developments of the RCN will be it is impossible to say.' Rather, he thought the expansion of the air force would appeal to most Canadians, and would form the bulk of any Canadian contribution in future war.

Taylor's commentary was close to the mark. Although the RCN budget received a boost as war closed in, Prime Minister Mackenzie King's Liberal government poured more funding proportionately into the Royal Canadian Air Force than any other service. Despite British concerns about the role Canada might play if war broke out, in a private conversation in June 1939, King told the Commander-in-Chief of the Americas and West Indies Station that he 'could count on Canadian help in case of war.' Canada did not automatically go to war with the rest of the Commonwealth on 3 September 1939, but when the House of Commons held its war vote on 10 September, Canadian participation was not in doubt.[17]

Out of the Shadows

The February 1944 edition of *The Naval Review* included a response of the First Lord of the Admiralty to a Parliamentary query about the Canadian contribution to the anti-U-boat campaign. 'The remarkable expansion of the Canadian naval and air forces engaged in the Battle of the Atlantic', A V Alexander observed, 'and their skilful deployment and gallant handling in appalling weather conditions have been one of the prime factors enabling the United Nations to get the measure of the U-boat.'[18] Echoing Lieutenant Rahill's words from decades earlier: 'Just so.' The RCN had expanded some fifty-fold during the war, and contributed magnificently to victory in the Battle of the Atlantic. Some ten thousand sailors and 128 warships and minor war vessels participated in the invasion of northwest Europe, RCN warships were deployed into virtually every theatre of the war, and Canadian sailors on loan to the RN fought wherever British ships served in the war at sea.[19]

As the war unfolded, readers of the NR had little difficulty keeping abreast of this remarkable story. Articles following the progress of the war routinely mentioned RCN affairs. The 'Naval Diary of the War' in the May 1941 edition noted it had been 'officially announced in Canada that patrol vessels of the whale-catcher type would in future be known as corvettes', and 'HMCS *Margaree* (ex-HMS *Diana*) lost by collision.'[20] 'Notes on the War at Sea' in May 1943 explained that the 'new frigates' – seventy of which would be constructed in Canada – were 'doing good work in the Atlantic', and, alluding to the creation of Canadian Northwest Atlantic Command in April 1943, 'that the North Atlantic U-boat warfare is to be taken on by ourselves and Canada.'[21] Two articles reflected on the significance of the re-establishment of a Canadian naval college and what that might mean to the future of the RCN. According to 'V':

> This was a development which will give the greatest pleasure in this country. Canada has made an effort at sea in this war far beyond anything that had been expected of her, and this effort, combined with the decision to found a naval college, is an earnest of the determination of the Dominion that that great and powerful member of the British Commonwealth is not going to allow a repetition of the processes by which the scattered sea Empire was denuded of its strength at sea in the years of delusion that followed the victory of 1918.

Apart from waxing romantically about a rosy future, V hoped the new college would find space for *The Naval Review* in its library; presumably to inculcate RN ideals and thinking.[22]

The NR provided little analysis or comprehensive study of RCN operations during the Second World War, even though the service had grown to become one of the largest navies in the world. As will be seen below, that would not come for some forty years when the first rigorous histories of the RCN's wartime experience began to appear. However, in the years following the war occasional accounts of Canadian aspects of the war appeared, many of which dealt with the tragic 1942 raid on

Dieppe. In the 1963 Jubilee edition, for example, Admiral of the Fleet Lord Mountbatten, then Chief of the Defence Staff, provided a comprehensive justification for the raid – interestingly, there was no comment from Canada.[23] Some of the accounts in the years following the war illuminated Canada's role and proved of value to Canadian historians. A 1946 article by 'EC' on the North Atlantic convoy commodores sheds important light on their experiences and identified some of the key individuals on the RCN side of the organisation.[24] Likewise, two articles written by Captain Basil Jones, leader of the 10th Destroyer Flotilla, described the operations of his unit in the English Channel and approaches in the summer of 1944, including insightful tactical analysis that helped explain the considerable achievements of the flotilla, which, at various times, included four Canadian Tribal class destroyers, who met with significant success, and became an important part of Canada's naval heritage.[25]

Postwar Evaluation

It is interesting to consider the wartime success of Canada and the RCN in the context of a 1948 article in which 'Uno' saw two alternatives to imperial naval defence: 'Firstly, the Dominions to strengthen, maintain and co-ordinate their Navies with the Royal Navy; secondly, all the present British naval forces to be merged into one Royal Navy, the nations of the Commonwealth contributing to its upkeep in proportion to their means.' Uno had no doubt as to the appropriate course:

> The second alternative would involve sweeping changes in which the newly won traditions of the Dominion Navies would be absorbed into one greater tradition. There would be many difficulties in such a merger, but they would be outweighed by the advantages: a more powerful force for less money; a better dispersal of strength, directive, and industrial resources; by recruiting from all the Commonwealth nations a better understanding of each other by the different peoples; and, finally, a Royal Navy which would once again be supreme on the seas. The world is moving swiftly into the atomic age, in which there will be NO place for small isolated Services. *The private navies must be replaced by one Combined Empire Navy.* [Emphasis in the original.][26]

Such thinking would be anathema to Canadian politicians, and to the great majority of those who had served in the RCN. To suggest that Canada take a step back and join an empire fleet after the breakthrough towards autonomy derived from its wartime experience showed a gross misunderstanding of national ambitions. Yes, the RCN would continue to pursue close relations with the RN but the idea of a unified imperial – or Commonwealth – fleet had no chance. The RCN was quite prepared to revel in its British roots but was unwilling to surrender its hard-won autonomy.

This tempered nationalism is evident in two insightful articles contributed in the early 1950s by a Canadian naval aviator. In probably the best survey on the RCN's development to appear in the journal, Lieutenant George W Noble, who had graduated from the RCN naval college in 1945, presented a well-thought out examination of the various factors that had shaped the Navy's growth in Canada. Most interesting was his analysis of the three minor RCN mutinies that occurred in 1949 and the findings of the Commission that investigated these 'incidents', especially the steps taken to 'Canadianize' the RCN; in other words make it less British:

> During and after the war, a great wave of nationalistic feeling swept across the Dominion, which influenced almost all the Government services with the exception of the Navy, which had always tended to be conservative and rather aloof. This was brought out in the answers of a great many of the men questioned [by the commission], who did in fact reflect the opinion of most of the men in the service. When the 'Canadianization' plan was recently carried out, it appeared to some that the aim was to throw out anything that had any connection with the RN, and much was made of this in the British Press and in the [House of] Commons. This is unfortunate, because if some of the measures seem at first to be rather trivial in themselves, it must be remembered that they are only a small part of a larger policy, the beneficial effect of which will not be felt for several years, when the measures will have been forgotten.[27]

Noble noted that the Commission's report, despite recognising the need to 'Canadianize' the service, admitted to 'an abiding admiration and respect for the grand traditions and institutions of the Royal Navy and for their continuing and beneficent and steadying force wherever British and Canadian ships may sail.'

That Noble wanted to retain a connection with the RN while maintaining RCN autonomy was evident from his 1953 article 'The Commonwealth Navies in War'. Written in the context of the establishment of NATO, and the United Nations mission to Korea, Noble argued against 'small but self-sufficient navies such as now exist in the dominions' but recognised 'complete internationalization of naval forces would be even more impractical, and perhaps not even desirable.' Noble presented a 'compromise ... in the form of an integration of the

British Commonwealth of Nations.'[28] Among other unifying measures he proposed that the individual dominions form unbalanced fleets that met specific capabilities, that general policy be guided by a central staff, that some Commonwealth bases be reallocated, and that ships, weapons and training be standardised. Noble acknowledged disadvantages – in particular, 'In the dominions the loss of a vestige of their hard-won political autonomy is contemplated with horror' – yet he was convinced of the advantages: 'It is not suggested that there be a drastic upset of present plans or even a universal pooling of resources, but simply that we employ the forces and natural advantages at the disposal of the various Commonwealth nations in an intelligent manner; and more important still, that we co-ordinate our future planning in order to remedy our present deficiencies.'

Captain P W Brock, RN, writing as 'Beaver', delivered a spirited riposte to Noble from 'the Canadian standpoint'. Interestingly, although Brock proclaimed himself a Canadian, and in this instance used the country's national symbol as his pseudonym, he had not lived in the country nor served in its Navy since graduating from the RCN College in 1920.[29] The crux of Brock's opposition was that Dominions such as Canada were too far down the road of autonomy to buy into a Commonwealth Navy, and, for smaller navies, organisations such as the UN and NATO were the best vehicles for combined naval defence and deterrence.[30] Responding to Brock, Noble revealed for the first time that he, too, was a Canadian, but was writing from a broader, Commonwealth perspective in his original article. In language a junior officer could only direct at a senior through a pen name, he noted Beaver's 'almost paranoic [*sic*] tendency to assume that whenever I wrote "Commonwealth" I really meant "British".' Turning specifically to Canada, he submitted his country would perhaps gain more 'by working in closer harmony with the rest of the Commonwealth' rather than the US, whose interest in her was 'fundamentally economic', and he thought that the Commonwealth would endure longer as an effective organisation than 'other present military alliances.' It is interesting that a Canadian of Noble's generation would take such a position, and, despite his long absence from Canada, Brock was more in touch with the Canadian outlook. Sadly, shortly after this exchange, Noble died in a flying accident and thus the RCN was deprived of a young, intelligent voice.[31]

The mid 1950s turned out to be the apogee of Canadian interest in the NR. In a membership analysis written in 1954, 'Sirius' noted that while RN subscriptions had fallen since 1950, the RCN's had more than doubled, expanding from thirty-four to seventy-three. Sirius described this as 'the most striking change of all' in the past four years, and concluded 'The wealth and prosperity of Canada must combine with her geographical situation to enhance her importance in world affairs, and one has long seen this coming; evidently, world affairs include naval affairs.'[32] This was an over-optimistic assessment, and the spike in RCN membership was probably due to the influence of one senior officer rather than any general increased interest in the NR. In a message to the officers of the RCN's Atlantic fleet, Rear Admiral Roger Bidwell, RCN, Flag Officer Atlantic Coast and an enthusiastic Anglophile who had gleefully commanded the RCN's Coronation Squadron, exhorted:

> I would also point out that membership in *The Naval Review* carries with it advantages which a keen and ambitious naval officer will be quick to realise. For apart from being able to read completely free discussions and criticisms from all levels of the Royal Navy, on such subjects as strategy, tactics, naval operations, administration, education and any other subject affecting the fighting efficiency of the Navy, he may also add his own voice for the ultimate benefit of the whole.[33]

Then, after citing the tribute from Sirius quoted above, in a second message Bidwell urged, 'I feel that there must be many more officers in this Command interested in those important aspects of our calling ... Membership of *The Naval Review* will help to encourage constructive thought and discussion on naval affairs, which will stand both the officer and our Navy in good stead.' It was this exhortation by Bidwell, with perhaps an assist by an interest in things British peaked by the Coronation – the RCN had sent the largest Commonwealth task unit, a light fleet carrier, cruiser, destroyer and two frigates, to the fleet review – that was responsible for the increase in membership.

But the spike was temporary. Despite the sentiments of officers like Bidwell and Noble, the RCN was increasingly moving into the orbit of the United States Navy, and by the mid 1950s the USN was its closest ally, a relationship cemented by bilateral defence agreements, common procurement and personnel exchanges. Although there are no statistics to support this, there is no question that Canadian officers interested in a forum on naval affairs would increasingly turn to the United States Naval Institute *Proceedings* rather than *The Naval Review*.[34] This would only strengthen over time.[35] The fact that, from the mid 1950s, Canadians no longer undertook officer training with the RN also had an impact. Although interest in the NR would not shrink to pre-war numbers – there had been only four RCN subscribers in 1937 – it would never again reach the heights of the mid 1950s. Correspondingly, any influence on the RCN from the *NR* decreased as well.

Nonetheless, Canadian content continued to appear. Lieutenant Commander Peter J E Lloyd, a British officer on loan to the RCN, contributed two articles that described the unique features of the icebreaker HMCS *Labrador* and then described its successful transit of the Northwest Passage, the first by a deep draft vessel. As *Labrador*'s navigator on her famous 1954 voyage across the Arctic, Lloyd knew the subject well.[36] In 1956, 'FF-H' authored a piece on contemporary anti-submarine warfare that included, among other things, discussion of 'The new factors [in ASW] which make nonsense of the continued existence of Coastal Command.'[37] Most readers would not have known that FF-H, Captain A B Fraser Fraser-Harris, DSC*, was an RCN officer heavily engaged in a battle over the control of Canadian maritime land-based air – as in the United Kingdom, the RCN failed to achieve control of the RCAF's maritime aircraft, which, over the long term, placed Canadian naval aviation in jeopardy.

The 1950s also featured a dispute over the role of the RCN in the Battle of the Atlantic. Commenting on Rear Admiral W S Chalmers's biography of Admiral Sir Max Horton, Captain J D Prentice, RCN, a former Canadian escort leader, pointed to 'certain inaccuracies both of major fact and minor detail, made by direct statement and by inference, which shake my faith in the book as an entirely accurate historical document.'[38] Along with disagreeing with analysis of his own tactics and the lack of mention of successful training procedures adopted by the RCN, Prentice complained that Chalmers, who a quarter of a century before had written on the RCN as BX, ignored Canadian Rear Admiral Leonard W Murray who, when as Commodore Commanding Newfoundland Forces (1941–43) and as Commander-in-Chief Canadian Northwest Atlantic (1943–45), had played a major role in controlling operations in the western Atlantic. In his rebuttal Chalmers saluted Murray, but observed he had not been writing a history of the entire battle. Somewhat cheekily, in a jab at Canadian sensibilities he also noted that the official account of the RCN in the Second World War had made no mention of Admiral Horton.[39] Prentice's efforts for a fair appraisal of the RCN's role in the Battle of the Atlantic appear to have had no influence whatsoever as indicated in an article by C G Brodie, who served as a Convoy Commodore during the battle. Describing his experience of one convoy, Brodie observed 'our Canadian escort were enjoying themselves by chasing imaginary submarines in all directions, which made me feel rather old and bored and inclined to tell them to look for

icebergs instead.'[40] Such stereotypic disparagement could not endear
the *NR* to Canadian officers.

Unification

If its history did not always get fair treatment, the 1960s saw
considerable attention paid to the contemporary RCN and the 'Naval
Affairs' section of the journal routinely covered Canadian events in
considerable detail; a 1964 article, 'The State of the RCN', gave a
particularly valuable account of the service's requirements.[41] Of course,
the Unification of the three Canadian services in the mid 1960s was the
main feature – some would say debacle – of the decade and, not
surprisingly, this received relatively extensive attention. One must
observe, however, that the coverage was not as insightful as it might
have been. A case in point is a lengthy 1966 article describing the
measures of the 1964 Defence White Paper, which included Unification.
The article is presented in a style overwhelmingly complimentary to
Defence Minister Paul Hellyer, who introduced the controversial policy.
What is not stated, however, is that the author, Group Captain William
M Lee, RCAF, was Hellyer's chief public affairs apologist, and the bête
noire of virtually all Canadian naval officers.[42] Perhaps the editor
should have smelled a rat: it was only two editions later that 'Half-
Back', in a letter applauding the efforts of Canada's military leaders to
save money through limited integration, revealed Lee's actual identity.[43]
Also in 1966 'Crapaud', who abhorred the loss of naval identity he
thought would stem from Unification – particularly if sailors lost their
traditional uniforms – tried to spark debate on the subject, but, in an
interesting twist, wanted to limit it to Canadians:

> I hope non-Canadian members of *The Naval Review* will forgive me
> if a peculiarly Canadian problem is aired. I trust they will find the
> discussion interesting and believe it may prove instructive, since
> arguments advanced for unification can often be applied with equal
> validity to most Commonwealth countries. All the same, my article
> is addressed to Canadian members and I hope others will bear with
> us and leave any further correspondence on the subject to
> Canadians, since the present situation can only be worked out in the
> Canadian context.[44]

Crapaud undoubtedly expected to ignite a storm of protest, but it was
not to be. In the *only* response to his appeal, 'Nevill' dismissed the idea
that droves of sailors would leave the Navy over their uniform. Rather:

> Let us take a positive approach in striving for highly motivated
> fighting units, ably led and well equipped. If unified force

organisation can best achieve this, let's get on with it. If poor
organisation or administration is the result of unification let us
change it or stop short of unification but let us not use the rather
shaky emotional argument of 'uniform identification' to retard what
may be a courageous move towards efficiency and economy.[45]

The debate over Unification rested there until 1974, when Captain John
Caldicott Littler, a self-described 'vintage' RCN officer who had retired
well before Unification, challenged Nevill as to the health of the Navy.
'Some years ago', Littler wrote, 'a Canadian naval officer ... asked us
all for forbearance, so that the political conception and birth of the new
Canadian forces would be given every chance of success. Since then
silence has reigned ...' Clearly embittered, Littler requested 'someone
now serving' answer four 'provocatively' framed questions, including
'Do you now have a proud elite force as good as its forebears, or have
they now largely become just people in uniform?'[46] Littler received no
reply, which is hardly surprising since six years had passed since
Unification had been enacted in 1968 – presumably wounds had healed
and most were 'getting on with it'.[47] But the lack of debate over
Unification is instructive about the relationship between Canada, its
Navy and *The Naval Review*, and it seems telling that the most
contentious event in the history of the RCN attracted such little
attention from either side of the Atlantic.

That trend endured. Over the next forty years, the *NR*'s content on
the issues related to the Canadian Navy did not become the focus of
debate or discussion. Even seemingly obvious subjects, such as Canada's
flirtation with nuclear submarines in the late 1980s which saw the RN's
Trafalgar-class in competition with French *Rubis*-class boats, received
little or no comment.

Despite the lack of intellectual sparring, the *NR* did keep its readers
apprised of naval events in Canada. A 2005 analysis of the fire in the
submarine HMCS *Chicoutimi* (formerly HMS *Upholder*) is a useful
case in point.[48] (Whether out of respect for the former service or out
of ignorance, the authors of several of these pieces referred to the
'RCN', an institution that had not existed since 1968 – an error which
would certainly raise the eyebrows of Canadian officers.[49]) Others
also considered the Canadian context when it applied to issues facing
the RN. In 1981, 'Ivy' considered whether new Canadian procurement practices, which allowed the contractor to 'flannel [his] way
through the over-expenditure after the event', and which proved
effective for Canada's acquisition of CF-18 fighters and City-class
frigates, would work for the RN:

Would *Invincible* in its present form and cost be afloat today under such a system? Perhaps under such a system, cheaper and more cost-effective ships with the same capability in greater numbers, would just be commissioning. You pay your money and take your choice, but with finite limits to our bags of gold which would you prefer?[50]

Another subject concerned the role of the Navy in helping to enforce maritime sovereignty in co-operation with other government departments. In a 1993 study, Michael Ranken concluded that the UK could learn from Canadian initiatives in this regard, a view supported by a former exchange officer to Canada who provided practical detail of how the system worked.[51] Two years later, Ranken looked at Canada's involvement in the North Atlantic fisheries disputes, when the Navy was involved in confrontation against foreign fishing vessels on the Grand Banks.[52]

A few Canadians also made an effort to bring Canadian issues before the readers of the *NR*. Admiral Robert H Falls, Chief of the Defence Staff (1977–80), submitted two articles on the strategic situation confronting Canada and its military. Falls was the first naval officer appointed CDS and he was clearly taking the opportunity to explain Canadian security matters before a naval audience.[53] Twenty years later, in an argument familiar on this side of the Atlantic, naval analyst Peter Haydon observed, with the Navy's capital programme under close political scrutiny, the country still had yet to really study the fundamental question of what Canadians wanted its Navy to be able to do.[54]

Through the Lens of History

But during this period, Canada's Navy received by far the most attention in the *NR* through the lens of its history. Canadian naval history entered a renaissance with the 1985 release of Marc Milner's *North Atlantic Run: The Royal Canadian Navy and the Battle for the Convoys*, and from that point a steady stream of high quality scholarship – some authored by official historians, some by academics – appeared on various subjects related to the history of the RCN. Many of these books were the subject of comprehensive and thoughtful analysis by knowledgeable reviewers such as Admirals Brock and Hill, and a newcomer to the stage, Jeremy Stocker, in the review section of the journal, and on occasion they ignited the type of debate that was absent when issues concerning the contemporary Canadian Navy were brought forward. For example, four years after the publication of Milner's *North Atlantic Run*, James Goldrick (qv) wrote a review essay

delineating a number of the issues that Milner thought had hampered
RCN operations in the North Atlantic, including substandard
equipment and training, and lack of support from the RN.[55] This seized
the attention of Captain Littler, whom we have already met. Writing
from the 'but I was there' perspective, Littler deprecated much of what
Milner and Goldrick put forward. As just one example, after describing
his corvette's successful experience at the RN training centre at
Tobermory, he jabbed 'Oh yes, Marc Milner, we were looked after by
the Royal Navy to the very limit of our own endurance and
absorption.'[56] In Littler's mind, the experience of one ship could stand
for all. Goldrick responded with a long essay that focused on the
importance of appreciating the difference 'between the conclusions
resulting from theoretical study of events and the conclusions derived
by those who experienced them at first hand.'[57] Goldrick could have
added a third dimension – the interpretation and research ability of the
historian and reviewer – but his commentary nonetheless contained
valuable discussion of issues at the heart of much of the historic content
that regularly appeared in *The Naval Review*. Interestingly, Milner
abstained from the discussion but was moved to become a member of
the organisation.[58] Although there was not again that level of discussion
around the other reviews of Canadian naval historiography that
continued to appear, their sheer comprehensiveness and understanding,
provide the most valuable insights of the Canadian Navy that appeared
in the last two decades of the *NR*.

The Canadian Naval Review

So what impact did *The Naval Review* have on the development and
understanding of the Canadian Navy? A survey of a small number of
Canadian naval officers who served between the 1950s and the present
confirms the view that *The Naval Review* was not all that relevant in
the Canadian context. Commodore Jan Drent, who retired in 1990,
perhaps put it best:

> I have been a happy *NR* subscriber since 1958 and have had much
> enjoyable reading. However, I believe that the reality is that the
> Canadian Navy has been only a peripheral and intermittent presence
> in its pages and *NR* has not had a substantial influence on the
> thinking of Canadian naval officers.[59]

The previous pages certainly bear out that view. But *The Naval Review*
has had one important, enduring influence. When a group of academics,
retired officers and naval enthusiasts looked to establish a forum for
the exchange of ideas on Canadian naval and maritime affairs, *The*

Naval Review was a model they sought to emulate. Since *The Canadian Naval Review* first appeared in the spring of 2005, it and its accompanying website, has proved a vibrant forum on naval subjects.[60] If imitation is indeed the sincerest form of flattery, *The Naval Review* can be proud of its Canadian legacy.

13 From Offspring to Independence: The Royal Australian Navy

Dr David Stevens

IT has to be stated up front that the Royal Australian Navy (RAN), and indeed wider questions of Asia-Pacific maritime defence, have seldom achieved particular prominence in the pages of *The Naval Review*. This is not to suggest the RAN has been entirely ignored. The original Naval Society welcomed Dominion members from the outset, and at least one relatively recent issue of the *NR* possessed 'a distinct flavour of marsupial', as the then editor put it. Nevertheless, for more than half a century the journal's focus has been largely NATO-centric, while even before the Cold War it remained more generally concerned with European issues.[1]

There are clearly logical reasons for this, including the simple matters of threat proximity, relative membership size and the pressing issues surrounding the changing nature and capabilities of British sea power.[2] Yet, even as strategic partnerships have waxed and waned, there has remained a continuing undercurrent of interest in Australasian affairs. Considerable shared experience exists, and although combined operations might now be less common, a century of exchanges and loans has ensured that members of the key Commonwealth Navies, if not as directly interchangeable as they once were, still identify with and benefit from a shared heritage. The *NR* has played a small but important part in strengthening this mutual understanding.

Coincidentally, both the *NR* and the RAN recognise 2013 as an important centenary, for it was on 4 October 1913 that the RAN's new 'Fleet Unit', three light cruisers and three destroyers led by the battlecruiser HMAS *Australia* (I),[3] first arrived at its new home port of Sydney. Australians of all persuasions flocked to see a naval spectacle that many perceived as their national coming of age. Just a dozen years after achieving nationhood, the fledgling federal administration found itself the possessor of a most valuable and flexible tool. Having expended considerable national treasure on acquiring an independent oceangoing Navy, expectations of increased influence in imperial decision-making ran high. Claimed one Australian senator, 'It is the destiny of the dominions to uphold the trident in the Pacific, and Australia has pointed out to her sister dominions their duties and responsibilities.'[4]

Still, behind the fine words of welcome nagging doubts remained. Beyond vague statements concerning naval diplomacy in peace and imperial control in war, there had been little real discussion or agreement on the RAN's strategic rationale. An ongoing concern in Australia, and indeed one of the local drivers in acquiring the fleet, had been the fear that British imperial and Australian security priorities might not always coincide. What might happen, for example, should the Admiralty in London insist on a wartime concentration in the North Sea and a threatening Pacific power seek to take advantage of Australian weakness? That the privately circulated *NR* could offer a safe forum for professionals to air such questions, was deliberately highlighted in the journal's first introductory article, and in the same issue 'War Thought And Naval War' discussed the need for a greater study of strategic factors as well as the more popular material and technical matters:[5]

> A community which has never studied its own development and the causes which have led to change and reform within finds itself severely handicapped when some new development is required, and our shortcomings are clearly reflected in the conflicting views and opinions current with regard to the duties of the Canadian and Australian navies.[6]

One early member of the Naval Society who took up the challenge to contribute was Commander W H C S (Hugh) Thring, RAN,[7] who in late 1912 had accepted a position as assistant to Rear Admiral Sir William Creswell,[8] the First Naval Member of the Australian Commonwealth Naval Board (ACNB). A thoroughly professional officer with a background in gunnery and intelligence, Thring was also an inveterate inventor and prolific writer, with a particular interest in Pacific affairs. Having resigned from the Royal Navy in 1911, his promising career cut short by the fallout from the Fisher-Beresford dispute, Thring clearly believed that Australia's Navy offered renewed opportunities.[9]

Arriving at Navy Office, Melbourne in mid March 1913, Thring immediately accompanied the Second Naval Member of the ACNB and the Chief of the General Staff on an inspection tour of northern Australia.[10] Directed to prepare a report on the future of Thursday Island in the Torres Strait as a fortified outpost, the group soon determined that their mission was futile without a general Australian war strategy, and so decided to expand the study's scope. Most importantly, they readily agreed on Australia's need to embrace an alternative maritime strategy; one that accounted for the Pacific's unique circumstances and that, if necessary, could function independently of imperial needs. It was Thring who originated the general idea of a naval frontier or 'advanced line' which became the central theme of the team's strategic plan. Either countering or deterring any potential attack through a combination of early warning, forward basing and high technology, the plan represented the first attempt to detail the potential functions of an independent Australian Navy and its relationship to other aspects of national power.

The strategic principles presented in the finished paper displayed many parallels with the work of the great maritime strategist Sir Julian Corbett.[11] While attending the naval War Course Thring had certainly listened to Corbett's lectures, and his plan almost certainly represents the first attempt to put some of Corbett's theories on the limitations and employment of maritime power into practice. However, by challenging existing Australian defence policy and, even more, Admiralty intentions, it did not gain ready acceptance in Navy Office. Staffing delays followed by the outbreak of war in August 1914 reduced the immediate need for action but, undaunted, Thring had already published the plan's fundamentals in the *NR* in an article titled 'The Pacific Problem'.[12] He then further refined his proposals while serving as the RAN's Director of War Staff.

Eventually much of this strategic work, and particularly the sections on regional naval co-operation, operating concepts and fleet basing, found their way into Admiral of the Fleet Lord Jellicoe's 1919 review of imperial naval defence.[13] That these plans became increasingly unrealistic in the straitened environment of the early interwar period do nothing to diminish either the *NR*'s role in stimulating thoughtful debate, or their importance in the history of the RAN's intellectual development. Thring went on to write many other articles during the 1920s, several focusing on the need for an Empire War Staff, but having retired through ill-health in 1922 his ability to remain current on strategic topics inevitably declined.[14] His last major contribution to the *NR*, was a multi-part work on 'Trade Routes and their Influence', appearing between 1928 and 1929.[15] Thring died in 1949, sixteen years after Creswell, who had himself received the rare honour of a *NR* obituary.[16]

As we shall see, until the late 1970s the RAN produced few, if any, authors to rival the breadth of Thring's contribution. Without the presence of a thoughtful strategic mind, or at least one willing to write, Australian representation progressed from introductory articles on the logic behind the formation of Dominion Navies, through to various reprints of official and semi-official wartime reports. The light cruiser HMAS *Sydney*'s[17] dramatic victory over the German commerce raider SMS *Emden*[18] in November 1914 provided the background to several of these accounts, including a comprehensive narrative by the Australian ship's surgeon,[19] but even the more routine proceedings of *Australia* in 1914–15 were deemed worthy of recording.[20] Personal recollections written specifically for the *NR* were far less common, but two concerning the First World War period are deserving of mention, if only for their insights into how Royal Navy officers then perceived Australia and its Navy.

The first piece, written in 1921 by Creswell's obituarist and former Second Naval Member of the ACNB, Admiral B M Chambers, offered a somewhat droll account of his role in providing chaplains to the RAN in 1911, and the problems he experienced in encouraging Australian sailors, 'not accustomed to the church habit', to attend a religious service.[21] Apparently the latter far preferred the opportunity to enjoy a quiet smoke. Australia's lack of a state church added to his difficulties, and Chambers related a lively discussion on the pros and cons of compulsory church attendance that he had with the Anglican Archbishop of Brisbane, who particularly objected to the Australian Navy's plan to allow Nonconformist chaplains to minister to members of the Church of England. Chambers eventually capitulated, in theory if not in practice, but the experience provided a rare opportunity 'for the exchange of theological broadsides between a naval officer and an arch-bishop.'[22]

The second piece, a letter which did not appear in the *NR* until some fifty years later, dealt with the short-lived *Australia* mutiny in June 1919. The author, Commander Cecil C M Usher, RN, had been a regular contributor to the *NR* and on retirement had taken up residence in Australia. In 1919 he had been a lieutenant on loan in the RAN flagship and his contribution provides a rare eyewitness account of the incident. Certainly, it is the only report to mention the central role of the 'FIF' (F... I've Finished) Party.[23] The party evidently found its home among some of the time-expired members of the ship's company, who argued that since the war had ended they had no obligation to continue serving. Having enjoyed a little too much hospitality during a first visit to Fremantle, several of these men managed to prevent the ship from sailing on time and five were subsequently found guilty of mutiny. But it was the perceived severity of their sentencing that provoked controversy.[24] The end of the war and the circumstances of their insubordination aroused much public sympathy, and assertions were later made in both parliament and the press that the Royal Navy's system of discipline, under which the RAN was administered, was harsh, cruel, and unnatural in the Australian context.[25] This response was undoubtedly an over-reaction, but initial intentions had been for members of the Dominion Navies to be entirely interchangeable with the Royal Navy, and the furore surrounding the mutineers highlighted how national attitudes might differ on a number of levels.

Not surprisingly, the issue of discipline has been a favourite theme of wardroom and classroom discussion between RAN and RN officers for decades.[26] The *NR* was not immune to involvement. The most clearly identifiable instance appears in a review of the RAN volume of the Australian *Official History* of the First World War. Appearing in 1929, and again written by Admiral Chambers, plainly the *NR*'s then RAN expert, the review took issue with the author's comments on the difficult living conditions experienced by RAN crews engaged in the patrols off India and China in 1915–17. The official historian evidently sympathised with the men, characterising a refusal to obey orders by seven stokers in the elderly Australian cruiser *Psyche*[27] as 'a foolish and regrettable display of indiscipline', but pointing out that the ships were 'never ... designed for either war services or tropical voyages.'[28] Chambers would have none of it:

> The old time British Blue would smile at such a description ... for was not half his service on the East Indian and China stations served in just such ships and under such conditions without ever or hardly ever grumble? The standards of comfort demanded by young Australia are certainly different, and the result points to the advantages of long disciplined training and the hardening of the old school.[29]

Accepting that such differences of perspective are real and have the potential to create misunderstandings, one might have expected that articles of the compare-and-contrast type, perhaps written by a Royal Navy officer after a period of exchange or loan, would have become a staple of the *NR*. But this does not appear to have been the case. Just a single article providing a direct comparison, 'Australia and Her Navy Today', appeared between the wars. Nevertheless, the author, Captain W S Chalmers, was an experienced observer, and his personal insights and detailed descriptions of life in Australia and RAN operational practice in the early 1930s make this contribution particularly valuable.[30] Royal Navy officers at times felt that by accepting an RAN appointment they were at best putting their careers on hold and, conceivably *pour encourager les autres*, Chalmers did his best to belay the colonial stereotypes that were already so firmly entrenched:[31]

> Had I believed all I heard I might have formed the impression that the country was almost barren except for a few gum trees and coarse grass suitable for sheep, and that the inhabitants were uncouth and rude, that the naval ratings were difficult to handle and that life in the Navy was one long joy ride spent in visiting the coastal cities. All this is far from the truth, and I am glad to have the opportunity of conveying through the medium of *The NR* a little information which I hope will dispel any illusions readers may have about this intensely loyal Dominion.[32]

Notwithstanding this apparent loyalty to the Empire, the RAN was steadily becoming less a direct reflection of its parent. With the post-war contractions, any semblance of balanced fleet capabilities had gone, and although Australia's declared policy held that the RAN would be maintained as 'an effective and contribution to Empire Naval Defence',[33] in practice it never received resources sufficient for such an undertaking. Nevertheless, the two new heavy cruisers, *Australia* (II) and *Canberra*,[34] remained a core RAN capability and were not only included in the Admiralty's calculations for trade defence, but also expected to replace older British cruisers in the main fleet once this deployed to the Far East. On occasion the NR reflected this professional interest. An article on 'Some Questions Concerning Australian Defence' by Vice Admiral Richmond, one of the founding members of the Naval Society, appeared in 1929, and did much to reinforce the argument that the Australian Navy's – and hence also the Admiralty's – priorities with regards to maintaining the cruiser capability were correct.[35]

The NR meanwhile, still managed a watching brief on broader aspects of Pacific defence. Echoing Thring's favourite theme, an early post-war article by Richmond had taken as its subject 'The Problem of the Pacific in the Twentieth Century'.[36] With admirable prescience and straightforward argument Richmond highlighted Japanese expansionist policies and the difficulties these might cause for the Western powers. An article by 'SDS' from 1935 titled 'The Pacific Problem' did much the same, but perhaps with a greater sense of urgency, describing European affairs as 'child's play' for statesmen, as compared with the mounting problems of Japan, China and the Western Pacific.[37] Australians at home might feel increasingly neglected by London, but at least the *NR*'s readership was not blind to the threats facing the outer reaches of the Empire.

Two articles in succeeding years provided more specific comments on Australian defence issues. The first, 'Australian Defence', appearing in 1936, and again authored by Richmond, delivered a thorough rebuttal to the arguments contained in two recent Australian books dealing with improvements to local defence. Both authors, while noting the increased danger from Japan, advocated making Australia's principal defence in the air.[38] Richmond naturally stressed the importance of global trade and sea power to the Empire's continued prosperity and security, but the existence of such discussions perhaps gave some readers the impression that Australia was wavering in its imperial responsibilities.

Possibly to correct this notion, the second article, 'Australian Co-operation in Imperial Defence', consisted of a reprint of the Australian Defence Minister's speech to Parliament in November 1936.[39] This contained an announcement of the largest budgetary outlay on defence in any year since 1918, and included suitable foundation statements on the centrality of naval operations to Empire defence, while also noting the RAN's important role in the support of British sea power. The speech might have mollified some media commentators in the United Kingdom, but in fact the Admiralty was already having reasonable doubts. In 1938, prompted by continuing uncertainty as to when, or if, Australian politicians would release RAN warships in times of crisis, the Admiralty chose to remove the uncertainty. Instead of providing reinforcement for the British main fleet in the Far East, the RAN's object thereafter became solely the defence of trade in Australian waters.

Despite these reservations over Pacific defence, in 1939 the crisis in Europe came first and RAN warships were rapidly placed under Admiralty control. Ships and men went on to serve all over the world as an integral part of the RN, much as they had done in the previous war. Only after the loss of Britain's intended deterrent to the Japanese, Force Z, were RAN ships sent hurrying home from distant stations. Thereafter, the Japanese onslaught allowed Australians no choice but to turn over their defence to the more powerful American forces. Little of this experience was reflected in the pages of the *NR*, however. With the war so large and expansive, and Australian naval participation so dispersed, descriptions of the RAN's achievements were generally found in a succession of book reviews and footnotes to Allied operations rather than in dedicated articles. This was unfortunate, because in addition to the operations of their own warships, Australian officers and sailors, and particularly reservists, played a vital role in less obvious fields in Home waters, notably explosive ordnance disposal and anti-submarine warfare. Indeed, one estimate has it that 20 per cent of the Commonwealth officers involved in the Battle of the Atlantic were trained at the RAN anti-submarine school at HMAS *Rushcutter*.[40] Ironically, with the addition of these RANR and RANVR officers with extensive Royal Navy operational experience, the *NR*'s Australasian membership was probably reaching its peak.

Regrettably, a similar pattern seems to have played out during the early years of the Cold War. In truth, and notwithstanding joint actions in Korea, Malaya and elsewhere, British and Australian regional interests were inexorably diverging. Although SEATO (the South East Asia Treaty Organisation) went some way towards achieving Australia's aim of bringing Britain and the United States together in the region, it did not provide a context for joint action. Moreover, it never approached the importance and longevity of NATO. Instead, Australia's most important security agreement became the ANZUS (Australia, New Zealand, United States) Treaty, which reinforced the move towards the United States and finally gave Australia the formal defence alliance it had always sought for the Pacific. Even with little in the way of direct discussion, the *NR*'s contents mirrored this changing strategic landscape. Significantly, in the 1939–75 index, references to the Royal Navy's NATO partners far outnumber those for the RAN. There are likewise just two index entries for SEATO and none at all for ANZUS.

Yet there did remain interest and a continuum of sorts. The regular 'Naval Affairs' column offered readers snippets of intelligence on both Allied and Commonwealth forces between 1956 and 1973, while in 1954 a younger Commander Usher provided a quite detailed report on 'The Royal Australia Navy: Background to Australia's Defence Problems'. Written from the perspective of an Australian resident, but outside observer, this article began with a review of the political and financial difficulties under which the Australian forces laboured, and then reprinted a speech on naval matters made by a current MP and naval reservist.[41] The speech made much of the continuing importance to Australia of her sea communications, and the vital role of her two new light fleet carriers in providing protection for shipping. In all it offered an optimistic view of the RAN's future, but the editor's postscript to the article brought back the reality of changing government priorities and the prohibitive cost of maintaining carrier aviation: 'Since the above was written the Australian Government has issued a Statement on Defence. The RAAF is to be increased at the expense of the RA Fleet Air Arm.'[42]

A decade later Commander Usher returned to print with a similarly themed contribution, but in the intervening years the *NR*'s members had been treated to another of the very rare views of the RAN at work from a serving Royal Navy officer.[43] Authored by a Lieutenant K R J Arnold, the 1961 article, 'Australian Vignette', was written when Britain still believed it had a major security role in southeast Asia, and began in a suitably dramatic fashion:

> The growing power of Communist China is now being recognised. There is to be a rearrangement of our forces to meet this threat. In the process Australia will become a most important factor in Far Eastern Defence. Thus, Britain has an increased incentive to keep Australia within the Commonwealth and to encourage her high degree of loyalty.[44]

That there might still be doubts over Australia's continued loyalty in the Cold War era was put down to a number of factors. The most important of these being: the influx of non-British immigrants; suspicions of continued British exploitation, notably common after the loss of Singapore in 1942 and the poor deals surrounding the acquisition of the light fleet carriers; and finally, the threat of American influence. Within the RAN, an obvious determination to outdo the parent Navy and rather pointed admiration of American equipment, might irritate traditional Royal Navy observers, but could not simply be dismissed. What was needed, Arnold argued, was recognition that the nature of the relationship had changed. Australia was now comparatively prosperous and increasingly independent, and the parent might soon have something to learn from its offspring. Fifty years ago this was apparently the sort of statement that could still shock many Britons.

The RAN's movement away from the Royal Navy and towards the US Navy is generally seen by historians in technical and equipment terms, particularly with Australia's rejection of the British County-class guided missile destroyer[45] in favour of the US Navy's superior *Charles F Adams* class[46] in the early 1960s. But there also existed an intellectual element. In seeking to find their own path, RAN officers were increasingly looking to establish their own professional forum and, though the formation of the *Australian Naval Institute Journal* in 1975 achieved this aim, it also tended to replace the need for maintaining separate membership of the *NR*. Demonstrating that the Royal Navy was by then less easily shocked, the *NR* would soon come to comment favourably on the Australian *Journal*'s contents, much as it did regularly for the US Naval Institute's *Proceedings*. Still, in 1976 the *NR*'s only apparent mention of Australia came about through a typographical error that, as one correspondent pointed out, conceivably threatened to poison relations.[47]

Australians, and presumably Austrians, are actually quite used to such literary confusion, but any suspicion that the NR might have by now have lost touch with RAN issues was firmly removed in 1978 when Midshipman James Goldrick, writing as 'Master Ned', produced his first 'Letter From Australia', undoubtedly the longest continuously running series by a single author in the NR's hundred-year history.[48] Goldrick, then working through the final year of his undergraduate degree, was already an unusually mature observer of maritime affairs and proved in his initial article that he had the necessary skill and confidence to provide a concise and insightful comment on current Australian naval developments. More importantly, he saw it as just the beginning of the journey and, where appropriate, soon elected to contribute directly to debates on many issues of common maritime interest.

Other RAN, RNZN[49] and RN authors have since provided the occasional commentary on matters Australasian, but James Goldrick is by far the most thoughtful, and the only one to have stayed the distance. Set against the background of more than three decades of strategic change, budgetary constraints and Australian politics, his regular letters to 'Commander M' offer a unique and coherent narrative from a progressively more senior and experienced naval professional. One hopes that the now Rear Admiral Goldrick will continue to write after his retirement from the service he understands so well, for the series, which at the time of writing amounts to thirty-four letters and more than 80,000 words, has become an important historical resource. Certainly, this author has been grateful for its existence, and has dipped into it for insights on many an occasion. Unfortunately, the series is probably better known in Royal Navy circles than Australian, but perhaps one day it will form the basis for an even better book.

This article began by remarking that there remains a strong bond based on shared heritage between the Royal Navy and its Commonwealth offspring. Deliberate or not, the NR has managed to reflect this bond in terms ranging from the strategic to the quirky, but always with affection. So perhaps there is no better way to conclude than by looking again at the 2000 'marsupial' issue noted in the first paragraph. In addition to 'Letter From Australia XXIV'[50] and an article on RAN hydrographic surveying, provocatively titled 'Swimming with the Crocodiles',[51] this issue contained a commentary on a selection of pressing and not so pressing issues from Australian and New Zealand defence journals.[52]

The point made by all three authors, either specifically or by implication, was that the issues and problems facing the British and

Australian Navies were all still very similar. Constrained resources, organisational change and the difficulty of explaining the complexities of sea power to politicians seeking simple solutions, are common to all maritime forces. What tends to differ is the relative positions of the two Navies on the endless bureaucratic cycle of prosperity or crisis. Thus, while in 2000 the Royal Navy contemplated the prospect of new carriers and the Type 45 destroyer, the RAN stood at the crossroads wondering where its strategic future might lie. Just over a decade later, the tables seem to have turned, with the Royal Navy facing an uncertain future and the RAN contemplating the introduction of major new capabilities. If this trend continues, then the lessons arising from the opposing juxtaposition further highlight the benefits of both Navies maintaining an open exchange of doctrinal and maritime strategic thinking. Since 1913, *The Naval Review* has been playing its part. Let us hope that the relationship continues for a second century.

14 Simon's Town and the Cape Sea Route

Rear Admiral Allan du Toit, RAN

THE naval base at Simon's Town, which sits astride the strategically important sea route around the Cape of Good Hope, regularly featured in the pages of *The Naval Review*, particularly in the years leading up to the termination of the Anglo-South African Simon's Town Agreement in June 1975.[1]

Early articles in the *NR* discussed the importance of Simon's Town and the Cape Sea Route, life on the station and the conduct of operations in the South Atlantic and Indian Oceans during wartime. The thrust of debates in the late 1960s and particularly during the early 1970s, however, increasingly focused on the importance of the Cape Sea Route, the strategic value of Simon's Town, the vexed issue of arms sales to South Africa, and the political liability of maintaining naval links with the Republic of South Africa at a time when Britain was withdrawing from East of Suez, and South Africa was becoming increasingly isolated internationally because of its apartheid policies.

Simon's Town as a Naval Base

As part of Great Britain's global presence, Simon's Town was progressively developed as an important naval base and dockyard during the nearly 150 years that it was a base for the Royal Navy. After the second British occupation of the Cape in 1806, which finally ended Dutch rule, the Royal Navy established a shelter for the ships of the Cape of Good Hope Station in Simon's Bay, in order to control one of the world's most vital trade routes and the only practical sea route to India and the Far East prior to the opening of the Suez Canal. As the importance of the Cape Sea Route increased, the small port at Simon's Town was slowly developed, eventually reaching the stage in the late 1800s where significant expansion of the harbour and base was required. The extensive new dockyard which included a graving dock and sheltered tidal basin was finally completed in 1910, the year that the four Southern African colonies joined to form the Union of South Africa, and Simon's Town became the principal base for the vessels of the Cape of Good Hope Station.[2]

An article in the July 1967 edition traced the development of the station which changed names several times during its long history. In 1857 the Cape of Good Hope Station became the Cape of Good Hope and West Coast of Africa Station, but reverted to its original name in 1903. In 1919 it was changed to the Africa Station, which it remained for the next twenty years. When war broke out in 1939 the name was changed for the fourth time to the South Atlantic Station. The station was not again renamed until 1956, when with the reduction of the America and West Indies Station, the Commander-in-Chief was given responsibility for the major portion of the waters surrounding South America and the title assumed its last form, the South Atlantic and South America Station.[3]

First World War

One of the first articles to appear in the *NR*, which discussed Simon's Town and the importance of the Cape Sea Route, was a lengthy report from the Cape of Good Hope Squadron in 1915. Published anonymously, it described in detail operations under the command of Rear Admiral H G King-Hall in Cape waters and in support of operations against German Southwest Africa and German East Africa, including the destruction of the German cruiser *Königsberg* in the Rufiji delta.[4]

In a subsequent article on operations after the destruction of the *Königsberg*, the author made the point that he was writing not so much on account 'of the interesting nature of the work carried out by the Cape Squadron, but as an attempt to fill in a small part of the background in the naval picture whose central figures are in the North Sea.' It was the author's 'hope that similar records of outlying operations all over the world would be obtained by the *NR*, so that by the time the war is over the whole work of the Navy since August, 1914 may be made clear.' The pages of the *NR* in the First World War and shortly afterwards suggest that this worthy aim was well and truly achieved.[5]

Between the Wars

In 1925, Midshipman W R Gordon provided useful insight into the importance of the Cape Sea Route and South Africa's contribution to imperial defence following the world cruise of the

Special Service Squadron and HMS *Hood*'s historic visit to the Cape in December 1924.

In addition to familiarising the personnel of the squadron with the trade routes and important ports of the Empire, two important objectives of the Special Service Squadron World Cruise, as stated by the Admiralty at the time, were to enable the people of the Dominions to see fleet units of the latest type and to bring about a better realisation of the importance of naval defence to the Empire.

Gordon contributed to this debate by observing that the inhabitants of the Cape gave the squadron a very hearty welcome and that there was considerable discussion during the visit on the strategic importance of the Cape and the problem of contribution to imperial defence. Gordon made the valid point that the population of South Africa is not maritime and that the provision of personnel to man an indigenous navy would be no easy task. He believed that 'in the future, the Cape route will be an important Imperial consideration as it was in the last war', and owing to its comparative security the provision of fuelling and docking arrangements at Simon's Town and other Union ports may be rendered necessary. He observed that 'South Africa is fortunate in her remote position from potential naval enemies and that the strategic role of her sea forces in war will be that of commerce protection, for which purpose light cruisers and sloops are the most suitable craft.'[6]

Indeed, Admiral of the Fleet Lord Jellicoe had recommended shortly after the First World War that South Africa should provide and maintain a squadron to keep open the trade route round the Cape. The Union Government, however, considered this to be beyond South Africa's limited human and financial resources. Although a small full-time naval service was established in 1922, with the arrival of the country's first three naval vessels from Britain,[7] this nascent service was short-lived and South Africa remained almost entirely dependent on the Royal Navy for the protection of its commerce and shores between the wars.[8]

An interesting article in 1970 by 'Onlooker', 'Navy Week in South Africa 1936–37', provides further insight into the importance of the Cape Sea Route and concern over the state of South Africa's seaward defences between the wars. He wrote that South Africa at the time, which lay far away from both the Far Eastern latent threat and the growing German menace, had 'little understanding of sea power' and had 'no realisation of how much their country depended upon its sea links with the outside world or what, in consequence, an effective Royal Navy meant to them.' As a result, he observed, the then Commander-in-Chief Africa Station, Vice Admiral Sir Francis Tottenham 'consistently devoted himself, whenever opportunity came his way, to explaining the role of the Royal Navy and its relevance to the security of South Africa' and that 'if something could be done to improve public understanding, much else would fall into place.'[9]

Second World War

The importance of Simon's Town and the Cape Sea Route was once again highlighted during the Second World War. As the war escalated in Abyssinia and the Western Desert, after the fall of France and Italy's entry into the war, the Cape Sea Route became of vital importance to the Allied cause after shipping routes between Gibraltar and Suez were severely disrupted. In December 1941, when the Japanese declared war on Great Britain and the United States, the Commander-in-Chief South Atlantic, who had moved his headquarters to Freetown in Sierra Leone when war broke out, returned once again to set up his headquarters in Simon's Town.[10]

Although German raiders operated in Cape waters early during the conflict, and also laid mines, the submarine threat in South African waters did not become a serious problem until October 1942 when the enemy launched widespread submarine attacks on shipping using the routes round the Cape. Thirteen ships were sunk in the first four days of the offensive.[11] Despite the enormous distances between Germany and South Africa, German records show that no fewer than twenty-nine U-boats operated in South African waters at various times during the war.[12]

Regrettably, little was written on the subject in the *NR* at the time, although a few articles appeared during the ensuing decades giving some account of the work of the Royal Navy in the war protecting the sea route round the Cape. This included a detailed account by Commander C C M Usher, who had served on secondment as Staff Officer, South African Naval Service (SANS) in the 1930s, in which he traced the development of the South African Naval Forces during the Second World War.[13] Although South Africa had no navy of her own at the outbreak of war in 1939, the establishment of an efficient seagoing force and the rapid expansion of the South African Naval Forces (SANF) during the conflict was quite remarkable, and at the peak period of hostilities in 1944, the South African Fleet consisted of seventy-eight vessels.

The Immediate Post-war Years

Towards the end of the Second World War the South African government decided to retain a permanent seagoing fleet for the defence of South Africa and the sea route around the Cape after hostilities ended. With the onset of the Cold War and the developing conflict in the Middle East, which threatened the alternate sea route via the Suez Canal, the strategic importance of the naval base at Simon's Town gained in importance. After coming to power in the 1948 general election, the Nationalist Government in South Africa, under Dr Malan, pressed with growing urgency for the Royal Navy's base at Simon's Town to be transferred to South African control. Following protracted negotiations, and at times considerable reluctance on the part of the British Government, a series of letters, collectively referred to as the 'Simonstown Agreement', were finally exchanged by the South African and British Governments in 1955.[14]

The Simon's Town Agreement

The Simon's Town Agreement established a special relationship between the Royal Navy and South African Navy and served as a very useful force multiplier in the South Atlantic and Southern Indian Ocean region. As Onlooker observed in his comprehensive article 'The Simonstown Agreement' in 1971, 'it was a plainly sensible arrangement ... and, moreover, something of great comfort to those responsible for the security of the Cape route', which not only provided for the transfer of the base at Simon's Town to South African control but also the significant expansion of the recently renamed South African Navy and maritime elements of the South African Air Force to assume an increasing responsibility for the collective defence of the vital sea route around the Cape of Good Hope.[15]

The agreement was mutually beneficial to both parties, but particularly favourable to Britain. Although it met the South African Government's strong desire to have the last British military base on South African soil transferred to South African control after a 150-year British presence, it importantly provided for the continued use of the base at Simon's Town by Britain and its Allies in peace and war, even in a war in which South Africa was not involved. It significantly increased commonality and interoperability between the two Navies and in time of war placed South African maritime forces under the command of the British Commander-in-Chief South Atlantic.[16]

The developing South African Navy vacated its base on Salisbury Island in Durban and moved to Simon's Town, and on 2 April 1957, the First Lord of the Admiralty, the Earl of Selkirk, represented the government of the United Kingdom at a ceremony marking the transfer when the British flag was lowered at HM Naval Dockyard, Simon's Town. In a speech at the ceremony, printed in the 'Naval Affairs' section of the NR, the First Lord said that the South African Navy 'had grown from modest beginnings to play a distinguished role in the Second World War, and today it was equipped with modern material of the highest quality and manned by men of great ability and sense of duty. We are confident that they will play the essential role which has always fallen to navies, the maintenance of free communications by sea', he said, adding, 'We believe the agreement we have reached in these matters is thoroughly sound, will operate to our mutual advantage and promote closer understanding – if that is possible – between the South African Navy and the Royal Navy.'[17]

As Onlooker noted, the Simon's Town Agreement initiated an era of unprecedented expansion and modernisation of the South African Navy between 1955 and 1963; 'effective professional co-operation was enhanced by the fact that both navies possessed ships with similar performance and fighting equipment.' The growth of the fleet also progressively led to the expansion of the Simon's Town naval dockyard.

Based on the experience of two world wars, and in the light of an increasing Soviet threat, the expansion of the South African Navy was almost exclusively focused on the acquisition of anti-submarine and mine countermeasures capabilities. It resulted in the rapid expansion and development of a small but highly professional, efficient and well-equipped Commonwealth Navy which was well able to train and effectively take its place alongside the Royal Navy and other Commonwealth and Allied Navies during the Cold War.

The Winds of Change

In the 1960s, as the National Party's racial policies began to create more and more ill-will abroad, South Africa was increasingly isolated from the international community. When South Africa became a republic in 1961 and left the Commonwealth, numerous African states were in the process of achieving independence. These states began to call for an arms embargo against the new republic and the cancellation of the Simon's Town Agreement. The threat of Communism and Communist-inspired insurgency in Africa also appeared to be growing. But, as Onlooker observed, South Africa's withdrawal from the Common-wealth 'in no way affected the defence agreements, it being fully accepted that both Great Britain and South Africa had a common interest in maintaining naval collaboration.'[18]

However, after the election of the Wilson Labour government in 1964, Britain refused to supply further arms to South Africa. Whilst this ban included any new orders for maritime aircraft and naval vessels and equipment, the British government was still prepared to honour existing contracts and to provide spares and ammunition within the terms of the Simon's Town Agreement. In spite of its determination not to enter into arms sales with South Africa, the strategic importance of the naval base at Simon's Town remained undiminished. As a result, the agreement continued and links between the Royal Navy and South African Navy remained strong.

Closure of the South Atlantic and South America Station

The Simon's Town Agreement was modified by mutual agreement in 1967 following the 1966 British Defence Review which resulted in the closure of the South Atlantic and South America Station as part of a steady contraction of the Royal Navy's overseas commands. As a result, on 11 April 1967, the last Commander-in-Chief South Atlantic and South America (CINCSASA), Vice Admiral J M D Gray, hauled down his flag.[19] At the same time, the prestigious Mediterranean Command was abolished and the C-in-C Home Fleet was expanded to cover command of all ships West of Suez.[20]

To mark the closure of the command after more than 170 years, the Admiralty Board sent a signal marking 'the manner in which the high traditions of the Royal Navy have been upheld, which has played no small part in helping to foster goodwill in this large and important area. The Admiralty Board notes with pleasure that this goodwill and the long and friendly association between the RN and SAN'. The signal detailed future arrangements including that the part of the old station in which South Africa lay would became the responsibility of the C-in-C Home Fleet, under whose command a senior British naval officer of the rank of commodore, to be known as the Senior British Naval Officer South Africa (SBNOSA), would act as his representative in South Africa and continue the existing liaison with the South African Navy.[21]

At the same time the last remaining Royal Navy frigate stationed at Simon's Town, HMS *Lynx*,[22] returned to the United Kingdom and the Chief of the South African Navy assumed the additional appointment of Commander Maritime Defence (COMMARDEF) and took on greater responsibility for the South African area in times of war. Most of the other provisions of the Agreement, however, remained unchanged, except that a caveat was made which required mutual agreement between the governments of the United Kingdom and South Africa before the facilities could be used in a war not involving South Africa.[23]

Increased Importance of the Cape Sea Route

The strategic importance of the Cape Sea Route and the naval base at Simon's Town was reinforced not long afterwards when the Suez Canal was closed during the Six Day War of June 1967 in the Middle East. Although the long retreat from Empire was well underway, significant commitments East of Suez remained. The Royal Navy consequently made considerable use of South African ports to support the constant deployment of ships required to meet these commitments, and continued to do so even after the withdrawals from Singapore and the Gulf were effected in the early 1970s.

During the prolonged closure of the Suez Canal, there was significant and lively debate in the pages of the *NR* about the political complications in the Middle East and Africa, together with the recent changes in British defence policy and force levels East of Suez, all of which impacted on Simon's Town and the importance of the Cape Sea Route.

In a far-sighted article entitled 'Sea Power Today', based on a lecture at Britannia Royal Navy College in June the previous year, Captain Stephen Roskill added considerably to the debate. He argued that 'the maintenance of overseas bases is not only extremely costly but is incompatible with the nationalistic aspirations of most of the countries in which they were situated.' He did not regard the loss of overseas bases as a disaster, arguing that the American Sixth Fleet had never had a fixed base in the old sense in the Mediterranean. His view was that fixed bases attracted antagonistic political overtones which meant that in many cases their value was 'highly dubious'.[24]

Although he considered that some overseas bases, such as Malta, Durban, Simon's Town, Singapore and the Falklands could be reactivated fairly easily if the need arose, he contended that Britain had to recognise that their future use was uncertain. He rightly foresaw that in coming years, Britain would depend almost entirely upon afloat support. Although he deplored the decision to withdraw from East of Suez, and found it hard to believe that the decision would be allowed to stand, he believed that Britain would in fact maintain a naval presence in the western Indian Ocean after 1971, and that it was essential to do so, or Russia would fill the vacuum. In his view, the probable availability of Simon's Town, as well as Durban, Mauritius and Addu Atoll to support a British presence made it 'perfectly feasible'. Furthermore, he strongly believed that stability in the Persian Gulf was of vital interest to Britain and he correctly foresaw that there would be yet another war in the Gulf following Britain's withdrawal. He also correctly predicted that China would develop its sea power, including a credible submarine and nuclear capability in the future.

In the very next edition of the *NR*, Onlooker, in his preface concerning the importance to Britain of the sea route via the Cape, argued that 'the importance of ensuring the security of the Cape route in the years ahead cannot be in question.' This, he argued, was implicit in the terms of the Simon's Town Agreement and readily accepted by South Africa notwithstanding its decision to sever its other connections with the British Crown. However, he contended that the continuance of the agreement 'is now in jeopardy in consequence of the refusal on the part of the United Kingdom to permit the export of the equipment needed, and preferred, by the South African Navy.' He made the point that, 'were the agreement to be unilaterally abrogated and South Africa were to turn elsewhere for the ships, aircraft and modern equipment it is determined to have, future effective co-operation at sea would be at a discount if not lost entirely.' He also contended that the dislike in some quarters of South Africa's internal policy was 'irrelevant to this issue' and posed the question whether 'in our own interests alone cannot common-sense prevail?'

'RGO', in 'Defence of the Realm' in January 1971, argued that 'Paradoxically the closing of the Suez Canal, for so long regarded as our essential lifeline to the east, is now a blessing rather than a disaster, since it makes Russian reinforcement in the Indian Ocean less easy.' He made the point that it had also forced Britain to build bigger and faster tankers specifically for the Cape route. He warned, however, that the Labour Government's attitude to South Africa endangered the Royal Navy's continued access to Simon's Town to protect the sea lanes around the Cape.[25]

Australasian Views

In 'Indian Ocean Strategy' in January 1971, 'Usher', writing from New South Wales, provided an Australian perspective on the Cape Sea Route and the Simon's Town Agreement. He argued that sea communications in the Indian Ocean and particularly via the Cape were of vital concern to Britain, but that they were also important to Australia 'as an isolated island continent which lives by what comes to and goes from her in ships.' He wrote that although Australia would not sell arms to South Africa and had no intention of entering a defence pact with the Republic, the Australian Prime Minister, Mr Gorton, had told the Australian Parliament that 'this agreement is designed to protect sea lanes from England into the Indian Ocean' and 'This protection also benefited Australia.' 'If Britain comes to some agreement, we have no intention of expressing opposition to it.'[26]

Two editions later 'JFA' digressed from his usual survey of New Zealand's maritime defence, in order to study the wider implications of the security of the Cape Sea Route on New Zealand.[27]

Royal Marine commandos land under fire at St Aubin-sur-Mer, Normandy shortly after H-hour on 6 June 1944.

oyal Marines of the 4th Commando rigade land at Westkappelle Dyke: after a erce battle between the narrow strip etween the sea and the floods inland, the aarines stormed the batteries dominating ie Scheldt estuary.

Royal Marines who took part in the battle for the Vietri defile at Salerno exhibit their battle trophies.

oyal Marines of the 3rd Commando rigade wade ashore on to the Myebon eninsular, Burma, during one of the ndings which concluded the Arakan ampaign.

Captain Peters

Commander Miers

Captain Sherbrooke

Lieutenant Roberts

Captain Warburton-Lee

Commander Ryder

Lt Cdr Stannard

Petty Officer Sephton

Captain Fogarty Fegen

Some recipients of the Victoria Cross in the Second World War, from a montage from *The Naval Review*.

nglo-US friendship: on 13 August 1945 the Admiralty Board held a farewell dinner at Greenwich for
dmiral Harold R Stark GBE (hon). Here Stark and the First Sea Lord are seated in the upper hall of
ie Painted Hall.

he Royal Canadian Navy emerged from the Second World War as a blue water navy with a global
utlook, a status it maintains today. This is the modernised light fleet carrier HMCS *Bonaventure*
itering Grand Harbour, Malta, in the late 1950s. (National Museum of the Royal Navy)

The modern Task Force evolved during the Cold War and grew into a potent force package – self-sustaining, flexible, with global reach and able to operate across the widest spectrum of military tasks. The Taurus 2009 Amphibious Task Group deployment, illustrated here, with 40 Commando Group RM embarked, conducted a wide range of activities, including maritime security operations, anti-piracy patrols, and carried out amphibious and anti-submarine warfare exercises, culminating in a multi-national amphibious and jungle training exercise in Brunei. At its maximum strength 3,300 personnel took part in the 20,400-mile (32,800km) six-month round-trip deployment, training together and building relations with seventeen nations. Seen here: HMS *Bulwark* (LPD); second row (left to right), HMS *Argyll*, HMS *Ocean* (LPH), RFA *Fort Austin*, HMS *Somerset*; third row, FNS *Dupleix*, RFA *Mounts Bay* (LSD), RFA *Wave Ruler*, RFA *Lyme Bay* (LSD), USS *Mitscher*; rear, Submarine HMS *Talent*.

The RAN's first true aircraft carrier, HMAS *Sydney* (formerly HMS *Terrible*), conducts a RAS with RFA *Wave Premier*, USS *Nicholas* and HMS *Alert* during the Korean War. A shared command structure and long-practised ability to operate with ships of Allied nations allowed RAN units to be sent to Korea within three days of the outbreak of war. (Sea Power Centre, Australia)

MAS *Sydney* operated as a troop transport later in her career and is seen here on her way to etnam accompanied by the destroyer HMAS *Duchess* and tanker HMAS *Supply*. The lack of British volvement in the Vietnam War added impetus to the need to ensure that the RAN was distinctly entifiable as Australian. This included the adoption of an Australian White Ensign in 1967. (Sea ower Centre, Australia)

Rear Admiral Sir William Rooke Creswell, KCMG, KBE, RAN (1911–1919), First Naval Member, Australian Commonwealth Naval Board. (Sea Power Centre, Australia)

Admiral Sir Richard Webb, KCMG, CB (1870–1950), the second editor of *The Naval Review* 1931–1949.

Admiral Sir Herbert Richmond, KCB (1871–1946), in an uncharacteristically diffident pose.

Admiral Sir Bertram Ramsay, KCB, KBE, MVO (1883-1945), one of the 'Sea-Kings' who awaits a full-blown biography.

HMS *Killecrankie* (aka *Bickerton*) of Forth Division RNR, named after a battle in which the Highland Scottish clans supporting King James VII of Scotland (James II of England) defeated the troops of William of Orange in 1689, during the first Jacobite uprising.

HMS *Curzon* (aka *Fittleton*) entering Shoreham, the base for Sussex Division RNR. Later manned by Sussex and London Division RNR she was sunk in a collision in the North Sea when twelve volunteers lost their lives.

Throughout the Cold War, the RNVR (RNR after 1959) manned a flotilla of minesweepers, and their ships took local names.

The Cold War saw the Royal Navy operate a large number of anti-submarine ships: here the Type 12 frigate HMS *Rothesay* with a Russian Whisky-class submarine in the foreground. (US Navy)

HMS *Eskimo*, a successor to the successful Tribal class of the Second World War; though this new generation of ships were single screw, their combination of steam and gas turbines gave them long range and they were used to extend the arm of the Royal Navy. (National Museum of the Royal Navy)

Whilst not arguing the intricacies and imponderables of the arms for South Africa debate, JFA gave an insightful view of the importance of the Cape Sea Route from a New Zealand perspective. He argued that New Zealand would find distance a much diminished shield in the future and that although 95 per cent of New Zealand's European trade went via the Panama Canal, this could be easily disrupted in time of hostility, which would necessitate a reliance on the Cape route, particularly if the Suez Canal was simultaneously closed. It argued that the 'Cape is the crossroads of the only all-weather deep sea route open to shipping in all seasons connecting the Atlantic seaboards of America, Europe, and Africa with the Indian Ocean and Pacific shores of Africa, Asia, and Australasia', adding that ice bars the northern coasts of Canada for much of the year and Cape Horn is a hazard.

JFA made the valid point that unlike the other old Dominions – Canada, Australia, and New Zealand – South Africa had no defence arrangement with the United States, her sole formal treaty with the western powers being the Simon's Town Agreement. He argued that this pact should be safeguarded 'to the advantage of the maritime group of nations forming the Western Alliance, and to the embarrassment of any Power which seeks to encroach on the freedom of the Oceans of the Southern Hemisphere.'

Arms Sales to South Africa

Following the election of a Conservative government under Edward Heath in June 1970 the British government stated its intention to rebuild Britain's vital defence interests in South Africa and to resume limited arms sales to help the Republic defend the sea route around the Cape in accordance with the spirit of Britain's obligations under the Simon's Town Agreement.[28]

Whilst the Heath government, which was under considerable pressure from within the Commonwealth not to sell arms to South Africa, was considering accepting naval orders from South Africa, the Labour opposition stated that any South African orders placed in the United Kingdom would be cancelled if they were returned to office.

Two comprehensive articles which took opposing views on the issue of arms sales to South Africa appeared in 1971. The first, 'Arms for South Africa', by 'Garefowl' and the second, 'The Simonstown Agreement', by Onlooker. Both engendered debate, particularly the article by Garefowl which drew spirited criticism in the letters pages, most notably from Captain T Wheeldon who thought that it was a 'blatant piece of rationalisation' and that the article 'introduced an unpleasant political note' rather than an entirely military view of the matter more befitting the *NR*.[29]

Garefowl argued that Mr Heath's desire to sell arms to South Africa for the defence of the Cape route 'provided an exceptional example for a study of the art of politics at various levels' and 'of the pressures that can be brought to bear on political decisions.' He contended that the strategic and military arguments for and against the sale had been less well aired and that the debate was taking place almost entirely on the political level. He cited that the key reason produced by the British government for selling arms to South Africa was to provide for the defence of shipping using the Cape, at a time when Russian penetration into the Indian Ocean was thought to be putting commerce at risk, particularly the flow of oil from the Middle East.

He asserted that 'the prime purpose of naval strategy is to pass your shipping and troops safely where you will and to stop the enemy doing likewise.' He believed that too much was being made of the importance of the Cape Sea Route and took the view that 'there is no need to defend sea lanes, in a way which implies keeping them open in all circumstances and conditions.' He argued that sea lanes were merely conveniences for shipping in peacetime, and that in war, if one's own ships remain protected and unharmed, it does not matter how many of the enemy's vessels are about you.

Garefowl therefore suggested that Britain should look very closely at what the Russian capability (rather than intention) may be off the Cape of Good Hope. He concluded that 'the nature and strength of the Russian naval presence in the Indian Ocean is not one that was primarily directed against the west and that selling arms to South Africa in order to counter it would be a very inappropriate way of meeting the so-called threat', for it would only encourage the Russians to seek a foothold along the African shore, which was one of their subsidiary aims.

Although Onlooker in his article made a reference to the Government's abhorrence of apartheid, and that 'no South African can be under any delusions over that', he wrote a plea for arms to be sold to South Africa, and for the continued use of Simon's Town, based on sound military thought. He acknowledged that the controversy over selling arms to South Africa had 'bedevilled us for a considerable time, with those averse to this provision especially vocal' and he contended that 'the intrusion of party politics has, moreover, not helped towards a rational understanding of the subject.'

In supporting the sale of arms to South Africa, Onlooker firmly believed that there was a vacuum in the South Atlantic and Indian Oceans at a time of increased Soviet maritime expansion and a diminishing Royal Navy worldwide presence, which reinforced the value of the South African Navy in helping to ensure that the vital Cape route would remain unmolested, adding that 'It is as much in our own interests as those of South Africa that the deterrent to interference in the freedom of the seas is effective.'

He observed that apart from the three new Type 12 frigates purchased in the sixties, the remainder of the South African Navy's British-built destroyers and frigates were over twenty-five years old. He considered that Britain had a legal obligation to replace these out-of-date vessels and that it was important that they be built in British yards to ensure effective interoperability at sea should occasions arise in which both Navies were involved. He argued that this was 'plain common sense and entirely in the spirit of the past agreements deliberately made with a view to future maritime defence co-operation.'[30]

Finally, Onlooker warned that if sensible requests for maritime arms were refused, 'South Africa might well feel justified in terminating the two-way agreement' with the resultant loss of base facilities at Simon's Town having significant consequences for Britain.

While South Africa duly ordered an additional seven Wasp helicopters and various items of naval equipment from Britain, the Conservative government made it clear that it was not politically opportune to accept orders for frigates at that time. The South African Navy was meanwhile also having second thoughts as it was not prepared to run the risk of ordering frigates which would not be completed before the next general election in Britain. This subsequently proved to be a wise decision.

Termination of the Simon's Town Agreement

Although regular combined exercises with the Royal Navy and Royal Air Force continued unabated, and indeed markedly increased throughout the early 1970s, and South African personnel continued to attend Royal Navy courses, relations between the two signatories of the Simon's Town Agreement steadily worsened following the return of a Labour government at the April 1974 British general election. 'Operationally necessary ship visits' to politically sensitive countries, including South Africa, came under closer scrutiny as well as the vexed issue of arms sales to the republic. The Government quickly reimposed a total arms embargo and cancelled the Wasp order which resulted in the last aircraft not being delivered.[31]

Although the Labour government initially allowed ship visits and combined exercises to continue in order to demonstrate Britain's adherence to the Agreement, it finally decided, after international press coverage of an operational group visit and extensive combined weapons training period in Cape waters caused a political furore in the United Kingdom, that the political disadvantages of doing so outweighed any military advantage.[32] In reaching this decision in October 1974, the British cabinet argued that 'although the defence facilities available to us under the Simon's Town Agreement were useful in peacetime and could be of importance in war, their value was not such as to justify continuance of the Agreement in view of its political objections.'[33]

This decision culminated in the termination of the Agreement through an exchange of letters between the two signatories in June 1975 and the subsequent withdrawal of SBNOSA and the closure of HMS *Afrikander* in February 1976. This finally closed the chapter on 180 years of British naval presence in South Africa and effectively ended the traditionally close relationship between the South African Navy and Royal Navy and by extension, South Africa's window into NATO.

After the vigorous debate on the importance of the Cape Sea Route in the pages of the *NR* during the mid 1970s, and the ongoing Soviet maritime threat, it is surprising that the only subsequent discussion on the subject was in October 1982. In an article on the strategic importance of the Falkland Islands, Hugh Rogers argued that British interests in both the South Atlantic and the important route round the Cape of Good Hope were increasingly being threatened by Soviet maritime expansion and presence on the west coast of Africa. He argued that if the ships of the NATO nations were unable to use the Cape Sea Route the effect would be serious, as 70 per cent of NATO's strategic material and 80 per cent of its oil was moved round the Cape. He also observed that following the Labour government's decision to terminate the Simon's Town Agreement, the Chief of the South African Navy had announced in 1978 that the South African Navy would no longer be responsible for the security of the Cape route and would concentrate entirely on defending the coasts and harbours of South Africa.[34]

On Reflection

In reflecting on how far the *NR* predicted or influenced the outcome of the prolonged debate on Simon's Town and the defence of the Cape Sea Route through its pages, it is worth pondering the observations of 'Benbow' following the decision to terminate the Simon's Town Agreement.

In his regular column in the January 1975 edition, just prior to the release of the 1975 Defence Review, he provided some interesting insights into the kind of political thinking that went into the debate. He observed that the question of whether or not Britain should make use of facilities at Simon's Town was a genuinely political one, commenting that

It can be argued that Simonstown is vital to the protection of our oil and trade-route round the Cape of Good Hope. It can also be argued that Simonstown could cost us a great deal of good will amongst the black states of Africa. Some say that we would certainly use Simonstown in the event of war, whatever agreements we may or may not have in peace. Others say that black Africa is far less concerned about what we do in Simonstown than we think ... it all depends upon what political view you take.

He cited a speech made by the Defence Under Secretary for the Navy, Frank Judd, at Portsmouth during the debate in which he said:

It is necessary to evaluate how far the (Simonstown) agreement may actually evoke an expansion of Communist influence in Africa and the Indian Ocean basin. It is necessary to evaluate how far it is sensible to locate defence facilities in an area of increasing instability, with the inherent danger that we may be drawn into positive support for the political status quo. But far more significant than any of these arguments, vital though they may be, is the whole question of the fundamental credibility of the Labour movement both in Britain and abroad.

Benbow further observed that whilst this speech was greeted by a certain amount of hilarity in the Tory press, and that many *NR* members may have thought that Mr Judd's remarks were preposterous, 'we must give Mr Frank Judd the credit for speaking the honest truth. To a socialist the credibility of the Labour movement here and abroad *is* more important than Communist expansion in Africa and the Indian Ocean, *is* more important than placing defence facilities of any kind anywhere, and infinitely more important than the future of the Navy'; but that 'they should remember that Mr Frank Judd happens to be a member of the party in political power, to which the armed forces are rightly subordinate.'[35]

In essence, notwithstanding the vigorous debate that occurred in the pages of the *NR*, largely based on sound military thought, logic and strategic argument, which in all likelihood informed and perhaps even influenced senior officers dealing with the issue at the time, it was ultimately a political decision that resulted in the termination of the Agreement; made all the more easier by the completion of Britain's withdrawal from East of Suez, the reopening of the Suez Canal and an increasing focus on the United Kingdom's NATO commitments.

Conclusion

The subject of intense political controversy in Britain and within the Commonwealth for much of its existence, the 1955 Simon's Town Agreement remarkably continued for some twenty years, largely because of the continued belief by both signatories in the strategic importance of the naval base that sat astride one of the world's most vital trade routes linking the United Kingdom and Europe with the Middle and Far East. Whilst financial savings were a consideration when Great Britain negotiated the agreement, Britain's prime interest was in maintaining unfettered access to Simon's Town in peace and in war for both her and her allies, at little or no cost, together with the concurrent development of the South African Navy's capacity to assume an increasing role for the defence of the Cape Sea Route in close co-operation with the Royal Navy.

For South Africa's part, the transfer of the naval base at Simon's Town to South African control, almost at any cost, was largely politically driven and a long-standing issue of national pride and sovereignty. The growth and development of the South African Navy, which Britain pushed so hard for, was initially of secondary importance to the South African government. The rapid transformation of the South African Navy into a small but highly competent blue-water force, together with the increasing strategic importance of Simon's Town and the Cape Sea Route, particularly following the closure of the Suez Canal and increased Soviet presence in the Indian Ocean, however, enabled the South African government to use the Agreement as a means to maintain close links with the anti-communist Western alliance.

Although the Simon's Town Agreement was finally terminated in 1975 for political reasons, long after South Africa had left the Commonwealth, and at a time when Britain was increasingly focusing on its NATO commitments, the agreement served the national interests of both nations and the broader Western alliance well; and at the operational level, it remains an excellent practical example of Commonwealth naval co-operation and interoperability.

Strangely though, for all the talk of the importance of the Cape Sea Route for so many years, the subject just seems to disappear from the pages of the *NR* over the last thirty years!

15 Fortress Singapore: British Naval Policy in the Interwar Years

Professor Greg Kennedy

AFTER the First World War, the British Empire was the dominant maritime global power. That dominance was not unchallenged, however, with America and Japan both possessing larger regional naval power, as well as increased merchant marine capacity. The continued instability of China, combined with the continued presence of Soviet Russia and France, along with German and Italian interests in the Chinese mainland, meant that the most important potential source of friction for future international relations was in the Far East.[1] Post-war articles in the *NR* pointed out the naval nature of the Empire's future defence in that region, as well as the need for collective measures for the provision of defence. At the farthest extremity of the Empire, provision of adequate naval forces, as well as the protection of trade and commerce, would be expensive. Furthermore, actions in the Far East that were seen as being pro-British Empire ran the risk of antagonising the emerging regional power, Japan, as well as providing a source of friction with the United States, a nation with a greater trade and economic presence in the region due to the dislocation of British dominance in areas such as shipping, banking and commerce.[2]

In this new balance of power environment, the Royal Navy was the linking force for the far-flung bits of Empire. Underpinning these economic and commercial elements of the imperial interests were the interconnected issues of race and democracy. As the Asiatic peoples embraced the power of democracy, the supremacy of the white races to rule the region would be challenged. That Asiatic nationalism, combined with growing economic and demographic power, made continuing the exploitative and advantageous position of British interests and the maintenance of the status quo in the region unlikely.[3] Any challenge to Britain's interests in the region would have to be dealt with by a mixture of naval power, diplomacy and economic leverage. In that formula, the key element was the ability to project effective and capable naval power, which, in turn, required the establishment of a permanent, modern, first-class naval base. Most often unstated and left as an obvious, unspoken given in the arguments made in the NR, the establishment of a secure and fortified Singapore was seen as the lynchpin around which all other modes of deterrence, coercion or force projection in the Far East were hinged. This was particularly true in light of the American and Japanese moves to provide fortified naval establishments in the region.[4] However, the question of Britain investing in the development of Singapore as a major base was still an unresolved policy issue in the first half of the 1920s, an age of economic austerity and limited defence spending. The articles appearing in the journal in the 1920s should be seen then as having been part of a lobbying and education campaign, aimed at a political-policymaking readership who were assessing if British interests in the Far East needed defending, and if so, how was that to be achieved.

The uncertainty of the relationship between established and emerging powers in the Far East was the source of much speculation in books reviewed by the NR, as well as specific articles. As details of the Washington Naval Conference began to be taken into account, many commentators, particularly foreign authors, pointed to the increase in American fortifications being constructed in the Pacific and how the terms of the treaty would work in favour of the defensive power: Japan. Hector Bywater and Vice Admiral Mark Kerr, USN, were just two of the prominent foreign naval analysts and practitioners of the age to highlight the impact the Washington Treaty would have on the Western powers' ability to project and protect naval power in the Far East. Singapore and the British strategic position were compared to the America basing position all in an effort to explain which locations were best placed to serve as strategic naval bases. Singapore was judged against the suitability of Sydney, while Guam, Manila, Pearl Harbor and Honolulu were all subjected to an analysis of their geo-strategic and tactical placement for fulfilling such roles. All pundits agreed that the basing issue was now the crux of the strategic situation in the Far East: any nation not possessing fortified and developed naval bases would find great difficulty in maintaining and sustaining an effective fleet in the region.[5] Opinions on the predictive worth of some of the books being published in the 1920s on the inevitability of a war between Japan and the West, and in particular America, did not so much challenge the likelihood of frictions occurring between Britain or America and Japan, but rather were less appreciative of the biases shown towards the superiority of American naval power. A scathing review of Hector Bywater's *The Great Pacific War: A History of the American-Japanese Campaign of 1931–33*, illustrates the support felt by some of the contributors to the *NR* to the mission of the League of Nations. The review derided Bywater's prejudices regarding the absolute certainty of an American naval victory, despite the glaring strategic advantages of position and defence accorded the Japanese. More importantly, the reviewer proclaimed it 'a mischievous book, and never should have been written at all' for presenting such a clash as inevitable and for the inflammatory and provocative emotions its content could evoke.[6] Still, the voices supporting the League views of collective security and restraint were few and far between in the *NR* volumes. Japan was almost unanimously hailed as a future threat to British interests in the articles appearing in the *NR* and the Singapore base question was a statement of providing security over the true, long-term, aggressive intentions of Japan.[7]

During the First World War Japan was a proven ally of Great Britain, having contributed men, money, intelligence and material to the war effort, as well as fulfilled its role as a naval partner in safeguarding the Far Eastern sea-lines of communication (SLOC) so vital to the imperial war effort. Japan also was a growing trading partner and industrial competitor, producing many goods more cheaply than could be done by British companies. The Pacific power had built its naval power on a template of the British imperial example, with technical, professional and industrial advice and assistance being supplied to the Imperial Japanese Navy by the Royal Navy itself.[8] The most prevalent example of the Japanese aggression and expansionist spirit was seen to be its attitude and policies towards China.[9] If Japan wished to deny Western nations access to China's resources and markets, and Great Britain refused to be deterred from continuing to do so, one method of Japanese retaliation was to use its growing naval power to threaten the Far Eastern oceanic trade and communications routes of the Empire. This perception of Japan having a tendency towards reducing Western interference in Far Eastern affairs was viewed by the *NR* contributors as a destabilising influence on the balance-of-power structure in that region.[10]

The Washington Treaty system, with its call for reduced armaments and limited fortifications, assured the Japanese of their position and right to have a greater role in Far Eastern affairs without having to fear isolation or containment from an Anglo-American maritime coalition. However, the terms of the treaty did nothing to address the issue at the heart of the growing rivalry, that of control over Chinese markets. Japan's ambitions in that regard had not been lessened by the mid

1920s, nor had a violent earthquake and the costs of repairing the damage done to the nation in that natural disaster affected Japan's position as a great power:

> Her Army and Navy ... are as strong as ever, her agriculture, which employs two-thirds of the population, is unaffected, and the more important industrial districts ... are unharmed. Japan's credit is excellent and she has an enormous gold reserve. Her problem of over-population though relieved for a year or two remains, and her ambitions also remains.[11]

After the First World War Japan was seen as a more aggressive, less submissive part of the international community, a fact recognised by the array of agreements present in the Washington Treaty system aimed at managing its newly derived place in the world. However, one of the more worrisome aspects of this new Far Eastern condition was the spectre of Great Britain having to choose between Japan and America, if the two nations found themselves at loggerheads in the region. This uncertainty of what Japan's policies were, and why they existed, were the most troublesome aspect of Japan's activity in the international arena of the mid and late 1920s:

> It may be that Japan and America eventually fall out over some action by Japan, in China, or in the Pacific, or even in Southern America. The quarrel may in no way directly concern Great Britain. Our interest might even be opposed to American interest. Yet this country would be forced to make its choice. If America and Japan are ever driven by public opinion in either country into war could Great Britain remain neutral?[12]

The tensions in Anglo-Japanese relations were just one of the variables regarding Japan's foreign policies that drove the continued belief in the need for a powerful British Far Eastern naval base. As the new world order of 1920 came to light, however, there were many questions about Japan's true intentions, particularly regarding its continued observation of the Open Door policy in China.[13] If an expansionist and aggressive Japan would no longer tolerate western powers encroaching on its Asiatic domain then conflict was inevitable:

> The disturbing influence in political waters will be Japan, and the cloud on the horizon, now no bigger than a man's hand, is an alliance between Germany and Japan arising out of the similarity of their aims. Both nations possess a population, vigorous and disciplined, too large for their own territories, but lacking colonies into which they may overflow, and the British Empire contains the

Naboth's vineyards which these modern Ahabs covet. The natural result of this will be to drive the two nations into each other's arms and compel the other great maritime and colonial empires – Britain, France and America – to combine. It is doubtful whether these actual combinations will have taken place in ten years' time, but all strategical problems will be based on that assumption.[14]

The theme of Japanese militarism was prevalent in the analysis provided in the *NR* articles in the early 1920s. Almost all were agreed that Japan could not, and would not, maintain the status quo in the balance of power system that was providing security in the region. Almost all observers believed that Japan's internal conditions of greater industrialisation, increased population growth and the opportunity to dominate a weak and divided China, made for conditions which demanded territorial and economic expansion in the near and distant future. Japan's reputation for aggression and as a potential enemy did not improve throughout the 1930s. The 1932 crisis between China and Japan, followed in 1934 by the Amau declaration of Japanese dominance in the region, and Japan's final acts of international disrespect for the place of other nations in the Far East: refusing to continue the 1930 London Naval Treaty aimed at limiting the impact of any potential naval arms race and the invasion of China in 1937, were the steps to a gradual but seemingly inevitable decline in Anglo-Japanese strategic relations.[15] By 1938 there was little faith that Japan's activities would in any way be beneficial to the British strategic condition. The *NR* articles dealing with Britain's Far Eastern policy and strategy all believed that Japan would at some point be a real, as opposed to potential, naval threat to the Empire. Whether relations broke down over China-related issues or with regard to Japan's growing Navy and its ability to threaten the security of the sea lanes linking Britain to its other Far Eastern possessions, at some point a showdown would take place.[16]

Japanese military commitments to mainland China meant that it was reliant on a large degree of sea-control for its SLOCs for sustaining that presence, as well as being dependent on the ability to use the sea for raw materials, foodstuffs, and trade. In order to protect this seaborne empire, Japan required an inner line of defence from its south coast on a line through to the Aleutian Islands, and over to Formosa and the Pescadores. A further layer following through the Marshall, Carolines, Pelew and Mariana Island groups provided a naval defence in depth, or, if desirous of more offensive actions, a staging area that allowed Japanese forces to reach all French, American and British possessions.[17]

The ability of the Japanese to project naval power into the sea lanes of the Pacific was a situation that Great Britain could not ignore.[18]

In order to safeguard Britain's strategic position and trade, the Singapore base, along with substantial naval basing facilities at Hong Kong, and major ports in Australia and New Zealand, allowed a strategy of containment and blockade of the Japanese home islands to be contemplated. This strategy was a counter to any Japanese attempts to oust the British from mainland China, as well as a means of protecting regional oceanic trading interests. With a ring of naval bases around the Japanese home islands, all hinging on the invulnerability of Singapore to attack, a SLOC interdiction strategy was a viable deterrent strategy against any potential threat from Japan. If Singapore were intact, and a substantial and capable fleet operating from it, then Japan would not be willing to risk challenging British sea power:

> If Singapore were to fall to an enemy, Hong Kong could scarcely be held against a determined attack, but if Singapore is well guarded, Hong Kong, if sufficiently armed to hold out for some weeks, is reasonably safe. Thus the protection of Singapore is vital to the security of our commerce on the China coast. Singapore also covers our possessions in India and around the Indian Ocean, from attack by Pacific powers. Perhaps the most important function of Singapore, but one which is less obvious because less complete, is the protection it would afford to Australia, New Zealand and other British possessions in the South Pacific. Throughout Naval history ... the importance of a flanking port, one from which enemy communications can be threatened, has been clearly demonstrated.[19]

Singapore, along with a garrison at Hong Kong and Australasian naval forces, would provide security for British imperial communications in the Far East. That protection was necessary, however, because of the belief within the British strategic policymaking elite that the Japanese were a threat to Chinese sovereignty and the Open Door,[20] and thus, British Far Eastern interests.[21] The protection of those interests, therefore, was tied to the development of a major naval fortress that could support a Far Eastern fleet. Questions arose in the interwar period, however, as to just exactly what sort of power would be projected from the Singapore base.

The topic of just what sort of base would be available to house any British naval forces in the Far East, especially given reduced defence spending, was as important to the Singapore issue as was the place of Japan on the list of potential threats.[22] Furthermore, there was some concern over the use of Singapore as the main Far Eastern base. These concerns were associated with the fact that Singapore was not a naturally good base, with limited approaches, resources and a large liability in the shape of a whole peninsula at its back that would need defending to prevent the base from being overrun by land forces. Many commentators, especially British Army officers, voiced their concerns very early on about the threat land forces poised to any base at Singapore. Such fears were dismissed and ridiculed as being fanciful musings of minds ignorant of the power of the Royal Navy to sweep all enemies before it on the high seas. In these debates questions of how Japan would declare war, how long the fleet would have to get to Singapore before Japanese forces arrived, and whether or not the British fleet would have to fight its way in to relieve the fortress or use it to stage raids and blockading actions abounded.[23] Throughout the 1920s, as questions of funding and whether or not the base would be completed to an appropriate size continued, articles in the *NR* continued to make the case of the need for a base able to house and protect dry docks capable of repairing battleships and the rest of the infrastructure required for sustaining a major battle fleet.[24]

By October 1926, British Prime Minister Stanley Baldwin was able to confirm that dedicated funding and a long-term commitment to the development of the Singapore base was a reality. However, funding for the base would come from not only Britain but imperial partners. The Federated Malay States would contribute £2,000,000 towards the cost of the base, the land itself was a gift from the Straits Settlement, and Hong Kong would contribute £250,000. At the Imperial Conference of 1926 Baldwin kept the construction of the base front and centre at the event, saying,

> This development is most urgently needed at the present time from the point of view of Imperial Defence. We would therefore ask those Dominions which are specially interested in the Far East to consider most carefully whether there is any way in which they can co-operate in the development of Singapore ... there could be no more valuable contribution to the defence of the Empire as a whole.[25]

Only New Zealand was considered likely to make such a contribution, since Australia had undertaken to establish a shipbuilding programme when the British Labour government had stopped the Singapore base idea in 1924. Canada reflected the post-war tendency to spend money on naval defence within its own borders and not for the Empire as a whole, thus not wanting to be tied to such grand imperial projects as the construction of a Far Eastern fleet base.[26] Funding for the base was the least, however, of the troubles facing the development and operation of this new lynchpin of imperial security in the Pacific. Along with the fiscal restraints on the ability to build and maintain a Far Eastern fleet to send to the Far East, as well as to build Singapore's infrastructure up to the size and scale that would allow it to operate a major fleet, there was the issue of whether or not naval power was still the best vehicle for the projection of military power into the Pacific. The increasing capabilities and performance of aircraft created many questions about whether or not Singapore should be more airfield than naval base.

This question was linked to the ongoing battleship versus bomber debate that dogged the interwar Royal Navy's attempts to acquire sufficient funding to meet the growing strategic demands being made on it for a force capable of protecting Britain's global strategic interests in the Far East.[27] The question of adequate funding being available for the Navy and its needs was a direct result of the amalgamation of the Royal Flying Corps and the Royal Naval Air Service into the independent Royal Air Force. With the defence budget now split three ways between the Army, Navy and the new Air Force, and the latter being technologically dependent and therefore expensive (given the experimental state of aircraft design and the rapid transformational nature of building air forces), the RN no longer had a monopoly on its ability to deliver global, strategic effects. Experiments by the United States Army against captured German battleships in the first half of the 1920s lent momentum to those who wished to argue that air power had now supplanted naval power as the supreme manifestation of military power and its ability to shape the battle space and influence all mediums: land, sea and air.[28] In Britain, the outcome of these new issues was a confused and unco-ordinated approach to the problem of putting air power to sea. That position was the result of the inability of the RN to settle on an informed and embracing internal attitude to the naval air power possibilities, as well as the admirals' inability to fight the political battle in Whitehall with the RAF adequately.[29]

Foreign naval officers writing in the journal were enormously critical of the lack of imagination, technical aptitude and doctrinal knowledge regarding the use and utility of air power at sea.[30] Unencumbered by a historically driven, Trafalgar/Jutland, battleship mentality that limited the ability of senior naval leadership to deal honestly and competently with new technologies, the USN led the way in the interwar years in aircraft and aircraft carrier development. The result of the lack of a firm decision on how to prioritise sea power and air force was a continued inability to decide whether to project air power or naval power from Singapore.[31] This need for the Navy to control air force at sea, as well as to ensure it controlled supporting shore-based aircraft tasked with the defence of major ports, provision of vital operational reconnaissance, and tactical air support to fleet units was a recurring and passionate part of the writings in the *NR* that analysed the worth of the Singapore base.[32]

That condition, of an uncertain future for naval power in light of the new technologies threatening it, as well as the expenses associated with having to build a major naval base at such a distance, combined to delay the building of the Singapore base. More importantly, however, the inability of the British strategic policymaking elite to deal with the need to create appropriate air forces, while building a significant Far Eastern Fleet, meant that even when the Singapore base was finished there was grave doubt as to what naval forces would be available to use it to deter Japan. One option was to base the United States Navy at Singapore.[33]

As the international situation in the Far East gradually deteriorated, British strategy became more and more reliant on the United States to help deter and contain Japanese aggression and expansion.[34] Although no outright policy of basing the American Pacific Fleet was ever articulated, the articles in the *NR* (some even written by Americans), revealed the growing desire for closer and more overt Anglo-American naval co-operation. Some of those writings, however, saw this closer co-operation as an illusory and fickle objective, bemoaning the passing of the Anglo-Japanese alliance which had safeguarded Britain's Far Eastern interests for so long and the need for the less than guaranteed support of the United States. As well, there was doubt as to the ability of America to take a more outgoing and interventionist role in world affairs, as opposed merely to lecture Japan, the European powers, and spin jingoistic slogans. Many of the articles criticised the United States for lacking a proper warrior spirit, which was in evidence during the Spanish-American war when American naval power had played a major role, particularly in the Far East. Still, the strategic reality apparent in many of the articles, particularly those written after September 1939, was that American naval power had become a more integral and needful part of the imperial defence planning process. Basing American vessels in Singapore would not only make operational sense, but would certainly send a loud and unambiguous message to the lurking Japanese: British interests were American interests and to threaten one was to threaten both.[35] The suddenness and decisiveness of the way in which the Japanese Navy dealt with the Anglo-American naval units protecting those interests in the Pacific, by 15 February 1942, came as an unexpected and overwhelming shock to the readers of the *NR*.

The fall of Singapore, the loss of *Prince of Wales* and *Repulse*, as well as the combined ABDA (America, Britain, Dutch and Australian) force in the Java Sea, all before March 1942, created a host of tactical, operational and strategic topics in failure for historians to study for generations to come. Interestingly, it was a decade before the debate began to be taken up in the pages of the *NR*. At that point the topic was more one of leadership and technical appreciation than it was about general British Far Eastern strategy and the role of Singapore.[36] Overall, given the range of useful and appropriate lessons for the Royal Navy of the 1950s and 1960s to learn from the Singapore affair, such as adapting to changing international relations, the need for a comprehensive service approach to a given strategic aim, technical innovation (revolution or evolution in military affairs) and inter-service rivalry, the lack of such analysis is interesting in itself. Unlike the interwar Royal Navy and readership of the *NR*, post-war members of the *NR* were not all that interested in the Singapore question per se ....

The writings in the journal during the 1920s and 1930s were only tangentially applicable to questions about the Singapore strategy. Indeed, given the volumes available and the importance of the topic, it is more a question to ponder why the readership was so disinterested in events in the Far East and this particular basing issue. Was a sense of superiority the reason for the neglect, or an overall ignorance of the Far East as opposed to European matters where the Navy was concerned? Were the political difficulties involved in waging an internal war with the RAF over control of the RN's aviation assets, and the impact of that technology on naval operations in the Pacific, something that was avoided by a conscious act on the part of the editors and contributors, or merely a topic ignored by senior naval leadership at all levels? Finally, how much analysis could be provided on the Singapore problem given the secrecy surrounding the topic at the time? With historical hindsight it is easy to say that more should have been debated or discussed, but would that have exposed more of the British weakness in the Pacific than was wise to show in public?

Overall, the study of the Singapore problem from the pages of *The Naval Review* is a limited and unsatisfactory endeavour for a modern historian looking for a detailed or sophisticated analysis of the role of the base in British Grand Strategy, due mostly to the lack of importance of the contributors and the limited analysis provided. However, as a vehicle for presenting a range of topics, both directly and indirectly linking the British Far Eastern strategic condition of the 1920s and 1930s to its readership, it was a job well done. Anyone able to read both on and between the lines of the *Review*'s pages would have seen the pitfalls awaiting Britain's Far Eastern Empire when at war in

Europe. As for the speed and decisiveness of the early Japanese victories, no one else really got that right, either. But where the *Review* discussed the deep and lasting strength of Empire, economics and the mobilisation of the nation for industrial warfare, as well as alliance and coalition efforts between the United States and Great Britain, it got things very right.

16 Anglo-American Naval Relations

Michael Simpson

RELATIONS between the Royal Navy and the United States Navy were hostile from the Revolutionary War (1774–83) to the conclusion of the War of 1812 (1812–14). An era of coolness then set in, as Herbert noted in the 1989 *The Naval Review*: 'Certainly right through the nineteenth century there was a scarcely veiled antagonism stemming initially from the War of Independence and carried on with suspicion and intrigue.'[1] The situation began to change with the dramatic events in Manila Bay on 1 May 1898. An American squadron arrived to seize Manila and the rest of the Philippines from the Spanish, part of the Spanish-American Cuban War. The Americans had little difficulty in defeating the rather decrepit Spanish squadron they found there but the real drama occurred in its aftermath. When the Americans sought to occupy the town of Manila, a German squadron under Vice Admiral von Diederichs proved an irritant, but, allegedly, was thwarted by a British squadron commanded by Captain Sir Edward Chichester, who 'placed his Squadron between the US Fleet commanded by Rear Admiral Dewey and a German Squadron.' This action 'gained the undying friendship of Admiral Dewey ... and brought about a great change of attitude by the Americans.' The truth was much more sober than the myth, Chichester merely observing protocol while Diederichs did not, but the myth, as so often, proved more long-lasting and persuasive than reality. It served the purpose of later statesmen and sailors in explaining the change of attitude of the two navies towards a closer relationship, briefly intimate in the First World War (1917–18) and, more permanently, since 1939.[2]

From its earliest days, writers in the *NR* sought to associate the United States with John Bull's defence of the British Empire, 'the white man's burden', and the cause of world peace and order under the leadership of an Anglo-American condominium. For example, an author discussing 'The Pacific Problem' in 1914 asserted that 'the interests of America, Canada and Australia are the same' and advocated a formal Anglo-American alliance (something the Americans regarded as anathema until 1941).[3] Close co-operation ensued only with American entry into the Great War in April 1917, though even then the Americans retained a certain degree of independence, intervening against the Central Powers not as an ally of Britain but only as an associated power. American entry, moreover, 'did not alleviate the shipping situation'[4] and it was only with the introduction of Atlantic convoys later in 1917 that the perilous situation facing these islands was averted, for 'the success of these convoys was phenomenal.'[5] A particular help was the Anglophile commander of USN forces in European waters, Rear Admiral William S Sims, and 'in all this work the good fellowship and liaison work with the American authorities in Grosvenor Gardens was excellent.'[6] Wartime amity, however, hid a deeply bitter suspicion among some USN officers about Britain's imperial and naval ambitions. The Americans sought parity with the British in all classes of warship and spent the interwar period establishing this, initially against Britain's reluctance to yield her historic maritime supremacy and rights of search and blockade. This confrontation of an irresistible force and an immovable object led to the 'Naval Battle of Paris' during the peace negotiations in Paris in 1919.[7]

In the 1920s, the *NR* concentrated on the issue of maritime rights. British policy was to exercise a distant blockade of an enemy and to stop, search and if necessary seize neutral ships suspected of carrying goods destined ultimately for Britain's enemies. This was regarded as a fundamental weapon, exercised by the Royal Navy from at least the eighteenth century, and in a century of total war, considered to be even more vital, undermining an enemy's will and capacity to carry on the war. It conflicted with the equally long-standing American doctrine of freedom of the seas, under which neutral ships should be able to sail the seven seas without let or hindrance, in war as much as in peace. Given America's status as the leading neutral carrier and that country's growing might and ambition, it was inevitable that the two doctrines should clash again once the need for wartime co-operation was over, and indeed the issue had led to rumours of war between the English-speaking peoples in 1915–16. An article on 'Freedom of the Seas' quoted the *American Journal of International Law*, which claimed that 'Freedom of the Seas means abolition of the doctrine of contraband and of commercial blockades and of the right of capture and destruction of enemy vessels.'[8] In the era of the League of Nations, it was felt that the League alone should exercise the right of blockade. The British position was that 'Great Britain shall exercise sea power in every possible direction so as to shorten the period of the present war.'[9] The dispute spluttered throughout the 1920s and there was always blue water between the two nations. In 1923 an article declared that 'it is clear that Great Britain should refuse to bind herself to any limitation of belligerent rights' and claimed that 'a belligerent has the right to prevent overseas supplies reaching the enemy.'[10] The issue remained unsettled and contentious down to 1940, when President Franklin D Roosevelt began to edge America to Britain's side.

There was a related dispute, too, on the issue of cruisers. The Americans were wedded to a score of 10,000-ton, 8in-gun, long-legged cruisers, chiefly for offensive and scouting work across the Pacific. The British, mindful of their dependence for prosperity and indeed existence itself on a global carrying trade, wanted a host of 5–7,000-ton, 6in-gun, short-legged cruisers, operating from Britain's worldwide web of bases, to defend trade against surface raiders. The question was left unsolved by the Washington conference of 1921–2 and at Geneva in 1927 an abortive and ill-tempered effort was made to bridge this gap. As Admiral Sir Reginald Custance expressed the difference, 'the United States went to Geneva under the belief that the Washington principle [the 5:5 ratio between the US Navy and the Royal Navy] holds for all classes of ships. We went there to declare that the principle does not hold for cruisers.'[11] Admiral Sir Herbert Richmond rebutted the American arguments in a learned article, which in itself is a justification for the *NR*'s existence, while another writer in the same issue stated bluntly but succinctly, 'the United States is still thinking of her rights as a neutral and not of her responsibility as a Great Power.'[12] The dispute was settled, in 1929–30, by two pacifically-minded statesmen, President Hoover and Prime Minister MacDonald, who sidestepped the question of maritime rights by reducing Britain's cruiser requirement from seventy to fifty. As the *NR* put it in 1932, 'at the root of the trouble was American fear of Japanese ambitions in the Pacific.'[13] This became a major concern for both the Americans and the British by the time the next limitation conference was in preparation and relations between them were undoubtedly much warmer; in the event, the 1935 London Naval Treaty was essentially an Anglo-American agreement in the face of Japanese ambition, intransigence and imperialism.[14]

The British, faced with the looming nightmare of simultaneous war in the Atlantic, Mediterranean and Pacific against Germany, Italy and Japan with little reliable or major support, acknowledged that 'for the time being, America has little value.'[15] The USA was bound up in domestic concerns and the Senate would not sanction any intervention in European affairs. If it came to a war on three fronts, Britain knew that she had a Navy large enough to deal only with two. There was, however, increasing solidarity in China in the face of Japanese aggrandisement and the Royal Navy and the USN co-operated in the defence of trade, the protection of civilians and, in the aftermath of the Japanese bombing of the US gunboat *Panay* in December 1937, the rescue of naval personnel.[16] The China situation exercised many contributors in the interwar period and there were several reminiscences of service there. As early as 1924 it was claimed that the Washington Conference of 1921–2 'staved off war', dealing with 'the problem of rivalry between America and Japan for the Far Eastern markets.' Prior to 1920, it was alleged, the Western powers 'let Japan do as she pleased in China as long as she did not interfere or hamper us.'[17] Dire warnings of Japan's imperialist ambitions, and the increasing likelihood of war, were given by writers in issues throughout the 1920s and 1930s. The United States, however, proved slow to anger, while Britain, pre-occupied increasingly with German and Italian aggression, felt unable to take a firm stand. As 'Hellespont' expressed it in 1938, 'any working up of the American people to an active bellicose state of mind against the Japanese has a long way to go in the absence of any exceedingly provocative act, although it can be done', noting that 'in fact, a stiffening of the public attitude is already strongly in evidence.'[18] Even so, Admiral of the Fleet Sir Ernle Chatfield remarked that if it came to a shooting war, one could be quite certain that the Americans would stand aside.[19] There were, nevertheless, many examples of the Royal Navy working with the USN along China's broad rivers, shepherding its busy commerce, in amongst its teeming population, and, above all, dealing patiently with China's eternal disorganisation and the simmering Sino-Japanese conflict, which finally erupted into all-out (but undeclared) war in 1937. In the face of internal warfare, HMS *Wivern* and USS *Paul Jones* evacuated Western civilians from Chungking in 1927 and HMS *Wolverine* and USS *Ford* were engaged in fire-fighting at the same time.[20]

As late as 2008, the memories of an officer on the cruiser *Danae*, stationed at Shanghai in 1937, were recorded, revealing a very acute insight into the Japanese mentality, government and aims, and he pointed out the dominance of naval and military influences. He observed the fighting in the city and its environs between Chiang Kai-Shek's Nationalist forces and the proud and cruel Japanese. In consequence, the British and American warships on station once more provided a humane service.[21] In letters from Swatow in 1939, Lieutenant Commander H G de Chair wrote home to his father, a retired admiral, that he and his American confrères had to undertake much diplomatic wrangling with the Japanese in order to keep Western trade flowing. 'My main object', he declared, 'was to show the Japanese what a close liaison we have with the Americans.'[22] Perhaps, but Swatow was not Washington or London. Amicable relations did not translate into an alliance or even an entente. 'GPDH', a midshipman on the pre-war West Indies Station recalled that Americans 'held Britain in high regard' but, for all 'their extraordinary level of hospitality', there was little sign of American naval assistance for the increasingly worried British.[23] American policy, especially in the Far East, remained 'nebulous and contradictory.'[24]

When war did come in 1939, Britain and the Commonwealth found themselves virtually alone after the first six months. President Franklin Roosevelt, aware that the United States had a direct interest in the war's outcome, steadily nudged his country towards meaningful support of the British. The first notable step towards a close relationship between the two Navies was the destroyers for bases deal of September 1940: *The Naval Review* thought it significant enough to print the text of the agreement. In exchange for fifty over-age American destroyers, Britain leased to the USA several bases in the West Indies and North America. Commenting on the agreement, the review observed that 'the US thus undoubtedly do well by the arrangement, but, even without the transfer of the 50 destroyers, we also stand to gain a lot', though the gain was less obviously a purely naval one than a diplomatic triumph for Churchill, who saw it, rightly, as the end of American neutrality and a major step towards an eventual alliance.[25] In the next few months, the United States extended its patrol areas in the Atlantic, 'a decided step in American aid to our fight in the Atlantic', and instituted Lend-Lease in the spring of 1941, following this with an undeclared maritime war with Germany by the autumn of 1941.[26] Secret talks between planning staff representatives of the two countries, the ABC conversations of early 1941, were followed by the Atlantic Charter meeting between the two former naval persons, appropriately on board warships, in August 1941. British warships were repaired in American Navy yards; 'much of what happened to us', wrote 'Ensee' in the *Review*, 'will have been common to all British ships.'[27] Noting that 'a most helpful attitude was apparent', he recalled that 'the United States naval officers could not have been nicer to us.'[28] America continued to support Britain, however, by all means short of war, Roosevelt declaring that his 'sole purpose is to keep war away from our country and people.'[29]

The transition from neutrality to belligerence was dramatically swift and traumatic. Ensee, whose ship was repaired at Bremerton Navy Yard, Washington State, in August 1941, was still there on 7 December when the full horror of Pearl Harbor struck home. He observed that 'incredulity was the prime emotion, followed by rage, followed by something like panic.'[30] The Japanese attack on Pearl Harbor was as shattering to the American psyche as the terrorist attack on New York and Washington of 9 September 2001. 'Fauteuil', who wrote the regular column 'Notes on the War at Sea', expressed the British reaction, which was one of disbelief that a modern power should have been caught out by a lethal surprise stroke: 'how anyone in responsibility can let it be an actual surprise in fact passes man's understanding', he wrote.[31] Many rumours surround the Pearl Harbor air raid; they have been emphatically disproved many times, the *NR* setting the record straight in 1989, when 'Parcener' acknowledged that both the British and the Americans had broken the relevant Imperial Japanese Navy code, JN25, and knew a task force was about to sail, but could not fathom its destination. The general belief in both countries was that the Japanese would move southward (which they did, as well as eastward). In the welter of messages, the Americans were unable to understand the relevant signal. It is demonstrably untrue that Roosevelt deliberately left the fleet at Pearl Harbor, knowing it was going to be attacked, and, moreover, was supposed to have kept the information secret from his service chiefs, as he was anxious to get the United States into the war. It is also manifestly untrue that Churchill kept prior information of the attack from the Americans in order to propel them into the war.[32] The Americans were nevertheless in the war, pitched into it by as grim a declaration of hostilities as can be imagined, and many Royal Navy personnel, like their Prime Minister, slept the better for that blood-soaked fact.

For the last month of 1941 and the first five months of 1942, however, the Japanese ran riot in practically all points of the compass. The British Commonwealth, Americans, Dutch and French proved utterly unable to defend their imperial possessions: it was the beginning of the end for colonial rule in the Orient.[33] Other than Pearl Harbor and the equally great shock of the sinking of the *Prince of Wales* and the *Repulse*, the early months of 1942 saw the comprehensive Allied defeat at the battle of the Java Sea, in which a substantial but scratch force of Allied ships was destroyed totally by a well-trained, cohesive Japanese squadron which profited from blanket air coverage, Long Lance torpedoes of great range and enormous destructive power, skill at night-fighting, and effective communications and leadership.[34] Despite a draw at the Coral Sea in May and decisive victory at Midway in June, the USN still struggled to keep a grip on Guadalcanal. They were helped to do so by the unique and reliable coast watch organisation, staffed mostly by Australians, who provided invaluable intelligence from behind enemy lines; of them, Admiral Halsey remarked that 'the Coast Watchers saved Guadalcanal and Guadalcanal saved the South Pacific.'[35]

In the Atlantic and European war, Anglo-American naval co-operation was most notable in the series of great amphibious landings conducted between 1942 and 1944. Admiral Sir Geoffrey Blake, himself the principal liaison officer with USN forces in European waters, commanded by Admiral H R 'Betty' Stark, wrote authoritatively about 'The Origins of Operation TORCH', noting the confusion, bad feeling, over-eagerness to open a second front, and the various changes in the plans which characterised its gestation. The operation itself was, overall, a great success, though it could have done with more landing craft, the bottleneck in all the great landing operations.[36] Commander James Humphrys noted that the United States 'took some persuading that the Mediterranean was worth military intervention.'[37] Strategically, the Americans were right: the Mediterranean was a dead end. Tactically, however, it is difficult to see how the Allies could have landed success-fully in northwest Europe without the invaluable experience they gained around the middle sea. Later landings proved as successful as Torch but that at Salerno in September 1943 hung in the balance for several days. Captain Roskill, in paying tribute to Admiral Sir Geoffrey Oliver, who commanded one of the naval task forces there, asserted that he steadfastly staved off disaster by refusing to contemplate evacuation.[38] Admiral Kent Hewitt, USN, in overall command of the expedition, endorsed Admiral of the Fleet Sir Andrew Cunningham's conclusion that 'it was the naval gunfire, incessant in effect, which held the ring when there was danger of the enemy breaking through to the beaches and when the overall position looked so gloomy. More cannot be said.'[39]

The greatest of all the landings was Operation Neptune, the maritime precursor to Overlord, in June 1944. The British continue to take great pride in the fact that it was a largely Anglo-Canadian enterprise, 78 per cent of the forces being British or Canadian against 17 per cent for the Americans. Even so, said Commander Wilson on the fiftieth anniversary of the Normandy landings, 'it was a truly joint affair, with Royal Navy ships carrying US troops, and vice versa, and with US ships under Royal Navy command, and vice versa.'[40] Acting Captain Dolphin, responsible for Mulberry harbour construction, remembered boarding an American LST, saying without shame that 'We chose an American one because we knew that they would have plenty of food and stores.'[41] That remark encapsulates the fact that it was the last hurrah for the British as equal partners in the Second World War. Britannia had already ceded Neptune's trident to Columbia a year earlier.

It was, however, in the Pacific that the greatest discrepancies were to be seen and where American naval might, in ships, planes and marine landing forces, had its major triumphs, with only marginal assistance from the Royal Navy and those of the Commonwealth and other nations. Captain Conley extolled the Americans' remarkable *guerre de course* waged by their submarines in the waters around the island nation of Japan, noting that neither Britain nor America realised Japan's vulnerability to a blockade. The US effort, characterised at first by teething troubles, especially with malfunctioning torpedoes, hit its stride in late 1943, virtually eliminating Japanese seaborne trade and effectively starving the enemy and strangling her industries. Technically advanced submarines, habitable, deep diving, fast on the surface, employing sophisticated tactics, long ranging, and supplied with splendid radar and the invaluable Ultra decrypts, were well deployed in this remarkable campaign. The forces employed, including aircraft, were relatively small but, thanks to the boldness, courage and skill of individual submarine crews and their skippers ('an aggressive, highly competent elite of submariners') were highly effective. The Japanese contributed to their own defeat by failing to take adequate anti-submarine measures and did not move to organise their merchant shipping and cargo and oil requirements until late in the war.[42]

The American air effort, particularly by Marine squadrons and carrier planes, was equally effective in driving the Japanese out of the host of islands they had occupied in the first six months of 1942. The Japanese began with a well-trained, well-equipped naval air arm but dissipated it quickly on wide-ranging operations, and aircrews succeeding the Pearl Harbor fliers were hurriedly trained. The Americans, however, went from a state of shock to one of over-whelming triumph. Their aircrew were of high quality, as were their aircraft, their industrial base was highly efficient and dwarfed those of all other belligerents put together, while they conducted effective research. The American aviators and their commanders kept their nerve and executed several bold moves. Midway in June 1942, for example, 'was a victory of pre-battle intelligence allied to courageous decisions.' By July 1943, the Americans had developed fast carrier task forces, supported by fleet trains which enabled them to keep the sea for two months at a time.[43]

When the Americans closed the Japanese homeland in early 1945, plans were laid for a massive invasion, due to take place from 1 November 1945 to 1 March 1946, with great landings in Kyushu and then Honshu. Some 4.5 million US troops were to be committed. Heavy American and Japanese casualties were expected but were avoided by the dropping of two atomic bombs, though it is debatable whether Japan could have survived much longer, owing to the submarine and air offensives cutting off her supply lines.[44]

The British were desperate to join in the final assault on Japan and initially proposed to offer all three arms but in the end Britain, already gasping, could send only a fleet. It was large by British standards but was no more than a Task Group in the mighty American armada. In the Pacific war, the British found themselves playing catch up and second fiddle to the Americans. The Senior Service was now very much the junior partner, welcomed, tolerated and indulged, rather than necessary. The British realised they had much to learn in this new game and despatched a team post-haste to Washington to find out what they required and how it should be used. They placed themselves under American command and adopted American signalling, sensible measures, but they noted that the US had invested heavily in 'R and D', making use of its universities, and they found the Americans had sophisticated radio and radar.[45] The British Pacific Fleet (BPF) was required to be self-sufficient and Admiral Fraser, the C-in-C, recalled that 'doubt as to our ability to operate in the Pacific was somewhat naturally in American minds.'[46] Somehow, a fleet train was cobbled together and, on a wing and a prayer, the BPF went into action in the spring of 1945. It had its plus side, for 'the toll taken by the suicide bombers of the more lightly armoured American carriers led to an increase of the proportionate effort provided by our carriers', which had armoured decks.[47] Admiral Fraser was well aware, however, of the inferiority of British ships to American vessels 'in operational capacity and mobility' and ordered a young Louis Le Bailly to report on the discrepancies.[48] The British ships had poor habitability, lacked air conditioning, and were short-legged and slow in refuelling. They kept the sea, said a contemporary officer only by the 'dedication and continuous 36-hours a day nursing of the machinery in awful conditions by every stoker, artificer and Engineering Officer available', adding, 'the misplaced superiority felt by many of us towards the Americans was based on sheer ignorance.'[49] Whereas American machinery was economical and reliable, operated by hostilities-only men, British machinery lacked reliability and efficiency and was poor in design and construction, ventilation and insulation, suffering from vibration, with poor damage control and deficient in adequate electrical equipment.[50]

The war ended with the Royal Navy back at school as it sought to assimilate certain American practices, but the conflict had also shown up basic differences between the two navies. In an article which must have satisfied *The Naval Review*'s founders, the American Rear

Admiral Bradley Fiske, the USN's leading light around 1914, noted that the US Naval Institute, the *Review*'s American equivalent as an intellectual ginger group of naval officers, had been 'the most stimulating single agency that has existed for the development of an American navy.' It highlighted for the NR 'the importance that is attached, in the US Naval service, to the dissemination and discussion of ideas.'[51] As is argued elsewhere, the US Naval Institute has had more impact on the American Navy than *The Naval Review* has had on the Royal Navy. Fiske's successor as the chief thinker in the US Navy, Rear Admiral William S Sims was well versed about the Royal Navy and outlined the USN's promotion methods, modified in the twentieth century in a bid to recognise great ability, leaving the NR to lament that 'we are sometimes reluctant to admit that there is anything we can learn from other countries.'[52] Sims, like many American officers, however, was a victim of the slow promotion (in his day chiefly only by seniority) which afflicted his service, its subservience to civil authority being insisted upon by successive Secretaries of the Navy.[53]

Britain led the way in the development of naval aviation but was surpassed by the USN by about 1930 in terms of numbers of aircraft, their quality, launching technique and, most crucially, the rule that commanding officers of carriers should be qualified fliers. In 1936, 'Vates' remarked wistfully that 'the US Naval Air Service of well over 1,000 aircraft forms a striking contrast to our 250 or so'. A year later, 'Osprey', who visited a US naval air base, remarked that 'a very pronounced feeling was shown against having any officers in naval aviation who were not *both* naval officers *and* active pilots. I was told that their future policy was to have a carrier commanded and officered by naval aviators only, as far as executive duties were concerned.'[54] Later in that year, 'Teeoh' observed with envy, 'the success of their system of complete control, with its absolute identification of their naval air units with other naval units, as an integral part of one Service, and the markedly superior efficiency of their naval air service to ours, is a proof that it is the one that will produce the best results.'[55] The USN's battle doctrine was, like that of the Royal Navy, however, still founded on the primacy of the battle fleet, the air playing only a supporting role. When that traditional assumption was reduced to a heap of scrap iron at Pearl Harbor, there was nevertheless a well-honed force of seaborne aviation, led by men with practical understanding of its operation in blue water able to take over the conduct of hostilities and eclipse the Navy's rebuilt dreadnought battle fleet in subsequent Pacific operations. The Americans had also moved well ahead of the British in countermeasures against hostile aircraft, their anti-aircraft

gunnery being built on substantial development ashore, a core of
Advanced Ordnance Officers, and the successful Mark 37 Director
System together with a highly-effective dual-purpose 5in gun.[56] The
source of this encomium was Captain Stephen Roskill, in a position to
know about the approach of both countries. In contrast to the
Americans' experimentation and willingness to incorporate new ideas,
the Admiralty proved obstructive to improvements, criticisms and
evidence of progress across the Atlantic.[57]

Radar had been a British development which the Americans had been
slow to adopt (had they pursued a more urgent learning process, they
might have averted the Pearl Harbor tragedy), but once they did so,
they were keen to learn from British wartime experience and soon
produced outstanding sets of their own. Their seaborne radar drive
encapsulated their general approach to problems afloat. There was, one
Royal Navy officer in wartime Washington wrote, a can-do mentality,
slick office procedure, energy in abundance, a willingness to learn, a
strong R & D base and an immense industrial capacity.[58] At the same
time, US officers were frequently amazed by the strong inter-service co-
operation evident in the British armed forces; there was a story current
among British naval officers serving in the United States that the US
Navy had three enemies: in order of priority, these were (1) the US
Army; (2) Japan; (3) anybody else (allies included).

Despite their differences in method and ultimately in scale, they got
on well together when the sailors met and forged effective associations,
strengthened by mutual friendships in two world wars. Even between
the wars, when there was much rivalry, suspicion, haggling over maritime rights and force levels, there remained an undercurrent of
amicability and free sharing of views and information. One could not
have expected more from two Navies who spent much of the nineteenth
century in frosty formality, replaced in the twentieth, fortunately, by a
willingness to be, as Churchill said, 'somewhat mixed up together.'[59]

Obedient to the historic doctrine 'Peace, commerce and honest
friendship with all nations, entangling alliances with none', the US was
reluctant to commit itself to post-war commitments.[60] In naval matters,
this meant that the USN was unwilling to continue the wartime
partnership with the Royal Navy. This attitude began slowly to change
as the Cold War developed from 1947 onwards. In part, the Cold War
was due to a perceived threat from the Soviet Union in Atlantic and
Mediterranean areas, seeming to demand a collective maritime
response. In part, the US was forced to act because of the manifest
weakness of the Western European powers, including the one
unconquered and victorious nation, Britain. Growing American

commitment to Europe and its maritime approaches was formalised in the establishment of NATO in 1949. Anglo-American co-operation was further strengthened by the mutually combative response to hostilities in Korea in 1950. In more recent times, American and British naval forces have worked together in the operations off Kuwait, Iraq, Afghanistan and most recently (2011) Libya.

However, an important aspect of the wartime relationship survived the initial, official post-war American indifference: numerous personal contacts persisted and they are prominent today. As co-operation became systematised, command structures, common procurement programmes, linked training schemes, exchanges of intelligence, the institution of common communications procedures, and task force exercises, became the norm. Co-operation was especially close and fruitful in the areas of naval aviation, submarine and anti-submarine warfare operations, notably in the equipment and deployment of nuclear missile-carrying submarines. Thus, as it enters a second century of warm and effective association, the Anglo-American naval relationship is firmly established and has been strongly featured in the pages of *The Naval Review* over the past century.

17 Life at Sea and Ship Organisation

Rear Admiral James Goldrick, RAN

L IVES at sea and ship organisation have been recurrent but not constant subjects within *The Naval Review*. This chapter seeks to examine only efforts to treat these issues in a contemporary context; while there are many retrospectives within the *NR*, their value has been for historians rather than advancement of the naval profession. Our interest is in periods during which the press of events has created feeling that change is necessary and when the *NR* has identified that the contract between the nation and the people who man its Navy has become unbalanced. Many times, articles have described problems and proposed changes not only well considered but often implemented soon after their publication. While it is difficult to specify whether such commentary served as a catalyst or simply reflected changes already in train, any Second Sea Lord would have been well repaid by close attention to the pages of the *NR*.

The First Assessments of Life at Sea

The first article on naval life is one of the most challenging. Chaplain G H Hewetson provided 'A Contribution to the Study of Naval Discipline' in August 1913.[1] He believed that the wardroom and the lower deck had drifted too far apart and that officers confused their knowledge, limited as it was, of ratings in their own branch with understanding of the whole. Change in the Navy over the previous half century had been profound. The organisation which had emerged to meet the new requirements of technology did not reflect the all-of-a-company outlook of the old Navy of sail. Hewetson's point was not only that ratings had become much more educated and self-aware, as well as more in touch with events ashore, but that the internal cultures of the various specialisations were so different that generalisations as to their outlook could be very dangerous.

236

Pulling no punches, Hewetson claimed that two pervasive problems in the Navy were sodomy and corruption and that the disciplinary system (particularly the ships' police) worked only to support a conspiracy of silence, creating unwillingness on the part of good men to intervene. More recent analysis largely confirms Hewetson's bleak judgements.[2] Above all, Hewetson urged officers to become more involved, to seek opportunities such as lectures (much appreciated if delivered in an informal environment), and to create a greater degree of confidence in the better men that they would be supported. The belief that the wardroom was too remote was echoed in February 1914 by Commander W A Egerton[3] and had, outside the NR, already been commented on by witnesses to the committee on disciplinary problems chaired by Rear Admiral F E E Brock in 1912.[4]

There was a consciousness that the lower deck (particularly the technical branches) had an increasingly trade-unionised outlook. Encouraged by the First Lord, Winston Churchill, and against Treasury resistance, the Admiralty attempted to improve pay and conditions in the years immediately before the Great War. Nevertheless, Captain W D H Boyle was prescient when he wrote in 'Welfare of the Personnel' in November 1915 of the need for the Navy to get ahead of the expectations of its people to avoid agitation and dissent.[5] Boyle even recommended that a Commission be established which should include experts from outside the Navy. Apart from this unusual readiness to seek counsel elsewhere, Boyle's article was notable for the robustness of his views (particularly given his rank). He not only acknowledged the lack of sympathy for the aspirations of ratings but also strongly criticised the disparity between officer and sailor accommodation. Boyle believed that the Royal Navy did not compare well to other navies and was the first to sound a note strongly heard thirty years later: 'As regards the ships of the United States it is hardly possible to make a comparison.'

Comes the Great War

Many campaign accounts contained vignettes casting light on life at sea. Two of the most telling observations after battle experience were made by Lieutenant Commander H E H Spencer-Cooper. He noted the need for a system of action messing and for ear protection to be provided to gun crews, and particularly to the internal telephone system operators, who were so deafened by gunfire as to become useless.[6]

The Royal Navy moved from a two-watch organisation to three as the reality of the long war dawned. A proposal for the new system rather than the classical two/four arrangement had already been raised within the *NR* in August 1913 by Commander J F Warton.[7] His argument was that it would allow more time for rest while still ensuring that sufficient armament was at readiness. Captain W R Hall has generally been acknowledged as the innovator of the system in the *Queen Mary* (commissioned in September 1913).[8] Warton's commentary suggests that Hall experimented with it well beforehand, when he commanded the armoured cruiser *Natal* 1909–11 and Warton was his executive officer. In November 1915, Lieutenant A F Pridham, serving in the light cruiser *Weymouth*, made a plea for the permanent adoption of three watches for both war and peace.[9]

The same insistence that the Navy needed to be organised in peace the way it would fight in war was apparent in Lieutenant Commander R L Edwards' article in the same issue. He was critical of the unsuitability of many ships' fittings for war, particularly in the use of wood.[10] He recognised, however, that there had been a real effort on the part of officers to look after their ratings, 'getting up lectures, singsongs and diversions of various sorts, all of them of the simple and popular variety. It is earnestly to be hoped that this precious spirit of comradeship and common sense will be allowed to continue.'[11]

After the Great War

Edwards' contribution was the forerunner of a barrage of articles that followed the post-war revival of the *NR*. They shared a determination to improve the relationship between officers and men and to ensure that the aim of the Navy was fighting efficiency. Given the events at Invergordon only twelve years later, it is significant that several took up Boyle's earlier plea for the Admiralty to remain in touch with lower deck feeling. Many were conscious that the example set by officers to an increasingly sophisticated lower deck needed to improve. Lieutenant Commander H S H Manley commented in November 1920 that the propensity of officers to employ naval stores for private purposes (even the piece of codline employed to lash a damaged car back together) was viewed with particular disfavour, given the severity with which ratings were dealt with if detected in similar transgressions.[12] This was not the first such intervention. A contribution in May 1920 from Lieutenant Commander Hilton Young, not only an MP but much decorated, was highly critical of the fixation on competitive evolutions at the expense of drills which could practise ships' companies for battle.[13] In the same issue, a former hostilities-only Able Seaman, William Lang, expanded upon his book *A Sea-Lawyer's Log* with the suggestion that officers and men were not a band of brothers, whatever the wardroom might like to believe, and that there was a deeply resented disparity in living conditions which seemed to be ignored by the officers. He cited as an example that officers in destroyers were able to take a daily bath while ratings had insufficient water with which to wash themselves. Lang's piece, which conveyed some affection for the Service (Lang emphasised that he himself had never been the subject of disciplinary action and had no personal axe to grind), met with little disagreement.[14]

Much more controversial was a review of Charles Morgan's novel *The Gunroom* in 1920.[15] The writer did not accept the bleak picture of bullying in pre-war gunrooms which Morgan painted, particularly of his first ship (the armoured cruiser *Good Hope* only superficially disguised; his second, the *Monmouth* was happier) but he was taken to task in May by Lieutenant E H Cameron who stressed that there was a case to answer and that what had been good enough before would not be good enough in the future, 'In the next war we shall be the smaller fleet. Very few people have fully realised that yet.'[16] In subsequent letters Lieutenant G H Jocelyn-Evans reported that his experience (albeit in wartime) as a midshipman had been much better than Morgan's while a ferocious response came from Lieutenant Commander H T Baillie-Grohman, who had served in *Monmouth* in the same commission.[17] Ironically, Morgan, who had left the Service as a midshipman, joined the RNVR during the war and was a member of the *NR*.[18] Few of the contributors seem to have been aware that he was one of their readers. Sadly, other than Baillie-Grohman, none were still on the active list in 1939.

May 1920 saw 'Ginger' Boyle return to the charge, expressing his concern at the unrest pervading the Navy.[19] He too emphasised the need for better links between officers and men and urged a greater emphasis on sports, competitive activities and lectures. Sports had already been the subject of a lively exchange after an ill-judged declaration in November 1919 by Commander W P Mark-Wardlaw which correlated proficiency at games with achievement of flag rank, a dubious proposition soon contradicted by Lieutenant Commander C H Rolleston (who also complained about officers who used afternoon sports as an excuse to neglect their duty)[20] and demolished by Rear Admiral H W Richmond's list of great admirals who very definitely had *not* been great sportsmen![21] Returning to the subject in May 1920, Rolleston also disagreed with the accepted wisdom of the role of games in maintaining morale in the bleak environment of Scapa Flow. While many officers had taken advantage of the facilities ashore, he doubted that this had included more than a small proportion of ratings.[22]

Games developed into one of the recurrent subjects of the interwar era. It is clear that there was a need to create opportunities for officers

and ratings to combine in an environment in which seagoing time was
limited and had to be husbanded to achieve maximum benefit,
particularly for weapon practices. There was also a consciousness that
making work for work's sake had to be avoided. At the same time, the
departure of coal burners from the seagoing fleet removed one of the
binding elements for ships' companies, the arduous and dirty 'coal ship'
from which only a handful were ever excused. Games and sporting
competitions were a logical substitute to develop ship spirit.

While there were several contributions (including the first by
Lieutenant Royer Dick) in 1921 complaining about the lack of opportunities for junior officers, it appears as though the Navy settled into
an effective peacetime routine.[23] Given the improvements in pay in
1919 and the fact that the national employment situation soon turned
sour, this is not surprising and the years 1922 to 1927 created a
relative lull in the NR for matters of life at sea, despite Treasury
forcing a pay cut for all new entry personnel in 1925 on the grounds
of the reduced cost of living. In this period, there is only one serious
indication of serpents in the garden, in August 1923, when Lieutenant
John Hughes-Hallett (who, with his brother Charles, was a mainstay
of the NR in the years ahead)[24] complained at length that the School
of Physical and Recreational Training's (P&RT's) ideas of discipline
had become predominant, being too focused on the idea that sports
would provide the perfect bond between officers and men. This meant
that sporting achievement had not only become too important a
consideration for promotion but that it came at the expense of
fighting efficiency.[25]

In February 1928 an article by Lieutenant Commander J Mackenzie-
Grieve sounded a warning that obsession with measurement and
reporting of results was creating increasing problems.[26] As promotions
tended to depend upon a ship's results relative to its squadron mates, a
tendency to use only the first eleven had developed. Furthermore, there
were too many officers and a failure to delegate responsibility. This
article was followed by a number expressing concern that drills had
become too rigid and unrealistic while sharing the unease at micro-
management. In January 1929 Lieutenant P W Brock (another key
contributor in the future) claimed that watertight integrity was 'a
whited sepulchre that wants attention.'[27] His assessment of big ship
efficiency was partly disputed in August by Captain E R Bent, who
compared the realism of drills and exercises very favourably with the
pre-war Navy but admitted that the staff could be better focused on
what really mattered. Bent also implicitly criticised the apparent
stranglehold of the PR&T branch by recommending in the main fleets

the replacement of the PR&T staff officer with a fleet executive officer at commander rank.[28] A slightly lighter note was struck by John Hughes-Hallett in May 1931: while the transition to 'talkies' was presenting challenges, it was clear that films were now an integral part of ships' recreational programmes. Hughes-Hallett observed shrewdly that they would play an important role in keeping men content during the restricted routines inevitable in war.[29]

Invergordon – Before, During and After

Significantly before the disturbances at Invergordon, Rear Admiral R A R Plunkett-Ernle-Erle-Drax asked, 'In what way (or ways) can we produce the greatest increase in fighting efficiency in the Royal Navy?' He cast out the bait to the membership, commenting that young officers needed much more support to develop their leadership, and that there might be too much drinking in the wardroom.[30] The latter suggestion sparked a lively debate but the problem of ship organisation started another volley of complaints about over-centralisation and over-large staffs. Drax tied his own colours to the mast with 'A Disease and the Remedy', declaring that executive officers were overworked in a grossly over-centralised system – he knew of four who had broken down under the strain.[31] A sharp response followed from retired Admiral Sir Douglas Nicholson who entitled his reply 'An Imaginary Disease and a Questionable Remedy'. This was less well judged than many of Nicholson's other contributions and showed the risks that retired members run in commenting on the contemporary service.[32] Drax's response was unambiguous; he asserted that any survey of executive officers in the fleet would confirm the effects of excessive 'competition, intensive training and "promotionitis".'[33]

In the aftermath of Invergordon there was much more on relations with the lower deck and micro-management. Fixation on sport was again criticised, John Hughes-Hallett noting in February 1932 that 'an entirely wrong attitude has grown up, in which men play as a favour, sometimes at the price of concessions which are little short of blackmail.'[34] Sail training also received considerable attention, although there seemed to be confusion as to what it was intended to achieve, whether a better sea-sense than was possible under power, or the development of self-reliance and initiative.[35] This lack of clarity suggests that Admiral Chatfield was wise to abandon the Admiralty's plans for a sail training squadron.[36]

Another view of lower deck (and wardroom) attitudes came with John Hughes-Hallett's review of *Clear Lower Deck* by Stanley Knock in May 1932, the memoir of a rating serving from 1903 to 1924.[37]

Some of Knock's many criticisms were accepted, although Hughes-Hallett was too quick to reject others (such as Knock's dislike of chaplains) and their potential causes. Most fascinating is the reviewer's surprise at 'the small amount of reference to officers' and Knock's view that feelings of fellowship amongst the ratings were strictly confined to the lower deck. In concluding, Hughes-Hallett commented that the writing 'conceals under a veneer of education a narrowness of outlook which is almost frightening.' Indeed.

Running a Big Ship

For the remainder of the 1930s there is a sense that balance had been restored. Personnel matters only became heated again after the favourable review in May 1937 of Captain Rory O'Conor's *Running a Big Ship on Ten Commandments*.[38] This brought a furious reply in February 1938 from Baillie-Grohman who felt that O'Conor's liberal approach, which included making Sunday largely a day of rest, was 'pandering to the ship's company'.[39] Baillie-Grohman's grasp of working-class life proved vague when he asked 'does he really suppose that there is no work going on in the average sailor's home after 0930 on Sunday?'. As a later contributor noted, whoever was working in a sailor's home on a Sunday, it was not the sailor! Baillie-Grohman's views were generally panned by a strong team, which may have included Admiral Sir William James and certainly included F T B Tower, O'Conor's captain in the *Hood*.[40] They attested to the outstanding success which *Hood*'s commission had been and it is fair to say that O'Conor's book was to have a significant influence for many years. More recent analysis suggests, however, that Tower's successor was not impressed by the cleanliness of the ship when he joined, while the amount of paint that had to be removed at the outbreak of war indicates that *Hood*'s focus had not been quite as much on fighting power as it might have been.[41] On the other hand, Captain B H Smith commented very favourably on the efficiency and professionalism of the Mediterranean Fleet in August 1938 from his perspective as a guest of the C-in-C. He was particularly impressed by the realism of the gunnery exercises (including an accurate high speed throw off shoot by *Warspite* and *Hood* incorporating multiple torpedo attacks by the opposition forces).[42]

The Experience of the Second World War

The onset of war drove life at sea from the pages of the *NR*. Not until 1943 did a flow of articles on the future of the Navy resume. At this time, our knowledge of the identities of the contributors becomes less certain, but the evidence suggests that the *NR* still enjoyed a reasonable range of rank and specialisation amongst its authors.

Habitability was severely criticised.[43] The Pacific experience highlighted just how much the Royal Navy had been a service of the narrow seas. The combination of a protracted oceanic war in extremes of climate and exposure to the United States Navy demonstrated the very real limitations of the British approach. There was rueful acknowledgement of how much more money had been available to the Americans in designing their ships and providing for their people, but also recognition that there had been too little innovation, particularly in improving lower deck conditions. Notably, internal cleanliness was recognised as having declined.[44] The Royal Navy no longer compared well with the USN or with other services, such as the Dutch, even when the latter were operating British-built ships. That the RN's standards really had deteriorated is evident from other sources. The First Sea Lord, Admiral Cunningham, was unimpressed by the light cruiser *Arethusa* in June 1944[45] while the Australian veterans of the N-class destroyers, operated by the Royal Australian Navy from completion until their exchange for Q-class destroyers of the same vintage, were scathing about the latter in late 1945.[46]

Centralised messing received much attention. Its proponents recognised the challenges, particularly finding sufficient space, but there were more potential benefits than just better meals and more flexible action messing. In particular, removing the need to eat in messdecks created the potential for the latter to be developed into proper living spaces, with permanent, comfortable seating, and areas for games and reading. This was highlighted by Charles Hughes-Hallett, in an article on *Implacable*'s experience in the Pacific in 1945, which supplemented a 1947 contribution about the peacetime commission of the cruiser *Glasgow*.[47] The author of the latter admitted that the ship had the advantage of two hangars for dining (and as cinemas) but also noted that the new arrangements allowed better alignment between the divisional organisation and accommodation.[48]

After the War

As early as May 1946 concerns were raised about the rapid deterioration of damage control training.[49] This was a continuing theme until early 1948, culminating in an unfavourable comparison between the damage control organisation in the Dutch (but ex-British) aircraft carrier *Karel Doorman* and that of the Royal Navy.[50] The speed of decline owed something to war weariness but more to very rapid demobilisation. By May 1948, a new note appears in the declaration that, while there was some way to go, efforts had been made to raise standards anew.[51]

The same tensions between the social progressives and the conservatives apparent in the debate over *Running a Big Ship on Ten Commandments* manifested themselves in arguments over the Labour Government's decision to abolish compulsory divine service and the amount of leave that personnel were allowed. The latter question had been highlighted by the dreadful period in which lack of funds and personnel forced the effective immobilisation of practically the entire Home Fleet in 1947–8, described elsewhere by one Captain (D) as 'a horrible time' during which only one weekend leave could be taken a month, despite the inactivity of the ships concerned.[52] The puritanical (and class-ridden) attitudes apparent in the 1930s were still occasionally manifest, but the tenor of most contributions was that naval personnel were not being well treated.[53] One article even suggested that ratings were getting approximately half the days off that their civilian counterparts enjoyed.[54]

Another issue of social justice concerned alcohol – available duty-free and at lunchtime and after secure for officers, but only in the form of the midday tot for ratings.[55] Part of the push was for beer to be available to the ship's company in the evening,[56] particularly during extended periods away from shore, and plaints that storage would be too difficult were quickly rejected.[57] But there was another concern, a view that alcohol provided a release from the tensions and the extreme discomforts of sea service and that it should therefore be available to the rating as well as to the officer.[58]

As the war receded, a theme became the deterioration of standards. At least part, such as mess life, was due to changing social conditions (and a lack of money), but there was also an acknowledgement that the majority had no idea what peacetime standards were, the youth of ship's companies being the subject of frequent comment.[59] Cleanliness, individual appearance, adherence to routines and ceremonial standards all caused concern. Yet there were signs that improvements were possible. An August 1949 article urged a Service-wide focus on improving noticeboards, commenting that they deserved the same attention that had recently and successfully been given to bathrooms. Habitability was not being ignored.[60]

Coping with a Changing Society

A growing concern with excessive demarcation between departments developed as the 1950s drew on. The challenges of naval aviation also received attention, notably in a 1955 article entitled 'Two Worlds' on the differences between serving in a flying squadron and a destroyer.[61] A key issue, perhaps partly a result of the rash of sabotage attempts which the Navy experienced between 1953 and 1955,[62] was a worry that the way in which sailors were managed was no longer appropriate.[63] Another factor was the increasing proportion of ratings (and junior officers) who were married,[64] although there was still an occasional implicit suggestion that marriage and the Navy, at least for junior personnel were and should be incompatible.[65] Discipline issues resonated over the next few years, with a debate in 1958 over punishment statistics, when senior members expressed concern over the appallingly high figures compared with those of the 1930s.[66] Their strictures seem justified and it is clear that the Navy had edged by degrees into acceptance of the unacceptable. Leave-breaking, particularly by very junior personnel, was a major topic in 1959–60.[67] Baillie-Grohman suggested that one cause might have been the mixing of under-age juniors with adult sailors; his experience was that their being messed separately reduced minor offences significantly but the greater influence seems to have been the combination of money in the pocket and cheap alcohol.[68]

A November 1955 article, entitled 'A Piece of Cake' by 'Nibs', was hard hitting, foreshadowing the need not only for a more flexible approach to sailors' engagements, but wholesale reductions in the officer establishment (soon accomplished through the 'Golden Bowler' scheme): 'I think the sailor's life is one of poor food, poorer living conditions, petty bureaucracy, departmental jealousies and, for the most part, intensely boring work. The officer is worse off ...' To be fair, many of the reforms proposed by Nibs did come and ships with the habitability and automation he wanted would enter service within a decade.[69]

Into the 1960s

A new focus on life at sea was triggered in April 1962 by 'Vermis' in 'Worm's-eye View', describing the general service commission of a *Daring*-class destroyer a few years before. He painted a warts-and-all picture of poor serviceability, inadequate and badly organised dockyard support, over-full ships' programmes, over-manned wardrooms and an over-staffed and over-admiraled Navy.[70] The picture was not all bad, but raised issues that demanded answers. The debate which followed supported more of Vermis' thesis than it contradicted, although the Captain (D) concerned was sufficiently galled by some of the more general criticisms of the *Daring* squadron as a whole that he contributed a crushing and largely dismissive reply,[71] justly criticised by Stephen Roskill for breaching the spirit of the *NR*.[72] Other contributors

commented that there had been some improvement since Vermis'
commission, notably through establishment of the Flag Officer Sea
Training organisation at Portland and reduction in the *Darings*' officer
complement, but the extent of over-admiraling and over-staffing was
acknowledged – one noting that in the 1950s he had witnessed an
eleven-ship assembly at Gibraltar at which there were five flags afloat.[73]

To complete the picture, Vermis should be compared with two articles
from the previous April. The first, perhaps written by Vice Admiral Sir
Peter Gretton, explained the new formula for proving readiness for
operations. The five-day task force, multi-threat scenario clearly
provided a much better mechanism for confirming the achievement of
a worked up state.[74] The second, by 'Constant Reader' made the point,
amongst others, that the sustained replenishment of the ships around
Iceland during the Cod War showed that the Navy (and, by association,
the RFA) possessed new skills of seamanship to replace the old.[75]

Certainly the late 1950s and early 1960s were a time of transition.
The evidence suggests that vessels in this period reached a peak of
complexity and difficulty and that they represented a level of challenge
greater than in the past. Valve and electromechanical technologies were
soon to be overtaken by solid state and digital systems. However, even
after the new ships arrived, problems of poor shore support, over-
stressed ships' programmes, and too many layers of staff would be
commented upon sufficiently often in the decades ahead to suggest that
the Royal Navy did not (or could not, by press of circumstances)
address them properly.

The other feature of the opening of the 1960s, as noted by Constant
Reader, was that ships went to sea and, perhaps for the first time outside
the great wars, stayed there, for up to two or three times longer than
once customary. The January 1962 'Naval Notes' record the rapid
recommissioning of the frigate *Rocket* from reserve in October 1960
to replace *Undine*. She was at sea within ten days and deployed to the
Far East within a month. *Rocket* returned to Portsmouth in October
1961 her crew having (as a ship's company) steamed over 76,000 miles
since the *Undine* had first commissioned in April 1960.[76] In 1968, it
was noted that the frigate *Zest* had steamed nearly as far (179,000
miles) over the last five years as in the preceding nineteen of her service
(428,000 in total over twenty-four years).[77]

It may be that this greater intensity of effort at sea highlighted the
fact that seagoing service had become financially less advantageous than
shore service, particularly accompanied overseas postings. There was
also an increasing sense that bases and dockyards had lost their focus.
This refrain was to continue well into the 1970s, with 'Lucky Jim's'

satire 'Lumbago Goes Right' in 1970 being particularly scathing. A protagonist in Lucky Jim's three-part play made the point: 'One of the great changes that has taken place in the last thirty years has been in what might be termed "the balance of brass", in other words the relative seniority of the seagoers to the shoreside.'[78]

One of the more visionary articles in the *NR*'s history appeared in January 1965. In 'Go Seventies Now', 'Asp' urged reform of the WRNS. He believed that they should receive equal pay and abandon many of their special privileges and 'feminine' ways. This was in the context of their contemporary employment, but Asp went further, declaring, 'I can see the day in which women will give valuable service at sea in mixed complements, contributing their special skills and discharging full responsibilities ... The day is yet to come, for the majority of our population is too sexually juvenile for it to be possible now.' He also argued for a seagoing allowance![79]

That problems remained was apparent from continuing plaints over engagements, conditions and workloads, but Captain R D Franks contributed a more optimistic note in January 1968 with his report of three days in the new guided missile destroyer *Glamorgan*. In retrospect the size of the ship's company in this class allowed more of the procedures of the old Navy to be maintained than Franks realised, but he was nevertheless greatly impressed by the habitability of the ship and the professionalism of her crew.[80]

The Legions Recalled

The next few years saw the Navy manage the withdrawal from East of Suez. Commitments in the Far East had clearly created significant strains, but a new note entered the debate as contributors contemplated becoming a European Navy with much greater limits on deployments. As early as 1969, 'Decision for Life' asserted that the Royal Navy had become too confined.[81] At the same time, there were renewed complaints about excessive strain. While there was little doubt that professional standards had improved significantly (25 per cent over ten years, according to a retired Flag Officer Sea Training after a sea day),[82] there were also suggestions that the FOST organisation was too rigid in its outlook.[83]

Many of the traditional routines of ship life were coming under the microscope. The rum ration's days were numbered, while there was increasing dissatisfaction about the demands placed on ships' companies in harbour, with little support from the shore in terms of telephones or transport (or parking) and rigid duty watch arrangements that saw junior ratings one in four (and officers with watchkeeping certificates sometimes even less). Significantly, the newly commissioned two-crew Polaris missile submarines were able to claim the certainty of their programmes and time off as an attraction for their people.[84] Certainly, the experience of these submarines with their dockyard support was happier than the remainder of the fleet. It was claimed that a key reason for the replacement of formal commissions in 1969 by continuous commission with trickle drafting had been the inability to complete refits on time.[85]

In 1976, then Commander G F Liardet provided an analysis of the performance of the 390-strong ship's company of the guided missile destroyer *Bristol* during a year in European waters. Out of sixty offences that could be considered serious, only eighteen were not related to alcohol. On the other hand, venereal disease rates had been extraordinarily low, with only three minor cases, less than the national average for the age group. This compared well with the past: a destroyer in the Far East only a decade before had experienced 100 cases out of a crew of 280 over eighteen months. As an aside to the removal of the rum ration a few years earlier, Liardet also noted that about 60 per cent of junior ratings took their daily beer ration of three cans.[86]

In 1976 the march of technology also created the first suggestion in the *NR* of a generation gap in which it was the professional standards of senior personnel which were in question, rather than the young. 'RW' in 'To Re-Silvering the Mirror', suggested that junior personnel became disillusioned 'when they observe their superiors unable to carry out correctly the simplest of drill tasks, for example to extract some basic information from the computer which had been stored there carefully just for the command's use.'[87]

Other themes that appear at this time include developing concerns over minimum manning and the load of cleaning and maintenance tasks. Whether the division between operators and maintainers should continue also began to receive attention. There were also indications that pay for the military had fallen even further behind. Just how far astern inflation and lack of Treasury support had put the Royal Navy was indicated by the heroic measures required to redress the situation. As 'The View from the Commander's Table' noted in April 1982, junior ratings had a 32 per cent pay rise in June 1979, a 14 per cent pay rise in May 1980 and a 10 per cent pay rise in May 1981.[88]

The Falklands and After

The challenges of the Falklands conflict were described in January 1983 by 'Sub Lieutenant RN' in 'Life in Two Yankee'.[89] This made clear the rigorous securing for action and damage control procedures which had been put in place. He lamented the absent Chinese laundrymen, implying that the Navy had been too slow to develop alternative methods for communal laundry, and acknowledged that synthetic action working dress had proved unsuitable to face battle damage and the inevitable fires.

The impression of increasing pressure is confirmed by a succession of articles in the late 1980s complaining about excessive administrative loads, cumulative deterioration in conditions of service as a result of attempts to achieve cost efficiencies and over-stretched ships' programmes. Notably, the majority, such as 'A Tale of Two Navies' (1987),[90] 'A Note of Caution for the Cost Effective Navy',[91] and 'A Letter to a Friend' (1988),[92] were written by lieutenants. The last also complained that junior officers did not feel that they were spoken to candidly by their seniors as to the problems faced by the Navy. Such articles were symptomatic of the increasing difficulty that the Royal Navy (and other navies) was facing in retaining junior officers. The plea for more 'can't' rather than 'can do' continued into the 1990s, with Commander Mark Kerr's article 'Desperate Diseases' in January 1990 pointing to the dangers of exploiting the dwindling goodwill of ships' companies to get their units out of refit and operational on time by working all the hours available.[93] In the same year, there was commentary on the decision to arm sentries in ships alongside, the first sign of the increasing threat of terrorism that would soon become a primary concern.[94]

The 1990s and Social Change

October 1991 saw 'Aeneas' assess the integration of women into seagoing ships. No supporter, he nevertheless provided a judicious review of this profound change for the Navy, and for the WRNS in particular. The take-up of seagoing opportunities by the WRNS (at only 10 per cent) had been much less than predicted, but 'Aeneas' noted that the WRNS had held a very feminised view of their functions. There was probably truth to his inference that many enjoyed (particularly in their inner office roles) the influence that came with those positions more than the potential authority that would come with progression up the ladder of seagoing careers. Aeneas also identified the challenge that the desire to have children would represent for a navy, up to 20 per cent of whose people were females. The expectation of many older WRNS that spinsterhood would be an acceptable price for high rank simply would not stand. The next two decades were to prove him right.[95]

Other articles in 1992 and 1993 gave more details of the seagoing experience of mixed gender. Some myths were quickly dispelled, with assurances that the females pulled their weight in operational deployments.[96] The difficulties came rather with the absence, as yet, of experienced females to act as role models, and that relatively few seemed interested in remaining at sea, however much they valued their service.[97] In April 1994 Aeneas returned to the fray to suggest reasons why the expected expansion of female numbers had not taken place. He, too, noted that female retention rates were lower than male.[98] Midshipman E R Hayman made a balanced survey in July 1994 in 'Women at Sea'. This acknowledged the demographic reality of an increasingly constrained recruiting constituency as being the key driver for extending the role of women and acknowledged that the attitudes of many had made it difficult for females to be fully accepted. On the other hand, the reality of life at sea had been a shock for many women, particularly junior ratings, and the discomforts of their situation probably contributed much to the aversion to a second sea posting.[99] Both commented that the combination of improved retention (partly due to an economic recession) and a post-Cold War reduction in the size of the seagoing fleet had eased the demographic pressure. The question was, for how long would this be true? Matters were a little confused by the mixed picture presented in the TV series on HMS *Brilliant*. This showed that all was not well with gender relations at sea, but the discussion in 1995 and 1996 also revealed that at least some of the tension between the sexes was set up – or at least encouraged – by the production crew in search of good footage.[100]

Aeneas in October 1995 led a change of focus in 'The Homosexuality Inquiry', prompted by the Government's decision to examine whether sexual orientation should continue to be a factor in military employment.[101] His contribution was one of the most balanced in the battery of articles and letters that followed. His identification of the dark side of the ban on homosexuality, the potential for blackmail and the witch hunts, or at best highly suspect investigative procedures, associated with it was accurate and, in retrospect, a compelling reason for ending the ban. There was a hysterical note to some contributions and a tendency to confuse homosexuality with corruption of the young through the abuse of power and proximity, a problem as much hetero- as homosexual.[102] Perhaps this was because much of the experience of homosexuality in the old Navy had been the result of men being confined together for lengthy periods without sufficient avenues for physical and emotional release.[103] Notably, the subject did not arise again after the Government's decision to end the ban. As with other navies, and perhaps largely because mixed-gender ships were now commonplace, the change caused barely a ripple.

Into the Twenty-First Century

The last fifteen years have seen rather fewer contributions on major issues on life at sea. That there have been improvements, particularly in shore support, has been acknowledged, although a claim in 1999 that the old (1979) horrors of inadequate telephones had ended was firmly contradicted in 2002.[104] Notably, this was despite the arrival of email. In this context, October 1998 and an article by Captain James Burnell-Nugent on *Invincible*'s deployment to the Adriatic and the Gulf marked the end of an era in that the ship's company communicated with their families by telephone.[105] This itself was a great advance from previous decades, but, by 2003, Rear Admiral David Snelson was commenting on the requirement to manage email security and the importance of the constant connection with home.[106] In 2005, Commander Toby Williamson in 'Executive Business' described the challenges when a ship's company have access to information sources ahead of their leadership.[107] Other articles, such as 'How to be Well Connected' by Kevin Rowlands, suggested the need for much more discipline in the use of email for administration.[108] His implied criticism of the staff ashore suggested that the development of improved communications had also resulted in increased bureaucracy. While some of this was the inevitable result of the increased governance requirements of occupational health and safety and environmental management, to name but two, there was clearly a view in the fleet that matters had gone too far. This was particularly the case, as noted by Sub Lieutenant Tim Montague in August 2009 because ships, notably minor war vessels, had very limited access to satellite bandwidth.[109]

The first decade of the new century saw the issues of over-stretch, retention and a generation gap resurface repeatedly. Just how much the officer corps had changed was indicated by the 2008 article on 'The Admiralty Interview Board' by Captain David James which noted that the average age of officers *on entry* was twenty-three.[110] Some of the potential problems were highlighted by 'Blackbess' in February 2009 in 'A Right Proper Fix We're In', particularly the difficulty of getting enough seagoing service out of officers who would be facing multiple personal demands and external pressures at the age of twenty-eight.[111]

The Iranian capture of HMS *Cornwall*'s boarding party in 2007 received less coverage in the *NR* than might have been expected, perhaps because by this time the wardroom bar in the *NR*'s website provided a safety valve. There was no doubt, however, of the depth of concern over the performance of the personnel concerned, not only on scene but in the bungled handling of the associated public affairs. This was confirmed in October when the First Sea Lord felt it necessary to provide reassurance to the membership as to the state of the Navy and his determination to renew its focus on training and operational standards.[112]

Conclusion

Two tendencies are apparent in the articles on life at sea within the *NR*. One, and it is reactionary, albeit well meaning, is romanticising the past. This deserves the *1066 and All That* label given to the Cavaliers of being 'Wrong but Wromantic' and particularly manifested itself in discussions about the lost art of seamanship and its role within a Navy of a more virtuous age. What is striking about many of these contributions is the uncertainty of the logic applied and the extent to which sentiment was important rather than necessity. The question which some of the enthusiasts concerned should have been trying to address was the extent to which the modern Navy supported the development of the qualities of initiative which had been vital under sail and which translated so well into the demands of war. All too often, however, this was not apparent within their strictures and the demand seemed to be for more discomfort and less efficiency. Another facet of this outlook has been that of younger members who have claimed that the Royal Navy of their present day works harder and has less fun and relaxation than that of the past. They have had more justification for their complaint, but not quite as much as they might believe.

The second is that of thoughtful senior officers who have had the chance to see the fleet at sea years after their own retirement. Their affection for the Service may add a tint of rose to their glasses, but their commentaries show no loss of grip and the changes that they comment on are just those which should be expected. Above all, they mention again and again, and independently, the greater professionalism and operational focus than the Navy of their own time. This tendency is also apparent in contributions of serving senior officers. In this case, while there may be some element of self-serving, there is more often a similar humility and respect for the young in their commentaries.

Nevertheless, the fact that the Navy has been able to get so much more from its people has come at a price, not always recognised either early or sufficiently enough. The pages of the *NR* have included many perceptive contributions which have identified problems and posed imaginative solutions. And many of those solutions, however the Service finally arrived at them, were the ones which would eventually be implemented. If the Royal Navy was often too slow to address its problems, and perhaps remains so, the direction of its effort was generally correct. Concerns continue to be raised within the *NR* and this suggests that there is no room for complacency in its second century. The bargain with the Royal Navy's people must be met, even as its elements change.

A last article on life at sea to be reviewed for this study is Commander John Craig's assault on shorts as uniform rig in 'Short Finals' in May 2010.[113] His comments on the cultural issues and the aesthetics involved were well chosen, but perhaps more significant was his note that shorts are too cold for wear inside air-conditioned ships. Veterans of service in the tropics in previous eras would acknowledge that this says a lot, albeit unconsciously, about just how much life at sea really has changed over the last hundred years.

18 From Selborne to AFO 1/56

Commander James McCoy

THE subject of officer structure and training became a recurrent theme in the pages of *The Naval Review* even before the first flush of articles about operations in the First World War was over: by 1924 well over a hundred thousand words had been written on the subject. Contributions varied from the philosophical to the political, pompous to pragmatic, often polemic and occasionally downright deranged. But early on two consistent threads emerged: the rise and fall of Dartmouth as an educational and training establishment, and the right to career and command for seaman, engineering and other specialists. There were plenty of impulses to the debate: for example, the original Selborne scheme, the 'Great Betrayal' of 1925, and Admiralty Fleet Order 1/56. Here the author attempts to show where the threads crossed, or more frequently became tangled and confused, in the *NR*.

A favourite stamp in the author's boyhood collection was issued in 1897. With a tiny map of the world, much of it pink, it asserted 'We hold an Empire greater than has been', while the Golden Jubilee Fleet Review the same year 'had instilled in Englishmen a spirit of bursting pride and confidence in their Navy'.[1] Thenceforward, by erosion of possessions, or of wealth, or of influence, or of confidence, a process of decline set in. The bloody nose inflicted upon the British Army by the Boers was followed by the German Navy Laws of 1898 and 1900 which announced the coming threat to the supremacy of the Royal Navy. Other cracks were appearing in the stable, even complacent social facade of the nation and Empire. The Navy was not immune to this uncertainty, and into this volatile atmosphere, the appointment of the fiery and hyperactive Admiral Jacky Fisher as Second Sea Lord in June 1902 burst like a mine in a goldfish pond.

One System of Supply, One System of Entry, One System of Training

Fisher was unusually senior for the post, more normally held by a Rear Admiral, and by December he had launched a major reformation of officer entry and initial training. Till then, seaman officers' initial training was conducted over four terms' study in *Britannia*, a hulk moored at Dartmouth. Having entered aged between fourteen and fifteen, they joined the fleet as midshipmen at about seventeen.[2] Engineers entered separately, through the Royal Naval Engineering College at Keyham, which had opened in 1888, and students started there between the ages of fourteen to sixteen for a five-year course in the rank of engineer student, equivalent to naval cadet in *Britannia*.[3] On graduation from Keyham they went to sea as assistant engineers, but, notwithstanding the acceptance of engineers as officers in 1847 and their admission to the wardroom in 1876, they were still classified as civil or non-combatant officers, as opposed to military or executive officers.

In social circles many could not accept that men who worked with machinery could be gentlemen, no matter how intelligent or well-educated, and in the Navy they were ranked separately and subordinate to their upper-deck colleagues. Naval engineers had become increasingly discontented, and there were too few candidates of suitable quality.[4] The national engineering establishment took up the cudgels and an acrimonious debate ensued. It was held as justification that the prevailing attitude in the Navy towards engineering had led it to fall behind the technological advances of the time, and this was of great concern to the then First Lord of the Admiralty, Earl Selborne, and to Fisher.

Fisher's solution was radical to the point of revolution: to remove all distinctions between the engineer and the executive officer by incorporating engineers into the main body of military officers, with similar prospects of promotion and command. Henceforward the engineer would become an executive officer specialising in Engineering (E), just as the Gunnery (G) or the Torpedo (T) specialist. The key phrase in the Selborne Memorandum of 16 December 1902 was: 'The result aimed at is … a community of knowledge and lifetime community of sentiment. The only machinery which can produce this result is early companionship and community of instruction. These opportunities will be secured by a policy of One System of Supply, One System of Entry, One System of Training.'[5]

Officers would join together, train together, and follow a common syllabus until promoted lieutenant, by which time all would have gained both bridge and engine room watchkeeping certificates. The memorandum continued: 'engineer officers will be assimilated to the corresponding ranks of executive officers and … will wear the same uniform and bear the same titles – sub-lieutenants (E), lieutenants (E) … rear admiral (E) … every endeavour will be made to provide … opportunities equal to those of the executive branch.' All would be eligible to command ships and no distinguishing cloth was to be worn between the stripes to distinguish engineers of the new scheme.

The construction of proper educational facilities had been decided upon in 1896, with the purchase of Mount Boone in Dartmouth, upon which a new college was to open. The Royal Naval College Osborne, a largely hutted camp in the grounds of Osborne House, opened in 1903 to give a rapid launch to the scheme where cadets entered at thirteen for two years before going on to Dartmouth for a further two. The syllabus was heavily tilted towards technical and mathematical subjects. However, the engineering syllabus was largely devoted to workshop training, and little, if any, to systems, design, capabilities and limitations. Then followed eight months in a training cruiser. Candidates subsequently joined the fleet as midshipmen aged sixteen to seventeen for about three years, and on promotion to acting sub lieutenant continued to obtain their watchkeeping certificates. Dependent on seniority gained, all became lieutenants at about twenty. Osborne and Dartmouth combined thus to form a type of naval public school, and, indeed parents were required to pay fees, albeit much less than the total cost of the education provided.

The Selborne scheme satisfied public opinion at a stroke by abolishing social divisions between Engineer and Executive. Within the service it caused marked divisions. The more progressive welcomed it whilst reactionaries opposed it fiercely. Some were opposed through misunderstanding, supposing it to be identical to the USN 'Line' officer introduced in 1898. That the issue of interchangeability between 'deck' (G, T, and N) specialisations and 'engineers' (E) remained unclear was due to Fisher's implacable and vindictive hostility to any who questioned his plans; but since the point at which this fatal flaw of the scheme became apparent lay many years ahead, the nettle was left ungrasped.

The fatal flaw was however to form the basis of endless debate and controversy in the public press as well as the *NR*.

The Early Years (1913–1916)

The year 1913 was a remarkable one for the Royal Navy. The naval arms race had escalated to the point at which war seemed inevitable. The Selborne scheme was capable of producing no more than about 250 officers a year, and to increase the intake a new Special Entry scheme was introduced to enter cadets on completion of their public school education aged about eighteen. After undergoing a shorter, intensive naval training they joined the fleet as midshipmen after just a year's training. The Public School entry, as this scheme became known, was announced in March[6] and the first cohort, forty-two strong, entered in September 1913.[7]

The first issue of the *NR* had appeared in March that year, and it would have been extraordinary if the question of officer entry, training and career progression had not formed part of the debate in its pages. Indeed, the first issue contained a thoughtful essay by one of the founding fathers, Commander the Hon Reginald Plunkett, 'Naval Education'.[8] He wrote seriously but with many amusing figures of speech. He fulminated against rote learning and the inability of the system to encourage the creative and spontaneous. His conclusion was that excessive effort was expended in cramming the brain with details suitable for regurgitation at examinations, and insufficient to training in imaginative and analytic processes. However, no clear plan for correcting this emerged.

Next to the crease came the senior of the founding fathers, Captain Herbert Richmond. Although initially a firm supporter of Fisher, and a keen proponent of the Selborne scheme, in this first of many contributions, he deplored the level of theoretical cramming seemingly necessary to train a young officer, and in particular the high proportion of this training devoted to engineering. He sought to reduce the engineering syllabus for the new Special Entry cadet, quoting the introductory memorandum for the scheme before disparaging it: 'The course of training ... will consist largely of instruction of a practical kind in naval engineering and in the service application of electricity ... Is engineering instruction so much the most important to an officer who is going to be a lieutenant, who will have to keep watch, to handle a torpedo boat or destroyer, to command a turret or a battery of guns ...? For these are among the principal duties we want the lieutenant to perform.'[9]

This extract reveals, perhaps surprisingly, that he did not conceive that an engineer could also be a lieutenant. Two other key points of future conflict emerge. First, he foresaw serious difficulties emerging when Selborne officers entered the zone for promotion to commander: 'When the lieutenant becomes a commander does he require a knowledge of engineering? I think not. I can think of nothing in a commander's duties which demands of him such knowledge ... and, besides, if he has been a deck officer throughout his lieutenant's time ... without having anything to do with [engines he] will have become both rusty and out of date.' Second, he suggests that if the new scheme is shown to be a success, then for reasons of economy all officers should be entered by this system and the thirteen-year-old entry – and the Osborne/Dartmouth system abolished. This latter debate continued in the pages of the review for the subsequent forty years.

Richmond returned to the attack in a letter published in the subsequent edition: quoting the *Report of the Committee on the Training of Midshipmen,* 'Every officer of the military branch should have experience of the engine-room department, and be able to take charge of an engine-room watch should the need arise', he commented: 'I have been at sea a good many years, and I have never yet seen the need arise for one of the lieutenants to relieve or replace the engineer officer in his duties, even if he had been able to do so'.[10]

Other pre-war contributions confirm the confusion over the career progression intended by the Selborne scheme. Dewar, another founding father, replying to Plunkett, disparaged the extent of engineering training: 'The Education Committee's statement, that every officer of the executive branch should have experience of the engine-room department and be able to take charge of an engine-room watch, would have been more convincing if it had explained when deck officers will be called upon to perform this duty'.[11] Others also opposed the Selborne scheme, and only one, Captain Trevelyan Napier, wrote in support of it;[12] whilst a pragmatist suggested that we are where we are and should make the best of it:

> One of the most valuable qualities of a seaman (in the wide sense of the term) is his custom ... of making the best of things as they are: not questioning the wisdom of those who provided him with impossible leads for his cables, turrets with tricky loading hoists, torpedoes with obscure abdominal symptoms, or feed pumps that will not heave; but endeavouring, generally ... to keep things going ... Naval Education might be approached in this spirit, accepting the principles ... for good or ill.[13]

The First World War and Its Aftermath: To Catch 'Em Young – or Not

The war disrupted training and made it impossible to evaluate the Selborne scheme. Naval College training was curtailed from four to three years, plus a term at Keyham College before officers joined their first ships as midshipmen aged sixteen. In the Fleet, the first Selborne officers had only recently reached lieutenant's rank, and, since the first new Keyham course for engineers had only started in October 1913, no graduates were yet at sea. But the anomaly that they would become notionally superior (albeit not senior) to some five hundred old-scheme engineer officers led to a reorganisation of the officer corps into five branches: military (seamen and engineers), medical, accountant, instructor, and artisans (the latter being warrant rank). Military command authority and the executive curl to their stripes (but with purple distinguishing cloth between them) was granted to all engineers on 1 January 1915.[14]

Wartime conditions led to many provisions of the Selborne scheme falling by the wayside, and training suffered. The author's father's E190[15] (the 1910 version) includes the requirements that all (including seamen) should obtain certificates that they have acted as 'as Stoker Petty Officer of a Stokehold'; 'satisfactorily taken charge of (a) an Engine room and (b) all the Boiler Rooms'; and become 'qualified to perform … duties of a Junior Engineer Officer'. Yet despite serving in a flagship (HMS *Lion*) from 1916 to 1919, where an exemplary training regime should have prevailed, his certificates are all blank.

Post-war the debate reopened promptly, but the context had changed. During the war, the Navy had not exactly failed, but it had not – in its own eyes – succeeded. There had been no decisive denouement with the German High Seas Fleet. Over-manning in the post-war Navy was obvious, and 'Geddes' axe'[16] was to follow in 1921 and 1922. The curious conditions of the Armistice (neither peace nor war) meant most had time on their hands. And the generally good performance of the Special Entry officers, of whom there were some four hundred in the fleet by the end of 1918, provided much fuel for argument. The debate opened with an important article co-authored by the editor and a distinguished former public school headmaster.[17] Originally published in the *Fortnightly Review* in April 1914, it was long and closely argued but it alluded to a time before the effectiveness of the Public School entry had been tested, and before the debate in the *NR* had taken shape. The stimulus of the article was the Custance Report which had found serious faults in the operation of the Selborne scheme.[18] Custance was a renowned opponent of Fisher, and the main argument he advanced was that it was impossible to judge the suitability of a pre-teenage boy after a short interview and that too many candidates were inadequate. This was compounded by an education too heavily biased in favour of engineering and mathematics, and that by trying to provide both a school education and naval training the system failed – expensively – at both.

It was held as the parents' task to educate their boys, and the Navy's to train them. The article concluded:

> that candidates for the Navy (like … the Army) should pursue their
> general education at the public schools up to the ages of 16 to 17;

... that their selection should be determined by examination and by personal interview combined with the usual medical safeguards; that the selected candidates should spend 18 months at Dartmouth before going to sea, and that their work at the colleges should be exclusively devoted to the groundwork required for a sea officer – to that and nothing more.[19]

If the editor's aim was to revive the debate he succeeded magnificently. Over the next six years the NR contained over thirty contributions on the topic. The basic division between the two camps (let us call them 'Pubs' and 'Darts') was straightforward: the intellectual and idealistic wanted to abandon the youthful Dart entry and concentrate on entry at eighteen. The others, perhaps more reactionary and pragmatic, whilst accepting the need for a proportion of Special Entries saw the Darts as providing the base load with the Pubs making up a minority – with a capability to surge if required. No one picked up on Henderson's point that at the suggested age of sixteen to seventeen, a boy's general education could hardly be considered complete.

Given that the Dart scheme was an established system, the Pubs had perforce to act as the prosecution, which they did, with great energy, leaving advocates of the Darts to defend the status quo. The principal argument against the Dart was that the Pub was a more rounded type with a broader view on the world than the boy who had been in uniform since thirteen. The Dart response was first, improve the quality of the education at Dartmouth. More responsibility and more individuality were counselled. Second, and more tellingly, it was argued that unless recruits were caught young, there would never be enough willing to join at eighteen, and that the brightest boys (of whom the Navy required its share) would instead go to university.

A further point made in favour of the Pubs was that at eighteen, a boy would be more likely to know what he wanted from his career. The Dart scheme was castigated as expensive (no thought here to sunk costs) but against that, because the education offered was state-subsidised the Dart entry offered a way into the Navy for those of modest means (such as sons of naval officers and vicars) who would struggle to put children through public school. Also early entry and hence longer training would open the demographics of entry to some of the labouring classes, citing the

> constant pressure ... to open the career of a naval officer to all comers ... the door must be opened wider. Now the two qualities in an officer which obtain the respect of his men are, (a) he must know his job thoroughly, (b) he must behave like a gentleman; a word which should convey a definite sense of upright conduct rather than that of dress and formal convention ... behaviour depends to a very

large extent on ... upbringing. If it be necessary to eradicate undesirable habits or bad manners ... a boy who is to be trained as an officer must be brought under the proper educative influences at a receptive age – as soon as possible ... 17½ years of age would be too late.[20]

A good summary of the case was provided by a writer in 1925 who concluded: 'Early entry for the majority and public school entry for those who have missed the earlier chance give, in the writer's opinion, the golden mean.'[21] He also pointed out that whereas most of the opponents to the Dartmouth scheme appeared to be the older Britannia entries, those arguing for the college were its – presumably – satisfied customers.

Great War to 'Great Betrayal': The Unstitching of Selborne

The end of the First World War also led to a complete reappraisal of the career structure for deck and engineer officers. Since 1915, all had been military, specialising as required in (G), (T), (N) or (E), but now the impending promotion of the first Selbornes to commander started to focus minds on the fatal flaw: how were lieutenant commanders (E) to be reintroduced to the upper deck as commanders, having spent perhaps twelve continuous years on engineering duties? Fisher's scheme had always caused considerable doubts on this score and, it seems, never intended to offer complete interchangeability between (E) specialists and others.[22] But it had clearly promised as an inducement to gain more (E)s, a clear passage to ship command, and was the intention as late as 1912. Post-war this principle came under threat.[23]

Throughout 1918 and 1919 the career paths of new-entry engineers were progressively changed. Whilst all would enter through the same schemes as the deck officers ('Darts' and 'Pubs' alike) their paths would divide on completion of initial training with the engineers going to Keyham for their three-year course and the deck officers to sea. The formal Admiralty decision came in July 1920: 'There is a definite distinction both as regards knowledge and capabilities between those ... trained in the science of naval war ... and those ... to deal with the upkeep and maintenance of engineering and mechanical appliances ... Each side requires a special study and for this reason final separation of the branches is essential.'[24]

A series of interim schemes were introduced for those Selborne engineers who still had expectation of, if not actual entitlement to, sea command and thus separation was effectively achieved, if not yet absolutely consummated.[25]

Then followed a spate of contributions to the *NR* concerning the age of entry, and training syllabi. Most of these were philosophical rather than practical, and many called for a reduction in the engineering syllabus at Dartmouth in favour of the liberal arts. At the end of 1920, the editor had called for a synthesis of the various ideas and a concrete proposal for reform of the officer structure, reproducing as his model a recently published and detailed US Naval paper.[26] This covered an officer's career from graduation from Annapolis through to his first small-ship command at the age of about thirty-five, together with a complex diagram illustrating each step of the way.

The response was swift. Two young engineer officers, Denys Ford and Bernard Greathed, writing as 'KGF', produced a detailed proposal which was published in 1921.[27] Their proposal suggested dividing the military officer corps into two main branches, one operational and the other technical, at the age of twenty-one to twenty-one and a half, after some eight years' common training (four for Special Entries). They proposed that at about twenty-one all sub lieutenants should enjoy a break for six months at university, before their career paths diverged. The majority of officers of both branches were required to take a series of requalifying or refresher courses in each rank up to commander. This was a thoroughly modern approach and showed, for the first time Electrical or (L) officers as a specialist engineering 'dagger' course.[28] The article was accompanied by an equally detailed progression diagram which (greatly simplified) is reproduced at Figure 1.

In the same issue were published a 'Critique'[29] and a 'Criticism',[30] which responded to KGF in different ways. The 'Critique' complained that in formulating the proposed scheme the author had paid insufficient attention to financial and administrative difficulties, and argued semantically for the retention of the 'executive' (rather than 'operations') branch. The author of 'Criticism' was less moderate in his approach, starting with an insulting rebuttal followed by a restatement of the official policy for officer entry, training and specialisation. He concluded pompously: 'The Admiralty system ..., in which the whole experience of the war has been given due weight, adheres to the following principle (a) Common Entry and a Public School education at Dartmouth [and] (b) Separation of Executive and Engineering Officers on completion of the Dartmouth training ... and it was on this basis that any proposals for improvement should be made.'[31]

Subsequent issues contained a series of articles and letters, for and against, together with further vigorous pieces by the pair defending their thesis – which mostly illustrate the difficulties of carrying out a debate in the pages of a quarterly journal! KGF argued cogently that the

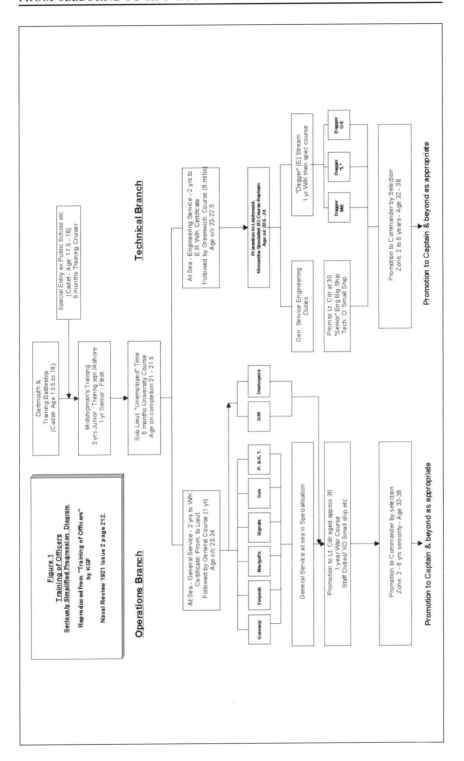

Figure 1
Training of Officers
Seriously Simplified Progression Diagram

Reproduced from "Training of Officers"
by KGF

Naval Review 1921 Issue 2 page 212.

Technical Branch

Operations Branch

Special Entry ex-Public School etc
(Cadet - Age 17.5 - 18)
6 months Training Cruiser

Dartmouth &
Training Battleship
(Cadet - Age 13.5 to 18)

Midshipman's Training
2 yrs Junior : Training sqn /Ashore
1 yr Senior - Fleet

Sub Lieut "Unemployed" Time
6 months University Course
Age on completion 21 - 21.5

At Sea - Engineering Service - 2 yrs to
E.R.Wk Certificate
Followed by Greenwich Course (6 mths)
Age o/c 22 - 22.5

Promotion to Lieutenant.
18 months Specialist (E) Course Keyham
Age o/c 22.5 - 24

"Dagger" (E) Stream
1 yr Wk then spec course

Dagger
O/E

Dagger
"L"

Dagger
M/E

Promotion to Commander by Selection
Zone 2 to 6 years - Age 32 - 36

Promotion to Captain & beyond as appropriate

Gen Service Engineering
Duties

Prom to Lt Cdr at 30
"Senior" Eng Big Ship
Tech. O Small Ship

At Sea - General Service - 2 yrs to Wk
Certificate: Prom. to Lieut
Followed by General Course (1 yr)
Age o/c 23 - 24

Gunnery | Torpedo | Navig'n | Signals | Gas | P. & R. T. | S/M | Destroyers

General Service at sea in Specialisation

Promotion to Lt Cdr aged approx 30
1 year War Course
Staff Duties/ XO Small ship etc

Promotion to Commander by selection
Zone. 2 - 6 yrs seniority.- Age 32-36

Promotion to Captain & beyond as appropriate

disruption caused by the war meant Selborne had been given no chance to settle down, won the debate on points.

Mackenzie-Grieve, now a gunnery specialist, argued powerfully for engineer's status: 'young officers specialised in "E" under the pledge of equal status with other specialists [and] it should in justice follow, that those who have been and are devoting their careers to Engineering under the scheme started in 1902, should not be deprived of the conditions pledged to them.'[32] He noted that while 'the top cadet of this first [Selborne] term has just been promoted to commander, being the first of the common entry to reach this point, the promotion of the first cadets who specialised in E in that term is held over',[33] and concluded that the Selborne scheme, though it had never been given a fair trial, was now starting to bear fruit. Most importantly, he noted there was a false assumption that all naval officers should be engineers rather than that all engineers must be naval officers.[34]

The last, spirited, and intelligent word in favour of what would later come to be called the General List engineer was in 1925. A distinguished, old-style engineer ridiculed the notion that the branch could be run entirely by commissioned artificers, any more than the upper deck could be run entirely by boatswains. He pointed out that in a large ship the engineer officer controlled almost as many men as the executive officer, and that their morale was as least as important as that of those serving the gun batteries:

> An engineer officer should be just as much an officer of the Service as any other – as any purely upper deck officer; there ought to be no invidious distinctions ... So often the engineer officer is treated as alien to the Service; he should have as much interest in the traditions, the general work, the amenities and welfare of the Service as any other officer ... He should know for certain that all the conditions of service for him are considered and settled with a sympathy, fairness and an intelligent knowledge of his outlook, just as it is for any deck officer ... ponder for a moment on the American scheme ... the American Navy goes on and progresses ... they produce results ... they are perhaps more mechanically minded, and most important of all they have no illusions as to the 'gentility' of engineering as a profession.[35]

However, contributions supporting the engineer were too little and too late to influence the outcome. The officer structure was reorganised in November 1925. The five branches established only seven years before were replaced by twelve categories: Executive, Engineer, Medical, Dental, Accountant, Instructor and Chaplains, who were commissioned officers; and Shipwrights, Ordnance and Electrical officers, School-masters and Wardmasters who held warrant rank. This re-organisation, announced in AFO 3241/25 and which became known by as 'The Great Betrayal', effectively unwound the remaining provisions of the Selborne scheme.[36] Engineers were deprived of the right to command at sea (and of military command) and insult was added to injury by requiring engineers to wear 'a more distinct shade of purple' between their stripes of rank.

A junior engineer who – after leaving the service – achieved eminence in the marine engineering field described the reaction:

> certain people do not consider that the 'officer class' is required below at all. They argue that the promoted ERA should be quite adequate to do all the work of an officer in charge of a ship's propelling machinery ... undoubtedly there are very many ERAs who could take the *Hood* round the world as Chief Engineer. There are also many coxswains who could make a pretty good fist of circumnavigating [the globe] and several GIs who could control the fire in a full calibre 15in shoot with tolerable success! It is in danger, difficulty and uncertainty that the real officer will make the differ-ence that counts ... the scheme was a failure because it was not allowed to be a success. About three years before the original volunteers came to the seniority for promotion, it was suddenly found that the scheme was a failure – without even a trial! If these officers had reached the stage of being considered for promotion, there would have been even more of a crush ... than there is under present conditions ... these (E) officers were the victims of the economic situation created by the great war.[37]

Thus, after twenty-three years, the Selborne scheme died.

The Great Depression, Invergordon and the Run-up to the Second World War – 1929–1940

The next tide of words on the officer structure arrived in the early 1930s. Again, it was a time of economic depression, social turmoil and low national morale. Successive naval treaties between 1922 and 1930 had eroded British naval supremacy, while the financial crash of 1929 had seriously depleted the savings of the middle classes, ie, the source of most naval officers. The officers' lists were grossly overcrowded and the Navy was found to have made the mistake of granting too many permanent commissions in wartime, and despite 'Geddes' axe' there were still far too many officers to man the reduced fleet.[38] 'The present excess of officers represents the most serious naval problem of the day

... In the first place there is insufficient work to go round ... the lazy officer flourishes, because he can often complete his work quite efficiently in about two hours per day, and gain a reputation for quiet and even-tempered efficiency, which would soon come to grief were he faced with hard work'[39] The Invergordon mutiny was exacerbated in its effects by big ship officers with too little to do having lost touch with their men.[40] This period was described in the *NR* as the 'Low Tide of the Royal Navy'.[41]

Richmond, recently retired, returned to the fray. In three articles in the *Fortnightly Review* in summer 1932 he rehearsed his arguments for later entry of officers and the reduction of Dartmouth to a training establishment.[42] Most of it had been written when he was Director, Training & Staff Duties in 1918, and his arguments presented little new. He received powerful support from the new editor, Admiral Sir Richard Webb, describing them as:

> a masterly analysis of the whole question of the entry and training of officers ... [suggesting] that the process of patchwork has been so long at work that the time to look at the structure as a whole has come ... [he] disposes of the fiction that it is necessary to send a boy to sea young ... in order to teach him to become a seaman.[43]

Richmond abhorred the allegedly monotypical Dartmouth product created by the combination of education and training for four years: 'The herd instinct is the commonest in mankind. It is very difficult for many men to escape from the herd, and it becomes particularly difficult when a boy enters, at an early age, a herd from which he will never fully escape. ... It is not the wearisome "reiteration of type" we require but the freshness of outlook.'[44] He had no time for the argument that in service life a certain uniformity of outlook might be an advantage, and failed to distinguish, it seems, between 'herd instinct' and 'team spirit' – not an unexpected opinion by Richmond and others for whom intellectual independence of thought is a virtue beyond others. Richmond's articles were reissued in a book published in mid 1933, which received a sycophantic review from Admiral Henry Thursfield.[45]

The supporters of Dartmouth responded with a veritable flood of words. Richmond's attack had been followed by an article in the *Daily Telegraph* predicting its imminent closure, but in presenting the naval estimates for 1933–4 the First Lord, Sir Bolton Eyres-Monsell, dismissed this as conjecture: 'Some months ago reports appeared in the Press that Dartmouth College was to be abolished. We immediately took steps to contradict the rumour, because I for one am convinced that we should never get a sufficient number of cadets of the right calibre in any other way.'[46]

The Headmaster of Dartmouth mounted a well-reasoned defence of the college, drawing on a recent report by the Board of Education which had found the college a thoroughly effective establishment.[47] Another contributor quoted from their report:

> Dartmouth is a highly efficient educational institution of which the Admiralty may well be proud ... The report, which runs into 20 pages, deals with every side of the education given at Dartmouth, and in their concluding observations the Inspectors state [that] The college is doing admirable work as a place of education for naval cadets. The Inspectors would indeed view <u>with dismay</u> any proposal to restrict its scope or <u>lessen the contribution it makes to the education of naval officers</u>. While the course at the college is designed to meet the special needs of those who will enter the naval service <u>it is in no sense narrowly conceived</u>. On the contrary it provides, in the view of the Inspectors, <u>a kind of education which would be very suitable for many of the cadets' contemporaries who have no intention of entering the Navy</u>. [underlining in the original][48]

Moreover, although some fees were paid, they were sufficiently low to allow naval officers who might have been unable to send their sons to public school to enter their boys for Dartmouth. The questions of relative costs between Darts and Pubs were addressed in an article by a paymaster writing as 'PLC'. He concluded that the difference in total costs for a Dart and a Pub were very similar. Little detail is provided as to how his figures were obtained (and some calculations seem a little spurious) but he had recently served at Dartmouth so may be presumed to be authoritative.[49] A light-hearted but very telling intervention, 'The Missing Light', covered the improvements in Dartmouth education made over the previous fifteen years. Having noted this piece as significant, it was no surprise to this writer subsequently to discover the author as one of the Navy's foremost thinkers, Rear Admiral (later Admiral Sir) William James.[50]

Richmond ended this phase of the debate with a petulant and pedagogic rebuttal including lengthy comments on the working class movement, and how, if the social intake was not broadened, the socialists would force an entry.[51] He did not elaborate on how entry at seventeen and a half (at a time when school-leaving age was fourteen) favoured the 'people' – and one wonders what this product of the Victorian artistic establishment really knew of the lower class. A contrary view had been aired some years earlier.[52] Richmond's alarmist view was, in the early 1930s, not unreasonable, and would in due course be vindicated. But he failed to recognise the improvements and fine-tuning in the Dartmouth syllabus subsequent to the 1921 reforms. To this author it seems the magisterial nature of Richmond's writing far outweighed the power of his arguments.

The dispute sputtered on to the end of the decade. A polemic anti-Dart article[53] was answered by a former Captain of the College[54] and the Head of History & English.[55] Lastly, a spirited defence of Dartmouth and its product was mounted by a senior Royal Marines officer who concluded 'Is Dartmouth too expensive? Then cheapen it. The discipline too rigid? Then alter it. The curriculum too narrow? Then amend it. **But don't abolish it.** If the sacred flame burns dim it is surely better to put oil in the lamp than blow up the altar.'[56] The editor closed this chapter of the debate in the final issue of 1940.

Did the debate in the *NR* shift official policy regarding Dartmouth? Probably not, but if the combined intellectual weight of Richmond, Thursfield and Webb could not shift official policy what could? In fact no major changes were made at Dartmouth, except that in September 1938, the term system, under which each entry was strictly segregated from all others, was abandoned in favour of the house system as practised in Public Schools.

Command and Material – the Roles of Seamen and Technical Officers – 1932–1945

From about 1932 onwards a new thread began to emerge in the *NR*, related to the questions of training, branch identity and command, but different in emphasis and outcome. Steady increases in the complexity of weapon systems was driving a significant wedge between those seaman officers charged with their maintenance and operation, increasingly the gunnery (G) and torpedo (T) specialists but also the rather rarer signals (S) specialists, and their non-specialist or salt-horse contemporaries. The more intelligent and career-minded officer tended to opt for specialisation as a road to early promotion, while increasing complex technology led to ever-lengthening courses, growth in the number of officers required to teach them, and a consequent increase in shore time.[57] Meanwhile the salt-horse, unless he escaped to destroyers or submarines, was left pounding the teak in the major fleet units, and enduring much lower and later promotion. To add insult to injury, specialists received extra allowances.

The engineering branch, still smarting from the Great Betrayal, had quietly got on with its job of propelling the ships and generating the electricity, and there were few contributions to the *NR* from engineers in this period. An abortive attempt in 1920 to make electrical matters an engineering responsibility had failed and (L) matters had become almost wholly the sphere of the seaman torpedo specialist: 'An unsuspecting person might expect to find torpedo officers most conspicuous in the principal torpedo carriers, namely destroyers. Where you actually find them is busy with the electrical installations of battleships, a class of ship from which it is more than likely that torpedoes will be removed altogether.'[58]

Gunnery officers were also becoming increasingly technical, immersed in the hydraulics and mechanics of their turrets rather than the tactical use of the guns. This led to a proposal that executive officers be subdivided into 'command' and 'material' streams. The latter would comprise torpedo, gunnery and signals specialists whose work was very heavily concerned with their materiel; and the former the salt-horses, the destroyer and submarine officers plus navigators. This argument first emerged in the NR in two articles in the August issue of 1933, where one protagonist asserted that: 'specialists are concerned with the supply and maintenance of the materiel; their knowledge of men is supplementary to their knowledge of materiel; in a word their function is administration.'[59] This was echoed in a reprint of the text of a lecture given in HMS *Suffolk*.[60] Harking back some centuries, the author reminded readers that at one point the fighting of a ship was the responsibility of soldiers, whilst the seamen only manoeuvred her. The kernel of his argument was a

> proposal for the training and employment of executive officers ... selected for either side according to their ability to command or to their flair for technical administration. [Thus] the officer in charge of weapon machinery will be a real expert, instead of an ardent amateur, and the officer using the weapon will have time to study its application and capabilities confident that its functioning is in expert hands.[61]

This proposal, with its foreshadow of the division between wet and dry lists of AFO 1/56 twenty-two years later, was rejected with vigour, for many of the specialists who would thus be consigned to a second-tier career were both the brightest and also among those from whom the NR drew most of its contributors. Between 1933 and 1937, a stream of articles followed written by well-known names such as Charles Hughes-Hallett,[62] his younger brother John,[63] and Russell Grenfell.[64] They opposed the formal separation into 'command' and 'materiel' streams of the executive branch, but admitted the need to transfer some of the technical detail and developmental work to the

engineers or to a more administrative type of executive officer. The gist
of their argument was:

> the right policy is to regard the specialist executive officer as a
> trained administrator with sufficient technical background to enable
> him to take charge of his department in a ship, or to direct and co-
> ordinate the activities of expert civilian designers ashore. To fill this
> role an officer needs a better general education than he receives at
> present, less technical training at the 'schools', and more employ-
> ment at sea in an ordinary executive capacity.[65]

A further excellent contribution in 1937, written by a future member of
the Admiralty Board, foresaw the need for an electrical branch: 'There
appears to be something incongruous in an executive officer having to
spend so much time as an electrical engineer. Is it necessary?'[66]

But in 1939 the nation – and the *NR* – was again at war. This had
two effects on the specialist versus salt-horse debate. First, the ever-
accelerating pace of technical innovation, radar, improved Asdics, better
and more comprehensive communications outfits, and even rudimentary electronic warfare equipment took the technical demands of
maintaining – if not operating – new systems well beyond the scope of
the traditional (G), (T) and (S) specialists. Second, the demands of
training and development meant that specialists were spending an
increasing proportion of their time in shore jobs. One wrote grumpily
in 1942:

> my chances of a sea job as a commander are most remote – and, if
> I do attain it, I shall be lucky if it is for more than a year. Hence,
> supposing I am fortunate enough to be promoted to captain after
> six years as a commander – and supposing that we are still at war –
> I shall be lucky if I have served more than four years at sea out of a
> total of twelve.[67]

Simultaneously, because the war at sea became increasingly a small-
ship effort, the laurels were largely going to the commanding officers of
the destroyers and frigates who were, predominantly, salt-horse. The
specialists, drawn from the more intelligent and ambitious among the
officer corps increasingly saw the chances of wartime small-ship
command and distinction retreating with each further staff
appointment. Dissent, not to say a degree of bitterness, pervaded the
debate which continued through 1943 and early 1944.[68]

The Navy's response to the first of these issues was both pragmatic
and successful. Substantial numbers of new officers were recruited from
the technical industries, awarded commissions as RNVR Special Branch

officers, given a fairly rudimentary naval general training and sent to sea both to operate and maintain the new equipment, but the fundamental issue was not addressed.

The Revival of the Engineering Debate in the Naval Review – 1944– 1950

Having been largely silent since the 'Great Betrayal', engineers now found their voice, one complaining that whilst much debate in the *NR* concerned the entry and training of executive officers, nothing had been said about engineers and paymasters. His immediate concerns were that the executive house officers at Dartmouth were unlikely to encourage young gentlemen to become engineers and that the location of RNEC Keyham in Devonport acted as a further disincentive to those who might otherwise wish to become engineers: '[An Entrant] has to be prepared to spend the next three to four years at an establishment situated in a very restricted area in an unsalubrious [sic] quarter of a dockyard town, amidst all the noise and distasteful atmosphere which are to be expected from its proximity to the streets, the gas works and the dockyard. A very considerable period of his instructional time is to be spent in the dockyard itself … which should be quite unnecessary.'[69]

A further contributor, 'Spud', criticised the suggestion that seamen officers should receive deep technical training and suggested rather cynically that they be given 'a veneer of technical training of the type contained in a Ford handbook' as a foundation for their specialist knowledge. He rehearsed the Great Betrayal and the loss of military command which went with it. Thus limited, engineers could not even command shore establishments unless enabled by specific Order in Council. He proposes a new type of engineer with a career potential culminating as Engineer-in-Chief with four-star rank[70] and a seat on the Admiralty Board.[71] Continuing Spud's theme, 'Bish' deplored the fact that too many engineers were drawn from those who failed to become seamen, and were content to become 'steam bosuns'. He suggested the remedy lay in widening the engineering branch to include electrical and ordnance engineers. He recommended that the training be directed towards gaining professional qualifications for those who may at a later stage take specialised 'dagger' courses, or, if this could not be done, then a graduate entry would be the solution.[72]

Perhaps the most significant piece on the topic marked the return of KGF (now both established stars in the engineering firmament) to the debate to which they had contributed so significantly in 1921.[73] Writing in early 1945, their views had remained substantially unchanged over the intervening twenty-four years. They complained that each time a new technical challenge presented itself, the Admiralty responded by introducing a new specialist officer to deal with it, patching up the problem rather than reappraising the whole organisation. They drew attention to repeated previous attempts to solve the problem of increasing technical complexity, each of which for one reason or another had been abandoned. For the future officer corps they offer three options for improving the situation including their preferred one of reverting to the Selborne scheme:

> as under it the user (of all ranks) would have a real knowledge of his material – and its limitations – and we should perhaps abolish the peculiar brand of would-be '*Herrenvolk*' who imagine that the mere giving of orders (which they could not themselves execute in detail) confers on them some divine right to lord it over all those base-born ones who have the bad taste to show any interest in 'nuts and bolts' (or even amps and volts). The probable objections to this scheme are : (i) a woolly idea that anyone common enough to take any interest in machinery is *ipso facto* incapable of taking any part in administration or staff work, and still less capable of 'taking charge', and (ii) a still woollier idea that Nelson (or perhaps Drake) would have disapproved of it.[74]

The barbed reference to the master race came at a time when the country was still at war with Nazi Germany. Change followed. In October 1946 the electrical branch was set up, with its training headquarters at HMS *Collingwood* near Fareham and initially staffed by transfers from other branches, by officers from the RNVR Special Branch, together with a growing number of Special Entry officers. It assumed all responsibility for electrical distribution from the torpedo specialisation. All electrical officers (except those promoted from the lower deck) were to be graduates, and after initial training cadet entries were to be sent to Cambridge to take their degrees. Ironically, the last captain of HMS *Vernon* to have responsibility for naval electrical matters was Captain John Hughes-Hallett, who in the 1930s had opposed the introduction of a separate electrical branch. The seaman anti-submarine specialisation was merged with the torpedo specialists, and assumed responsibility for mine warfare: *Vernon* became the headquarters for all underwater warfare training.

Socialism, the Labour Government and Post-war Dartmouth

The Admiralty had entered the Second World War determined not to repeat the error of granting too many permanent commissions. So in 1939–40 the numbers were ramped up principally by recruitment of temporary officers into the RNVR, and in many cases highly successful they were. However, there remained a need to increase the intake of regulars, and in particular the coalition government of 1941 saw the need to widen the recruitment net. Accordingly, a limited scholarship scheme was introduced to encourage boys from national secondary schools to enter Dartmouth and to reduce the costs to parents. Twenty were awarded per entry, ten to state-educated boys and ten to the private sector. In early 1946, while the naval college was still in its wartime location at Eaton Hall, a *collegium* of House Officers – most of whom had held wartime destroyer command – submitted an article with generally favourable comments on the quality and the potential of the scholarship boys from state schools, albeit with some reservations:

> Firstly, the spirit of service is frequently lacking and work for the common good is less readily given than work for themselves. This habit is not easily or quickly dispelled; and our difficulties would certainly increase greatly should the proportion of scholarship entries be substantially increased. Secondly, when allowance has been made for the strangeness of the life, it seems likely that the proportion of potential leaders is lower in this form of entry than among the remainder.[75]

With the end of the war imminent, major societal changes were afoot. Among these, the 1944 Education Act was a catalyst for change in the education system, dividing secondary education into three tiers, grammar schools, technical schools and secondary modern (the technical schools proved weak and failed to take root). The means of dividing children among the tiers was the eleven-plus examination, which was a relatively simple test designed to sort out those with academic potential from the rest. And the Act also notionally raised the school-leaving age to sixteen – although successful grammar-school children could remain at school longer to qualify for entry to university.

Notwithstanding the opportunities offered by the scholarship scheme, Labour politicians elected in 1945 soon started to agitate for more egalitarian entry. An extract from the debate on the Naval Estimates in March 1946 claimed: 'the most serious fault is ... the whole question of promotion to commissioned rank ... Whereas merit and suitability should be the sole criteria, there exists in fact the strongest possible class bias ... This bias and this tradition are symbolized by Dartmouth ... an instrument for recruiting officers from a restricted social class.'[76] The speaker, a public school and Oxford-educated playwright and wartime naval officer, plainly had this bit well between his teeth – but he was not alone. Announcing the official solution to this problem, the sixteen-year-old entry, just over a year later, the Parliamentary Secretary to the Admiralty said: 'The new educational system ... makes it possible to afford the opportunity of becoming a naval officer to boys from all classes of the community who possess the qualities of mind and potential leadership required by the Royal Navy.'[77]

Entry to the Naval College at thirteen-plus had been tailored to the private school system in which preparatory schools taught children to the Common Entrance syllabus for entry to public school. This was a much more academic exam than the eleven-plus, and so state-educated children, although allowed to compete for entry to the Naval College and eligible for scholarships, were still at a disadvantage to prep school boys. The new entry at sixteen-plus was designed to allow grammar school boys better chances of achieving the necessary educational standard. With many acknowledgements to its general success, the thirteen-year-old entry was abolished, with the last cohort to enter in May 1949. The sixteen-year-old scheme to replace it was announced in January 1948, for entry that September. Class equality was to be ensured by abolishing tuition fees at Dartmouth, but means-tested maintenance charges were introduced for the better-off. The public school or Special Entry continued, with the initial single term's training of the Benbows, as they were now known, taking place at Dartmouth.

This effectively transformed Dartmouth from a naval public school into a sixth form college. However, the sixteen-year-old entry was unpopular in many quarters. Headmasters were not keen on losing boys at School Certificate/O-level stage, and were reluctant to encourage boys to sit the exams. From the candidates' viewpoint their education was broken just as they were entering sixth form and they were bounced to the bottom of the heap. Perhaps too much of the old Dartmouth routine was retained: chest flats, cold baths, Guff Rules,[78] doubling everywhere, regular caning, no shore leave and so forth. These were acceptable – even normal – restrictions for public school boys, but unsettling for grammar school boys away from home for the first time. The education, however, was first class. The general facilities – sport, river, food, and so on – were excellent, and once the new cadet had settled down, life was pretty satisfying.

However, there was a persistent shortfall of about 15 per cent of candidates in this principal method of entry, thus fulfilling the prediction made by the First Lord in 1933. Despite relaxing the entry regulations to allow two attempts, the Benbow entry had to be increased from the peacetime average of about seventy-five per year to over a hundred between 1949 and 1953 (figure 2). Moreover, halving the length of the course meant that Dartmouth was under-used, and efforts were made to take up the slack. Among other measures, upper yardmen were brought from their own college (HMS *Hawke* near Southampton) to the near-empty block hitherto known as Sandquay Barracks.[79]

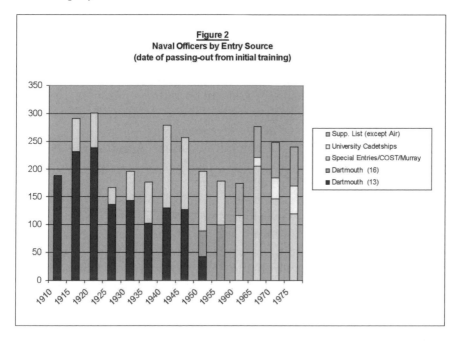

Figure 2
Naval Officers by Entry Source
(date of passing-out from initial training)

The writer contends that the sixteen-year-old entry was not a failure in training terms per se, and its products were at least as successful as the special entries – the last two full years of Darts (1953 and 1954) produced three Admirals, four Vice Admirals and three Rear Admirals from 229 entrants, while the Benbows entered in these years produced one, four and four respectively from 199 candidates. But its failure lay in its attempt at politically-based social engineering: it did not produce the answer required. It was unpopular with headmasters; the bespoke entry examination distracted candidates from their GCE studies; and it failed to attract as many grammar school boys as had been hoped. No one bothered to ask whether this failure was based on the grammar school boy's preference for a career in industry, commerce or the civil service over the privations of Dartmouth and the restrictions and demands of a naval life.

The Committee on Cadet Entry under the Judge Advocate of the Fleet, Ewen Montagu, was established in July 1952 to examine, yet again, the options.[80] Reporting in May 1953, it recommended that the thirteen-year-old entry should be reinstated to provide 25 per cent of the required intake; the sixteen-year-old entry retained to provide a further 25 per cent, and the remaining 50 per cent to come from the Special Entry. The report produced a storm of sanctimonious protest in the press, who were consequently invited to sit in on the interviews held in the summer term of 1953. Reintroduction of the thirteen entry was politically unacceptable: the Admiralty 'must have been aware of the attitude of the Socialist Party to it, and of the probability that, if they returned to office and found it operative, they would again sweep it away.'[81] Instead, they adopted a minority report written by a Labour educationalist from Yorkshire.[82] Political correctness prevailed, the baby was thrown out with the bath water and it was decided all cadet entries from May 1955 were to be at age seventeen-plus.

Also in January 1954, a committee under Admiral Sir Aubrey Mansergh was established to conduct a wide review of the entire officer structure. Because the Montagu report had been rejected, the first priority of the Mansergh committee switched to devising the training required for the new entry which became known as the COST scheme.[83] On entry aged between seventeen and a half and nineteen, cadets were first given two terms' initial training ashore, one term in the new Dartmouth Training Squadron and finally four terms at Dartmouth as midshipmen to include some education mixed with professional courses, and some sea time, following which they went to sea as acting sub lieutenants under training aged about twenty. All were given eighteen months to obtain appropriate certificates, of competence, bridge watchkeeping and (for seamen officers) ocean navigation. Engineers then went to Manadon, electrical officers to Cambridge University and the seamen and supply specialists to complement billets. Dartmouth thus evolved from a sixth form college into a college of further education.

The COST scheme did not last long. Although the professional training ashore was quite good – albeit not so 'deep' as the former sub lieutenants' courses, it meant that officers went to sea earlier, with a stripe on their arms, but lacking in what might be called naval nous – the sort of knowledge which is absorbed by osmosis at sea rather than in a classroom. (The present writer, when quite appropriately made officer of the day for his first Christmas in a ship, met the Aggie Weston's representative visiting the messdecks and invited him to the wardroom for a drink!)[84] And the quality of training the COST acting sub lieutenants received varied enormously from one ship to another.[85]

With almost indecent haste, the COST scheme was replaced by the Murray Scheme.[86] Yet another change drew some pretty critical reactions: 'Since the war ... training of junior officers has gained a reputation, second only to that of the Fleet Signal Book, for frequent and radical changes.'[87] The key elements of the new scheme, introduced in September 1960 were an annual entry with improved educational standards, and a year's sea time for midshipmen. The attempt to integrate academic and professional training was abandoned, and degree-level study was introduced for all engineering and electrical specialists. Under the Murray scheme, entrants would spend their first year at Dartmouth on basic naval training and academic levelling up, then join the fleet as midshipmen for their second year (but living in the wardroom as gunrooms had been abolished). Seamen and supply officers then returned to Dartmouth for a third, academic year followed by professional courses, whilst the engineers and electricals started their degree courses.

In its turn, the Murray scheme did not last long. The Robbins report on national education in 1963 recommended a massive increase in university education, and the conversion of polytechnics to universities.[88] Although the first seaman officers had commenced to read for degrees in civil universities in 1962, this change in educational emphasis, together with the zeitgeist of the 1960s essentially marked the end of Dartmouth as a place of education. The Murray scheme was superseded in 1972 by a naval cadet entry, a direct graduate entry and a wide range of expedients to fill gaps.[89] Thus Dartmouth changed into a training establishment with no real educational function; and the course has been reduced by stages through the years since to its current twenty-eight weeks.

AFO 1/56 and After: What Goes Around ... the Selborne Scheme Reborn

Articles cited earlier indicated widening dissatisfaction with the general structure of the officer corps. The edifice had evolved through a series of short-term reactions to developments in naval technology and tactics and needed a complete rethink. The numbers of shore appointments to support the fleet of the 1950s was increasing. Additionally, the growing dependence of ever more complex ships on the technical and supply branches (see figure 3) was happening without their receiving a commensurate degree of recognition and authority. And their career prospects remained dismal. A major manifestation of this dissatisfaction was amply illustrated by the disciplinary system, in that engineers and supply officers, denied military command, lacked the right to discipline their own men for minor departmental offences.

But this and other similar issues were just symptoms of a deeper malaise. Given that there were many more non-seaman officers, and

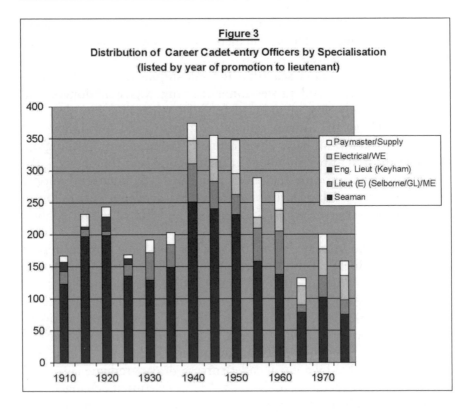

Figure 3

Distribution of Career Cadet-entry Officers by Specialisation
(listed by year of promotion to lieutenant)

their ratings formed a much larger proportion of ships' companies than in previous decades, these anomalies could not be endured. Today's officers may be unable to imagine the situation whereby the most junior seaman officer held authority over much older and more senior officers of the non-seaman branches. Engineers and supply officers were unable to act as officer of the day, not through lack of competence, but through lack of legal authority.

The Mansergh COST committee produced far-reaching recommendations for reform. Formal announcement was to await the beginning of 1956, but was prefaced in 1955 by the abolition of distinguishing coloured cloth between the stripes of engineer, electrical and supply officers. Advance notice of the outcome was trailed in the NR by an article apparently written by a member of Second Sea Lord's department in which the main reasons for the change, including the need to integrate Fleet Air Arm officers properly into the executive branch, the need to provide enough sea-time for senior seaman officers, and the need to improve career prospects for all were explained in some depth.[90]

The full scheme was launched at the beginning of 1956 in a seminal Admiralty Fleet Order 'The New Officer Structure'.[91] Recognising that it was over fifty years since the basic structure had been examined the introductory memorandum, printed over the names of the entire Admiralty Board, indicated three main objectives:

(a) ... the tendency has been for the executive officer to become more and more technical and for the technical officer to increase in numbers and, at the same time, to become more and more executive ... gone are the days when the executive officer told off the vast bulk of the hands for their day's work allocating a small proportion to the technical departments as he saw fit. To-day a very high proportion of the daily work of any ship's company is quite rightly controlled by the (E), (L) or (S) officer concerned ...

(b) we are not making full use of the experience and knowledge of the senior officers in the technical branches ... we believe that senior officers of the (E), (L) and (S) branches could and must play a more important part in the higher administration of the future Navy.

(c) The present chances of promotion to Commander offer insufficient career prospects... Any new structure must offer better prospects of promotion to Commander and must allow for the best candidate, be he Seaman, Engineer, Electrical or Supply, to reach the higher ranks.[92]

In order to achieve this, all cadet entries to the four major branches, Executive, Engineer, Electrical and Supply would be placed on a General List and: 'every cadet shall in future enter the Navy as "an officer" – which is his prime function, and that his early training shall be, to the greatest possible extent, common whether he is eventually to become a Seaman, an Engineer or a Supply specialist', and 'After special training for his specialisation every junior officer will take a part in the day to day duties of running a ship in harbour or a shore establishment.'[93]

The question of military command was resolved by awarding it to all on the General List, but now distinguished from sea command which would be reserved to Seaman specialists. Thus Engineer and Supply officers could now command establishments, but ship command was restricted to Seamen. Yet there were insufficient seagoing appointments for commanders and above to allow all Seamen officers an equal share, and so emerged the most unsatisfactory aspect of the whole scheme:

At the stage of promotion to Commander, the Seaman specialisation will divide. Seaman specialists will be selected ... either as Post List or General List Officers. Appointments in the rank of Commander and above in command of HM Ships at sea, or as Second-in-

Command at sea, or as Commander (Air) at sea and higher
appointments carrying operational responsibilities will be reserved to
Post List officers.[94]

This bombshell was not referred to in the introductory memorandum
but buried deep in the main text, and its effect on Seaman officers was
instant and deeply unpopular. Selection to the General List or 'dry' list
was seen as condemnation to a second-class career of desk-driving and
pen-pushing. (The Post List was soon known as the 'wet' list.) Whilst
most 'dry' selections were among the more senior in the promotion
zone, there were numerous examples where relatively early promotions
among perhaps the more cerebral officers were 'dry', thus preventing
them rising to the top for lack of sea command experience. A number
of good arguments against it were aired in the NR. It was seen as
inflexible and arbitrary: 'the Wet List is generally regarded as 1st XI
and the Dry List as very 2nd XI. That this is generally believed now is
indisputable, cankerous and unnecessary.'[95] It effectively signalled the
end of the line for many ambitious and able officers who resigned to
take their talents elsewhere.

The third main aim of the reorganisation was to provide greatly
improved prospects of promotion for cadet-entry officers. A 'career
factor' of 75 per cent chance of promotion to commander for General
List lieutenant commanders featured in the introductory memorandum,
and hence there was a need to bulk up the base of the officer pyramid.
The Special Duties List was created from the ranks of the Branch
officers (promoted from the lower deck), and the Supplementary List
for officers on short-service commissions (hitherto restricted to
aviators).

There was a considerable and wholly intended similarity to Selborne
which was plainly laudable. But their Lordships were keen to ensure
that this scheme was free from the fatal flaw contained in the Selborne
scheme of fifty-four years earlier. Engineers, Supply and Electrical
Officers could not aspire to sea command, and this was spelled out
clearly to members of the NR by 'Gradatim' who emphasised that the
aim was not to unify the officer corps as had been Fisher's in the
Selborne scheme but to consolidate it and improve the prospects for
the non-seaman.[96] As one used to remark in the cinema in the days
when shows ran continuously, 'This is where we came in!'

The system settled down quite well after the distinction between the
wet and dry lists for Seaman officers was removed in the late 1960s and
replaced by a performance-related system under which Seaman commanders and captains were assessed regularly by a Sea Appointments

Review Board. However, the failure to allow non-Seamen sea command, and shortage of opportunities of elevation to the highest ranks still rankled in some quarters, twenty years on. This writer was engaged in a minor duel of words with a close contemporary, with a similar naval background – but a Manadon rather than a Dryad graduate – in 1976–78.[97] But slowly seats at the top table – the Admiralty Board – and promotion to full admiral for non-Seaman officers began to come. Amongst others, Sir Francis Turner (an engineer) became Chief of Fleet Support (essentially the Fourth Sea Lord) in 1970, Sir Peter White (a supply officer) took the same post in 1978, Sir Brian Brown (another supply officer, but also a Fleet Air Arm pilot) became Second Sea Lord in 1988, and Sir Lindsay Bryson (an air electrical officer) was promoted full Admiral whilst Controller of the Navy in 1981.

Unfortunately, the catastrophic decline since in naval strength, accompanied by incessant reorganisation and rationalisation of the managing structure make further similar comparisons fruitless.

Conclusions

It is unsurprising that in a journal written by officers for officers, the production of officers should be a major topic. Nor that, given its literary nature, the preferences of *NR* authors should be for the humanities rather than the sciences. But the wheel in this, like in so many walks of life, was reinvented at regular intervals. It is impossible to determine which articles in the *NR* influenced development, but it is easy to see which ones made a good shot at forecasting the way ahead. Some of the outcomes were very much as recommended by authors, but after so long a delay as to render it unlikely that the policymakers had read them. A few of the best include those two brave engineers, Ford and Greathed writing as KGF in 1921 and 1944; 'BMW' (Lt Cdr B M Walker) and his seminal lecture in 1933, and the Hughes-Hallett brothers in the 1930s all clearly had influence. Only one plainly affected the outcome. 'Elba' suggested in 1954 that to avoid appointing turbulence and expense, selective promotions be announced six months in advance.[98] His suggestion was adopted with alacrity in AFO 1/56!

The 1970s marked the formal withdrawal from the Far East, and the revocation of the Navy's role in policing the Indian Ocean. It marked the commencement of a decline in strength, size and influence which continued for the next forty years. If the Royal Navy can be compared in its influence to the Roman legions, this was indeed 'recalling the legions',[99] and charted in the *NR* for May 2006.[100] Notwithstanding this shrinkage, from the abolition of the sixteen-year-old entry in 1955 the Navy has suffered from a continuous shortage of officers.[101] Scheme after scheme has been introduced to attempt to overcome these shortages, yet no system has been given a chance to settle before the next upheaval. For example, in this writer's last sea command, a frigate in the 1980s, there were billets for seven officers under training. By the time all were filled, they represented no less than five different schemes of officer entry and training, each with different backgrounds and different needs. Each change was accompanied by a series of reforms whose stated aims were modernisation, improvement or rationalisation, but in practice represented a cheapening, a reduction and a slip down the scree slope of expediency. And the training task was offloaded to the fleet.

In the Britannia Royal Naval College we – the Royal Navy – possess an unequalled training resource. The River Dart and the South Devon coast provide unrivalled opportunities for teaching young men and women the way of the sea. Nevertheless, it beggars belief that there in twenty-eight weeks we can make an officer out of a graduate of any university, however self-disciplined he or she may have been and however relevant his or her degree might be to the sea, to leadership, and to war fighting.

Teaching young officers sea sense in a bridge simulator may be inexpensive but it is not realistic. To teach them anchor-work aboard a decommissioned, stationary minesweeper is not enough. It may be possible to develop leadership by plodding around Dartmoor in the drizzle, but such training is no more appropriate to naval officers than it is to bankers or butchers – paintballing without the fun! Incessant changes to the entry routines, the syllabus, serious gapping of staff, and unavailability of suitable fleet units for a major part of initial training combine to make the current system unworkable, and are destroying staff morale.

It will always be difficult to recruit officers to make their career in a service which is shrinking, but this won't be achieved by reacting at every wind shift to the whims of accountants and politicians. Nor by downgrading the level of initial training. We need to decide what we require, and argue for it rather than cringing away into a solution based on the minimum acceptable. Has Annapolis compromised on its degree course by substituting a diploma? Has the French Navy reduced the excellence of the *formation* provided at the École Navale at Brest? I think not. How many changes have been made to the Sandhurst course over the past few years? They take forty-eight weeks to train an entrant who almost certainly starts his training with two essential attributes of Army service already in place – he can walk, and can run, and can probably drive. In the Navy we have to train our young officers to lead and fight in an alien environment – at sea. We surely cannot believe we are that much better at it than the Army.

Each reduction in naval strength and each vanishing capability has been followed by brave words from successive Chiefs of the Naval Staff along the lines that short-term reduction will secure the longer-term future. Has *The Naval Review* helped? It is difficult at this distance safely to attribute cause to effect: to link writing in *The Naval Review* to official reaction and policymaking. Sometimes the anonymity of authors makes it difficult to discern which of the authors are influential, who understand and are thus explaining the thrust of policy, and those who aren't and are merely seeking to influence it. But certainly the debate about officer training and structure has been thorough.

19 Teaching Naval History

Dr Harry Dickinson

THE establishment of *The Naval Review* coincided with the most intense period of officer educational reform in the Royal Navy's history. These were the years of the Selborne Scheme, Admiral Sir John Fisher's blueprint for a common training that attempted to abolish distinctions between the Executive and Engineer branches. No personnel measure, before or since, generated such passion and the prospect that the holystoned quarterdeck might somehow be tainted by the grime of the engine room, energised and divided not only the Royal Navy but wider British society as well. Educational reform was also evident everywhere. In 1902 a Directorate of Naval Education was formed under the leadership of Alfred Ewing who also served as Director of Studies at the Royal Naval College Greenwich.[1] At Greenwich the first Senior Officers' War Course was established and Julian Corbett was appointed the College's first Professor of History.[2] By 1906 the original War Course had transformed itself at Portsmouth into an autonomous Naval War College. The year in which the objects and regulations of *The Naval Review* were defined also saw the establishment, under the auspices of the War College, of the first Naval Staff Course.[3] It is hardly surprising then that even a glance through the early volumes of *The Naval Review* reveals much on the subject of officer training and education – the first edition alone included articles on general training, its effects on character and intellect, and possible future educational developments in the French Navy.

The early volumes of the *NR* also demonstrated an interest in naval history or more obviously in historical narrative, usually long on chronology and short on analysis. Designed to inform and entertain, these contributions seldom attempted to extract lessons relevant to contemporary operations or to see reading history as much more than a generally appropriate pastime for military men. There was certainly the feeling that history was 'valuable' and in some vague way 'useful' but little exploration of historical principles or their potential contemporary application. Nevertheless, early contributors were at ease with this, and one article in 1915, drawing comparisons between the respective Army and Navy staff courses, made a stout defence of the practice, noting that naval history which did not deduce theory or identify principles had 'the undoubted advantage of avoiding all danger of heresy and dogma'.[4] But exploration of the utility of the subject, whether it placed the intellectual cart before the horse or otherwise, was quite rare and readers of the *NR* up to the end of the First World War were apparently content with monographs extolling British naval greatness in general, and the feats of great men in particular. Officers with an interest in history, rather like officers with stamp collections, could adjourn to cabin or study for an untroubled evening pursuing a respectable and relevant hobby.

Early editions thus showed a considerable, if rather uncritical, interest in history and a similar, if somewhat more impassioned, concern for education. There was, however, little that suggested that one might be connected to the other. Comment on Osborne and Dartmouth was common but was invariably wide-ranging and discursive and although the value of naval history to the cadet was sometimes asserted there was little exploration of what that value might be, beyond some vague appreciation of 'a glorious heritage' or 'the importance of tradition'. Of higher education, perhaps surprisingly since the syllabus of both the Senior Officers' War Course and the War Staff Course already contained elements of history, there was little evidence of debate up to 1919. Indeed it was probably the refounding of the Staff Course at the Royal Naval College Greenwich in June of that year and the return of the War Course in October 1920 that finally prompted contributions in this area. The connections between the College and the *NR* were particularly close at this point. The first President of the War College at Greenwich, Herbert Richmond, was a founder member, as was the first Director of the Staff Course, the exotically named Captain the Honourable Reginald Ranfurly Plunkett-Ernle-Erle-Drax, who later served as temporary editor. It can hardly have been coincidence that with the return of the Naval War College to Greenwich came two seminal articles, 'The Study of Naval History'[5] and 'The Place of History in Naval Education'.[6]

The former piece was the work of Carlyon Bellairs, elder brother of Roger Bellairs, a founder member of the *NR*. It had originally appeared in the *United Service Magazine* more than twenty years previously and had presumably been reprinted with the opening of the Staff College in mind. It was an article of rare power and persuasion which criticised the current 'intoxication caused by the victories of naval science' and the tendency to be impressed by 'passing phenomena and surface appearances.' Yet at the same time the author argued, history should not be taught merely to emphasise matters which remained constant. Where history had a vital role to play in the professional development of the naval officer was in its ability to provide 'regulation of the imagination', the judgement or intuition that was the necessary complement to knowledge acquired by observation and teaching. Neither, and presumably this was why the editor felt the article apposite, could this be achieved by 'desultory reading without guidance' for such skills were best obtained from within the Navy and by organised effort. For too long, the author concluded, British naval history had been outside the educational courses of the naval profession and no one should have to plead in vain for so grand a story to be told.

The theme was taken up the following year in an article also presumably influenced by developments at Greenwich and more purposefully entitled 'The Place of History in Naval Education'. Here the anonymous author confessed himself satisfied with the history teaching for cadets but noted that at a higher level while excellent lectures were given in the college there was little opportunity or appetite for analysis by students. Listening had thus become synonymous with studying and, citing von Moltke and Foch, he argued that the 'reciprocal and quickening action' of combined study and discussion was missing in the current approach. The Navy compared to other professions was particularly guilty of pursuing knowledge without seeking to draw deductions and this was poor preparation for high command where 'habit of mind', powers of reasoning and imagination were essential. The author had little truck with the notion that such qualities might be inborn but even if they were, cultivation and development was still essential. In practical terms this was a process best conducted in the middle stages of an officer's career. He praised the current policy of sending sub lieutenants to study for a short period at Cambridge where the history course, devoid of any tactical elements, was the best medium for understanding the Navy as an instrument of national policy.[7] Such study should then be complemented in the Staff College where naval warfare, strategic and tactical principles would be taught. Above all it was important to engage an officer while he was still 'inquisitive, receptive, doubtful, perhaps iconoclastic but also capable of absorbing and developing ideas … and history should be the medium.'

These two articles certainly contained enough to stimulate discussion, not least because they ran quite counter to the familiar line evident so far, namely that for the young officer naval history was a source of inspiration and for seniors it should be a sort of library or vault from which episodes from the past might be drawn to support current debate. But in fact there was little evidence from the pages of the NR throughout the 1920s that the debate had moved on. Articles appeared from time to time often with somewhat singular titles, 'History without Tears' or 'Is History Any Good?', for example, but there was little evidence of a real shift in approach. Addressing the subject in 1922 one contributor acknowledged the quality of the arguments in previous articles but suggested that few would have been convinced that 'here at last was the road to knowledge.' To have any value history must surely be practicable, it must provide answers and 'it should be produced in a form which will appeal to the Service at large as suitable and useful ... if the right stuff is produced', noted the author, 'it will not lack readers.' Discussion of exactly what constituted the right stuff featured in several contributions in the 1920s, as practical men scanned the past in search of exemplary lessons which, defying all considerations of context, might provide a recipe for contemporary success.

Henderson's efforts to propagate the study of naval warfare through the medium of history only ceased with his death in his eighty-sixth year in 1931. He had made a remarkable contribution to the development of the subject, both as a founding member of the NR, via his editorship which he held to the end, and also as an early proponent of the Senior Officers' War Course. A friend and correspondent of A T Mahan, whose passion for history he shared, Henderson probably did more than any officer of the period to promote freedom of expression, particularly amongst younger officers. The editorship passed at Henderson's behest to Admiral Sir Richard Webb, a former President of the Naval War College, an early member of the Navy Records Society, and an officer with an acute understanding of the difficulties of encouraging discussion and debate in a cold economic climate.[8] Unsurprisingly, with a current membership of little more than a thousand, drawn from a Navy a hundred times this size, his early editorials stressed the importance of recruitment, retention, and above all the requirement not merely to read the journal but to contribute to it.

In fact, there was no shortage of articles in the 1930s. The question of arms limitation and the impact of international law on ship construction clearly engaged the readership and returned discussion to more materialist considerations. But there were also articles on naval training, although few showed much interest in its actual content, and some pieces clearly generated more heat than light. An intense debate over training was initiated by a paper circulated to naval colleagues by the Labour politician A V Alexander, First Lord of the Admiralty from

1929 to 1931. Somewhat provocatively entitled 'Democratisation', it argued the case for extending the catchment for cadets to a broader cross-section of the population and, perhaps predictably, was not well received in naval circles. Nevertheless, Alexander persisted and established a committee to examine whether the present system gave boys 'belonging to all classes of the community a fair opportunity of gaining cadetships.'[9] A particularly contentious issue was the age of entry, not least because setting it at sixteen, or for the Special or Public School entry at eighteen, would bring the value and position of Dartmouth into question. The spectre of the closure of the college duly brought a flood of articles in the NR addressing age of entry, length of training, promotion prospects and a vigorous discussion of the qualities that supposedly applied to 'Darts', 'Pubs' or, heaven forbid, the products of what were baldly termed 'other secondary schools'.

The readership remained fixated by forms of education rather than substance and by the summer 1940 the editor's patience was sufficiently tried for him to close the correspondence noting that 'enough has now been said to enable us to leave this important subject.'[10] With the pace of war quickening, Webb now urged serving officers to use the NR as a clearing house for discussion of current problems and as 'stimulant to thought towards their correct solution', advice which unsurprisingly stimulated much consideration of the here and now. Undeterred, it was again Sir Herbert Richmond who as both a naval officer and a distinguished historian, sought to emphasise the connection between historical study and contemporary activity. In 'The Modern Conception of Sea Power', he urged government ministers, the press and other writers to return to history to gain a proper grasp of the potential of sea power and avoid an understandable but unhealthy concentration on material matters, in particular naval strength measured solely by numbers of ships. While history undoubtedly emphasised the importance of the fighting element, it also demonstrated that bases, merchant fleets and shipbuilding facilities constituted a vital triumvirate contributing to control of the seas. Richmond also deplored what he saw as the current taste for 'segregation' in the application of sea power, particularly the tendency to draw artificial distinctions between the effects achieved by ships and aircraft. Recourse to history, he claimed, would clearly show the advantages of both unity of command and the requirement to integrate all the elements of sea power.

Notwithstanding Richmond's efforts and a brief flurry of discussion about the effects of the 1944 Education Act on future officer entry, the subject of history and officer education took something of a back seat during the war and indeed for some years afterwards This was probably due to the editor's desire to concentrate on operational matters (in 1947 he identified specific topics that potential contributors should address) but it also coincided with the passing of several stalwart supporters of the subject – in particular, Captain B H Smith, the architect of the early Portsmouth Staff Courses and a frequent contributor, and Admiral Sir Herbert Richmond, the outstanding naval historian of the age and without doubt its most influential and vigorous champion. As Richmond's obituary in *The Times* noted, he combined a passion for history, a keen sense of its importance to understanding the nature of sea power, and an unflinching determination that this should be better understood by his fellow officers. The cause of naval history was dealt a further blow in January 1950 when Admiral Sir Richard Webb, editor of the *NR* since 1931, and an energetic supporter of free expression and the vigorous exchange of ideas, also died.

The new editor was Admiral Sir Gerald Dickens, grandson of the author and a former Director of Naval Intelligence who, like his predecessor, occasionally gently directed members towards specific matters of interest.[11] In one instance he wondered what would be the effects of the recent war (and also the prospects of a new Cold War) on the nature of officer education. 'Clio' duly offered his thoughts in May 1952 with 'On the Education of Naval Officers', where he noted that future wars might see 'the spoken word' claim equality with physical weaponry and that the Service should invest in a knowledge economy that no longer relied either on automatic assimilation, or vague assumptions that rank should dictate learning requirement. The training of the mind in an understanding of strategy and policy, for example, must start long before officers reached a position to decide such matters – and the study of history was the bedrock of this process. The Cold War, which Clio observed presciently, would be with us for years to come and would make stern demands on the study of human behaviour which could not be confronted by merely increasing technical efficiency. It was only when disciplined historical study was provided at *all* levels of training and education that officers would be able to meet these complex demands and become true masters of their profession.

This theme, together with some broader consideration of contemporary defects in command, administration and training, was pursued in a series of articles throughout 1955 and 1956 under the generic title 'Naval Reform'. The discussion was initiated, under his own name, by retired Vice Admiral Kenneth Dewar, a famously independent-minded officer, a founder member of the *NR* and a long-standing and vitriolic critic of the Royal Navy's training and education regime. Perturbed by what he saw as increasingly anodyne analysis of the conduct of the recent war, Dewar called for the adoption of the proper historical study he believed was the basis of successful staff work. He extended Clio's original point by suggesting that this had not happened so far because there was still a general belief in the Service that strategic competence was somehow 'the natural and undeniable attribute of rank, rather than the product of study and research.' As long as it was assumed that certain subjects belonged solely to senior officers and that all others should confine themselves to 'technical and executive work', the prospect of a properly educated officer corps would remain a distant one. The present system of staff training which discouraged officers from writing anything which might, even indirectly, criticise the actions of senior officers was in his view producing cautious and repressive attitudes.

The response was both immediate and predictable although the defence of the status quo came not from senior staff but from two relatively junior staff-trained officers – a fact that Dewar would have doubtless argued exactly proved his point! In the first article a somewhat exasperated 'SDS' claimed that the admiral's views might have had some value forty years ago but were now quite out of date. Ironically, while stressing how much things had changed, he invoked perhaps the most ancient of the anti-intellectual arguments, namely, that for naval officers 'one year's experience of war would be of more value than ten years' study of it.' Clearly a man with a taste for the artificial dichotomy SDS concluded by declaring that historical analysis would do better to concentrate on the causes of success, rather than dwelling on the conditions of failure. Similar sentiments were contributed by 'Commander' who, adopting the tone of the senior officer he evidently hoped to become, declared baldly that while freedom of thought, discussion and expression had their place, 'confidence will be undermined unless the principle of (Flag Officer's) infallibility is in general preserved.' With a disingenuousness that would have driven Dewar and the founders of the NR to apoplexy, if not despair, he noted that, anyway, executive officers of ships were far too busy to have time for 'higher thought'.

By the summer of 1960 the editor, Sir Aubrey Mansergh, was warning members that 'serious professional articles seem at present to be in short supply' and while he was still receiving sufficient contributions these were no substitute for the 'serious discussion that the journal seeks to promote.' Of necessity his policy was therefore to accept lengthy articles (one 1962 book review was nine pages long!) and to tip the editorial balance in favour of reminiscences and historical narrative, often without much context. While this may have filled the pages, it was unpopular with members and probably did the cause of naval history, certainly with younger officers, few favours. Neither did the sort of extended article on Jutland by Kenneth Dewar, now in his eighty-second year, but written in his usual coruscating style, which criticised the conduct of a raft of senior officers and the system of education and training that produced them. Members were discomfited and the summer 1963 edition contained no less than eight letters in response, ranging from a measured examination of the arguments by the historian Captain S W Roskill to the heartfelt deprecation of the 'wounding remarks about individuals whom I was brought up to revere', by correspondent 'MG'. While, of course, this discussion was in a sense fully in accordance with the objects of the *NR*, the prospect of a bunch of senior officers, just about in control of their tempers, disputing the events of almost fifty years ago could hardly have inspired the young officers of the nuclear age to turn to the study of naval history. The problem, the editor admitted, was also a more general one: long articles by senior officers deterred junior officers from contributing, thus 'contemporary' articles were scarce, which meant that thought was not stimulated, which meant that junior officers would not join, which meant less contributions and too many long articles by senior officers.[12]

Most editors over the years would have recognised this difficulty but fortunately help was at hand as the Royal Navy of the 1960s attempted to grapple with significant changes in officer education. The first of these was the introduction of the Murray Scheme at BRNC Dartmouth and the introduction of two A-level passes for General List entry – a move largely welcomed without much debate by readers. Far more contentious was the notion of graduate entry to the Seaman branch first raised in a 1963 article by Captain S W Roskill but prompted by the recent publication of the government-sponsored Robbins Committee on Higher Education.[13] This envisaged a transformation of the university system and a huge expansion in the numbers of undergraduates from 216,000 in 1963, to 560,000 by 1980. Roskill, at this point a Fellow of Churchill College, Cambridge, concluded that unless the Service quickly embraced graduate entry, particularly to the Seaman branch, the educational standard of the naval officer in relation to that of the nation as a whole was 'virtually certain to decline.' It was a measured article founded on statistical evidence and one that initiated a long-running debate which roamed widely across the educational landscape for the following three years. While there was some support for a graduate entry and a grudging recognition of having to move with the times, what is striking now is the number of readers who still felt that non-technical officers required little further education – that once military skills and powers of leadership had been instilled, those capable of reaching high rank would emerge naturally and under their own steam. Despite the arguments that the Service would always need to attract the best candidates and there would inevitably be a vast expansion of the graduate population, many felt that the Royal Navy could stand apart from the general trend. The appropriately named 'Spartan', writing in the autumn of 1964, summed up the view with his observation that time at university was time the Service could ill afford and concluded, perhaps rather obtusely, that 'nothing approaches or can ever approach the education of the sea.'[14]

The graduate debate, in common with a number of others, only came to a close with the publication of the 1966 Defence Review and in particular the announcement of the cancellation of the aircraft carrier CVA-01 – a decision of such consequence that, to the apparent despair of the editor, it effectively monopolised contributions for years to come.[15] It also ushered in a long period of despondency characterised by a dearth of scholarly articles and a series of dismal assessments of a carrier-less future – 'The End of the Road', 'The Illusion of Power', 'The End of an Era', etc. Complaint followed complaint and even the various historical narratives seemed to centre on accident and disaster. In 1971 a future editor, Richard Hill, noted that the January edition of the *NR* had been the most depressing in thirteen years and members really should now dispense with bitterness and despair and take the opportunity for a major intellectual rethink about Britain's naval future. His words had little effect for, while there were sporadic attempts to raise the level of debate, they were largely drowned out by correspondents identifying the Navy variously as 'stumbling from crisis to crisis' ('PRCJ'), 'suffering from chronic sickness' ('Cecil') with 'no one ... in charge' (Cecil again). Even a change of editor did little to affect the mood, one correspondent informing the new incumbent, Vice Admiral Sir Ian McGeoch that his first (and it has to be said carefully considered and modestly advanced) editorial was in fact 'arrant rubbish'.[16]

One of the effects of these dark days, which also saw the distribution of the *Review* disrupted by strikes and paper shortages, was that significant developments in officer education and the place of history within it were either ignored or under-reported. Thus recommendations by a Select Committee of MPs that the Staff Course should consider moving from Greenwich to Camberley, or that the Senior Officers' War Course should be abolished, passed unnoticed.[17] Similarly, the end of the Murray Scheme, arguably the last coherent educational (as opposed to training) programme to be conducted at Dartmouth, prompted no comment. Even the publication of the Howard-English Report on Service Education which recommended the abolition of the academic departments at Greenwich, the transfer of all staff training to other locations, the removal of the nuclear training to Shrivenham or Manadon, and the establishment of a federated tri-service Royal Defence College awarding its own degree, stimulated just two responses. 'Lancaster', endorsing these radical proposals and invoking the Fisher spirit, asked whether the Royal Navy had someone 'ruthless, relentless and remorseless' to adopt the new scheme – to which the answer, as far as readership of the *NR* was concerned, was apparently 'No'.[18]

In the meantime naval history within the officer training and education syllabus at all levels was fading fast. At Dartmouth, while most academic subjects were still being taught in relatively small classes, the naval history programme – now just thirteen general lectures – was given to students assembled en masse in Caspar John Hall. Here in upholstered comfort, exhausted young officers slumbered while lecturers of the calibre of Geoffrey Till, Eric Grove and E L Davies diligently cast their pearls into the snore-ridden, sock-scented, semi-darkness. It was hardly surprising that, in the parlance of the day, many young officers must have concluded that the medium was indeed the message. At Greenwich things were hardly any better. Apparently fearing that the History and English Department (later the Department of History and International Affairs) might disappear completely, a succession of professors including Michael Lewis, Christopher Lloyd and Bryan Ranft, all men who had established reputations writing and teaching naval history, silently complied with the requirement to make courses more 'relevant', more 'vocationally orientated', and above all more compliant with the notion of 'useful knowledge.' Discretion may well have been the better part of valour, but it still seems remarkable that for almost two decades nobody was prepared to speak up, either in the pages of the *NR*, or anywhere else, for teaching the history of an organisation whose record of military success belonged with the armies of Alexander and the legions of Rome.

By 1979 Captain Godfrey French (GAF) evidently decided enough was enough and asked why the teaching of naval history was now so neglected and whether this was a result of deliberate policy.[19] In the resulting correspondence Peter Nailor, Professor of History and International Affairs at Greenwich since 1977, suggested a number of causes, not necessarily consistent, but tending to push in the same direction. The first was an instinct that naval warfare had changed so fundamentally that the value of historical study had diminished. The second was the discovery of management as a quasi-intellectual discipline and its subsequent intrusion into almost every professional syllabus, usually at the expense of more traditional subjects. Most of all, Nailor attributed the present low stock of naval history to a general loss of confidence by the Royal Navy about its assured place in the scheme of things, and a consequential turn away from the customary studies that had provided this reassurance. Novelty took precedence over stability, and thus naval history ceased to be fashionable, with the resultant danger that officers lacking any sense of historical continuity would eventually lack proper professional cohesion as well. Not a very satisfactory state of affairs, admitted Nailor, but equally not one that could be addressed without some more wide-ranging review of the value of education and training, and a coherent vision of what was really required to turn silk purses into brass hats.

This exchange did not promote discussion but the general theme of the intellectual development of the officer corps was eventually taken up in a lengthy exchange of correspondence initiated by Dr Nicholas Rodger in the autumn of 1986. His point was a familiar one in the pages of the NR, namely, that while the Royal Navy had traditionally trained its officers superbly, it had devoted little thought about how they should be educated.[20] Technical competence and strength of character was seldom in short supply but too little had been presented which tended to broaden the mind or develop powers of informed judgement. In such circumstances it was perhaps unsurprising that those who skilfully navigated the oceans had difficulty plotting a safe course through the corridors of Whitehall. Predictably, a flood of correspondence followed with a number of members (including a future First Sea Lord)[21] keen to contest the issue and to emphasise that while Dr Rodger's point may have been true historically, the modern naval officer was infinitely better intellectually equipped and professionally aware than his predecessor. Any shortcomings in the current presentation of the 'naval case' could not be attributed to a failure to understand the intellectual fundamentals of the profession. The Director of the Royal Naval Staff Course, the then Commodore J J Blackham disagreed, citing a recent survey showing that on arrival at Greenwich less than 5 per cent of students had ever read a work by Mahan, Corbett, Brodie or Roskill, and that less than 1 per cent were subscribers to the NR, USNIP, RUSI or other relevant learned journals. The simple conclusion he felt was that the Royal Navy did not think it important to encourage in early training the habit of professional, philosophic and strategic study, or indeed reading, of either standard or current literature.

Perhaps unwittingly confirming the point, in July 1987 it was announced that Britannia Royal Naval College Dartmouth was to abandon naval history as a separate subject and incorporate it 'into the wider field of defence studies with the aim of relating past lessons to contemporary affairs.'[22] As we have seen, by this point the subject had virtually disappeared as a meaningful part of the young officer syllabus anyway but the *Daily Telegraph*, and subsequently *The Times*, decided that its demise should at least be accorded full military honours. Both papers duly ran leaders – the *Daily Telegraph* largely inaccurate but deeply heartfelt, *The Times* more measured and prepared to see some value in the change if sensitively handled.[23] Various correspondents deplored the decision, Captain John Moore, editor of *Jane's Fighting Ships* feeling the situation to be 'quite horrifying', and Eric Grove, lately a Dartmouth academic staff member, foresaw the little history remaining as likely to be squeezed out by other subjects. Nicholas Rodger, at this point the secretary of the Navy Records Society, wrote to the *Daily Telegraph* reiterating the sentiments originally expressed in the *NR* and deploring the failure to arouse an interest in young officers that might bear fruit in the intellectual breadth essential to high command.

Curiously, despite national press exposure, there was little comment on the matter in the pages of the *NR* although it wasn't long before the whole question of the educational regime at Dartmouth, was again being discussed – with 'Areopogus', leading the way.[24] Areopogus (or Areopagus, the rock adjacent to the Acropolis where in classical times murderers were tried), in a withering critique of Dartmouth training and education, argued that while the College paid lip service to education, the activity was almost totally marginalised by the pressure of other duties – sport, social functions, divisional matters and the supervision of juniors, which all conspired against serious applied study. He argued that this situation was exacerbated by divisional officers' distain for academic staff and that such attitudes were quickly assimilated by young officers. When combined with inadequate classroom facilities and a lack of proper teaching resources, the picture was a gloomy one and reflected a view that the Dartmouth task was not to educate, but merely to train young officers to a minimum baseline before passing them to the next level. There seemed to be an assumption, noted Areopogus that most would leave the Service within a few years anyway, and thus no deeper investment was required.

Down at Dartmouth the Training Commander (R St J S Bishop) was duly instructed to respond, and his 'Dartmouth the Cradle: Rock it Don't Knock it!' constituted an energetic and emphatic defence of the status quo.[25] Claiming to be delighted that Areopogus had raised the issue, Bishop skilfully conceded a number of small points, but argued resolutely that it was not the College's job to nurture and develop academic skills –

'that is not what the Fleet needs or wants.' In essence he confirmed that all BRNC could reasonably do was 'point the way' and that, for example, the current Term One Defence Studies Course (which now included just six naval history lectures all based on episodes from the Second World War) provided 'just enough' to help a young officer explain 'why we need a navy and what its role is.' Anyway surveys of trainees returning from sea had shown, claimed Bishop, that Defence Studies was 'less important' than other parts of the syllabus – although quite how three months in the Dartmouth Training Squadron imparted such wisdom was not explained. BRNC, the article concluded, could only *prepare* (underlined in the original) officers for their training and there were many later opportunities to gain an appreciation of history and strategy.[26]

These two articles represented an interesting counterpoint, not least because they didn't really disagree about the current training and education landscape or, for that matter, the place of history teaching within it. For Areopogus, the reduction of the young officer's syllabus to a series of inputs and outcomes, where only the measurable was admissible and practical utility was the ultimate consideration, was a sign of weakness. For Bishop, an advocate of the just-enough-just-in-time philosophy, whether it applied to sandwiches or students, the elimination of inputs not derived from analysis, design, and implementation was a sign of strength. While it was true that for many years at Dartmouth concepts of training and education had co-existed in a difficult and uncomfortable accommodation, by 1990, in a world where training was utterly dominated by objectives, they were viewed as almost mutually exclusive – a system centred on practical application had come to see anything requiring critical analysis as a distraction.[27] In such a world there was little place for the disciplined study of naval history and the student timetable merely reflected that fact.

For the decades straddling the millennium the subject of naval history and its place in officer education figured only sporadically in the pages of the *NR*. Rear Admiral Richard Hill, continuing the long tradition of editorial support and interest in the subject, contributed a masterly review article, reflecting ruefully that while general interest in naval and maritime history had expanded over the years it had virtually disappeared from the naval officers' training syllabi.[28] Perhaps unsurprisingly, the prospect of Trafalgar bicentenary celebrations prompted a lengthy and somewhat predictable exchange of correspondence, loosely gathered under the heading of naval history and young officers. One seagoing captain reported that his young officers' ignorance was 'breathtaking' – one was unable to name Nelson's flagship at Trafalgar, another could not cite the dates of the

First World War and a third was certain that the Spanish Armada had been destroyed in 1888. As usual and as so often over the years, the correspondence rumbled on with members variously 'shocked', 'depressed', and 'anguished' at this account – one simply refused to believe it and was convinced the captain must have been the 'victim of a wind up'! Again, as usual, there was no shortage of suggestions as to how the situation might be addressed including ship's history quizzes, wardroom discussions, young officers' breakfasts, issuing books from the ship's library, and so on. Perhaps significantly, no one was prepared to suggest that the disciplined study of naval history should become a core component in the formal training regime.

The bicentenary of the Battle of Trafalgar was marked in the November 2005 edition of the *NR* with a collection of specially written essays from several of Britain's leading naval historians – Geoffrey Till, N A M Rodger, Colin White, Eric Grove and Andrew Gordon. In the words of its promoters the official celebrations, Trafalgar 200, had set out to ensure that the legacy of the battle, the influence of Nelson and the importance of the sea would remain in the minds of a wide audience, and that the profile of the Royal Navy and its importance to the life of the nation would be suitably enhanced. In the midst of all the razzmatazz, a fleet review, a son et lumière of Southsea, drumhead ceremonies on Southsea Common and the International Festival of the Sea, the commissioning of these original papers ensured that the *NR* played a modest but characteristic part in this process. How far the popular and successful celebrations really made the general public more aware of the importance of Nelson and his achievements remained a moot point. But for those prepared to enquire within, it was found that the *NR* provided some of the gravitas and the cultural and doctrinal context to advance a genuine understanding of the great man's achievements.

For a hundred years naval history and its place in naval education have seldom been far from the minds of members of the *NR*. The former, of course, can only be properly understood in the context of the latter and over more than a century this changed considerably. Higher education for naval officers, those activities associated with various levels of staff training, for example, seems to have retained some of the characteristics of its formative period. Clearly, the style and the environment has changed greatly but the requirement for command, analytical and communication skills, and minds that were flexible and able to analyse and conceptualise in a military context, would have been recognisable even in the early days. Ironically, the demand for a wider understanding of individual component characteristics by the three Services has ensured that more naval history is being studied in the

modern joint environment than in the old days of single Service staff
training. In initial training the changes have been more drastic and
perhaps less encouraging. Reacting to significant shifts in gender, entry
age, social background and educational attainment, and sorely pressed
by reduced training times, budgetary restriction and convenient
assumptions that education could be now be left to schools and
universities, the Service has largely abdicated responsibility for any
personal development in an early career beyond that defined by the term
training. Thus naval history at Dartmouth, unable to justify its utility
in the closed vocabulary of training objectives and measurable outcomes, has generally been consigned to the metaphorical dustbin, to be
rummaged through only prior to Trafalgar Night, a VIP visit or the
departure of a divisional officer for the Staff Course.

It is clear that over the years the subject of naval education, and in
particular the value of naval history, has been a hot topic. For a long
period there was little argument about its importance, but it was
assumed, rather than intellectually determined, that new entry and mid-
career officers should be instructed in the past achievements of their
profession. While there was always a debate about what *sort* of naval
history should be taught, there was no real questioning about its general
place in the scheme of things. In later years as this assumption fell away
and the drive to make all training immediately purposeful prevailed, it
was replaced by more general concerns – about the '*uses*' of history,
about the sense that operationally as well as doctrinally not enough
attention was being paid to the past and, although this seemed to
assume some previous 'golden age', about the quality of historical
scholarship itself. As ever, the articles and correspondence columns of
the NR revealed deeply held convictions and many differing views and,
of course the extent that such musings influenced the development of
policy must remain unclear. Yet regardless of the outcome, positive or
otherwise, the preponderance of contributors to *The Naval Review*
were on watch to affirm that the face of war had not changed so rapidly
that the experience of former times can be neglected and that society is
not changing so rapidly that a hard-won reputation for professional
competence has no relevance today.

20 Law, War and the Conduct of Naval Operations

Professor Steven Haines

'THE business of the navy is war and the peculiarity of our business is that we are never at it.'[1] So states the opening sentence of the first substantive article to appear in the inaugural issue of *The Naval Review* in 1913. Captain Dewar, the then anonymous author of those words, must surely have regretted their inclusion some months later as the European powers succumbed to the first general multilateral great power war for over a century.[2] The fact that just over a year after *The Naval Review*'s first appearance, the principal powers of European civilisation would carelessly initiate what would become an extended period of seventy-five years of ideological conflict – what Niall Ferguson has termed *History's Age of Hatred* – was not to be predicted.[3]

While its opening sentence was perhaps unfortunate, the general theme of that first ever *NR* article, written as Anglo-German naval antagonism intensified, has largely stood the test of time. Its author implied that naval officers must not be wholly preoccupied with the technical detail of their daily business or allow themselves to eschew abstract thought on strategic, tactical and other vital themes. We wholeheartedly agree. The article goes on to state that 'The subjects mentioned as suitable for discussion cover an ample field, including strategy, tactics, command, staff work, operations, discipline, education and naval history.'[4]

In that otherwise fairly comprehensive list, there was no mention of the law governing naval operations. Perhaps the relevance of law was implicit in both 'strategy' and 'tactics'. Whether implicit or not, it certainly and promptly became clear that law was firmly on the membership's agenda. While the opening salvo of the journal contained no specific mention of the law, the actual experience of general great power war at sea in the months following provoked

299

strong comment on certain pre-war legal developments. Almost a hundred years later, as this chapter is being written, the Royal Navy is committed to counter-piracy operations in the Indian Ocean and Gulf of Aden. Not surprisingly, those operations and the legal issues they have generated have certainly featured in the pages of the *NR* in the run up to its centenary.[5]

It is surely right that those responsible for the conduct of operations are able to articulate their concerns about the influence of the law on their ability to deliver. The journal's first engagement with vitally important operational legal matters, almost immediately after it first appeared, is mirrored in coverage today of the demands of counter-piracy operations; the *NR* continues to provide a medium through which important legal issues can be raised. But what has happened during the intervening years? Have legal matters featured prominently throughout the one hundred volumes? How has the membership regarded the law since 1915? These are good questions and, although they can by no means be answered fully, there is an interesting story to tell about how the law has developed (or not, as the case may be) and how this has been dealt with in the pages of the journal.

The Law Framing the Conduct of Naval Operations

With what precisely are we dealing? Historically there have been two distinct bodies of law providing the principal legal framework for naval operations: the Law of the Sea, and the Laws of War at Sea.[6] They are not the same thing. Strictly speaking, the former was a part of what was traditionally described as the 'Law of Peace' while the latter was the maritime element of the 'Laws of War'. In theory the line of distinction was clearly drawn, with the Law of Peace/Law of the Sea governing the use of the oceans for peacetime activities, while the Laws of War at Sea regulated the conduct of warfare between belligerents as well as their relationships with neutral powers. Once a state of war was either declared or had broken out, the Law of Peace gave way to the Laws of War.

In practice, of course, no such theoretical distinction has ever been so clearly drawn, given the need for neutrals to conduct their dealings with each other in accordance with the Law of Peace at the same time that belligerents are applying the Laws of War, both to each other and to neutrals. Today, it is regarded widely as being more appropriate to describe both the Law of the Sea and the Laws of War at Sea as component parts of the broader body of law known as the Law of Maritime Operations.[7] Within that, the Law of the Sea and the Laws of War at Sea interact and overlap in the regulation of the complex mix of contemporary operations that range across a spectrum from benign peacetime operations, through constabulary (or law enforcement) operations, to the conduct of armed conflict at sea.

The Law of the Sea and the Laws of War at Sea have developed separately in the past and are unlikely to do otherwise in the future. In the one hundred years since the *NR*'s launch, that separate development has been quite marked and the focus of effort on the development of the two bodies of law has been far from coincident. As we shall demonstrate, there was great interest in the Laws of War at Sea from the early years of the twentieth century to the Second World War, from which point interest seemed markedly to wane. In contrast, the Law of the Sea developed hardly at all until the years after the Second World War, with the main developmental activity taking place during the 1970s and early 1980s.

Preparing the Law for War: The Hague and London Conferences

A mere six years before the journal was launched, the 1907 Hague Peace Conference had produced an important series of naval-related conventions. These dealt with such vital naval war-fighting issues as: the status of enemy merchant ships; the conversion of merchant ships to warships; the laying of automatic submarine contact mines; bombardment by naval forces; the right of capture in naval war; the establishment of an international prize court; and the rights and duties of neutral powers in naval war.[8] Two years later, in 1909, came the London Declaration Concerning the Laws of Naval War and, in the very year of the *NR*'s first appearance, 1913, the Institut de Droit International adopted the *Oxford Manual of Naval War*.[9]

Legal developments negotiated in The Hague and in both Paris and London were by no means uncontroversial. The 1909 Declaration of London represented a British Government attempt to establish rules to be applied by the International Prize Court proposed in 1907 Hague Convention XII, and to clarify aspects of the rights and duties of neutrals contained in 1907 Hague Convention XIII.

The rules relating to neutral versus belligerent rights in economic warfare terms was reflective of the contrast between Britain's recent trading experience and more traditional naval opinion. To quote one commentary that appeared after the Great War:

> The long period of peace at sea enjoyed by Great Britain had developed intensely this commercial view of sea-borne trade, and some of the incidents of the Russo-Japanese War (1904–5), in which British ships were seized or destroyed by a belligerent, caused a rude

shock. In consequence, at the Hague Peace Conference of 1907 and at the London Conference of 1909 the British Government's instructions to its delegates reflected the neutral commercial view more strongly than that of a belligerent naval view.[10]

The long experience of Pax Britannica, during which the British Empire controlled most maritime trading routes, had caused a shift in opinion within Britain from the requirements of naval war-fighting towards the commercial desire for the free movement of goods. This affected policy and diplomacy. British delegations to The Hague and London conferences reached agreements with other major maritime powers that reflected the commercial bias. Subsequently, though, the Government found it impossible to ratify these:

> The Declaration came under the consideration of Parliament in 1910 when a Naval Prize Bill was introduced ... to which had been added provisions to give statutory approval to the 12th Hague Convention, ie, to the establishment of an International Prize Court and the British share of expenses therein. The House of Commons by passing this Bill signified approval to the Declaration of London but the Bill was thrown out by the House of Lords, largely owing to the adverse criticisms promulgated by Mr Gibson Bowles. Neither the 12th Hague Convention nor the Declaration of London was, therefore, ratified by Great Britain.[11]

Commercially minded members of the House of Commons were easily whipped into support for the Liberal government's position; more Conservative and independently minded peers were not. The Admiralty was convinced of the need to pursue a policy of 'capture at sea'[12] and naval lobbying convinced Peers that the 1909 Declaration imposed unacceptable restrictions on both Britain's right to determine what was and what was not contraband and the Royal Navy's ability to impose an effective blockade. Despite this, on the outbreak of war in 1914 Asquith's Liberal Government went ahead and adopted the 1909 Declaration.

This intense focus on the Laws of War at Sea in the first decade or so of the twentieth century was prompted by increasing fear that general war may well break out and the belief that it would be sensible to reach agreement about how that war would be conducted at sea before hostilities commenced. All the conventions agreed in The Hague were effectively 'tested' between 1914 and 1918 during the first general and sustained naval war for over a century. This Great War also provided evidence of state practice, including in one particular sense that caused considerable concern – the use of submarines, especially for *guerre de course* (the interdiction of merchant shipping on the high seas).

The First World War

The first shot in the naval war between Britain and Germany was fired on 5 August 1914 off Harwich by the British destroyer HMS *Lance* against the German minelayer *Königin Luise*; the latter was sunk.[13] There were to be several skirmishes of this sort but no major naval action during the first weeks of the war. By February 1915, however, the gloves had come off and Germany's U-boats were preparing for unrestricted attacks on merchant shipping in the seas around the British Isles.[14] It had taken a few days less than seven months of war for laws endorsed merely seven years before to be consigned to the waste bin in Berlin.

   If the outbreak of hostilities in 1914 initiated a test of what had been agreed in The Hague in 1907, then the law did not stand up well. As Admiral Sir Herbert Richmond reflected long after the war was over, in 1929:

> International agreements ... were made in plenty at The Hague in 1907. Neutral territory was not to be violated, hospital ships to be immune, mines were to be laid only under defined conditions and in defined places, prisoners of war were to receive proper treatment, open towns were not to be bombarded, merchant ships were to be treated in an agreed manner. Every one of these was broken by Germany without a protest from any neutral power except in cases where their own interests were involved: and the breach, in some cases, notably the invasion of Belgium and the mining of commercial ports, was not even made under the stress of impending defeat but was planned in the cool atmosphere preceding the war.[15]

Similar views had emerged when the war was in its early stages. In August 1915, the *NR* contained a passionate critique of legal restraints on sea power. The anonymous author, Commander Plunkett, entitled his piece 'Sea-Power or Sea-Lawyers?' He made it very clear from the outset what his answer to that question would be.[16] Plunkett regarded the London Declaration, the output of The Hague conferences, and even the 1856 Paris Declaration[17] as anathema:

> Each [document] adds further to the long list of lawyer's parchments which no one, not even England, will really be bound by when vital interests are at stake, though England would very possibly handicap herself by being the last country to depart from them. Each one definitely puts a premium on national dishonesty, by offering great advantages to that Power which first breaks the law or bribes a

neutral to do so in her interests. Each one adds more to the
perplexities of the Naval Officer and the juggling powers of
International lawyers. And each one, in its construction affords
golden opportunities for the representatives of one Power to fool
and hoodwink those of the others.[18]

There was immediate support for this strongly worded assault on both
the law and the lawyers responsible for it in a paper submitted to the
editor before the end of 1915. Its author firmly endorsed its
predecessor's critical tone and asserted that 'the Declaration of London
and its earlier prototype the Declaration of Paris are dishonoured and
unsung'.[19] The decision by the government on the outbreak of war to
adopt the 1909 Declaration, and its negative effects at sea, prompted
the critical articles submitted to the NR in 1915.

While the law seemed to be attracting negative comment, we can be
more positive about the role of the NR: the journal was doing precisely
what it was intended to do – providing a medium for the articulation
of informed professional naval opinion on matters of crucial importance to the Service. Those first two legal articles could also be viewed
as representing not so much an attack on the law in general but an
operational critique of certain legal proposals that had seemingly
ignored some vital practical consequences for the British Empire.
Indeed, there was strongly implied support for the law as it had existed
prior to those changes negotiated in The Hague and in London – and
in Paris over half a century before. Evidence for this emerged in the
government's reaction.

By May 1915, Asquith had been forced to take Conservatives into a
coalition government. The combination of the realities of economic war
at sea and this effective change of government led to Britain
withdrawing its support for the 1909 Declaration. The explanation
given was that: 'the rules laid down in the Declaration could not stand
the strain imposed by the test of rapidly changing conditions and
tendencies which could not have been foreseen.' It went on to state that
Britain was returning to 'the historic and admitted rules of the Law of
Nations.'[20]

While there is certainly no evidence that the two articles submitted in
1915 to the NR were influential in relation to this 1916 shift in policy
(the second was not even published until 1919), they do serve as useful
indicators of naval opinion at the time – opinion that was eventually
influential at the highest level. Law was not to be dismissed in 1915 but
it had to be the right law and it needed to be related to both strategic
objectives and operational realities.

Although the difficulties the RN was experiencing with the generality of economic warfare at sea were thereby resolved, in one specific area it continued to prove problematic: the regulation of submarine warfare, notably that of an unrestricted nature.[21]

In February 1915, Germany declared the waters around the British Isles a war zone within which all merchant ships would be destroyed with no guarantee as to the safety of crews or passengers. German resort to unrestricted submarine warfare clearly breached the customary law on the targeting of merchant vessels. While restrictions were reimposed by Berlin later that year, they were again lifted in the aftermath of Jutland, with a clear return to unrestricted submarine attacks on merchant traffic from 1 February 1917.[22] The fact of unrestricted submarine warfare certainly raised questions as to the legality of the German use of this method of warfare. Was it regulated by existing rules restricting the actions of surface warships, or were submarines so fundamentally different that new rules would be required, informed by practice during the war then being fought? This question was not resolved to any degree, however, until after the war was over.

Before we move on to the interwar years, it is well worth reflecting on one view expressed during those years about the state of the law during the war by then over. While Admiral Richmond may well have reflected negatively about the law, its influence and its enduring relevance, Paymaster Captain Manisty had something slightly more positive to say:

> the law of nations is not reduced to nullity by being sometimes broken, any more than the law of the land becomes a mere dream because many habitual criminals disregard it with impunity every day. The rule of force, and force alone, is a sign of barbarism all the world over. The more backward the community the less does it observe any command which cannot be driven home at the moment by sinews or weapons. Rear Admiral S S Hall, CB (who was Commodore of British Submarines during the Great War), stated in October, 1919, in a paper on Submarine Warfare, 'I would like to outline briefly the general features of the German submarine campaign, in order to show how it failed and why it failed, and in the end provided perhaps the finest vindication of International Law in history'.[23]

The Interwar Years

Wartime compliance with the law was of serious concern and generated a good deal of post-war debate, some of which was mirrored in the pages of the *NR*. In the interwar years, the journal contained several informed contributions, including two substantial collections. Between 1926 and 1928 a series of six articles over as many issues, totalling 150 printed pages, on the subject of international law were submitted by Paymaster Captain Manisty. This was effectively a serialised textbook on law as it affected naval operations.[24] The year immediately after this series completed, a special issue was devoted to a debate on the 'freedom of the seas'.[25]

In addition to these 'collections', several individual articles with a legal theme appeared through the years between the First and Second World Wars. The first of those wars remained a relatively recent experience. As the years passed, however, thoughts were increasingly turning to the possibilities of another general great power war in Europe, one likely to result in extensive and sustained naval action. As a precursor, the Spanish Civil War generated legal issues and a set of naval arrangements (the 1937 Nyon Arrangements) for dealing with non-intervention, unattributable and unrestricted submarine activity, and the maintenance of vital sea lanes in the Mediterranean.

Subjects addressed in the journal included general disarmament at sea, chemical warfare, the regulation of bombardment, the arming of merchantmen, the legality of naval actions during civil wars, the 1930 London Treaty, the 1936 Montreux Straits Convention, the 1936 London Naval Conference, and aerial warfare.[26] There was clearly solid interest in the Laws of War at Sea, with plenty of views expressed about their value in relation to the actual conduct of operations.

Interestingly, however, the bulk of articles dealing with aspects of economic warfare at sea concentrated on the generality of that subject rather than on the specifics of the notably controversial unrestricted use of submarines. This must be regarded as a little surprising.

One of the principal international concerns, following the Paris Peace Conference, was with naval armaments in general and the potential for a naval arms race in particular. The major naval powers met at the Washington Naval Conference between November 1921 and February 1922 to address these issues. Much was discussed and agreed and several treaties negotiated.[27]

Britain argued for a total ban on submarines, possibly only as a bargaining chip against France, and this was opposed, principally by France. Absent a complete ban, a separate treaty was agreed that constrained the use of submarines in operations against merchant traffic. Articles 1 to 4 of the 1922 Washington Treaty Relating to the Use of Submarines and Noxious Gases in Warfare represented an attempt to reaffirm the long-established customary principles forbidding the sinking of enemy or neutral merchant shipping on sight and requiring the crews of ships being legitimately destroyed at sea to be placed in safety.[28]

The four articles stressed that submarine commanders were to conduct warfare according to the same rules as commanders of surface warships. While the Washington Treaty never entered into force (the French withheld ratification), the rules contained therein were substantially adopted at the London Naval Conference in 1930 and subsequently included in the 1936 London Protocol.[29] By the outbreak of war in 1939 there were forty-nine parties to the London Protocol, including all the major naval powers: the UK, the US, the USSR, Germany, Italy, France and Japan.[30]

The absence of a significant debate in the *NR* about the legitimacy of submarine warfare is difficult to explain. One would have thought that some members would have become engaged, in particular one or two of those belonging to the submariner community. What did attract some attention was the generality of economic warfare – and the vexed issue of the 'freedom of the sea', a variation on the pre-First World War debate between traditional naval and commercial interests.

In the context of the Paris Peace Conference, the second of President Woodrow Wilson's famous Fourteen Points was: 'Absolute freedom of navigation upon the seas, outside territorial waters, alike in peace and in war, except as the seas may be closed in whole or in part by international action for the enforcement of international covenants.'[31] It is worth teasing out what this meant and how it was dealt with after the Peace Conference. As remarked upon already, the editor of the *NR* decided to devote an entire issue to the topic a full decade after the conference.

There was a clear strand of international political idealism in evidence following the Great War. Another of the Fourteen Points – the fourth – provided for 'Adequate guarantees (to be) given and taken that national armaments will be reduced to the lowest point consistent with domestic safety.' Disarmament was seen as a way towards eliminating the scourge of war: rid the world of the weapons to fight aggressive war and there will be none. The first substantial attempt at disarmament came at the Washington Conference. It was generally successful, and it is positively regarded today, despite a great deal of criticism in between times.[32] That criticism came principally because the process of disarmament did not progress beyond the conference. One proposal to encourage it was to lay stress on the Freedom of the Seas.

Colonel Edward House, confidant of President Wilson, championed this in an article published in the special issue of the *NR*. He remarked that:

a way to peace might be found through a revision of the sea laws which would permit merchantmen, be they neutral or belligerent to sail the seas in war-time as in time of peace undisturbed by seizure or search ... a combination of the proposals made by the British and American Governments at the Hague Conference in 1907.[33]

Rear Admiral J D Allen, who provided a preface to Colonel House's paper, asserted that:

If we can only bring about a revision of the laws relating to the seas, laws which can be agreed to by all the maritime Powers, that will be a very great advance towards the prevention of war. Then it will be possible to make better progress towards a reduction in armaments.[34]

Essentially, if economic warfare at sea and the methods used to conduct it (*guerre de course* and belligerent blockade) were banned, the wartime role of navies would be much reduced and substantial naval disarmament would be possible. The argument was further refined following the coming into force of the 1928 Kellogg-Briand Pact which sought to outlaw war.[35] In an extract from a *Times Literary Supplement* book review reprinted in the *NR*, the reviewer noted that:

[the author] maintains that the renunciation of war as an instrument of policy involves a reformulation of the doctrine of the freedom of the seas in terms suitable to our own day. He points out that certain British politicians and publicists have declared in favour of the reversal of the entire history of British naval strategy, and while fully recognising the reasons for this strategy in the past and the peculiar position of Great Britain as an island Power with an Empire scattered over the seven seas, he holds that the elimination of the right of 'private'[36] war has made it safe for her to renounce those belligerent rights at sea which in the past have strained her relations with the United States to breaking point.[37]

Idealism and the genuine desire to end war are admirable qualities. Even if naval officers possess a streak of idealism (which thankfully, many do), this is usually tempered by sound common sense born of realism. Such was reflected in the contribution made by Captain Alfred Dewar to the 1929 special issue, in which he dealt with the subject of blockade. As he noted:

Another suggestion is that the weapon of blockade shall be used only in a League of Nations war and a League of Nations war is termed a 'public' war while the Great War and other wars are merely 'private' wars. This is a bastard and absurd phraseology. The League has never waged a war and has no organisation for war. A League war is a purely hypothetical conception.

In what in 1929 was a rare footnote, Dewar remarked:

> those who use (them) ... will find a correct definition of 'public' and 'private' war ... (if they) ... consult Wheaton, Pearce Higgins and a score of other jurists of every nation, who use the words 'public' and 'private' in their correct sense. It is really a specimen of cheap cunning in the use of terms, by which some members of the League of Nations Union try to push half baked views.[38]

There has never been any convincing evidence that war as a general phenomenon can simply be eliminated through an international treaty. As we now well know, neither the League of Nations Covenant nor the Kellogg-Briand Pact stood the test of time; they certainly did not prevent the second major conflagration of the twentieth century.

The Second World War

During the Second World War there was no departure from the existing law sufficient to suggest a general change in state practice capable of establishing new customary norms or requiring a substantial amendment to conventional law. That is not to say there were no breaches in the law; there emphatically were. While Captain Langsdorff of the *Graf Spee* complied faithfully with the law on *guerre de course* between September and December 1939, on 17 February 1940 Churchill authorised a breach of Norwegian neutrality for Captain Vian in HMS *Cossack* to intercept the *Graf Spee*'s tender, the *Altmark*, as it lay in Jössingfjord in Norwegian territorial waters on its way to its base port in Germany.[39]

The most noteworthy breaches of the law, however, concerned – once again – the use of submarines against merchant shipping. The early decision by the German High Command to order its U-boat commanders to commence unannounced attacks on merchant vessels, in late November or early December 1939, most certainly breached the 1936 Protocol and the customary rules it had codified.[40] Ultimately, while the International Military Tribunal at Nuremberg held Admirals Raeder and Dönitz responsible for the violation, it did not pronounce them guilty of a war crime. Their principal defence was that they had issued the order by way of reprisal. It was, of course, also the case that both the UK and the US had similarly breached the Protocol; if Raeder and Dönitz had been convicted it would have raised serious questions, in particular about the conduct of Admiral Nimitz, the US Pacific Fleet commander. Realising this, Dönitz's defence counsel skilfully argued that the British and American authorisation of unrestricted submarine warfare clearly suggested that the customary law relating to attacks on merchant shipping had actually shifted – in which case neither Admiral Nimitz nor his own client, Admiral Dönitz, could be judged to have breached the law.[41]

Despite the renewal of controversy over the legality of submarine operations and legally interesting events such as the cruise of the *Graf Spee*, the Battle of the River Plate and the *Altmark* incident, during the war only three articles appeared with an operational legal flavour. One was an historical piece on the arming of merchant vessels.[42] The second dealt with an unrealised proposal for a 300-mile neutral zone around the American continent.[43] The third was a straightforward account of the international law relating to mines.[44] The membership of the journal during the Second World War appears to have been insufficiently concerned with the legal framework for operations to submit legal articles for publication. One can only assume that the pre-war debates about economic warfare at sea and submarine operations had been satisfactorily resolved. The law itself seems to have provoked little controversy, even if breaches of it occurred. Or perhaps the comment made to the author of a review, published in 1943, of Pearce and Colombos's classic text on *The International Law of the Sea* is the reason: 'Why on earth read that nonsense now ...? It is simply a set of copybook maxims that nobody pays the slightest attention to in these days [of war].'[45]

Post-War Developments 1945–1970

The only post-Second World War treaty with a principal focus on warfare at sea is the 1949 Geneva Convention II. This important convention is not about the actual conduct of hostilities but about the protection and humanitarian treatment of war's victims. Remarkably, when it comes to the regulation of combat at sea, there has been no formal development of the conventional Laws of War at Sea for almost eighty years.

This might be regarded as surprising, given the evidence of state practice and lessons learned during the Second World War, coupled with both technical and tactical developments since. Missile technology, for example, is a post-war phenomenon and other developments to do with sensors have increased tactical distance markedly since 1945, with consequences for remote targeting. Politico-legal factors that might have resulted in the development of the conventional Law of War at Sea include the coming into force of the UN Charter and the process of review and development of the Law of the Sea, which commenced formally in 1958 with the First UN Conference on the Law of the Sea (UNCLOS I).[46]

Despite the trial of Admiral Dönitz at Nuremberg, raising the issue of the legality of unrestricted submarine warfare, and the beginnings of a significant shift towards extensions of coastal state jurisdiction at UNCLOS I, between 1945 and 1970 there was just one article published in the NR about the Laws of War (a polemical assault on the principle that illegal superior orders should not be obeyed), and nothing about the Law of the Sea![47] The quarter of a century following the Second World War was a barren time indeed for the law in the NR.

It is difficult to explain why this should have been necessarily so. Apart from the beginnings of the UNCLOS process (of which more below), there was no absence of war and there was also the beginning of the development of constabulary operations. Suez in 1956, the US (and Australian) involvement in Vietnam which had interesting legal dimensions, the Six Day War in 1968 and the mounting of the first ever UN mandated economic embargo operation off Mozambique (Beira Patrol) by the RN from the mid 1960s; none prompted legal comment (indeed, any comment) in the pages of the NR. It is perhaps sufficient merely to express surprise.

The UNCLOS Era

As already related, the focus in the earlier periods of the NR's publication was on the Laws of War at Sea. These have not prompted substantial comment since 1945, let alone since 1970. These have not been subject to any formal review, which might explain this. The negotiation of the two 1977 Protocols Additional to the 1949 Geneva Conventions were generally focused on land warfare. No developments in naval weapons technology have attracted regulation. There has also been little in the way of state practice to inform the development of customary law. Unfortunately for the development of the law – but fortunately in every other sense – there have been very few conflicts involving general naval war since 1945, and certainly none in which economic warfare at sea became a significant method of warfare, something that prompted the present author to comment as follows in 2011:

> While the Graf Spee's operations in 1939 may have been legally acceptable and understood at the time, it is difficult to imagine them being regarded as uncontroversial in that sense today. It is arguably inconceivable that a warship patrolling the high seas, seeking out and deliberately sinking merchant ships in that manner, would now

be considered generally to be engaged in acceptable behaviour. Times
have changed and attitudes have done so as well.[48]

The naval dimensions of wars have been largely restricted to sea control
operations against other maritime forces and power projection
operations in support of principally land or air campaigns. For the RN,
of course, the 1982 Falklands War stands out.[49] Indeed, it is arguably
the only substantial and sustained naval war, in the generally
understood sense (if a few weeks can be regarded as 'sustained'), to
have been conducted since 1945. There have been other conflicts with
a notable maritime dimension since 1970, including the Indo-Pakistan
War of 1971, the Battle of the Paracels between the Chinese and
Vietnamese Navies in 1974, the Iran-Iraq War of 1980–88 (which
included significant attacks on neutral shipping), and the two Gulf Wars
of 1991 and 2003. Nevertheless, the Laws of War at Sea have simply
not attracted general attention or prompted development.[50]

Despite the absence of developments in both the conventional and
customary Laws of War at Sea, there has been one significant initiative
worth noting. In 1987, the International Institute of Humanitarian Law
in San Remo, Italy initiated a series of meetings of international lawyers
and naval experts to assess the need for a modernisation of the law
applicable to armed conflict at sea. Eight years later the results were
published as the *San Remo Manual*.[51] Important though this is, it is not
an authoritative statement of the law; it is neither a treaty nor strictly
a codification of existing law. Nevertheless, it is an important
document. It was, for example, used as the basis of the 'Maritime
Warfare' chapter in the UK's own *Manual of the Law of Armed Conflict*
published in 2004.[52] Despite the manual's significance, no article on this
subject was published in the *NR* following its publication; it seems to
have gone unnoticed, perhaps because legally aware members were by
1995 preoccupied with the Law of the Sea rather than the Laws of War
at Sea.

From the early 1970s to the early 1980s, the Law of the Sea underwent a radical review leading to the 1982 United Nations Convention
on the Law of the Sea (1982 UNCLOS). There have been two
operationally important features of the resultant legal regime. First, the
convention ushered in substantial extensions and enhancements in
coastal state jurisdiction. Second, the 'package deal' at the heart of the
convention balanced the extension of jurisdiction with the protection of
navigational freedoms, allowing for the free movement of shipping
(both merchant ships and warships) through areas of the oceans
previously part of the high seas. From the coverage given to UNCLOS

related issues in the journal, the most significant development for members was that dealing with the development of the 'offshore estate' (principally to do with the newly defined 200 nautical mile Exclusive Economic Zone) which created new roles for navies. These were mainly of a constabulary nature to do with the maintenance of good order at sea within coastal states' maritime domains. The potentially wide ranging tasks associated with this were first referred to in a perceptive article in the journal, published in 1974, as the 'Offshore Tapestry'.[53] From that point on, the principal focus of articles in the NR dealing with the legal dimension of maritime operations was about coastal and offshore policing and the forces necessary to conduct it.

In 1976 there was a brief but notable 'exchange' on the Law of the Sea, between a pseudonymous author ('IL') and one 'JRH' (the NR's subsequent editor, Captain Richard Hill). The former saw sense in coastal states extending jurisdiction, into what he termed a 'patrimonial sea':

> it would lie in the UK's and the West's interests to have a 200 mile patrimonial sea which would greatly deny the seas to the Eastern bloc countries. With the Third World so strongly in favour, I believe this will eventually happen. With the West's support, it would come about much quicker and I believe bring greater benefits to the Free World.

JRH was somewhat less enthusiastic, seeing such patrimonial seas as motivated by extremes of nationalist opinion:

> There were chances a few years ago, of true international co-operation growing at sea ... with the recent access of nationalism these hopes have faded. We will do well to keep them alive, for excessive nationalism will lead only to conflict.[54]

The latter's position more closely reflected the outcome of UNCLOS III. Between these two contributions was another piece dealing with patrol tasks in expanded British waters.[55] Following that, a speech by then First Sea Lord, Admiral Sir Edward Ashmore, delivered at the US Naval War College in 1976 was published.[56] Clearly the subject was attracting serious comment by significant members of the NR's membership and it is encouraging indeed that the then First Sea Lord himself was not only clearly interested and concerned about the consequences of legal developments but was also keen to use the NR as a vehicle for articulating his views.

These interventions came just before the establishment of the UK's Extended Fisheries Zone on 1 January 1977. They were written with the recent 'Cod War' against Iceland as a backdrop. Britain effectively lost that so-called war because pressure to establish coastal state regulation of fisheries on the relatively shallow waters of the continental shelf was becoming irresistible. The 'offshore tapestry' became a reality for the UK that January. Nevertheless, from that point on, the debate seemed to wane. The extension of coastal state jurisdiction was a reality and, although 1982 UNCLOS was not opened for signature until late 1982, the inevitable had already become obvious through the various iterations of the conference negotiating texts.

Somewhat paradoxically, immediately following the end of the Cold War attention turned briefly to the ways in which the Law of the Sea was affecting traditional naval mobility. Two articles addressed this in successive issues in 1991, since when coverage has been slight.[57] As the 1990s progressed, it became increasingly clear that 1982 UNCLOS had established a relatively stable regime for the oceans, with little call internationally for further significant change. Arguably, the membership's lack of engagement serves to confirm this.

Admiral Sir Ian Forbes, Chairman of the Trustees as the NR reaches its centenary, commented in 2010 on the extent to which the law had become a progressively more powerful influence on the conduct of operations during his own four decades of service.[58] He contrasted the late 1960s and early 1970s (during which the law was not an especially prominent consideration for those operating at sea in peacetime) with the 1990s and beyond, by which time seagoing commanders often needed (and also received) immediate legal advice from experienced specialist operational lawyers deployed on their staffs. By 2012, it was not the Laws of War at Sea that were important so much as the much broader Law of Maritime Operations, a significant element of which is the Law of the Sea that developed apace during Admiral Forbes's career.

One element of that broader body of law deals with the maintenance of good order on the high seas. It includes the law relating to piracy. As this chapter is being written, the RN is committed to counter-piracy operations in the Indian Ocean and Gulf of Aden. Piracy was once rewarded with brutal summary justice executed by deployed and independent naval commanders. In contrast, the law to be applied today can appear to confound rather than facilitate an effective response. Off Somalia, for example, the NATO rules of engagement for counter-piracy operations, influenced by such considerations as the constantly developing jurisprudence of the European Court of Human Rights, certainly restrict commanders' options. As the Chief of Staff of the NATO counter-piracy Task Force 508 noted in the NR in May 2011:

you have some pretty tight Rules of Engagement (ROE) imposed ... for the right reasons of course, but all quite limiting. Mother ships can't be disabled ... if there is any danger that hostages might be harmed; and that can never be guaranteed. If you want to disable a skiff tied to a dhow, you have to drag it away first. And all of this, generally, has to be done with warnings and minimum force.[59]

The legal constraints on the application of force today are greater than they have ever been. Perhaps it is the fact that this chapter's present author is himself a lawyer that he senses the membership does not give quite as much attention to this as they might.

Conclusions

So, what might we conclude about *The Naval Review* and the law? To start with, the subject has by no means dominated the agenda. It reared its head at the outbreak of the First World War and prompted debate during the years immediately following its conclusion. From the 1930s onwards, however, the Laws of War at Sea seem to have attracted almost no interest, with few articles devoted to the subject through to the present day. Following an almost complete lack of publishable interest in the 1940, 1950s and 1960s, the UNCLOS process began to generate opinion once the Third Conference got underway in the early 1970s. A flurry of interest as that conference proceeded, another as the 'offshore tapestry' was established, and a brief dip into aspects of traditional naval mobility as the Cold War ended.

Should we be concerned about the apparent lack of legal coverage? Perhaps surprisingly, this author thinks not. The pattern of articles and the subjects covered do reflect the pattern of developments in the law. The articles published also seem to have covered the most important themes that defined the wider debate about the law at the times they were published. Most naval officers are not lawyers, even if professionally they may have a more than passing interest in the law's content and effect. Those that have commented include amongst their number some who are lawyers and some, like our distinguished former editor, Rear Admiral J R Hill, who understand it as well as those who are. In the sense that *The Naval Review* also serves an important purpose in informing its membership, one concludes that the journal and its contributing membership have done their duty – no more but certainly no less.

21 The Development of British Naval Thinking

Professor Geoffrey Till

O N occasional display at Tate Britain, there is a monumental, life-size sculpture by the society artist, Sir William Reynolds-Stevens, called *A Royal Game*. Produced in 1906 and bought for the gallery by the Chantry Bequest in 1911, it shows a naval chess game between Queen Elizabeth I and King Philip II of Spain. The Queen knows exactly what she's doing; she sits tall, imperious, proud, and even haughty, a galleon in her hand as, below her, an anguished Philip crouches over the chessboard desperately seeking an escape from imminent defeat. Sir William's message of 1906 was crystal clear. The absolute superiority of the Royal Navy, its ships, its ideas and its strategy, over all comers – Germany included – was the country's ultimate safeguard. Naval arms race or not, Britons could rest assured; they and their interests were safe.

The founders of *The Naval Review*, however, were not so sure that any of this was true. They worried about the paucity of *modern* strategic naval thinking and its consequences for the structure of the fleet and the conduct of future operations. There was, they thought, a clear need to develop the higher side of the profession, to sift theory, to debate tactics, strategy and history and to explore the sublime aspects of war, which they thought had been sadly neglected in the nineteenth century.[1] The first editor, Admiral Henderson, had an uneasy suspicion that foreigners might be doing it better and that in consequence the crouching Philip IIs of the future could in fact be developing cunning and hidden plans to confound the complacent British. They inveighed, in particular, against what Henderson called 'the cult of the practical', the obsession with the material means rather than the strategic purpose of naval operations. 'In tactics, strategy and history', wrote Henderson, 'The cult of the practical has been characteristically sterile.'[2]

316

The Aim of the Exercise

Accordingly, the long-term aim of the *NR* was to develop British naval thinking for it 'is only when sound theory has full sway that the utmost useful developments of practice can be expected. Theory and practice are complementary, the one without the other must be ill-balanced.'[3]

The problem was, the founding fathers of the *NR* thought, that the British were a profoundly pragmatic people with a demonstrable capacity to respond effectively to the consistently unexpected, and so were apt to rest on the laurels of ultimately successful extemporisation. Commander Plunkett recalled that he had gone to one of London's leading reference libraries and found only five books on naval strategy, none of them by a Briton. 'I think', he concluded, 'that we must admit that Army Officers take these questions of theoretical education more seriously than we do.' He added, 'Until the Navy can evolve a "school of thought" based on very careful training and study, it will never be able to enjoy continuity of policy or unanimity of opinion [on the principles of war]. Moreover the authorities at headquarters, and flag officers afloat, will never be able to inspire the full confidence of their subordinates.'[4]

It was, moreover, particularly important that junior officers understood the principles too. One day they would be 'authorities at headquarters and flag officers afloat' and in the meantime they needed to understand the bigger picture. 'Modern war', commented Major Halliday in 1914, 'calls for an intelligent use of initiative by subordinates, and it is certain that the subordinate who most clearly grasps the broad situation will solve the local situation most intelligently.'[5]

The Plan of Campaign

The editor was sure that it was through the processing of previous experience, naval history in other words, that enlightenment would come. Contributors therefore focused their gaze on the richest source of such experience, not Sir William Reynolds-Stevens' Armada period, but the golden age of British sail in the eighteenth century and what they confusingly tended to call 'the Great War' – the wars between Britain and France between 1783 and 1815.

In the second edition of the *NR* Captain Harding kicked this process off with an exploration of fire control, concentration, morale and manoeuvring tactics in the battle of Trafalgar and their significance for the early twentieth century:

> In studying the evolution of naval tactics during the eighteenth century, it is exceedingly interesting to notice that the necessity for methods of concentration of force was the commonplace of tactical

thought to a degree quite comparable with and, in many respects, similar to corresponding modern ideas. What ought to be done, what promised great advantage or heavy risk was as clear then as today. But the basis of the theories was essentially geometrical, and, then, as now, the parries were obvious, and when necessary were successfully executed in practice. The practical problem was not what to do but how to do it. In applying the results of history to modern practice, the differences between past and present conditions are the factors of major importance in reaching a right conclusion. There is little doubt that steam and modern construction have rendered far easier the concerted movements of fleets. It seems probable that the differences in the standard of execution will be less than in the days of sails. The counter manoeuvre is easier than ever.[6]

Whatever we might make of this particular conclusion, the intelligent study of the history of the Royal Navy (including both its similarities and its differences with the early twentieth century), together with the recent experience of other navies and the views of British and foreign strategists, was seen as the antidote to an undue preoccupation on the development of the technological means at the expense of proper consideration of the tactical, operational and strategic ends.

Early Days

What could be reasonably called strategic thinking appears in the pages of *The Naval Review* in a wide variety of guises. Some articles, and indeed sequences of articles through several issues, deal with the subject directly and rely heavily on the processing of the history of the sailing era; in many, and often the most stimulating, cases it appears as occasional paragraphs and working assumptions in articles apparently addressing such other issues as command style, training and education, the idea of building a canal from the Forth to the Clyde, the nature of orders and instructions and so on. It appears also in the gradually increasing tendency to review relevant articles and books.

In the period up to and including the First World War, two major if interconnected themes emerged along lines which had no doubt been anticipated by the founding fathers. The first was indeed a focus on the balance of attention that should be struck between the accumulation of better material in the shape of guns, torpedoes, submarines and aircraft on the one hand and on the methods by which these could be used effectively to achieve the aims of policy on the other. One correspondent seeking to address the future potential of the long-range torpedo, for example, lamented that the chief difficulty in dealing with this problem, as perhaps with all our most important war problems, is that we have no tactical or strategical doctrine. If our fleet goes out to-morrow to fight a powerful enemy we have no knowledge of what are the main principles of tactics by which our Commander-in-Chief would be guided, and our research must therefore be conducted somewhat in the dark.[7]

Instead of simply generating bigger and better fighting instruments, more attention needed to be paid to how they should be used, and with what end. Hence a strong interest was expressed in command systems, especially in the question of centralised and decentralised control,[8] and the connected issue of the extent to which the fleet should resort to divisional tactics rather than the line of battle.[9] At Trafalgar, readers were reminded, Nelson 'did not intend to work the fleet as a whole. Each divisional leader had to work his division in such a manner as would best give effect to the known intentions of the commander-in-chief.'[10] Because Nelson had done it, the inference was, every other fleet commander should at least think about following suit.

There was as much focus on a second area of concern, and this had to do even more with the ultimate purpose of naval operations, and in particular on the question of the need for battle (and therefore for offensive operations more generally) as an end it itself (the destruction of the enemy's main fleet) and as a means to an end (the ability to exploit command of the sea both in defence of one's own trade and territory and in the attack of the enemy's). The emerging consensus of the Young Turks who were the most avid supporters of the aims of the *NR* was that there was a tendency amongst the less enlightened to focus too much on battle at the expense of its ultimate purposes:

> It must be clearly understood that victories at sea, however decisive and however glorious they may be, will not of themselves *compel the nation* whose forces are defeated to make peace. If by some miracle the German *or* the Russian Navy were to-morrow obliterated from the earth, no German or Russian citizen would by that fact be one penny piece the worse off; indeed, he would be the better off, since he would be relieved of the expense of maintaining the fleet.[11]

Instead, Lieutenant Taylor went on to say, the critical issue was the Royal Navy's capacity to inflict a decisive blockade on Germany. Winning command, the implication was, did not in itself matter – but being able to go on to exploit it successfully most certainly did. In a way, this wariness about the wholehearted pursuit of decisive battle was reinforced by two further considerations. The first was the admittedly controversial notion that the advent of the submarine would make it much more difficult to win command, in the conventional sense of the word, in the North Sea anyway, and that in the meantime the Navy would need to get on with other priorities.[12] The second was an acute awareness demonstrated by some correspondents that the enemy might not be too willing to contribute to his own demise by accepting battle against the Royal Navy. Correspondents to the *Review* were notably prescient in anticipating that this would indeed be Germany's response in what they often seemed to assume would be the coming war. Thus Captain K Dewar who wrote a gold medal-winning article for the *NR*:

> Now for this imaginary campaign, we must imagine a German plan of action, and it might be assumed that her main fleet would concentrate in the Heligoland Bight refusing decisive action in the early stages of the war, while submarines and mining craft endeavoured to reduce our supremacy in larger ships. Against our trade, a systematic *guerre de course* might be executed by small squadrons, single cruisers and armed merchantmen, with occasional raids directed against the east coast.[13]

Captain Dewar concluded that the function of the Grand Fleet should be to focus on the blockade of Germany, only venturing into the southern North Sea if the prospect of an imminent German invasion made for realistic prospects of a decisive clash with the German fleet.

Once the war started, this article and others like it seemed to justify the view that

> it is interesting to observe how little comes to light that might not have been known before. There are of course the plans and tactics of the enemy, and a few points about material, but it is quite clear that intelligent study and research in peace will generally solve quite nearly enough all our most important problems. Even the enemy's plans required only imagination and a little study to reveal their main features. The same applies to his tactics.[14]

As is discussed elsewhere, the *NR*'s capacity to review the unfolding events of the First World War and indeed into the early post-war period were severely circumscribed, and the editor had to make up the pages by the inclusion of much material actually written before the war.[15]

The Interwar Period

Unsurprisingly, reviewing the lessons coming from the experience of the First World War became a major preoccupation of both the editor and his contributors, as soon as they could tackle them. A whole set of inter-related issues arose. Probably the most contentious of them all remained the balance the Navy, and especially the Grand Fleet, had struck between its various offensive and defensive functions. The extent to which the Grand Fleet pursued a decisive battle with the High Seas Fleet shaped the composition and distribution of the fleet, its manner of operations, and the Navy's readiness and capacity to do other things such as support and conduct expeditionary operations, defend British trade and blockade Germany's.

Initially, Plunkett wrote that the war at sea *was* going broadly according to plan. In October 1914 in 'With the Grand Fleet' he wrote that 'To sum up, the British navy has achieved, practically without fighting, all that a Navy has ever been expected to perform.' The country had been secured from invasion, its forces safely transported overseas, its food supplies assured, Germany's colonies were under assault and an effective blockade was in train.

> Having cleared the outer seas we work inwards towards the centre and gradually concentrate an ever-increasing force in the area where the decisive issue must eventually be settled ... [but] ... we will not easily risk battle ... We already possess everything that sea power can give ... [thanks to the Grand Fleet] ... lost to view amid the Northern mists ... silent, unsleeping, and as yet unchallenged.[16]

This almost complacent vision of the overall strategic situation in the North Sea came under increasing strain, even in the inevitably circumscribed pages of the *NR* during the war, as problems arose elsewhere. The failure of the Dardanelles campaign, the seriousness of the U-boat threat to trade and even the deficiencies in the Grand Fleet at Jutland all challenged the vision.

The pages of the *NR* saw three broad schools emerge. The first was close to the conventional wisdom, arguing that for all its faults the Admiralty's distribution of resources and effort had in the end proved successful. Another body of thought, in which Corbett figured, concluded that too much attention had been paid to the pursuit of battle and too little to the exercise of sea power through the defence of trade and the conduct of expeditions. A third school agreed that more should have been made of the actual exercise of command but argued, often stridently, that this required the speedy settlement of the situation in the North Sea through a far more aggressive and offensive pursuit of decisive battle with the German Navy, especially when it became clear that the threat of German torpedo aircraft to the free operation of the Grand Fleet was nothing like as serious as had been feared before the war.[17]

One of the most thought-provoking articles to this effect appeared in the 1917 edition of the *NR*. 'Considerations of the War with Germany' by Captain Richmond spanned both the last two schools:

> it is even possible now, after four years of war, to find people speaking of the diversion of naval strength from its 'military duties' to those of escorting merchant ships and patrolling areas, and saying that a vigorous fleet action gives 'command of the sea', even at a time when the submarine attack on trade has been endangering our very existence. It is to be hoped that this matter will be better understood in the future.

But, at the same time, Richmond went to great lengths to point out all the operational and strategic benefits that would have flowed from a more decisive action at Jutland.[18]

This particular theme ran deep into the interwar period too and became intermingled with what was essentially a long debate about the tactics employed at Jutland. Much of this was implicitly critical of Jellicoe's allegedly over-cautious approach, which some attributed to an excessive focus on technology and an absence of initiative and others to the supposedly malign influence of Corbett. This came out with particular clarity in the rather pained, perverse and patronising review of the third volume of Corbett's *Naval Operations of the War* which appeared in 1924, after the author had died. 'No review of this volume can be complete without a mention of the great loss suffered by Naval History in the passing of the writer. And yet we cannot think that the present volume will ever rank in the forefront of his works. His fame rests on securer foundations.' The problem was, Captain Dewar thought, that

> some of it is so entirely opposed to sound tradition and modern staff opinion that the Admiralty have evidently felt bound to attach a special disclaimer to the volume, stating that some of the principles advocated are directly in conflict with their views. This probably refers to the clear indications in it of the doctrine which depreciates the place of the battle in naval war – doctrine peculiarly Sir Julian Corbett's own, which he never relinquished, and which brought him into sharp conflict with the followers of Captain Mahan. It is evidently this opinion of the secondary place of the battle in war, which colours Sir Julian Corbett's view.[19]

This kind of thinking, much associated with the offensive approach adopted by Admiral Custance and his followers, was scathingly attacked by Richmond, as only he could, in the pages of the journal of the Royal United Services Institute: 'Neither skill nor talent is indicated by treating the offensive as a trump which will win every trick; in fact, its use may be merely an outward expression of an inward inability to think out a situation.[20]

But what might be termed the Jellicoe school gained paradoxical support from those who pointed out that many of the problems encountered in the conduct of expeditionary operations or the defence of trade had in any case precious little to do with the situation in the North Sea, anyway. A whole shoal of articles in the interwar period argued that the Dardanelles campaign had failed largely through muddled strategic thinking on the one hand about whether it was intended 'as a diversion which might be converted into a decisive blow which would eliminate Turkey, or as a decisive stroke from the beginning', and on the other a consequent and lamentable failing in joint thinking about how the campaign was best conducted operationally.[21]

The particular theme of producing what Corbett called a properly maritime approach so as to avoid such failures in the future became a significant focus of attention in the early post-war period. Sir Julian's own posthumous article 'United Service' in the May 1923 edition attracted much interest and was accompanied by a number of other articles, including one that won the Gold Medal for Naval History in 1922 for a review of the Navy's support for military operations on land in the Napoleonic era.[22] An impressive article on 'Joint Strategy' in 1924 extended the concept of much more inter-service integration into the air, while others argued for what we would call Joint Force Commanders in foreign stations.[23]

In rather the same vein, while it is true that a shortage in escorts caused in part by Grand Fleet priorities contributed to the difficulties in defending trade against German submarine attack, the real problem lay in the principled rejection of the notion of convoy in the age of steam that had taken place well before the First World War, a failure to accumulate the kind of data needed fully to comprehend the problem, and a huge underestimate of the German readiness to take the strategic risks associated with the conduct of unrestricted submarine warfare.[24] Many of the key issues emerged in book reviews of Admiral Jellicoe's *The Submarine Peril* and Lloyd George's war memoirs, which appeared in 1933.[25] A more decisive outcome at Jutland may not, in itself, have significantly helped resolve any of these difficulties (although the release of destroyers from the Grand Fleet would certainly have helped solve the convoy problem). Accordingly, there was less need to take risks and force the pace in the North Sea than some of Jellicoe's critics were inclined to assert. Instead, the operational deficiencies of both campaigns needed to be addressed directly, and this process began in the pages of the *NR* before the war had even ended.

Accordingly, the importance and best methods of defending trade became a major focus of interest, with Captain W H C S Thring providing a sequence of articles that demonstrated the centrality of this task in the history of the Royal Navy.[26] Despite this, Richmond wrote, 'we were found unprepared, in doctrine and in material, for the submarine campaign … We had not thought out the problem.'[27] Drawing the proper conclusions from all this for the future protection of trade became a major preoccupation in the interwar period.

But, returning to the Battle of Jutland, all three bodies of thought were inclined to agree that a number of avoidable technical and tactical deficiencies had combined to produce a less decisive result on 31 May 1916 than the nation had expected and the Navy hoped for. The question was why? Many correspondents were inclined to fall back on the criticism of the 'cult of the practical' that had inspired the founding of the *NR* in the first place. 'Materialism', the tendency to rely over-much on having bigger and better guns and ships, and implicitly to accept the deterministic impact of technology, had been a characteristic of the pre-war Navy and was widely blamed for a failure to think through the issue of how that technology should properly be used.[28] This together with a tendency to overrate the technological prowess of the adversary's torpedo craft (both submarines and destroyer flotilla) conspired to an overly cautious approach to battle, and paradoxically, some notable tactical-technical failings in the battle itself. Some, indeed, concluded that the biggest failing of materialism under Admiral Fisher was that the movement did not in the end produce even the equipment and procedures that the Grand Fleet needed.[29]

Moving into the Future

But for all the dangers of materialism, correspondents of the *NR* continued to explore the connections between technology and naval strategy. This came out in a variety of different forms; one was the exploration of the complex relationship between the Navy and its roles and the impact of air power. Articles on the future roles of air power at sea, the developing relationship between the Admiralty and the Air Ministry and the vexed issue of who should own the Fleet Air Arm became a staple of the *NR* in a manner which should finally consign the old canard about naval conservatism to the wastepaper bin. Another, much related issue was the future size and role of the capital ship, defined both as battleships and battlecruisers. This was a major focus of Admiralty policy and attracted much attention in the *NR* since its readers well understood that answers to such questions would determine the shape of naval spending in times of increasingly constrained resources for defence, Britain's approach to the ongoing naval disarmament negotiations that started in Washington after the war and dragged on into the mid 1930s, and finally, of course, the nature of British naval operations in any future war. The displacement and weaponry of the capital ship accordingly became a major focus of attention, with Admiral Richmond, one of the *NR*'s founders leading the charge for much smaller capital ships than the 35,000-ton vessels painfully achieved through the Washington and later naval arms control negotiations.[30] Some balance to all this interest in technology was provided by Admiral Custance's long, not to say interminable, series of articles that started in 1922 entitled 'A Study of War'; one of the leading lights of the so-called historical school, the admiral made sure that his successors had little excuse to claim they knew nothing of history and of the Royal Navy's continuing absolute requirement to engage in offensive operations against the enemy's main forces.[31]

Interpretations of the past inevitably affected expectations of the Royal Navy in the future. One of the most interesting themes to emerge in the interwar pages of the *NR* was a concern for Britain's ability to impose a commercial blockade with the success that most, but by no means all, correspondents thought it had during the First World War.[32] It was hard for the survivors of the gruelling First World War *not* to recognise the critical importance of the economic dimension of war. Although the issue had appeared before, it arose particularly clearly in the later 1920s when the whole issue of the 'freedom of the seas' against the historic 'right of capture' appeared as a major international issue – most obviously between Britain and the United States. The US claim that all merchant ships, neutral and belligerent 'should sail the seas in wartime as in peace, undisturbed by seizure or search' was seen to threaten the Royal Navy's capacity to impose a commercial blockade.[33] Not only would this deprive sea power of one of its most effective weapons, but the readiness of the Germans to disregard convention in 1917 by unleashing unrestricted submarine warfare suggested that any such international agreements would be impractical anyway. Thus, Admiral Sir Richard Webb, a future editor of *The Naval Review* in 1929: 'To adopt the Freedom of the Seas is for this country to renounce the power to make war, with the weight in the World which that power gives, while leaving untouched the same power in the hand of those Powers which maintain armies.'[34]

Connected with this, of course, it was clear that the defence of British trade needed to be handled better next time than it had been in the First World War, especially as it now faced new threats as well as old ones – not least from the air. The first response, after the searing experience of 1917 was convoy, of course. Given the general view that Asdic had significantly improved the technical/tactical balance between the submarine and the surface ship, it was perhaps not surprising that there were still those who pointed out that convoy was but a part of the solution to the problem. A very detailed review of independent routeing in 1934 was followed by a number of articles exploring options other than convoy, especially because of a probable shortage in the number of escorts available. Remarked one correspondent: 'there will still be those who, remaining unconvinced, will bubble with indignation that convoying is not to be universally and immediately enforced.'[35] The speech by Lord Stanley, Parliamentary Secretary to the Admiralty, when introducing the Naval Estimates in 1935 was seen to confirm the view that full convoy might prove both unnecessary and unlikely to be strategically affordable and so reignited the debate.[36] The success of convoy, in short could not be taken for granted.

Another major theme of the period was the push for a reanimation of Corbett's maritime approach in which the efforts of all three Services were to be co-ordinated and used in imaginative ways that would achieve national ends while avoiding the ghastly costs of a continental commitment. The appearance of a shoal of books in the 1930s provided an arena in which this issue could be debated in the pages of the *NR*. There was Admiral Richmond's own writing to discuss, and his reviews of other important books of the time by Basil Liddell Hart and David Lloyd George, as we have already seen.[37] The Dardanelles campaign had failed, certainly, but this was due to the manner in which it was carried out, not because of the idea behind it. 'Why! Oh why! did the Navy and the Army never attack together?' lamented the reviewer of volume II of Brigadier General Aspinall-Oglander's *Official History of the Gallipoli Campaign* in 1932. From now on, such grotesque errors must be avoided and a combined maritime strategy followed so that Britain could properly enjoy the benefits of its sea power. This Corbettian approach to an explicitly *national* strategy gained further traction as war approached.[38]

At the same time, there was also an increasingly explicit acceptance that there was much more to a proper understanding of sea power and maritime strategy than simply fighting battles with peer competitors.

One of the earliest clear-cut expressions of this appeared in a 1930 article, 'The Navy as a Police Force', which stressed the importance of showing the flag. This theme was taken up, and to some extent challenged by a thoughtful article which pointed out some of the limitations of naval strength.[39] A growing focus on the implications of international affairs for British naval policy likewise drew attention to the fact that there were 'gaps in the study of strategy' even as explored by Julian Corbett, its great master of the period, in the need to reflect on the requirements of what we would call naval diplomacy, deterrence and maritime security. 'It really should not need much arguing to show that, unless an officer has thought a great deal about the trend of international politics and the significance to be attached to their various manifestations, he cannot expect to get a quick grasp of the situation when diplomatic manoeuvring has to give way to military action.' Nelson, after all, exemplified the successful conduct of all these wider functions of sea power as much as he did prowess in battle.[40] Strategists, in short, should reflect on the implications of contemporary economics, law, imperial relations, and so forth. There was also a growing sense that it was particularly important to do this in relation to the developing situation in the Far East.

Reviewing the Review

So what are we to make of the *NR*'s attempt to raise the bar on the understanding of naval strategy in the Royal Navy up to the end of the interwar period? The first thing we must remember is that the general understanding of what strategy meant, and what it was actually about, started out in 1913 rather differently from the way in which we understand the term now. Much of this derived from the lack of a clear sense of the operational level of war. Interestingly, Captain Harding came up with a threefold division of what he called 'battle tactics': namely Grand/Major Tactics which had to do with the 'conceptions, plans and methods of execution of supreme leaders'; below this came Minor Tactics, 'the work of the subordinate leaders in the battle handling of their divisions'; and finally 'Fire Tactics ... the application to battle of weapon technique.' In his conception of grand tactics Harding was clearly groping towards our idea of the operational level; they covered, he thought, 'the vague territory between strategy and what we usually understand by tactics.'[41] Minor and fire tactics on the other hand were about the 'movement of forces and the application of force on the field of battle.'[42]

Even in the early days, some articles focused on what we would call the strategic level of war, namely the issue of how naval policy

contributed to national purposes. They included debate on how the
Dominion Navies might contribute to imperial defence and the
emerging challenges in the Pacific. What we would call the military
strategic level of war got an airing too with articles on the relative
importance of the defence of trade, and the competing advantages of
the offensive and defensive approach.[43] There was virtually nothing
on naval diplomacy, maritime security and the rest of our pre-
occupations with what is now generally, if inaccurately, known as
non-traditional security.

Before the First World War there was little on the great debate of the
balance to be struck between the continental and maritime schools, or
for that matter on the balance to be struck between defence
preparations and the health of the economy that so preoccupied the
policymakers of Britain, 'weary titan' of the time.[44] Strategy was
debated in largely military terms and in a far narrower way than we
would today. Indeed, one fairly typical definition of it argued that 'the
great aim of strategy (and tactics) is to bring the greatest possible force
to bear at the point and time where and when the main blow is to be
struck.' From the start, though, there were those arguing for a wider
conception of what strategy meant and that 'International politics
should be the peculiar study of naval officers.'[45]

Instead, there was more of a focus on the operational and, especially,
the tactical levels of war. Operational issues included debate on the role
and effectiveness of the Patrol Flotilla in the North Sea (including where
it should operate), the operational threat of the submarine, the
competing priorities of attacking transports or escorts in the defeat of
hostile invasions, the distribution of the fleet in the North Sea and so
forth. The bulk of strategic articles, though, were clearly about the last
two of Captain Harding's levels of battle tactics, a tendency which
much increased during and immediately after the First World War when
the editor was able to publish many fascinating battle narratives of the
war. These had the great advantages of topicality, human interest and
general readability which earnest, overlong and often ponderous
accounts of the lessons of previous wars did not.[46]

This tactical focus may help explain what tends to surprise modern
readers – namely the conundrum of a journal set up to encourage
strategic thinking which, especially in the early days, makes so few
references to the great masters of the time, Mahan and Corbett. Mahan
gets some attention, by no means always totally admiring. Lieutenant
Commander Dewar warned his readers in 1914 that, 'though Mahan
is illuminating as an exponent of certain principles, he must not be
regarded as an infallible authority. He never had the opportunity of

consulting the Admiralty orders and dispatches in our Record Office, and his book must be looked on as a general outline of naval history and not as an authoritative treatise.'[47]

Despite Rear Admiral Richmond's laudatory obituary in 1923 and the occasional very fair review of his ideas, Corbett sometimes often got even shorter shrift.[48] An article describing the study of naval strategy in 1909 at the War College observed that 'we have a course of lectures in Naval History and as ... a precaution against faulty academic deductions the lecturer is a civilian. Though a most able historian, his knowledge of naval warfare is necessarily so limited that he can make no attempt to dispense maxims and precepts.' Articles in 1924 and 1931 were even more scathing, as we have seen, effectively blaming Corbett for some of the naval disappointments of the First World War, particularly the alleged lack of drive in the pursuit of decisive naval battle. Bearing in mind the sheer intellectual horsepower, limpid prose, majestic breadth and powerful exposition of Corbett's very occasional appearances in *The Naval Review*, this lacuna was regrettable.[49] But at least it does demonstrate that the *NR* was a genuine organ for debate and not simply a sounding board for views that its founders would have found sympathetic.

In any case, as the interwar period continued, the broad outlines of what I have elsewhere described as the Corbett-led British School, were clearly falling into place, with a special emphasis on the need to develop the capacity for a combined/maritime strategy and a much broader appreciation of the importance of sea power in national policy.[50] The adversities of the period, economic problems and an acute shortage of defence resources, the public's longing for peace and disarmament, the promise and then the failure of the League of Nations, and the deteriorating situation in both Europe and of increasing significance for the Navy of the Far East, combined to encourage reflection on what the Navy was for and what its priorities were. Paradoxically perhaps, the Invergordon mutiny of 1931 was something of a tipping point.

'The events at Invergordon in September, politely but inadequately termed "Unrest" must give all naval officers furiously to think', wrote one correspondent. 'That our service should have done such appalling damage to our country is a bitter thought.' Another added, 'If recent articles in the *Naval Review* are taken as a guide, it would seem that the Navy is passing through a period of profound introspection ... [and] reveal something akin to disquiet.'[51] Perhaps as a result, there was increasing attention paid to the overall context in which the Royal Navy would need to operate, a point illustrated by the growing provision of book reviews, and indeed coverage of journals such as *International Affairs*.

Most of the books reviewed, though, were closely related to the naval profession. A couple of naval authors, both at the Staff College in the late 1930s, merit special attention, Commanders Russell Grenfell and John Creswell. Their books, Creswell's *Naval Warfare: An Introductory Study* and Grenfell's *The Art of the Admiral* were both very competent and warmly reviewed by Captain Bertram H Smith in 1936 and 1937, the latter, 'it is satisfactory to note, simply exudes the spirit of the offensive.' Smith went on to point out the appearance of such people and their books was 'hardly a sign of the suppression of original thought and its expression by junior ranks in the Service. It is certainly a contrast with one's own time; not that we did not think, or try to think, on strategy; but the effort to think seems nowadays a more conscious one, and the would-be thinker has at his disposal more definite guides ... to help him.'[52]

Naval strategic thinking (as we would understand the term in the early twenty-first century) was alive and well by the arrival of war in 1939. The objectives of *The Naval Review*'s founders had been realised. Bearing in mind the extent to which the more well-known of the contributors to the journal wrote their own books and articles elsewhere, participated in official policymaking and had significant roles in professional military education, it is impossible to gauge the independent impact *The Naval Review* had per se on this crucial process, but at very least it helped. And perhaps it is not too fanciful to detect in this a partial explanation of the Royal Navy's superior performance in the Second World War and indeed in facing up to the challenges of the nuclear age afterwards.

22 Facing the Realities of Medium Power, 1945–2001

Rear Admiral Richard Hill

SIR James Cable, in a memorable stricture, wrote 'Sixty articles in five consecutive issues of *The Naval Review* included precisely one devoted to naval strategy.'[1] As was quickly shown by research into this subject, his sample was not representative, but in any case the premise, inherent in the word 'devoted', was shaky. It is difficult to write an article embodying maritime strategy, particularly one addressed to practitioners, purely on that topic; inevitably human, operational and materiel aspects will be discussed, for the nature of sea power is bound up with the instruments used to exercise it.

Thus, time and again, over the fifty-five years covered by this survey, a *NR* article concluding with a recommended size and shape for the nation's maritime forces was found to begin with arguments for, or assumptions concerning, the strategy that the United Kingdom was, or was thought to be, or should be, pursuing. Many others primarily addressed the matter of strategy without much conclusion as to forces or organisation.

This did not make the job of the author of this chapter any easier. Over two hundred articles in those fifty-five years (*pace* Cable) had a strategic element of the kind described, and the ideas have been marshalled within three periods, and within each period, under six headings.

I From Empire to Nation-State, 1945–1966

Chronological Background

The Royal Navy ended the Second World War with over 850,000 personnel and a vast fleet of ships, submarines and aircraft, many of them war-worn. It had fought with conspicuous success in the Atlantic and the Narrow Seas, somewhat less decisively in the Mediterranean and with mixed fortune East of Suez. It had benefited greatly from Allied, mostly American, support. Its strategic experience during the war was based upon the maintenance of sea communications and, latterly, of massive amphibious operations; and these coloured its outlook for many years, though the Korean War (1951–53) and operations in support of the emerging Commonwealth (1960–66) placed increased emphasis on the projection of maritime power from a position unchallenged at sea. The politico-military limitations of such use were highlighted by the Suez operation of 1956.

Domestically, the national budget was incapable of supporting the scale of maritime forces to which the services had become accustomed. The Korean War gave some boost to provision, but the Sandys Review of 1957 set a downward trend that was steepened by the advent of a Labour government in 1964.

The Nature of Conflict

In the immediate aftermath of a global, and essentially maritime, war, concluded by the advent of a weapon of unprecedented destructiveness, it was understandable that early essays on the nature of future conflict should lean heavily on recent history. Thus articles in 1946 emphasised the effect of nuclear weapons – even though these tended to be regarded at first simply as more effective ways of causing devastating explosions.[2] More sophisticated views, including the notion of strategic deterrence, gathered strength as the period went on.[3]

The Korean War appears to have had surprisingly little effect on thinking. Two developments that commanded more attention were the Atlantic Alliance (the Cold War was first mentioned in 1952) and limited conflict East of Suez, in the aftermath of empire.[4]

British Interests and Resources

Throughout the period, in spite of the evidence that Britain carried less strategic weight than she had done up to the end of the Second World War, contributors to the NR generally regarded her as an independent great power, and many clearly assumed that she had resources to match appropriate aspirations. The coldest douche to such views came from the NR's most eminent member: in November 1951 Lord Chatfield wrote that Britain was 'almost bankrupt', but reiterated that 'the security of the sea is basic to all our planning.'[5]

As the late 1950s and 1960s went on, the problem of matching resources to perceived strategic needs became more prominent in NR articles. The most committed advocates of sea power – and that was the great majority of contributors – acknowledged that budgetary constraints would increasingly exert pressure on naval provision, although there were one or two hardy souls who insisted that such provision should be made 'regardless of cost'.[6] The consensus view nevertheless (and in spite of Suez, whose implications were covered in some strategic, but more tactical, depth)[7] was that Britain was to remain mistress of her strategic destiny, and that sea communications remained at the heart of the national interest.[8]

Few contributors ventured upon an analysis of Britain's economic interests. One or two noted the importance of access to Middle East oil supplies and more broadly, of sea trade, but such statements tended to be in general terms, with facts and figures lacking.[9] The preservation of the Commonwealth was regarded by some as a vital interest,[10] but the majority of contributors took the view – often unstated – that a strong Britain, with emphasis on strength at sea, would provide the backbone necessary for Commonwealth survival.[11]

Threats

In the late 1940s and 1950s, discussion of threat in the NR tended to be in material rather than strategic, and general rather than specific, terms. The existence or potential of certain systems – nuclear weapons, guided missiles, fast submarines and pattern running torpedoes – was viewed by one 1952 contributor as a theme for tactical investigation,[12] without attributing them to any particular threat navy; and when in the same year Lord Chatfield touched upon the Soviet threat, he did so in general terms and indeed as an argument for giving appropriate weight to Army and RAF claims for resources.[13] While Soviet power at sea gained increasing emphasis as the fifties and early sixties went on,[14] the impression holds that contributors regarded it during this period as a latent threat, able to make mischief by its influence on emergent nations but not dominant. Threats from other navies or naval air forces were seldom discussed in specific terms.

Alliances

It was little wonder therefore that alliances did not figure prominently in the period before 1966. The concert of nations in the Korean War appears to have been taken almost for granted – after all, it was only six years since the final coalition against the Axis powers had been under the aegis of the United Nations, and here again was the same title applied against a different adversary.

The NATO alliance, however, was a new structure and this was under early discussion. Scepticism emerged almost at once,[15] and was a recurring theme.[16] The geographical limits of NATO's area of interest, and the crudity of its earlier operational concepts, came under question and criticism. Even less credence was given to ideas of multi-manned ships, especially in the nuclear context. Nevertheless the necessity for an alliance of NATO's general character and composition, and in particular the formal engagement of the USA, appears to have been generally accepted.

There was even less reliance on the other alliances in which Britain was involved. The political inconsistencies of CENTO and SEATO were stressed by one contributor, and their operational weakness noted. The Commonwealth was regarded as a stronger support, but with diminishing emphasis as time went on.

Policies and Strategies

It is unsurprising that in the aftermath of the Second World War, defence policies advocated in the *NR* were little different from those that had carried that war to a successful conclusion, even though an enemy in the form of the Axis powers no longer existed. Thus up to and some way beyond 1950, contributors emphasised amphibious warfare and the security of sea communications,[17] in the context of an unspecified interstate war. The *tour d'horizon* so much favoured by later writers (to the extent that the term became a cliché in many strategic circles) was only occasionally apparent. By the late 1950s, however, the focus changed and became sharper; senior officers, not necessarily writing for but certainly quoted in, the *NR* emphasised the growing strength and numbers of the Soviet Navy and its capacity for sea denial, with the corollary that Western, and specifically British, maritime forces must have the capacity for sea control.[18]

However, there was little apparent desire to focus on the Soviet Navy to the exclusion of other potential opponents. 'Lampray' stated the aim of armed forces in the Cold War as 'to promote stability by creating confidence in both friendly and neutral countries', going on to advocate training and development of local forces. Increasingly, deterrence was seen as a concept operating at all levels of peace, tension and conflict, not confined to one potential opponent, and not confined to nuclear instruments. In all these areas the Navy was seen as having a vital role, and the gloom that accompanied the 1957 Sandys White Paper was lightened.[19]

Arms control, especially the control of nuclear weapons, figured in *NR* articles in this period principally through the efforts of two contributors: Admiral Sir Anthony Buzzard, and a member writing under the pseudonyms of 'Moryak' and, later, 'Willow'.[20] They expressed considerable doubt about many aspects of both tactical and strategic weapons and particularly British possession of them. They will be addressed in more detail in another chapter of this book. It is necessary simply to state here that they did form a substantial part of policy discussion, and that many other contributors, quoted above, addressed their concerns in passing – generally to support British possession of nuclear weaponry.

The Wherewithal

It is probably natural that military practitioners should be more comfortable when discussing the tools of, and organisation for, their trade than in addressing the policy and strategic aspects of it. This preference was apparent in most of the articles throughout the history of the *NR*, and was not lacking in the period considered here. However, there were clear limits, apparently largely self-imposed, to the extent of discussion. Pure technicalities had indeed been precluded from the earliest days as a matter of editorial policy,[21] but most contributors carried the limitation further, to the extent of avoiding material detail regarding specific systems or their salient characteristics, and being singularly cagey about their likely, or recommended, tactical employment.

There were reasons for this. Ingrained in most officers' minds were the necessity for confidentiality and the requirement for reticence on all operational and tactical matters. Fleet Operational and Tactical Instructions, the guiding document in this area, were classified 'Confidential' or higher, and when they were issued, so were similar NATO publications. Intelligence material generally carried an even higher classification. Members were not schooled in the art of finding an unclassified reference in the public domain, and most would have been uneasy in using one even if they found it. Thus, even though many articles concluded as their authors would have wished, with a recommended size and shape for maritime forces, they were often in general terms. This did not mean they were short of controversial ideas.

While, as already noted, atomic matters were early brought into discussion, means of combating them varied; and as notions of deterrence gained ground, so did the possibility of non-nuclear war at sea. In consequence, the provision of maritime forces for the more traditional forms of warfare was a more usual route for contributors to take. Here there were wide variations. 'Nico', writing very soon after 1945, had advocated a fleet including forty-five aircraft carriers; others, more realistically, stressed a balanced fleet, still to include aircraft carriers but comprising all arms.

Questions of balance predominated for the rest of the period. The claims of carriers and nuclear-powered submarines, guns and missiles, amphibious operations and trade protection were extensively discussed, with excursions into wilder ideas of missile-armed battleships and fighter submersibles.[22] Surprising omissions were detailed discussions of communications and action information systems. Shore bases were often mentioned as essential, in a way that now appears old-fashioned.[23] No consensus emerged, to the extent of an agreed party line, but the maintenance of a fleet developing in the way planned by the Admiralty (the department was succeeded by MoD (Navy) only in 1964) appears to have been generally endorsed.

II Finessing the Cold War, 1966–1989

Chronological Background

CVA-01, the Navy's project for a new generation of fixed-wing aircraft carriers, was cancelled by the Labour administration in February 1966. There followed a period of strategic uncertainty, in which some residue of the previous East of Suez policy remained, until January 1968 when a decisive change occurred, whereby British forces were in the future to be dedicated to, and justified by, their roles within the NATO alliance.[24] This was to be the official UK defence policy until the fall of the Berlin Wall, and the break-up of the Soviet Union in 1989.

The new policy made planning for maritime forces along accustomed lines singularly difficult. Now, if the policy was rigidly interpreted, they were to be predicated upon a single role against a single threat, within a defined geographical area, responding to a single scenario. It did not always work rigidly; the efforts of the naval staff in Whitehall saw to that, and so did events, most notably in the Falklands War of 1982.[25] Nevertheless the constraints are apparent in many of the NR articles written during this period, as are members' efforts to break through them.

The Nature of Conflict

The shift in focus for United Kingdom defence policy moved many Naval Review contributors towards an emphasis on deterrence. If, after all, the opponent was a massive military power with a growing and diverse navy, it made sense for that opponent to be convinced that war was not a rational option. Thus articles in the late 1960s and throughout the 1970s and 1980s very generally stated deterrence as a tenet.[26] There was an important gloss, however: deterrence was regarded by the great majority of contributors as an all-level affair, not at all confined to strategic nuclear systems.[27] The change in NATO strategy from Massive Retaliation to Flexible Response was generally endorsed. The corollary, that it was therefore necessary to plan for a relatively prolonged maritime campaign (because it was impossible to envisage a successful outcome to a short NATO war) was less often mentioned. The possibility of a 'totally wet war', confined to a Soviet assault on western sea lines of communication, although raised by some, was generally discounted.

At the other end of the scale of conflict, the growing importance of Britain's offshore estate, and the means of ordering and safeguarding it, received a good deal of attention.[28] Contributors generally advocated evolutionary development of the current organisation rather than radical centralisation on the US Coast Guard pattern.

An attempt was made to draw together all these strands in a major series in 1976–7, which sought to formulate a modern and generalised theory of sea power from the standpoint of a medium-sized nation-state.[29] It introduced, in particular, the concepts of levels of conflict and of reach. While not specifically directed to the British situation, it clearly had relevance to that case.

British Interests and Resources

Mention of British national interests was unfashionable in official defence circles during this period. It was, often implicitly, assumed that the British strategic interest was subsumed in that of the NATO alliance.[30] That assumption was not generally held by members of the NR. This was to be expected in articles in the wake of the carrier decision,[31] but more mature consideration continued the theme throughout the NATO decades.[32] Even those with a more alliance-based view of British interests acknowledged that national considerations must often be taken into account.[33]

Consciousness of resource constraints was far more marked, and far more realistic, than in earlier years. This was an effect partly of the public language and rhetoric of the defence establishment, particularly during the ministry of Denis Healey, but also of the increased exposure of members to work in Whitehall, finance-driven as it was. One article described in detail the budgetary process, so that no reader could claim ignorance of the system.[34] While many chafed at the limitations, and almost all argued for their relaxation, the impression remains that most contributors were resigned to straitened circumstances.

Threats

As followed inevitably from the calling-home of the legions, the threat from the Soviet Union achieved prominence, to the detriment of all others, in the years after 1968. Controversy over this threat, and particularly that from the Soviet Navy, was possibly the fiercest of all arguments in the *NR* during the second half of the twentieth century.

One view, from a position of authority gained during deep study, access to intelligence information and knowledge of the Russian language, was put forward by Michael MccGwire.[35] The author saw Soviet naval policy as essentially reactive, if not defensive; it was held to be based upon protection of the Soviet Union against nuclear attack, whether from carrier aircraft or submarine-launched ballistic missiles. Spurred by previous articles from this author, one contributor had already hotly contested these conclusions.[36] Argument continued throughout the period.

Analysis of the many comments on the capabilities and intentions of the Soviet maritime forces, suggests that the more alarmist view was increasingly dominant, although few assessments came down to one extreme or the other.[37] In some respects opinions followed the evidence of Soviet deployments, which became more enterprising as the century went on, and the writings of the Soviet Commander-in-Chief, Admiral S G Gorshkov,[38] which could be interpreted as advocating a policy which, though still based upon the defensive, allowed some proactive operations in support of Soviet interests. This was acknowledged by MccGwire in his later articles. There was still extensive disagreement about the possible employment of Soviet attack submarines: in the event of war, were they to be used against sea transport in the Atlantic, or to defend the SSBN bastions, acknowledged to be in the Arctic? Not unnaturally, most contributors opted for the former.

Alliances

Throughout the period, NATO remained the prime alliance in *NR* discussions, as it did in official pronouncements. But scepticism, and often downright criticism, was a common sentiment among *NR* members. The rigidity and continental bias of the alliance was a fairly constant theme,[39] as was distrust of the United States' commitment to the security of Western Europe.[40] All that said, there was acceptance that NATO was the best alliance the UK could get, and that its procedures, concepts and strategies, however questionable in detail, must be harnessed to justify the best maritime fighting force that Britain could contribute. As was argued in a comprehensive article in 1979, 'British strategy must be wholly compatible with the alliance.'[41]

It was not unnatural that other alliances, on which some reliance might have been placed in previous years, receded into the background. The decline of CENTO and SEATO – both formally in existence for over a decade after 1968 – was scarcely noticed in the pages of the *NR*. The Five Power Defence Arrangement found some support, as did more flexible and ad hoc combinations, particularly as the eighties wore on.[42]

Policies and Strategies

As already noted, *NR* contributors were very uneasy with the (largely implicit) NATO strategy of Massive Retaliation, and more comfortable with its more explicitly stated successor, Flexible Response. Occurring as it did in the late sixties, this change set the scene for the plethora of articles over the next two decades which sought to interpret the strategy to the maximum advantage of the Royal Navy and its development as a viable, balanced force.

All-level deterrence remained the bedrock of most thinking, with escalation theory supporting it. The need for strength 'within measurable distance of the Warsaw Pact' was stressed by one ex-chairman of the NATO Military Committee,[43] and was generally echoed by many contributors. A recurring theme was the focus of strategy on the NATO sea area, limited by the Tropic of Cancer in the Atlantic, which many found unrealistic and inconsistent with the realities of Western interests and growing Soviet assertiveness 'out of area'. Even the articles that sought to address strategy in general, rather than contemporary, terms touched upon this factor.[44] Some comfort was found in the introduction of NATO Standing Maritime forces, though there was less reference to the Maritime Contingency Plans being formulated at that time.

At the beginning of the 1980s, a less defensive-reactive policy was apparent. An important article, by a contributor clearly well-versed and influential in NATO affairs, advocated a 'mobile strategy', aimed at 'preventing the Soviets from being able successfully to implement a sea denial strategy against us.'[45] That this appeared in January 1982 is significant; though it seems to anticipate the US Navy's Maritime Strategy, which was published in 1986,[46] by four years, it is known that the latter document was some years in gestation and probable that the author of the *NR* article was involved with it.

In any event, the US Maritime Strategy occupied the attention of many *NR* contributors between 1986 and 1990. Some were sceptical[47] but most accepted that something of the kind would put the Soviet Navy on the back foot, and that this would have the effect suggested in the earlier article.[48] To some extent this discussion sidelined a topic that recurred over the NATO decades, the question of convoy. Discounting the few who rejected the idea that shipping protection was any longer relevant, *NR* opinion was divided between those who supported the principle of convoy, often based upon historical principle and precedent, and those who argued that systems had changed so much that it was no longer valid.[49]

Arms control, linked in these decades with the morality of the use of force, was addressed at intervals. In the wake of the Falklands, concerns focused on the individual sailor.[50] Later in the eighties, more formal issues were addressed: the Chief of Defence Staff himself wrote 'The Impact of Arms Control' in the seventy-fifth anniversary issue,[51] and this was extensively discussed in a subsequent article.[52]

The final word in this section should perhaps be awarded to Sir James Cable: in July 1982, after the Falklands War, he wrote: 'The function of navies is to provide the instrument of appropriate force at or from the sea'.

The Wherewithal

The provision, or reprovision, of combat air power at sea was a principal topic for the *NR* in the decade before 1975. After the initial, and understandable, outburst of anger following the decision not to proceed with CVA-01, discussion quickly settled into consideration of the capability needed and the means of providing it.[53]

There was general agreement on the need for anti-submarine capacity, and that this would include helicopters capable of search and attack. This alone would require ships of some size and sustainability. Greater controversy surrounded fixed-wing aircraft – essentially, V/STOL aircraft, since the revival of catapulted aircraft quickly receded. Here, some early contributors thought V/STOL incapable of carrying out significant military tasks. But, more or less in line with Ministry of Defence (Navy) thinking, the case for V/STOL gained ground, culminating in an *ex cathedra* justification by the then First Sea Lord.[54] Thus, the evolution of the *Invincible* class of aircraft carriers proceeded with general approval from *NR* members (although one, perhaps not alone, called them a 'palliative for sentiment'[55]).

There was even less disagreement about the continued production of nuclear-powered fleet submarines. On their effectiveness, relative to that of other naval units, there was considerable difference. Some regarded them as 'capable of commanding the sea', or 'the master weapon of sea warfare', or 'the most effective ASW systems'. But some pointed to limitations: 'it doesn't know and you can't tell it', and submarines are 'not capital ships'.

As a topic, the need for specialist amphibious shipping scarcely figured in the *NR* during the 1970s. Partly this was because the ships, though ageing, were there, and partly because the Royal Marines felt reasonably secure in their Arctic role and few contributed to the *Review*. This changed quite sharply after the Nott Review of 1981: an article by an ex-Marine Member of Parliament[56] raised the alarm, and subsequent discussion – influenced by the Falklands experience – often brought amphibious forces into consideration.

Finally, some mention should be made of questions that should have been raised in the *NR*, but were not, or hardly at all. One sin of omission was the failure to provide Airborne Early Warning, for which such a heavy price was paid in the South Atlantic. Hardly any mention can be found in the *Review* during the seventies. Secondly, no one pointed out the deficiencies of the Batch 2 'Leander'-class conversions which, with no gun or anti-air (or surface) missile, and only the untried Ikara/ light helicopter ASW system, were undeployable as independent frigates. Finally, only one article[57] could be found questioning the expensive, single-role, soon to be outdated, 'Upholder'-class conventional submarines. Surely the Young Turks of the membership could have done better.

III Into a Turbulent Future, 1990–2001

Chronological Background

The fall of the Berlin Wall was predicted by one contributor,[58] but even he did not foresee the extent of the collapse of the Soviet Union and the Warsaw Pact. The end of the Cold War precipitated the world into a condition that was, to some, uniquely diffuse and troublesome; to others, perhaps with a longer view of history, it was a reversion to a more normal state in which many interests, both national and sectional, competed for power and influence.

The management of this situation, or set of situations, was the preoccupation of defence analysts in many fields beyond those of the *NR*. In November 1995, Professor Lawrence Freedman made an important distinction between wars of necessity and wars of choice,[59] and this underlay the numerous employments of force that occurred in the nineties: the war to liberate Kuwait in 1991, the Balkan conflicts of the mid 1990s, precautionary deployments in the Gulf and interventions further afield. It also informed discussion and decisions about the future of force structures: notably in the British case, the Strategic Defence Review of 1998.[60]

The Nature of Conflict

Contributors to the *NR* were not slow to point out that the sea must play its full part in the new defence environment. The geographical spread of concern was prominent,[61] as also was the requirement for amphibious planning and operations.[62] More generally, the notion of expeditionary warfare, so long the butt of critics who regarded it as a sentimental reversion to Victorian ideas, revived in a way that in many cases significantly anticipated the 1998 Strategic Defence Review.[63]

It was generally accepted that the level of conflict, when it did occur, was likely to be lower than that planned for in a NATO/Warsaw Pact scenario.[64] However, numerous warning notes were sounded: it would be unwise to plan only for low intensity operations, since escalation was a likely contingency, nor for conflicts of short duration. Sustainability was a recurring theme.[65]

So, overwhelmingly, was the objective of stability: in international affairs generally,[66] and in the context of maritime trade in particular.[67] It counted too in the discussion of offshore tasks around the United Kingdom, where the theme of the Offshore Tapestry recurred from time to time.

There were counter-currents to the general flow of thought in the direction of a new orthodoxy of maritime conflict. Contentions that the UK was 'Too Big for our Boots',[68] or simply incapable of conducting operations in the way to which we aspired,[69] were not lacking, but they were substantially outweighed by argument that the nature of conflict in the new world order, or disorder, gave British maritime forces an important part to play for which they could be well suited.

British Interests and Resources

In the early 1990s, the British government turned quite rapidly from a strategic direction based upon its Atlantic alliance to one founded upon the national interest.[70] But, as previous sections of this study have shown, many contributors to the *NR* had not lost sight of national priorities during the whole of the NATO period, and there was a distinct air of 'I told you so' in some of the articles in the final decade of the century. It was mixed with relief, because the new direction gave the Navy a more secure philosophical foundation than the 'contribution to NATO' that had preceded it.[71]

Thus, in numerous articles, the national interest was stressed, though variously described. Some, somewhat naturally given the character of the journal, emphasised the maritime element;[72] more took a broader view embracing economic and political factors;[73] and a few adopted a more Eurocentric outlook, linking the national interest closely with that of other Western nations.[74]

Resources, however, were a constant concern. Curiously, a peace dividend accruing from alleged victory in the Cold War was seldom mentioned in terms, but consciousness of the ever tightening grip on British defence budgets was an abiding factor. Some contributors used the known constraints as leverage for their own hobby horses, and some chafed against them more or less ineffectually, but most made a serious effort – from varying levels of inside knowledge – to assess how best to deploy the resources available.[75] World resources were looked at from a broader standpoint by those who addressed the scene in that way, and even by the early 1990s the possibility of conflict over water resources, and the security effect of climate change, were already being mentioned.[76]

Threats

Probably the sharpest distinction between the previous period and that after 1990 lay in the threat with which the armed services might have to deal. As the decline in Soviet forces and the breakdown of the Warsaw Pact became apparent, the obvious conclusion was drawn by many contributors that threats elsewhere must take centre stage. The then editor argued indeed that since threats would in future be 'diffuse, diverse, changing and hard to predict', it was no longer appropriate to base strategy upon them, but rather on the ability to meet a wide range of contingencies with as balanced a force as could be managed.[77]

Others were more specific. Terrorism was early addressed by several contributors[78] and the theme of Islamic terrorism was later taken up by one highly knowledgeable author, whose understanding of the complexities tempered any possible 'us or them' conclusions.[79] Balkan problems were seldom addressed in terms of threat, rather as politico-military contingencies to be managed operationally in accordance with the directives of the government, the alliance, or the United Nations.

The threat of state-on-state conflict took a back seat. In the early years contributors were cautious in accepting that Soviet capabilities presented no serious problem for the foreseeable future but such caveats receded as the decade went on.[80] The capabilities of small navies, particularly those with modern systems, were sometimes raised but mostly in general terms. The maritime power of China had scarcely yet risen above the horizon, and only one article addressed it with any degree of concern.[81]

Alliances

In the startling new conditions, it was natural that the NATO alliance, which had been predicated upon a Soviet threat and had so dominated

European defence thinking over the past decades, should come into question. The most extreme view came from a long-time and much-respected contributor to the *NR*: in 'NATO Must Go' Sir Peter Stanford contended that NATO's 'strategic goals are now obsolescent' and that a new structure, accommodating 'a wider constituency', was needed.[82] He saw in the western European Union 'a ready and convenient vehicle' that could form a contractual basis with the USA and Canada.

Scarcely any other contributors went so far. Though nearly all saw a need for change with, understandably, a wider geographical outlook and a more flexible approach to conflict at all levels and against all adversaries, most thought British policy should remain formally tied to the alliance.[83] Some, probably from a standpoint within NATO headquarters, described developments in the alliance that were already occurring or expected to take place; the word 'transformation' was first seen in 1991.[84] Others noted the factors surrounding NATO enlargement and some of the possible pitfalls.[85]

Other formal alliances received relatively little attention. The demise of CENTO and SEATO was noted without great regret. The role of the United Nations as a generator of requirements was accepted, though its limitations in both organisation and operational nous were acknowledged. The trend throughout the decade was moving towards ad hoc coalitions.

Policies and Strategies

The legendary remark of British statesmen and officials over the centuries – 'our policy is to have no policy' – might be thought to apply to the 1990s more than to most decades. It would not be entirely just, however. The objective of international stability has already been noted; it was often mentioned in the *NR*, as creating the conditions in which national well-being could flourish. More than this, though, the phrase 'a force for good' was beginning to enter the vocabulary, in the wake of – or sometimes preceding – operations that had altruistic elements or objectives. Kuwait, Bosnia, Kosovo and Sierra Leone – all, in Freedman's words, wars of choice – strongly demonstrated a desire to set the world to rights.

It was a set of objectives that found endorsement in *NR* articles over the decade. References are almost too numerous to mention, but Larken, Ranken, Till, Eberle and Blackham were among the most prominent protagonists.

As to how, in the maritime field, these objectives were to be met, there was more difference of opinion. A balanced force was a common enough starting point, but the strategies to give it effect were expressed in various ways. Deterrence, presence, readiness, fighting strength and capacity for maritime manoeuvre were the most common elements, but further than that, some placed emphasis on amphibious capability, while others gave the direct protection of trade a higher priority. The golf-bag approach, giving options for a mix of systems and capabilities and typified by a carrier group operating jointly with units from the other services, was strongly supported.[86]

Arms control in the materiel sense gave way to unilateral reductions on cost grounds.[87] Confidence-building measures in the operational field were advocated.[88] Against the run of thinking at this time, some doubts about the legality of intervention operations were voiced.[89] Correspondents, before and after, sought to rebut these.[90]

The Wherewithal

The 1998 Strategic Defence Review decision to replace the *Invincible* class with two large new aircraft carriers was without doubt the most striking announcement of the decade, so far as the Navy was concerned. It had been anticipated in several *NR* articles, including one by a midshipman in 1990.[91] In the final years of the nineties opinions on the new project were numerous. One contributor expressed doubt as to whether financial resources would sustain a full-blown force on accustomed lines, and advocated vessels that would in effect be mobile airfields with minimal facilities beyond those needed to operate aircraft.[92] Others, while still acutely conscious of resource constraints, looked to the more orthodox design of carrier.[93] The latter articles were notable for quite detailed discussion of the characteristics of aircraft, a topic that would have been unlikely a generation before.

Specialised amphibious ships occupied less space in the pages of the *NR*, but this was not unnatural considering that a new generation of such vessels was coming into service; they were generally acknowledged as a core capability. Anti-submarine warfare received little detailed attention and in some articles was distinctly downplayed. Nuclear-powered submarines were considered to be key units, but in terms of their general potency rather than a specific anti-submarine role.

Other enablers were not always mentioned in detail but acknowledged to be important parts of the package. They included the Royal Fleet Auxiliary, mine countermeasures and maritime patrol aircraft. Less attention appears to have been paid to command, control and communications, and to surveillance and intelligence systems; even with the evidence of the Falklands, the need for airborne early warning in the future received little mention.

One proposed maritime role for the future, albeit US-led, received some attention. This was the provision of theatre ballistic missile defence. One experienced commentator believed it was 'a role that beckons.'[94] another took the view that it was primarily a device to preserve the US Navy.[95] A more neutral view, based upon deep study, was later available.[96]

Overall, the consensus of articles over the post-NATO decade was that in the new strategic situation, the shape of extant and planned maritime forces was about right. There was far more concern about size: whether numbers would be sufficient to support the operations that were needed, in the present or even more so, given resource constraints, in the future.

Summary and Conclusions

Readers of this chapter may be irritated by the voluminous endnotes, which occupy almost as much space as the text itself. They should not be. The titles of the articles referred to, and, where it is allowed, their authorship, demonstrate the depth and breadth of the *NR*'s treatment of topics that were profoundly central to the Navy's business. The shoulder headings in the sections above, and the coverage indicated by the endnotes supporting the text, show just how earnestly the membership discussed its core concerns, from the nature of conflict through policy and strategy to the means by which the nation's interests could be preserved and promoted at and by sea.

Discussion was increasingly helped, as the century went on, by a wider spread of membership and the readiness of academics, politicians and civil servants to add their voices to those of serving and retired officers. These latter were drawn from all ranks, from midshipmen to admirals of the fleet, with equal status given to all; it was a matter of pride to at least one editor that he had never refused an article by an officer of lieutenant's rank or below. Debate was further enriched by contributions from overseas members: Australia, Bangladesh, Canada, India, New Zealand and the USA were all represented.

It would also be valuable to look not only at the names of authors, where they appear, but at the dates on which their topics were addressed. It will often be found that they anticipated, often by some years, the appearance of the issues in the public domain or official pronouncements. The prescience of some contributors was truly remarkable. On the other hand, their reluctance to expose some of the sillier projects coming from within Whitehall, or its failure to pursue sensible ones, was unworthy of a professional journal, even one that regarded itself to some extent as self-censored.

With such a diverse set of authors and opinions, it is no easy matter to derive a set of conclusions about the main stream of naval thought as it appeared in *The Naval Review*. Some however can be identified. First, it is clear that the national interest of the United Kingdom was the driving force behind the great majority of the articles. Even when official UK policy appeared to have been subsumed almost entirely in that of the Atlantic Alliance, that interest was apparent – often overtly, sometimes implicitly. Second and following from this, a Navy of substantial autonomy was generally judged to be the most appropriate for this nation; and third, again following, it should be a Navy of balance and versatility.

Whether this stream of thinking influenced the naval and defence staff in Whitehall will be for others to judge; this writer's conclusion is that it could hardly have failed to do so, particularly as so many of the authors either were, or had been, or became, key figures in that staff. The Navy that resulted, often in the face of official resistance, was the Navy that won the South Atlantic war in 1982 and operated successfully in a myriad of contingencies and deployments before and after that date. It represented the outcome of a mainstream of naval thinking which, in spite of some backwaters and cross-currents, helped to bear the service along in a time of constant stringency: and it was truly strategic in nature. Sir James Cable's criticism, which began this chapter, could not have been more wide of the mark.

23 The View from Bath: A Naval Constructor's Perspective

Professor David Andrews, RCNC

I was very pleased to be asked as a former naval constructor, who is still active in the design of naval vessels, albeit now in academia, to contribute an article to this centenary edition of *The Naval Review*. I believe it is important that the readership of *The Naval Review* hears from a naval constructor, given the view of many that the Royal Corps of Naval Constructors (RCNC) was a relatively early casualty in the decline of the Royal Navy from its pre-eminence a century ago. I would like to conclude this article with a personal view as to why, I believe, this occurred to the RCNC and furthermore why the Navy has suffered severely for letting this happen, almost without realising it. Before we get to that I thought it best to make some general comments from a perusal of the back issues of the *NR* and to make some reflections on some significant ship design related issues.

A publication that I had reason to read recently in producing a review of '150 Years of Ship Design' for the Royal Institution of Naval Architects (RINA), the professional body for merchant and naval ship designers, seems highly pertinent to my theme.[1] This was a comprehensive summary by K J Barnaby of the learned papers published in the *RINA Transactions* to commemorate that body's first hundred years (1860–1960).[2] Barnaby did not just summarise the papers presented but also the discussions on them, which are recorded in the *Transactions*. Barnaby's century was one of intense technological advance and those discussions were noticeable in that they included significant contributions from leading Royal Navy officers of the day, alongside those provided by naval constructors and other members of the naval architectural profession. These debates, which were largely on the merit of a given design being presented, were far from polite affairs. Thus for example the 1873 discussion on the 'extraordinary

HMS *Devastation*' was extremely heated.[3] Such debates were characterised by the Chief Constructor of the Navy (that post then became that of the Director of Naval Construction (the DNC) from 1875 to 1960) having to defend the design of the latest new ship against 'an annual pillory' (DNC Sir Nathaniel Barnaby) by the profession and senior naval officers. This peak was reached in the great Sir William White's 1889 consummate defence of his *Royal Sovereign* design, the discussion on which was chaired by Lord Hamilton, then First Lord of the Admiralty.[4] As Anglo-German naval rivalry and the post-*Dreadnought* arms race reached its pre-1914 apogee, detailed debate on specific designs became more circumspect, and debate then seemed to focus on a discussion of general principles; however, the contribution from naval officers to that debate on naval ship design continued well into the twentieth century.

In contrast, over sixty years later I and my co-author, Arthur Honnor, in presenting to RINA a paper on the *Invincible*-class 'aircraft carrying ships',[5] considered we were exceptionally fortunate to have two senior captains contribute extensively to that paper's published discussion. Both, Mike Livesay, the ship's first commanding officer, and the subsequent commanding officer of the ship in the Falklands War, Jeremy Black, spoke extensively. That two such outstanding naval officers of the day provided a direct RN contribution to the discussion of a radically new class of naval vessels greatly enhanced the largely technical discussion and showed what an opportunity for a design-related dialogue has generally been lost in the last few decades. That this constituted such an exception could be seen to be symptomatic of the drifting apart of the senior naval fraternity and their constructor colleagues.

Given the 'object of the Naval Society in founding a REVIEW [was] to encourage thought and discussion on such subjects as strategy, tactics, naval operations, staff work, administration, organisation, command, discipline, education, naval history, and any other topic affecting the fighting efficiency of the Navy, *but excluding the material aspects of the technical sciences*; it is hoped that it will help to build up that body of sound doctrine which is so essential to success in war, and to provide a means of expression and discussion within the Service',[6] I sought in the annals of *The Naval Review* for debate on ship design, at least amongst the seagoing naval community, as a major topic of concern appropriate to an organ of naval matters.

It is true that, largely in the context of naval arms limtiation in the 1920s and 1930s, there was debate in *The Naval Review* about the size of battleships including their speed,[7] what dictates the size of a warship,[8] a running debate which included a corporate contribution by the RCNC,[9] what destroyers should be designed for,[10] and even the meaning of the term battleship.[11] Readers may have been puzzled by the irony of Captain Acworth who advocated an 18-knot coal-burning battleship of 8 x 13.5in guns and 18,000 tons.[12]

Most of the issues were summed up in a long review of one of Admiral Richmond's books by Captain Smith who discussed the size and shape of the battle fleet and of the high level arguments regarding the requirements of ships, a discussion which stopped well short of raising any direct technical issues.[13] However, the debate petered out in the late 1930s with the battleship question,[14] a paper on how the Suez Canal limited the size of ships,[15] and a parallel and somewhat recidivist argument on coal and oil.[16]

In contrast, I note a vigorous debate on ship design does continue in the US Naval Institute Proceedings and, in what might be considered the naval equivalent of the RINA Transactions, the US Naval Engineers' Journal. However, neither of these openly published American journals record debates of the passion of our Victorian forebears, even if they do maintain a dialogue on the course of naval ship design which neither of the separate British journals now seem to be able to provide.

Truly the debate in the NR has been very sparse. A substantial paper in 1921 on the 'correct relationship' between ship design and the ship's role, focused on the primary characteristics sought in (again!) battleships (guns/armour/speed) and then the protection of seaborne trade (by convoy).[17] Little was said that might directly help the ship designer, though this reader was left with the strong impression that the perceived future of naval warfare (the Second World War) was likely to be more complex and multifaceted than in 1914–18. This in hindsight seems quite prescient, and even typical of the modern fleet (2012) which is numerically minuscule in comparison, yet the naval ship designer still has to provide for a wide range of warship types, albeit in tiny handfuls. Another paper in 1930 debated the size of battleships but, rather than a design analysis, considered the Royal Navy's dilemma of producing vessels that would not be outclassed by any 'existing capital ship', while meeting Britain's need for more battleships than other navies, in order to defend the far-flung Empire.[18] Of design interest was the early comment in that paper which conceded that 'a failure to sufficiently narrow down the questions left for experts [by which I presume he meant DNC and his constructors] to decide.' More recent historical papers addressing the 'battlecruiser con-troversy'[19] and air power versus battleships[20] seemed to show that between the wars the debate on design, in the first instance, ignored the losses at Jutland of the battlecruisers as being due to the lack of sensible anti-flash precautions and in the other case an over-confidence in the effectiveness of anti-aircraft gunnery.

In passing, Geoffrey Till, in the second of these papers, quotes Philip Watts' successor as DNC in the First World War (Sir E Tennyson d'Eyncourt) as concluding in 1919 that the future air threat was likely to be so severe that capital ships should 'submerge for protection',[21] proving once again that the Admiralty Board's principal technical adviser (the DNC) was far from technically hidebound.

In musing as to whether I was wrong, as a mere ship designer, to consider ship design to be fundamental to a navy's well-being and effectiveness, I reread Admiral Lord Hill-Norton's 1982 book *Sea Power*, where he defined sea power as 'essentially about navies, which comprise different types of warship.'[22] Thus the titles of seven of his ten chapters are those of the main ship types from battleship to submarine and gunboat. So it is not just the naval constructor who sees the types of naval vessels and their differing design issues as being that which makes naval warfare unique. Unfortunately, it may also be a significant aspect that makes it hard to articulate the necessity of sea power to a sea-blind political, administrative and media-dominated establishment. All the more reason why the seagoing Navy and the naval design community should better communicate with each other in order to articulate to the wider nation the importance and subtlety of sea power.

It might now be informative to consider some of the key issues that have arisen in the last century of naval development, as I believe they reinforce this sorry state of affairs. The editor of *From Dreadnought to Daring* suggested I start with the advent of the submarine – which to me exemplifies the lesson that technology advances can't be resisted. Now, while there were comments over a hundred years ago, still dragged out by the media, to the effect that submarines were 'damn un-British', many, not least Jacky Fisher, saw the Holland boats as potentially battle-winning vessels. Even he could not have imagined fifty years later USS *Nautilus* (or probably more accurately USS *Skipjack*, being the true amalgam of *Nautilus*'s nuclear propulsion and *Albacore*'s teardrop hull-form) as the first real submarine when compared to previous, air-dependent submersibles. Another clear lesson I take from this is that, as with the 1905 *Dreadnought*, the leading navy of the time needs to quickly embrace innovation – as clearly the RN did when it was pre-eminent, and before that mantle was taken up by the US Navy. A more recent innovation, closer to both the naval and academic parts of my career, is that of the oceangoing trimaran ship, developed initially in the 1990s through the RCNC-sponsored course at University College London.[23] This concept was then taken up by the Ministry of Defence, in its new procurement home of Abbey Wood, Bristol, leading to the production of the two-third scale prototype (of a UCL produced 5,000-tonne destroyer design) demonstrator, the Research Vessel *Triton*.[24] However, with the Ministry of Defence's current obsession with risk reduction, too readily encouraged by the shipbuilding producers, any exploitation of this concept now seems to be left to others. In contrast, the US Navy have a class of trimaran Littoral Combatant Ships coming into service – sadly drawing on the Australian fast ferry derivative of the UCL concept rather than the original UK design. Is this yet another story of stifled British engineering inventiveness?

An obvious naval design example historically is that of the decline of the battleship and its succession by the aircraft carrier. The British naval ship design community can reflect with pride on the leading role it played pre-war, with the first modern carrier design of the 1938 HMS *Ark Royal*, and post-war the development and incorporation of several post-war British innovations which enabled jet aircraft to operate off such mobile air stations. The latter innovations were then splendidly developed by the US Navy in their supercarriers – probably the ultimate demonstration of Mahan's arguments about sea power.

I was also asked to comment on the 'short fat ship' controversy of the mid 1980s, which I suspect many naval officers, without the benefit of naval architectural theory or subsequent practice in ship design, may feel shows a resistance to innovation by the constructor fraternity. Leaving aside the clear evidence that, historically, the British naval record is one of innovative technical adoption rather than resistance to it, any proposal has to be qualified by a clear demonstration that a given proposal is technically justified and good value for money.

So any new ship design proposal needs to follow the scientific practice of being presented, preferably in an open forum, to a suitably broad range of informed professionals able to objectively assess its merits from the evidence. The proponents of the 'short fat frigate' proposal never presented this proposal to the naval architecture discipline, as can be seen from the written discussion to Admiral Sir Lindsay Bryson's paper on 'The Procurement of a Warship' in the 1984 *RINA Transactions*.[25] While the public debate about 'short fat' turned on a legal issue, the private debate in the pages of *The Naval Review* was technically illiterate.[26] In fact the hull form drew on small craft practice, namely the published National Physical Laboratory's guidance on such (Marwood Bailey) planing forms, which are valid up to 200 tons displacement but not for frigate-size vessels operating at typical frigate speeds when the vessel is over ten times heavier than the NPL limit.[27] Elementary knowledge of the effect of Froude number ($V/\sqrt{(gL)}$) on a ship's wave-making resistance would have ruled out such a form for frigate size and speed.[28] Furthermore, the dynamic stiffness of frigate-sized vessels, given such a wide beam and a practical weight distribution, would have been such that the configuration would be highly likely to have too stiff a motion to operate in a seaway.

The whole saga was more an example of the low status professional engineering is given in the UK when compared to our continental *Ingenieur* equivalents, plus the manner in which miracle cures are grasped by peacetime governments under fiscal pressure. In this case it was doubly ironic that the first scientifically (if not technically) educated Prime Minister, Margaret Thatcher, fostered a government attitude that positively distrusted professional advice, especially if the experts were in public service. That neither the Navy nor the MoD seemed to strongly support its own professionals, when (as I observed at the time from my NATO colleagues) no professional ship designer could understand the lack of official support for the professional engineering advice, says more than a little about the UK's decline from its former position of being the leading industrial power.

As already remarked, the underlying motivation that led to a lengthy consideration of such a technically incoherent proposal was that of fiscal pressure on the defence budget. Sadly, that pressure has got progressively worse in the last three decades. In naval ship design terms this means a desire for ever cheaper ships, which is another spin on the debate of quantity versus quality. At about the same time as the 'short fat frigate' saga, a colleague and I in the Controller of the Navy's Forward Design Group produced a conference paper on the design of cheap warships.[29] We pointed out that, almost without exception, when a cheap single role design has been produced alongside a marginally (and this can be just a few per cent on initial cost) more expensive, more generously designed, longer life, multi-role, and superior quality design, then the latter ends up being much better value for money through the life of both classes. Examples of this include the R-class versus the *Queen Elizabeth*-class battleships, the Flower Class versus the Black Swans/Loch escorts, the Type 14 *Blackwood* class versus the Type 12 *Whitby* (or even better the Canadian *St Laurent*) frigates, the USN FFG7s versus the *Spruance* class, Type 21 versus Type 22 frigates. Many of the cheap solutions involve taking out both growth margins (for ensuring design performance is maintained despite unplanned weight gain through life) and Board margins (allocated to accommodate currently unplanned future updating). Such savings on margins end up being a false economy.[30] Furthermore, retention in the fleet of such tight designs means they absorb more of the budget in their difficult refits, and this then has consequences on the Navy's funds for future new-build programmes. This initially 'cheap ship' approach also leads to adopting commercial standards in materials (such as for pipework), which are not intended to last the thirty or more years when government and Treasury subsequently decide that 'short life' ships have to run on. Two examples of this are, first, the Type 42 destroyers, which the design director (K Purvis, RCNC) said would be too tight and not readily refittable – sadly all too obvious in their refit budget over-runs. Second, the Type 23 frigate, which was predicated on an eighteen-year life as the ASW unit in the Greenland–Iceland–UK gap, yet the class has instead been employed as the RN's main general purpose, worldwide peacekeeper, which it was never designed to do, and is now planned to be in service for some thirty years (I speak as the original concept designer). The naval staff deserve some credit for realising in the 1990s that steel is cheap, and air free, even if against the odds.[31]

So we might ask why were the ship design professionals respected by their naval peers in the times of DNCs Sir William White (1880s), Sir Philip Watts (pre-1914) and Sir Stanley Goodall (WWII), while in more recent years their successors appear to have been marginalised? There have been some notable exceptions: thus Lord Mountbatten greatly respected the ship design talents of Rowland Baker, RCNC, before and during the Second World War, such that he subsequently made him Technical Director for both *Dreadnought* and then the Polaris project – both of which finished on time and within budget. Follow-on successes to these projects were the subsequent submarine designs, *Swiftsure* and *Vanguard* classes as, arguably, exemplars of their types. The former was readily developable into the *Trafalgar* class and beyond, because it was a generous design with margins for growth and upgrade – not an easy thing to achieve in submarine design. Perhaps it could be argued that senior submariners, in general, have been much closer to the engineering of their vessels than their surface ship equivalents, for obvious reasons, and have had a closer relationship with submarine constructors. Additionally, submarine designers can use the 'safety card' to more easily deflect political, administrative and, even, naval arguments of 'gold plating'. But also other excellent warship designs have been produced, such as the highly innovative *Invincible* carriers and the novel composite structure of the Hunts, perhaps also the stealth and zoning features of the Type 23s could be seen as notable achievements, especially in a cost-capped design with the nonsense of the imposition of its intended short life and, also, arbitrarily, reduced complement (resulting in no Training & Advancement margins and the complement not being based on proper complementing studies).

These examples show that balanced first-rate designs have been produced, often when there is an open dialogue at the crucial early stages of the design between the naval staff and the ship design team. Such practice needs to be unfettered by contractual barriers – not just straight commercial ones but also artificial 'customer-supplier' internal barriers set up in the Ministry of Defence – especially when the warship project team is subsequently going to be the technical authority and 'material owner' of the ship class through its life. This does mean that commercial barriers mitigate against both parties striving for best value for money, both for the Treasury and the Navy, rather than one of the parties being driven by short-term company profit. Such organisational and commercial barriers have contributed to the persistent delays to the Future Surface Combatant programme over the last decade, resulting in a lack of strategic thinking, so that the consequential extensions to the 'short-life' Type 23 class were excluded from the equation when the cost of delay to the FSC programme was being considered. Another nonsense that arose from this 'customer-supplier' internal market was that the ship/submarine technology research programme became no longer managed by the ship design organisation, which understood the technology balance and design implications. Thus, while combat system research priorities could be set by the requirements staff, the same was not appropriate on the ship technology research in setting research priorities for (say) developing submarine pressure hull structural design codes or trimaran hydrodynamic and structural investigations.

So am I arguing that the role the RCNC had a hundred (or even fifty) years ago should be restored instead of continuing with a policy that seems to assume, provided the Navy spells out what it wants, industry can provide? I am afraid I am, because warship design is not a straightforward process, like high street shopping. Working out what is possible for something as complex as a modern warship, within ever greater constraints, requires what I have called a 'requirements elucidation'[32] process. This is essentially a dialogue of equals under the Navy umbrella, namely the (naval) staff and the concept design team. Going back to the 1921 *Naval Review* paper mentioned earlier it states:

> The [designer's] task is to design a ship which, as nearly as possible, will meet the requirements of the naval officer ... Thus the tactician must be responsible for the general principles of the design, which

the constructor works out in every detail, and the two must work in close co-operation if the best results are to be achieved.[33]

This relationship sounds co-operative but is sequential and is akin to the current relationship between the defence staff producing detailed non-material requirements, which industry then endeavours to meet materially. That this is a nonsense for naval ship design and acquisition I have addressed elsewhere (see note 32). This is partly because it is very poor systems engineering practice, not just for ship design, but also leads to poor guidance to ship design teams in particular. What is actually required to obtain coherent requirements, and coherent and affordable ship designs, is a dialogue of equals where the ship designer's exploration (using modern computer-assisted design tools) of potential material solutions informs the naval staff's evolving requirement, so that it can meet as many of the desired capabilities that are affordable and deliverable. The UK has not been unique in going down this blind alley; the US Navy went down a similar track to the UK in devolving more of the ship design role to industry but has now backed off and is reconstituting its in-house warship design capability. Thus in 2007, the (then) Secretary of the Navy, Dr Winter, issued a clear intent that the US Navy (which includes the NAVSEA design directorates) will take the lead in directing and managing warship acquisition and will be resourced to do so.[34]

Now, it could be argued that the RN has become too small to justify such a commitment; however, the consequences of no longer being able to technically manage both the tasks of design authority and acquisition of warships get worse as the budget is squeezed ever tighter. The imperative in achieving best value for money is to coherently work out and then spell out what is wanted, followed by adequately controlling how it is produced. This means producing concept designs to elucidate what is needed and affordable, at a sensible level of risk. Knowing what this is enables the MoD as the customer of industry to spell out and then manage what it wants. This, it could be argued, was done for the submarine programmes from *Dreadnought* to *Vanguard* class and indeed for something as novel as the *Invincible* class. Such programmes were delivered to time and cost. So why was the model discarded?

Sadly, the answer comes back to my opening remarks that the RCNC, which in large part – but not exclusively – made those programmes such a success, was allowed to be emasculated. That occurred both in regard to its design and ship acquisition role but also in its organisational autonomy, which was first granted to Sir William White, as the first Head of the Royal Corps, in 1883. So the superb training scheme, including six months' sea-time in uniform, and its pre-eminence in retaining the senior naval acquisition and design authority posts, achieved through clear and responsible career pathways, was allowed, by the Navy, to be destroyed by a jealous administrative Civil Service. (Only the MSc course in Naval Architecture at UCL remains of the RCNC cadetship scheme.) That jealousy was in part due to the RCNC being seen as a model for a technically capable alternative to the 'Sir Humphrey' generalist, called for by the 1970s Fulton Enquiry, but wilfully destroyed by the then head of the Civil Service, Sir William Armstrong. The Navy was preoccupied with fighting, if not for survival, then certainly for the retention of a genuine ocean-wide capability, and seemed to see the emasculation of an elite dedicated naval constructor corps as affordable in the midst of inter-service rivalry. Rather, I would argue the loss of the Corps' grip on warship design and acquisition has accelerated the Navy's decline, with recent warship programmes becoming more and more incoherent, over-spent and late. This has then weakened the Navy's case for an adequate fleet size and mix.

Perhaps if the RCNC had (as Sir Rowland Baker argued at the time) joined the uniform branches immediately after the Second World War, it would now be akin to the US Navy Engineering Duty Officers' Branch, which runs the NAVSEA Command – along with the strong support of some excellent civilian naval architects. Alternatively, the RCNC could have had the support of all the services to establish a *Corps de l'Armament* as the French achieved by building on their corps of naval constructors, itself founded by Colbert. Of course, the French corps has the advantage of its members being *ingenieur* graduates of the Ecole Polytechnique, a starkly engineering-educated national elite, in marked contrast to the Oxbridge-produced generalists, who populate the British administrative civil service and the political elite. Either route for preserving the capabilities of the RCNC might have resulted in a more coherent and affordable suite of naval vessels than the current dwindling order of battle. This might then have enabled the RN to lead a European naval community that the USA would see as a more effective partner in the current century – but I stray from mere ship design matters, or do I?

24 The Empire Strikes Back: The Battle of the Falklands in 1914 and the Falklands War of 1982

Commander David Hobbs

THE Royal Navy's two twentieth-century conflicts in the Falkland Islands and the seas surrounding them were separated by sixty-eight years in time, but by an even more significant gap in terms of weapons, tactics, and even the way in which the Royal Navy perceived itself.

There were obvious similarities in that both conflicts involved a Task Force despatched from the United Kingdom to achieve a specific aim and obvious differences since the earlier conflict involved a battle at sea and the latter included a hostile invasion force that had to be defeated on land by amphibious forces carried into theatre and sustained by sea. Both were excellent examples of the flexibility and usefulness of sea power in defending the national interest decisively and with little warning.

In 1914 *The Naval Review* was new and had yet to establish itself as a vehicle for officers to write about their experience of battle. By 1982 *The Naval Review* remained a primary vehicle for officers to write about professional matters and to express their opinions. However, there was a change in outlook between the different generations of correspondent. In 1914 the Royal Navy was an expanding force at the height of its power. The recent loss of Admiral Cradock's squadron off Coronel was the only defeat in an era that had seen nothing but victory since the days of Nelson and his contemporaries over a century before. Imperial defence was one of the Navy's primary roles and there was clearly no need to explain what and where the Falkland Islands were and why Britain was defending them. The Royal Navy of 1982 had suffered decades of decline, the cancellation of the CVA-01 aircraft carrier project in 1966, the withdrawal of the Far East Fleet in 1971, and, only months before the war, the infamous Nott Defence Review which had identified many of the ships that made up the Task Force for disposal, condemning the Service to a limited role within the NATO area.[1] Imperial, colonial or even Commonwealth defence was no longer on the agenda.

The Battle of Coronel, off Chile, had seen the cruisers *Good Hope* and *Monmouth*, the former being the flagship of the Rear Admiral Sir Christopher Cradock, sunk by Vice Admiral Graf von Spee's German East Asia Squadron, formerly based in Tsingtao. The action was a one-sided affair in which Cradock, with his inferior ships, had engaged the enemy with the hope of causing damage which would limit the enemy's subsequent course of action. The light cruiser *Glasgow* managed to get away with slight damage and one of her officers wrote details of the action in a letter to *The Times* which was published on 11 December 1914 and subsequently reprinted in *The Naval Review*. Written eight days after the battle on 9 November 1914, it is upbeat and begins 'we are at this moment steaming gaily along at 17 knots ... our five men slightly injured by pieces of shells now quite recovered and none the worse.' After describing the action and the loss of the armoured cruisers he wrote 'I cannot understand our deliverance; none will ever. We were struck at the water-line by in all 5 shells out of the 600 directed at us but, strangely not in vulnerable places, our coal saving us on three occasions.'[2]

He saw the ship's withdrawal from the action as necessary to warn the old battleship *Canopus*, which was making her way north to join Cradock's squadron,

> to turn and run ... we were some hours getting through to her because of the continual jamming by the enemy's wireless ... It would have been a needless and useless sacrifice of our ship and our 370 odd lives to have remained and engaged the enemy's ships again; some 1,600 lives had already gone in the *Good Hope* and *Monmouth*. Luckily our engines and boilers were intact and we were able to push through the heavy seas at 24 knots ... and warn the *Canopus* who, although she no doubt would have fought gallantly, could hardly hope to successfully fight five ships. We all thanked God for our miraculous escape after a very severe action against great odds.[3]

For the majority in *Glasgow* this had been their first experience of action and the loss of two cruisers and the admiral must have been a severe blow but the setback was thought to be temporary. If the anonymous correspondent is typical, no one doubted that the German squadron would be brought to action and defeated. The letter to *The Times* was strikingly frank and contained information that a later generation would consider to be of use to the enemy. The accuracy and effect of German gunnery, the fact that German wireless operators could detect and jam British transmissions at close range, and that 'we only had two guns ... that would pierce their armour – the *Good Hope*'s two old 9.2's, one of which was out of action 10 minutes after the start', must have been read with interest in Berlin.

In 1914 the correspondent took it for granted that the readership knew of the islands as an isolated colony, important then as a coaling station on the global system of imperial sea routes. In 1982, however, Hugh Rogers felt he had to explain where the islands are and their significance.

> Before the Argentine invasion it is probable that comparatively few people in the United Kingdom knew much about the activities of the Falkland Islanders or about the size, climate, terrain and communications of the country they inhabited. Now, as the result of the publicity from the press and television during the military operations, the people of England, at any rate, must be far better acquainted with the Falkland Islands than they are with the Outer Hebrides.[4]

There are other differences in outlook. The deployment of the battle-cruisers *Invincible* and *Inflexible* with their attendant light cruisers to the South Atlantic to seek out and destroy von Spee's squadron after Coronel was exactly the role the battlecruisers had been designed for.[5] Able to operate at long range with communications that could receive the latest intelligence information, they could dictate the terms of battle and were the epitome of Fisher's transformational reforms for the Royal Navy. Significantly, the decision to deploy them came soon after Fisher returned to the Admiralty as First Sea Lord in October 1914. Their superiority over the German squadron was taken for granted so no one felt compelled to write about it in *The Naval Review*. In stark contrast, the Task Force of 1982 was not carrying out its primary mission. Out of its key ships, the recent Nott Defence Review had decided to sell the new *Invincible* to Australia and dispose of *Hermes* together with the amphibious assault ships *Fearless* and *Intrepid*, as the politicians saw no use for them in a continental NATO strategy. The Far East Fleet, a balanced strike force deployed in the South China Sea and Pacific was only a memory, and for over a decade the Royal Navy had concentrated on anti-submarine warfare in the Atlantic. Fortunately, there were enough officers with experience of strike warfare to make the difference as the Task Force sailed south.

The requirement to support a fleet operating many thousands of miles from the UK had declined significantly by 1982 but recovery was still possible and this significant achievement was described in *The Naval Review* in an article put together from a number of contributions from the staff of the Chief of Fleet Support:

> It has been said that logisticians are a sad, embittered race of men, very much in demand in war but sinking into resentful obscurity in peace. Before that decline develops in the aftermath of the Falkland Islands campaign (Operation Corporate), it is appropriate to review the part logistics played in the operation. To most people logistics sounds dull and is thought of in terms of fuel, food and stores. There is, however, much more including maintenance and repair, ammunition supply, transport (land, sea and air) and medical services. In war logistics is far from dull and is the very lifeline of operations; indeed logistic constraints may well determine the conduct of operations.[6]

This was not new; the British Pacific Fleet's contribution to USN operations off Japan in 1945, only thirty-seven years earlier, had been severely constrained by the lack of logistic support but in the intervening years the Royal Navy had declined with frightening rapidity into a small force of limited reach and the lesson had, largely, been lost.

In one of those chances that so easily affect the outcome of conflict von Spee delivered the German squadron into action on 8 December 1914 by closing Port Stanley with a view to destroying the signal station, on the day after the British battlecruisers had arrived. After he was sighted from a lookout post on a hill, his flagship, the armoured cruiser *Scharnhorst*, was engaged by *Canopus* which had been moored to act as a static fort in the harbour. The other British ships were at reduced notice and were taking on coal but managed to raise steam in short order and settled into a stern chase to overhaul the German squadron which made off to the east when the tripod masts of *Invincible* and *Inflexible* were recognised in harbour. They, together with the light cruisers *Cornwall*, *Kent* and *Glasgow*, were soon able to work up to maximum speed; HMS *Bristol*

> had her fires out for repairs to machinery, as well as the [armed merchant cruiser] *Macedonia*, and did not leave harbour till an hour later, when they were ordered to destroy three enemy transports which had been sighted from a look-out station some miles to the southward. They only succeeded in finding two ships which proved to be colliers and sank them. The preliminary feature of the action resolved itself into a stern chase with the two battlecruisers in the

van. At about 1.0 pm they opened fire at a range of 17,000 yards on the enemy's light cruisers which caused the German admiral ten minutes later to signal his fleet: 'I will engage enemy's battlecruisers AS LONG AS I AM ABLE, light cruisers are to use every endeavour to escape.'[7]

The message must have been sent in plain language and was intercepted and read in the British ships. It shows that von Spee held out little hope of fighting a successful action against Admiral Sturdee's force.

The British viewed the prospect of action with exhilaration.

As she cleared the harbour the flagship hoisted the signal for 'general chase'. The German ships were gradually joining forces, steaming in an easterly direction, and could now begin to make out their opponents. As described by a survivor from the *Gneisenau*, they at first tried to believe that there were no battlecruisers but those ominous tripod masts convinced the most determined unbeliever: then they thought that the ships must be Japanese; but at last they realised the precise force from which they were running. They then went to prayers. From the bridge of the *Kent* the scene was most exhilarating to behold. The five German ships with their funnels only showing over the horizon, a sight which still seemed almost too good to be true; the two battlecruisers close together belching forth smoke, their snowy wakes creeping up their sterns, a perfect presentiment of modern power.[8]

... On the forecastle of the *Kent* was collected the entire ship's company not otherwise employed. Little had to be done to prepare for battle and soon all hands were free except the stokers on watch down below. The men were all cheerful, almost hilarious, and when presently firing commenced they cheered and clapped each shot as it was fired, and again as each shot fell about half a minute later. It was like a football match for them, the finest relaxation since leaving England. The chase started at 9.00am. At 1.00pm the *Invincible* and *Inflexible* opened fire on the rearmost ships at a range of 16,000 yards. For once the Germans seemed to be out-ranged and there was no reply until about 2.00pm when the *Scharnhorst* and *Gneisenau* turned to port in line ahead to meet their fate. The light cruisers turned to the south-east and continued to run ... Being about four miles astern of the big ships at the commencement of the action, we obtained the finest possible view of a modern big ship action; we were, as it were, in the front row of the stalls, so close that we could almost touch the actors on the stage, yet so far that no stray missile disturbed the comfort of our view.[9]

The fast-paced action described by correspondents to *The Naval Review* in 1914 contrasts with the longer drawn out explanations in 1982. The predominant early emotion was surprise that conflict could have happened so quickly in such a place. The much longer run-up to war in 1982 was explained rather well by 'Felix in Undis' who gave his own breakdown of events prior to HMS *Invincible* sailing with the Task Force, starting with a drawn out period alongside in Portsmouth beforehand.[10]

The journey south, use of Ascension Island as an intermediate base, failure of political negotiations, and the commencement of hostilities were all written about in some detail. Hostilities, when they started, extended over a period of weeks rather than hours and involved aircraft, missiles and electronic warfare on a scale that would have been difficult for the earlier generation to imagine. They were all described along with action working dress, feeding arrangements at action stations and many other professional subjects brought to the fore by the fleet's lack of recent combat experience.

Captain Hart Dyke of HMS *Coventry* described his perspective of the opening stage of the conflict.[11] 'On 1 May 1982 HMS *Coventry* with her sister ships *Sheffield* and *Glasgow* formed an advanced air defence screen to protect our two carriers and entered the Total Exclusion Zone (TEZ)'. The two carriers and their embarked Sea Harrier fighters and Sea King helicopters were, of course, the key enablers without which the British could not seriously have considered the liberation of the Islands. He continued, 'Our task was to control the Sea Harriers and to guide them into action against incoming air raids. On 1 May the air battle went decisively in our favour. Seven aircraft were shot down by the Sea Harriers and we suffered no losses.' He explained that after *Sheffield* was sunk on 4 May and *Glasgow* put out action by bomb damage a week later, only *Coventry* was left to do the front line work and this she did by day and night.

On our first mission close to the enemy's south coast we shot down two Skyhawk fighters escorting a supply Hercules aircraft. We achieved this with one missile fired at its maximum range. An hour or two later we shot down a troop-carrying helicopter with another missile at a range of thirteen miles. After this action the Argentinians were forced to land supplies on a grass strip on the West Falklands. This successful action with Sea Dart missiles was the first ever in Royal Navy history.

Missiles had not completely replaced the gun in British warships in 1982 although many had advocated that they should do so. The

Falklands War was to show that medium guns were still important in giving warships flexibility, and new designs, including what would become the Type 23 frigates and the Batch 3 Type 22s were recast to include a 4.5in gun mounting.

By 1982 the Lynx helicopter had replaced the Wasp in a number of destroyers and frigates but by no means all. *Coventry* had one of the first Lynx flights to be equipped with Sea Skua air-to-surface missiles and used them to good effect. Hart Dyke wrote:

> In the early hours of 3 May my Lynx helicopter armed with two Sea Skua missiles detected two enemy ships heading for Port Stanley – presumably with supplies for the army ashore. The helicopter scored two direct hits with its missiles and totally destroyed one of the targets. The explosion as the vessel blew up was seen thirty miles away by other ships in the Task Force. The second vessel was later severely damaged by a Lynx helicopter and its missiles from *Glasgow*. This was the first surface action of the war. A second surface action took place a day or two later when *Coventry* and *Glasgow* formed up in poor visibility to take on two small fast-moving radar contacts assessed as fast patrol boats. Both ships fired twenty or thirty rounds of 4.5 inch shell and destroyed the targets. Later we discovered we had been engaging a group of albatross but this was a very real action and in war any contact that is not a known friendly unit is attacked without hesitation.

Later, on 25 May *Coventry* was herself attacked by enemy aircraft and sunk.

> We came up against a very brave and determined attack by four aircraft who sprang at us from behind the land and flew very fast and low the last ten miles or so over the sea to our position north west of Falkland Sound. We engaged with everything we had got, from Sea Dart missiles to machine guns and even rifles, but one of the aircraft got through delivering four bombs – three of which went into the port side of the ship and exploded. However, we hit at least one aircraft with guns and we learnt later that two aircraft did not get home to their bases ... The operations Room, low down in the ship where I and some thirty men were controlling the battle, was devastated by the blast and immediately filled with very thick smoke.

The ship had, subsequently, to be abandoned and Captain Hart Dyke paid tribute to the bravery of his crew.

> A young officer directing the close-range guns from the very exposed position of the bridge wings did not take cover when the enemy

aircraft were closing at eye-level and straffing the ship with cannon fire. He stood there for all to see and ordered the guns' crews to stay at their posts and engage the enemy until he gave the order to stop. This order was not questioned by the very young sailors manning the guns and they kept firing despite their totally exposed position. At least one aircraft was hit and two were turned away by the barrage of fire. A rating in the engine room hearing a large thump looked round to see a bomb which had come into the ship a few feet from where he was standing. He did not run but went to a telephone and reported this fact to damage control headquarters; he described the bomb, the whereabouts of the hole in the side and the nature of the damage to the machinery. The bomb then blew up as he was still talking. Miraculously he was shielded from the blast by a bit of machinery and walked out unharmed. Others were killed outright.

As the ship was abandoned, 'two Chief Petty Officers, separately and on their own initiative, revisited smoke-filled compartments when everyone else was on the upper deck and the ship listing dangerously over to port; they ensured that everyone still alive was got out of the ship.' One had found a senior rating unconscious with his clothes on fire and saved his life, the other helped two very frightened young sailors climb past a hole in the deck, through which flames were issuing, to save their lives.

Every captain in both conflicts would have felt the loss of their ship and their people keenly. Captain Hart Dyke spoke for them all when he wrote:

I can never forget the brave people in my ship who fought so well. Nor can I forget those nineteen equally brave men who lost their lives and who also contributed to the battle. They did more than their best continuously for at least four weeks of intensive and dangerous operations ... Our Nation, our Navy, has a priceless inheritance which has given us men of great quality who have fought so well down the ages and not least in the South Atlantic in 1982.

All British warships have close ties with cities and institutions ashore and these have proved especially important in wartime. *Kent* in 1914 and *Coventry* in 1982 illuminate two minor but interesting issues, trophies and affiliations. When *Coventry* had first commissioned, the city after which she was named presented her with three medieval nails from the bombed cathedral which were formed into the shape of a cross and mounted on a wooden plinth. It was kept in a prominent place in the ship in a display cabinet. It was not landed before the war and went down with the ship, which is now a war grave. The aircraft carrier

Invincible landed all her trophies in Portsmouth before sailing, except one. The Supply Officer elected to retain on board a silver toast-rack that had been on board the battlecruiser *Invincible* at the Battle of the Falkland Islands in 1914 to give a feeling of continuity. On 12 December 1914 Captain J D Allen of HMS *Kent* wrote to the Secretary of the Association of Men of Kent and Kentish Men to give details of the battle and the part *Kent* had played in it.[12] He added that

> the silk ensign and jack presented to the *Kent* by the ladies of Kent were flying the whole time. They were both torn to ribbons, but I have got them both safe. I carefully collected every bit I could, as they were torn to pieces and some pieces were caught in the rigging. I am afraid they are past repair, but nearly all the pieces intact. They can never be flown again. Will you be so kind as to ask the ladies of Kent what they wish done with them? They can be sewn up, though some pieces are missing. Meanwhile I will keep them here for the present.

Among many advances in naval capability between the conflicts, that of lifesaving equipment stands out. In Captain Allen's letter he says that

> no sooner had she [*Nürnberg*] sunk than the *Kent*'s men displayed the same zeal and activity in endeavouring to save life as they had done in fighting the ship. Boats were hastily repaired and lowered, manned by men eagerly volunteering to help. Unfortunately the sea was rough and the water very cold so we only succeeded in picking up twelve men, of whom five subsequently died.

In another anonymous report in *The Times* which was printed on 20 January 1915, the author described the sinking of the *Gneisenau*.[13]

> About 5.15pm ... She heeled over very slowly till she got to about 70 degrees, then she went over with a rush, there was a large cloud of steam, she cocked her stem up in the air and disappeared. As soon as possible we got out what boats we had left to pick up the survivors, and threw lifebuoys and any available bits of wood to them. The flagship and the other cruiser had come up and were doing the same, but a lot of them were drowned as we were short of boats and the sea had started to get choppy. We picked up the Commander of the *Gneisenau*, seven officers and about fifty men and between the three ships managed to save about one hundred and fifty men.

By contrast the lifesaving kit in *Coventry* worked well and the presence of winch-equipped helicopters in the Task Force made a huge difference. Hart Dyke wrote:

All the starboard side life-rafts were in the water and people were helping each other to put on their lifejackets and once-only [survival] suits ... the life-raft I was in was sucked in against the overhanging port side of the ship and was punctured by the sharp nose of a Sea dart missile that was till in the launcher. About thirty-five men, some badly burnt, ended up back in the water when the life-raft sank underneath them. The injured, who were unable to swim, were held up above the sea by their courageous colleagues until some helicopters arrived and were able to lift them to safety. One helicopter actually landed on the ship's side to pick up people who had had to scramble back on board; by this time the ship was burning red hot inside. These men were all rescued.

The most obvious difference between the two conflicts was the widespread importance of aircraft in 1982, both in terms of the embarked Sea Harriers and helicopters in the Task Force and air bridge from the UK to Ascension Island which became, for a time, the world's busiest airfield. The support given to the fleet by the RAF air transport organisation and the eventual deployment of Harrier ground-attack aircraft to the Task Force led to an article in *The Naval Review*, one of the first to be written by members of another of another Service and perhaps an indication of the increasing jointness of operations.[14]

Like so many others, the war started for 801 Naval Air Squadron (NAS) early in the morning of 2 April when the Senior Pilot initiated the cascade recall system to get everyone back to RNAS Yeovilton from leave. Reinforced by part of 899 NAS, the training unit, 801 embarked in HMS *Invincible* and settled into a war footing on the voyage south. Then on 1 May 'two of our aircraft engaged a pair of Mirages high over West Falkland; one of these Sea Harriers claimed the first kill of the war when he downed a Mirage with a stern shot. The second Mirage fared no better as it was also hit by a missile en route to the nearest friendly cloud.' Lieutenant Commander Ogilvy went on to describe how Sea Harriers shot down a Canberra bomber at low level that evening 'at the end of the day it was a nice feeling to know that we had bloodied their noses without loss to ourselves.' The Sidewinder missile

proved to be a most formidable weapon and it retained its reliability throughout the war. After this hectic start life settled down into a regular pattern of Action Stations and Combat Air Patrol (CAP) during daylight hours as we continued to patrol the TEZ, with long periods of deck alert at night. For the Squadron the most poignant event of that period was the tragic loss of Lieutenant Commander Eyton-Jones and Lieutenant Curtis in appalling weather conditions on 6 May 1982.[15]

The flying programmes were worked out by the Air Operations Officers in the two aircraft carriers. Lieutenant Cairns described how

> We worked eight hours on watch and eight hours off, changing over at noon, eight in the evening and four in the morning ... if I was going on watch at 4.00am I would wake at 3.30, go for a quick shower, don my overalls and anti-flash gear and take over on the hour in the Air Ops Office where my opposite number would give me a brief on what was happening, what should be happening but wasn't, and what was happening when it shouldn't have been. Signals would be read and sorted and Ops 2 would start on the next twelve hours flying programme based on tasking from the Admiral's staff in HMS *Hermes*. The overall requirement for aircraft would be sent by a signal known as the Opgen 'C' which outlined the numbers and type of aircraft needed to counter the expected threat. The exact timings, weapon loads and callsigns were all included in another signal the Opgen 'F'. Despite a myriad of signals winging their way between ships, it very often became necessary to speak to the Admiral's staff on an encrypted radio circuit known as the 'bubble-phone'. Many potential problems and unexpected changes were sorted out by Ops 2 getting on the 'bubble-phone' and 'discussing' the problems with varying degrees of vehemence.[16]

In both conflicts equipment was found to have suffered from a lack of operational input during decades of peacetime operations. In 1982 soft furnishing, carpets, wood panelling and other materials used to make living spaces in warships more comfortable were found to be flammable and emergency measures had to be taken to strip them out as far as possible after the loss of HMS *Sheffield* to fire. The problem was not a new one:

> The burning question of the hour points to the necessity for the invention of some non-inflammable material in lieu of the linoleum and corticene now in use in the Service, which only adds fuel to any fire caused in action. The Germans had their iron-work scraped practically bare, and the linoleum stripped, leaving the decks also bare; yet their very bulkheads seemed to burn: this seems to indicate the advisability of trying to ascertain the main causes of fire in action.[17]

At least in 1914 uniforms were made of wool and cotton which are naturally fire-retardant but by 1982

> it was realised that the normal issue action-working rig was an unviable proposition. This was due to it being made from man-made fibres which melt in the heat from an explosion and cause

lethal burns. Therefore a new rig was introduced, colloquially known in my ship as 'Falklands Fighting Order' or 'FFO'. This consisted of a set of flame-resistant overalls, anti-flash hood and gloves, and steaming boots. All of this continually worn over the top of warm clothing made up the rig. In fact during the period of hostilities it was never taken off, and one even had to sleep in it. At all times one had to carry a life-jacket and a once-only survival suit. Most of us also found it worth while to carry extras such as a torch and a seaman's knife. Everybody also had to wear an identification tally around the neck and carry a Geneva Convention Identification Card. After the initial sinking of ships, an optional extra was introduced, the personal survival kit, this was a kit in a handy container consisting of a change of underclothes, toothbrush, razor and other extras one required. All in all we were rigged and ready for any emergency.[18]

Both conflicts saw weapons that had been developed and tried in peacetime used for the first time in action. Inevitably, after the battles, correspondents wrote their views on the lessons that had been learned. Gunnery had dominated the 1914 battle when the anonymous writer in HMS *Cornwall* had noted that 'with the long ranges at which this action was fought, great difficulty was experienced in seeing whether shots were going over the enemy or were hitting him.' He also observed that 'another great obstacle that must be overcome by the spotting officer, which does not occur in peace-time, is to differentiate between the flash of the enemy's gun and the burst of one's own shell.' Control of ships' guns from a director was new in 1914 and allowed the British ships to engage the enemy at long range, hitting less frequently but not being hit in return. Commanding officers and their gunnery lieutenants still yearned to bring the enemy to close action, however, the technique which had allowed the Royal Navy to dominate its nineteenth-century opponents with the weight and volume of fire.

> The *Kent* now gained ground very quickly, and bent on sinking her opponent in the least possible time, closed in to a mean range of 5,000 yards as she wished to take advantage of what might only prove to be a temporary reduction of speed. Rapid salvoes were exchanged by both sides, so the *Kent* finding that she was being hit, closed in still further to a final range of 2,500 yards. To sheer weight of her heavier armament together with the accuracy of her aim may be attributed the fact that she sank the *Nürnberg* about 7.10pm.

The results of long-range fire caused several comments. 'Sidelights on the Battle' continued 'At extreme ranges requiring high-angle fire, the deflections actually used were far in excess of what might have been expected'. 'As the bursting qualities of lyddite have been called in question, it may be of interest to remark that the German prisoners were unanimous in stating that they burst efficiently and regularly, creating tremendous havoc.' Clearly, when interviewed the survivors had revealed more than their name, rank and number. Plunging fire had never been encountered and analysed before and it was noted that 'on several occasions, the enemy's projectiles fell within five yards of our ships without causing any damage whatever. This was naturally due to the high-angle fire.' Both battlecruisers found deviations of as much as two points in their magnetic compasses after the action, caused, it was presumed, by sub-permanent magnetism due to the 'shock of discharge of their guns.' They were fortunately able to rely on gyro compasses after the action. The article ended with conclusions which are as relevant today as they were in 1914 and 1982. 'An organised system, by which food should be supplied to the ship's company while at stations for action, should be introduced throughout the Service. It is suggested that this should be of a portable nature.' The need to reduce the amount of flammable material in ships and wear clothing that could protect the wearer from flash has already been quoted but Sidelights also suggested that 'all men stationed at or near guns should be com-pelled to wear some form of protection against deafness. If properly used this will increase the efficiency of telephone services.'

Some form of camouflage to masts and funnels to make range-finding more difficult was suggested together with the beneficial effects of keeping men informed of what was happening, especially those below decks in machinery spaces and magazines. Although written by the commanding officer of a cruiser forming part of the largest Navy the world had ever known, Sidelights ends by saying that 'the object with which it has been written is to supply food for thought and con-sideration on points of which the British Navy has had no experience, and that appear to be of more than passing interest.' This was precisely the sort of article *The Naval Review* was created to put into print.

'Bystander' took a somewhat less specific view in 1982.

In principle, there are no lessons from the Falklands. It remains another twelve-inches-to-the-foot example of the political utility of sea power. That it happened to the British suddenly and out of a clear sky at about the same time as the 1981 Defence Review is coincidental, but it does not materially affect the truths of maritime strategy, truths which the United Kingdom will continue to ignore at its peril.

He did comment on some practical lessons from a material perspective that should not have needed to be relearned. These included what he considered to be self-evident facts that 'only ships can carry heavy weights long distances over water; a maritime force requires organic air power including Airborne Early Warning and nuclear submarines present a severe threat to surface forces but cannot conduct air defence nor naval gunfire support.' Bystander emphasised that the South Atlantic Campaign of 1982 'was a famous victory and it was won by the surface ships of the Royal Navy. Or, put in another less partisan way, the operation would not have been possible at all without the surface ships of the Royal Navy.' Included with those surface ships were the aircraft that operated from them and the Royal Marines and other amphibious forces they carried into action because he amplified his comments by saying 'our surface ships wrote off a medium power's gallant air force in a matter of days and a mere four hundred miles from their bases, allowing a very considerable amphibious operation to take place with minimal casualties to the landing force.' His article also looked at diplomacy, the unthinkable consequences of defeat and the presence in ships of so many representatives of the media.[19]

The Falklands War of 1982 was the first in which reporters and camera crews sailed with a task force and digital broadcasting techniques allowed moving pictures to be sent back to the UK in near real time. We can now see it as the dawn of our current information age in which the press and public not only expect but demand instant access to events and an explanation of what their armed forces are doing. Many officers at sea considered that information that would be useful to the enemy might be handed over too easily but few realised the need to maintain public support as a critical factor. In hindsight, this view that military activity must all be kept secret seems a more distant attitude than that of the gunnery officers off the Falkland Islands in 1914. 'KRJA' wrote an article giving his views on a House of Commons report on the handling of press and public information during the Falklands War, claiming 'that too much was revealed and that a lot more was revealed too soon.' He stated that 'war is a nasty business: to televise it probably serves no practical military purpose. It is merely pandering to the public's morbid desire to witness blood and gore and should not be allowed. It may be "good TV", but it is in execrable taste.'[20]

It is clear that in 1914 officers were expected to inform the public of their activities and they wrote to the press with frank descriptions of combat. How else would the public know what their Fleet had done 8,000 miles away? Some of those letters were subsequently picked up and used by the editor of *The Naval Review*. The development of more immediate reporting techniques was viewed with aversion by at least some members of the 1982 Task Force although subsequently the Service has learnt that it must be able to cope with them. Operational Sea Training now includes simulated press visits during work-up to accustom command teams to the need.

The author was in the Ministry of Defence in 1982 and cannot recall his own view of the press at the time but like most others he has subsequently recognised the important role of the media in showing the justice and legitimacy of British actions. Indeed, the media can be said to have changed the concept of warfare, especially with regard to the collateral damage caused by aerial bombing. Stateless terror groups have been quick to televise civilian casualties after bombs and missiles have hit urban targets in the many campaigns that have followed the Falklands War, and if Western forces had maintained the silence advocated by KRJA in 1982 they would appear, to the world community, to be at best accepting, or at worst attempting to hide, guilt.

In contemporary operations individual officers will find their every move reported upon and analysed by press and television, but while they may now be forbidden from writing to *The Times*, they may, of course, still write for *The Naval Review*.

25 Nuclear Matters

Rear Admiral Guy Liardet

WHEN Yoshio Nishina, the best known of the Japanese atomic scientists, was asked by a journalist from the official news agency on the morning of 7 August 1945 whether he believed the American broadcast that an atomic bomb had been dropped on Hiroshima, he was greatly alarmed. The journalist hoped it was mere propaganda. But Nishina replied that it was quite possibly true. At dawn that day, the Deputy Chief of the General Staff, General Kawabe, had also received a report that was at first incomprehensible: 'The whole city of Hiroshima was destroyed instantly by a single bomb.' As soon as Nishina appeared at headquarters, Kawabe asked him whether any defence was possible. He was able to make only one suggestion, to shoot down every hostile aircraft that appeared over Japan.[1]

Subsequent to the bombardment of Nagasaki, the Japanese government on 11 August offered unconditional surrender, concluded on 14 August.

Members of *The Naval Review* serving in the Pacific theatre were, naturally enough, much relieved by the cessation of hostilities. E V B Morton was a naval doctor on board the 'Woolworth' carrier *Pursuer* which was preparing for Mountbatten's Operation Zipper, the invasion of Malaya. Echoing the opinion of many others,[2] he wrote: 'In retrospect there can be little doubt therefore that thousands of British and Allied lives (possibly my own included) were probably saved by the atomic bombs being dropped on the Japanese mainland on 6th and 9th August, and I for one am grateful for that cataclysmic intervention by the Americans.'[3]

The coercive power available to a nuclear weapon state over a non-nuclear weapon state had been ruthlessly demonstrated. Atomic, or nuclear, weapons (the nomenclature changes about 1956) have been present for exactly two-thirds of the life of *The Naval Review*. It is unsurprising that in the some 250 issues between the autumn of 1945 and 2008 can be found more than 120 articles, book reviews, parliamentary extracts and editorials concerning nuclear weapons. The subjects covered include war-fighting considerations, weapon effects, deterrence philosophy, proliferation, arguments concerning budgetary allocations, morality, legality, the contribution of arms control to security, inter-service rivalry and many other issues. Here, much selectivity will be required and much fine writing will have to be ignored.

There is a belief abroad, a suspicion, hardly discussed, but pervasive, that the Royal Navy never took nuclear weapons seriously, coming to an early and, one might say, a sophisticated opinion that they were unusable and irrelevant to the business of exercising sea power in a post-war world of superpower stasis where the major threats to a balanced fleet seemed to be more budgetary than strategic, the opposition nearer to home than a few kilometres of intra-German border. Indeed, in his doctoral thesis on the Royal Navy's nuclear policy, Richard Moore says:

> It will be a central part of my argument that throughout the period under review – roughly the first Cold War and the 'golden age' of academic nuclear strategy – the Royal Navy was less than enthusiastic about nuclear weapons. This lack of enthusiasm was far from moral and few in the senior service would have had any truck with those of the Campaign for Nuclear Disarmament who marched on Aldermaston, still less with their successors in the peace camps of the 1980s ... Instead, then, their lack of enthusiasm was practical, nuclear weapons were largely irrelevant to their major concerns.[4]

Harry S Truman became president of the United States on 12 April 1945. On 25 April the Secretary of War, Henry L Stimson, warned Truman that other nations would be able to make atomic bombs and that such possession would be either a threat to or a guarantor of peace. Robert Oppenheimer, scientific leader of the Manhattan project, forecast that the Soviets would rush to build the atomic bomb and the result would be an arms race, while General Groves, military project manager, predicted it would be twenty years before they caught up, a huge overestimate. In October, during a discussion about relative rates of disarmament, Truman's budget director Harold Smith said, 'But you have the atomic bomb up your sleeve.' Truman replied, 'Yes, but I am not sure it can ever be used.' Without the bomb, American policy might well have been more conciliatory and less confident after VJ Day, but possession proved disappointing and did not allow her to shape the world as she wished; practicalities, morality and public opinion would never support its use against a recent ally to 'save' Eastern Europe, even though the freedom of Poland was Britain's *casus belli*. Briefed by the atomic spies, Stalin's studied indifference to Truman's revelation at Potsdam was echoed by Soviet policy during the subsequent negotiations, never claiming to be threatened and publicly minimising its strategic value. Here, unilateral possession did not seem to coerce. The decision not to trust and involve the Soviet Union in post-war control of atomic energy is seen as contributing to the Cold War.[5]

Thus by the end of 1945 many of the issues that were to flower in later years were already becoming apparent – mutual deterrence, morality, competition, the effect on the level of 'conventional' forces. How did *The Naval Review*'s editors and contributors shape up to this New Atomic Age? How can the role of *The Naval Review* best be described? Did it advance the intellectual level of debate as the arcana of nuclear strategy piled higher and higher? Was it a vehicle for informing a wider naval audience about the issues? Did it influence policy formation in nuclear matters?

From Dispersal to Deterrence

In the August 1945 issue, the editor, Admiral Sir Richard Webb, quoted a letter received from 'Fauteuil'[6] which explains that 'Election landslide, atomic bomb, surrender of Japan' are such momentous events that they cannot be dealt with by means of an updating footnote to his series 'Notes on the War at Sea', but that 'everything be left for treatment in the next number.' In the next number, 'H' speculated in 'The Atomic Bomb' on the need for dispersal:

> The Navy's main weak spot will be at home. Large factories and shipyards will be useless owing to vulnerability to enemy weapons. Owing to this lamentable state of affairs the yards and factories supplying the navies of the Commonwealth will have to be sited in the Colonies ... Surely, even more than ever before, our strength lies in the world-wide distribution of our forces, including the resources to maintain and produce them. Should we not set up, in all of our Colonies and Dominions, rocket batteries which can be directed to shower upon any aggressor a hail of 'V20' missiles?

H also called for 'Anti-atomic-bomber fighters, which, to my mind, would be specially streamlined heavy fighters built almost entirely of some asbestos material and armed with a single large atomic rocket which would be launched from battleships and cruisers and land back on carriers.'[7] While these sentiments early recognise the prospect of an atomic-equipped enemy, the winds of change that have blown since 1945 render them nothing short of quaint.

In the May issue of 1946, 'Nico' studied a 'size and shape' for a fleet in the atomic age, setting out a range of politico-military objectives and, inter alia, calling for ten fleet carriers, seventeen light fleet carriers and eighteen escort carriers.[8] Nico's article is all of a piece with an absurdly ambitious culture within the naval staff relative to national near-bankruptcy – a theme strongly identified by Eric Grove in the first chapter of his comprehensive history of the post-war Royal Navy.[9]

The air and underwater bursts of the first of the series of American tests at Bikini Atoll on 1 and 25 July 1946 occasioned a certain amount of optimism in *The Naval Review*. 'Teaboat' summarised the report of the Joint Chiefs of Staff to the President:

> In the dispositions used when carriers are operating, ships are not normally within a mile of one another, so it seems that one atomic bomb would never sink or heavily damage more than one ship, and there would perhaps be a 50 per cent chance of all ships in the formation escaping without heavy damage. Taking a convoy in the disposition normally used in the last war, the maximum number of ships in the 500-yard circle would be three, and in the 1,000-yard seven.[10]

In the same issue Nico forecast ballistic missile delivery of atomic weapons which might also, by being 'far more powerful than either of those dropped at Bikini', destroy a convoy. He postulated concentrated vitamin food pills and 'huge steel containers towed across by specially designed submarines' as ways of feeding the nation.[11]

In the January issue of 1947 'SWR' took the worldwide dispersal of bases still further and carried the actual text of the Joint Chiefs of Staff report of the Bikini trials as an appendix.[12] In the May issue of 1947 'Mate' poured scornful cold water on the possibility of dispersion, 'If money is of comparatively little account in war, its influence in peace is only too well known. From where, then, will it come to finance this gigantic exodus of men and materials to the far corners of the Empire?' For the first time within these pages some of the wider consequences of atomic warfare were raised: 'Is it morally defensible or even worth while to mortgage our souls and all that makes life worth living for an existence devoted to an end that at best is unlikely to offer anything better than mere survival in a Wellsian aftermath of devastation, where the most ardent optimist could hardly hope to distinguish victor from vanquished?'[13] This thought is echoed by 'Tite-Barnacle' in a discussion of the future of maritime air power: 'If both sides bombard each other with atomic missiles the victor's plight will not be much better than that of the vanquished. The resultant peace will not be worth having.

Is it really supposed that we should start that form of warfare or accept its inevitability?'[14]

In the autumn of 1946 Britain had decided to build its own bomb. In 1947 one of the worst of the post-war economic crises resulted in savage naval cuts and an accelerated scrapping programme. In May 1949 the North Atlantic Treaty was signed and the Federal German Republic proclaimed, while Stalin grudgingly lifted the Berlin blockade, a failed gambit which had made the Soviet Union appear brutal and incompetent. But on 29 August 1949, as predicted, Russia became an atomic weapon state.

Appearing in the November issue of that year, 'Sirius', in his review of *The Absolute Weapon: Atomic Power and World Order*,[15] edited by Bernard Brodie, wrote: 'I am not convinced that it is altogether a good sign that there should have been relatively little discussion of this question in *The Naval Review*, for that seems to be a somewhat disquieting pointer to the curious conventionality of the military mind, of which more will have to be said later – though not by me.' Perhaps a little unfair, given the coverage noted above, but it is true that Sirius drew attention to several of Brodie's postulates written as early as 1946 and which represented an advance on the level of thought seen heretofore. Briefly, these were: no adequate defence against the bomb exists, nor is it probable that any will be found; the atomic weapon puts a high premium on the development of new types of carrier and greatly extends the destructive capability of existing carriers; air superiority fails to guarantee security; superiority in the numbers of atomic weapons held does not guarantee strategic superiority; there is no shortage of raw material and other powers will have the ability to produce the bomb in quantity within five to ten years.

The institution of a New Prize Essay Competition in the May 1952 issue entitled 'More Forethought' generated a lengthy essay in November by 'Credo' which discussed the nature of a Cold War and the circumstances under which it might become 'hot', particularly in the context of the Korean War currently being fought by the United Nations coalition. Interestingly, he believed that Russia would be better contained by the reunification of Germany and the rearming of Japan. The hydrogen bomb was mentioned (the first American test of which obliterated a Pacific island on 1 November 1952 – the critical test in the Pacific that got out of control with a yield of fifteen megatons and widespread radioactive fallout did not take place until 1 March 1954). Credo wrote: 'Considering the nature and dispersal of vital areas, Britain and America may be more vulnerable to atomic attack than Russia, but this vulnerability is more than offset by a larger stock of atom bombs. It is not improbable, therefore, that Russia might be quickly knocked out by atomic attack and the way paved for the internal upset of her Government and Communist regime …'. Some of his speculations about the role to be played by 'the Empire' during a European atomic war and his belief that 'it may be necessary to move during the course of the war over ten million Britons to Canada, Australia and New Zealand' lay in the realm of fantasy.[16]

In the August issue of 1953, 'ADT' provided a long and detailed account of the efficient planning and execution of the test of the first British atomic weapon in the Monte Bello Islands off northwest Australia in October 1952.[17]

During 1953 and under conditions of intense downward pressure on the defence vote, the war-fighting potential of atomic weapons gave rise to much Government argument centring around the likelihood of a 'short war' of six weeks, a scenario supported by the then Minister of Supply, Duncan Sandys: 'only those forces that contributed in peacetime to Britain's position as a world power and which were relevant to the first six weeks of war should be maintained.'[18] Such a stark analysis was softened by the concept of a 'broken-backed war' during a 'survival period' after the atomic exchange, a concept favoured by a naval staff concerned about maintaining a fleet which would be capable of projecting maritime power worldwide. Grove described how Rear Admiral Sir Anthony Buzzard, Director of Naval Intelligence (DNI), in July 1953 had started to question the 'mass destruction policy' based on immediate use of American strategic air power, and denounced counter-city attacks – which in the future would be termed 'countervalue' – as likely to bring devastating retaliation, suicidal for the UK, while suggesting the retention of a deterrent force to prevent attack on Western urban areas.[19]

In February 1954, 'Porthole' found it astonishing that there had been so little reference to atomic power so far in *The Naval Review* and gloomily discussed how atomic weapons might be used and made reference to the hydrogen bomb which he called 'The Monster', expressing doubts about its applicability to naval warfare. 'The Bikini' he sees as useful against both land and sea targets but very certain to provoke counterattack. 'The Tactical' he believes might not do so: 'It is a very different matter losing a few million lives in an already over-populated country than having all one's cities and industries reduced to rubble.' Defence against 'The Tactical' is – once again – dispersion. He worried about 'Mines' and 'Time Bombs': 'Out go our sweepers the next morning and start exploding the mines by their magnetic sweeps. Suddenly the atomic mine is exploded. All the sweepers are sunk.

Sheerness is almost totally destroyed, or rendered radio-active due to spray, and the Medway is blocked.'[20]

Marshal of the RAF Sir John Slessor's book *Strategy for the West* was reviewed in the important November 1954 issue by 'PWB':

> Even if antidotes were more nearly in sight than they are now, anything approaching effective defence is not a practical economic proposition. No one can now expect to 'win' a war, in the old sense of profiting by it: all alike will suffer so grievously that the threat of atomic air power should prevent war, provided that it has been made clear that it will be used without hesitation against any aggressor.

Inaccurately described by Moore[21] as 'a lone visionary in the pages of *The Naval Review* (who) concluded that the H-Bomb had ushered in an era of mutual deterrence', the writer 'EHS' countered[22] the irrational and hugely expensive 'dispersion' proposals made by 'Hornli' in the same issue.[23]

What can we say about *The Naval Review*'s contribution to the debate thus far? With a certain hand-wringing tenor to the writing, it has not been alone in a struggle to integrate the war-fighting characteristics of atomic weapons with any sort of a credible third world war scenario with its generally unexplored but catastrophic political, social, economic and cost-benefit consequences, the unrealistic 'broken-backed' warfare concept being an example. With others, it had failed. The hydrogen bomb and concomitant mutually assured destruction ushered in a quest for security either by treaty, by overkill or by a careful matching of capability – a 'golden age' of academic nuclear strategy.

Polaris and Flexible Response

In the May 1955 issue, Admiral Buzzard's splendid article 'Must We Mass Destroy Cities?' took further his theme exposed above when he was DNI and introduced fresh concepts to the pages of *The Naval Review*: declaratory policy and negotiated arms control. Typical of his thinking was:

> Finally, a statement by the Western Powers that they would only attack cities with weapons of mass destruction in retaliation for such attack, would, surely, be a further welcome step along our present course of reducing tension, and do something to counter the very real fears in the minds of the masses on both sides of the 'Iron Curtain', planted there by Communist propaganda, that the USA is bent on a war of mass destruction. In particular, it would be an assurance of our sincerity in the disarmament discussions.[24]

Contrapuntal to all this arid debate, readers were properly reminded of the horrors of atomic warfare in *Hiroshima Diary*, a journal by the physician Michihiko Hachiya, the first full-length eyewitness account to be published in the English language and here reviewed by 'PH'.[25]

In an article reprinted from the *Spectator* of 9 March 1956, Anthony Buzzard, taking some words by John Foster Dulles, introduced the idea of 'graduated deterrence', calling for a 'strong and representative body' to establish the distinctions between tactical and strategic nuclear weapons which would have the best chance of holding in wars of limited aims.

In 'A Lieutenant Looks at the Navy', 'PM' drew attention to the US Strategic Air Command's alarming hair-trigger posture and Field Marshal Montgomery's declaration that NATO intends 'first use.' The Navy lacked a capable strike aircraft and was unable to contribute to this policy of 'Defence by Deterrence'. He suggested an atomic and a conventional division of the fleet's resources.[26] The May 1957 issue, while much devoted to the Suez operation, continued with an article by 'Blob' on morale in a Navy affected by atomic weapons. 'Thus the bewilderment and rather ill-defined feeling of impotence that existed in the immediate post-war years is being replaced by one even more damaging; that the Navy, as at present constituted, is of little importance in the ordering of world affairs.'[27] Later in the year, the editor wrote:

> a lot of members have simultaneously arrived at the same thought, which may be expressed in the questions: 'Are we right to be spending such a high proportion of our defence vote on "The Great Deterrent" – thermonuclear bombing at the expense of conventional forces? Is our insistence on contributing our tiny share of these unspeakable weapons to the NATO armoury based on anything more substantial than muddled thinking and *amour propre*.'

In January 1959 the editor deplored the 'pitiful size' of the Navy.

In June, the Royal Navy's first nuclear submarine, the *Dreadnought*, was laid down and launched ten months later. But it is in the July 1958 issue that the Parliamentary Secretary to the Admiralty, Mr Robert Allan, mentioned the word 'Polaris' for the first time in these pages:

> The tactical superiority of these submarines may be minimised by new defensive devices, but their strategic value, especially when armed with Polaris (the American ballistic missile), is incalculable. Polaris is now being developed in the US for launching from a submerged submarine. It is stated that it will have a range of some 1,500 miles and be armed with a megaton warhead. Nuclear

submarines thus armed – and I have heard it said that they can carry up to 20 or more missiles – will be able to place themselves within missile range of almost any target in the world, with little fear of counter attack, or indeed of detection.[28]

Mountbatten had arranged a close link with the American Polaris programme, but issues of credibility and cost produced 'distinctly limited enthusiasm' within the Admiralty and within the submarine service who saw their hunter-killer nuclear submarine building stream being affected. Despite an aggressive anti-Polaris lobby by the RAF, the developmental failure of the Skybolt (an air-launched ballistic missile) led to the Nassau Agreement of January 1963 and the creation of the Polaris Executive.[29]

Anthony Buzzard continued his series of far-sighted articles in November 1959 with a long discussion of the relationship between defence and disarmament, making the point that 'we are in such a mess in both' because they are usually considered separately. He deplored the disarmers as being likely to break up the NATO Alliance, suggested arms limitation talks with 'the Communists' and seeking agreements from other countries not to join the 'nuclear club' – foreshadowing Non-Proliferation Treaty ambitions – and expressed a determination to 'escape from our position of having to be the first to resort to tactical atomic weapons', thus identifying many of the issues that were to dominate future years.[30]

Prominent amongst these, of course, was the essential weakness of NATO's strategy of 'flexible response' formalised nearly ten years later by Military Committee document MC14/3 dated 16 January 1968 and the thinking behind which Professor Lawrence Freedman attributed to the 'graduated deterrence' ideas 'formulated in Britain in the mid-1950s'[31] as a reaction to the incredibility of Eisenhower's 'massive response' doctrine. Under 'massive response', a weakness in conventional force levels in Europe would (possibly) be countered by first use of nuclear weapons thereby escalating the conflict to a higher level of what, given Soviet theatre nuclear force numbers, may also be weakness and with the risk of further escalation to strategic exchanges. To quote Freedman's pungent concluding line: '*C'est magnifique, mais ce n'est pas la stratégie.*'

In the next issue, PM cogently argued against the H-bomb and Britain's nuclear-based defence policy, saying that our aspirations towards being a great power damaged our relations with medium powers: 'If the West is to regain the offensive in the worldwide battle between freedom and tyranny it must re-approach the whole problem of defence. It must escape from the idea that security can be provided only by the creation of ever more expensive and destructive weapons ... the offensive must be taken with the less destructive weapons of political ideals and economic aid.'[32]

The Cuban missile crisis, which broke in October 1962, was the most alarming of the twenty-one 'nuclear threats' issued by the superpowers between 1948 and 1969, most of which 'were not very influential.'[33] The crisis merely rated two brief mentions in the 'Naval Affairs' series in subsequent issues, lauding the use of sea power.

For the first time, the European dimension is raised by 'Willow' in the 1962 August issue, with particular regard to our historically damaged relations with France, not improved by her record during the Second World War and the pro-Nazi elements of Vichy policy. Willow postulates an 'Anglo-Saxon conspiracy', which it is believed, reduces the ability of Europe to function geopolitically:

> In nuclear weapons, by insisting that our special status required us to have an independent strategic deterrent, Britain gave France every reason to follow the same expensive and unnecessary path. Even if we allow the questionable assumption that it is necessary for the European nations to have a deterrent separate from that provided by the United States, it would at least have been less costly and more effective if Britain and France had joined forces in the project.

There is a link between this article and a fiery editorial in the issue celebrating the fiftieth anniversary. The editor explained that the day of the manned bomber as a national deterrent was over and that this would have effects on the purpose of the RAF.[34] He said:

> There is a popular belief that the Prime Minister got quite a good bargain at Nassau but this seems very doubtful; in place of 'Skybolt', to be fitted to our existing and highly efficient bomber force, we are to be allowed to buy 'Polaris' missiles to be fired by huge submarines which do not yet exist and the building of which is likely to absorb the whole of the Navy's share of the Defence vote. If this is a good bargain the writer will eat the editorial hat.[35]

The independent deterrent was a ridiculous pretension, given the strength of the American Minutemen ICBMs. Better spend the money on proper ships.

A suitable corrective to a number of similar articles in the mid 1960s is provided by 'Onlooker' in August 1963 who warmly welcomed the deterrence duty placed upon the Royal Navy and, in explaining to the sceptical the anti-submarine facts of life, introduced the stabilising value of an invulnerable second strike capability: 'Not only is the Polaris missile first-class, but by employing the submerged "vehicle" an enemy's chance of destroying the source of the deterrent by surprise is reduced to negligible proportions.'[36] But the fact that navigational inaccuracy and lack of missile mid-flight guidance presupposed 'countervalue' targets is not mentioned.

Elsewhere, the first Soviet nuclear-powered ballistic missile submarine of the comparatively primitive Hotel class was commissioned in November 1960 and the more numerous Yankee class was in service from 1967. The USS *George Washington* began its first strategic deterrent patrol on 15 November 1960; HMS *Resolution* fired her first test Polaris missile on 15 February 1968 at 1115 Eastern Standard Time, creditably only 15 milliseconds late on a plan formed as early as 1963.[37]

These developments naturally took away some of the fears about pre-emptive counterforce strikes by either side. 'DJSW' in his lengthy 'British Sea Power in the Next Decade – A Study of the Roles of the Navy' stated that 'a credible second strike capability will be an essential element of Defence Policy',[38] and this opinion became dominant amongst the increasingly rational, professional and well-argued articles in *The Naval Review* of the later 1960s. In his 1968 article 'Submarine Matters', Ian McGeoch, with his lips moving slowly so that all can follow, irrefutably sets out the case.[39]

From Polaris to Trident

A decade of silence is loudly interrupted by 'Bels' in April 1979 who asked in an important article whether Britain needs a successor to Polaris.[40] With appropriate source material, he explained that Soviet and US strategic forces now have similar counterforce and countervalue postures, remarking that the Soviets compensate for less counterforce accuracy with larger yields. Both nations were hardening silos. Drawing on an Institute for the Study of Conflict working party report, Bels produced a chilling analysis, with quotations from Soviet periodicals and official statements, of their unending campaign of hatred and xenophobia and constant boasting about their military invincibility and moral infallibility. The Soviets' drive for strategic superiority and the role of force within society and as an instrument of foreign policy were exposed and compared with President Carter's softer line – cancellation of the B1 bomber, deferred deployment of the neutron bomb and his swiftly rejected disarmament proposals; 'the current SALT II talks are uniquely significant and a misjudgement by President Carter could jeopardise the existence of the United States and with it the survival of the free societies of the West.'[41] The Soviet attitudes to peaceful co-existence, détente and correlation of forces were described; success in the Findlandisation and decoupling of Europe from the United States would be a huge step towards Marxist world domination. Drawing attention to an Adelphi paper by Mr Ian Smart,[42] Bels pointed out the command and control difficulties inherent in any Anglo-French co-operation in Europe's name before agreeing with Mr Smart that the British replacement will depend on the *conviction* that an independent 'last resort' deterrent is *essential* coupled to a judgement that Britain has the *technical and economic capacity* to deploy a force able to exert the necessary deterrent influence on Soviet leaders.

In the November 1980 issue, editor John Nunn announced the government's decision to adopt the Trident system.

> The country now knows that it is to have a strategic force that has sufficient substance to pose a potential threat to key aspects of Soviet state power. I find it interesting and refreshing that the government in naming a foreign power has departed from the traditional formula of 'potential aggressor.' Plain speaking is needed if deterrence is to deter. But what about the cost?

In April 1981, this author surveyed the contemporary situation, explaining the necessity for, yet the inconsistency of, the NATO doctrine of flexible response and making the rarely seen point that NATO's three nuclear powers (one outside the Integrated Military Structure) represent three centres of decision making, thus complicating any Soviet démarche.[43] It's not only the mind of the President that had to be influenced.

Inter alia, he covered linkage with tactical systems at sea and the rationale for the NATO Theatre Nuclear Force Modernisation programme which was unanimously agreed in Brussels on 12 December 1979 and which drew so much media attention subsequently, making the point that 'single-key' American release of these weapons, despite their foreign basing, was strongly coupling to American strategic systems, the whole object of the exercise.

A couple of pages were spent on exploring the position of the Campaign for Nuclear Disarmament (CND), dissecting the ten essays collated and edited by E P Thompson and Dan Smith in *Protest and Survive*,[44] a title intended to parody the derided government civil defence pamphlet *Protect and Survive*. Fundamental anti-Americanism was clear, E P Thompson writing: 'The United States seems to me to be more dangerous and provocative in its strategies which press around the Soviet Union with menacing bases. It is in Washington, rather than Moscow, that scenarios are dreamed up for "theatre" wars; and it is in

America the "alchemists" of superkill, the clever technologists of advantage and ultimate weapons, press forward the politics of tomorrow.' CND completely ignored the differences between a totalitarian state and a democratic one in terms of the influence of public opinion and the availability of information. Its objective appeared to be unilateral disarmament by the West. At one point this author wrote: 'it is cheap to accuse CND of being in the pay of Moscow, but they will have to do better than ... (etc, etc)'. (Not quite so cheap, given the more recent revelations by defector Vladimir Bukovsky. Perhaps Lenin's useful idiots fitted better.)

The article concluded by saying: 'But CND has *heart*, there is a very real fear of nuclear war abroad to-day which needs to be answered by perhaps more sympathy and sound counter argument than is apparent at the moment so that emotion can be separated from cerebration.'

Decisions on the size and shape of the Trident submarine force had been taken by late 1981. In October 1981, the obsolescent Soviet Whisky-class submarine S363 ran aground in Swedish national waters – a radiographic survey indicated it was carrying a nuclear-tipped torpedo, causing alarm that such weapons should appear so low down in the Soviet order of battle. In 1982 Chevaline, the improved Polaris warhead with its extra decoys and improved penetration against Soviet ABM systems came into service hugely over budget; the target was still the Moscow criterion, the assured destruction of the Soviet capital.

The year 1981 was also the one that the BBC chose 'The Two-Edged Sword', delivered by Professor Laurence Martin, for its Reith Lecture series, marking some sort of apotheosis of academic nuclear strategy. Amongst many points made by Professor Martin was his paradoxical 'People Good, Weapons Bad', essentially saying that the accurate counterforce capability of 'Pershing 2' missiles was destabilising, giving rise to 'use or lose' and therefore more dangerous than to threaten centres of population.[45]

The Falklands war of spring 1982 had no nuclear weapon inputs save the erratic accusation by Mr Tam Dalyell, MP, that Britain had deployed a SSBN and some media whispers that warships and RFAs had had to disembarrass themselves of nuclear weapons before sailing south.

Ethics, Legality, Morality, Arms Control

With weapon procurement decided and Allied strategy (more or less) set in aspic since the Harmel Doctrine of December 1967,[46] it was natural that *The Naval Review* should now dwell upon supplementary topics – ethics, legality, morality, arms control.

In July 1982, the ethics of nuclear deterrence were argued with great force and precision by the Rev Dr Malcolm McCall, a naval chaplain,[47] who quoted the esteemed Sir Michael Quinlan, sometime Deputy Under Secretary (Plans and Programmes) in the Ministry of Defence and who, as the MoD's leading nuclear theorist and a prominent Roman Catholic, carried some weight in this field. McCall concluded that nuclear pacifism is not the morally right response to the international state of affairs.

> This paper has aimed to show that nuclear disarmers are in fact seriously misled on four main counts. First, they are wrong in an over-optimistic assessment of unredeemed human nature. Secondly, they largely ignore the sociopolitical requirements for adequate restraining force to deter aggression and prevent anarchy. Thirdly, they are unrealistically utopian in hoping for new forms of international relationships, based on 'good' populist pressures ... Fourthly, they fail to recognise the essentially untruthful and evil nature of Marxism-Leninism ...

In January 1984, Lieutenant J R Stocker raised several interesting questions:[48] how does the higher accuracy of the Trident missile affect the investment balance between seaborne and land-based systems; whether Trident is seen as a potential first-use counterforce weapon by either side or by disarmers; and is the invulnerability of the SSBN at risk by reason of recent advances in passive acoustics? He perhaps made too much of this last – while it was for a period indeed possible broadly to track a proportion of SSBNs by passive means, a fire-control solution on all or many was another matter altogether.[49]

A contribution from Captain A G Y Thorpe, Chief Naval Judge Advocate, made the point that, despite CND's warning that handling nuclear weapons is illegal, the possession of nuclear weapons has never been outlawed.[50] He listed the several controlling treaties that implicitly recognised their possession as lawful. He pointed to NATO's declaration at the Bonn Summit of June 1982 which forswore 'first use' of any weapons and ended by saying that in the propaganda battle it would be important to make sure that servicemen were fully aware that to obey proper orders regarding nuclear weapons is not in any way illegal, a motif taken up in the correspondence pages of subsequent issues.

In 1988 the seventy-fifth anniversary issue of *The Naval Review*, with its graceful Royal foreword and conspicuous red cover, contained an article by Admiral Sir John Fieldhouse, Chief of Defence Staff, on arms control which described the success of NATO's INF

(Intermediate Nuclear Forces) treaty negotiations:[51] a 'twin-track' approach which removed the threat of Soviet medium-range missiles from Europe and achieved asymmetric reduction in tactical warheads in NATO's favour; 'there was no prospect of removing the threat by arms control unless NATO had comparable systems to trade – a point readily overlooked by ... the so-called "peace movement".'After a survey of the rest of the field, Admiral Fieldhouse concluded by saying that he saw no early prospect of arms control leading to significant savings in defence expenditure.

From his knowledge of the Soviet Union and its officials, Admiral Sir James Eberle[52] remarked: 'As senior Soviet officials readily admit, it is all too clear that "our" system is doing very much better than "theirs".'[53] Sure enough, but to nearly everyone's surprise, on 9 November 1989, the Berlin Wall fell as political control in the communist German Democratic Republic disintegrated, Gorbachev's perestroika and glasnost ran away with him and the Soviet Union's Warsaw Pact allies began to revise their futures. Bilateral treaty negotiations threatened to become chaotic, the West pushing for a bloc-to-bloc agreement while there was still someone on the other side with whom to negotiate.

Professor Lawrence Freedman reviewed Admiral Richard Hill's book *Arms Control at Sea* in August 1989, praising his clarity of thought and argument, noting that much of the book describes why a series of favoured proposals such as ASW sanctuaries and zones of reduction were non-starters, although he did identify possible starters where he could find them. He made a strong case for cutting back on Western tactical nuclear weapons at sea, recognising that verification will be particularly difficult – points later well made by Commander H L Foxworthy in October.[54]

In a long and comprehensive paper reproduced from his Royal College of Defence Studies essay in the Seaford House Papers, Captain A B Ross identified the difficulties inherent in maritime arms control: asymmetries between the needs of sea-based NATO and continental Russia and in their naval forces – Russia does not have large carrier battle groups – militate against trade-offs.[55] He saw as plausible the complete removal of tactical nuclear weapons from the sea and the institution of a variety of confidence-building measures aimed at preventing incidents.

Throughout this period it became apparent from the Royal Navy's point of view that 'arms control reductions' would be 'structural' and budget-driven in search of an evanescent 'peace dividend' rather than negotiated.

In November 1995 Willow's expert paper opened with the thought that the decades-old role of nuclear weapons as the cornerstone of Western defence policy is coming into question, quoting authoritative figures who believe that possession diminishes rather than enhances US security.[56] He wrote: 'We have reached an unusual juncture in world affairs. One distinct and turbulent era has come to an end. The next has yet to take shape. We have the opportunity to make a real choice about the future of nuclear weapons.' He worked his way round the nuclear weapon states, quoting statements that each have made about disarmament and explaining how the security of each could be improved in a nuclear-free world. He believes in a reinforced Non-Proliferation Treaty and that 'break-out' could thereby, with 'world opinion' solidifying, be controlled.[57] His arguments were persuasive but depend upon some favourable developments in international relations.

Over two issues in 1997,[58] Stocker, now promoted and a reservist, authoritatively covered the recent history and present capabilities of the worryingly large number of nations that possess land-based ballistic missiles of various ranges and capabilities.

> There is also some European scepticism as to whether available technologies do offer credible defences that are remotely affordable. NATO and Western European Union[59] studies have failed to produce any tangible results, and given the universal and steep decline in defence budgets, America's main allies appear to wish the whole subject would go away.

Stocker provided a compellingly interesting account of First Gulf War anti-Scud[60] measures and an analysis of all possible counters to such weapons and their possible weapons of mass destruction, from deterrence through counterforce to various inflight and point defence solutions. The Royal Navy, he thought, might have a minor role if fitted with a capable anti-missile system. Not a happy picture.

Possibly because of security classification issues, tactical nuclear weapons at sea have hardly featured amongst *The Naval Review*'s writings. The subject was very fully discussed by Matthew Allen in a fascinating article appearing over two issues in 2001.[61] Allen clearly had inside knowledge of American weapon systems and doctrine. The dominant question was, of course, linkage to land-based nuclear systems and the fear of escalation. Allen speedily discounted any thought that nuclear weapon use at sea could remain isolated, making the point that several maritime nuclear capable systems are land-based, notably maritime anti-shipping and ASW aircraft. Amongst many cogent points, Allen said: 'Nuclear war fighting would only end after a tactical exchange at sea if the maritime dispute had been sufficiently important for one side to take the risk of escalation and yet unimportant enough for the defeated side to be able to accept failure without escalation.'

We close this chapter with a mention of three articles by Professor Steven Haines that delineate the future – 'Replacing Trident – A New Nuclear Debate';[62] 'Trident and the Non-Proliferation Treaty';[63] and 'The Real Strategic Environment'.[64] Haines rehearses the arguments now abroad against the renewal of the *Vanguard*-class submarines but he, an academic lawyer, says: 'I must say that when it comes to the issue of nuclear weaponry I am not convinced that the law has real utility (or relevance) in the shaping of strategic posture.' He is reassuring about the position of UK as a founding nuclear weapon state signatory of the Non-Proliferation Treaty. His survey of the shifting tectonic plates of power worldwide is a useful reminder of what has happened since the fall of Communism and '9/11'. 'Public enthusiasm for "force for good" humanitarian intervention has been profoundly undermined by unwise military adventurism in Iraq. The effects of this are likely to be long lasting.'

Haines concluded:

> But to be a stabilising influence requires successive governments to ... recognise Britain's great power status and the responsibilities it brings with it to effect some measure of equilibrium within what is still an inherently unstable system. Second, they need to ensure that status is retained. Divesting Britain of military capabilities, particularly those of most significance in great power terms, is not a responsible way forward. Here lies the rationale for nuclear weapons ... Relatively minor investment to cope with the immediate threat of terrorism is not what the overall defence budget is about.
>
> *Verb sap.*

Summary

It will be recalled that Richard Moore was quoted above as saying that the Royal Navy's 'lack of enthusiasm was practical, nuclear weapons were largely irrelevant to their major concerns.' That may be true of naval attitudes in the wider world, but within the pages of *The Naval Review* the subject of nuclear weapons has received almost continuous attention and with a noticeable flavour of sometimes passionate involvement.

It is noted above that Professor Lawrence Freedman attributed the concept of 'graduated deterrence' to British thinking in the 1950s, this evolving towards the long-lived NATO doctrine of 'flexible response'.

While it is not possible to show conclusively whether *The Naval Review* influenced national or Allied policy, Anthony Buzzard's far-sighted and widely-read articles on this particular subject were ahead of their time. Some of the better informed, more scholarly, submissions have been reprints from elsewhere. In keeping the membership up to speed, *The Naval Review* has performed well – there are very few topics that have not been identified within its pages in a timely fashion; the magazine has matched the evolution of nuclear strategy. One does have to say, however, that an evolutionary process in the quality of writing and argument is very apparent and this may be true of *The Naval Review* as a whole. Some of the earlier contributions have earned the epithet 'quaint' or 'fantasy' while talk of 'Empire' and 'the Colonies' reveal an ignorance of the post-war realities even as early as the late 1940s. All can agree that the quality of argument in the last thirty years or so has been outstanding.

26 The Reserves

Captain Martin Reed, MN, Captain Peter Hore,
and Captain Jeremy Stocker, RNR

Part I: Captain Martin Reed, MN

The Royal Naval Reserve

THE history of the Reserves has been well recorded in the pages of *The Naval Review*.[1] In brief, after the difficulties of manning the fleet during the Russian War 1853–56, the First Lord of the Admiralty, Sir John Pakington, set up a Royal Commission on Manning the Royal Navy which recommended more training ships for boy seamen, free bedding and mess utensils for new recruits, free uniform for continuous service entrants, and an improved scale of victualling, improved pay for seamen gunners; and, most importantly, the formation of a Royal Naval Reserve (RNR).[2]

The Royal Naval Reserve (Volunteers) Act of 1859 established a reserve of professional seamen from the merchant service. In 1862 it was extended to include Merchant Navy officers who adopted a distinctive lace consisting of stripes of interwoven chain, known as the 'rocky stripes'. In 1865, to support their representation for an undefaced blue ensign to be flown by merchant ships commanded by an officer in the RNR, the Registrar General of Shipping and Seamen informed the Admiralty that there were 117 lieutenants and sixty-five sub lieutenants with RNR commissions.

The Hungry Hundred and Famishing Fifty

In the 1890s the Navy urgently needed more lieutenants and 100 officers were recruited from the Merchant Navy, ninety of whom were RNR officers who accepted permanent commissions. A condition, however, was that these officers were not eligible for promotion beyond the rank of lieutenant, except for war service. They became known as the 'hungry hundred'. Three years later, with the shortage of lieutenants continuing in the RN, a further fifty RNR officers were given similar permanent commissions. They were inevitably known as the 'famishing fifty'.

In 1910, the RNR (Trawler Section) was formed to actively recruit and train fishermen for wartime service in minesweepers and minor war vessels, and the rank of Skipper RNR(T) was established, with enrolment into the force beginning in Grimsby and Aberdeen in 1911.

The success of Pakington's vision was shown soon after the outbreak of war, when a report from HMS *Kent* at the Battle of the Falklands in 1914 showed that 'three-fifths of her complement [were] Fleet Reserve men or Royal Naval Reserve [and] five men in every Seamen's 6in guns crews were Scotch fishermen.'[3]

Officers and men of the Reserves would serve in destroyers, submarines, armed merchant ships and Q-ships, and fishermen of the RNR(T) saw their ships fitted out as minesweepers. Some RNR officers flew in the Royal Naval Air Service (RNAS), and many more served ashore in the Royal Naval Division, where the Navy suffered 40 per cent of its losses. Merchant Navy officers and men in hospital ships, fleet auxiliaries, and transports were also entered in the RNR.

The Royal Naval Volunteer Reserve

The RNVR could trace a somewhat skimpy line back to the Sea Fencibles, established in 1798 and on through the Naval Coast Volunteers of 1853 and the Royal Naval Artillery Volunteers of 1873. In amongst these appeared the Royal Trinity House Volunteer Artillery of 1803 manning moored frigates on the Thames as a defence against a French invasion. However, in 1903 the RNVR was refounded as a reserve of civilians. Within fifteen years it more than proved its worth:

> That a force 10 years old, and a small one at that, should have expanded to such enormous proportions and served with distinction in almost every quarter of the globe, afloat, ashore, and in the air, is a magnificent achievement of which it has every right to be proud. It had no great traditions of its own to live up to. None of its forebears had ever seen active service. Almost, in a sense, it had a stigma to live down, in that previous naval volunteer organizations had come to untimely ends because they had proved unsuitable for the purpose for which they had been raised. The RNVR rose superior to every difficulty and made for itself an imperishable tradition which is a very real factor in the esprit de corps and keenness of the RNVR today.

It will give some idea of the numbers involved when it is realized that at the end of the war, 6,665 held commissions in the RNVR,

while, exclusive of the pre-war force, the total number of RNVR
ratings enrolled during the war approximated 60,000, of which
15,000 were taken for the RN Division prior to its recruiting being
undertaken by the War Office, leaving 45,000 for purely naval
services. That the RNVR proved a link of the utmost value between
the Navy and the non-seafaring civilian population of the country is
an outstanding fact.[4]

Masters of all Trades

Come the First World War, the RNR had an exceptional war record,
earning over five thousand honours including eleven Victoria Crosses.

> The RNR Officers have proved themselves invaluable, and without
> them we would not have had nearly enough lieutenants to
> commission all our ships. In fact, in ships employed on the trade
> routes they are in many respects more suitable than naval officers
> because they know all about merchant ships and merchant shipping,
> whereas most naval officers are profoundly ignorant of such
> matters.[5]

But Pakington's scheme had almost been too successful and there was
a surplus of Reserves who, under the direction of a youthful and
energetic Winston Churchill, then First Lord of the Admiralty, were
formed around a cadre of Royal Marines into the Royal Naval
Division and went on to fight with distinction, earning battle honours
ashore at Antwerp, Gallipoli and on the Western Front: 'The Division
suffered casualties of 582 officers and 10,797 other ranks killed, and
another 1,364 officers and 29,528 other ranks wounded. But between
them they won 923 decorations with eight VCs, 42 DSOs, and 555
Military Medals.'[6]

Articles in the early copies of the *NR* reported many areas where the
Reserves were involved and the following extracts indicate some of the
strange places and people involved, but foremost of all at Gallipoli:
'The *Talbot* picked up a Greek refugee on the coast and took him on
board the *Lord Nelson* to interview Lieutenant Palmer, RNR, late
British Consul at Chanak ... he gave us some useful information
regarding the forts and damage done inside the Straits.' (Nothing like
having a little local knowledge, but one wonders how the Consul
became a Lieutenant RNR?) The same article noted that five VCs were
given to the Navy on V-beach during the landing on 25 April.[7]

And Gallipoli again: 'We are taking up to the East a Commander
Campbell. He is a Commander RNR now, but a very short time ago
was a cavalry colonel. He is a yachtsman with his own yacht and has

been minesweeping in the North Sea all the winter. He apparently wants a change, so has left his yacht at home and come out here on a loose end.'[8] (Some loose end! There must be a further story to tell here.)

Even, in the early part of the war, armoured cars:

> In the early days of the war, armoured cars were found to be of great use during the time the front was in a state of flux, and the RNAS [Royal Naval Air Service] squadrons operating out in Flanders and Belgium were able to do very good work with cars fitted with extemporised protection.
>
> So successful were they that it was decided to form a body of officers and men specially trained in armoured car work and equipped with the best cars and specially designed armoured bodies. One squadron was originally contemplated, but in the course of a year the force had grown into 18 complete squadrons of heavy and light armoured cars, motor machine guns, and three landship squadrons were forming. The officers were mainly RNVR, and the men the pick of the motor mechanics and drivers in the country. ... The whole force was part of the RNAS and at one time when it had grown to 250 officers and 2,500 men, was the larger portion of it.[9]

And elsewhere, here in the Cameroons, a force consisted almost entirely of officers of the Reserves:

> In the evening we proceeded outside and anchored 5 miles south of Ambros Island, rendezvous for craft arriving tomorrow ... The flotilla arrived during the day and consists of: IVY (Governor of Nigeria's S Yacht, Com Hughes RNR, BALBUS (Steam Tug), Lieutenant Martin RNR, WALRUS (ditto), Lieutenant Richmond RNR, VAMPIRE (Steam Launch), VIGILANT (ditto) Lieutenant Henderson, RNR, ALLIGATOR (Motor Launch) Lieutenant Ford RNR, CROCODILE (ditto), TROGA (small collier), One lighter full of gelignite.

One wonders about the lighter full of gelignite! And when eventually convoys were started until 1917:[10]

> In May it was approved to send a Commodore RNR, of the White Star Line, to America, with the object of collecting an experimental convoy of 12 ships from Newport News ... The following month, a number of Lieutenant Commanders, RNR, were appointed for duty as Commodores of the various stream-line convoys, and 200 signal ratings were appropriated to the Mediterranean to improve the means of communication between ships in convoy.

Between the Wars

In 1921 Captain Sir David Wilson-Barker reminded all that the real purpose of the RN was in being a security for such as pass on the seas upon their lawful occasions. Wilson-Barker also called for something that sounds like a non-executive member of the Board of Admiralty: 'a Royal Naval Reserve officer ... who could take his place ... whenever questions concerning the two Services [RN and MN] in co-operation or otherwise were being dealt with, no matter how slight the connection.'[11]

The success of the Reserves in the war led to some seemingly odd suggestions such as 'a limited amalgamation of the Royal Naval and Merchant Service personnel, more particularly in the deck and engineer ranks and ratings', but sober analysis showed that the apparent advantages were outweighed by the difficulties to be overcome.[12] As the Navy suffered inevitable peacetime cutbacks, others speculated: 'the smaller our Navy the less we can afford to dissipate our resources; the reinforcement of our naval or military resources in war by withdrawing personnel or ships from the Merchant Navy must necessarily correspondingly reduce the resources of the latter; this must be borne in mind when considering the Merchant Navy as a Reserve for the Royal Navy.'[13]

Others were worried about the size:

> as the Second Sea Lord remarked last year, the existing Naval Reserve is rapidly becoming depleted, for there has been an alarming decrease in the number of trained seamen and a still more alarming decrease in the number of our fishermen ... Let us pray that ... when we do awake we may find our house set in order, particularly that portion of it whereof the doors are labelled 'NAVAL RESERVES'.[14]

Replying, an anonymous contributor commented to the editor that 'the writer of the article entitled "Naval Reserves" in your November issue stated that he speaks "without any very special knowledge" [and] after perusing his article I am forced to agree with him', before delivering some hard facts, including a swipe at the modern system of Naval Regional Officers: 'Your correspondent's suggestion of a number of Staff College Trained Captains, who are to organise the various areas aided by patriotic gentlemen (and ladies), and are in due course to hoist their flags, is too fantastic to merit serious discussion in these days of rigid economy and is not, presumably, intended to be taken seriously.'[15]

The editor intervened by publishing a lecture which started by declaring that 'the Royal Naval Reserve and the Merchant Service are almost synonymous terms' and continued, in case anyone was asleep at the back of the classroom, 'The Merchant Service is and always has been, the Reserve of the Royal Navy, ever since the days, not so long ago historically, when a Royal Navy was formed for the business of fighting. For centuries before that date, the Merchant Service had been accustomed to do all its own fighting, and to fight for the nation with the assistance of soldiers sent afloat when the occasion arose.'[16]

The editor also republished an essay from the *US Naval Institute Proceedings* in which one Captain Chester Nimitz described how the US was going about creating a corps of reserve officers, the Naval Reserve Officers' Training Corps, commenting that it had only been in existence 'some year or 18 months ... and it [was] too early for the author to give details of actual results. The principles are however both novel and interesting and such as might with advantage be considered for possible adoption in this country.'[17]

Others asked the more practical question of what are the Reserves for? 'What is required of an RNVR officer in wartime? To what is his peacetime training leading? It is suggested that the answer can be found in the single word "Replacements". It should be able to take on the work of naval officers, in small craft especially, in order to release fully trained officers for more important work.'[18]

Whatever the source of Reserve officers and men, 'When it is remembered how severely and progressively the Navy and its personnel have been reduced, it is evident that the importance of the Reserves has correspondingly increased. It therefore seems safe to assume that the RNVR, which met so successfully the tremendous calls of the late war, will continue to be regarded as an essential part of the country's system of naval defence.'[19]

Another writer made a specific bid for a Fleet Air Arm Reserve, though the reference to a high mortality rate would, presumably, not have appeared on any recruiting poster:

> The only Fleet Air Arm Reserve that exists at present consists of those regular and ex-shore service RAF officers who have qualified as deck landing pilots, and who have done a period of service in aircraft carriers. There are in addition a very small number of RN pilots who have for one reason or another permanently reverted to general service; but as most of these have not been kept in general flying practice they can hardly be considered as a reserve. The FAA would play a large part in the early stages of any war, and it is reasonable to suppose that the casualties among the officers would be high, particularly in torpedo-bomber aircraft, and it is for this type of aircraft that it takes considerably longer to train efficient personnel, owing to the amount of experience that a torpedo-bomber pilot requires before he can be reasonably certain of his torpedo hitting the target.[20]

There was also a prophetic article which called for the creation of university naval clubs which would be a particular kind of 'special volunteer reserve [which would] spread a leaven of naval thought and history throughout the universities, and through them to the educated classes in the Empire as a whole [and] build up a reserve of partly-trained, well-educated gentlemen, who would be available to join up as temporary officers in time of war.'[21] Something which sounds vaguely like the modern University Royal Naval Units, if not the language which a modern spin-doctor would use.

Many of the same arguments, though dressed in different language, would occur in the next post-war period.

The Reserves Leavened by the Regulars

In his history of the Reserves Murrison recorded: 'On commencement of hostilities in the Second World War, the RN once again called upon the experience and professionalism of the RNR from the outset to help them shoulder the initial burden until sufficient manpower could be trained for the RNVR and "hostilities only" (HO) ratings.'[22]

The Admiralty had already taken steps:

> To avoid a shortage of executive officers ... consequent on the rapid expansion of the fleet ... a large number of warrant officers will be promoted to lieutenant, additional officers of the RNR, 250 of whom have already been passed into the Navy, will be transferred and ... officers of the Merchant Navy ... will be entered, irrespective of the fact that they have not had any RNR experience ... Temporary employment in the fleet for a period of three years will also be offered to suitable officers of the RNVR and to members of the RNVSR.[23]

Looking back in 1959 the editor noted,

> By the start of World War II the RNR had expanded in a number of directions, notably the Patrol Service with its headquarters in Lowestoft. Some 5,600 officers and men were available on mobilization and the peak number of 57,000 in this part of the Reserve was reached in 1944. Most notable development was, however, in the Royal Naval Volunteer Reserve ... and at one time 44,000 of the 68,000 officers in naval service held RNVR commissions. The Fleet Air Arm and the Coastal Forces depended particularly on the RNVR and in 1940 the Submarine Branch was opened to this Reserve. RNVR officers eventually attained command of these craft and at least one submarine went to sea with an all RNVR Wardroom.[24]

Significantly: '98 per cent of the officers in the wartime coastal forces had served in the RNVR or the RNR.'[25]

Minesweeping became another Reserves speciality:

> 1,553 ships were employed, 1,228 being RN manned, 236 Dominion manned, and 69 Allied manned. 263 minesweepers were sunk; nearly one in five – a startling figure which shows how much was owed to the personnel ashore and afloat, 57,055 in all, of the British minesweeping service, little heard of, and little seen except by coast dwellers when apparently cruising leisurely and aimlessly in the offing. Of its 4,205 officers, 63 per cent were RNVR, 34 per cent RNR, and 3 per cent RN.[26]

Indeed:

> To get some idea of the Reserve/Regular balance, Lieutenant (Lord) Astor's speech to the House of Commons in 1943 ran: 'I do not know whether the House realises to what extent the Navy is now manned by men of the various Reserves. It has authoritatively been said that the war is no longer being fought by the Royal Navy, assisted by the RNVR and the RNR, but by the RNVR with a small leaven of the Royal Navy. We are going to win the Battle of the Atlantic and the Naval War in so far as we use all the talent available in the Reserves to the best possible advantage.'[27]

For example, a major part of the success of the breakout from Normandy in 1944 was the supply of fuel and lubricants which was achieved by PLUTO (Pipe Line Under The Ocean):

> Through this line over 600,000 tons of petrol was pumped, adding in the Cherbourg and Port-en-Bessin pipe supplies, Force Pluto put over three quarters of a million tons of petrol across the Channel. The compact little force of men drawn from the ships and streets of a few great ports, officered almost entirely from the RNR and the RNVR, to whom no amount of work, difficulty or disappointment could act as a damper to their faith and spirits, formed a 'Band of Brothers' in the Nelsonian tradition. And so it was done.[28]

RNR and RNVR officers again found themselves in command of destroyers, frigates, sloops, landing craft and submarines, or as specialist navigation officers in cruisers and aircraft carriers. In convoy work, the convoy commodore or escort commander was often an officer of the Reserves. As in the First World War, the Reserves acquitted themselves well, winning four VCs.

ll three South African Type 12 President-class frigates were extensively modernised at Simon's Town between 1968 and 1977. This included fitting long-range air-warning radar, a modern gunfire control system, Mk 32 torpedo launchers and the capability to carry a Wasp helicopter to counter submerged submarines detected by their medium-range sonar outside the radius of their Limbo mortars. Pictured here is the Clyde-built SAS *President Steyn* after her conversion. (Allan du Toit)

During 1955 a series of letters, collectively referred to as the Simon's Town Agreement, were exchanged by the South African and British governments which resulted in the naval base at Simon's Town being transferred to South African control on 2 April 1957, with Britain retaining certain privileges and the South African fleet being significantly expanded to assume an increasing responsibility for the collective defence of the Cape Sea Route. (Allan du Toit)

The hunter and the hunted: the Type 12 anti-submarine frigate SAS *President Kruger* and the A-class submarine HMS *Alliance* exercising in False Bay during July 1963. The Simon's Town Agreement enabled the South African Navy to develop into a professional, efficient and well equipped force well able to take its place alongside the Royal Navy and other Allied Navies during the Cold War. (Allan du Toit)

Within the terms of the Simon's Town Agreement, South Africa purchased four frigates, ten coastal minesweepers and five seaward defence boats from Britain between 1955 and 1963, which virtually trebled the size of the Fleet. Pictured here are the last two of Ton-class units to be transferred to South Africa, SA Ships *Mosselbaai* and *Walvisbaai*, being commissioned at HMS *Diligence*, Hythe, on 20 September 1959. The South African Navy was the largest operator of Ton-class minesweepers after the Royal Navy. (Allan du Toit)

S *Canberra* trialling her newly installed replenishment-at-sea gear by refuelling from RFA *Tidepool* n their way south to the Falkland Islands in 1982 (Martin Reed)

he assault ship HMS *Fearless* and her landing craft in San Carlos Water, Falklands. (Royal Navy)

HMS *Invincible* arriving for a visit to Naval Station Jacksonville, Florida in 2004. (US Navy)

Today's Royal Marines: Operation Volcano, January 2007, Kajaki, Helmand, M Company, 42 Commando Royal Marines. An iconic photograph during 3 Commando Brigade's second deployment in Afghanistan. Balancing the competing demands of sustained land operations against maintaining and training contingent amphibious capability has been a repeated dilemma since the end of the Second World War, exacerbated by an understandable desire by RM not to miss out on operations, the Army to use them to augment their forces, and the RN to question 'Royals' maritime commitment.

RFA *Black Rover* docked at Falmouth in 2007 (MoD UK)

chard Hill

Jeremy Blackham

The Sea Harrier or jump jet, despite not being a high performance aircraft was the backbone of the Navy for many years, which helped so significantly to win the Falklands War, and as the Sea Harrier FA2 and armed with AMRAAM (Advanced Medium-Range Air-to-Air Missile) was Britain's best air defence fighter. (US Navy

(Left) On 13 June 1982 two 800 NAS Sea Harriers, with insufficient fuel to return to HMS *Hermes*, were unable to land at the airstrip ashore and recovered to HM Ships *Intrepid* and *Fearless*. Lt Cdr Neil Thomas is seen here being refuelled on the flight deck of *Fearless* in San Carlos Water. (David Hobbs)

The first of a new generation of nuclear-powered submarines, HMS *Astute* entering the Clyde estuary bound for her home port of Faslane. *Astute* will be followed in due course by her sister submarines *Ambush*, *Artful* and *Audacious*, and will be armed with torpedoes and land-attack cruise missiles. (MoD UK)

Over hundred years ago the American naval strategist Mahan wrote about what he called the 'Anglo-Saxon consortium', meaning the navies of the USA and of the British Empire: in the new century HMS *Daring* is seen here operating in the Indian Ocean with the USS *Abraham Lincoln*. (US Navy)

There has been a *Dragon* in the Royal Navy since the early sixteenth century. Seen here is HMS *Dragon*, the fourth ship of the Type 45 destroyers, the latest class of destroyers. At over 7,000 tons she is as big as a cruiser of the Second World War. (US Navy)

Part II: Hore, P G, Z/005160, Ord, RNR

Wartime Planning

A little more than a year into the Second World War contributors to the *NR* were thinking about how the Reserves could be better organised after victory. 'Alpha' asked, 'How can we make the RNVR larger, more efficiently trained, and more attractive?'[29], 'Carthusian' theorised about the better training of RNVR midshipmen specifically,[30] and 'WHR' asked about the training of RNVR officers in general:[31] both articles sparked correspondence in the *NR* which lasted over several wartime editions. All were agreed about the quality of those officers, 'Fauteuil' noting that:

> Another help to the nation's realization of sea power is that there should be a measurable element in civil life whose war experience may enable them to fill the gap till a younger generation is educated and able also to exert a strong enough influence to foster and support that generation's education. This is where the educated 'Hostilities only', the RNVR officer and man, will come in. The temporary element is far more really absorbed in the body of the Navy than was the case in the last war. In fact this war's Navy seems to be run by a temporary personnel with a regular stiffening. Instead of finding duties to fit the civilian, the civilian is fitted to true naval duties.[32]

Nor did the RNVR lack opinion: as 'AWB' noted, 'It has been encouraging to see ... RNVRs and RNRs bursting into song. The war at sea is largely being fought by our reservists, and it must be all to the good that they should contribute some words as well as deeds to the struggle.' He added, 'The subject of their training after the war should be one of much interest to all RN officers ... Had we had a larger trained reserve perhaps we should have been able to delegate much of this training to the RNVR themselves after mobilization, so that we, the whole-time experts, could get on with the job at sea.'[33]

As was his style Fauteuil was able to sum up the debate pithily: 'The permanent RNVR, given liberal treatment and supply of practice craft in peace, can get their training for their war-time work ... [while] The development of material and methods ... will require the regular professional ... It is therefore important that the [RNVR officer] should get practical war-time experience now so as to use it himself and pass it on to his successors of after-war entry.'[34]

'Navalteer' had mused, 'I do not think it is unreasonable to hope that we may see an RNVR officer on the Board of Admiralty before the war is out.'[35] That did not happen but by 1945 it was noted that RNVR officers were in the majority in the fleet (in fact 65 per cent)[36] and that RN officers would in peacetime be the caretakers: 'a complimentary term because the RN officers [had kept] the Service at a high state of efficiency throughout the peace years.' Post-war it was thought that RNVR officers, 'who have proved themselves such splendid seamen and such good leaders of men', would in their turn 'take up the honourable task of caretakers by ... sacrificing some of their leisure hours to help the Sea Cadets.'[37]

All were agreed that 'the need for well-organized Reserves by the Royal Navy was one of the lessons of this war that stands out a mile,'[38] and, though the subject had been mooted four years before, 'the present time may not be too early to give some thought to the organization of the RNVR after the war.'[39] It was assumed that conscription would have no place in the scheme of things, but that there would be an increase in the size of the present Reserve divisions and in their number and geographical spread: 'a couple of Nissen huts would serve, if nothing better is to be had' and 'the more exacting the requirements the better the type of officer and man who will want to take part'. The future of the University Royal Naval Units which we know today was outlined in an article which outlined how in 1936 the principal of St Edmund's Hall, Lt Cdr Emden, RNVR, with others had started naval training in one of the college barges, though he had not received official approval, and the project had been dropped and not reopened until October 1942, when the University Naval Division was started.[40]

'Blondin' was more decided, if less realistic, about how the Navy might be manned in future: anti-submarine forces, aircrew and air direction personnel should be 80 per cent permanent Navy, carriers might be well diluted with RNR, and monitors with retired RN. Combined operations should be RNVR and minesweeping about 50 per cent RNR.[41]

Other themes emerged: Navalteer thought that 'If we are too poor to maintain a strong Navy we can at least do our best to form a healthy RNVR, a form of Reserve which costs exceedingly little in time of peace', while 'Jumbo' thought that on the outbreak of nuclear warfare there would be no time for further training and the 'Active Service, Emergency List, RNR or RNVR must all be ready. In other words, let us Think Wisely, and Plan Boldly, so that we are in a position to Act Swiftly.'[42] By the 1950s one quarter of members of *The Naval Review* were RNVR or RNVSR and it was surely a healthy sign that Jumbo could quote *NR*'s strap line to its readers.[43]

Unification

The Admiralty was not deaf to all this discussion, and took early opportunity to reform the RNVR Divisions, and to increase the number of establishments. However, before the war the RNVR had been a gentleman's navy: 'Recruitment then was often from well-to-do men, and in many Divisions a large percentage of well-educated men were also to be found on the lower deck ... their technical efficiency was never particularly high ... [but] They proved themselves well worthwhile.' However, 'during six years of war there had been considerable loss among members of the RNVR, and in any case the wavy stripes had been awarded to every single one of the temporary, hostilities only, officers, and the RNVR were thus completely swamped beyond recognition and lost their true identity.'

Post-war, 'there was at once an enormous response from experienced commissioned officers of all ages, but a disappointing response from the lower deck', and many Reserve Divisions 'found themselves struggling to maintain reasonable standards in attendance at drill, customs of the Service and extra voluntary training such as cruising at week-ends, sailing, boat pulling and shooting.' Nevertheless the Admiralty set an ambitious target of twelve RNVR Divisions, several RNV(W)R Sub-Divisions, and five RNVR Air Divisions with a strength 15,000 officers and men.[44] In addition there were 9,000 officers in the RNVSR, whom it was not possible to include in the peacetime RNVR.[45]

These high ambitions also marked the high tide of the post-war RNVR. Many Divisions were filled with veterans of the war and not with 'true volunteers and [needed to be] much stronger in active young officers, petty officers and leading rates of high quality', and the assistance they gave in the pre-National Service training of the Royal Navy was largely to the exclusion of their own training: 'although RNVR divisions are splendidly equipped, and with fine new sea tenders attached, very few divisions are able to take proper advantage of this advanced equipment, because much the greatest commitment they have is to take in lads for new entry training for drills for a year or so before they go for conscription, and this in spite of the fact that in very many cases the men concerned do not re-join their RNVR divisions afterwards.'[46]

Nevertheless, 'Adsum' promptly called for greater parity with the RN and higher expectations of the RNVR, calling them not reservists but 'the spare time RN': some, Adsum thought, would 'think that this change is bad, in losing the old RNVR esprit de corps, but I have suggested that in losing some of this, it [would gain] the wider and more significant "standard of the Royal Navy" with all that that implies in efficiency and objective success.'[47]

Be careful of what you wish for! In 1952 the Admiralty abolished the distinctive lace which had given the RNVR its nickname of 'Wavy Navy', an event which Solent Division RNR marked with a mock funeral.[48] In 1957 the Admiralty announced that it was 'compelled by financial and manpower considerations to agree to the disbandment of the Air Branch of the RNVR ... a step is necessary to ensure the replacement and re-equipment of the Fleet as a whole within the limit of Navy Votes which our economy can stand.' Some four hundred pilots and observers, about three hundred other officers and 420 ratings were affected.[49] And later the same year Admiralty announced another carefully disguised economy measure: all the present volunteer reserve forces, viz, RNR(GS), RNR(PS), RNVR, RNV(W)R, RNVSR, Postal Reserve, WRNVR and a new Headquarters Reserve would be integrated so that 'a greater interchange between the professional experience of the RNR and the resources of the RNVR could take place.'[50]

Anxious to avoid legislation which might delay budgetary savings, the Admiralty fell back on the Royal Naval Reserve (Volunteer) Act of 1859 which referred to the Royal Naval Reserve, senior officers of the RNR and the RNVR were consulted, the shorter title was thought to be self-explanatory and 'So RNR it is.'[51] (The 900-strong Royal Marines Force Volunteer Reserve did not change its name, to Royal Marines Reserve, until 1967.)[52]

For some the centenary dinner of the 1859 Act, held in the Painted Hall of the Royal Naval College, Greenwich, on 3 November 1959 with the Duke of Edinburgh as the principal guest, and a service in St Paul's the next day, were muted affairs.

Cold War Stability

The next quarter of a century of the *NR* are – comparatively – silent on the subject of the Reserves, except to observe their regular participation in naval exercise such as in the summer 1967 when the 10th Mine Countermeasures Squadron assembled at Plymouth and visited Gibraltar, Casablanca and Lisbon,[53] or two years later paid a squadron visit to Nantes,[54] and in 1970 when eleven MCM of the RNR deployed to the Mediterranean. Perhaps this silence was because the Reserves had settled to their task, the war veterans had retired, there were many former national servicemen available to join, and the RNR was recruiting people whom the old RNVR would have recognised: eg, the training officer of Tay Division was not a veteran but had been in the RNR since 1946,[55] and the occupations of the minesweepers' crews were 'extremely varied, ranging from bankers to bus conductors, crane drivers and bricklayers, and were supported by Reserve engineer, supply, communications and administrative staffs and included 20 members of the Women's Royal Naval Reserve.'[56] [As a schoolboy this author was recruited via an uncle, and became a CW candidate in 1962.]

However, though re-equipped with some new ships, the Reserves did not escape frequent rounds of defence cuts, and they atrophied despite the fine words of governments that reserve forces would be expanded as the regular forces were reduced. A correspondence started following the publication of 'The Royal Naval Reserve – Today and Tomorrow', after the government had announced in 1984 that the strength of RNR was to be increased by over 40 per cent, though 'Trenstow' noted that this announcement produced 'virtually no discussion in the press nor in the columns of *The Naval Review*.'[57] However, there was no commitment to any timescale for this increase, and after a flurry of letters even *NR* members lost interest in what was evidently wishful thinking – by all parties.

There was one exception to this tale of long-term decline and neglect – as long as a British-officered Merchant Navy existed. After the 1959 unification of the Reserves, Merchant Navy officers continued to serve within the RNR as 'List 1 Officers' with their own separate 'Commodore List 1'. Commander Fairthorne, reminiscing in 1982 on a lifetime at sea, commented that 'on recall in 1939 I found a welcome change in attitude towards the RNR and RNVR. The old saying that the former were sailors but not gentlemen, and the latter gentlemen but not sailors, had gone out.'[58] He might be surprised to learn that the sailors of 'List 1' have led a charmed existence: even while his reminiscences were at the printers, 'List 1' officers were at Fleet Headquarters in Northwood coordinating Ships Taken Up From Trade (STUFT) for the Falklands War, and twenty-two Royal Fleet Auxiliary ships and forty-nine merchant ships, some with RNR officers as masters, served in support of the task force. Since the Falklands War 'List 1' officers have been nominated as Senior Naval Officers in future STUFT, and an Amphibious Warfare (AW) Branch was established, manned largely by 'List 1' officers.

Thirty years apart, two articles with similar titles, 'Royal and Merchant Naval Liaison' in 1953[59] and 'Royal Navy – Merchant Navy Liaison' in 1984,[60] worried about the links between the RN (the 'Senior Service') and the MN (which one correspondent characterised as the 'Fourth Service'):[61] in retrospect it seems that those links were more at risk from the decline in the two Services themselves than from any other cause. However, one of the first articles in the *NR* after the Falklands

War was a reprint from *Seaways*, the international journal of The Nautical Institute, which had published the experiences of Captain Martin Reed, Chief Officer of the luxury liner *Canberra* which had been requisitioned as a troopship.

The end of the Cold War would bring further changes in the structure of the RN's reserves.

Part III: Captain Jeremy Stocker, RNR

Renaissance

The end of the Cold War had obvious implications for the future of the Reserve Forces. The 1991 Defence White Paper stated that

> We attach great importance to the Volunteer and Regular Reserves of all three Services, who will continue to have a key role to play. We shall be examining more closely our requirements in this area, including the roles, size and number of Reserve units. Our plans ... require a wide-ranging study of the balance between Regular and Reserve forces ... best matched to anticipated tasks, reduced readiness requirements and extended warning and preparation time.'[62]

Twenty years later that process was still underway.

The RNR had suffered reductions under the 1990 'Options for Change' programme along with the regular Navy. This occasioned little comment in the *NR* until October 1992 when Lt Cdr Collins initiated some correspondence.[63] Captain Stewart in the next issue suggested that the RNR was an easy target as few in the RN really understood what the Reserves did.[64] This impression may have been reinforced, albeit unintentionally, by Cdr Taylor who lamented the demise of the Degaussing Branch.[65]

In 1993 'Rookie' provided the first comprehensive look at the RNR's current and future role:

> Renewed pressure on the defence budget has once again brought the future size of our reserve forces into consideration. The RNR, whose manpower is currently less than 10 per cent of that of the RN, feels itself particularly vulnerable to cuts, and looks with envy at the TA which is far better understood by its parent service, and insofar as its manpower is half that of the Regular Army, far more integrated and important to it.

He noted the cost-effectiveness of the RNR, its twin tasks of regeneration in time of war and augmentation during peacetime and the importance of civilian employers' attitudes, all factors in the 2011 Future Reserves 2020 (FR20) review some eighteen years on.[66] He also foresaw the loss of the RNR's dedicated ships, the *River*-class minesweepers, which was indeed announced later the same year.

This measure, driven by the demise of their specialised Extra Deep Armed Team Sweeping (EDATS) role as much as budgetary cuts, was a watershed event for the RNR. It meant the end of a dedicated seagoing role but also a greater integration with the rest of the Navy, albeit much of it ashore. Personnel numbers were cut substantially and it remains a raw memory for some Reservists, a decade and a half later. 'Flook' marked the passing of much of another aspect of the RNR, its shore establishments.[67] Reduced to 3,500 personnel, the RNR was now half its 1980s size, a much greater proportional reduction than in the RN. The shedding of roles, capabilities and units had not, as yet, been matched by new tasks.

The 1990s saw further adjustments to defence, including the 1994 Front Line First and the 1998 Strategic Defence Review. Discussion of these in the *NR* did not include the RNR, probably because it didn't feature much in either review. The SDR did promise a 10 per cent increase in the strength of the RNR but this was never achieved.[68] Numbers actually continued to fall as resources never matched expectations and Reserve units became more vigilant in weeding out those who did not fully contribute so as to concentrate limited spending on personnel who did.

Revealingly, an explanation of a new manning concept developed by Project Topmast contained not a single reference to Reserves.[69] Nor did a detailed proposal for a Naval Intelligence Branch, despite the RNR having intelligence specialists working at the strategic (Defence Intelligence Staff (DIS)) and tactical (Operational Intelligence (OPINT)) levels.[70]

After the events of September 2001 the 'war on terror' took on a new importance. How this might play out for the RNR was suggested by the ever-loquacious 'Steam Trap':

> a presence that can be activated around our coast, together with allies worldwide, based at major ports and with outstations in the minor ones and a roving 'as required' role in those where a full-time presence is unjustified. The role would primarily be to bridge the knowledge and awareness gap between civilian users and the 'military authorities', providing support, but most importantly giving guidance and reassurance to the former ... The role needs to be aligned not only with naval operations but with others closely involved with the 'land/sea interface' ... Those involved would

include Police, Customs and Excise, Immigration, Coastguard, harbour authorities and shipping owners and agents ... On the military side there would need to be the command and communication infrastructure in place ... This requirement is ideally suited to the RNR, as it can be activated and de-activated as the 'threat' cycles.'[71]

Steam Trap pointed out that much of this liaison function had previously existed in the NCS organisation.[72] He was ahead of his time, however, as it was not until 2011 that the RN was invited to examine the role of the Reserves in coastal security.[73] In the following issue Richard Pothecary assured Steam Trap that NCS was still alive, though now under the guise of Naval Co-operation and Guidance for Shipping (NCAGS), with a UK organisation then (as now) deployed in the Middle East.[74]

In 2003 the RNR celebrated another centenary. This was marked by 'Le Commissaire' with a potted history, concluding that 'the RNR is alive, healthy and raring to go – it's not just words and spin – they've just proved it in the Gulf working alongside the RN, the Army, the RAF and Coalition Forces.'[75] The founding date of the modern RNR is taken from the 1903 Naval Forces Act and the establishment of the Royal Naval Volunteer Reserve (RNVR) though other forms of Reserve, largely based on Merchant Navy personnel, date back earlier.

Despite publicity surrounding the centenary, and a parade on Horseguards, the RNR still seemed to be the most silent of the Silent Service. Articles on NCAGS and Intelligence in 2004 managed to avoid any reference whatever to the RNR.[76] Two years later the First Sea Lord outlined a future for the RN which despite reference to flexible career structures and opportunities overlooked the RN's part-time element.[77] Also neglected in the pages of the NR was the formation of the Maritime Reserves (MR), bringing together the RNR and the RMR under a single one-star commander, initially Commodore Elliot Reynolds, RNR. The RMR has remained even more hidden with barely a mention at all in the NR, though its regular counterparts are not often featured either.

Steam Trap appeared again in 2009 on the subject of Dad's Navy.[78] Fortunately for the image of the RNR this was not about a naval Home Guard! To further confuse the NR's readers Cdr Murrison's history of the Reserves started in 1859.[79] This RNR was merged with the later RNVR in 1958 to form a single Royal Naval Reserve though today, with fewer Merchant Navy officers available, it more closely resembles the RNVR of old.

As the decade drew to a close some of the RNR's specialist roles got better exposure, including Lt Cdr Stewart's description of Forward Logistics Sites (FLS).[80] The Maritime Reserves were fully engaged on operations in Iraq and Afghanistan as well as further afield. The RMR provided individual Marines to augment the regulars whilst the RNR supplied air branch, submarine operations, medical, logistics, amphibious warfare, force protection, intelligence, maritime trade, media, mine warfare, and information operations personnel. Since 2005, over half the trained strength of the RNR and about three-quarters of the RMR have been mobilised, many more than once. Lance Corporal Matthew Croucher of the RMR was awarded the George Cross in 2008 for his service in Afghanistan,[81] and in December 2011 Air Engineering Technician Michelle Ping was awarded the title Best Reservist at the Sun Military Awards (the 'Millies') for her work as a paramedic, also in Afghanistan.

The Future Reserves 2020 (FR 2020)

The Reserve Forces were excluded from the 2010 Strategic Defence and Security Review (SDSR). Instead, the Prime Minister commissioned a separate report undertaken by the Vice Chief of the Defence Staff (VCDS), Julian Brazier, MP, and Sir Graeme Lamb, a retired general. The scale of reductions in the regular force, the political sensitivity of the Reserves especially the TA, and the natural synergy between the Reserves and Prime Minister David Cameron's 'Big Society' agenda, all suggested a rejuvenated role for the Reserves.

The Future Reserves 2020 (FR 2020) Report was published in July 2011. The RNR emerged as something of an example of best practice, being described as 'a taut and effective Reserve, well structured, manned and deployed against a clearly defined and current operational requirement.'[82] The RMR fared less well and is sometimes compared unfavourably, and somewhat unfairly, with the TA's 4 PARA.

At the time of writing it was too soon for the NR to respond to FR 2020, the great majority of whose recommendations have been accepted by the MoD. But it is appropriate to close with a brief summary of where it will take the MR.

Overall, the Maritime Reserves are to grow from 8 per cent of the Naval Service to around 12 per cent (the TA will constitute almost a third of the entire Army). This means the RNR has to expand its trained strength by around 50 per cent by 2018. No expansion in the RMR is envisaged, other than to make up the current shortfall in numbers (around 20 per cent). The MR will take on new roles and capabilities mainly in the C4ISTAR[83] area and allow a limited substitution for regular manpower. More radical options, such as those being implemented in the Army, were rejected in view of the high readiness required of all operational naval units.

The RN was also invited to examine a significant Reserves role in coastal security, echoing Steam Trap's earlier musings. There is much that could be done here, but without a clearly articulated policy requirement for the Navy to do more than it already does in areas like fishery protection it will need a broader mandate than just FR20. The RN itself remains ambivalent about an essentially domestic role which is seen as a distraction from its core missions. There are also several other government departments with fingers in this particular pie.

The growth targets for the RNR, in terms of numbers and capabilities, are ambitious. If met, they will represent a real renaissance after years of neglect and decline. The Reserves certainly enjoy a higher profile within the Navy, and the headquarters in particular, than possibly they have ever done. No doubt this will be reflected in the pages of the NR in the years to come.

27 The Royal Marines: From 'Er Majesty's Jolly to Amphibious Commando

Brigadier Jeremy Robbins, RM

AS *The Naval Review* observes its centenary, the Royal Marines (RM) are finalising preparations to mark their own anniversary two years later, 350 years since the raising of the Admiral's Regiment in 1664.[1] Such significant milestones invite retrospection, inquisitive examination and a degree of forward looking. This chapter endeavours to review the extraordinary transformation in the fortunes of the RM over the last hundred years, examining their core roles and relationship with the Royal Navy – as illustrated primarily in the *NR* – and where this may lead next. Whilst focusing on the years since the Second World War, the contextual background is very much set at the turn of the last century, coincident with the establishment of the Naval Society and *NR*.

The Royal Marines Today

The contemporary comparative standing of the Royal Marines has never been higher, providing a unique, ubiquitous and, given their small size, a disproportionate contribution to British maritime and defence capability.[2] This is a bold but supportable claim.[3] Firmly embedded within the Fleet, the Corps contributes a significant proportion of UK high readiness contingent forces. Just 3 per cent of uniformed service manpower, they currently provide 43 per cent of the UK Special Forces Group. The RM provide land and amphibious assault forces as a core part of amphibious capability, which today is at the heart rather than the periphery of British maritime doctrine, and at the cutting edge of wider joint expeditionary capability.[4] With inherent flexibility, adaptability and versatility, amphibious forces provide options across the full spectrum of military intervention, in operations which are quintessentially joint,[5] involving force elements from all three services.

Contingent capability is balanced against meeting enduring commitments. At the time of writing, the Commandant General Royal Marines (CGRM) has just completed fourteen months commanding the European Union Naval Force counter-piracy operation off Somalia, the sixth command since the creation of his operational role as Commander UK Amphibious Forces in 2002, along with his namesake Fleet battlestaff.[6] 3 Commando Brigade RM is completing its fourth operational tour in Afghanistan, whilst a commando group contributes to contingent amphibious capability. A Royal Marine officer will be the next three-star Chief of Joint Operations, and the Corps has provided three-star deputies in Iraq and Afghanistan. With only three tied one-star and one two-star posts, the RM fill fourteen such posts across defence. Military Assistants to the Prime Minister (PM), Defence Secretary and Vice Chief of Defence Staff are at present RM.[7]

An eclectic and cosmopolitan recruiting base is imbued with the Commando ethos at the Commando Training Centre.[8] Here, uniquely in the UK services, basic officer and non-commissioned recruit, command and some specialist training are collocated,[9] and consistently proven to provide cost-effective, operationally relevant training to admirably high standards. And the RM Band Service is widely regarded as the acme of military band service, as well as conducting secondary operational duties.[10] As near a meritocracy as exists in the services, the camaraderie and esprit of the Corps – including the many attached naval, army and occasional RAF personnel who also serve within the Fleet, battle staffs, Commando Brigade or Amphibious Group – truly reflects Nelson's band of brothers.

It has not always been thus. The red and blue Marines (respectively RM Light Infantry and RM Artillery) of 1912 were a very different entity, with a very different standing to those who wear the Globe and Laurel cap badge on their green berets today. Whilst proud, their position had been one of social and professional inferiority to both the Army and Navy. For officers in particular they had limited career prospects, few chances of higher level operational command, and the Corps had been an unfashionable choice of service career, 'a poor man's regiment'.[11] It is the improvement in RM fortunes which makes study of their transformation of interest – in particular to a naval service whose own fortunes and standing have been in relative decline. And, notwithstanding all the above, as in the past there is much uncertainty concerning the future of around 20 per cent of today's naval service.

Soldier An' Sailor Too?[12] – *The Fisher Legacy and First World War*

As a notable contributor to the *NR* observed, 'if it had occurred to Fisher to ask "what are the Marines for" he would have replied, "to man the guns of the Fleet."'[13] The original roles of the eighteenth- and nineteenth-century Marines and RM – to preserve good order and discipline on board, provide musketry and boarding parties, and take part in landing operations – had long been overtaken by a professional rather than pressed Navy, precision rifled long-range engagement, and making good any shortfalls in naval personnel at sea. The emergence of mine and submarine threats saw limited enthusiasm and planning for coastal landing and raiding, in a Navy that was in any case more preoccupied with Mahanian command of the sea and decisive fleet engagement,[14] rather than Corbettian application of maritime power linked with operations on land.[15] And Fisher's view was that 'the British army should be a projectile to be fired by the British navy.'[16] Fledgling plans for landings to seize forts and islands in the Frisian Islands and Baltic in any war against Germany were ill prepared. Similarly, RMLI battalions were rarely permanently constituted, and sending them to train with the Army ceased. It was only in 1912 that a committee considered the organisation of a marine advanced base force, in 1913 extended to raiding and covering the landing of a large force on a hostile shore. But no decision to implement the latter decision was made before the outbreak of war.

Whilst the early twentieth-century Marine was more often gainfully but misemployed as a gunnery sailor rather than sea-soldier, the officer had few responsibilities beyond the administration of his men. In characteristically forthright prose Fisher wrote of the Marine officer as 'an anachronism ... totally unsuited to the combatant and executive work of the ships – an encumbrance to the Service and a humiliation to themselves.'[17] To Lord Selborne he wrote in 1902 'the only officer we can never train is the Marine Officer ... he is worse than useless because he occupies valuable space on board! ... we must get rid of his military training or, ... get rid of him altogether!'[18] He almost did. The Selborne scheme, which saw executive and engineer cadets enter and train together before specialisation, was extended to the Corps. Unsurprisingly with such bias, the unattractive Marine option was shunned by cadets, with only two entrants to the Corps whilst the scheme ran between 1907–12. This ensured that the Corps entered the First World War with a deficit of nearly 120 trained subalterns.

On mobilisation in August 1914 over 10,000 of a combined RMA/RMLI strength of 18,000 were at sea, primarily in the Grand Fleet, and by the Armistice the Corps strength was 55,000.

Notwithstanding often distinguished tactical service,[19] Marines had a generally frustrating war, exacerbated by 'vagueness of roles, the pre-occupation with base defence and the often challenged participation in fighting on the Western Front.'[20]

What about the Dardanelles?[21]

The War Council decision on 13 January 1915 had directed 'that the Admiralty should prepare for a naval expedition in February to bombard *and take* [author's italics] the Gallipoli Peninsula with Constantinople as its objective.'[22] Marine landing parties accompanied the naval bombardments on 25 February 1915, with more substantial landings on 4 March.[23] There are hints in the *NR* that an early opportunity was missed, before the controversial attempt at forcing the narrows on 19 March, or the combined landings on 25 April. 'The original landing parties met virtually no opposition … indicative of what might have been if a real occupation operation had been put into force.'[24] 'For some unexplained reason, a strong force of marines from Lemnos, detailed to protect the demolition parties, was not available on 26th February.'[25] And the Turkish official account recorded that 'up to 25 February, it would have been possible to effect a landing successfully at any point of the Peninsula and the capture of the Straits would have been comparatively easy.'[26] There was speculation in the *NR* on what may have been achieved in the Dardanelles (and elsewhere) if there had been a naval concept of 'Land Operations in Maritime Warfare'.[27] With no more than a division defending the Gallipoli peninsula, Major General Julian Thompson contemplates:

> What might have happened had all the Marines in the Dardanelles Squadron, some 1,200, been landed … reinforced by leading elements of the RM Brigade (some 2,000 men), who were in ships off the Dardanelles on 25 February … plus some 5,000 Australians who arrived at Mudros on 4 March. Given the strength of the Turks they could perhaps have held a bridgehead from which to develop operations. Carden probably never considered it. Like most naval officers of his generation, major amphibious operations, as opposed to landing parties, were beyond his competence, indeed probably never formed part of his tactical thought-process … Had a Marine suggested it, he would probably have been thought to be getting above himself.[28]

Maybe too much conjecture, but the conceptual and institutional failings highlighted were to have long standing ramifications for the development of both the RM and combined/amphibious operations.[29]

The Interwar Years and Second World War

The Armistice and demobilisation saw the Corps rapidly revert to the status quo ante in numbers and role. From their wartime level of 55,000 they were reduced to 15,000 in 1919, and a further reduction to 9,500 directed by the Admiralty in 1922, albeit not the total abolition that the Treasury called for. The economies demanded forced the amalgamation of the RMA and RMLI to reform as a single Corps, the RM, in 1923, and 'the age old question of whether Marines were necessary at all arose again.'[30]

In 1924 a committee chaired by Admiral Sir Charles Madden reaffirmed that the RM were an integral and essential part of the RN, and specified roles in priority order: detachments for larger ships manning their share of gunnery armaments; independent forces for seizure/defence of temporary bases, and raids on enemy's coastline and bases; and, a connecting link between the Navy and the Army, and provide units for special duties requiring naval experience. Madden recommended creation of a brigade-sized striking force, together with a training centre and regular exercises with the Fleet. But with an overriding emphasis on the first recommendation, neither the economic nor strategic environment favoured raising such forces, and once again 'naval gunnery was regarded right into WWII as the primary role of the RM.'[31] And the three major deployments of RM in the interwar years reinforced in the Navy's mind the role of base defence over that of combined/amphibious operations.[32]

And so the opportunity to forge a more significant and relevant role for the RM (and RN) in developing combined/amphibious operations, as the United States Navy and Marine Corps[33] – and the Japanese[34] – were doing, was to a large extent lost. The NR entered the debate both for,[35] and against.[36] 'Combined operations! Have we ever had a war in which combined operations, the landing of troops especially, have not always figured and on which have often depended great strategical issues? Is it not certain that … we will have to do these things again?'[37] But the prevailing official view was negative, and as late as 1938 the First Sea Lord told the Chiefs of Staff Committee that he 'did not foresee a combined operation being mounted in the next war.'[38] And where combined operations were developed it was with the Army.[39] There was study of combined operations at the staff colleges,[40] and one of few major interwar amphibious exercises was conducted at Slapton Sands in July 1938. 'Probably no more visionary exercise [was] carried out in Britain than this combined forces assault landing',[41] but still 'at the pulling cutter-steam-piquet boat stage',[42] in which the harsh judgement was that 'no progress in technique had taken place since the

Crimea.'[43] And 'there had been set up in 1938 a very small Inter-Service Training and Development Centre at Eastney, with an officer from each of the three Services and a Royal Marine Adjutant. Their job had been to give thought to amphibious landings (and they had indeed produced a total of nine landing craft), but on the outbreak of the Second World War they were immediately disbanded.'[44]

The Second World War

And so on the outbreak of the Second World War the RM were in a similar position to that of the First. The immediate priority was manning the Fleet, engaged early in operations. Only on mobilisation was the creation of a brigade ordered, subsequently expanded to a division, and only in January 1940 that the full RM group of two Mobile (which they weren't particularly) Naval Base Defence Organisations (MNBDOs) approved, although many constituent parts were already deployed. Neither were fully operational by May 1940, nor was the brigade available for the Norway campaign. And after the fall of France the priority became one of defence, in Britain and further afield. This priority meant that when Prime Minister Churchill put the Adjutant General RM, Lt Gen Bourne, in charge of commando raiding operations (proposed by Lt Col Dudley Clarke, Military Assistant to Chief of the Imperial General Staff) in June 1940, it was the Army that seized the emerging commando role (although in 1942 the all-volunteer 40 RM Commando was raised). His request to relinquish the AGRM role to focus on combined operations denied, Bourne was replaced by Admiral of the Fleet Sir Roger Keyes as the first Director of Combined Operations a month later, temporarily remaining as deputy.

Meanwhile, the story of the RM brigade and division was not overall a happy one. The brigade was despatched to West Africa in August 1940 on the abortive Dakar operation.[45] Repeated attempts to employ the RM frustratingly came to naught. Churchill noted in June 1942, 'I have heard nothing of the Royal Marine Division since … Dakar … There should be good opportunities for well trained, lightly equipped amphibious troops.'[46] In truth there were, but they were not in the mind of the Admiralty, even though 'in Madagascar 50 Marines had turned the scale at … a critical moment in the attack on Antsirane.'[47] The faults were not one sided; '[when] the ball was placed fairly and squarely at the [RM] feet … and only needed the smallest kick to fly into the goal of establishing themselves in new and larger fields … instead they nearly always took their eye off the ball to pursue a strictly military object and … eventually found themselves back where they started.'[48] It was not until early 1943 that decisions were made that started shaping the RM in a direction that we recognise today, based on commandos and amphibious assault.

By early 1943 over half of the Corps had seen and had little prospect of seeing significant action, and an observer criticised 'the 'diffuse, ill-sorted tasks which fell to their lot' and the fact that 'this beautifully disciplined corps' found itself habitually saddled, by other people, with diverse and unrewarding chores.'[49] As Chief of Combined Operations Vice Admiral Mountbatten saw the danger and opportunity and, although 'against the opposition of certain senior officers',[50] but with the support of the AGRM, Lt Gen Hunton, he proposed the break-up of the RM division and conversion of RM battalions into commandos. Concurrently, the Admiralty faced the challenge of manning the large number of landing craft required for the Normandy landings, and proposed to break up the MNBDOs to crew them. Both proposals were approved by the Chiefs of Staff, and supported in the NR. 'Lampray' welcomed both moves. He also thought there was little the RM did at sea that should not be done by sailors, and that RMs should train: 'how to embark in, to operate and to disembark from landing craft; how to storm a beach; how to use ground cover; how to scale a cliff; in short, all the thousand and one problems which a sailor or soldier must learn to master to become an amphibian: a Royal Marine'[51] – in fact a commando. And former RMLI officer and cabinet secretary Lord Hankey observed 'as the three Services come to be recognised as forming one co-ordinated fighting whole, the Royal Marines, amphibious by reason of their comprehensive training in all arms, and possessed of a sea sense deep down in their bones, should come into their own, in the words of their motto, *per mare, per terram*.'[52]

D-Day involved over 17,500 RM, crewing landing craft, six RM Commando units (a further three in the Far East), and manning ships' detachments and guns of the Fleet. The remainder of the war saw the RM engaged in all theatres, with a fine record admirably recorded in the NR.[53] But was this wartime transformation to the commando and amphibious roles to be consolidated?

Post-Second World War

With extraordinary rapidity within a few months of the end of the war, Army Commandos were disbanded. After some discussion, the commando tradition and role was retained solely in the RM Commandos, and so too was RN/RM responsibility for amphibious strike forces.

By 1948 the Corps had dropped from a wartime strength of 74,000 to 13,000, less than 2,000 at sea, and 2,200 in the Commando Brigade based in Malta, having moved from Hong Kong, with Commando units in Palestine. Once again the role and position of the RM came under scrutiny, and the *NR* had already entered the debate. 'The primary role of the Corps remains, as it has always been, to man their share of the gun armament of the Fleet ... A Marine is an amphibious soldier and should therefore be used as such';[54] 'The Royal Marines should take over naval gunnery.'[55] The Harwell Committee, examining the structure of the services, suggested abolition, and the Admiralty countered by proposing that RM strength should be proportional to naval requirements alone, but suggested disbanding the Commando Brigade. Déjà vu!

It fell to the CGRM, General Sir Leslie Hollis, to persuade the Admiralty that the amphibious commando brigade should be retained, leaving him to find savings from elsewhere in the Corps.[56] The Corps was to stand at just over 10,000, including 1,750 national servicemen, from 1950–57. However, as Hollis himself acknowledged, almost constant land-based operational commitments by 3 Commando Brigade[57] militated against training for the amphibious role. It was RM ships' detachments who were to land in British Honduras in 1948, as well as on the shore of Malaya. And 41 Independent Commando RM was raised from volunteers for raiding operations in Korea, reminiscent of the often ad hoc raising of RMLI battalions in the past.[58] A wide ranging *NR* article by Hollis concluded with comments on post-war amphibious operations, referring to the success of the US Inchon landings, and highlighting the need for Britain to 'keep in being at least a small but highly trained amphibious force – and this means material as well as men.'[59] The hint of concern in his words over what today is called amphibious readiness was to be borne out by the Suez experience.

Suez 1956

Suez was both a cathartic and rejuvenating experience. As a campaign it exposed to the world the UK's changed strategic circumstances, an example again of the dangers of a lack of politico-military clarity, unanimity and honesty. Tactical success in the face of political pusillanimity probably saved it from the same disapprobation as after the Dardanelles. Operationally, only eleven years after the end of the Second World War, it also exposed the limited amphibious capability,[60] not so rapidly augmented by ships from the mothballed reserve, and the fragility and perishable nature of amphibious expertise. Moved from Cyprus back to Malta in August 1956, 3 Commando Brigade reacquainted itself with amphibious operations and prepared for an amphibious assault, initially planned on Alexandria, but finally conducted on Port Said on 2 November 1956.

The politico-military, operational and tactical unfolding of events are told elsewhere.[61] Judgement on the amphibious element of the Suez campaign was mixed: conventional amphibious operations were perceived to be slow and lack tempo; but the helicopter assault by 45 Commando from the training carriers *Ocean* and *Theseus* in Sycamore and Whirlwind helicopters was a new development, at least for the UK.[62] Whilst not the catalyst, the experience of Suez gave further impetus to work carried out by Major General Moulton, then Major General RM Portsmouth and a former Fleet Air Arm pilot, and others, based on the US concept of a helicopter carrier, which had been presented to the staff colleges and service chiefs. This led in 1957 to Admiralty approval for conversion of the light fleet carrier HMS *Bulwark* to a commando carrier,[63] and the start of an exciting modernisation of amphibious capability, not lost on the *NR*. 'In this new era the Corps will have more to offer the Navy than ever before. Wherever practicable Marines will continue to serve afloat. A fairly large proportion of the Corps will be employed ashore, but seldom out of sight of the sea. The Navy's voice in the affairs of the nation may be strengthened in consequence.'[64]

East of Suez

Moulton was appointed Chief of Amphibious Warfare in London in 1957, the post-war successor to the Chief of Combined Operations, a more powerful position from which to promote the amphibious case, but frustrating in the face of still largely disinterested single Services. But to him and his staff, the Sandys 1957 Defence Review (which inter alia directed a limited war and intervention capability East of Suez, ideally suited to amphibious group capability) and a dollop of Lady Luck, lies much of the credit for the further modernisation of amphibious capability. Design studies had developed the UK concept of a Landing Platform Dock (LPD).[65] Comparison with US amphibious developments, and then a timely demonstration of amphibious utility when pre-emptive landings in Kuwait in July 1961 deterred probable Iraqi invasion (42 Commando landed from *Bulwark,* armour from amphibious squadron LSTs, together with air reinforcement), supported the case.[66] Approval followed in 1961 to convert the carrier HMS *Albion* as a second commando carrier, the order was placed for HMS *Fearless,* the first of two LPDs, as well as the first Landing Ship Logistic (LSL) RFA *Sir Lancelot.*[67]

And so the 1960s saw a buoyant Royal Marines, and whilst numbers reduced to just under 9,000, further reductions in service at sea enabled re-activation of 41 and 43 Commandos (in UK), to join 40, 42 and 45 (all based East of Suez), against a backdrop elsewhere in the Services of significant cuts. Reorganisation and augmentation took place, with the addition of 29 Commando Regiment Royal Artillery to the Brigade, and the Corps continued to cement its post-war reputation with continuing operational service in Brunei, Borneo, Tanganyika and Aden, often utilising amphibious shipping, and supported by naval helicopters. The *NR* continued to debate where the RM were best placed, variously in the Army, substantially increased within the Navy, and in one case suggesting they should absorb the whole of the Army![68] And the arrival of the first LPD (and LSL) alongside the LPH in Singapore in mid 1966 saw a true amphibious theatre mobile reserve, the new capability described enthusiastically in an *NR* article which concluded by saying that 'in the late sixties, the debate should not be on "what use are they", but "have we enough of them?"'[69]

The withdrawal from Aden in November 1967, 45 Commando by air and 42 Commando by helicopter to HMS *Albion,* indicated a shift in defence policy and the start of the withdrawal from East of Suez announced in the Healey Defence Review. 45 Commando returned home after twenty-one years' continuous service abroad, to be followed by the remainder of the Brigade by late 1971.[70]

A NATO Role

The RM and newly acquired amphibious capability required a new role supporting the defence priority – NATO. Deft lobbying saw an emerging amphibious task, alongside the US, of increasing the mobility of NATO forces and strengthening the northern and southern flanks.[71] Operations in Northern Ireland and exercises on the peripheral – literally and metaphorically – NATO flanks were to be the RM staple in the 1970s.[72] But given the Navy's focus on anti-submarine warfare, countering the Soviet submarine threat, maintaining the new deterrent, and protecting the transatlantic bridge, amphibious capability was not a high naval priority, in a decade of shrinking resources.

The *NR* recorded some of the prevailing sentiment and drift. The 1973 RN Presentation highlighted the NATO ASW focus of the RN, with no mention of the RM and just these two words on 'amphibious operations.'[73] A thoughtful contribution on the future of the RM in the naval service argued that securing the landward flank of Norway supported the ASW focus of the RN, but questioned the RN commitment to updating the necessary amphibious lift, although concluded by stating the RM were best placed within the naval service.[74] The ensuing *NR* correspondence did not necessarily agree. One referred to 'an expensive amphibious force of ... doubtful value ... the Corps in spirit divorced from the Navy ... irreversible trend ... highlighted by ... Ireland, is toward pure soldiering ... best recognised by the transfer to the Army.'[75] Defence of amphibious capability and the RM was not overwhelming. One argument for RM retention was that the RN would not keep the money. And there was cold comfort in the well-meant observation 'If they were ever to become tragically lost, it would be better if the Marines were abolished [rather than transferred to the Army] because it is the fact of being the Navy's soldiers which makes every Marine feel so special.'[76] More telling and perhaps foreboding was the lack of any mention whatsoever of the RM or amphibious capability in an article exhorting the RN to organise for results![77]

Nevertheless, in 1979 the First Sea Lord was to give a more positive overview in the *NR*:

> The Royal Marines form an integral part of the naval service, and total just under 8,000. As the Navy's seasoldiers they form the backbone of our amphibious forces and provide RM Detachments for sea service in RN ships, and for many other tasks ... Maintaining an amphibious capability to reinforce the Northern Flank of NATO is their primary role, [with] a Commando Brigade comprising a Brigade HQ and four RM Commando units with full combat support ... This force ... would deploy as early as possible in a time of tension in our amphibious ships. These include the carriers HMS *Bulwark* and *Hermes* and the amphibious ships HMS *Fearless* and *Intrepid*, together with their embarked naval helicopters and landing craft.[78]

Fine words from a great man, but the reality was: HMS *Bulwark* shortly to be decommissioned, without replacement; HMS *Hermes* having been an ASW platform, was to be converted to operate Sea Harrier to assist introduction of the *Invincible* class, with no replacement; one LPD had been employed more often as the Dartmouth Training Ship[79] and the other was at extended readiness; and the fourth Commando was shortly to be disbanded. The fear in the RM was that in the face of further defence cuts, the amphibious capability would be first to be sacrificed by the RN, and with that the rationale for the RM.

RM fears appeared to be realised in the 1981 Nott Defence Review, recorded in the *NR*:

> The logic escapes me and the mind boggles ... 'We will maintain the three RM Commandos since we place great value on their unique capability in and beyond the NATO area.' followed by this 'We will dispose of the two specialist amphibious ships earlier than planned and without replacement.' I need hardly remind the reader that it is those two ships which play a large part in giving the RM their

unique capability. So we value their capability and are therefore going to deprive them of it.[80]

There was in fact a temporary reprieve for disposal of the LPDs in late 1981, but with no planned replacement the future still looked bleak, and the new First Sea Lord, Admiral Sir Henry Leach, told the Brigade Commander in early 1982 'that in the future there would be no more amphibious assaults by the British.'[81] The prognosis for amphibious operations, and by extension the RM, had reached a post-war nadir, as had RM trust in the RN to fight their corner. And in the NR it was an Army officer who argued for an offensive maritime strategy.[82]

The Falklands

The denouement was to be driven by events rather than policy, in the South Atlantic. It is beyond the scope of this chapter to describe events on another close-run campaign. Suffice to say that maritime sea/air control, amphibious capability, 3 Commando Brigade RM, and a logistic feat of arms were essential components on which a Corbettian maritime campaign to retake the Falkland Islands and South Georgia was successfully built. Despite a plethora of articles, there was surprisingly little examination of the amphibious and subsequent landing force operations in the NR other than in book reviews.[83] Disappointingly, there was also little immediate dividend for the amphibious capability, beyond reprieve for the LPDs. It took nearly three years of hard argument and staff work, with CGRM's department in the vanguard, to endorse a Chiefs of Staff paper, CDS 10/85, a conceptual statement of the desired UK amphibious capability (nearly achieved some twenty years later). Some argued persuasively in the NR to look beyond NATO, for more balanced and general purpose capability, including amphibious shipping.[84] Others still contended that 'in light of alliance priorities ... amphibious operations [were still] least secure of all',[85] with business (NATO, ASW-orientated) as usual. It was to take another totemic change, the demise of the Soviet Union, before policy was to significantly change, and the shibboleth of stove-piped single-service operations, that had grown around the separable NATO tasks of the individual Services, be replaced by a renaissance in complementary joint operations – the very tactical space occupied by amphibious forces.

Beyond NATO

Options for Change[86] set about transforming the UK armed forces from the certainty of the Soviet-based threat towards a more joint capability.

Building on the Falklands experience, the language of the 1990s vision for the RN started to become more expansive, reflected in the *NR*. Amphibious forces were 'readily available, rapidly deployable, immediately self sustaining' in one contribution arguing for two Commando brigades;[87] although another questioned whether we could afford amphibious shipping, with the incorrect assumption that air portable forces were less expensive.[88] Whilst the Gulf War did not involve British amphibious forces, the US example was cited in support of new maritime force structures,[89] and another article called for an intervention capability with amphibious forces at its centre.[90] New concepts of littoral and land warfare were developed,[91] and the First Sea Lord saw amphibious forces as a core capability.[92] In 1993 a replacement LPH, HMS *Ocean,* was ordered,[93] and the case for the LPD replacement continued to be made.[94] US naval concepts in 'From the Sea' (1992) and 'Forward from the Sea' (1994), which spoke of dominating the littoral and projecting power ashore, influenced the development of the RN maritime contribution to joint operations (MCJO).[95] And in posing the question 'does the USMC provide a role model for the future', there was clear praise for their form of jointery.[96] Perhaps there was a missed opportunity in not following the rebranding exercise when USMC force packages were redesignated from Marine *Amphibious* to Marine *Expeditionary* (Unit, Brigade, Force),[97] to capture the expeditionary epithet for RN and RM maritime forces before others.

With hindsight the 1998 Strategic Defence Review (SDR) now looks like a high water mark for contemporary British maritime expeditionary power projection.[98] It endorsed a brigade-sized amphibious force and gave approval, at last, to replace the two venerable but increasingly fragile LPDs with new ships, HMS *Albion* and *Bulwark,* (although still a finely fought battle, after more scrutiny than any other comparable area in defence). It committed to replacing the LSLs with four of the significantly more capable and flexible *Bay*-class Landing Ship Dock (LSD). And of course it also committed to plans for two carriers to eventually replace the *Invincible* class.

The Bastard Child of the Naval Service?[99] Amphibious/ RM Command

A less headline-grabbing but equally significant change had taken place between the late 1980s and early 2000s. A US observer noted in 1948 that 'since [British] amphibious operations are not squarely the responsibility of one service, the subject tends to take on the aspects of an orphaned child dependent on the indulgence and generosity of the older members of the family.'[100] This was to be perpetuated post-war, with three unequal family members, the Admiralty, a subordinate RM and the Chief of Amphibious Warfare (as well, of course, as the Treasury).

The influence and frustration in the post of Chief of Amphibious Warfare has been described earlier. Answering through the Vice Chiefs of Staff up until 1962, the post became Director Joint Warfare Staff in 1963, incorporating Army–Air as well as Navy–Army cooperation, working to CDS. But this did not materially strengthen the position, and with much of its subordinate work focused on joint doctrine and education, the role never again achieved the impact it did under Moulton, and became increasingly marginal.[101]

A 1945 NR article identified the RM position. 'The pre-war organization of the Corps was that the RM Office, with the Adjutant General RM at its head, functioned as an Admiralty Department responsible to the 2nd Sea Lord.'[102] The title changed during the war from AGRM to CGRM, with direct access to the Navy Board.[103] But still

> the Corps is controlled by the Board of Admiralty without being represented on it, and one can hardly expect the Sea Lords to give equal thought to semi-military operations as to Fleet actions. The solution would seem to be that the CGRM should run his own department at Board level (cf the FAA), ... having a seat on the Board ... in a position to argue his case, with his own separate element of the Navy vote.[104]

The first and last elements of this proposal were to occur, but not Navy Board membership.

The problem was that this would have pitched the Department of CGRM, which existed up until 1993 in London, and the Navy as protagonists for different parts of a complementary capability. But with different priorities, and ever tighter resources, the danger was that protagonists became antagonists, as evident in the events of the late 1970s/early 1980s. 'Onlooker' was wrong when he said, 'Here then is the case for the "Jollies". I am sure that it could have been put better had it been presented by a Royal Marine.'[105] The case needed to be owned and championed by the Navy and the Navy Board. The Falklands produced the shock required to prevent total divorce (or infanticide). Subsequently, it was largely the vision of Lt Gen Sir Henry Beverley, CGRM from 1990–93, who saw the future had to be a closer RM relationship within the naval service. CGRM's Department moved to Portsmouth as HQRM in 1993 as a standalone subordinate to Fleet, and was integrated within the Fleet HQ organisation in April 2002.

Responsibility and advocacy for all elements of amphibious capability were finally fully aligned in the Fleet, fifty-one years after Moulton had suggested this in the *NR* in 1951![106] But Navy Board membership was more elusive, and only in 2010 did CGRM start to serve on the Navy Board, in an advisory role – the first time that an RM officer has served on the Navy or Admiralty Board in any capacity.

A corollary to that of Fleet command and Navy Board representation is that of RM senior promotions and appointments. The low esteem and bias against RM officers evidenced in Fisher's comments at the start of this chapter are history.[107] But there remains a contemporary perception of a glass ceiling within the naval service. A recent debate in the House of Lords highlighted the issue:

> exceptionally able Royal Marine officers' careers come to a grinding halt after they reach two-star level ... no Royal Marine officers have been appointed to three or four-star Royal Navy only appointments. This is extraordinary because, anecdotally Royal Marine officers distinguish themselves at the highest levels on operations and are held in the highest regard ... by our allies ... I very much hope ... that we have a fair system of promotion and appointment ... that does not exclude or discriminate against some of the most talented and able officers in all of the services.[108]

The fact is that in the seventeen years since the RM started to move towards a closer relationship with their parent service, and nine years since complete integration, *totus porcus*, within the Fleet, only two two-star RM appointments other than CGRM have been made within the naval hierarchy. The remainder have been made in the joint arena, where RM compete well. A telling comparison is with the sister Royal Netherlands Marine Corps, who were fully embedded in the Royal Netherlands Navy in 2005.[109] Since then the former Commander of the RNLMC has held the position of Deputy Commander RNLN. The position of Commander is statutorily held by a Vice Admiral or Lieutenant General, and Lieutenant General R L Zuiderwijk, RNLMC, was Commander of the RNLN from 2007–10. Clearly they struck a better pre-nuptial agreement.

The New Millennium

By the turn of the century there was broad agreement with the *NR* editor's assertion that 'few things could be more important than our amphibious capability and its organisation and back-up.'[110] The ability of amphibious forces to move in-stride from exercising in the Gulf to an operational footing off Afghanistan in late 2001 proved once again maritime/amphibious agility and utility.[111] But it was unfortunate that when the planning started in autumn 2002 for operations to seize key strategic objectives on the Iraq Al Faw peninsula, the availability of UK amphibious shipping was again at a low. Nevertheless HMS *Ark Royal,* reconfigured in the LPH role, led an extemporised amphibious operation.[112] But memories are short, and both campaigns have come to be associated with the slog and sacrifice of enduring land operations, ignorant of the assured access guaranteed in the Gulf by nineteen years of naval presence, and that 'force protection of the sustainment effort [in Afghanistan] continues to be a naval role in all but the last 500 miles ... [and] more than half of all close air support missions ... launch from maritime platforms.'[113] The heresy of in any way decrying these operations, in which the RN and in particular RM have played their part, and expended blood and treasure, made it all the more difficult to shape strategic thinking towards the maritime in the build up to a much needed defence review in 2010.[114]

'The Royal Marines are here to stay. They do a fantastic job and will go on doing so,' Prime Minister David Cameron[115]

So what of the future? Despite the PM's assurance, 'the RM has never been an organisation blessed with the luxury of being able to rest on its laurels.'[116] With a defence review underway, in Geoffrey Till's words the hope was for 'an outcome in the SDSR [Strategic Defence and Security Review] possibly to the advantage of maritime conceptions of expeditionary operations.'[117] Some even hoped for 'a maritime strategy and vision in which the Army and RAF were supporting [the RN]'.[118] It was not to be.

Calling for adaptable, agile and versatile forces, the SDSR confirmed 'we will retain the Royal Marine brigade, and an effective amphibious capability.'[119] And then '3 Commando Brigade will provide one key element of our high readiness Response Force. They will be able to land and sustain a commando group of up to 1,800 personnel from the sea from a helicopter platform and protective vehicles, logistics and command and control support from specialist ships, including landing and command ship. It would allow us to conduct an operation such as Sierra Leone in 2000.'[120] More detail followed, which further reduced the coherence of maritime expeditionary and amphibious capability: the loss of maritime patrol aircraft, the loss of Harrier GR9 aircraft, and, despite long term commitment to new carriers, the dangerous – 'In the short term, few circumstances we can envisage where the ability to deploy airpower from the sea will be essential.'[121]

So the outcome in the SDSR was that, whilst espousing expeditionary joint operations, there was a significant reduction in a major instrument for its delivery. Just as the second recapitalisation of the amphibious fleet since the Second World War was completed, the UK is to dispose of one LSD (to Australia) and place one LPD and LSD at the far extreme of extended readiness. And for the first time in nearly sixty years (overthrowing CDS 10/85 and the 1998 SDR) the level of amphibious ambition is no longer based around a brigade-equivalent landing force, but on the Commando Group – arbitrarily pegged at 1,800 because that was the capacity of the remaining shipping – beneath that of many of the UK's major peers, to whom the UK had been an exemplar. And all this was surrounded by rumours that at one stage more was on the cutting table, and this was only the result of a late deal. As Moulton was to say in a similar context 'no strategy, no forces; no forces, no strategy'.[122] On a 2010 visit to Australia the editor of the *NR* drew a striking picture of a prime minister who understood their maritime geo-strategic context, resulting in a maritime focused defence strategy, not dominated by the Navy but providing coherence and focus for all three Services – and a key role for amphibious capability.[123] Have the long-time Australian contributor to the *NR*, Master Ned, and his contemporaries been more persuasive and better understood in espousing the maritime expeditionary case?

The challenge now for the Fleet will be to make the amphibious force package as flexible, versatile and potent as possible. The commitment to retain 3 Commando Brigade should ensure that essential functions in which the RM have led (command and control, joint fires coordination, information exploitation, logistic support) are maintained, and available to task organise in the Commando Group. 3 Commando Brigade should be the UK's one-star expeditionary Land Component Commander – as well as alternative Joint Task Force Commander – of choice, as the natural bridge between maritime and land expeditionary capability (a modern expression of the 1924 Madden role). A final issue is that of the comparative size of the RM. Fluctuations in RM numbers have not always been in parallel with the RN or the remainder of defence. As the naval service faces a mandated reduction to 30,000, it is hoped that operational output, and not an arbitrary percentage cap, is the criterion on which RM numbers will be determined.[124]

Postscript

To what extent has the *NR* had a bearing on the role of the RM and the amphibious case? In the opinion of this author, not as much as it could have. Despite the copious footnotes to this chapter, there has not been a consistent debate, and the conceptual battleground has been elsewhere. Indeed, for the broader maritime case to thrive it must engage an external audience, not just preach to the choir. With some notable exceptions the RM themselves have not been great contributors.[125] This uncharacteristic reticence may have been from a desire not to 'expose the sometimes frantic trick-cycling required to ensure ... survival as a corps of naval infantry.'[126] Undoubtedly, the effort and time was being expended elsewhere. And they are of course only part – but a key part – of delivering amphibious capability. But as a core warfare area this author thinks the lack of engagement has been a mistake. Broader engagement may have seen safer passage through some of the rocky years with more mutual understanding, if not mutual support – but then it may have only confirmed prejudices! Perhaps the last word should remain with comment from a *NR* institution, written just before the Falklands War when amphibious and RM fortunes were unquestionably low. 'A word of apology is needed for the absence of the amphibious element, and particularly the Royal Marines, from this article: but they are the perennial addback, the great survivors, and they'll get through.'[127] Let us sincerely hope that they continue to get through, but, with the help of a second century of *The Naval Review*, based on more than serendipity.

28 An External Audit

Professor John B Hattendorf

A N audit from overseas of *The Naval Review* may be likened to comparing apples and oranges. While apples and oranges have seeds, are edible, produce sweet juice, grow on trees, require sunshine, and respond well to extensive cultivation, those trees, the climates they require, as well as the fruits they produce are all distinctively different. There may be a difference of opinion as to how far one would want to apply this analogy to American and British naval journals, but suffice it to say that, not unlike apples and oranges, the origins and purposes of our different professional journals have been nurtured in different historical circumstances, in the context of similar and related – yet distinctive – professional cultures, and have been designed to focus on different varieties and levels of professional commentary and literature. They are different, even if they are also professional and naval.

Alongside *The Naval Review*, there are two American professional naval journals that immediately come to mind: the United States Naval Institute's *Proceedings* and *The Naval War College Review*. In recent years, readers of *The Naval Review* have benefited from member contributors who have written useful summaries with brief commentaries on articles of mutual interest that have appeared in these two journals. This has become a regular and valuable feature in *The Naval Review* that encourages and promotes increased professional discussion. The differences between these two American naval journals and *The Naval Review* can be traced in a large part to their historical origins, the purposes for which they were originally developed, and the circumstances and specific context under which they have each since grown and matured.

The oldest of the three is the United States Naval Institute *Proceedings*, established in 1873 as a private organisation with dues-paying members. It was founded at Annapolis, Maryland, by a group of fifteen naval officers, most of whom were assigned to the staff and faculty of the US Naval Academy. The creation of both the Naval

Academy and the Naval Institute were steps in the larger and growing trends of professionalisation in the nineteenth-century USA. Until the late nineteenth century, no occupational group in the United States had yet developed a sense of professional group identity that had led it to establish formally a professional association with journals that promoted a specialised and theoretical knowledge for their own group. American lawyers, doctors, engineers, and educators – even historians – all began to form such professional occupational groups and to create journals of their own in the last quarter of the nineteenth century. The Naval Academy, established in 1845, was an earlier part of this development. It had taken a difficult half century to establish the Naval Academy, even though the US Army had established its Military Academy at West Point in 1802. Despite the professional advantages to be gained for the US Navy, a significant portion of the larger American public remained suspicious of such institutions for the Armed Forces and was unwilling to allow the Federal government to proceed too far in the development of permanent institutions that could help form elite officer groups within the Army and Navy.[1]

The Naval Institute and its *Proceedings* were not the first professional naval organisation or journal for the United States Navy. One of the most important precursors of the Naval Academy had been the establishment of the US Naval Lyceum in 1833 at the New York Navy Yard. As its name suggests, it was inspired by the ancient Greeks. The name was derived from that of the building where Aristotle taught in Athens and it was part of the larger Greek revival cultural movement in North America. Aside from these cultural origins, the lyceum movement joined with other contemporary trends that sought to propagate useful and practical knowledge for national advancement. The work of the lycea was typically focused around libraries, lectures, museum collections, and publications. Separate naval lycea were established at New York, Boston, and Annapolis, but the naval application of the lyceum movement was relatively short-lived, lasting until the late 1860s and early 1870s. Its journal, the *Naval Magazine*, appeared only for two years, 1836 and 1837.[2]

After the US Naval Institute was established in the autumn of 1873, it eventually absorbed the collections and activities of several of the naval lycea. Although established as a private professional organisation that was self-supporting and not an official agency within the US Navy, the Naval Institute fairly quickly evolved to establish a permanent physical presence at the Naval Academy, acquired an office, meeting rooms, and a staff, all of which were part of the academy. For a time, an officer was even ordered to the duty as secretary.[3]

428

Interestingly, the American officers involved in the establishment of the various American naval lycea had a British model in mind: the *United Service Journal and Naval and Military Magazine* that dated to 1829. Those officers who established the US Naval Institute four decades later were well equally aware of the leading professional journal of their day: the *Journal of the Royal United Service Institution*, today's *RUSI Journal* that dates to 1857. Many American officers were also aware of the French Navy's official journal, *La Révue Maritime et Coloniale* (published from 1861), while fewer may have seen the Italian Navy's *Revista Marittima* (from 1868), or the Russian Navy's *Morskoi Sbornik* (from 1848). Later they would become aware of the German Navy's official *Marine Rundschau: Zeitschrift für Seewesen* that began publication in 1890, nor even the oldest of all the *Tidskrift i Sjövasendet* founded by the Royal Swedish Society of Naval Sciences, a branch of the Royal Academy, in 1771.

For the US Naval Institute, the model of the Royal United Service Institution was particularly important. Interestingly from our perspective at the beginning of the twenty-first century, American naval officers were not so much interested in replicating the RUSI's approach in which military and naval men could share ideas within a common organisation. While today we think that such opportunities for 'jointness' in professional thinking might be very valuable – or even essential – both the founders of the Naval Institute and *The Naval Review* wanted a strictly naval organisation. Each organisation had different reasons for taking this view. For the late nineteenth-century group of American naval officers, one principal reason was the relative lack of higher level professional activity within the Navy. A decade and a half later in 1886, one of the founders of the Naval Institute, Stephen B Luce wrote 'knowing ourselves to be on the road to that leads to establishment of the science of naval warfare under steam, let us confidently look for that master mind who will lay the foundations of that science, and do for it what Jomini has done for the military science.'[4] A dozen years later in 1899, Luce wrote on his copy of this article, 'He appeared in the person of Captain A T Mahan.'[5]

The desire to deal with the underdeveloped nature of naval thought was certainly a factor in creating a purely American naval group in 1873, but this did not stop the Naval Institute's founders from borrowing directly from the RUSI in the format of their meetings. At the outset, the Naval Institute held formal meetings at which members presented prepared papers that were written out and which led to debate and discussion among members present, as was the practice at the RUSI. This format was widened with the expansion of the same approach to branch chapters of the Naval Institute that flourished for a time. Additionally, the direct connection of the Naval Institute to the Naval Academy reinforced an academic approach to its meetings. This practice is what created the original character of the Naval Institute's *Proceedings*. It was these formal papers that became the first articles in the *Proceedings*, the very first of which to appear in print was an examination by Captain Stephen B Luce on 'The Manning of our Navy and Mercantile Marine'.[6]

The original publication plan was to circulate the proceedings of meetings to members as pamphlets at intervals when the Institute's committee on printing and publication had gathered together 100 octavo pages of material. Dependent on obtaining this type of a formal paper that could meet the formal standards of the day, *Proceedings* was published only intermittently until 1881. The first volume appeared in 1875, although dated 1874, and the next two volumes appeared in 1876 and 1877, with two numbers appearing in 1878. The Naval Institute's *Proceedings* was not the only American professional journal of its time. Since 1863, William Conant Church had been editing his *The Army and Navy Journal*, a weekly with anonymous articles by military and naval officers. Five years after the founding of the Naval Institute in 1879, two additional journals were established, *The Army and Navy Register*, and *The United Service*, a commercial monthly journal established by Lewis Hamersley, who later became well known for his registers of officers' services that remain so valuable for researchers on American naval history. In 1879, the Army's similarly named United States Military Institution also began to publish a journal. While the Naval Institute was the older organisation, the simultaneous appearance of these other new publications may well have been the catalyst that encouraged the Naval Institute's publications committee to regularise the appearance of their own *Proceedings* in that same year. In 1879, the Naval Institute issued five numbers and then in 1880 settled into a quarterly pattern that occasionally reached five issues a year in 1883 and 1890. It remained a quarterly journal until 1914, when it became a bimonthly. Three years later in 1917, *Proceedings* became a monthly and it has remained so since that time.[7]

The founding membership of the Naval Institute also identified it as an organisation that was somewhat different from the founders of *The Naval Review*. From the outset at Annapolis, there were two distinct types of members. On the one hand there was the small group of younger more intellectually inclined officers, led by William T Sampson, Caspar F Goodrich, and Stephen B Luce, and Naval Academy academics, such James R Soley, who together formed the first leading core of activists within the organisation and contributors to

Proceedings.[8] On the other hand, the group of founders sought legitimacy for their work by trying to attract the leaders of the naval establishment as members and officers for the organisation. Secretary of the Navy George M Robeson was named Patron, while Admiral of the Navy David Dixon Porter became the first President of the Naval Institute, while its Vice President was Rear Admiral John L Worden, then Superintendent of the Naval Academy, and who earlier in his career had commanded USS *Monitor* in her world-famous engagement with the Confederate ironclad *Merrimack* in 1862. Additionally, the Institute established a Board of Regents, from 1884 called the Board of Control, made up of prominent senior officers including the flag officers who were the serving chiefs of the naval bureaus in Washington. While these were all honorary positions and had no requirement for daily management responsibilities, Rear Admiral Daniel Ammen, then Chief of the Bureau of Navigation, became a major supporter and active proponent of the Institute's work.[9]

The placement of such high-ranking officers with direct responsibility for current naval policies and management established a clear potential for conflict over the free expression of opinion in the *Proceedings,* but this did not become an issue in the early decades of the Naval Institute. At first, the wider range of American naval officers did not welcome the Naval Institute. Initially, growth in membership was slow and limited, but not unimpressive. In 1878, only 20 per cent of the naval officer corps – 245 members of some 1,200 officers in the US Navy – joined the Naval Institute. By 1899, the number had risen to 666 regular members, or about half of the officer corps, with another 187 associate members who were civilians and foreign naval officers. For much of the Naval Institute's history, associate members have out-numbered regular members. For example at the organisation's centenary in 1973, there were 20,000 regular members and 40,000 associate members.[10] While those outside the US Navy showed great interest in the organisation and its journal, one of the Naval Institute's early members and one of the US Navy's innovative thinkers of the time, Bradley A Fiske, believed that in its early years the Naval Institute was in a precarious position and that it did not gain general acceptance with the US naval officer corps until after 1904, some thirty years after its establishment.[11] Today, the Institute has more than 100,000 members in the United States and around the world.

Throughout its history, the Naval Institute *Proceedings* has insisted on signed contributions from both authors and commentators. Unlike the earlier American publication, *The Army and Navy Journal,* or *The Naval Review,* anonymous contributions and contributions from authors using pen names were not accepted. The original founders certainly encouraged freedom of thought and expression as a fundamental aspect in their work to further naval professionalism. The Institute's basis as a private, self-supporting, non-governmental and non-profit organisation was intended to place it in a position in which it could encourage and cultivate professional intellectual independence. An organisation built on such principles could not help but to come into conflict with those who supported opposing views. The Institute's use of the names of the Navy's most prominent senior serving officers in its organisational hierarchy, albeit in positions that were intended to be honorary, was a recipe for conflict with conservative forces within the Navy. In the history of the Naval Institute there have been a number of documented cases of censorship. As one author adroitly described it in the 1970s, the Naval Institute's claim to be an open forum required 'a very delicate balance in self-censorship exercised by the Editor, the Board of Control and co-operation with the Navy Department in matters of security.'[12] One of the Institute's founding members, Caspar F Goodrich put the issue a different way in judging the indiscretions of an author: 'punish him for conduct unbecoming an officer and gentleman if an author exceeded the bounds of common courtesy or confidentiality'.[13]

Over the span of nearly 140 years, both the Naval Institute, as an organisation, and its *Proceedings,* as a journal, experienced much growth and change. While its original purposes remained the guiding principles, the Naval Institute first began to widen its publications as early as 1898, when it published its first book. Initially, the Institute published basic guides for service use. The most famous of these remains the *Blue Jackets' Manual,* first published in 1902, for the use of seamen. Over the years, the book arm became known as the Naval Institute Press and it has become one of the largest publishers of general interest naval books of all types in the world. In 1984, it published its first work of fiction, Tom Clancy's *Hunt for Red October.* Today, its list of current titles include how-to books on boating and navigation, operational combat histories, naval biographies, ship and aviation guides, professional manuals, a series of classic works of fiction and non-fiction, and audio books.

In 1985, the Naval Institute revived its attempt a century earlier to create local branches, but in its modern application its takes the form of conferences open to the public, as well as to members, focused on current specific defence-related issues. In recent years, there have been three conferences a year, meeting away from Annapolis at places where there are a large numbers of naval officers: San Diego, Virginia Beach, and Washington, DC.

In 1987, the Naval Institute began to publish a second journal, *Naval History*. This bimonthly seeks to bring a range of popular, but authoritatively written, illustrated articles on naval history to a wider audience. At the same time, the Institute has developed into a major resource with its own collection of some 450,000 historical photographs that it makes available for sale. In addition, since 1969 it has developed an important oral history programme. This has produced more than 230 bound transcripts of interviews with key naval figures that are made available for sale, with additional interviews awaiting transcription.

In developing financial support for carrying out the Naval Institute's mission of advancing professional, literary, and scientific knowledge in the naval and maritime services, The Naval Institute Foundation, Inc, was established in 1992. Designated as a charitable educational foundation under a clause in the US Tax Code, the Naval Institute Foundation accepts tax-deductible contributions from individuals, corporations, and foundations that support the work of the Naval Institute.

While all these organisational changes and developments have occurred in the organisation that produces *Proceedings*, the journal itself has also changed in physical appearance as well as in the source of its articles. The shift away from papers that had been presented at formal meetings of the society began quite early with the establishment of the General Prize Essay contest established in 1879. From the outset, the essay written by the prize essayist was published as well as those who received honourable mention. Among the founding members who competed in 1879, writing on the set theme of naval education, Lieutenant Commander Allan D Brown, later President of Norwich University in Vermont, was the winning prize essayist. Commander Caspar Goodrich, later a rear admiral and a key figure in the early years of the Naval War College, won first honourable mention, while Commander A T Mahan, the future historian and strategist, won second honourable mention. The quality of the contributions and contributors to the Prize Essay Contest established in 1879 has continued to the present, but as a contest, it too has changed. In 1985, the contest name was changed to the Arleigh Burke Essay Contest in honour of the World War II hero, former Chief of Naval Operations, and President of the Naval Institute. In 2008, the name reverted back to the General Prize. It currently honours the first, second, and third best articles published in *Proceedings* in the twelve-month period between October through September. Selection from this period allows the winning prize essay to be featured in the January issue of the following year. The practice of presenting papers at meetings gradually faded away and eventually shifted entirely to contributions that authors sent directly to the editor-in-chief for consideration and selection for publication by the editorial board.

The Naval Institute *Proceedings* has been much more highly affected by the changing fashions in the publishing world than *The Naval Review*. The cover of *Proceedings* first changed significantly in 1911 by placing the table of contents within a decorative coloured border frame on the title page and adding the US Naval Academy's crest alongside that of the Naval Institute; the size of paper was increased slightly in both height and width with the January 1927 issue. This formula served until 1949, when with its seventy-fifth volume, *Proceedings* changed its cover design from a traditional one with a list of the contents on the cover and in its place began to use covers with photographs. Then, it June 1970, it changed the paper size again to an even larger format that was consistent with those of others in the glossy-cover magazine market.

Like *The Naval Review,* which published an index to its past issues in 1976, *Proceedings* published a cumulative index in book form in 1982, covering the years 1874 to 1977. Today, *Proceedings* is published in digital format as well as a traditional paper copy. Its website has a searchable archive of past issues back to 1987, with selected earlier issues currently going back to 1882. Similarly, digital editions of *Naval History* are published with an online digital archive of that magazine's entire run back to its first issue in 1987. One can even have a discounted membership when one no longer wants a paper copy, but prefers only a digital copy of the magazines.

A far younger sister to *Proceedings* is the *Naval War College Review*. This journal has a very different background addressed to a different level of audience. The Naval War College was founded in 1884 at Newport, Rhode Island, as the US Navy's highest level of professional military education. It formally became a graduate-level institution in 1991 when it was officially accredited to award its own Master of Arts degree in national security affairs and strategic studies. Since its founding, the College has graduated more than 24,000 mid-career US military and international officers as well as hundreds of senior federal service civilian executives. In 2011, the Naval War College could count a total of 331 heads of other navies among its graduates and thirty-one current heads of navies around the world. With a current resident study body of about six hundred students, there are several thousand students enrolled in a variety of the College's off-campus programmes that include faculty-led evening seminars at various major US naval facilities, a web-enabled programme, and a CD-ROM based correspondence programme.

There are a number of separate strands in the development of the Naval War College that have led to this current broad level of academic activity. As early as 1894, the College published its first book, a volume on international law. In 1914, it developed its first correspondence programme and began to reach students who were not physically present on the Newport, Rhode Island campus. After World War II, these numbers had expanded significantly. Additionally, College leaders were becoming increasingly interested in expanding the College's reach beyond the classroom at a time when the numbers of officers who could be made available for a year of study were declining.

In early 1948, the Chief of Naval Personnel, Rear Admiral Thomas L Sprague, suggested to the commandants of all the joint service colleges and to the President of the Naval War College, Admiral Raymond Spruance, that each college establish a publication that could distribute selected lectures, thereby making a key educational component at the college available to the officers who, for one reason or another, were not available for year-long educational assignments. Responding immediately to the suggestion, Spruance reported that the Naval War College was prepared to proceed immediately with the plan, upon approval of funding.

Lectures at the Naval War College have traditionally been delivered on a 'not-for attribution' basis, thereby allowing visitors as well as faculty to discuss freely the full range of aspects and issues with the students. The new publication, initially named *Information Service for Officers*, first appeared in October 1948 featuring as its lead article a lecture by Vice Admiral Robert B Carney, 'Logistical Planning for War'. Distributed by the College's Correspondence Course Department, it was initially classified as 'Restricted' and issued only to individual officers in the grades of commander and above, not to naval activities or commands. The first monthly issue had a circulation of 3,000 copies and was provided to recipients free of charge at government expense. In 1949, the College announced that it had been authorised to distribute copies to officers in the grades of lieutenant commander and Marine Corps major and above.[14]

In its fifth year of publication, *Information Service for Officers* had reached a circulation of 6,000 copies monthly and was being distributed to major commands as well as to individuals. At that point, the name was changed to the *Naval War College Review*. Shortly thereafter in December 1953, the publication was downgraded to 'For Official Use Only.' In 1958, Chief of Naval Operations Admiral Arleigh Burke complained that 'Our Naval War College publications are For Official Use Only and, consequently, have practically no influence on civilian thought.'[15] Despite Burke's complaint, the security classification remained in effect until September 1964, when it was removed entirely. From this point onward, anyone interested in receiving the journal could receive a subscription to it at no cost. One merely had to return a postcard each year to confirm one's continuing interest in receiving it.

Further changes in editorial policy to allow the *Naval War College Review* to publish articles by civilian academics did not occur until the editorship of Commander Robert M Laske, between 1968 and 1975, when a dearth of publishable material from lectures forced him to search for contributors at meetings of the American Political Science Association and the Inter-University Seminar on the Armed Forces and Society. When Vice Admiral Stansfield Turner was President of the Naval War College in 1972–74, he revolutionised the College's curriculum, basing his new approach on the tutorials he had experienced as a Rhodes Scholar at Exeter College, Oxford, in the later 1940s. Along with his complete change to the curriculum, he initiated a wide range of other administrative and educational innovations. In establishing the College's first permanent civilian faculty, he sought to instil an enquiring academic spirit in the faculty that would result in renewed research and an increase in their scholarly publications. As part of this effort, he strongly encouraged both War College faculty and student contributions to the *Naval War College Review*, making it a bimonthly that emphasised locally produced articles, while at the same time widening circulation by allowing naval lieutenants and above to obtain personal subscriptions. Simultaneously, he established the College's first off-campus seminars that allowed active duty officers to obtain a College diploma without being in residence in Newport. One side effect of the off-campus programme was to increase readership for the *Naval War College Review*, adding these additional students and faculty to the distribution list.[16]

At this point, Turner established the Naval War College Press to publish both the *Naval War College Review* as well as a wide range of books on professional naval subjects. He created two series of book publications, an historical monograph series and a general book series, and immediately invited authors to begin work for these books, which began to appear from 1975 onward. Earlier, in 1969, the Naval War College Foundation had been established as an educational charity to provide supplemental financial support for the Naval War College in addition to the funds it received from the Department of the Navy. One of the areas that the Naval War College Foundation supports is the College's publication programme. With Admiral Stansfield Turner's reforms, the *Naval War College Review* reached the fundamental form in which it can be seen today. In contrast to the Naval Institute's *Proceedings*, operated by a private organisation with subscription-paying members for a general naval audience, the *Naval War College Review*, produced with government funding and distributed free of charge, became a graduate-level academic journal that reflected the Naval War College's research and academic interests. Its current official description makes very clear the academic values of the *Review* as:

> A forum for discussion of public policy matters of interest to the maritime services. The forthright and candid views of the authors are presented for the professional education of the readers. Articles published are related to the academic and professional activities of the Naval War College. They are drawn from a wide variety of sources in order to inform, stimulate, and challenge readers, and to serve as a catalyst for new ideas. Articles are selected primarily on the basis of their intellectual and literary merits, timeliness, and usefulness and interest to a wide readership. The thoughts and opinions expressed in this publication are those of the authors and are not necessarily those of the US Navy Department or the Naval War College.[17]

Meanwhile, the physical appearance of the *Naval War College Review* began to change. In September 1967, the editorial staff did away with the old format and began using colour photographs and artwork in place of the traditional list of contents. In 1999, the College decided to change the look of the *Review* as it entered the twenty-first century. As the Dean of the Center for Naval Warfare Studies at the Naval War College, Alberto R Coll, announced 'it was time for the Review to make a new start, in the new century, and to set itself a new goal – to become not only the best of the military periodicals but one of the nation's finest scholarly and policy quarterlies.'[18] With the issue for Winter 2000, the journal changed from being a bimonthly to a quarterly and appeared for the first time in a larger size (changing from 9in by 6in to 10in by 6¾in) with a new typographical design and with a large cover illustration that appeared sideways on the title page. This design only lasted for three issues, when it was entirely redesigned and began to appear in its current format with the Autumn 2000 issue. With these changes, the height remained the same at 10in, but the width was reduced by a quarter of an inch to 6½in. In recent years, the Naval War College has been improving its website. Readers may now find indices by author, subject, and book reviews in all issues since its establishment in 1948 as well as the current issue of the *Review* and nearly every issue back to 1948. Similarly, many of its book publications may be found on the website, although the Government Printing Office has taken some titles to sell through its outlets, in e-book as well as print format, and these are not currently available at the Naval War College.

Looking at all these journals together, one concludes that each is very different and each addresses different audiences at different levels of professional discussion with different and complementary purposes in mind. One who reads them all may conclude that it is not just comparing apples and oranges, but enjoying and savouring an apple, an orange, and a peach.

29 Coda

Vice Admiral Sir Jeremy Blackham

A S the editor of *The Naval Review* over the past decade – only the eighth editor since its foundation – it falls to me to write a coda to this celebration volume. Under the rules of the journal I cannot quote from authors during this past ten years but, having been a member of *The Naval Review* for half its life, I can offer some reflections on the journal, its past, present and future.

The historical importance of the Royal Navy to our nation brooks no dispute. For three centuries from the late seventeenth century the Royal Navy was a world-class organisation; for much of that time in a class of its own. Our empire, our national prosperity and prestige were built and maintained largely by its efforts and during that time no other nation successfully challenged British command of the oceans. *The Naval Review* was founded, in 1913, at the peak of that power and has watched and commented on the period of decline from that date to the rather precarious position that the Royal Navy occupies at the time of writing (early 2012). Throughout that century, *The Naval Review* has effectively represented the Royal Navy 'at prayer', reflecting on its deepest concerns about national maritime and naval security and the ability of the Royal Navy to match these tasks. It has dwelt on the things that have both interested and worried its own people, often putting forward novel ideas for addressing those issues which have deserved more attention than they have sometimes received. There are, as this volume has shown, many subjects which have resonated across the whole century and the development of professional thought about them is documented here.

In particular, the journal and its members have greatly benefited from the unique privilege granted to members of *The Naval Review* – a group whose eligibility has always been tightly controlled – to publish in the journal without obtaining official approval; this is its so-called exempt status. It has allowed authors of all ranks to explore and bring to bear their experience as well as their intellects on a range of ideas which were counter to official or received wisdom, without fear of sanction, using pseudonyms if they chose. Without this important licence, it would not have been possible for the journal to have debated effectively many of the issues this volume discusses.

Inevitably, the membership of the journal has always been drawn from amongst the more thoughtful and able of the cadre of officers and supporters, although the long-standing naval tradition of anti-intellectualism has taken its toll too. Not all senior officers have encouraged membership, and over the years some have been actively opposed to the journal. Even so, there has always been a consistent membership from serving officers. One of the useful by-products of the present volume has been the opportunity it has provided to see who thought what, and when, and what they did about it when they reached senior rank.

Nevertheless, the relatively small catchment pool has always made it difficult to attract a very large membership which, for many years, has hovered around, sometimes above and often below, the two thousand mark. At the time of writing, it is around 2,200, historically a high number. Perhaps more interestingly, the current active service membership, though smaller in absolute numbers than in the past, represents a higher proportion of the active officer corps than at any previous time. One might conclude from this that interest in and intellectual curiosity about naval and maritime matters is higher than it used to be, unsurprisingly given the much higher proportion of the contemporary officer corps who are university graduates.

It is impossible not to hope that this is so given the enormous difficulty that the Royal Navy seems to face in persuading either the public or the government of its critical value to the nation. Indeed, there has rarely been a time when it has been more important that naval officers should be thinking about the role and value of their profession, its relevance to the modern world and how this should be reflected in personnel, training, force structures and modes of operation. The Navy's central national position can no longer be taken for granted; rational debate and sound intellectual argument, especially amongst the serving community and above all amongst those serving at sea is of vital importance to our naval, and therefore national, future. The rather Victorian idea that thinking was the prerogative of senior officers whilst doing (and obeying) was the prerogative of junior officers seems outmoded in a Navy where very few officers above the rank of commander are at sea, where society is freer and less subservient than hitherto, and where the Royal Navy contains a far higher proportion of university graduates.

The founding document makes it clear that this function has, since its foundation, been the *raison d'être* of *The Naval Review*. It is this that makes it so important in today's world. And this is precisely how it is currently being used to serve the defence of the realm.

It has not always been an easy path to tread. There have always been some in authority who would prefer that officers did not think too deeply about their profession and certainly should not publish articles about it if these thoughts happened to run counter to current official opinion. This sentiment found its highest expression in 2011, in the remark of the Prime Minister David Cameron, 'You do the fighting, I will do the talking.' We live in an era where political correctness and rigid adherence to a fixed government line to take has tended to dominate official discussion. In this climate, *The Naval Review* has more than once been threatened with closure, or with the withdrawal of the exempt status which is so critical to its purposes.

The occasions for these threats have been various; most recently in 2007 following an incident in the Gulf where a boarding team from HMS *Cornwall* was captured by the Iranian Revolutionary Guard. In the aftermath of this shocking event, and some curious handling of the press interest in the story, a Ministry of Defence review of relations with published media initially, and possibly inadvertently, included *The Naval Review* in a blanket requirement for any statement or article by serving personnel to obtain official approval. Inadvertent or not, it was a clear threat to the main purpose of the journal and it is greatly to the credit of the Ministry that, when representation was made about this matter, the exempt status was eventually confirmed.

As a consequence it has always been necessary for the editor to ensure as far as he can that the rules of *The Naval Review* are properly respected by members and to be aware of the potential risks of publishing controversial articles. One solution to this is to expand the membership as far as possible to suitable people to limit the risk of improper access by naval enthusiasts who are not members and therefore not bound by the rules. It is a source of satisfaction that, over the last decade or so, the existing process of spreading membership to other categories of people and to other nationalities in a careful and sensible way has, if anything, accelerated and the journal has members from the USA to Australia and New Zealand and from the Falkland Islands to the Baltic States, with an increasing number coming from the Indian subcontinent, where interest in naval and maritime matters is strong and increasing. It has also spread eligibility to warrant officers and plans to go further than this, at a speed with which the Royal Navy is comfortable. This spread can only broaden and improve the standard of debate which remains encouragingly high despite the travails of the contemporary Navy.

A particular feature of the last ten years has been the creation of a website, with both a (limited) public side and a much more comprehensive members-only side. The site has a number of features providing a noticeboard, an obituary section, various reference libraries and an opportunity to publish articles which, for whatever reason, do not achieve publication in the journal. The site has been an undoubted success, but easily the most important and most visited part of it is the forum, appropriately entitled the 'Wardroom Bar'. Here members can float ideas, mount campaigns, respond to events, engage in strong but polite (and well refereed) argument and debate.[1] Many of the comments are of course ephemeral and many are knee-jerk reactions; some of the threads have a tendency, as do bar conversations, to wander off the main point and start a new thread without resolving the original issue. Nonetheless many comments are valuable contributions to the naval debates of the day, and are much more immediate, although the fact that not all members have joined the site means that the debates are less full than those the journal can host.[2] Disappointingly, but perhaps unsurprisingly, one of the consequences of the success of the Wardroom Bar has been a significant decline in the correspondence columns of the printed journal.

There is no question that the website has been greatly welcomed by many members in this electronic era. *The Naval Review* is now giving careful thought to the question of e-publishing, and to its benefits and disadvantages, as well as to the value to future researchers of an e-archive. By the time this volume is published, a decision on this is likely to have been reached.

But the heart of *The Naval Review*, as it has been for the last hundred years, is the printed quarterly journal, divided today as for many years into editorial material, articles by members, lively correspondence columns, a section today called 'International Maritime Digest', drawing together naval and maritime information from a number of international sources, and reviews of recently published books on relevant subjects. It is in members' articles that the founding purpose of *The Naval Review* as an educational instrument – one of its main claims to charitable status – finds its clearest and most important expression. These articles shine a spotlight on those issues and questions which have been at the heart of naval policy and professional debate in the very difficult first decade of the twenty-first century.

And what are these issues? As has always been the case, there has been a wide range of subjects in the seven hundred or so articles published in that time. As well as articles on subjects of vital professional interest, there has been a number of historical articles, many on subjects that have not been exhaustively written about elsewhere, many of them eyewitness accounts of important events, making them important primary source material. Such, for example, have been accounts of Japanese assault of Shanghai in the Japanese-China war of the late 1930s,[3] or an account of the early experimental work with hydrogen peroxide submarines.[4] A particularly original contribution was a most unusual piece describing the distant escort support given by a submarine to the ill fated Second World War convoy PQ17.[5] There are many personal reminiscences of the Navy, some of them purely anecdotal, but many of them describing events and experiences that have not been published anywhere else and which make a significant contribution to our understanding of some of the most important events of their, and our, times. And there is humour of various sorts, much of it illustrating perfectly the ability of sailors to find something to laugh at in the most trying circumstances and recalling to many of our readers their own experiences. There have been over six hundred book reviews and review articles, ranging from critical reviews of important maritime and naval publications to summaries of other journals published in several countries and providing a handy digest of contemporary information about the maritime scene internationally.

However, the main course in this varied menu is undoubtedly composed of the professional articles. The maritime debates of the last ten years have been dominated by a variety of issues: deployed operations in the Middle East, the problems caused by piracy and the extraordinary pressures to which the Royal Navy and its force structure have been subjected despite the increasing demands placed upon it to conduct live operations. Needless to say, all these subjects have been strongly represented in the journal.

Operations in Iraq, Afghanistan and Libya have inspired articles on a range of issues. These have included the importance of psychological warfare,[6] the handling of media relations,[7] the legal basis of operations,[8] the training of indigenous forces and the way in which various operations should best be conducted,[9] all of them providing lessons of much more general value, in most cases written by officers with actual operational experience in the region. There has been discussion of the value of maritime forces in containment, with some authors suggesting that this is a more effective policy than full-scale military activity with its attendant risks.[10] In the same category, though of more obviously general application was the reaction in the journal to the shocking, and very damaging, incident in the Gulf in 2007 when a boat from HMS *Cornwall* was captured by the Iranian Republican Guard and the Navy was forced to re-examine a great deal of its training and indeed its entire fighting ethos – an embarrassment for a Navy whose public 'strap line' had for some while been 'A world class Navy, ready to fight and win.' *Naval Review* members were predictably and understandably angry and concerned and were able to express this in a forum where other naval members could read it, without their comments being publicly aired.[11]

The issue of piracy has run throughout the decade. It made its first appearance in its latest incarnation in my first edition in 2003 and has run continuously since then throughout a decade in which more and more international naval effort has been devoted to trying to contain or defeat the problem.[12] Few editions of the journal have made no mention of the subject – an indication perhaps of how the surface fleet actually spends a large part of its operational time. Many different operational and tactical aspects of it have been considered and their success assessed, and much of the material has come from serving naval officers on the various anti-piracy patrols spawned by the problem, as well as from representatives of the commercial shipping sector who, of course, are the potential victims of the pirates.

Discussion of this type of very traditional maritime security task has naturally enough led on to debate about the ideal structure of a Fleet no longer large enough to own the range of capabilities needed to cover every contingency, although this last fact has sometimes been denied in official statements. In particular, there has been discussion about the ideal balance between high-intensity warfare capable ships and those needed for less demanding but far more frequent maritime security tasks. This particular debate in its latest form was launched by an angry article from a junior officer, 'Escorts: The Naked Emperors', arguing that the expensive surface escort was of little value and that emphasis should instead be placed firmly on high intensity capabilities, and particularly the planned new aircraft carriers.[13] This led to an ongoing debate over the value, or otherwise, of building smaller, cheaper and therefore less capable ships for these lower level tasks in order to obtain the numbers of ships necessary for a global role, some members favouring this whilst others were firmly in the 'high intensity capability (aircraft carrier) at all costs' camp. The debate was given added piquancy by the *Cornwall* incident which some members felt was a demonstration of the lack of the right kind of ships. At the time of writing this debate, a very old chestnut in the Royal Navy, was still unresolved but the continuing and future pressure on resources will ensure that it continues.

The RN hierarchy's own view became pretty apparent during the Strategic Defence and Security Review (SDSR) of 2010 where they were consistently clear that the preservation of the highest levels of war-fighting capability was their goal, and that they were ready to surrender both ship numbers and lower-level capabilities to achieve this. They were buoyed, as were members of *The Naval Review,* by the confident belief at the start of the review that naval capabilities were particularly well matched to the global geo-strategic situation. 'The Future is Bright: The Future is Dark Blue?' was the title of one senior contribution.[14] Yet the SDSR ended with the Navy and its supporters feeling bemused, battered and even angry about the huge, and seemingly incoherent, cuts inflicted on the Navy after a decade or more of snipping and pruning at the edges. Unsurprisingly, every edition of the journal from late 2010 has carried articles on the outcome of the SDSR, most of them expressing concern either that the SDSR had been dominated by short-term considerations, and in particular by the long-lasting commitment to Afghanistan or that it was bereft of serious strategic analysis altogether. This latter view was most powerfully and intellectually expressed in a striking article entitled 'Strategy in an Age of Inevitability'.[15] Given that there are now to be formal strategic defence reviews every five years, one can expect this particular subject to run and run.

A wide range of other issues have made an appearance, some of them several times. Particular mention should be made of the thirty-four 'Letters from Australia', written by Rear Admiral James Goldrick, RAN, throughout his distinguished career in several different ranks and keeping members current on the development and, more recently, growth of the Australian Navy with shrewd and penetrating observations, many of which apply with equal force to the RN. There have been many articles examining possible future causes and regions of naval conflicts, and the appropriate force structures to meet their demands. Naval manpower and training requirements have been frequent subjects of debate as, naturally, has equipment acquisition. Virtually no area of naval interest has been left untouched in this decade.

A particular and welcome new feature has been a substantial increase in articles from Indian contributors (and indeed in Indian Navy members); India has the fastest growing navy in the world at the time of writing and such an increase in contributions is therefore both appropriate and educational.[16] An article by an RN officer who had served on an exchange appointment,[17] claiming that the USN was not all it claimed to be caused a slight flurry and received a swift and robust rebuttal from a USN member;[18] fortunately it was written before the

HMS *Cornwall* incident which would have quickly exploded any RN claim to superior knowledge, tactical skill or training but it also further demonstrated the international flavour of the journal. And two high-quality series, full of humour, but also full of shrewd observation and occasional biting and accurately targeted satire deserve recognition. A serving officer, 'GoCo', has produced a great deal of high-class, very entertaining but very sardonic and realistic comment on the way in which defence policy is developed and defence is administered. 'And finally ...', his own title, 'DittO' has produced a final article to every edition in the last decade, drawing on some contribution to the previous edition and illustrating some key aspect of it with an always highly pertinent, and often very amusing, anecdote.

This is a rich menu indeed, with no sign of diminishing quality or commitment to intellectual examination of maritime and naval questions.

One cannot resist the feeling that much of the material published represents a striking collection of intellectual effort on behalf of the Navy and that it could and should have been of great, if not mandatory, interest to the Naval Staff. I am in no doubt that would have repaid far greater attention than it appears to have received, not least because it is composed in less frenetic and less politically restrictive conditions than those under which the Naval Staff themselves seem always obliged to operate. The only reaction, however, that I have ever received from any First Sea Lord was that the journal was 'a useful vehicle for letting off steam'. This seems to me to indicate that neither he, nor his staff, can have taken the trouble to read it very carefully. It is certainly true that senior serving officers have always had mixed views on the place of *The Naval Review*, some regarding it as a valuable source of debate and education whilst others have seen it as almost improper, even as a risk to discipline, since it appeared to encourage more junior officers to question the decisions of their seniors, and even of the Navy Board. This too is a long-running debate, but it would be wrong to fail to record that contributors to the journal have on a number of occasions been right when their seniors have been wrong. And all of them have the good of their Navy firmly in their minds.

In today's world of dramatic change, accelerated technological advance and smaller ships, when overwhelmingly the seagoing part of the service is relatively junior, the senior rank at sea in really substantial numbers is Lieutenant Commander, and the number of Captains at sea can easily be counted on one's fingers, the carefully considered views of more junior officers serving operationally at sea would seem to be of considerable significance and potential value. With the best will in the world, it is less easy for senior officers whose sea experience may well be a decade or more behind them, to maintain an informed view of the operational detail at sea. This puts an onus on giving those with current operational experience, who in this day and age tend to be the more junior officers, the opportunity and encouragement to debate it in a relatively free, if unclassified, way. That was the aim of the founders of *The Naval Review*, effectively approved by the Admiralty Board of the time in their granting of special status. The Navy of today, under greater pressure and challenge than that of 1913, can hardly afford to overlook this rich body of professional thought. The principles enunciated by Lord Haldane upon which the founders built, and which are still printed in every edition of the journal are surely still as true and as important as they were in 1913:

> It is only by the possession of a trained and developed mind that the fullest capacity can, as a general rule, be obtained. There are, of course, exceptional individuals with rare natural gifts which make up for deficiencies. But such gifts are indeed rare. We are coming more and more to recognise that the best specialist can be produced only after a long training in general learning. The grasp of principle which makes detail easy can only come when innate capacity has been evoked and moulded by high training.

This is the continuing aim of *The Naval Review*. Perhaps it is best summed up in the encouraging words of a letter I received in 2011 from a junior officer member:

> May I also say that I have found *The Naval Review* essential reading in recent years, and I have found the debates surrounding the recent SDSR and, having recently returned from the Middle East, the articles regarding service members' experiences of counter-piracy operations most illuminating. I can only agree wholeheartedly with the analogy which was drawn for me at Dartmouth when I applied for *Naval Review* membership, that *The Naval Review* was the RN officer's equivalent of the doctors' *Lancet*. There are few places where an honest and confidential discussion of service matters can take place, and an insight into the bigger picture is always appreciated.

I could not put it better.

Notes

Introduction

1 See Captain Stephen Roskill, *Hankey, Man of Secrets: vol I 1877–1918* (Collins, 1970), pp102–3. The Agadir crisis of 1911 was one of a series turning on German colonial ambitions at the expense of the French, which threatened war between the *entente cordiale* of Britain and France, and Germany, Admiral of the Fleet Sir Arthur Wilson's performance at a meeting of the Committee of Imperial Defence (the then equivalent of the 2010 National Security Council) on 23 August 1911 was 'halting, unprepared, and utterly unconvincing.' His namesake General Wilson, 'with a perfect obsession for military operations on the continent ... and [the need for] a conscript army', gave a polished and expert explanation of War Office plans. Arthur Wilson's audience, who were predisposed to his case, were appalled, and he was eased from office. Nevertheless, Britain was set on the road to participation in the murderous war of attrition on the Western Front in 1914–18.

2 'British Strategy after Afghanistan: What would Corbett have said?', *NR* (2011) 4, 323–7, by Professor Geoffrey Till.

3 A recent exception is Robert L Davison, *The Challenges of Command: the Royal Navy's Executive Branch Officers, 1880–1919* (Ashgate, 2011).

1 The Founders

1 Richmond diary entry of 27 October 1914, cited in Arthur J Marder, *Portrait of an Admiral: The Life and Papers of Sir Herbert Richmond* (London: Jonathan Cape, 1952), p89.

2 The author contributed 'The Founders and the Early Years', *NR* (1988), 75th anniversary issue, 56–62. This article expands considerably on that piece with the benefit of his own research and of the substantial scholarship undertaken into the period by other naval historians over the last quarter century.

3 Letter, Dewar to Richmond, 13 June 1911. RIC/12/1 Richmond Papers, National Maritime Museum.

4 The remainder of the course included Commander Arthur K Betty (later Vice Admiral), Lieutenants Charles Ennals (later Commander), Archibald Gilbert (later Commander), Frederic Peile (later Commander), Leonard (later Commander) Robinson, Basil Poe (later Commander) and Arthur Jameson (lost at Coronel). Royal Marine officers included Captains Walter Huntingford (later Lieutenant Colonel), Bernard Gardiner (later Lieutenant Colonel) and William Godfrey. Godfrey became a full General and Adjutant General of the Royal Marines. The success (albeit in a 'bloody war') of the survivors of the course but the generally (bar Betty and Godfrey) greater success of the quartet enlisted by Dewar suggests both that good officers were selected to undertake the staff course and that, despite his later strictures – see his autobiography *The Navy from Within* (London: Gollancz 1939), p154 – Dewar had a shrewd eye for quality.

5 Marder, Arthur J, *Portrait of an Admiral*, p89.

6 Who later took the surname Plunkett-Ernle-Erle-Drax and will henceforth be described as 'Drax' in the remainder of this chapter and 'Plunkett' elsewhere.

7 Dickinson, H W, *Educating the Royal Navy: 18th and 19th Century Education for Naval Officers* (Abingdon: Routledge, 2007), p164.

8 Reginald Henderson was another Young Turk who in his work in the Admiralty Staff from December 1916 to early 1919 and as Controller of the Navy from 1934 to his death in 1939 probably had the greatest influence on the Navy as a whole of any in the faction.

9 James, Admiral Sir William, *Admiral Sir William Fisher* (London: Macmillan, 1943), p2.

10 James, Admiral Sir William, *The Sky Was Always Blue* (London: Methuen, 1951), p5.

11 See James Goldrick, 'The Irresistible Force and the Immovable Object: *The Naval Review*, the Young Turks and the Royal Navy, 1911–1931', James Goldrick and John B Hattendorf (eds), *Mahan is not Enough: The Proceedings of a Conference on the Works of Sir Julian Corbett and Admiral Sir Herbert Richmond* (Newport: Naval War College, 1993), pp83–102.

12 'Free Expression – A Commentary', *NR* (1988) 75th anniversary issue, 71–81, by Cdr P G Hore.

13 The part played by Richmond and Dewar in the events of 1917 is difficult to assess exactly. Professor A J Marder's fourth volume of *From the Dreadnought to Scapa Flow: 1917: Year of Crisis* (Oxford: Oxford University Press, 1968) deals with this at length but probably gives too much weight to the activities of the Young Turks, particularly Lieutenant Commander J M Kenworthy, later Lord Strabolgi. Nicholas Black, *The British Naval Staff in the First World War* (Woodbridge: Boydell Press, 2009), provides a different perspective in his sixth chapter, 'The Jellicoe Era', which emphasises the expansion of the Admiralty staff during the period and its legitimate efforts to master the complex issues of the naval war. However, key questions that remain to be assessed are the extent to which matters may have been over-centralised *into* staffs (a source of particular concern in the 1920s in *The Naval Review*) and over-centralised *within* staffs, with senior officers (such as Jellicoe and, later, Backhouse and Pound) still involving themselves in too much detail and trivia and not leaving enough to their subordinates.

14 Henderson, Admiral W H, 'The Naval Society and Review and an Historical Abstract of other Service Periodicals', *NR* (1922) 3, 386–402. See especially 388–90. See also Andrew Lambert, *The Foundations of Naval History: John Knox Laughton, the Royal Navy and the Historical Profession* (London: Chatham, 1998), pp40–1.

15 The National Archives (formerly PRO, henceforth UKNA), ADM 196/86: Henderson.

16 Richmond, Admiral Sir Herbert, and Admiral Sir Richard Webb writing anonymously, 'Admiral Sir W H Henderson: Strategy and Tactics for Young Officers', in *The Times* of 30 April 1931. This was reprinted in *The Naval Review* (1931), 201–4.

17 'Admiral Sir William Hannam Henderson, KBE', *NR* (1931) 2, 200, unsigned by Ad Sir Herbert Richmond.

18 Letter Richmond to Henderson, 3 March 1913, RIC/7/1 Richmond Papers, National Maritime Museum. After service on the Australia station in the *Nelson* (just missing Richmond who joined the ship as a Midshipman the year after Henderson left), he brought back an Australian wife, Sarah MacCabe.

19 'Editorial Note', *NR* (1913) 1, unnumbered page, by Adm Henderson.

20 'The Action off the Falkland Islands: A Letter from the *Invincible*', *NR* (1915) 2, 252, unsigned by Mid S G McEwan. The first critical (rather than narrative) article by a midshipman was by E M Evans-Lombe (later Vice Admiral Sir Edward) writing anonymously in 1920 with (unsurprisingly) 'A Suggestion for the Practical Training of Junior Officers', *NR* (1919) 3, 360–3. He was followed in 1921 by John (later V Adm) Hughes-Hallett writing anonymously with 'Training and Instruction of Junior Officers', *NR* (1921) 4, 584–95, another unsurprising choice of subject but a much longer and more thoughtful piece. Evans-Lombe and Hughes-Hallett are two of the three officers known to have reached flag rank after contributing to the *NR* as midshipmen, but there must have been others.

21 'Thoughts on the Service: An Older Point of View', *NR* (1921) 1, 55–9, unsigned by Adm Henderson.

22 'Review of *Portrait of an Admiral* by Arthur J Marder', *NR* (1952) 3, 339, signed SWR by Capt Stephen Roskill.

23 Black, Nicholas, *The British Naval Staff in the First World War*, provides a comprehensive analysis of the organisation and development of the naval staff in the First World War. Andrew Lambert's chapter 'The Naval

War Course, *Some Principles of Maritime Strategy* and the Origins of "The British Way in Warfare"' in *The British Way in Warfare: Power and the International System, 1856–1916* gives a balanced analysis of the educational effort involved in RN war courses and staff training.

24 Davison, Robert L, 'Striking a Balance between Dissent and Discipline', *The Northern Mariner*, XIII: 2 (April 2003), 47.

25 Ibid, 49.

26 Admiral Sir Frederic Dreyer's autobiography *The Sea Heritage: A Study of Maritime Warfare* (London: Museum Press, 1955) was intended as a reply to *Portrait of an Admiral*, although it was careful, despite many peculiarities in its narrative, to avoid criticising Richmond directly and mentioned him only once (p280) in connection with the establishment of the IDC. See Barry Hunt, 'Richmond and the Education of the Navy', James Goldrick and John Hattendorf (eds), *Mahan is not Enough*, pp66–7.

27 'Richmond', *NR* (1952) 3, 335–8 by Adm Sir Gerald Dickens.

28 UKNA ADM 196/89: Richmond.

29 Richmond diary entry of 27 October 1912, A J Marder, *Portrait of an Admiral*, p87.

30 UKNA ADM 196/98/Richmond: Extract of report dated 3.12.1919.

31 Stephen, Adrian (with an introduction by Quentin Bell), *The 'Dreadnought' Hoax* (London: Chatto & Windus, The Hogarth Press, 1983), pp49–50. See also Andrew K Blackley, '*Dreadnought* and her People – Some Additional Thoughts', *NR* (2006) 2, 143–8. To be fair to Fisher, having the Stephen family as cousins must have been something of a trial. Dewar describes his part (with no suggestion that he had penetrated the disguises at the time) in *The Navy from Within*, pp120–1.

32 Richmond Minute of 8 May 1918. Cited Nicholas Black, *The British Naval Staff in the First World War*, p231.

33 Hunt, Barry D, *Sailor-Scholar*, p107.

34 'Richmond', *NR* (1952) 3, 335, by Admiral Sir Gerald Dickens (who was the first senior naval directing staff member of the IDC and who worked with Richmond and Dill to set up the College). Barry D Hunt, 'Richmond and the Education of the Royal Navy', James Goldrick and John B Hattendorf (eds),

Mahan is not Enough, pp65–81 expands upon his book *Sailor-Scholar Admiral Sir Herbert Richmond 1871–1946* (Waterloo, Canada: Wilfrid Laurier University Press, 1982), particularly in relation to the IDC. Hunt's work on Richmond provides a much more balanced view of his strengths, weaknesses and actual achievements.

35 Hunt, Barry D, *Sailor-Scholar*, p150.

36 CB 973 *Naval War Manual (Provisional) September 1921* replaced by CB 973 (later OU 5394) *Naval War Manual 1925*. See UKNA ADM 186/66. Albeit limited in scope, these are more substantial works than suggested by Arthur Marder in his essay, 'The Influence of History on Sea Power: The Royal Navy and the Lessons of 1914–1918', Arthur J Marder, *From the Dardanelles to Oran: Studies of the Royal Navy in War and Peace 1915–1940* (Oxford: Oxford University Press, 1974), p36.

37 Richmond diary entry of 10 November 1920, cited Arthur J Marder, *Portrait of an Admiral*, p364.

38 Field, Andrew, *Royal Naval Strategy in the Far East 1919–1939: Preparing for War against Japan* (London: Frank Cass, 2004). See pp130–5 for the influence of Drax and Richmond on the development of tactical thought in the early 1920s.

39 Hunt, Barry D, *Sailor-Scholar*, pp144–5.

40 Admiral Sir Herbert Richmond writing as 'HWR', 'The Modern Conception of Sea Power', *NR* (1943) 1, 24.

41 Mahan, Alfred Thayer, *The Influence of Sea Power upon History* (London: Sampson Low, Marston & Co, 1890), p7.

42 Particularly in the campaign that started in 1929. See Admiral Sir Herbert Richmond writing anonymously 'What is it that Dictates the Size of the Fighting Ship?', *NR* (1929) 3, 409–33 and 'The 10,000 Ton Cruiser', *NR* (1929) 3, 457–63.

43 See Eric J Grove, 'Richmond and Arms Control', James Goldrick and John B Hattendorf (eds), *Mahan is not Enough*, pp227–41, for an excellent summary of the story of Richmond's efforts on these subjects, together with the discussion that followed (pp243–64). Also Barry D Hunt, *Sailor-Scholar*, pp167–207.

44 Chatfield, Admiral of the Fleet Lord, *It Might Happen Again*, volume II of *The Navy and Defence* (London: Heinemann, 1947), p61.

45 Cited in Robert L Davison, 'Striking a Balance Between Dissent and Discipline', op cit, p53.

46 UKNA ADM 196/43: Richmond: Extract from CW 2788/30. He had already served as President of the International Conference on the Safety of Life at Sea.

47 Roskill, Captain Stephen, 'Richmond in Retrospect', NR (1963) 1, 25–6 for the best analysis of Richmond's achievements at Downing College – written by one who also became closely associated with Cambridge.

48 'The Modern Conception of Sea Power', NR (1943) 1, 23–30, signed HWR by Adm Richmond and 'The Royal Canadian Navy and the Royal Canadian Naval College', NR (1944) 1, 34–6. Richmond published a study of the junior officer problem in 1933 (Naval Training, Oxford: Oxford University Press). This recommended replacement of the thirteen-year-old entry with an adult one. At the RAN College (which had a thirteen-year-old entry based on the RN system), the book was placed carefully within the 'staff section' of the College library – and not made available to cadet-midshipmen!

49 Anonymous, 'An Admiral's Criticisms: Training the British Naval Officer', Review of The Navy from Within, in The Straits Times, 27 March 1939, p10.

50 UKNA ADM 196/90 Dewar: Extracts from reports of 15.2.23 (Admiral Sir William Pakenham) and 24.6.24 (Vice Admiral Sir Michael Culme-Seymour) and 6.27 (Rear Admiral Alan Hotham – notably, Hotham had been the executive officer of the Dreadnought, serving with both Richmond and Dewar. He was one of the less well known but more influential of the Young Turks).

51 Dewar, K G B, The Navy from Within, p115.

52 Roskill, Stephen, Admiral of the Fleet Earl Beatty: The Last Naval Hero, An Intimate Biography (London: Collins, 1980), pp33–5. See also Andrew Gordon, The Rules of the Game: Jutland and British Naval Command (London: John Murray, 1996), pp545–6.

53 Between Rear Admiral Cecil M Staveley, RA First Battle Squadron and Captain Francis A Marten, Flag Captain in the Resolution in 1926. Neither was employed again. There are references to Marten's 'failure' in a letter from Admiral Sir Henry Oliver (C-in-C Atlantic Fleet) to Admiral Sir Roger Keyes (C-in-C Mediterranean Fleet who had passed on that information to Oliver) dated 29 November 1926 (Paul G Halpern, The Keyes Papers: Selections from the Private and Official Correspondence of Admiral of the Fleet Lord Keyes of Zeebrugge, vol II, 1919-1938 (London: George Allen & Unwin/Navy Records Society, 1980), p195). Keyes endorsed Staveley's unfavourable report on Marten (UKNA ADM 196/96: Marten. Letter dated 14.11.26) and reported well on Staveley (UK NA ADM 196/89: Staveley. Letter dated 20.11.26). However, Admiral of the Fleet Sir William Staveley, Cecil Staveley's son, understood that the clash with Marten had contributed to his father going no further on the active list. Noting that Marten had been very well reported on by senior officers such as Sir Charles Madden (who was soon to become First Sea Lord) this is possible. The affair is touched upon by Leslie Gardiner in his study The Royal Oaks Courts Martial (Edinburgh: Blackwood, 1965), p39.

54 There are two books on the affair: Leslie Gardiner's work and the more recent Robert Glenton, The Royal Oak Affair: The Saga of Admiral Collard and Bandmaster Barnacle (London: Leo Cooper, 1991).

55 'Book Review: The Navy from Within', NR (1939) 2, 316–19, signed BHS by Capt B H Smith. 'Letter: The Navy from Within', NR 2 (1939) 3, 596–9 by V Adm K G B Dewar.

56 UKNA ADM 196/45: Dewar.

57 'The Training of Officers: A Critique', NR (1921) 2, 219, unsigned by Capt R M Bellairs.

58 In fact he joined the Fleet Flagship, then the battleship Neptune as early as January 1913 but at this stage was also the ship's torpedo officer. It then became apparent that the combination of duties was too much and he reverted to the torpedo officer role alone. UK NA ADM 196/49: Bellairs. Bellairs' time on the staff much more closely resembles the progression 'on the hog's back' of contemporaries in the Paymaster Branch who became flag officers' secretaries and could follow their masters – if the right ones were picked – through a succession of increasingly senior appointments.

59 As remarked to his term-mate, H G Thursfield. Captain A B Sainsbury,

RNR, letter to the author, 17 June 1987.

60 Roskill, Stephen, *Naval Policy Between the Wars, II: The Period of Reluctant Rearmament* (London Collins, 1976), pp110–11.

61 Whinney, Captain Reginald, *The U-Boat Peril: An Anti-Submarine Commander's War* (London Arrow, 1989), p40. Whinney was closely involved in the events of the mutiny.

62 UKNA ADM 196/91: Bellairs. Undated (but probably January 1932) extract of report by Admiral Sir John Kelly.

63 The best biographical study of Drax is Robert L Davison, 'Striking a Balance between Dissent and Discipline', op cit.

64 'Home Defence – A Reply', *NR* (1914) 3, 165–70, signed RX by Plunkett, gives a well-reasoned response to Richmond's critique of his original article.

65 An enthusiasm of Drax's for many years – he developed and installed a solar-heated swimming pool on his estate.

66 Plunkett, Lt R A R, *The Modern Officer of the Watch* (Portsmouth: Griffin & Co, 1904; fifth edition by Gieves, 1918).

67 See Robert L Davison, 'Striking a Balance between Dissent and Discipline', p50.

68 Murfett, Malcolm H, 'Admiral Sir Roger Roland Charles Backhouse', Malcolm H Murfett (ed), *The First Sea Lords: From Fisher to Mountbatten* (Westport: Praeger, 1995), pp177–80.

69 'Mission to Moscow – Part I', *NR* (1952) 3; 'Part II', (1952) 4; 'Part III', (1953) 1. Also a follow-up letter in *NR* (1955) 1, and a final article, 'Mission to Moscow', *NR* (1958) 4, by Drax.

70 'Quo Vadis', *NR* (1930) 3, 567, signed RX by Drax.

71 'Advice to the Young: A Few Notes for a Dartmouth Cadet', *NR* (1945) 3, 234–5, signed RPE-ED by Drax.

72 'Letter: The Battle of Jutland', *NR* (1960) 3, 382–4, by Drax.

73 UKNA ADM 196/142: Thursfield. Remarks on inspections of *Invincible* by Rear Admiral the Hon Stanley Colville, 16 November 1910 and 14 & 20 January 1911. *Invincible*'s electric systems were replaced by hydraulic machinery between March and August 1914. See John Roberts, *Battlecruisers* (London: Chatham, 1997), pp84–6.

74 As expressed to his son, Patrick Thursfield (although the latter muddled the story in his old age). See Allan Ramsay, 'Patrick Thursfield: The Last Tangerine', *Contemporary Review,* April 2004.

75 UKNA ADM 196/91: Thursfield. Letter by Vice Admiral Sir William Fisher of 22 May 1931. There is a reluctant but full endorsement by Admiral Sir Ernle Chatfield in a covering letter of 25 May 1931. He had been the subject of earlier reports by Chatfield and Tyrwhitt when in *Comus* and Pound when Director of the Tactical Division which indicated uncertainty as to his drive and power of command.

76 For example, Thursfield's last contribution was 'The New Ministry of Defence', *Brassey's Annual: The Armed Forces Yearbook 1963* (London: William Clowes, 1963). *Brassey's* became 'Joint' in 1950. Thursfield's articles in *Brassey's* ranged widely over naval questions. The 1946 edition included 'Lessons of the War' (pp1-12) when he prophetically gave more emphasis to the importance of guided weapons for the future development of naval forces than to nuclear weapons. In 1955 he wrote a very balanced piece on 'Living Accommodation in HM Ships' (pp302–7) which rejected old-fashioned ideas as to the moral virtues of austerity and discomfort.

77 'Book Review: *Fear God and Dread Nought (Volume II)*', *NR* (1957) 2, 221–3, signed HGT by R Adm Thursfield. Thursfield's suggestion that the selection of letters by Professor Marder may have been on the basis of what was entertaining rather than what was significant bears consideration.

78 'The Naval Review Jubilee, 1963', *NR* (1963) 1, 27 by R Adm H G Thursfield.

79 UKNA ADM 196/125: Fisher. The Acting promotion was never confirmed and he retired as a Commander, ironically because the nature of his service (ashore on the staff) could not justify an honorary promotion on retirement.

80 Musk, George, *Canadian Pacific: The Story of the Famous Shipping Line* (Newton Abbott: David & Charles, 1981), p35.

81 Sumida, Jon Tetsuro, *In Defence of Naval Supremacy: Finance, Technology and British Naval Policy 1889–1914* (Boston: Unwin Hyman, 1989), see pp 48–50, 83–4, 90–1, 95–8, 121, 123 & 132.

82 Friedman, Norman, *Naval Firepower: Battleship Guns and Gunnery in the Dreadnought Era* (Barnsley: Seaforth, 2008), p21.

83 'Studies in the Theory of Naval Tactics, Part I', *NR* (1913) 1, 12–25; 'Part II', (1913) 2, 82–95 (citation from p95), and 'Part III', 4, 208–23, signed CQI by Capt E W Harding.

84 UKNA ADM 196/62: Harding. Extract from confidential report of 4.8.16 (may be 4.8.15).

85 'Book Review: *Fifty Years in the Royal Navy*', *NR* (1921) 2, 318–20, unsigned by Col E W Harding.

2 The Sea-Kings of Britain 1913–2013

1 *NR* (1930) 1, 151–202: three articles; signed Convectus by A H Pollen; signed ACD by A C Dewar; and by W H Henderson: and *NR* (1930) 2, 324–45, 'Lord Fisher's Critics in the February Number', three letters; by Fred C Dreyer, Sydenham of Combe, and D R L Nicholson.

2 *NR* (1931) 2, 199–204, unsigned by Richmond. The same issue carried a copy of *The Times* obituary, which carried the subtitle 'Strategy and Tactics for Young Officers'. A wider appreciation of Henderson's work is contained in the chapter called 'The Founders'.

3 *NR* (1933) 3, 543–55: 'Pioneer and Creator of the Royal Australian Navy', by B M Chambers. For a wider appreciation of his work, see the chapter called 'From Offspring to Independence – the Royal Australian Navy'.

4 *NR* (1935) 4, 681–5, 'An Appreciation', signed HWWH by H W W Hope.

5 *NR* (1936) 1, 2–30, 'Admiral of the Fleet Earl Jellicoe and JRJ: an Appreciation', by R F Phillimore and H L Heath. Other writers were Roger Bellairs and H W E Manisty.

6 *NR* (1936) 2, 203–32; Tribute by the Archbishop of Canterbury, letter to *The Times* by Ernle Chatfield; memoirs by Roger Keyes, Walter Cowan, and signed RPD.

7 *NR* (1937) 3, 411–15, 'The Undefeated Spirit', by L S Amery.

8 *NR* (1943) 4, 281–6, exchange of letters; two signals; two unsigned memoirs.

9 *NR* (1945) 1, 1–3, 'Two Personal Tributes': signed LGD by L G Dawson; and signed GEC by G E Creasy.

10 *NR* (1947) 1, 1–8; three memoirs by Richard Webb, Alfred C Dewar and H G Thursfield, and the address delivered by G M Trevelyan at the memorial service. A wider appreciation of Richmond's career is contained in the

chapter called 'The Founders'.

11 *NR* (1950) 1, 9–10, unsigned.

12 *NR* (1952) 1, 4–5, signed RABP by R A B Phillimore.

13 *NR* (1963) 3, 260–3, signed DML, PLV and JAGT, by D M Lees, P L Vian, J A G Troup.

14 Addison, *The Campaign*, line 219.

15 The *Scotsman*, 13 June 1963.

16 *NR* (1980) 2, 102–8, 'Dicky Onslow', signed RDF by R D Franks.

17 *NR* (1979) 4, 259–64, 'Mountbatten the Leader', by Stephen Roskill; 'Mountbatten the Professional', by Peter Gretton; 'Mountbatten the Tri-Service Chief', by J L Moulton.

18 *NR* (1981) 1, 7–9, by Stephen Roskill.

19 *NR* (1981) 3, 191–2, text of memorial address delivered by Admiral Sir Henry Leach.

20 Readers – and contributors – to the *NR* should note that Roskill was commissioned to write *The War at Sea* – which started him on his second career as a Cambridge don – on the strength and quality of his pre-war articles for *The Naval Review*: see Barry Gough, *Historical Dreadnoughts: Arthur Marder, Stephen Roskill, and Battles for Naval History* (London, 2010), p143.

21 *NR* (1983) 1, 3–8, 'An Obituary', by A B Sainsbury; 'An Obituary from Australia', by James Goldrick.

22 *NR* (1984) 4, 287–90, 'Fighter for Naval Air Power', signed DCEFG by Donald Gibson.

23 *NR* (1992) 2, 98–100, by Richard Hill.

24 *NR* (1993) 1, 3–5, by Ian McGeoch.

25 *NR* (1999) 2, 95–9, 'A Man of True Resolution', by Roddy Macdonald and Tony Sainsbury.

26 *NR* (2001) 2, 99, by Richard Hill.

27 *NR* (2011) 1, 5, by Jeremy Blackham.

28 Command 8288, *United Kingdom Defence Review 1981*. John Nott, the Secretary of State, was widely criticised by the Royal Navy chiefs for his decision to cut back on government naval expenditure.

29 *NR* (2011) 4, 207–8, by Richard Hill.

30 Wilson, *NR* (1924) 2, 301–4, unsigned; Troubridge, *NR* (1980) 4, 301–7, by Godfrey French; Webb, *NR* (1950) 1, 1–8, signed HGT, LGD, JSC and PB, by H G Thursfield, L G Dawson; Hughes-Hallett, *NR* (1986) 2, 97–9, signed A B S by A B Sainsbury; Mansergh, *NR* (1990) 4, 292–3, by A B Sainsbury; Stanford, *NR* (1991) 3, 187, by James Eberle; Staveley, *NR* (1998) 1, 97, by

Richard Hill; Nunn, *NR* (2010) 2, 113, by Guy Liardet.

3 Sir Julian Corbett and the Naval War Course

1 'The late Sir Julian Corbett', *NR* (1923) 1, 14, by R Adm Herbert Richmond.

2 Salvemini, G, *Historian and Scientist: An Essay on the Nature of History and the Social Sciences* (1939), p3.

3 Lambert, A D, *The Foundations of Naval History: John Knox Laughton, the Royal Navy and the Historical Profession* (1998).

4 Schurman, D S, *Julian S Corbett, 1854–1922: Historian of British Maritime Policy from Drake to Jellicoe* (1981).

5 Marder, A J, *From the Dreadnought to Scapa Flow: Volume 1. The Road to War, 1904–1914* (1961). Basing his analysis on memoirs and reminiscences Marder ignored the relevant archives, did not assess the aims and objectives of the programme, or even count how many officers attended.

6 Hunt, B, *Sailor-Scholar: Admiral Sir Herbert Richmond, 1871–1946* (1982).

7 Capt Henry May (1853–1904), appointed to the Royal Naval College, Greenwich in 1900, promoted R Adm in 1902, and died in office. He gave the first lectures of a Naval Strategy Course which grew into the War Course 'on the broad lines of the American Naval War College but altered to suit the different conditions under which the work was to be carried out.' See Keith Neilson & Greg Kennedy, *The British Way In Warfare: Power and The International System, 1856–1956* (2010), p221.

8 Henry May to Corbett 19.9.1902, RNC Greenwich: Corbett Papers, National Maritime Museum, Greenwich (henceforth CBT) 13/3/50.

9 Lambert, A D, *The Foundations of Naval History: John Knox Laughton, the Royal Navy and the Historical Profession* (1998), pp200–1, 235–7. Dewar, K G B, *The Navy From Within* (1939), pp134 & 137, noted using these books to study tactics. He ignored Corbett, the editor of the material, because of the bitter post-war feud over Jutland.

10 H J May to Corbett, 27.8.1902 RNC: CBT 13/3/51.

11 Corbett, J S, 'The Teaching of Naval and Military History', *History* (April 1916),12–24.

12 Vice Admiral Philip Howard Colomb (1831–1899) naval historian and inventor (his younger brother Sir John Colomb was also a strategist); his naval experience included operations against piracy in Chinese waters, the Burmese War of 1852–3, an Arctic expedition in 1854, the Baltic Sea during the Crimean War, including the attack on Sveaborg, and the suppression of the slave trade off Zanzibar and Oman. Colomb was a precursor to and then contemporary and collaborator with Alfred T Mahan. Due to his prolificacy, Jacky Fisher unkindly called him 'column and a half'.

13 Fisher to Corbett 24.5.1905: Schurman, p43.

14 Admiral Sir Edmond Slade (1859–1928) was a commander on the staff of the War College in 1904 and Director of Naval Intelligence in 1907. In 1913 when the British Government bought a 51 per cent stake in the Anglo-Persian Oil Company, Slade became a director, a position he held until his death.

15 Bassford, C, *Clausewitz in English: The Reception of Clausewitz in Britain and America 1815–1945* (1994), p97.

16 Lambert, A D, 'The Principal Source of Understanding: Navies and the Educational Role of the Past', in Hore, P G (ed), *The Hudson Papers, vol 1* (London: Ministry of Defence, 2001), pp35-66.

17 Slade to Corbett 22.8.1905: Corbett MS Liddell-Hart Centre, King's College London.

18 Rawlinson to Corbett 25 & 30.8.1905: Corbett Ms LHC.

19 Henderson, G, *The Science of War* (London, 1904).

20 Schurman, D M, *The Education of a Navy, 1865–1914* (London, 1965), p164.

21 Schurman 1965, p167.

22 Schurman 1981, pp44–5, and discussions with Professor Daniel Baugh.

23 Corbett to Newbolt 31.1.1906: Schurman 1981, p47.

24 Chatfield, A, *The Navy and Defence: The Autobiography of Admiral of the Fleet Lord Chatfield* (1942), p91.

25 Ranft, B McI (ed), *The Beatty Papers*, vol I (1989), pp33 & 60.

26 Ranft, *Beatty* I, p59.

27 Schurman, p63.

28 Corbett 1910, pp247–54.

29 Corbett 1910, Preface.

30 Fisher to Corbett 17.3.1907: Schurman 1981, p67.

31 *The Nineteenth Century*, February 1907.

32 Barfleur, pseud Custance, R, *Naval Policy: A Plea for the Study of War* (London, 1907). Corbett's copy of this text contains significant marginalia. Chapter IX 'The Speed of the Capital Ship' was the target of Corbett's paper.

33 Corbett, J S, 'The Strategical Value of Speed', *JRUSI*, July 1907, delivered 6.3.1907.

34 *The Nineteenth Century*, June 1907: reprinted in Mahan, A T (ed), *Some Neglected Aspects of War* (Boston, 1907).

35 Schurman, p73.

36 Schurman, p67, referring to correspondence of March 1907 between Fisher and Corbett, leading to the pamphlet 'Some Principles of Naval Warfare'. The National Archives (TNA) ADM 116/1043B. Corbett, *Some Principles* (1988 edn), ed Grove, E, xxiv, including the 'Green Pamphlet'. Kemp, P (ed), *The Fisher Papers*, vol 2 (1964), pp318–45; Schurman, *Corbett*, Ch 3, 4 & 5.

37 Grove, 'Introduction', 1988, xxiv–xxv.

38 Schurman 1965, p182.

39 TNA CAB 45/1, contains notes and sketches for the CID project.

40 Corbett Diary 6.11.1913: Schurman 1981, p143.

41 Churchill at CID 3.3.1914: TNA CAB 38/26/11.

42 'Methods of Discussion', *NR* (1920), 322–4. A posthumous article 'United Service' was published in May 1923.

43 Course list reconstructed from ADM 203/100, a 200pp manuscript record book.

44 Hunt, pp107–20.

45 'War from the Aspect of the Weaker Power', *NR* (1920) 2, attributed to Lieutenant J S MacKenzie-Grieve, RN, 152–66, quote at 166.

46 For Wilkinson see Luvass, J, *The Education of an Army: British Military Thought 1815–1940* (London, 1964), pp253–90, at pp277–8.

47 Schurman 1965, p183; *Morning Post* 19.2.1912.

48 The vitriolic response to Jutland, in which he was publicly blamed for the inconclusive nature of the battle began in June 1916 and culminated in 1923, when the Admiralty published an insulting, stupid, disclaimer in volume III of the *Official History*, stating that they disagreed with his 'tendency to minimise the importance of seeking battle and of forcing it to a conclusion'.

49 Corbett, 'Methods of Discussion', 323.

50 Schurman 1981, pp45, 57–8.

51 Corbett, 'Methods of Discussion', 324.

52 Nietzsche, F, 'The Use and Abuse of History' (1873), 40.

4 The Problems of Convoys 1914–1917

1 'Strategical Principles and the Forth-Clyde Canal', *NR* (1913) 3, 229, unsigned by Cdr K Dewar.

2 'The Influence of the Submarine on Naval Policy I', *NR* (1913) 2, 147–50, unsigned by Capt S S Hall.

3 'The Influence of the Submarine on Naval Policy III', *NR* (1914) 1, 31, Hall.

4 'The Influence of Commerce in War', *NR* (1914) 3, 160, by Cdr K Dewar, winner of the Gold Medal Essay of the United Service Institution in 1913.

5 'The Protection of Trade in Past Wars', *NR* (1914) 4, 249, unsigned by Capt H W Richmond.

6 Moutray commanded the escort of a large convoy of merchantmen bound for the West Indies, India and China in 1780. Unfortunately the convoy fell in with a Spanish squadron under Admiral Cordoba and fifty-two merchant ships, including Government-chartered storeships and five valuable East Indiamen, were taken as prizes. Moutray ignored warnings of enemy forces at sea, and abandoned his charges. See p34 et seq, and p80, Richard Woodman, *Britannia's Realm, A History of the British Merchant Navy* (2009).

7 Suggestions that persons of mercantile expertise were at least consulted are largely anecdotal, but would seem sensible enough to give colour to the notion. Undoubtedly the fallout from the losses of Moutray's convoy, which amounted to some £2m, stirred the directors at East India House and much improved the arrangements for convoy during the long conflict between 1793 and 1815.

8 Terraine, J, *Business in Great Waters, The U-boat Wars, 1916–1945* (1989), p51.

9 Hurd, A, *The Merchant Navy, vol III* (1928), p371. Archibald Hurd (1869–1959) was on the editorial staff of the *Daily Telegraph* (1899–1929). He wrote extensively on shipping, including the official history of the Merchant Navy in the First World War. He was joint editor of *Brassey's Naval and Shipping Annual*, and on the Council of the Institute of Naval Architects, an Honorary Member

of RUSI and a contributor to the DNB. He was knighted in 1928: his papers are in the Churchill College Archives.

10 'With the Grand Fleet (4 January 1915)', *NR* (1915) 1, 2, unsigned by Plunkett.

11 'The Influence of Overseas Trade on British Naval Strategy in the Past and at Present – Part I', *NR* (1915) 1, 112, unsigned by Lt V H Dankwerts.

12 Ibid, 112.

13 'Some Considerations of Germany's Naval Policy', *NR* (1915), 235–40, unsigned by Capt R M Orde, RM, one of the first RM officers to write for the *NR*.

14 'With the Grand Fleet (1 July 1915)', *NR* (1915), 345–53, Plunkett.

15 'A Year of Naval Warfare', *NR* (1915) 4, 535–8, Arthur Balfour, later Earl of Balfour (1848–1930), Prime Minister 1902–5, leader of the Conservative party 1902–11, Foreign Secretary in David Lloyd George's coalition government 1916–19, and succeeded Winston Churchill as First Lord of the Admiralty 1915–16.

16 'With the Grand Fleet (4 October, 1915)', *NR* (1915) 4, 539–46, Plunkett.

17 'A Curious Analogy', *NR* (1915) 4, 574, unsigned by Lt Guy C Cooper.

18 'The System of Convoys for Merchant Shipping in 1917 and 1918', *NR* (1917), 42-95, Sir Norman Leslie.

19 Aware of mounting losses the Cabinet had proposed the Admiralty introduce convoy in March of 1917. This was refused by Their Lordships but revived by Rear Admiral Duff towards the end of April. Jellicoe finally relented on 27 April, supposedly on the threat of a personal visit by the Prime Minister, David Lloyd George.

20 Ibid, p49.

21 'The Navy and the Merchant Service', *NR* (1919) 1, 95–8, unsigned by Cdr P J Stopford.

5 Blue Oceans, Blue Ensign: The Royal Fleet Auxiliary

1 'Naval Affairs', *NR* (1969) 4, 358.

2 *The Naval Store Journal* (March 1952), 8. 'We have not seen the like of her capacious holds in any other ship, with every available piece of space occupied, with stowage plans carefully calculated to accommodate the maximum quantities.'

3 Being coal burners the battleships had no capacity to stow anything other than water.

4 'Obituary: Admiral Sir Dudley Pound, GCB, OM, GCVO', *NR* (1943) 4, 285, unsigned.

5 'The First RAS', *Naval Store Journal*, December 1963, 4, by JD.

6 Morison, S E, *History of US Naval Operations in World War II; vol 14 Victory in the Pacific* (1960), p103.

7 Winton, John, *The Forgotten Fleet* (1969), p281. In November 1944 the Admiralty requisitioned a further eleven store carriers but that order was rejected by the Ministry of War Transport.

8 'RFA *Bacchus* in the Fleet Train', *NR* (1993) 1, 55, by Lionel Hall provides an insight into the support undertaken to elements of the British Pacific Fleet at Leyte Gulf in 1945.

9 *History of US Naval Operations in World War II*, p159. The US Logistic Support Group off Okinawa once transferred 64,000 tons of cargo at sea in two days, more than the stevedores of a port like Boston handled in a week.

10 'Book Review: *The Forgotten Fleet*', *NR* (1970) 2, 175, signed CCHH, V Adm C C Hughes-Hallett. The quotation from Winton's book is from p269.

11 'The Mobility of the Fleet', *NR* (1965) 4, 325, Capt Louis Le Bailly.

12 *British Vessels lost at Sea 1939–45*, originally published by HMSO 1947; 1977 reprint, pp47–8.

13 'The Commonwealth Navies in the Korean War', *NR* (1951) 4, 426, signed Observer.

14 The ex-German supply ship *Northmark* seized 1945 and renamed 1947.

15 'Naval Affairs', *NR* (1959) 1, 101.

16 Naval stores, victualling and armament were separate departments of the Admiralty.

17 *Lyness, Stromness, Tarbatness.*

18 A *Dale* oiler carried 70,000 tons of oil to a *Leaf*'s 18,000 tons.

19 *Stromness* was the last to have a Chinese naval store working party, *Tarbatness* the last to have both a Maltese crew and working party, while *Tidereach* had a Maltese crew, as did the *Hebe*, while the *Bacchus* was Seychellois-manned. LSLs in the Falklands had a complement of Chinese.

20 'Naval Affairs', *NR* (1968) 1, 82.

21 'April Fool', *NR* (1983) 3, 189, signed JBD, who detailed the *Stromness* reactivation.

22 The first Harrier landing on a RFA was on *Green Rover* at the 1972 RN Equipment Exhibition.

23 Detail taken from *Flight Deck* (Fleet Air Arm) magazine, Falklands edition (1982), 50: 'The RFA goes to War', by WMW.

24 'RFA Sir Galahad – The Demise of a Gallant Knight', *NR* (1984) 1, 53, Capt P J Roberts, RFA.

25 'Removing Bombs from Sir Lancelot and Sir Galahad', *NR* (2008) 2, 142, Cdr John McGregor.

26 *Force Four* (RFA newsletter) (April 1983), 24, letter dated 1 July 1982. *The RN Supply and Transport Service Journal* (1983) 46, provides additional detail of the RFA workload during Operation Corporate.

27 Freedman, Sir Lawrence, *The Official History of the Falklands Campaign: vol II War and Diplomacy* (2005), p725: 'The great success was in naval air power, without which the operation would have been unthinkable.' 'Logistic Support for Operation CORPORATE', *NR* (1982) 4, 264, signed Supporter, provided an overview by Chief of Fleet Support staff.

28 Command 3999 Strategic Defence Review, 1998.

29 'The Gulf War – Logistic Support and Merchant Shipping', *NR* (1991) 3, 198, by Michael Ranken.

30 'Desert Shield/Desert Storm – The Right Flank', *NR* (1992) 1, 6, by Cdre C J S Craig.

31 'Desert Shield/Desert Storm – Command Priorities/Principles', *NR* (1992) 3, 244, by Ranken.

32 'The Fleet Train', *NR* (1946) 1, 32, signed Valor by Hughes-Hallett.

33 'Some Strategic Lessons to be drawn from the Second World War', *NR* (1952) 4, 435, by Roskill.

34 For ease of logistic support, the majority of the aircraft were American designs. Is there a lesson here?

35 'The Future of the Royal Fleet Auxiliary', *NR* (1950) 2, 134–5, signed Avis.

36 'Supplies to the Fleet', *NR* (1952) 2, 126, signed X.

37 NB: in 1994 Defence Cost Study Number 10 reversed this policy and as an economy, rationalised and consolidated storage back at the waterfront.

38 Jack immediately renamed the beer brewed at sea 'Davy Jones'.

39 'A View of Afloat Support and Sea Basing', *NR* (2004) 4, 314, signed St Emilion.

40 'The Royal Fleet Auxiliaries', *NR* (1979) 4, 327, by Michael W F Day.

41 'Letter: The Royal Fleet Auxiliary', *NR* (1980) 1, 74, signed Spider.

42 'Sea Time for the Asking (Being the Case for the Navalisation of the Royal Fleet Auxiliary)', *NR* (1955) 3, 269, by JWC.

43 'Sea Time for the Asking – A Reply', *NR* (1955) 4, 449, by DHT.

44 'Royal Fleet Auxiliary', *NR* (1955) 4, 510, signed Avis

45 'The Royal Fleet Auxiliaries', *NR* (1979) 4, 327, by Michael W F Day.

46 'The End of the Road for the RFA?', *NR* (1985) 2, 142, signed A.

47 'The End of the Road for the RFA? An Opinion from the Other Side', *NR* (1985) 3, 197, by MD.

48 Chaff: a short-range counter measure to decoy radar-guided missiles. 20mm guns: rapid fire close-in weapon system.

49 'Command System for Type 23 Frigate and Auxiliary Oiler', *NR* (1989) 4, 422, unsigned.

50 A naval officer specialising in supply and secretariat known as a purser (but written and spoken as 'pusser'.) Known collectively as the 'white mafia' or 'white mice' from the days when the distinguishing coloured lace on their sleeve was white.

51 'A Right Proper Fix We're In', *NR* (2009) 1, 22, signed Blackbess.

52 'The Shape of the Royal Navy in the Twenty-First Century', *NR* (1995) 3, 193, by Blackham.

6 The Long Shadow of the Dardanelles on Amphibious Warfare in the Royal Navy

1 Perhaps the most obvious exception to this was the Pacific campaign, 1941–45, in which the naval battles were essential, and very public, precursors to the amphibious advances.

2 *Dardanelles Commission: First Report* (London, February 1917), pp41–3. See also the dissenting note from W Roch, p59. For a modern assessment of the terrain and earlier assessments of the practicalities of an assault, see P Chasseaud and P Doyle, *Grasping Gallipoli: Maps, Terrain and Failure at the Dardanelles, 1915* (Staplehurst, 2005).

3 'Dardanelles: Narrative of Mine Sweeping Trawler 448 Manned by HMS *Queen Elizabeth*', *NR* (1916) 2, 184–97, unsigned by Lt H R G Kinahan; see also R Keyes, *The Naval Memoirs of Admiral of the Fleet Sir Roger Keyes: The*

458

NOTES TO PAGES 85–88

Narrow Seas to the Dardanelles, 1910–1915 (London, 1934), pp202–20.

4 Wemyss, Lord Wester, *The Navy in the Dardanelles Campaign* (London, 1924), pp216-18.

5 Corbett, J S, *England in the Seven Years War*, 2 vols (London, 1907) and J S Corbett, *Some Principles of Maritime Strategy* (London, 1911).

6 Bell, C M, *The Royal Navy, Seapower and Strategy between the Wars* (Stanford, 2000).

7 Maund, L E H, *Assault from the Sea* (London, 1949), pp1–23; B Fergusson, *The Watery Maze, The Story of Combined Operations* (London, 1961), pp35–45.

8 Pond, H, *Sicily* (London, 1962); S E Morrison, *Sicily–Salerno–Anzio: January 1943–June 1944* (Boston 1954), pp204–19. Cunningham was captain of the *Beagle*-class destroyer, HMS *Scorpion* which was converted into a minesweeper during the campaign. A Cunningham, *A Sailor's Odyssey* (London, 1951), pp60–9.

9 'Proceedings of HMS *Amethyst* while at the Dardanelles', *NR* (16) 1, 85–100, unsigned by Lt Cdr E L Morant; 'A Narrative of HMS *Agamemnon* in the Mediterranean', *NR* (1916) 1, 104–83, unsigned by R Adm A H S Tyler, CB, DSO; 'Dardanelles Notes: HMS *Prince George*', *NR* (1916) 1, 198–269, unsigned by Lt Cdr A R Hammick; 'An Account of the Operations in the Dardanelles in 1915: Notes from HMS *Prince of Wales*', *NR* (1916) 1, 270–92, unsigned by Lt Col G P Orde, RM; and 'Dardanelles Operations: a Narrative of Events from HMS *Lord Nelson*', *NR* (1916) 1, 293–7, unsigned by Lt K Edwards (NB This latter contribution is accompanied by the note 'Not passed by Admiralty for November 1915 number'.).

10 'Anzac Impressions of the Landings and 14 Weeks' Work on the Beach', *NR* (1916) 1, 298–319, unsigned by Cdr G C Dickens, CMG; and 'Some Notes on the Evacuation of Suvla and Anzac', *NR* (1916) 1, 320–3 unsigned by Lt H J Carnduff, DSC.

11 The unfortunate minesweeping trawlers were given the sobriquet of 'Harry Tate's Navy'. See 'The Work of a Trawler in the Aegean Sea', *NR* (1918), 13–67, unsigned by Petty Officer A H Craven. (NB the editor has noted 'This came into my hands quite accidently, the writer, a pensioner PO, did not write it for publication.').

12 'Dardanelles Details – Part I', *NR* (1936) 1, 81–91, signed BHS by Capt B H Smith.

13 'The Crushing Blow', *NR* (1931) 1, 34–5, unsigned; and 'Book Review: *A Glance at Gallipoli*, by Lt Col C O Head, DSO', *NR* (1931) 3, 576–8, unsigned by Adm Sir Richard Webb.

14 '*Les Enseignements Maritimes de la Guerre Anti-Germanique* – Part II', *NR* (1921) 3, 496, by Contre Amiral Daveluy, translated by Capt G L Parnell, DSO, OBE: in the form of a book review containing the quotation 'Definitely, let it be said that the experience acquired at the Dardanelles and in Flanders demonstrated that the relation between batteries ashore and afloat remains unchanged. The advantage lies clearly with the former, since forts are less visible and to reduce them each gun separately must be knocked out; whereas one lucky shot may suffice to put a ship out of action.'

15 Beginning at *NR* (1922) 2, 157, Custance serialised in the *NR* a series entitled 'A Study of War', and it was completed at (1924) 1, 11, the year of its publication for a wider readership.

16 See 'A Study of War', *NR* (1922) 2, 161, which contrasts with the initial reaction to the failure of 18 March, in which the loss of three expendable old battleships was seen as a reasonable price to pay for an attempt which, intrinsically, had prospects of success. See 'With the Grand Fleet', *NR* (1915) 3, 182, unsigned by Plunkett: 'We have lost, so far, three battleships which can very well be spared. Our own losses are quite insignificant compared with the issues to be decided.'

17 'Imperial Defence', *NR* (1921) 2, 171–7 unsigned by Capt W H C S Thring, CBE, RAN; and 'The Disadvantages of a Single Ministry of Defence', 178–84, by Capt A C Dewar.

18 In the light of this recurring debate, the current proposals to diminish the service chiefs' representation on the Defence Board should be viewed with extreme caution. See http://www.defencemanagement.com/news_story.asp?id=16704 (accessed 1 August 2011).

19 'Winston Churchill and the Dardanelles', *NR* (1924) 1, 25–39, by Alfred Dewar.

20 'Book Review: *The Mediterranean Muddle: the Navy in the Dardanelles*

Campaign by Admiral of the Fleet Lord Wester Wemyss', *NR* (1924) 3, 441–6, unsigned.

21 'Book Review: The Naval Memoirs of Admiral of the Fleet Sir Roger Keyes: *The Narrow Seas to the Dardanelles 1910–1915*', *NR* (1934) 4, 782–91, by Cdr J H Owen: 'In the light of our knowledge to-day, can anyone doubt that the forcing of the Dardanelles would have shortened the war by two years, and spared literally millions of lives?'

22 'Book Review: *The Official Review of the Gallipoli Campaign – volume II*, by Brig Gen C F Aspinall-Oglander', *NR* (1932) 4, 803–6, signed WWG by Col W W Godfrey, RM: 'Why! Oh, why! Did the Navy and the Army never attack together?' Oglander later became Keyes' post-war biographer. See C Aspinall-Oglander, *Roger Keyes : Being a Biography of Admiral of the Fleet Lord Keyes of Zeebrugge and Dover* (London, 1951).

23 'Book Review: *Gallipoli: the Fading Vision* by John North', *NR* (1936) 2, 373–8, signed BHS by Capt B H Smith. Smith noted that 'Judging by this book, it would have made little difference if we [the Navy] had done this better; if the stupidity of the soldiers had really been as great as here made out it would have been sufficient to ensure failure in any case.' This view was common, for a lower deck view see *NR* (1918) 1, 28, 'Our nation will now realise that good leaders for this military expedition cannot be made in a year. Naval officers start from childhood. I am sure our middies would make rings around most of them.'

24 'The Disadvantages of a Single Ministry of Defence', *NR* (1921) 2, 180–1, by Capt A C Dewar.

25 A recognition that a justified, if perhaps overdone, self-critical approach had crept into histories of the operation can be found in 'Dardanelles Details – Part III', *NR* (1936) 3, 487–8, by BHS.

26 'Fortification and Coast Defence – Part I', *NR* (1914) 1, 58–64; 'Part II', *NR* (1914) 2, 108–14; and 'Part III', *NR* (1914) 3, 181–5, unsigned by Col Sir G Aston, KCB, RMA.

27 'A Lesson from the Dardanelles', *NR* (1917), 253–6, unsigned by Cdr G C Dickens; quotation from 'With the Grand Fleet', *NR* (1915) 3, 350, unsigned by Plunkett.

28 'What Changes are Suggested in Naval Construction and Tactics as a Result of (a) The Experiences of the War? (b) The Development of Submarine and Aerial Warfare in the Future?', *NR* (1922) 1, 73–104, by Col J F C Fuller, the RUSI First Naval Prize Essay for 1920.

29 'The Influence in the Future of Aircraft upon Problems of Imperial Defence', *NR* (1922) 2, 231, unsigned by Plunkett.

30 Harding, R, 'Learning from the War: The Development of British Amphibious Capability, 1919–1929', *Mariner's Mirror*, (2000) LXXXVI, 173–85; 'Amphibious Warfare, 1930–1939', in R Harding (ed), *The Royal Navy 1930–2000: Innovation and Defence* (London: Frank Cass Publishing, 2005), pp42–68.

31 Richmond, H W, *Sea Power and the Modern World* (London, 1934), p173.

32 'Book Review: *If War Comes* by R Ernest Dupuy and George Fielding Eliot', *NR* (1938) 2, 377, signed PWB by Lt Cdr P W Brock.

33 'Book Review: *Japan Must Fight Britain* by Lt Cdr Tota Ishimaru, IJN', *NR* (1936) 2, 366–72, signed PWB by Lt Cdr P W Brock; *Recent Naval War Experience*, *NR* (1937) 4, 646–9, signed Alpha by Lt Cdr J Hughes-Hallett.

34 'Ships and Forts', *NR* (1934) 1, 19–21, signed OL by Capt B H Smith.

35 Even the options for landings on exposed beaches as happened at Cape Helles were reconsidered. For an unusual example see 'Landing upon an Exposed Beach', *NR* (1939) 2, 253–4, by B M Chambers.

36 'Talking about Dieppe', *NR* (1942) 4, 297–300, signed Berkeley.

37 'Notes on the War at Sea', *NR* (1942) 4, 276–8.

38 Operation Torch, the Allied invasion of North Africa, was acknowledged by reproducing the First Lord of the Admiralty's report to Parliament, 'Naval Operations in the Expedition to North Africa', *NR* (1943) 1, 31–2, by A V Alexander.

39 'Book Review: *Amphibious Warfare and Combined Operations* by Admiral of the Fleet the Lord Keyes', *NR* (1943) 3, 258–60, signed HWR by Adm Sir Herbert Richmond, the printed version of Keyes' Lees Knowles lectures at Cambridge. Keyes also emphasised the lack of planning that had gone into amphibious operations before 1914 and 1939. Richmond asserted that all the

lessons of the Dardanelles had been allowed to die in the interwar period. The editor's comment was 'Since this was written the expedition to Sicily has shewn what preparation can achieve.'

40 'Notes on the War At Sea: The Landing on Sicily', *NR* (1943) 3, 197–203 and 'The Mediterranean and Italy', *NR* (1943) 4, 290–1. See also R Harding, 'The End of the Amphibious Option? The Cancellation of Operation Chopper, Sicily July 1943', *Northern Mariner/Le Marin de Nord*, 15:1, 1–14.

41 An historical account of the Dakar operation appeared in *NR* (1979) 2, 142–6, 'Naval Operations against Vichy France (1)', by Hank Rotherham. Dieppe was reported at the time. See *NR* (1942) 4, 'Dieppe', 276–8, and in a number of book reviews. Dieppe also featured in the Jubilee edition of the *NR*, but only in the form of a justificatory article by the President, Earl Mountbatten. See 'The Dieppe Raid', *NR* (1963) 1, 35–40, by Earl Mountbatten of Burma. A review of the supplement to the *London Gazette*, dated 12 August 1947, on the Dieppe raid appeared in 'The Dieppe Despatch', *NR* (1947) 4, 313–17, by JDL.

42 'Book Review: *Years of Victory 1802–1812* by Arthur Bryant', *NR* (1945) 1, 74, signed HWR by Richmond. Richmond compared the lack of clear thinking at the Walcheren Expedition of 1809 with similar problems regarding the Dardanelles in 1915.

43 'Amphibious Air Mobility and the Ocean Air Group', *NR* (1992) 4, 381, by Major N E Pounds, RM.

44 'The Maritime Strategy – A View from Below', *NR* (1990) 4, 308–14, by R Adm K R Menon, IN; 'Planning the Royal Navy for the Future', *NR* (1994) 1, 3–9, by Cdre N R Essenhigh.

45 One of the earliest narratives of the Gallipoli campaign noted that the ships' boats used to land the troops were inappropriate and designs similar to the Japanese sampan would serve the purpose better. See 'A Short Description of the Landing of the Australians at Gabi Tepe [*sic*], Dardanelles on Sunday 25 April 1915', *NR* (1915) 4, 657, unsigned by I A S Hutton.

46 'With "ABC" in the Med – Part I', *NR* (1977) 2, 133–9, signed AGP; 'The Impact of Technology on the Relationship between Sea and Air Power', *NR* (1985) 1, 4–12, by Sqd Ldr

D M Moss, RAF; 'Book Review: *Why the Allies Won* by Richard Overy', *NR* (1996) 3, 291–3, signed ABS by Capt Tony Sainsbury, RNR.

47 Sheffield, G, *Forgotten Victory: The First World War: Myths and Realities* (London, 2001), pp86–7, 94–7; W Philpott, *Bloody Victory: The Sacrifice on the Somme* (London, 2009); J M Bourne, *Britain and the First World War, 1914–1918* (London, 1989), pp40–8.

48 'An Unusual Job', *NR* (1981) 3, 238–40, signed MLD. The perception that the amphibious specialism remains marginal still emerges occasionally in the pages of the *NR*. See also 'Albion de Bulwark' (1999) 2, 126, by Lt S J Shaw, the second navigator of an LPD: 'There is a great deal of "amphibious blindness" in the Royal Navy, which is staggering considering the capability of its platforms in service in both the RN and RFA.'

7 The Submarine as Commerce Raider

1 'Sea Power in 1913', *NR* (1913) 2, unsigned by Lt A H Taylor.

2 'The Influence of the Submarine on Naval Policy', *NR* (1913) 3, 147–50 and 4, 236–9, unsigned by Capt S S Hall.

3 'The Influence of the Submarine on Naval Policy III', *NR* (1914), 31–4, unsigned by Capt S S Hall.

4 *The Times*, 5 June 1914.

5 *The Times*, 10 July 1914.

6 'The Submarine and the Surface Vessel', *NR* (1914) 3, 172–7, unsigned by Capt H W Richmond.

7 'The Influence of Commerce in War', *NR* (1914) 3, 159–64, unsigned by Cdr K G B Dewar.

8 'Protection of Trade in Past Wars', *NR* (1914) 4, 249–57, unsigned by Richmond.

9 'The Influence of Oversea Trade on British Naval Strategy in the Past and at Present', *NR* (1915) 104–37, unsigned by Lt V H Danckwerts.

10 'Submarines', *NR* (1933) 1, 30–46, unsigned by Lt Cdr S M Raw.

11 'The Introduction of the Convoy System', *NR* (1935) 2, 306–17, unsigned by Capt B H Smith; Arthur J Marder, *From the Dreadnought to Scapa Flow* (1969), vol 4, p154.

12 'Considerations of the War at Sea', *NR* (1917), 7–41, unsigned by Richmond.

13 'The System of Convoys for Merchant Shipping in 1917 and 1918; As seen by the Ministry of Shipping', *NR* (1917),

42–95, unsigned by Sir Norman Leslie.

14 Sir Norman Leslie to Lord Maclay, 14 February 1933; cited Marder, op cit, vol 4, p165.

15 Marder, op cit, vol 4, p61.

16 Ibid, p154.

17 Leslie, op cit, 46.

18 Ibid, 54.

19 'After the Washington and Genoa Conferences; translated from the French of Rear Admiral Degouy', NR (1922) 4, 36–49, translated by Lt A J G Langley.

20 'The Employment of Submarines and their Future Development', NR (1920) 3, 378–84, unsigned by Lt John Creswell.

21 'Changes in Naval Construction and Tactics', NR (1921) 3, 420–38, by Lt Cdr R G Studd, DSO, Third Naval Prize Essay, RUSI (1920).

22 'The Defence of Trade', NR (1927) 4, 833–9, unsigned by Cdr B Acworth, DSO, reprinted from The Shipping World.

23 'What Changes are Suggested in Naval Construction and Tactics', NR (1921) 4, 596–618, Second Trench-Gascoigne Prize Essay, RUSI.

24 'On Pacifism and Internationalism', NR (1933) 4, 717–22, unsigned by Lt Cdr J Hughes-Hallett.

25 'Some Elements in Imperial Naval Defence', NR (1933) 3, 442–58, a paper read by Admiral Richmond to a meeting of the British Commonwealth Peace Federation, March 1933.

26 See Marder, op cit, vol 4, p170.

27 'Book Review: War Memoirs of David Lloyd George, vol III (1934)', NR (1934) 4, 773–81, signed HWR by Richmond.

28 'Book Review: The Submarine Peril: The Admiralty Policy in 1917 by Admiral of the Fleet Earl Jellicoe (1934)', NR (1934) 4, 760–72, unsigned by Adm W M James.

29 'The Introduction of the Convoy System', NR (1935) 2, 306–17, Capt Bertram H Smith.

30 'On the Theory of War and the Freedom of the Sea', NR (1928) 2, 185–92, by Adm Sir Reginald Custance.

31 Degouy, op cit, 643.

32 'On Commerce Warfare, Blockade and Blockade Breaking: A Study in the Economics of War', NR (1928) 4, 684–709, by V Adm Hugo Meurer, reprinted from Marine Rundschau, April 1927 (contributed by Naval Intelligence Department).

33 'The Submarine War and Foreign Politics, Extracts from The Submarine War 1914–1918, by V Adm Andreas Michelson, lately Senior Officer in Command of German Submarines', NR (1929) 3, 598–613, translated from the German into French by Lt de V R Jouan and from the French by Lt Cdr H B Crane.

34 'Book Review: Germany Prepares for War by Professor Ewald Banse (1933)', NR (1934) 2, 409–11, signed EBKS by Cdr E B K Stevens.

35 'The International Situation', NR (1935) 3, 495–503, signed Alpha by Cdr J Hughes-Hallett.

36 'The Anglo-German Naval Agreement', NR (1935) 3, 504–6, signed Agna by Cdr J Hughes-Hallett.

37 'The Naval Debate and Commerce Protection', NR (1935) 2, 241–53, signed Teeoh by Capt B H Smith.

38 'The Naval Debate: Commerce Protection – and "Many Things"', NR (1938) 2, 183–96, signed Teeoh by Smith.

39 'Modern Types of Warships: A German Naval Opinion', NR (1939) 2, 197–200, by V Adm Hugo Meurer reprinted from the German journal Militär-Wochenblatt (1938), with some comments signed R.

40 'Our Mercantile Marine in War, September–October 1939', NR (1939) 4, 615–18, signed ACW.

41 'Our Mercantile Marine in War – 1939', NR (1940) 1, 30–6, signed ACW.

42 'Postscript to Notes on the War at Sea', NR (1940) 4, 549–54, signed Fauteuil by Capt B H Smith.

43 'Notes on the War at Sea', NR (1941) 1, 2-19, signed Fauteuil by Capt B H Smith.

44 'The Battle of the Atlantic', NR (1941) 2, 231-2, unsigned.

45 'Notes on the War at Sea', NR (1941) 2, 183–201, signed Fauteuil by Capt B H Smith.

46 'Notes on the War at Sea', NR (1941) 3, 478–508.

47 'Notes on the War at Sea', NR (1942) 1, 1–19.

48 'Notes on the War at Sea', NR (1942) 2, 97–109.

49 'Notes on the War at Sea', NR (1943) 3, 185–204.

50 'The Battle of the Atlantic', NR (1945) 3, 204, a 'brief summary of the part played by British, Dominion and Allied Forces under British control in the Battle of the Atlantic was issued by the

Admiralty as a Press Notice on the 13th of July 1945.'

51 'Naval Science against the U-boats', *NR* (1946) 1, 42–4, 'The following account of Naval Science against the U-boats was issued by the Admiralty as a Press Notice on the 1st of December, 1945. As it was only very briefly reported in the Press, those members who are not in close touch with scientific naval progress may like to see the full text.'

52 'Convoy Diary', *NR* (1946) 2, 194–200, by Gerald S Graham (1903–1988) who was Professor of History at Queen's University, Kingston, Ontario, when he joined the RCN in 1942, and was appointed to the newly opened Canadian Naval College at Royal Roads to teach naval history. He spent academic breaks in Canadian destroyers in the Atlantic and in torpedo boats at Dover. Following the Allied landings in northern France in 1944, Graham served as a major in the historical section of the Canadian Army. Post-war he led a distinguished academic career.

53 'Radio versus the U-boats', *NR* (1946) 4, 362–4, signed GMB.

54 'The Navy Estimates in the House of Lords', *NR* (1950) 3, 235–9, signed W.

8 The Naval Aviation Controversy 1919–1939

1 In the most serious German air raid of the war, Gotha bombers had flown over London in broad daylight, killing 162 and injuring 432.

2 For air policy during the war see the documents in S W Roskill, *The Naval Air Service* (Navy Records Society, 1969).

3 'Naval Air Requirements', *NR* (1919) 3, 305–11, unsigned by Brig Gen Oliver Swann, RAF (he anglicised his name from Schwann in 1917), who had been involved in the original Mayfly airship project and had made a pioneering seaplane flight in the machine bought privately by those involved in the airship project at Barrow. He had commanded the fleet seaplane carrier *Campania* during the war and rose to the rank of Air Vice Marshal.

4 'The Air Ministry: a Suggested Policy', *NR* (1919) 4, 443–5, unsigned by Lt Col F L M Boothby, RAF.

5 'Air Policy of the Future', *NR* (1919) 4, 446–59, unsigned by Capt M D Briggs.

6 The RNAS was included in the Navy List as the Naval Wing of the Royal Flying Corps until the creation of the RAF. This accounts for its separate cap badge and rank structure.

7 'A Plea for a Naval Air Force', *NR* (1919) 4, 451–3, unsigned by Cdr W P Gandell.

8 'The Progress of Aircraft', *NR* (1920) 3, 408–21, unsigned by Lt G W Hooper.

9 'The Navy and the Air', *NR* (1921) 1, 71–3, unsigned by Capt G C Dickens.

10 'Naval Aviation, A Reform Required', *NR* (1921) 2, 269–73, unsigned by Lt G W Hooper.

11 This had recently been set up by Chatfield the ACNS much against the will of the Air Ministry.

12 'The Navy and the Air Parts II and III', *NR* (1935) 1, 11–28, signed Seagull by Cdr G A French.

13 'The Influence in the Future of Aircraft on Imperial Defence', *NR* (1922) 2, 220–47, unsigned by Plunkett.

14 'Aircraft with the Fleet in War', *NR* (1923) 1, 282–93, unsigned by Lt C H L Howe.

15 'Letters: The Future Relations between the Navy and the RAF', *NR* (1923) 4, 759–60, unsigned by Lt A E M Dodington.

16 'The Navy and Its Aircraft', *NR* (1924) 4, 646–8, unsigned by Lt M A Maude.

17 'The Navy and Air Power', *NR* (1925) 2, 250–6, by Col Lord Sydenham of Combe.

18 'Sanity in Aviation', *NR* (1925) 4, 773–8, by Lt Cdr Ralph Wood, USN, reprinted from the *USNIP* of July 1925.

19 'The Fleet Air Arm', *NR* (1926) 2, 315–17, unsigned by Lt H St J Fancourt, and 3, 595–612, Part III, signed CLH by Lt Cdr C L Howe.

20 'Fleet Air Arm Notes', *NR* (1929) 3, 557–66, unsigned by Lt Cdr C L Howe.

21 'The Fleet Air Arm', *NR* (1931) 4, 699–704, unsigned by Lt Cdr C G Thompson.

22 'The Fleet Air Arm To-Day', *NR* (1932) 1, 95–100, signed Sirius by Lt P Bethell.

23 'The Fleet Air Arm', *NR* (1932) 2, 311–15, unsigned by Lt J C Richards.

24 'The Fleet Air Arm Today and Tomorrow', *NR* (1932) 2, 316–22, signed Saturn by Lt Cdr F S Slattery.

25 'The Fleet Air Arm Today', *NR* (1932) 3, 522–33, Part I signed CGT by Lt Cdr C G Thompson, Part II signed Nobspil by Lt J C Richards, and Part III signed Ovian by Lt P Bethell.

26 'The Navy and the Air, Parts II and III',

NR (1935) 1, 27, signed Seagull by French.

27 Inskip had been Attorney General and Prime Minister Baldwin thought his lawyer's forensic skills would be at a premium in judging between the services.

28 'The Navy and the Air', *NR* (1936) 3, 409–24, Part I signed RAC by Wg Cdr R A Cochrane, Part II signed Vates by Lt Cdr V E Kennedy, and Part III signed Philistine by Lt Cdr W T Couchman.

29 'Navy and the Air: a Commentary on the Replies', *NR* (1936) 3, 425–8, signed Pegasus by Cdr J Hughes-Hallett.

30 'Wanted – A Fleet Air Arm Reserve', *NR* (1936) 3, 429–31, signed Osprey by Lt Cdr J Dalyell.

31 'The Navy and the Air: the Problem of the Fleet Air Arm', *NR* (1937) 1, 1–23, signed Teeoh by Capt B H Smith.

32 'The Navy and the Air: the Problem of the Fleet Air Arm Part II', *NR* (1937) 2, 215–33, signed Teeoh by Smith.

33 Ibid, 232.

34 'Air Cooperation in Naval Warfare', *NR* (1937) 4, 662–5, signed Ka by Cdr J Creswell.

35 'The Navy's Share in Co-operation in the Air', *NR* (1938) 1, 10–16, signed Teeoh by Smith.

36 'The Command of Aircraft Units', *NR* (1939) 2, 241–6, signed Kestrel.

9 The Post-1945 Struggle for Naval Aviation

1 The best general account of the Royal Navy in the post-1945 period remains Eric Grove, *Vanguard to Trident: British Naval Policy Since World War II* (London: Bodley Head, 1987).

2 'A Plea for Greater Interest in Naval Aviation', *NR* (1947) 2, 111–12, signed R; see also 'Air-mindedness', *NR* (1946) 4, 343, signed R.

3 'Editor's Notes', *NR* (1947) 4, 290.

4 'The Post-war Navy', *NR* (1945) 2, 122–3, signed Daw.

5 'The Fleet of the Future', *NR* (1945) 4, 286–7, signed Blondin.

6 'The future of seaborne air power', *NR* (1947) 4, 331–3, signed Mate.

7 'Doubts: Comments on the article "The future of seaborne air power"', *NR* (1948) 1, 33–6, signed Tite-Barnacle.

8 'The future of seaborne airpower: a reply', *NR* (1948) 2, 139–41, signed Mate.

9 For an account of the struggle in the early 1950s, see 'British Naval Aviation and the "Radical Review", 1953–1955', in Tim Benbow (ed), *British Naval Aviation: The First 100 Years* (Farnham: Ashgate, 2011).

10 'Aviators and Seamen', *NR* (1954) 2, 169–71, signed DAW.

11 'Arresting the Decline of the British Fleet', *NR* (1955) 3, 319–26, signed ERM.

12 'Tamino and the Air', *NR* (1954) 2, 162–8, signed Tamino.

13 'Air/Sea power in the future – an American view', *NR* (1948) 2, 141–4, signed Flat Top.

14 'Sea Power and the Air', *NR* (1951) 3, 244–9, signed AHTF.

15 'The Navy and the Hydrogen Bomb', *NR* (1954) 4, 442–6, signed EHS.

16 'Sea Power Today', *NR* (1955) 2, 226–9, by AF Sir Rhoderick McGrigor.

17 'The Aircraft Carrier Aspects of Musketeer', *NR* (1957) 2, 124–30, signed JS.

18 Cmd 124 (1957): *Defence: Outline of Future Policy.*

19 'Editor's Notes', *NR* (1957) 3, 251.

20 'The pressing need for Naval fighters of the highest performance', *NR* (1953) 2, 125–7, signed VVV.

21 'A Lieutenant looks at the Navy', *NR* (1956) 3, 314–21, signed PM.

22 'Naval Affairs: Formidable Addition to Naval Striking Power', *NR* (1959) 1, 100.

23 'Naval Affairs, Modernisation of HMS *Victorious*', *NR* (1958) 2, 228.

24 'Suez and Syracuse', *NR* (1959) 2, 131–7, signed RAC.

25 'The Navy We Need', *NR* (1962) 2, 163–5, by Derisley Trimingham.

26 'Naval Affairs: Press Conference on Navy Estimates 1960–61', *NR* (1960) 2, 234.

27 'Defence Policy in the Sixties', *NR* (1962) 2, 130–7, signed Taurus.

28 'New Carriers', *NR* (1962) 4, 378–81, signed LN.

29 The Admiralty was at this stage – and for most of the period of this article – still the operational headquarters and administrative centre of the Royal Navy.

30 'Naval Affairs: The New Carrier', *NR* (1963) 4, 456–7.

31 The name was formally proposed in March 1964 and was informally approved by Her Majesty the Queen in April: The National Archives: ADM1/29044.

32 'Britain's Defence Review', *NR* (1965) 4, 303–6, by Secretary of State for Defence.

10 Full Circle: *Queen Elizabeth* to *Invincible* and Back Again

1 'Part I of the Statement on the Defence Estimates 1966', *NR* (1966) 2, 94–102.
2 Grove, Eric J, *Vanguard to Trident: British Naval Policy since World War II* (London: The Bodley Head, 1987), p280.
3 'Letters: Carriers: The Essential Requirement', *NR* (1966) 4, 363–4, by Capt E F Archdale.
4 'Editor's Notes', *NR* (1966) 3, 179–80, by V Adm Sir Aubrey Mansergh.
5 'Where Do We Go From Here?', *NR* (1967) 1, 2–6, signed Matelot.
6 For a comprehensive account of the evolution of the escort cruiser concept, see D K Brown & George Moore, *Rebuilding the Royal Navy: Warship Design since 1945* (London: Chatham Publishing, 2003), pp61–9.
7 'Letters: VTOL for Aircraft Carriers', *NR* (1966) 2, 169–70, signed CEE.
8 'Maritime Forces for Non-Nuclear War', *NR* (1967) 4, 301–12, signed Piers.
9 'Defence Against the Submarine', *NR* (1970) 1, 9–13, by Lt Cdr F P U Croker.
10 'The Need for an Efficient Navy', *NR* (1971) 1, 17–22, signed PRCJ.
11 Childs, Nick, *The Age of Invincible: The ship that defined the modern Royal Navy* (Barnsley: Pen and Sword Books, 2009), p37.
12 'Everybody's Friend', *NR* (1971) 2, 119–23, signed Cecil.
13 'Conservation of the Eagle', *NR* (1971) 1, 22–4, Croker; 'Benbow's Column', *NR* (1971) 1, 2–11, signed Benbow.
14 'Sic, Sic, Sic', *NR* (1971) 3, 205–14, by Cdr (later R Adm) J R Hill.
15 'Editor's Notes', *NR* (1973) 3, 200–4, by V Adm Sir Ian McGeogh.
16 'The Great Through-Deck Mystery', *NR* (1973) 2, 151–4, Croker.
17 'How Big is Small?', *NR* (1980) 2, 127–30, signed D P Norman.
18 Cmnd 8288, *The United Kingdom Defence Programme: The Way Forward*, p11.
19 Childs, p130.
20 'Planning the Royal Navy for the Future', *NR* (1994) 1, 3–9, by Cdre (later Adm Sir Nigel) Essenhigh, First Sea Lord 2000–1.
21 'The Shape of the Royal Navy in the Twenty-First Century', *NR* (1995) 3, 189–95, by R Adm (later V Adm Sir Jeremy) Blackham.
22 'Letters: Letter to a Friend II', *NR* (1997) 1, 9–14, signed Nonius.

23 'The Strategic Defence Review [Extracts]', *NR* (1998) 4, 291–301.
24 'The Strategic Defence Review: Message from First Sea Lord,' *NR* (1998) 4, 289–90, by Adm Sir Jock Slater, First Sea Lord 1995–8.
25 'Carrier 2000: A Consideration of Naval Aviation in the Millennium – II', *NR* (1999) 2, 105–13, by Cdr D R James.
26 For example, 'The Future Aircraft Carrier', *NR* (2000) 1, 61, by J C Lawrence (a CVA-01 Chief Constructor), and 'Counterfactual Aircraft Carrier (Things That Never Were)', *NR* (2002) 4, 375–81, by Philip D Grove (a lecturer at BRNC).
27 'Fleet Air Arm 2000 and Well Beyond', *NR* (2001) 2, 100–2, by R Adm Iain Henderson; 'Joint Force 2000 – On Track or Coming Off the Rails?', *NR* (2003) 4, 349–53, by R Adm Scott Lidbetter.
28 Childs, p171.
29 Otherwise known as the Joint Strike Fighter (JSF).
30 'Perfect Storm?', *NR* (2009) 4, 337–9, signed GoCo.
31 'The Failings of Britain's Future Carrier Strike Programme', *NR* (2007) 4, 323–9, by Lt Cdr David South.
32 'An Open Letter to the New Secretary of State for Defence', *NR* (2010) 3, 244–7, signed Plowdew. Ironically, in order to reduce costs, the design selected is less capable than an earlier version.
33 'Dead Navy Walking', *NR* (2010) 2, 16–18, by David Mugridge.
34 'SDSR: A Badly Designed Camel', *NR* (2011) 1, 25–8, by Peter Freeman.

11 From the Honourable East India Company's Marine to Indian Navy

1 'The Indian Navy', *NR* (1953), 381–8, signed VAK.
2 'The Naval Development of the East India Company', *NR* (1924) 2, 251–64, unsigned by Lt Cdr K H Grant; and 'Possibilities for the Royal Indian Marine', 265–7, unsigned by Lt C A W Clarke.
3 'The Place of India in Naval Strategy 1744–1783', *NR* (1930) 3, 461–74; and 'The Maritime Defences of India Under The East India Company 1763–1783', *NR* (1930) 3, 475–82, by Adm Sir Herbert Richmond.
4 'The Royal Indian Navy', *NR* (1928) 3, 417–35, by Capt R H Garstin.
5 'Book Review: *Neptune's Trident Spices And Slaves: 1500–1807* by Richard

Woodman', by Mike Plumrose.

6 'Letters: Plumbers' Hundred', *NR* (1981) 1, 57, signed RJT.

7 'The Suppression of Piracy in the Gulf 1797–1820', *NR* (1996) 4, 378–83, signed Mewstone by Lt Cdr J B Claro; and 'Book Review: *The Pirates of Trucial Oman* by H Moyse-Bartlett', *NR* (1968) 1, 97–8, signed JENC.

8 'Book Review: *Warship 1993*, Robert Gardiner (ed)', *NR* (1994) 2, 186–8, by David Ellison.

9 'The Imperial Conference of 1926', *NR* (1927) 1, 7–30, unsigned by Cdr C A G Hutchison.

10 'The Royal Indian Navy', *NR* (1927) 4, 838–43, by Capt E J Headlam, RIM. Captain Sir Edward Headlam, Bt, CSI, CMG, DSO (1873–1943) joined the RIM in 1894 and served: Marine Survey of India, 1897–1914; British Expeditionary Force, China 1900–1; Naval Transport Officer, East African Forces 1914–17; Principal Naval Transport Officer, South And East Africa 1917–19; Director Royal Indian Marine, 1922–28.

11 See 'Book Review: *The Royal Indian Navy 1612–1950* by Cdr D J Hastings, RINVR', *NR* (1989) 2, 191, by Philip Towle.

12 'Notes on the War at Sea', *NR* (1943) 1, 3, 17 & 58.

13 'Commander A B Goord and his Contributions to the Royal Indian Navy', *NR* (2010) 2, 154–60, by Lt Cdr Yogesh Athawale, IN.

14 'Emerging Navies in the 1950s I: The Indian Navy and Vice Admiral Sir Stephen Carlill', *NR* (1996) 3, 238–9, R Adm Krishan Dev, IN; 'Book Review: *Blue Print to Blue Water* by R Adm Satyindra Singh, IN', *NR* (1993) 3, 282–3 by Capt R P Khanna, IN.

15 Quoted in R Adm Satyindra Singh of *The Indian Navy 1951–65* (Lancer International, 1982), p1.

16 See also Peter Hore, *Patrick Blackett: Sailor, Scientist and Socialist* (2003).

17 'Naval Affairs', *NR* (1961) 4, 398; 'Naval Affairs', *NR* (1960) 4, 485.

18 Mountbatten letter dated November 1965 to R Adm K Sridharan quoted in Sridharan, *Maritime History of India* (Publication Division Ministry of Information and Broadcasting, August 1965), and Adm Hiranandani, *Transition to Triumph* (Spantech & Lancer, 2000), pp8–9.

19 'Why the Indian Navy Did "Sweet Fanny Adams" in the 1965 War', *NR* (2010) 4, 379–84, by Cdre Ranjit Rai, IN.

20 'Naval Operations in the Indo-Pakistan War – 3 to 17 December 1971', *NR* (1973) 1, 14–22, signed ILMMcG by V Adm Sir Ian McGeogh.

21 'Indigenisation in the Indian Navy – a Progressive March', *NR* (2001) 2, 129–32, by Cdre M K Banger, IN.

22 'Indian Navy – Historical Perspective and Future', *NR* (1991) 2, 118–22, by Capt R P Khanna, IN.

23 'Admiral Gorshkov – a Day to Remember', *NR* (2003) 3, 239, by Cdre M K Banger, IN.

24 'Letters: A Letter to Master Ned', *NR* (1988) 3, 255–6, signed Cdr M by Cdr J A A McCoy.

25 'The Technological Growth of the Indian Navy – A Review', *NR* (2001) 4, 362–4, by Cdre M K Banger, IN.

26 'Management of Indian Naval Dockyards', *NR* (1997) 1, 39–43, by Cdre M K Banger, IN.

27 'Indian Navy – Historical Perspective and Future', *NR* (1991) 2, 118–22, by Capt R P Khanna, IN.

28 'Naval Power in South East Asia', *NR* (1974) 1, 40–6, by Mohan Singh.

29 'Letters: Maritime Reconnaissance Role Goes to Indian Navy', *NR* (1975) 4, 1975, by Mohan Singh.

30 'Membership of *The Naval Review*', *NR* (1951) 2, 204–9; 'Membership of *The Naval Review*', *NR* (1954) 3, 322–5 both signed Sirius by (presumed) Lt Cdr P Bethell; and 'An Analysis of Membership', *NR* (1957) 3, 336 unsigned.

31 'Book Review: *Suez Thrombosis: Causes and Prospects* by Capt P S Bindra (1969)', *NR* (1970) 2, 183–4, by George A Riding.

32 'Nafta and a Maritime Strategy', *NR* (1969) 4, 295, reprint of a lecture given at RUSI on 19 March 1969 by Dr Geoffrey Williams.

33 'Red China Goes Black', *NR* (1971) 4, 352, signed RH.

34 'Indian Navy – Historical Perspective and Future', *NR* (1991) 2, 118–22, by Capt R P Khanna, IN.

35 'Naval Power in South East Asia, *NR* (1974) 1, 40–5, by Mohan Singh.

36 'The Growth of Navies: Some Historical Lessons', *NR* (1987) 4, 303–7 and (1988) 1, 24–9, by Cdre Raja Menon.

37 'India's Naval Expansion', *NR* (1989) 3, 228–30, by Capt R P Khanna, IN.

38 'Book Review: *Maritime Strategy And Continental Wars* by R Adm Raja Menon (1997)', *NR* (1998) 3, 269–70, by Capt Peter Hore.

39 'The Royal and the Indian Navies Relationship – a Review', *NR* (2002) 3, 230–2, by Cdre M K Banger, IN.

40 'China's String of Pearls vs India's Iron Curtain in the Indian Ocean: it is a C3IC Issue', *NR* (2010) 1, 32–5, by Cdre Ranjit Rai, IN.

12 A Distance Beyond Geography: The Royal Canadian Navy

1 Chalmers (later Rear Admiral W S Chalmers) often contributed to the *NR*, and as an historian wrote biographies of significant naval figures such as Earl Beatty and Admiral Sir Max Horton, the latter which, as will be seen, drew Canadian criticism. In 1916 Chalmers became the brother-in-law of Captain R A R Plunkett, one of the founders of the *NR*.

2 Initially, Rear Admiral Charles Kingsmill and Minister Louis-Philippe Brodeur. For a general history of the Canadian Navy one can do no better that Richard H Gimblett (ed), *The Naval Service of Canada 1910–2010: The Centennial Story* (2010). For the early history see William Johnston, William Rawling, Richard H Gimblett and John MacFarlane, *The Seabound Coast: The Official History of the Royal Canadian Navy, 1867–1939* (2010).

3 The Royal Navy College of Canada was initially established at Halifax but was moved to Esquimalt as a result of the damage suffered from the 1917 Halifax Explosion. It was later closed as a part of budgetary reductions.

4 'Canada and the Navy', *NR* (1913) 2, 96, signed BX by Lt Cdr W S Chalmers.

5 'Australia and Her Navy', *NR* (1914) 3, 210, unsigned by Lt D Rahill.

6 'Contributions, Donations, or Dominion Navies', *NR* (1913) 2, 126, unsigned by Admiral W H Henderson.

7 For more on this period see Michael Hadley and Roger Sarty, *Tin Pots and Pirate Ships: Canadian Naval Forces and German Sea Raiders, 1980–1918* (1991).

8 'The Future of the Royal Canadian Navy', *NR* (1915) 3, 369, unsigned by Lt Cdr H B Pilcher.

9 For a commemoration of the reserve's role see Richard H Gimblett and Michael Hadley (eds), *Citizen Sailors: Chronicles of Canada's Naval Reserves* (2011).

10 'The System of Convoys for Merchant Shipping', *NR* (1917) 1, 68–71, unsigned by Sir Norman Leslie.

11 Later Vice Admiral Bertram Mordaunt Chambers, RN (1866–1945).

12 'Halifax Explosion', *NR* (1920) 3, 445–6, unsigned by Vice Admiral Bertram Chambers.

13 See J G Armstrong, *The Halifax Explosion and the Royal Canadian Navy: Inquiry and Intrigue* (2002).

14 The Chanak incident in September 1922 was the threatened attack by Turkish troops on British and French troops guarding a neutral zone in the Dardanelles. Ironically, although the Canadian government refused to provide forces, a number of RCN officers were serving in RN warships deployed to Chanak.

15 'The Canadian View of Naval Policy', *NR* (1934) 4, 634, signed SDS by Cdr S D Spicer, RCN.

16 'Some Canadian Aspects of Imperial Defence', *NR* (1937) 4, 643, signed Zeta by Cdr C R H Taylor, RCN.

17 For RN/RCN relations in the final years of peace see W A B Douglas, Roger Sarty, Michael Whitby et al, *No Higher Purpose: The Operational History of the Royal Canadian Navy, 1939–43* (2003), pp52–3.

18 'The Royal Canadian Navy and the Royal Canadian Naval College', *NR* (1944) 1, 34, signed HWR by Admiral Sir Herbert Richmond.

19 The starting point for the wartime history of the RCN are W A B Douglas, Roger Sarty and Michael Whitby et al, *No Higher Purpose: The Operational History of the Royal Canadian Navy, 1939–43* (2003); and *A Blue Water Navy: The Operational History of the Royal Canadian Navy, 1943–45* (2006).

20 'Naval Diary of the War', *NR* (1941) 2, 266 & 270.

21 'Notes on the War at Sea', *NR* (1943) 2, 104.

22 The Royal Canadian Naval College', *NR* (1942) 2, 157–8, signed V; 'The Royal Canadian Navy and the Royal Canadian Naval College', *NR* (1944) 1, 34, signed HWR by Richmond.

23 'The Dieppe Raid', *NR* (1963) 1, 35–40, by Mountbatten of Burma.

24 'Commodores of Ocean Convoy', *NR* (1946) 2, 127–33, signed EC by Rear Admiral Sir Edward Owen Cochrane.

25 'A Matter of Length and Breadth', *NR* (1950) 2, 136–42 and 'Birthday Party', *NR* (1950) 3, 292–6, both signed BJ by Capt Basil Jones. The Tribal HMCS *Haida*, Canada's most famous warship, survives as a museum in Hamilton, Ontario.

26 'Future of the Dominion Navies: One Combined Empire Force', *NR* (1948) 1, 28–30, signed Uno.

27 'The Development of the Royal Canadian Navy', *NR* (1951) 4, 377–8, signed GWN by Lt (P) George W Noble, RCN. Noble (1928–1953), born in Toronto, was no relation of Admiral Sir Percy Noble.

28 'The Commonwealth Navies in War', *NR* (1952) 3, 296, signed GWN by Noble.

29 Writing under several pen names, R Adm Brock was a regular contributor to the *NR*. His obituary was published in *NR* (1989) 1, 2–3.

30 'The Commonwealth Navies in War', *NR* (1953) 1, 115–18 signed Beaver by Capt P W Brock.

31 Noble authored a final article on Barbarossa that was published after his death: 'The Forgotten Admiral', *NR* (1955) 1, 61–6.

32 'Membership of "The Naval Review" – An Analysis', *NR* (1954) 3, 322–3, signed Sirius by Lt Cdr P Bethell.

33 'Editor's Notes', *NR* (1954) 4, 393.

34 The author's father, Lieutenant Commander J P Whitby, RCN, was one who in the 1950s and 1960s chose *Proceedings* over the *NR*.

35 Interestingly, during the late 1950s, Canadian naval historian Donald Schurman, urged on the RCN Chief of Naval Staff the need for a Canadian journal along the lines of *Proceedings* or *The Naval Review* without success. Schurman to Michael Whitby, 15 April 2009.

36 'HMCS *Labrador*', *NR* (1954) 4, 495–7, and 'Northwest Passage', *NR* (1955) 2, 190–5, both signed PJEL by Lt Cdr P J E Lloyd.

37 'The Flotilla – Battle Fleet of Today', *NR* (1956) 3, 272–80, signed FF-H by Capt A B F Fraser-Harris, DSC*, RCN.

38 'Letters', *NR* (1955) 2, 256–7, by Capt J D Prentice, RCN.

39 'Letters', *NR* (1955) 3, 374–5, by R Adm W S Chalmers: Chalmers referred to volume II of G N Tucker's, *The Naval Service of Canada* (1952).

40 'Ocean Convoy – VI, 1943–45', *NR* (1961) 2, 148, R Adm C G Brodie. Brodie had retired in the 1930s but was recalled as a convoy commodore in the Battle of the Atlantic .

41 'Naval Affairs, Canada: The State of the RCN', *NR* (1964) 1, 78–83.

42 'Background to the Canadian White Paper on Defence', *NR* (1966) 1, 2–12, Gp Capt William M Lee, RCAF.

43 'Organization of the Canadian Armed Services', *NR* (1966) 4, 369–70, signed Half Back.

44 'Unification – A Crisis of Conscience for Canadians', *NR* (1966) 3, 186–8, signed Crapaud.

45 'Letters: Unification – A Crisis of Conscience for Canadians', *NR* (1966) 4, 370–1, signed Nevill.

46 'Letters: How Are We Doing Canada?', *NR* (1974) 3, 265–6, by Capt J C Littler, RCN. Littler entered the RCN through the RCNR, and retired in 1962. His memoirs are *Sea Fever* (1995).

47 Perhaps to have some response to Littler, the *NR* later reprinted an article by a Canadian officer from another journal that reflected on leaderships aspects of a unified force, 'A Unified Armed Force', *NR* (1975) 1, 31–6, signed GMdeR by Commodore G M de Rosenroll, RCN.

48 'Book Reviews I: *The Marine Engineer's Review*, "RCN – HMCS *Chicoutimi* – Fire"', *NR* (2005) 4, 429–30, by Cdr R B Berry.

49 Such an error would no longer be an issue: in August 2011, the government officially resurrected the name Royal Canadian Navy from 'Maritime Command', as Canadian naval forces had been known since Unification.

50 'Defence, Micawber and Free Enterprise', *NR* (1981) 4, 318–20, signed Ivy.

51 'Maritime Sovereignty, the Offshore Estate and National Defence', *NR* (1993) 2, 135–40, by Michael Ranken; and 'Letters: The Canadian Navy – Support to Other Government Departments', *NR* (1993) 4, 420–1, by Lt Cdr A W Knight.

52 'United Nations' Legal Regime for Management and Conservation extended to cover High Seas Fisheries', *NR* (1996) 1, 28–33; and 'Rules of Engagement and Tapestry Tasks: Canada's Recent Experience on the Grand Banks', *NR* (1996) 2, 135, both by Michael Ranken.

53 'Canada's Defence', *NR* (1978) 4, 326–31, and 'Canada's Security', *NR* (1980)

2, 122–6, both by Adm R H Falls.

54 'The Canadian Navy at (Another) Crossroads', (2001) 1, 35–7, Peter Haydon.

55 'Reviews: North Atlantic Run Article', NR (1989) 1, 75–7, by Lt Cdr James Goldrick, RAN.

56 'The RCN in Wartime', NR (1989) 3, 278–80, by Capt John Littler, RCN.

57 'Learning From the Past', NR (1990) 1, 53–5, by Lt Cdr James Goldrick, RAN.

58 'New Members', NR (1989) 4, 439.

59 Commodore Jan Drent to Michael Whitby, 24 April 2009.

60 The Canadian Naval Review (CNR) website is at http.naval.review. cfps.dal.ca. The NR now includes coverage of CNR in its review section.

13 From Offspring to Independence: The Royal Australian Navy

1 Editorial, NR (2000) 1, 1, by R Adm Richard Hill.

2 A quick survey of the membership list published in the 1988 75th anniversary issue indicates that at most 2 per cent were members of the RAN or RANR. This percentage is unlikely to have increased in the years since.

3 HMAS Australia: battlecruiser, 1913; 18,500 tons, 8x12in; 16x4in, 2xtt, 23kts.

4 Senator Pearce, quoted in Sydney Morning Herald, 6 October 1913.

5 'Introductory', NR (1913) 1, 1–4, unsigned by Capt H W Richmond.

6 'War Thought and Naval War', NR (1913) 1, 6, unsigned by Capt A C Dewar.

7 Cdr (later Capt) Walter Hugh Charles Samuel Thring, RAN (1873–1949), entered RN 1886, RN retired list 1911, Assistant to First Naval Member ACNB 1913–18, Director War Staff 1914–18, RN Liaison Officer 1919–22, RAN retired list 1922.

8 R Adm (later V Adm) Sir William Rooke Creswell, RAN (1852–1933), entered RN 1866, RN retired list after being invalided 1878, First Naval Member ACNB 1911–19.

9 For a recent assessment of the dispute between Admirals Fisher and Beresford see R Freeman, The Great Edwardian Naval Feud: Beresford's Vendetta Against 'Jackie' Fisher, (Barnsley: Pen & Sword, 2009).

10 See D M Stevens, '"Defend the North": Commander Thring, Captain Hughes-Onslow and the beginnings of Australian

naval strategic thought', in D M Stevens and J Reeve (eds), Southern Trident: Strategy, History and the Rise of Australian Naval Power (Sydney, 2001).

11 See J S Corbett, Some Principles of Maritime Strategy (London, 1911).

12 'The Pacific Problem', NR (1914) 2, 102–7, and 'Force Required For The Defence of the British Possessions in The Pacific', NR (1914) 2, 237–8, both unsigned by Cdr W H C Thring, RAN.

13 For details on the Empire Mission and Jellicoe's Report see A Temple Patterson (ed), The Jellicoe Papers: Selections from the private and official correspondence of Admiral of the Fleet Earl Jellicoe, vol II 1916–1935 (London: Naval Records Society, 1968).

14 'United We Stand', NR (1921) 1, 2–5, unsigned by Sub Lt H C Guernsey; 'A Defence Organisation for the British Commonwealth of Nations', NR (1921) 1, 6–9, unsigned by Thring; 'Imperial Defence', NR (1921) 2, 173–7, unsigned by Lt L F Robinson; 'A Defence Organisation For the Community of the British Nations', NR (1922) 1, 53–72, unsigned by Thring.

15 'Trade Routes and their Influence, Parts I–IV', NR (1928); 'Parts V–X', NR (1929), unsigned.

16 'Vice Admiral Sir William Creswell, Royal Australian Navy', NR (1933) 3, 543–56, by Adm B M Chambers.

17 HMAS Sydney: light cruiser, 1911, 5400 tons, 8x6in, 2xtt, 26kts.

18 SMS Emden: light cruiser, 1908, 3600 tons, 10x4.1in, 2xtt, 24kts.

19 'The Wounded in the Action Between the Sydney and the Emden', NR (1917) 1, 243–52, unsigned, taken from Earl of Medina's Journal.

20 'The Royal Australian Navy: Itinerary of HMAS Australia and Narrative of her Proceedings', NR (1915) 1, 138–42 unsigned by C M Macintrer.

21 Adm Bertram Mordaunt Chambers (1866–1945) entered RN 1879, Second Naval Member ACNB 1911–13, retired list 1927.

22 'Naval Chaplains in the Australian Navy', NR (1921) 2, 283–6 signed R Adm B M Chambers.

23 'The Mutiny in HMAS Australia in 1919', NR (1972) 4, 388–9, signed CCMU by Cdr Cecil Usher, RN.

24 Each had received sentences of between one and two years' imprisonment, all with hard labour and dismissal from the service.

25 See D Stevens, 'The HMAS *Australia* Mutiny, 1919', in Christopher M Bell & Bruce A Elleman (eds), *Naval Mutinies of the Twentieth Century* (London: Frank Cass, 2003), pp123–44.

26 See, for example, Sir Henry Burrell's comments about his time in HMS *Devonshire* in 1937, *Mermaids Do Exist: The Autobiography of Vice Admiral Sir Henry Burrell Royal Australian Navy (Retired)* (Melbourne: Macmillan, 1986), p65. This author also recalls being instructed in the failings of the RAN disciplinary system by a RN exchange officer in the late 1970s.

27 HMAS *Psyche*: light cruiser, 1897, 2135 tons, 8x4in, 2xtt, 20kts.

28 Arthur W Jose, *The Official History of Australia in the War of 1914–1918, Volume IX, The Royal Australian Navy* (Sydney: Angus & Robertson, ninth edition, 1941), p218.

29 'Book Review: *Official History of Australia in the War of 1914–1918 Vol IX – The Royal Australian Navy* by A W Rose', *NR* (1929) 1, 155–61, unsigned by Adm B M Chambers.

30 Capt (later R Adm) William Scott Chalmers (1881–1971), commanding officer and flag captain HMAS *Australia* (II) 1929–32, retired list RN 1939.

31 Notwithstanding this comment, some very high quality officers served with the RAN during the interwar period, including the future Adm Sir Denis Boyd, the future Admiral of the Fleet Sir Philip Vian and the future Adm Sir Harold Burrough.

32 'Australia and her Navy Today', *NR* (1932) 1, 35–46, unsigned by Capt W S Chalmers.

33 Statement by the Prime Minister on Commonwealth Government's defence policy in light of the Imperial Conference, 24 August 1937, National Archives of Australia, Series MP1587/1, file 218AO.

34 HMAS *Australia* (II) & *Canberra*: heavy cruisers, 1928, 10,000 tons, 8x8in, 8xtt, 31kts.

35 'Some Questions Concerning Australian Defence', *NR* (1929) 4, 747–65, unsigned by Richmond.

36 'The Problem of the Pacific in the Twentieth Century', *NR* (1922) 3, 403–15, unsigned by Richmond.

37 'The Problem of the Pacific', *NR* (1935) 2, 294–305, signed SDS by Capt S D Spicer.

38 'Australian Defence', *NR* (1936) 1, 39–51, signed HWR by Richmond.

39 'Australian Co-operation in Imperial Defence', *NR* (1937) 2, 234–40, 'extract of a speech made last November by Sir Archdale Parkhill, Minister of Defence in the Commonwealth of Australia, now in England attending the Coronation and the Imperial Conference, during the Parliamentary Debate on the Defence Estimates, 1936–37, for the Commonwealth. It is here reproduced as showing clearly the Australian Government's policy of Defence.'

40 See Foreword by Rear Admiral G V Gladstone, RAN, in G R Worledge (ed), *Contact! HMAS Rushcutter and Australia's Submarine Hunters 1939–1946* (Sydney: A/S Officers Association, 1994), viii.

41 Lt Cdr F M Osborne, RANVR, MP, then a Member of the Foreign Affairs Committee of the Commonwealth Parliament.

42 'The Royal Australian Navy: Background to Australia's Defence Problems', *NR* (1954) 2, 195–203, signed CCMU by Usher.

43 'Australia's Defence and Foreign Policy', *NR* (1964) 2, 168–73, signed CCMU by Usher.

44 'Australian Vignette', *NR* (1961) 3, 266–72, signed K R J Arnold.

45 County class: guided missile destroyer, 1959, 5440 tons, 4x4.5in, 1x Seaslug, 2x Seacat, 1x helo, 32kts.

46 *Charles F Adams* class: guided missile destroyer, 1965, 3370 tons, 2x5in, 6xtt, 1x Tartar, 2x Ikara, 35kts.

47 'Austro-Antipodean Umpire?' *NR* (1976) 1, 79, signed GMB: 'According to the last issue of *The Naval Review* (October, p371): "From March 1917 until March 1918 H.M.S. *Sir Thomas Picton* together with another 12-inch monitor ... were based at Venice, bombarding the *Australians* [author's italics] in the Gulf of Trieste."'

48 'A Letter From Australia', *NR* (1978) 4, 313–15, signed Master Ned by Goldrick.

49 Space precludes discussion of the Royal New Zealand Navy's contribution to the *Review*, but note should be made of the 'By Ships We Live' series *NR* (1965–73), signed IWIK and JFA; and Cdr Richard Jackson's articles at intervals more recently.

50 'A Letter From Australia – XXIV', *NR* (2000) 1, 42–5, signed Master Ned by Goldrick.

51 'Swimming with the Crocodiles', *NR*

(2000) 1, 45–7, signed Lt Scott Preskett, RAN.

52 'Journal of the Australian Naval Institute, RNZN Navy Today & New Zealand Defence Quarterly', NR (2000) 1, 73–7, signed Cdre Peter Wykeham-Martin.

14 Simon's Town and the Cape Sea Route

1 Although the modern spelling is Simon's Town, earlier spelling used in many of the sources is Simonstown.

2 See Allan du Toit, South Africa's Fighting Ships Past and Present (Rivonia, 1992); C H Bennett and A G Söderlund, South Africa's Navy (Simon's Town, 2008), p39, and Denis Judd, Empire: The British Imperial Experience, from 1765 to the Present (London, 1996), p105.

3 'Naval Affairs: The South Atlantic Command', NR (1967) 3, 256–7.

4 'A Synopsis of the Doings of the Cape of Good Hope Squadron', NR (1915) 4, 637–43, unsigned by C D D Shakespeare.

5 'Naval Operations on the East Coast of Africa after the destruction of the Königsberg', NR (1916) 2, 345–51, unsigned by Lt Cdr E W A Blake.

6 'Special Service Squadron World Cruise, Being an extract from the diary of Midshipman W R Gordon', NR (1925) 1, 108–14, by Mid W R Gordon.

7 The nascent South African Naval Service consisted of a survey ship and two minesweepers to train members of the South African Division of the Royal Naval Volunteer Reserve (RNVR(SA)) which had been established in 1913. Although funded by the South African government, and constitutionally part of the Union Defence Forces, the RNVR(SA), which made a valuable contribution during the First World War, was to be placed at the disposal of the British Admiralty in time of war, and the Royal Navy's C-in-C, Cape of Good Hope Station, was responsible for the Division's peacetime organisation, training, administration and discipline.

8 In 1935, the South African Prime Minister, General Hertzog, made South African dependence on the Royal Navy, and the Government's acceptance of this position very clear. Indeed, this position prevailed well into the 1940s.

9 'Navy Week in South Africa 1936–37', NR (1970) 2, 155, signed Onlooker possibly by Capt A W Clarke who used

this pseudonym in 1963.

10 'Naval Affairs: The South Atlantic Command', NR (1967) 3, 256–7.

11 During the Second World War some 133 ships, totalling 743,544 gross registered tons, were sunk within 1,000 miles of the South African coast by Axis U-boats, whilst only three German U-boats were lost during this offensive.

12 South Africa's Navy, op cit, p23.

13 'Letters', NR (1970) 3, 296–7 signed CCMU by Commander C C M Usher.

14 See G R Berridge and J E Spence, South Africa and the Simonstown Agreements, in J W Young (ed), The Foreign Policy of Churchill's Peacetime Administration 1951–1955 (Leicester, 1988), p188, and Ronald Hyam and Peter Henshaw, The Lion and Springbok: Britain and South Africa since the Boer War (Cambridge, 2003), pp243–4.

15 'The Simonstown Agreement', NR (1971) 2, 146–50, signed Onlooker possibly Clarke.

16 The Agreement established a strategic zone approximating to the British South Atlantic Station, including the Mozambique Channel, in which both the RN and SAN would operate under the operational authority of the British Commander-in-Chief South Atlantic. Within this zone lay a South African Area which remained the direct responsibility of the SAN.

17 'Naval Affairs', NR (1957) 3, 349–50.

18 'The Simonstown Agreement', NR (1971) 2, 148–50, signed Onlooker possibly Clarke.

19 FCO 25/656, JS 10/10, Withdrawal of the British Commander-in-Chief from South Africa.

20 'Defence Policy 1945–1982 – II, The "Healey" Defence Review 1964–1966', NR (1992) 4, 374, signed Mewstone.

21 'Naval Affairs: The South Atlantic Command', NR (1967) 3, 256–7.

22 HMS Lynx: Type 41 anti-aircraft frigate, 1957; 2,300 tons; 2x4.5in; 2x40mm; 1xSquid A/S mortar; 24 kts.

23 FCO 45/1613, The Importance of the Simon's Town Agreement.

24 'Sea Power Today', NR (1970) 1, 16–19, 'a lecture delivered at Britannia RN College in June 1969 by Captain Stephen Roskill, DSC, MA, FRHISTS, Royal Navy'.

25 'Defence of the Realm', NR (1971) 1, 12–16, signed RGO.

26 'Indian Ocean Strategy', NR (1971) 1, 28–33, signed CCMU by Commander C

G M Usher.

27 'By Ships We Live – VI: The Cape Route', *NR* (1971) 3, 225–30, signed JFA.

28 Edward Heath, *The Course of My Life* (London, 1998), p319.

29 'Arms for South Africa', *NR* (1971) 2, 142–7, signed Garefowl; 'The Simonstown Agreement', *NR* (1971) 2, 148–50, signed Onlooker possibly Clarke; 'Letters: Arms for South Africa', *NR* (1971) 3, 289, by Captain T Wheeldon.

30 'The Simonstown Agreement', *NR* (1971) 2, 148–50, signed Onlooker possibly Clarke.

31 FCO 45/1613, op cit.

32 This task group, the most powerful British force ever to call at the Cape in peacetime, consisted of the helicopter-cruiser HMS *Blake*, flying the flag of V Adm Henry Leach, Flag Officer First Flotilla, six frigates, the nuclear-powered attack submarine HMS *Warspite* and three Royal Fleet Auxiliaries.

33 CAB 128/55/17, CC(74) 42, 31 Oct 1974.

34 'The Strategic Importance of the Falkland Islands', *NR* (1982) 4, 274–5, by Hugh Rogers.

35 'Benbow's Column', *NR* (1975) 1, 3–4, signed Benbow by Lt Cdr Ian Pratt, aka John Winton, the naval novelist and popular naval historian.

15 Fortress Singapore: British Naval Policy in the Interwar Years

1 Greg Kennedy, 'The Royal Navy and Imperial Defence, 1919–1945', in Greg Kennedy (ed), *British Imperial Defence: The Old World Order, 1856–1956* (London, 2008), pp133–52.

2 'Book Review: *The Problem of the Pacific in the Twentieth Century*', *NR* (1922) 3, 403–15, unsigned review of a book (1922, republished 2010) by General Nikolai Nikolaevich Golovin in collaboration with Admiral A D Bubnov.

3 'United We Stand', *NR* (1921) 1, 1–5, unsigned by Sub Lt H C Guernsey.

4 'The Singapore Base', *NR* (1925) 3, 463–9, by Col Lord Sydenham of Combe.

5 'After the Washington and the Genoa Conferences', *NR* (1922) 4, 636–49 translated from the French of Rear Admiral Degouy in the *Revue des Deux Monds* (1922).

6 'Book Review: *The Next Great Naval War*', *NR* (1925) 4, 723–35, by Sir Herbert Russell of Hector Bywater's *The*

Great Pacific War: A History of the American–Japanese Campaign of 1931–33.

7 'Composition of the Main Fleet in the Future', *NR* (1923) 1, 121–9, unsigned by Lt L W S Wright.

8 On the nature of the Anglo-Japanese Alliance in the post-First World War period see Keith Neilson, 'Unbroken Thread: Japan and Britain and Imperial Defence, 1920–1932' in Greg Kennedy (ed), *British Naval Strategy East of Suez, 1900–2000: Influences and Actions* (London, 2005), pp62–89.

9 One of the more positive and culturally oriented articles appearing in the *NR* that dealt with the nature of the Japanese was 'Modern Japan, Part I', *NR* (1925) 3, 470–4, signed SK-H by Lt Cdr Stephen King-Hall and 'Modern Japan, Part II', *NR* (1925) 4, 719–22. The review article, 'The Riddle of Japan', *NR* (1926) 1, 108–22, by Geoffrey Drage (reprinted from the *Edinburgh Review* of October 1925) struck a much more alarmist note, signalling the failure of the British government adequately to finance the building of naval units as a repetition of history that was sure to encourage further Japanese aggression and expansion in the Far East.

10 'The Menace of the Far East', *NR* (1925) 2, 244–50 by Brigadier General C D Bruce.

11 'China and the Policy of Japan from Past to Present', *NR* (1924) 1, 55–68, unsigned by Lt Cdr C J M Lang.

12 'The Menace of the Far East', 246–7 by Bruce.

13 The best general survey of the international situation in the Far East in the period from 1919–33 is provided in the relevant chapters of Zara Steiner, *The Lights That Failed: European International History, 1919–1933* (Oxford, 2005).

14 'Composition of the Main Fleet in the Future', *NR* (1923) 1, 122, Wright.

15 Greg Kennedy, 'The Challenge in the Far East, 1919–1941' in Gordon Martel (ed), *A Companion to International History, 1900–2001* (Oxford, 2007), pp195–207.

16 'The Far Eastern Crisis', *NR* (1932) 3, 491–500, unsigned by Lt Cdr J Hughes-Hallett; 'The Sino-Japanese Clash in Shanghai, 1932', *NR* (1933) 1, 1–29, unsigned by Adm Sir Howard Kelly; 'Some Elements in Imperial Defence', *NR* (1933) 2, 442–59, a paper read by

Adm Richmond to a meeting of the British Commonwealth Peace Federation in March 1933; 'The Problem of the Pacific', *NR* (1935) 2, 294–305, signed SDS by Captain S D Spicer; 'The International Situation', *NR* (1935) 3, 495–503, signed Alpha by Cdr J Hughes-Hallett; 'The Pacific Situation', *NR* (1936) 4, 615–21, signed Beaver by Lt Cdr P W Brock; 'The Far East', *NR* (1938) 3, 477–84, signed AHT by R Adm A H Taylor; 'The Situation in the Far East', *NR* (1939) 3, 461–3, signed AHT by Taylor.

17 'Imperial Defence', *NR* (1926) 1, 87–97, unsigned by Cdr B Acworth.

18 'British Trade and Maritime Strategy in the Far East', *NR* (1924) 4, 632–41, by Capt Alfred C Dewar (reprinted from the *Asiatic Review*, July 1924).

19 'Problems of the Western Pacific', *NR* (1923) 4, 664–9, unsigned by Capt W H C S Thring, RAN.

20 The Open Door was a concept in foreign affairs referring to a policy of the early twentieth century allowing multiple imperial powers access to China, with none of them in control of that country.

21 'Imperial Defence', *NR* (1926) 1, 87–97, by Acworth; 'The Imperial Conference 1926', *NR* (1927) 1, 9–30, unsigned by Cdr C A G Hutchinson; 'China', *NR* (1928) 1, 77–89, signed FX by Lt J R Henderson; 'China, Its Past and Present Situation', *NR* (1928) 3, 447–78, by Captain R B I Miles; 'Some Aspects of the Chinese Situation', *NR* (1928) 4, 659–73, by Lt Cdr C M Faure.

22 'Composition of the Main Fleet in the Future', *NR* (1923) 1, unsigned by Wright.

23 'Singapore', *NR* (1924) 1, 69–72, unsigned by Wright.

24 'The Singapore Base', *NR* (1925) 3, 463–9, by Sydenham.

25 'The Imperial Conference of 1926', *NR* (1927) 1, by Hutchinson.

26 Ibid. Articles appeared throughout the interwar period on the strength and ability of both the New Zealand and the Australian Navies, as well as the nature of the nations themselves and their willingness to contribute to the imperial defence system. See 'Australia and Her Navy To-day', *NR* (1932) 1, 35–46, unsigned by Captain W S Chalmers; 'New Zealand and Her Naval Forces', *NR* (1933) 4, 643–55, unsigned by R Adm Geoffrey Blake; 'India and Sea Power', *NR* (1933) 4, 656–61, unsigned by Adm Sir Herbert Richmond; 'Australian Defence', *NR* (1936) 1, 39–52, by Adm Sir Herbert Richmond; 'Australian Co-operation in Imperial Defence', *NR* (1937) 2, 234–42, extract of a speech by Sir Archdale Parkhill, Minister of Defence in the Commonwealth of Australia.

27 'The Navy and Air Power', *NR* (1925) 2, 251–6, by Sydenham.

28 Ibid, 254–5.

29 'Air Power and its Effect on Naval Operations', *NR* (1931) 3, 422–34, signed RL. This was a lecture given to sub lieutenants and midshipmen attending the Junior Air Course in HMS *Argus* during the autumn cruise of the Atlantic Fleet, 1929. 'Notes on the War at Sea', *NR* (1940) 1, 11–27, unsigned; 'Aircraft Carriers', *NR* (1940) 2, 233–5, unsigned.

30 'The Relation of Aircraft to Sea-power', *NR* (1928) 4, 728–45, reprinted from *United States Naval Institute Proceedings*, Lt Cdr Bruce G Leighton, USN; 'Italian Views on Air Co-operation with the Navy', *NR* (1928) 4, 746–7, contribution by Naval Intelligence Division.

31 'Some Problems of Imperial Defence', *NR* (1931) 4, 607–27, Adm Sir Herbert Richmond. For the complete story on the use of air power and the Singapore basing issue see John Ferris, 'Student and Master: The United Kingdom, Japan, Airpower, and the Fall of Singapore, 1920–1941', in Farrell and Hunter (eds), *Sixty Years On*, pp94–121.

32 'The Navy and the Air', *NR* (1936) 1, 65–71, by Cdr J Hughes-Hallett; 'The Navy and the Air – I', by Wg Cdr R A Cochrane; 'Part II', by Lt Cdr V E Kennedy; 'Part III', by Lt Cdr W T Couchman, and 'Commentary', *NR* (1936) 3, 409–24, by Hughes-Hallett; 'The Navy and the Air – Part II', *NR* (1937) 2, 215–33, by Capt B H S Smith; 'An American View of our Naval Re-armament', *NR* (1937) 3, 468–71, by Lt Cdr P W Brock.

33 Greg Kennedy, 'Symbol of Imperial Defence: The Role of Singapore in British and American Far Eastern Strategic Relations, 1933–1941', in Farrell and Hunter (eds), *Sixty Years On*, pp42–67.

34 Greg Kennedy, *Anglo-American Strategic Relations and the Far East, 1933–1939* (London, 2002); Ian Cowman, *Dominion or Decline: Anglo-*

American Naval Relations in the Pacific, 1937–1941 (Dulles: Berg Publishers, 1996).

35 'The Pacific Situation', *NR* (1936) 4, 615–20, by Brock; 'The London Naval Conference, 1935', *NR* (1936) 1, 31–8, by Maj H R Lambert, RM; 'The London Naval Treaty, 1936', *NR* (1936) 2, 259–77, R Adm H G Thursfield; 'Some American Impressions', *NR* (1936) 1, 100–11, by Brock; 'The Situation in the Far East', by R Adm A H Taylor and 'America's Foreign Relations', *NR* (1939) 3, 461–5 by Drax; 'The United States and the Far East', *NR* (1938) 2, 267–70, signed Hellespont; 'The Far East', *NR* (1938) 3, 477–83, by Taylor; 'The British-American Agreement', *NR* (1940) 4, 561–72, text of a White Paper 'Exchange of Notes Regarding United States Destroyers and Naval and Air Facilities for the United States in British Transatlantic Territories'; 'Notes on the War at Sea', *NR* (1941) 2, 183–201, signed Fauteuil by Capt B H Smith; 'Notes on the War at Sea', *NR* (1942) 1, 1–23, signed Fauteuil by Smith.

36 'The Loss of the *Prince of Wales* and *Repulse*', *NR* (1954) 4, 407–12, by S W Roskill.

16 Anglo-American Naval Relations

1 'The Start of the Special Relationship', *NR* (1989) 2, 165–7, by Peter Herbert.

2 See also 'Naval Operations at Manila', *NR* (1980) 1, 59–61, extract from the midshipman's log of Admiral Sir Percy Noble, kept when serving in HMS *Immortalité*.

3 'The Pacific Problem – I', *NR* (1914) 2, 100–7, unsigned by Lt W A Egerton.

4 'The Control of Shipping during the War', *NR* (1919), 2, 163, unsigned by Capt R G H Henderson.

5 'The System of Convoys for Merchant Shipping in 1917 and 1918', *NR* (1917), 42–95, unsigned by Sir Norman Leslie. Leslie (1870–1945), a partner in the firm of Law, Leslie and Co, and a member of the Baltic Exchange, volunteered for service in the Transport Department of the Admiralty 1915–16, and transferred to the newly formed Ministry of Shipping, where he was involved in inaugurating the convoy system 1917–18.

6 Ibid, 72.

7 'The Naval Battle of Paris', *NR* (2009) 3, 286–7, by Jerry Jones (reprinted from the *Naval War College Review* [USA],

Spring 2009).

8 'Freedom of the Seas – I', *NR* (1919) 1, 77, unsigned by Adm Sir E J Slade.

9 'International Law and Sea Power, II', *NR* (1919) 1, 66, unsigned by Capt M H Anderson.

10 'The Maritime Rights of Belligerents', *NR* (1923) 1, 71–3, unsigned by Capt K G B Dewar. See also the following articles: 'War Trade and Sea Power', *NR* (1920) 1, 36–9, unsigned by Cdr A H Taylor; 'International Law, VI', *NR* (1928) 1, 126–47, unsigned by Paymaster Capt H W E Manisty; 'The Freedom of the Seas', *NR* (1929) 2, 213–20, Col Edward M House (President Wilson's right-hand man).

11 'On the Theory of War and the Freedom of the Sea', *NR* (1928) 2, 188–9, by Admiral Sir Reginald Custance.

12 'The Freedom of the Seas: Some Comments on Colonel House's Pamphlet', *NR* (1929) 2, 221–36, Admiral Sir Herbert Richmond; 'The British Commonwealth and Freedom of the Seas', 266 (reprinted from *The Round Table*), anon.

13 'Naval Disarmament', *NR* (1932) 2, 266, unsigned by Lt Cdr J Hughes-Hallett.

14 'An American View of the 1935 Naval Conference', *NR* (1934) 3, 462–9, by Adm William Veazie Pratt, USN. (Pratt was the recently retired Chief of Naval Operations; this was an article in *Foreign Affairs* (USA), July 1934). See also 'Freedom of the Seas', ibid, 487–90, signed Helm by Cdr L E H Maund.

15 'The International Situation', *NR* (1935) 3, 501, signed Alpha by Cdr J Hughes-Hallett.

16 'Shanghai, 1937', *NR* (2008) 4, 386–97, from the papers of Capt P H E Welby-Everard; 'The United States and the Far East', *NR* (1938), 2, 268, signed Hellespont.

17 'China and the Policy of Japan from the Past to the Present', *NR* (1924) 1, 66–8, unsigned by Lt Cdr C J M Lang.

18 'The US and the Far East', *NR* (1938) 2, 267, signed Hellespont. See also 'Some Aspects of the China Situation', *NR* (1928) 4, 659–73, by Lt Cdr C M Faure.

19 Admiral of the Fleet Sir Ernle Chatfield (First Sea Lord) to Admiral Sir Roger Backhouse (C-in-C, Home Fleet), 6 October 1937, CHT 4/1, Chatfield Papers, National Maritime Museum.

20 'The Third Destroyer Flotilla in China, 1926–1928', *NR* (1930) 1, 99–110,

unsigned by Lt Cdr K R Buckley.
21 'Shanghai, 1937', Welby-Everard.
22 'Three Swatow Letters', *NR* (1984) 1,
   66, by Cdr H G de Chair. See also
   'Experiences in China, 1938–1941', *NR*
   (1943) 2, 147–50, signed SDH.
23 'Pre-War Recollections', *NR* (1991) 1,
   60, signed GDPH.
24 'The Pacific Situation', *NR* (1936) 4,
   618, signed Beaver by Lt Cdr P W Brock.
   See also 'The London Naval Treaty, Part
   II', *NR* (1936) 2, 269–77, R Adm H G
   Thursfield.
25 'British-American Agreement', *NR*
   (1940) 4, 566 (text of White Paper).
26 'Notes on the War at Sea', *NR* (1941) 3,
   485, signed Fauteuil.
27 'A Refit in a US Port', *NR* (1942) 3, 218,
   signed Ensee.
28 Ibid, 219.
29 President Franklin D Roosevelt, 'The
   Arsenal of Democracy' speech, 29
   December 1940.
30 'A Refit in a US Port', *NR* (1942) 3, 220,
   Ensee.
31 'Notes on the War at Sea', *NR* (1942,) 1,
   9, Fauteuil.
32 'Churchill's Responsibility (??) for Pearl
   Harbor', *NR* (1989) 4, 402–4, signed
   Parcener.
33 'The Beginning of the End of British
   Prestige in the Far East', *NR* (1997) 4,
   352, by Cdr James Humphrys.
34 'The Far East, 1940–1941', *NR* (1991)
   1, 47–54, unsigned.
35 'The Coast Watchers', *NR* (1960) 2,
   168, by Lt Cdr E A Feldt, RAN. Feldt
   was appointed Staff Officer,
   (Intelligence) at Port Moresby in 1939
   and directed the coast watcher
   organisation throughout Papua and
   New Guinea and the Solomon Islands
   until relieved because of ill health in
   1943: his article in the *NR* led to a book
   in 1979.
36 'The Origins of Operation TORCH',
   NR (1959) 1, 48–55, by Adm Sir
   Geoffrey Blake.
37 'The Mediterranean – World War II and
   Current Relevance, II', *NR* (1999) 1, 47,
   by Cdr James Humphrys.
38 'Admiral Sir Geoffrey N Oliver', *NR*
   (1981) 1, 7–8, by Capt S W Roskill.
39 'The Allied Navies at Salerno', *NR*
   (1954) 1, 45, by Adm H Kent Hewitt,
   USN (quoting Admiral of the Fleet Sir
   Andrew Cunningham), reproduced from
   Proceedings of the US Naval Institute,
   September 1953.
40 'Some Notes on Operation NEPTUNE,

May–June 1944', *NR* (1994) 2, 101, by
   Cdr A J W Wilson.
41 'The Normandy Landings', *NR* (1977)
   3, 246, by Acting Captain 'Fish'
   Dolphin; see also 'The Logistics of
   Operation NEPTUNE', *NR* (1994) 3,
   245–50, by Capt P G Hore.
42 'US Submarine Warfare in the Pacific',
   NR (2000) 1, 52–8, by Capt D Conley.
43 'Naval Air Operations in the Pacific,
   1941–1945', *NR* (1951) 1, 59–65, by C
   S G. See also 'Naval Strategy in the
   Pacific in World War II', *NR* (1950) 3,
   320–7, signed C S G; and 'Factors that
   Contributed to the American Victory at
   the Battle of Midway', *NR* (2006) 4,
   336–9, by Lt Cdr O Hutchinson.
44 'Operation DOWNFALL', *NR* (2000) 4,
   365–70, by Peter Wickham.
45 'The Elusive BPF', *NR* (1985) 4, 331–4,
   by Cdr H StA Malleson.
46 'The Contribution of the BPF to the
   Assault on Okinawa', *NR* (1948) 3, 229,
   by Admiral of the Fleet Lord Fraser.
47 Ibid, 229.
48 'Comments on Louis Le Bailly, *The Man
   Around the Engine*', *NR* (1991) 1, 68,
   by M Ranken.
49 Ibid, 68–9.
50 'The US Naval Institute', *NR* (1919) 3,
   268, 270, by R Adm Bradley A Fiske,
   USN, reprinted from the *Proceedings of
   the US Naval Institute*, February 1919.
51 'Comments on Rear Admiral William S
   Sims, US Navy, "Promotion: An
   American Opinion"', *NR* (1935) 4, 744,
   signed Piscis by Lt Cdr P W Brock.
52 Ibid, 744–5.
53 'The Navy and the Air', *NR* (1936) 3,
   419, signed Vates by Lt Cdr V E
   Kennedy, RAN.
54 'A Visit to the US Navy's Fleet Air Base,
   Caso Solo, PCZ', *NR* (1937) 1, 97,
   signed Osprey by Lt Cdr J Dalyell Stead.
   See also 'The Development of Naval
   Aviation in the British and US Navies',
   by Lt Cdr H M Dater, USNR, & 'Part
   II', signed DAW by Lt Cdr D A Waters,
   NR (1954) 4, 413–24.
55 'The Navy and the Air, II', *NR* (1937) 2,
   229–30, signed Teeoh by Capt B H S
   Smith.
56 'AA Gunnery between the Wars', *NR*
   (1978) 2, 129–33, by Capt S W Roskill.
57 Ibid, 129–33.
58 'When Radar was RDF', (2009) 3, 268–
   72, by Capt P H E Welby-Everard.
59 Mr Winston Churchill, the Prime
   Minister, House of Commons, 20
   August 1940.

60 President Thomas Jefferson, First Inaugural Address (1801). This policy formed the basis of US foreign policy down to 1941.

17 Life at Sea and Ship Organisation

1 'A Contribution to the Study of Naval Discipline', *NR* (1913) 3, 156, unsigned by Chaplain G H Hewetson.

2 See, for example, Christopher McKee, *Sober Men and True: Sailor Lives in the Royal Navy 1900–1945* (Cambridge, Mass: Harvard University Press), pp192–5 and p147.

3 'The Trinity of Efficiency', *NR* (1914) 1, 63, unsigned by Cdr W A Egerton.

4 Wells, John, *The Royal Navy: An Illustrated Social History 1870–1982* (Stroud: Sutton, 1994), p85.

5 'Welfare of the Personnel', *NR* (1915) 4, 553, unsigned by Capt W D H Boyle: 'Ginger' Boyle, later Admiral of the Fleet the Earl of Cork and Orrery.

6 'The Action off the Falkland Islands: Sidelights on the Battle', *NR* (1915) 2, 278–9, unsigned by Lt Cdr H E H Spencer-Cooper.

7 'Routines', *NR* (1913) 3, 151, unsigned by Cdr J F Warton.

8 See Admiral Sir William James, *The Sky Was Always Blue* (London: Methuen, 1951), pp78–9, and his article 'A Minor Revolution', *NR (1959)* 4, 441–3.

9 'Letters: Organisation', *NR* (1915) 4, 699, unsigned by Lt (later V Adm Sir Francis) A F Pridham.

10 See James Goldrick, 'The Impact of War: Matching Expectation with Reality in the Royal Navy in the First Months of the Great War at Sea', *War in History* (January 2007), 14:1, 33.

11 'The Shibboleths of Peace', *NR* (1915) 4, 547, unsigned by Lt Cdr R L Edwards.

12 'Discipline for the Wardroom', *NR* (1920) 4, 516, unsigned by Lt Cdr H S H Manley.

13 'Some Impressions of a Temporary Officer', *NR* (1920) 3, 325; Lt Cdr Hilton Young (later Lord Kennet), DSO, DSC*, RNVR, had an outstanding war record, including Zeebrugge and ashore in Flanders, and later in Russia. A financial expert of great standing, he also had extensive literary connections, notably with the Stephen family and the Bloomsbury Set as well as E M Forster.

14 'Lower Deck and Ward Room', *NR* (1920) 2, 147, by Able Seaman William Lang.

15 'The Gunroom', *NR* (1920) 1, 114, unsigned by Lt C H Drage.

16 'Letter: The Gunroom', *NR* (1920) 2, 311, unsigned by Lt E H Cameron.

17 'Letter: The Gunroom', *NR* (1921) 1, 164, signed S by Lt Cdr H T Baillie-Grohman who retired as V Adm and remained a frequent commentator on contributions to the *NR* for many years.

18 Morgan (1894–1958), novelist and playwright, was a member of the Royal Naval Division despatched to Antwerp in 1914 and spent the remainder of the war interned in the Netherlands.

19 'The Spirit of the Personnel', *NR* (1920) 2, 141, unsigned by Boyle.

20 'Letters: Games', *NR* (1919) 4, 567–8, unsigned by Cdr W P Mark-Waidlaw, and 'A Reply to the Above', 569, unsigned by Lt Cdr C H Rolleston.

21 'Letters: Games', *NR* (1920) 1, 127, unsigned by R Adm H W Richmond

22 'Games', *NR* (1920) 2, 208, unsigned by Rolleston.

23 'The Young Lieutenant', *NR* (1921) 1, 42, unsigned by Lt (later R Adm) Royer Dick.

24 The Hughes-Hallett brothers Charles Hughes-Hallett (1898–1985) and John Hughes-Hallett (1901–1972) both became V Adms. John became a Conservative MP and a junior minister in the government (1954–64). John first contributed to the *NR* as a midshipman, being one of at least three members to do so and later achieve flag rank.

25 'Officers and Men', *NR* (1923), 3, 486, unsigned by Lt John Hughes-Hallett.

26 'Results Count', *NR* (1928) 1, 123, signed QD by Lt Cdr J S M Mackenzie-Grieve.

27 'Our Present Enemy' *NR* (1929) 1, 139, unsigned by Lt (later R Adm) P W Brock.

28 'The Staff and its Relation to the Work of the Fleet', *NR* (1929) 3, 546, signed Walrus by Capt E R Bent.

29 'The Navy and the Cinema', *NR* (1931) 2, 312, unsigned by Lt J Hughes-Hallett.

30 'Quo Vadis?', *NR* (1930) 3, 566, signed RX by Plunkett.

31 'A Disease and the Remedy', *NR* (1931) 1, 129, unsigned by Plunkett.

32 'An Imaginary Disease and a Questionable Remedy', *NR* (1931) 2, 262, unsigned by Adm Sir Douglas Nicholson.

33 'An Imaginary Disease: A Reply', *NR* (1931) 3, 467, unsigned but clearly by the author of 'A Disease and the Remedy'.

34 'Officers and Men', *NR* (1932) 1, 80, unsigned by Lt Cdr J Hughes-Hallett.

35 'Training in Sail' (analysis of RUSI lecture by Sir James Thursfield in 1900 on sail training and the subsequent debate), *NR* (1932) 3, 445, unsigned by Capt H G Thursfield; 'The Training of Seamen', *NR* (1932) 3, 459, unsigned by Cdr H P K Oram; 'Sail or Steam', *NR* (1932) 3, 472, 'contributed by HMS *Warspite*' (presumably a team effort from officers onboard).

36 Chatfield, Admiral of the Fleet Lord, *The Navy and Defence; vol II: It Might Happen Again* (London: Heinemann, 1947), pp54–9.

37 'Review of *Clear Lower Deck* by Stanley Knock', *NR* (1932) 2, 368, signed JHH by Lt Cdr J Hughes-Hallett.

38 'Review of *Running a Big Ship on "Ten Commandments"*', *NR* (1937) 2, 387, signed JSC by Cdr J S Cowie.

39 'Quo Vadis?', *NR* (1938) 1, 38, signed Sea Arrow by Baillie-Grohman.

40 'Quo Vadis? – Three Replies', *NR* (1938) 2, 228; 'Reply I' by Epsilon (possibly Sir William James), 'Reply II (*Autres Temps, Autres Moeurs*)' by Sampan, and 'Reply III' by FTBT (R Adm Francis Tower). See also an exchange of letters, *NR* (1938) 3, 577, between Executive Officer and Baillie-Grohman still writing as Sea Arrow .

41 See Bruce Taylor, *The Battlecruiser* HMS Hood: *An Illustrated Biography 1916–1941* (Barnsley: Seaforth, 2008), pp165 and 182.

42 'The Musings of Methuselah', *NR* (1939) 3, 417, signed BHS by Capt B H Smith.

43 'About Sailors', *NR* (1945) 1, 45, signed K.

44 'Comparisons are Odious', *NR (1946)* 1, 53, signed Blake. Notably, this article was written in early 1944 but not submitted for publication at the time.

45 Diary entry of 16 June 1944, Michael Simpson (ed), *The Cunningham Papers, vol II: The Triumph of Allied Sea Power 1942–1946* (Aldershot: Ashgate & Navy Records Society, 2006), p207.

46 Conversation with the late Capt W F Cook, MVO, RAN, who as a Lt Cdr in command exchanged his 'lovely *Nizam*' for *Quadrant* in October 1945. His comments are supported by lower deck veterans of the N and Qs in RAN service. See also Cdre Dacre Smyth, RAN, *Pictures in my Life: an Autobiography in Oils* (Melbourne: self

published, 1994).

47 'Centralized Messing', *NR* (1948) 2, 180, signed Implac by Capt Charles Hughes-Hallett.

48 'Man-Power at Sea: The Importance of its Care and Maintenance', *NR* (1947) 4, 334, signed Peregrine.

49 'Basic Damage Control Training', *NR* (1946) 2, 183, signed Iota.

50 'Letters: Damage Control', *NR* (1948) 1, 99, signed BNLO.

51 'Letters: Damage Control in Peace-Time', *NR* (1948) 2, 216, signed Walrus (possibly Cdr G M Bennett).

52 Fisher, R Adm R L, *Salt Horse: A Naval Life* (Gartocharn: Famedrum), p187.

53 'Leave', *NR* (1948) 2, 189, signed Yorick.

54 'Letters: Leave', *NR* (1948) 3, 315, signed Bob. Even in the mid 1980s the weekend leave problem had not been properly solved in the fleet, with personnel living onboard RN ships over the weekend required to turn to on Saturday forenoons when alongside, while those who had family or accommodation ashore did not have to return onboard.

55 'Strong Drink', *NR* (1945) 1, 49, signed Daw.

56 'Strong Drink I', *NR* (1945) 2, 136, signed Task Force.

57 'Strong Drink II', *NR* (1945) 3, 238, signed Bacchus.

58 'Strong Drink I', *NR* (1945) 3, 237, signed Judex.

59 'Some Notes on the Running of a Small Ship', *NR* (1949) 2, 119, signed Nico.

60 'Letters: Notice Boards', *NR* (1949) 3, 317, signed Bashan.

61 'Two Worlds', *NR* (1955) 1, 38, signed B.

62 Wettern, Desmond, *The Decline of British Sea Power* (London: Jane's, 1982). These seem to have reached a peak in late 1953 (p86) and 1954 (p88).

63 'Manning Difficulties', *NR* (1954) 1, 53, signed T.

64 'Letters: Re-engaging?', *NR* (1953) 4, 483, signed Clean Sweep

65 'Marriage and the Navy', *NR* (1949) 1, 36, signed Spunyarn.

66 Initiated by 'Can we reduce our Defaulters?', *NR* (1958) 3, 343, by Hornli, based on recent experiences in a cruiser. A group of articles followed in the next edition, including 'Discipline – IV', *NR* (1958) 4, 411, signed JAGT by V Adm Sir James Troup.

67 Starting with 'The Problem of

Leavebreaking', *NR* (1959) 4, 434, signed OBS.

68 'Letter: 'The Problem of Leavebreaking', *NR* (1960) 4, 503, by Baillie-Grohman.

69 'A Piece of Cake', *NR* (1955) 4, 467, signed Nibs.

70 'Worm's-eye View', *NR* (1962) 2, 143, signed Vermis.

71 'Letter: Worm's-eye View', *NR* (1962) 3, 531, by Capt (later V Adm Sir Charles) C P Mills.

72 'Letter: Worm's-eye View', *NR* (1962) 4, 479, by S W Roskill.

73 'Letter :Worm's-eye View', *NR* (1962) 3, 352, signed Moryak.

74 'A Modern Method of Inspection', *NR* (1961) 2, 108, signed Hallmark (possibly V Adm Sir Peter Gretton).

75 'Some Remarks by a Junior Officer', *NR* (1961) 3, 132, signed Constant Reader.

76 'Naval Notes', *NR* (1962) 1, 97.

77 'Naval Notes', *NR* (1968) 3, 374.

78 'Lumbago goes Right – II', *NR* (1970) 2, 219.

79 'Go Seventies Now', *NR* (1965) 1, 22, signed Asp.

80 'A Visit to HMS *Glamorgan*', *NR* (1968) 1, 37, by Capt R D Franks.

81 'Decision for Life', *NR* (1969) 1, 49, signed Dreadnought.

82 'Letters At Sea with the Navy', *NR* (1971) 4, 383, by Ex-FOST (possibly V Adm Sir Peter Gretton).

83 'Sea View', *NR* (1970) 3, 227, signed RGK.

84 'Ships with Two Captains', *NR* (1970) 2, 99, signed Fritz.

85 'To Re-Silvering the Mirror', *NR* (1976) 2, 124, signed RW.

86 'Welfare in the Royal Navy: a Worm's Eye View', *NR* (1976) 3, 237, signed Tartarus by Cdr (later R Adm) G F Liardet.

87 'To Re-Silvering the Mirror', *NR* (1976) 2, 124, signed RW.

88 'The View from the Commander's Table', *NR* (1982) 2, 84, signed Cdr A J W Wilson.

89 'Life in Two Yankee', *NR* (1983) 1, 37, signed Sub Lieutenant, RN.

90 'A Tale of Two Navies', *NR* (1987) 1, 28, signed REY by Lt Simon Atkinson.

91 'A Note of Caution for the Cost Effective Navy', *NR* (1988) 3, 195, by Lt A D Traher.

92 'A Letter to a Friend', *NR* (1988) 3, 219, signed Pollux.

93 'Desperate Diseases', *NR* (1990) 1, 24, by Cdr Mark Kerr.

94 'Sailors with Guns', *NR* (1990) 3, 204, signed Ricochet.

95 'The Employment of Women in the Royal Navy: A Retrospective', *NR* (1991) 4, 328, signed Aeneas.

96 'Letters: The Employment of Women in the Royal Navy', *NR* (1992) 2, 165, by Cdr C S Hadden.

97 'Missing their Sea-Mummies?', *NR* (1993) 2, 141, by Cdr T R Harris.

98 'Coping with the Reality of Equal Opportunities', *NR* (1994) 2, 118, signed Aeneas.

99 'Women at Sea', *NR* (1994,) 3, 216, by Mid E R Hayman.

100 'Letters: Distort – To Misrepresent', *NR* (1995) 4, 385, signed Antonius by Capt Chris Craig; 'Letters: HMS *Brilliant*', *NR* (1996) 1, 77, by Capt James Rapp; 'Letters: HMS *Brilliant*', *NR* (1996) 2, 163, by Capt Peter Kim; 'Book Reviews: I Brilliant Television', *NR* (1996) 2, 180, signed John Winton by Lt Cdr John Pratt, novelist and popular historian; 'HMS *Brilliant*', *NR* (1996) 2, 183.

101 'The Homosexuality Inquiry – I', *NR* (1995) 4, 303, signed Aeneas.

102 For example, 'The Homosexuality Inquiry – II', *NR* (1995) 4, 305, signed Old and Bold. However, the majority of the remaining contributions (see 'The Homosexuality Inquiry III to X', *NR* (1996) 1, 39–45, all under pseudonyms) were more balanced.

103 'The Homosexuality Inquiry – V', *NR* (1996) 1, 41, signed Bels is particularly honest in its summary of the experience of the 1930s and 1940s.

104 'A View from the Bridge Card', *NR* (1999) 3, 212, by Capt (later Adm Sir) James Burnell-Nugent, Second Sea Lord 2003–5 and Commander-in-Chief Fleet 2005–7; and 'Make Like a Duck – Life in the Surface Flotilla', *NR* (2002) 2, 102, signed Foreigner (with contributions from colleagues).

105 'HMS *Invincible* in Operation Bolton', *NR* (1998) 3, 191, by Burnell–Nugent.

106 'Liberating Iraq – the UK's Maritime Contribution', *NR* (2003) 4, 323, by R Adm David Snelson.

107 'Executive Business', *NR* (2005) 3, 236, by Cdr Toby Williamson.

108 'How to be Well Connected', *NR* (2005) 3, 233, by Kevin Rowlands.

109 'Small Ship Logistics', *NR* (2009) 3, 257, by Lt Tim Montague.

110 'The Admiralty Interview Board', *NR* (2008) 3, 241, by Capt David James.

111 'A Right Proper Fix We're In', *NR* (2009) 1, 19, signed Blackbess.

112 'The Royal Navy in 2007', *NR* (2007) 4, 308, by Adm Sir Jonathon Band, Commander-in-Chief Fleet 2002–5 and First Sea Lord 2006–9.

113 'Short Finals', *NR* (2010) 2, 135, by Cdr John Craig.

18 From Selborne to AFO 1/56

1 Marder, Arthur, *From the Dreadnought to Scapa Flow* (1961), vol I, p6.

2 Dickinson, H W, *Educating the Royal Navy: 18th and 19th Century Education for Officers* (2007), and Admiral of the Fleet Lord Cunningham of Hyndhope, *A Sailor's Odyssey* (1951), pp15–17.

3 Penn, Geoffrey, *Up Funnel, Down Screw* (1955), p114.

4 *Educating the Royal Navy*, op cit, p191.

5 Admiralty memorandum dated 16 Dec 1902, issued 25 Dec 1902, and subsequently as Cmd 1385.

6 Admiralty Weekly order 139/13 issued on 28 Mar 1913, cited in John H Beattie, *The Churchill Scheme: the Royal Naval Special Entry Cadet Scheme* (privately published 2010), p16.

7 *The Churchill Scheme*, op cit, p20.

8 'Naval Education, its Effect on Character and Intellect', *NR* (1913) 1, 26–30, signed RX by Plunkett.

9 'A Suggested Training for Naval Cadets', *NR* (1913) 2, 76–81, unsigned by Capt H W Richmond.

10 'Letters: Engine-Room Training', *NR* (1913) 2, 128, unsigned by Richmond.

11 'The Training of Naval Officers I', *NR* (1913) 3, 180–7, signed AX by Cdr Kenneth G B Dewar.

12 'The Training of Naval Officers II', *NR* (1913) 3, 187–9, unsigned by Capt T D W Napier, Captain of RN College Dartmouth 1907–10, and again from Sept to Dec 1914 after mobilisation.

13 'Naval Education', *NR* (1914) 4, 274–7, unsigned by Cdr N A Sulivan (later V Adm, entered *Britannia* 1892. He was author of a booklet, *The Cradle of the Navy*, written as 'Navilus' which described life in the old ship).

14 Unpublished note by J D Brown, Head of Naval Historical Branch, dated 7 Sep 1987, cited in 'Who is to Command?', *NR* 75th anniversary (1988), 29, by V Adm Sir Ian McGeoch.

15 Form E190 was a 'Record and Certificates of Mr (N) during his service as Naval Cadet, Midshipman and Acting Sub-Lieutenant'.

16 A major round of post-war redundancies instituted following a manpower review conducted by Sir Eric Geddes, who had served as First Lord 1917–19, and who was appointed to chair the Committee on National Expenditure in 1921. This cut the defence budget by over 40 per cent. 2,000 officers including 350 captains, and the bottom 40 per cent from the cadet strength at BRNC were ejected with little recompense.

17 'The Training of Naval Officers: an Imperial Question', *NR* (1919) 2, 211–24, by Adm W H Henderson and H B Gray (late Warden & Headmaster, Bradfield College) reprinted from the *Fortnightly Review* of April 1914.

18 The National Archives, ADM 116/1288, Custance Committee on training of Midshipmen and Cadets, dated 1912.

19 'The Training of Naval Officers: an Imperial Question', op cit, 224.

20 'The Case for Early Entry', *NR* (1920) 3, 338, unsigned by Capt E Astley-Rushton. In 1919 Astley-Rushton was serving at the Admiralty as Deputy Director of Naval Training under Richmond, with whom, presumably, he disagreed.

21 'Early Entry v Late Entry', *NR* (1925) 1, 59, unsigned by Lt Cdr J S M Mackenzie-Grieve.

22 For an elaboration on this point, see Ruddock F Mackay, *Fisher of Kilverstone* (OUP, 1973), pp275–84.

23 '"E" or "Eng" – *Quo Vadimus?*', *NR* (1925) 3, 516–23, unsigned by Lt Cdr J S McKenzie-Grieve: he cited a call for volunteers from the first two terms of the new scheme officers to become the first engineer specialists on course at Keyham which had been due to commence in October 1913.

24 Statement on the 1920/21 Naval Estimates by the First Lord of the Admiralty, subsequently promulgated by AFO 2157/20, cited in John Wells, *The Royal Navy: An Illustrated Social History* (1994), p135.

25 For a complete summary of this process, see '"E" or "Eng" – *Quo Vadimus?*', op cit, 517–21.

26 'Report and Recommendations of a Board ... regarding the Instruction and Training of Line Officers', *NR* (1920) 4, 539–61, reprinted from the *United States Naval Institute Proceedings* for August 1920.

27 'Training of Officers', *NR* (1921) 2, 197–215, signed KGF by Lt (E) D C Ford and Lt (E) B W Greathed. They were both early Selborne entries in 1905

and 1906. Both were promoted commander (E) on 30 Jun 1926 prior to continuing to flag rank.

28 The 'dagger' symbol (†) was used to denote completion of advanced courses in a variety of specialisations, both seaman and technical, eg, N(†) indicated completion of the advanced navigation course required to navigate large ships.

29 'Training of Officers: a Critique', *NR* (1921) 2, 214, unsigned by Capt E Astley Rushton

30 'Training of Officers: a Criticism', *NR* (1921) 2, 216, unsigned by Capt R M Bellairs

31 Ibid, 219–20.

32 '"E" or "Eng" – *Quo Vadimus?*', op cit, 516–23

33 The first Selborne promoted was Oliver Bevir, entered BRNC ex-Osborne in first entry Sept 1905, was Cadet Captain and retired a Rear Admiral in 1945.

34 '"E" or "Eng" – *Quo Vadimus?*', op cit, 516–23.

35 'Entry of Cadets and Scope of Engineering', *NR* (1925) 4, 747–52, unsigned by Engineer R Adm R W Skelton, a submarine engineer who served as Fleet Engineer Officer, Mediterranean Fleet and was promoted V Adm, appointed as Engineer-in-Chief in 1928.

36 Cited in Wells, op cit, p135, and Geoffrey Rawson, *Earl Beatty: Admiral of the Fleet* (1930), p235.

37 'Letters: Engineer Officers RN', *NR* (1927) 2, 431, signed Lieutenant (E) RN by Lt (E) Peter Du Cane, who left the service in 1928 to become in 1931 the managing director and principal designer at Vospers, producer of the original Motor Torpedo Boat and other fast craft including *Bluebird* and the Brave-class Fast Patrol Boat.

38 'Results Count', *NR* (1928) 1, 123, signed QD by Cdr J S McKenzie Grieve.

39 'Remarks on a few Current Naval Problems', *NR* (1931) 1, 126, signed Credo possibly by Cdr H M Daniel who had used the pseudonym in 1928.

40 Cunningham, op cit, p150.

41 'Low Tide of the Royal Navy', *NR* (1932) 2, 290, unsigned by Cdr W G Tennant, later Adm Sir William Tennant, senior beach master at Dunkirk 1940, sunk in the battlecruiser *Repulse* in 1941, second-in-command Eastern Fleet 1943–4, C-in-C America and West Indies 1946–9.

42 Hunt, Barry, 'Richmond and the

Education of the Royal Navy', in Goldrick & Hattendorf, *Mahan is Not Enough* (1992); Admiral Sir Herbert Richmond, *Naval Training*, in *The Fortnightly Review,* June, July and August 1932.

43 'The Discussion on Naval Training', *NR* (1932) 4, 645–9, unsigned presumably by the editor.

44 Hunt, op cit, and Goldrick & Hattendorf, *Mahan Is Not Enough* (1992), pp69–70

45 'Book Review: *Naval Training* by Admiral Sir H W Richmond', *NR* (1933) 2, 350–7, signed HGT by R Adm Henry G Thursfield, naval correspondent of *The Times* 1936–52.

46 'Dartmouth', *NR* (1933) 2, 212, extract from the First Lord of the Admiralty's statement on the Navy Estimates 1933: the First Lord referred to rumours that Dartmouth might close and announced that 20 per cent financial savings had been found in order keep it open .

47 'Naval Training', *NR* (1933) 3, 474, signed WK by E W E Kempson, Headmaster of Dartmouth 1927–42.

48 'A Logical Case for the Retention of Dartmouth', *NR* (1933) 3, 668, signed NAW by Capt N A Wodehouse, then Captain of the College.

49 'Rival Systems of Entry – the Matter of Costs', *NR* (1933) 3, 463, signed PLC by Paymaster Lt Cdr H C Lockyer: he was Captain's Secretary at BRNC 1929–30, subsequently Cdr (S) and still writing for the *NR* in the 1960s.

50 'The Missing Light', *NR* (1934) 1, 59, signed M—S— by R Adm W M 'Bubbles' James: grandson of the painter Millais, James's portrait as a child was used to advertise Pears soap. He was active in the First World War in British naval intelligence and in the Second World War as C-in-C Portsmouth; he commanded Operation Ariel, the British evacuation from Normandy and Brittany in 1940.

51 'The Logical Case for the Retention of Dartmouth', *NR* (1934) 1, 46, Admiral Sir Herbert Richmond (he actually didn't believe there was such a case).

52 'Early Entry v Late Entry', *NR* (1925) 1, 59, unsigned by Lt Cdr J S Mackenzie-Grieve.

53 'Our Serial,' *NR* (1940) 3, 413, signed Sirius by Lt Cdr Peter Bethell.

54 'Dartmouth – I', *NR* (1940) 4, 583, by Captain F Dalrymple-Hamilton, Captain of the College 1936–39, subsequently

Admiral Sir Frederick Dalrymple-Hamilton, Flag Officer Second-in-Command Home Fleet during the Normandy Landings, and British Naval Representative Washington 1948–50.

55 'Dartmouth – III', *NR* (1940) 4, 591, by E A Hughes, Second Master & Head of History & English, BRNC, served on academic staff 1910–47.

56 'Dartmouth – IV', *NR* (1940) 4, 595, signed Gad, Sir! by an unidentified RM officer.

57 'Random Reflections', *NR* (1935) 3, 533, signed Phoenix by Lt Cdr Russell Grenfell, giving statistics which appeared to show that between qualifying and promotion or being 'passed over', only 55 per cent of Gunnery appointments were seagoing, Torpedo 62 per cent and Navigation, 78 per cent. 'Salt-Horses', Submariners and Destroyer 'specialists' would expect almost 100 per cent seagoing appointments at this phase of their career.

58 'Training of Officers', *NR* (1935) 1, 37, signed Comma by Lt Cdr Russell Grenfell.

59 'Executive Specialisation – its Effect on Leadership', *NR* (1933) 3, 492, unsigned by Capt A H Taylor.

60 'Command and Materiel – a Lecture given on board *Suffolk*', *NR* (1933) 3, 496, signed BMW by Lt Cdr B M Walker.

61 Ibid, 499.

62 Cdr C C Hughes-Hallett (1898–1985) joined via BRNC in 1911, specialised (G) in 1921, as V Adm was head of the British Joint Services Mission to Washington 1952–4.

63 Lt Cdr John Hughes-Hallett (1901–1972) joined via BRNC in 1915, specialised (T), was Senior Naval Officer for the Dieppe Raid (1942), retired as V Adm in 1954 and became MP for Croydon 1954–64.

64 Cdr Russell Grenfell, joined Osborne 1905, author and naval correspondent for *The Daily Telegraph*.

65 'Training & Advancement (I) What is Seamanship?', *NR* (1936) 4, 635, signed Sigma by Cdr J Hughes-Hallett.

66 'Specialisation in Torpedoes', *NR* (1937) 3, 476, signed L by Lt N A Copeman, a (T) specialist, Deputy Director of Torpedo, Mining and Anti-Submarine Warfare 1948–50, Captain of the torpedo school HMS *Vernon* 1953–55, Vice Controller of the Navy in 1956–58 and Fourth Sea Lord in 1958–60.

67 'A Specialists Problem', *NR* (1942) 2, 151, signed Specialist.

68 See 'The Salt-Horse Problem I–IV' and numerous others in the *NR* from (1942) 2 to (1944) 1.

69 'Entry and Training of Engineer Officers', *NR* (1944) 1, 44, signed Technician.

70 The star system is of American origin, and indicates flag ranks by the number of 'stars' worn in working uniform. A four-star officer is thus a full admiral or general, a three-star a vice admiral or lieutenant general and so down.

71 'A Constructive Criticism of the "E" Branch', *NR* (1944) 3, 221, signed Spud.

72 'On the Wider "E" Branch (With a Criticism of the Present Method of Entry)', *NR* (1945) 1, 38, signed Bish.

73 'Training of Officers', op cit, (1921) 2.

74 'New Schemes', *NR* (1945) 2, 132, signed KGF by R Adm (E) D C Ford (later V Adm Sir Denys, Engineer-in-Chief, 1947–50) and Capt (E) B W Greathed (later R Adm and ultimately founder of the Historic Houses Association): a pseudonym they had first used as lieutenants nearly a quarter of a century before.

75 'Dartmouth', *NR* (1946) 1, 13, signed RNC by a group of Naval College house officers.

76 *Hansard*, House of Commons, 7 Mar 1946, col 591, Mr Benn Levy, Labour MP for Eton & Slough who had served in the war as an RNVR.

77 *Hansard*, House of Commons, 17 May 1947, col 425, Mr John Dugdale, Parliamentary & Financial Secretary to the Admiralty.

78 The 'Guff Rules' issued at BRNC each term by the Chief Cadet Captain, were a code of petty restrictions and privileges designed to emphasise the importance of senior cadets and the insignificance of juniors.

79 'The Upper Yardman College', *NR* (1946) 4, 351, signed PFC.

80 Capt the Hon Ewen E S Montagu, CBE, QC, DL, RNR (1901–85), lawyer, writer and naval intelligence officer. Educated at Westminster School, Trinity College, Cambridge and Harvard University, conceived Operation Mincemeat, a major deception plan against the Germans popularly known as 'The Man who Never Was'.

81 'The New Officer Structure', *NR* (1956) 1, 6, signed Gradatim by an official of the Admiralty.

82 Barraclough, F, Chief Education Officer for the North Riding, cited in Jane Harrold and Richard Porter, *Britannia Royal Naval College, Dartmouth – an Illustrated History* (2005), p146.

83 COST or Committee on Officer Structure & Training.

84 Dame Agnes Weston, a Victorian lady, founded the Royal Sailors' Rests in the nineteenth century to provide a place for the sailor ashore to relax, free from the temptations of demon drink.

85 'Letters: Letter From A Failure', *NR* (1961) 4, 428, signed Wyncoll.

86 Named after Sir Keith Murray, Chairman of the University Grants Committee, who was in 1958 appointed to head yet another committee to resolve the issues thrown up by the COST Scheme.

87 'The Entry and Training of Naval Officers', *NR* (1960) 2, 168, by J J S Yorke reprinted from Brassey's Annual.

88 Higher education: report of the Committee appointed by the Prime Minister under the Chairmanship of Lord Robbins 1961–63, Cmnd 2154, 23 Sept 1963.

89 Harrold & Porter, op cit, p154.

90 'The New Officer Structure', 1955, op cit.

91 'The New Officer Structure', Admiralty Fleet Order 1/56: NCW 14542/55 (full text available as pdf file on the Naval Review website, www.naval-review.org.uk).

92 Ibid, Introductory memorandum, paras 3(a), 3(b) and 3(c).

93 Ibid, Introductory memorandum, para 4.

94 Ibid, main text, paras 38 and 39.

95 'Frank or Furtive', *NR* (1963) 4, 414, signed JMWM by Lt Cdr J M W Morgan, a salt-horse serving in his third command and selected 'dry', and 'Split Mentality', *NR* (1964) 2, 124, signed Chairborne.

96 'The New Officer Structure', op cit, p6.

97 See 'Whatever Happened to AFO 1/56', *NR* (1976) 4, 352, signed Snipe by Cdr Patrick Middleton, and 'AFO 1/56 – A Seaman's View', *NR* (1978) 4, 332, signed Seamus by Cdr James McCoy, and other contemporary articles.

98 'Some Comments on the System of Promotion to Commander and Captain', *NR* (1954) 3, 344, signed Elba.

99 See Eric J Grove, *Vanguard to Trident: British Naval Policy since World War Two* (1987).

100 'Below the Bottom Line', (2006) 2, 104,

by Muxworthy, Middleton, McCoy et al.

101 See, for example, 'Naval Affairs', *NR* (1960) 2, 230, and (1962) 4, 365, an appeal by the First Sea Lord for help recruiting, and 'Naval Affairs', *NR* (1963) 2, 219, Statement on the Defence Estimates for 1969, etc.

19 Teaching Naval History

1 Professor Sir James Alfred Ewing (1855–1935) a Scottish physicist and engineer, Director of Naval Education (1903–14), codebreaker in Room 40 during the First World War, Vice Chancellor of Edinburgh University (1916–29).

2 Sir Julian Corbett: see chapter 3.

3 The two earliest Royal Naval Staff Courses (1912 and 1913) were held in Portsmouth – the more familiar connection with the Royal Naval College Greenwich was not established until 1919.

4 'The Staff College', *NR* (1915) 1, 84–103, unsigned by Plunkett.

5 'The Study of Naval History', *NR* (1919) 3, 327–42, signed A Naval Lieutenant by Cdr Carlyon Bellairs, reprinted from the *United Service Magazine* of March 1896. Commander Carlyon Bellairs (1871–1955), specially promoted to Lieutenant in 1891 having obtained first-class certificates at all examinations, inventor, retired on failure of eyesight, 1902; MP (1906–10); lecturer at Senior Officers' War Course; declined a baronetcy in 1927; founded and endowed the Biological Institute of McGill University.

6 'The Place of History in Naval Education', *NR* (1920) 1, 1–13, unsigned by Captain Herbert Richmond.

7 For a detailed explanation of the scheme see S W Roskill, 'The Navy at Cambridge 1919–23', *Mariners Mirror* (1963), 49:3. The scheme commanded strong Admiralty support but eventually foundered in the face of Treasury opposition. One of the students to benefit from the arrangement was Sub Lieutenant Patrick Blackett who, as Professor P M S Blackett, would be awarded the Nobel Prize for Physics in 1948.

8 In 1924 Admiral Webb had been charged with examining the financial conduct of the Royal Naval College Greenwich – see National Archives (hereafter NA) ADM 203/16, Report of the Committee on Overhead Charges

and Accommodation at the Royal Naval College Greenwich (The Webb Report). Having carried out the investigation and recommended significant reductions, he was subsequently appointed as Admiral President and invited to implement them!

9 For a full discussion of a contentious issue see S W Roskill, *Naval Policy between the Wars* (London, 1976), pp32–5.

10 This seems to have been the first use of this measure in the history of the *NR*.

11 Admiral Dickens inherited a significantly more robust membership list than his predecessor – at 1,793 in 1951 it represented a 60 per cent increase over the immediate pre-war figure.

12 'Editor's Notes', *NR* (1961) 2, 95.

13 For an excellent compact discussion of the Robbins Report see Richard Aldrich, *An Introduction to the History of Education* (London, 1982), pp159–61.

14 'Letters', *NR* (1964) 4, 470, signed Spartan

15 'Editorial', *NR* (1967) 1. Admiral Mansergh felt it necessary to remind members that function of the journal was to promote debate and that the essence of debate was 'the presentation of *conflicting* (italics in the original) views.'

16 'Letters', *NR* (1973) 2, 181, D M Lees,

17 *House of Commons, Eighth Report from the Estimates Committee, Session 1963–4, Service Colleges*, (London: HMSO, 1964)

18 Ministry of Defence (MOD), *Independent Enquiry into the Service Colleges (The Howard English Report)*, (London: MOD, 1964).

19 'Naval History – The Roots of Our Tradition and Morale', *NR* (1979) 4, 284–6, signed GAF by Capt Godfrey French.

20 'Letters', *NR* (1986) 4, 392, by N A M Rodger.

21 'Letters: A Well Read Naval Officer', *NR* (1988) 3, 259, by M Stanhope.

22 'Dartmouth Drops Naval History', *Daily Telegraph*, 7 July 1987.

23 'Remember Nelson', *Daily Telegraph*, 7 July 1987. The leader writer seems to have confused Dartmouth with Greenwich – noting that the former was 'the seed bed of academic naval historiography' and that Sir John Knox Laughton had once been a member of staff there. Neither of course was true.

24 'Dartmouth: Cradle or Coffin of the

Navy?', *NR* (1989) 4, 360–6, signed Areopogus.

25 'Dartmouth the Cradle: Rock it Don't Knock it!', *NR* (1990) 3, 231–8, by Cdr R St J S Bishop.

26 In the some ways this was the weakest point in the article because it was patently obvious that such opportunities did *not* exist – at Greenwich for example the LGC only continued to train a fraction of the Lieutenant's list and the Royal Naval Staff Course saw an even smaller sample. In the late 1980s it was still common practice for officers to be appointed to staff positions without formal staff training.

27 For a further discussion of the training and education dilemma see H W Dickinson, 'Athens in Sparta: Making the Case for Naval Education', *NR* (2002) 3, 243–9, and 4, 337–41.

28 Jock Gardner, a member of the Ministry of Defence Naval History Branch, also considered the subject (*NR* (1995) 3 and 4) and agreed that while there was indeed much to celebrate, a real 'generational renewal' was required amongst naval historians – unless younger academics were encouraged to take up the subject it would soon wither and die.

20 Law, War and the Conduct of Naval Operations

1 'War Thought and Naval War', *NR* (1913) 1, 5–11, unsigned by Capt A C Dewar.

2 One should acknowledge, however, that Europe was certainly not at peace for a century. Wars between the European powers were a constant feature of nineteenth-century history, with a total of fourteen significant conflicts within Europe between 1821 and 1912. Nevertheless, none of these were general, multilateral great power conflicts generating significant naval activity (either economic warfare or major fleet engagements). See S Halperin, *War and Social Change in Modern Europe:The Great Transformation Revisited* (Cambridge: Cambridge University Press, 2004), pp5–9.

3 Ferguson, N, *The War of the World: History's Age of Hatred* (London: Allen Lane, 2006).

4 'War Thought and Naval War', *NR* (1913) 1, 5–11, unsigned by Dewar.

5 At the time of writing, the latest example is: 'All That Piracy: Why Can't We Just

... Deal With It!' *NR* (2011) 2, 114–16, by Cdr M Ewence.

6 There are other bodies of law that affect naval/maritime operations (including, more recently, human rights law) but these will not be discussed. Since 1945, the term 'Laws of War' has largely been replaced by the 'Law of Armed Conflict' or 'International Humanitarian Law'. All these terms are synonymous. For consistency over the time span being considered, in this chapter we shall refer throughout to the 'Laws of War at Sea'.

7 This is reflected in the RN's latest iteration of its principal reference on international law. This was originally a CONFIDENTIAL publication, *CB3012: Notes on Maritime International Law*, first published in 1929. A subsequent edition reflecting the four 1958 Geneva Conventions on the Law of the Sea was issued in the 1960s and it remained at that classification until reissued in 1992 in a RESTRICTED edition as *BR3012*. The present author produced a fully revised electronic (CD-ROM) edition in 2003 issued to operational staffs and units in preparation for operations against Iraq. He fully declassified the publication and changed its title to *BR3012: Handbook on the Law of Maritime Operations*, under which title it remains in its latest edition first issued in 2005.

8 1907 Hague Conventions VI (Relating to the Status of Enemy Merchant Ships at the Outbreak of Hostilities), VII (Relating to the Conversion of Merchant Ships into Warships), VIII (Relative to the Laying of Automatic Submarine Contact Mines), IX (Concerning Bombardment by Naval Forces in Time of War), XI (Relative to Certain Restrictions with Regard to the Exercise of the Right of Capture in Naval War), XII (Concerning the Creation of an International Prize Court), XIII (Concerning the Rights and Duties of Neutral Powers in Naval War). Convention X was also naval in that it extended the application of the 1906 Red Cross Convention to naval warfare. The texts of all these conventions, together with important commentaries on them, are included in N Ronzitti (ed), *The Law of Naval Warfare: A Collection of Agreements and Documents with Commentaries* (Dordrecht, Boston and London: Martinus Nijhoff, 1988). The conventions themselves may also be accessed via the worldwide web.

9 The texts of both the London Declaration and the *Oxford Manual* are also included in Ronzitti, *The Law of Naval Warfare*.

10 'International Law – V', *NR* (1927) 4, 779–804, unsigned by Paymaster Capt H W E Manisty.

11 'International Law – II', *NR* (1927) 1, 129–45, unsigned by Manisty.

12 Kennedy, P, *The Rise of the Anglo-German Antagonism 1860–1914* (London: George Allen and Unwin, 1980), p443

13 Halpern, P, *A Naval History of World War I* (London: University College London Press, 1994), p27.

14 Halpern, P, *A Naval History of World War I*, p293.

15 'The Freedom of the Seas', *NR* (1929) 2, 221–36, 'some comments by Vice-Admiral Sir Herbert Richmond on Colonel House's pamphlet issued by the National Society for the Prevention of War.'

16 'Sea Power or Sea Lawyers?', *NR* (1915) 3, 354–63, unsigned by Plunkett.

17 The Paris Declaration dates from the time of the Crimean War and remains to this day the basic document governing the conduct of economic warfare at sea (for text and commentary see Ronzitti, *The Law of Naval Warfare*).

18 'Sea Power or Sea Lawyers?', by Plunkett.

19 'International Law and Sea Power', *NR* (1919) 1, 65–71, unsigned by Capt M H Anderson (although submitted before the end of 1915, this article's appearance was delayed until 1919 by the interruption to the publication of *The Naval Review* during the First World War).

20 Taken from *Parliamentary Papers (Miscellaneous)*, No 22 (1916), quoted in D P O'Connell, *The International Law of the Sea Volume II* (Oxford: Clarendon Press, 1984), p1104. Even so, the Declaration was not formally cancelled until the Allies issued a formal memorandum to that effect on 7 July 1926 (see 'International Law – II', *NR* (1927) 1, 139–40, by Manisty).

21 For a brief yet good account of the issues associated with submarine attacks on merchant ships see H Levie, 'Submarine Warfare: With Emphasis on the 1936 London Protocol', together with comments by Vaughan Lowe and Dieter Fleck, in J Grunawalt (ed), *The Law of*

Naval Warfare: Targeting Enemy Merchant Shipping, being vol 65 of *International Law Studies* (Newport, RI: US Naval War College, 1993), pp28–85.

22 P Halpern, *A Naval History of World War I*, pp293, 338.

23 'International Law – I', *NR* (1926) 4, 759–69, by Manisty. In 1926, authors were not so committed to footnoting and referencing as they are today and the precise identity and location of Admiral Hall's paper was not noted. This is a pity as it would surely make for interesting reading.

24 'International Law Parts I–VI' over the six issues: *NR* (1926) 4, 759–69; *NR* (1927) 1, 129–45; *NR* (1927) 2, 335–62; *NR* (1927) 3, 541–70; *NR* (1927) 3, 779–804; and *NR* (1928) 1, 126–47, all unsigned by Paymaster Capt H W E Manisty.

25 The 'special issue' was published in 1929, as issue no 2 that year.

26 See 'Consideration of the Principles of Naval Disarmament', *NR* (1931) 2, 206–21, by Richmond, 'A paper read at the Institute of Politics, Williamstown, Massachusetts. August 1930'; 'Chemical Warfare', *NR* (1924) 2, 312–20, unsigned; 'The Regulation of Bombardment', *NR* (1938) 2, 259–66, by J M Spaight; 'Armed Merchantmen', *NR* (1931) 1, 9–25 by Henry Cabot Lodge (a speech in the Senate of the United States on 18 Feb 1916 'delivered at a time of great tension during the recent war'); 'Blockade in Civil War: a Commentary', *NR* (1922) 4, 548–55, unsigned by Lt Cdr C A G Hutchison; and 'Battle of Bilbao Bay', *NR* (1937) 3, 550–2, signed Jimmy by Lt R B N Hicks; 'The Fleet after the Conference', *NR* (1930) 3, 561–5, unsigned by Lt Cdr B W Galpin; 'The Straits Convention', *NR* (1937) 1, 61–7, signed HRL by Maj R Lambert, RM; 'London Naval Conference 1935', *NR* (1936) 1, 31–9, signed Una by Maj H R Lambert, RM; and 'Aerial Warfare, *NR* (1933) 1, 88–92, unsigned by Lt Cdr J Hughes-Hallett.

27 There were three major treaties: a Four-Power Treaty; a Five-Power Treaty (the Washington Naval Treaty); and a Nine-Power Treaty, as well as a number of lesser agreements. With one exception (on submarines, discussed presently) none of these was about the conduct of naval operations. They were about such things as the limitation of naval armaments, territorial issues and dispute resolution.

28 It also dealt (in Article 5) with the use of noxious gases, prompted by their use, principally in land warfare, during the past conflict.

29 Through Article 22 of Part IV of the 1930 London Treaty for the Limitation and Reduction of Naval Armaments. Although that treaty time-expired at the end of 1936, Article 22 of Part IV remained in force and was reaffirmed by the 1936 London Protocol.

30 It arguably remains in force today, although the practice of naval warfare during both the First and Second World Wars continue to raise doubts about the applicability of the rules contained therein. See A Roberts and R Guelff, *Documents on the Laws of War* (3rd edition) (Oxford: Oxford University Press, 2000), p170. The general thrust of the rules was included in the important assessment of the Laws of War at Sea conducted under the auspices of the International Institute for Humanitarian Law in San Remo, Italy in the early 1990s: L Doswald-Beck, *The San Remo Manual on International Law Applicable to Armed Conflicts at Sea* (Cambridge: Cambridge University Press, 1995).

31 Articulated in a speech to a joint session of the US Congress on 8 January 1918. This, together with the other thirteen points contributed to a vision of international relations after the Great War and had significant impact on the negotiations at the Paris Peace Conference. Through illness, Wilson was not able to take a full and decisive part in the Conference and his idealistic vision was somewhat watered down. It was also substantially rejected by the US Congress which refused to ratify and endorse US involvement in the resultant League of Nations system. See C Mee, *The End of Order: Versailles 1919* (London: Secker and Warburg, 1980), pp164–7; M Macmillan, *Peacemakers: The Paris Conference of 1919 and its Attempt to End War* (London: John Murray, 2001), pp21, 284, 498.

32 Steiner, Z, *The Lights that Failed: European International History 1919–1933* (Oxford: Oxford University Press, 2005), p377.

33 *The Freedom of the Seas*, NR (1929) 2, 214–20, by Col Edward House, US Army, with a preface by R Adm L D Allen, first published by the National

Council for the Prevention of War in the *Contemporary Review*.

34 Op cit.

35 Otherwise known as the Pact of Paris.

36 The term 'private war' as used here needs to be regarded in contrast to the term 'public war.' The former was describing war between states in pursuit of national interest (something 'outlawed' by the Kellogg-Briand Pact). The latter described a war conducted by forces authorised by the League of Nations, against another state or states in breach of the new international rules. In post-1945 UN terms, a 'public war' would be one waged by states authorised by a UN Security Council Chapter VII mandate against another state in breach of the UN Charter – eg, the NATO action against Libya in 2011 in accordance with UN Security Council Resolution 1973 (2011).

37 'The Pact of Paris and the "Freedom of the Seas"', *NR* (1929) 2, 332–3. Extract from a review of J Shotwell, *War as an Instrument of National Policy and its Renunciation in the Pact of Paris* (Constable, 1929).

38 'Freedom of the Seas and Modern Blockade', *NR* (1929) 2, 374–81, by Capt A C Dewar.

39 C Barnett, *Engage the Enemy More Closely: The Royal Navy in the Second World War* (London: Hodder and Stoughton, 1991), p101.

40 By Admiral Dönitz's War Order No 154 quoted in P Padfield, *Dönitz the Last Führer: Portrait of a Nazi War Leader* (London: Gollancz, 1984), p206.

41 Luban, D, 'The Legacies of Nuremberg', in G Mettraux, *Perspectives on the Nuremberg Trial* (Oxford: Oxford University Press, 2008), pp638–72.

42 'The Arming of Merchant Ships: An Historical Retrospect', *NR* (1939) 4, 619–25, signed RW.

43 'The Proposed 300-Mile Zone', *NR* (1940) 2, 239–45, signed BMC by Adm B M Chambers.

44 'The Mine in International Law', *NR* (1941) 4, 415–18, signed Sampan possibly by R Adm F T B Tower.

45 'Book Review: *The International Law of the Sea* by Pearce Higgins and C J Colombos (Longmans, Green and Co Ltd)', *NR* (1943) 3, 263–7, signed Little Bill Brown.

46 Which produced four conventions: 1958 Geneva Conventions on The Territorial Sea and Contiguous Zone; The High Seas; on Fishing and Conservation of the Living Resources of the High Seas; and The Continental Shelf.

47 An important principle in the context of Nuremberg but one of which the author clearly did not approve. See 'Superior Orders', *NR* (1951) 1, 12–15, by Russell Grenfell.

48 'Economic Warfare at Sea: Blockade and *Guerre de Course* in Maritime Doctrine and Contemporary International Law', *NR* (2011) 4, 315–22, by Steven Haines. The year before this article appeared, the Israeli imposition of belligerent blockade on Gaza had attracted worldwide attention when a number of protesters on a vessel attempting to breach the blockade were killed. Legal aspects of that situation were dealt with in 'Israel, Gaza and the Blockade: What About the Law?', *NR* (2010) 4, 313–19 by this author.

49 The Falklands War is regarded generally, and by the International Committee of the Red Cross, as a copybook example of war fought in accordance with the Laws of War. The only significant naval legal issues that arose concerned the zones established by the British around the islands (which were not legal zones and set no legal precedent), the sinking of the Argentine cruiser *General Belgrano* (which was entirely in accordance with the targeting rules contained in the Laws of War at Sea), and the fitting of encrypted radio equipment in hospital ships (which has initiated a shift in customary law and a departure from the law of the Geneva Conventions – see, for example, Article 171 of L Doswald-Beck (ed), *San Remo Manual on International Law Applicable to Armed Conflicts at Sea* (Cambridge: Cambridge University Press, 1995) – of which more below).

50 See N Ronzitti, 'The Crisis of the Traditional Law Regulating International Armed Conflicts at Sea and the Need for its Revision', in N Ronzitti (ed), *The Law of Naval Warfare*, pp1–58.

51 *San Remo Manual*, ix.

52 Ministry of Defence, *Manual of the Law of Armed Conflict* (Oxford: Oxford University Press, 2004). The present author chaired the editorial board of the *UK Manual* and was joint author of its 'Maritime Warfare' chapter. He accounted for the differences between the *San Remo Manual* and the *UK*

Manual in S Haines, 'The United Kingdom's *Manual of the Law of Armed Conflict* and the *San Remo Manual*: Maritime Rules Compared', in *Israel Yearbook on Human Rights*, vol 36 (Leiden/Boston: Martinus Nijhoff, 2006), pp89–118.

53 'The Offshore Tapestry', *NR* (1974) 2, 119–23, signed Weaver.

54 'The Law of the Sea', *NR* (1976) 1, 70–4, signed IL; and correspondence under the same heading in *NR* (1976) 3, 260–1, signed JRH by Capt J R Hill.

55 'Patrol Tasks in Expanded British Waters', *NR* (1976) 2, 130–7 signed RTRP by R Adm R T R Philips.

56 'The Royal Navy and U.N.C.L.O.S', *NR* (1977) 2, 125–33, signed EBA by Admiral of the Fleet Sir Edward Ashmore.

57 'How Might the Emergent Law of the Sea Affect the Operations of Traditional Maritime Powers?', *NR* (1991) 1, 3–13, by Lt Cdr M Alabaster; 'International Maritime Law – A Threat to Traditional Naval Activity?', *NR* (1991) 2, 104–8, by Lt Cdr Tim Thornton.

58 Forbes, Adm Sir I, 'Military Operations and the Law: An Operator's Perspective', Opening speech to the 2nd Annual Senior Officers' Security and Law Conference, Geneva Centre for Security Policy, 14–17 June 2010 (text in the author's possession).

59 'All That Piracy: Why Can't We Just … Deal With It!', *NR* (2011) 2, 114–16, by Cdr M Ewence.

21 The Development of British Naval Thinking

1 Many historians would argue that the founders of *The Naval Review* much exaggerated the intellectual torpor of their Victorian predecessors. It is of course, a characteristic of Young Turks to disparage Old Turks. See Andrew Lambert, *The Last Sailing Battlefleet* (1991), Roger Parkinson, *The Late Victorian Navy: The Pre-Dreadnought era and the Origins of the First World War* (2008), and Nicholas Black, *The British Naval Staff in the First World War* (2009).

2 'Editorial Note', *NR* (1913) 1, 7, by Adm William Henderson.

3 'Studies in the Theory of Naval Tactics', *NR* (1913) 1, 13, signed CQI by Capt E W Harding, RMA. This was the first of a series of opening articles in subsequent editions of the *NR* which were clearly

intended to spark debate.

4 'The Staff College', *NR* (1915) 1, 101, 102, unsigned by Plunkett.

5 'Notes on Appreciating a Situation', *NR* (1914) 2, 118–9, unsigned by Major L Halliday, RMLI.

6 'Studies in the Theory of Naval Tactics', *NR* (1913) 2, 93–4, signed CQI by Capt E W Harding, RMA.

7 'The Influence of the Long-range Torpedo on Battle Tactics', *NR* (1915) 1, 56, unsigned by Plunkett.

8 Many of the issues about this in the battle of Jutland are brilliantly explored in Andrew Gordon's *The Rules of the Game: Jutland and British Naval Command* (1996).

9 'Studies in the Theory of Naval Tactics – III', *NR* (1913) 4, 220, unsigned by Capt E W Harding, RM.

10 'The Fleet in Action', *NR* (1914) 1, 53, unsigned by Capt W R Hall.

11 'Sea Power in 1913', *NR* (1913) 2, 192, unsigned by Lt A H Taylor.

12 'The Influence of the Submarine on Naval Policy', *NR* (1913) 3, 149, unsigned by Capt S S Hall.

13 'The Influence of Commerce in War', *NR* (1914) 3, 160, unsigned by Capt K Dewar.

14 'With the Grand Fleet', *NR* (1915) 2, 172, unsigned by Plunkett.

15 Goldrick, Cdr James (as he then was), 'The Irresistible Force and the Immoveable Object: *The Naval Review, The Young Turks and the Royal Navy 1911–1931*', in James Goldrick and John B Hattendorf (eds), *Mahan is Not Enough: The Proceedings of a Conference on the Works of Sir Julian Corbett and Admiral Sir Herbert Richmond* (1993), pp91–5.

16 'With the Grand Fleet', *NR* (1914) 4, 309, *NR* (1915) 1, 2–3 and (1915) 3, 436, unsigned by Plunkett.

17 'With the Grand Fleet,' *NR* (1915) 2, 172, unsigned by Plunkett.

18 'Considerations of the War at Sea', *NR* (1917) 1, 7, unsigned by Capt H W Richmond.

19 '*Naval Operations of the War Volume 3: the Battle of Jutland*', *NR* (1924) 2, 286–300, unsigned by Capt A C Dewar. This review is interesting in that it treats Corbett as a historian rather than a strategist and much exaggerates Corbett's inclination to depreciate the role of battle. Corbett's essential point was that a decisive battle was merely a means to an end, and not an end in itself.

20 Richmond, Captain H W, 'Strategical Theories: A French Authority', *Journal of the Royal United Services Institute* (May 1933), 332 (a review of the work of Raoul Castex).

21 'Considerations of the War at Sea', *NR* (1917) 1, 29, unsigned by Richmond.

22 'United Service', *NR* (1923), 201–14, by the late Sir Julian S Corbett; 'Naval Operations in the Napoleonic War after Trafalgar as Illustrating the Use of Maritime Power Assist Operations on Land', by Lt C H Drage, First Prize, Admiralty Naval History Essay (1922.)

23 'Joint Strategy', *NR* (1924) 3, 446–53, unsigned by Cdr A H Taylor, and 'The System of Command in Naval Warfare More Especially upon Foreign Stations', 469–477, unsigned by Capt W P Koe. This was also a major theme of Richmond's book *Naval Policy and National Strength* (1934) reviewed in *NR* (1934) 3, 543–9, signed HGT by Capt H G Thursfield. Admiral Richmond's own review of B H Liddell Hart's *The British Way in Warfare* appeared in *NR* (1934) 4, 794–800, which he thought 'shows a clear appreciation of combined strategy'.

24 On the pre-war rejection of convoy, see Bryan Ranft, 'The Protection of British Seaborne Trade and the Development of Systematic Planning for War, 1860–1906', in Bryan Ranft, *Technical Change and British Naval Policy, 1860–1939* (1977), and Roger Parkinson, *The Late Victorian Navy: The Pre-Dreadnought Era and the Origins of the First World War* (2008), pp9–31, 82–8; 'The Influence of Overseas Trade on British Naval Strategy in the Past and at Present', *NR* (1915) 1, 104–37, unsigned by Lt V H Danckwerts, which carries the editor's warning that it was 'written before the War. Some of the deductions and assumptions may be examined in the light of our present experience'.

25 'Book Review: *The Submarine Peril: The Admiralty Policy in 1917* by Admiral of the Fleet Earl Jellicoe (1934)', *NR* (1934) 4, 760–72, unsigned by V Adm W M James, and *NR* (1934) 4, 773–81, 'Book Review: *War Memoirs of David Lloyd George Volume III* by David Lloyd George (1933)', signed HWR by Admiral Richmond.

26 'Trade Routes and their Influence', *NR* (1928) 3, 398, unsigned by Capt W H C S Thring, was the first of several articles on the subject.

27 'A Problem of Defence of Communications', *NR* (1934) 1, 10, unsigned by Richmond, who wondered here whether the Navy was going to be caught again by the air threat to merchant shipping.

28 Hamilton, C I, *The Making of the Modern Admiralty: British Naval Policy-Making, 1805–1927* (2011), pp206–12. See also the comments of the 1922 Keyes Committee, ibid, pp 276–7.

29 'Book Review: *Lord Fisher of Kilverstone* by Adm Sir Reginald Bacon (1929)', *NR* (1930) 1, 151–201, signed Convectus by A H Pollen, ACD by Capt A C Dewar, and by Adm W H Henderson. The editor invited 'further information or criticisms' which were printed under the initial heading 'Lord Fisher's Critics in the February Number', *NR* (1930) 2, 324–45, and perhaps pointedly all signed by V Adm F C Dreyer, Sydenham of Combe, and Adm D R L Nicholson.

30 'The Size of the Fighting Ship', *NR* (1929) 4, 661, signed V by Capt A H Taylor, makes for an arithmetical approach to this issue.

31 'A Study of War – X', *NR* (1924) 3, 381, by Adm Sir Reginald Custance provides a good summary of his views. This series can be compared with his *Naval Policy: A Plea for the Study of War* (1907).

32 For examples of scepticism, see 'The Influence of Oversea' by Danckwerts (note 24) and 'Finance and Naval Warfare', *NR* (1915) 2, 201–13, unsigned by Capt G P Orde, RM.

33 There were many articles to this effect in the *NR* in early 1929, including 'The Freedom of the Seas – Some Comments on Colonel House's Pamphlet', *NR* (1929) 2, 221–36, by Richmond.

34 'The Freedom of the Seas', *NR* (1929) 4, 733–46, a lecture delivered by Adm Sir Richard Webb at the University of London on 22 May 1929. Webb became editor of *The Naval Review* in May 1931.

35 'A Problem of Defence of Communications – Some Comments', *NR* (1934) 1, 206–7, signed PS by Lt Cdr P W Brock; 'The Pre-Convoy Defence of Trade', *NR* (1934) 3, 417, signed TEEOH by Capt B H Smith. For an at least complementary strategy see 'Independent Routeing of Merchant Ships', *NR* (1934) 2, 275–303, signed TEEOH by Smith.

36 'The Naval Debate and Commerce

Protection', *NR* (1935) 2, 241–7, signed TEEOH by Smith.

37 '*War Memoirs of David Lloyd George volume I*', *NR* (1933) 4, 806 signed HWR by Richmond, who was an evident admirer of David Lloyd George: 'If Mr Lloyd George was an amateur, one is inclined to ... wish we had had a few more such amateurs to direct the war.' This sentiment would have annoyed those correspondents who thought Lloyd George had grossly mistreated Admiral Jellicoe in policy at the time and in print later.

38 'Some Reflections on the Direction of War: the Trend Towards a Combined Staff', *NR* (1938) 3, 417–28, signed Central by Cdr G A French.

39 'The Navy as a Police Force', *NR* (1930) 4, 696–707, unsigned by Cdr R L Edwards; 'British Naval Strength and Diplomatic Influence', *NR* (1934) 3, 437, address given at The Royal Institute of International Affairs by Rear Admiral H G Thursfield on 10 May 1934.

40 'Gaps in the Study of Strategy', *NR* (1931) 3, 339, unsigned by Capt G C Dickens. Another interesting question was 'Are Some of Us Too Line-of-Battle-Minded?', *NR* (1937) 2, 257–60, signed Delta by V Adm Sir G C Dickens. These reflections followed the Royal Navy's conduct of several significant and demanding humanitarian operations in the period; see 'Smyrna and the Dardanelles 1922', *NR* (1935) 3, 467–80, signed Kopje by Cdr L B Hill; 'The Evacuation of Refugees from Bilbao by HMS *Esk* on Thursday 17 September 1936', *NR* (1937) 1, 85–9 signed W by Lt Cdr E W Wilson; 'In Aid of the Civil Power, Trinidad, June–July 1937', *NR* (1937) 4, 696–702, signed Osprey by Lt Cdr J Dalyell Stead.

41 'Studies in the Theory of Naval Tactics IV', *NR* (1914) 2, 123, signed CQI by Capt R M A Harding, RM.

42 'The Staff College', *NR* (1915) 1, 89, unsigned by Plunkett. The reference to 'movements of forces ... on the field of battle are infinitely more difficult and complicated than is the case at sea' is significant. To judge by the degree of reference to land strategy there was little emphasis in most articles of the distinctiveness of naval strategy.

43 'Notes on Appreciating a Situation', *NR* (1914) 2, 117–28, unsigned by Maj L Halliday, RM. One of the most stimulating, persuasive and prescient of

strategic level articles, in which Halliday says 'Strategy is the combination of the single battles of a war, in order to attain to the object of the campaign, or war'.

44 Sumida, Jon, *In Defence of Naval Supremacy: Finance, Technology and British Naval Policy* (1989) remains the clearest exposition of this issue.

45 'The Relative Importance of the Moral, Mental and Material Forces in Modern Naval War', *NR* (1918) 1, 10, unsigned by Lt Roland A Clark. This article was actually written in 1913.

46 See the plea at the end of (1915) 2, 342–3 for correspondents to be more concise and to 'lighten up'.

47 'The Fallacy of the "Enemy's Coast": a Criticism of "The Patrol Flotilla"', *NR* (1914) 3, 196, signed ADZ by Lt Cdr A C Dewar; on the other hand Danckwerts in 'The Influence of Oversea Trade' had been much more supportive.

48 'The Late Sir Julian Corbett', *NR* (1923) 1, 14, unsigned by Richmond; and 'Naval Strategy', *NR* (1928) 2, 278–85, unsigned by Lt T J H Hilken is a nice summary of Corbett's views, with a dash of Custance's for good measure.

49 'Naval Strategy in 1909', *NR* (1915) 3, 214–34, unsigned by Plunkett; 'Sea Heresies', *NR* (1931) 2, 222–36 by Lord Sydenham of Combe, and 'Some Notes on the Early Days of the Royal Naval War College', *NR* (1931) 2, 237–47, unsigned by V Adm D T Norris; 'United Service', *NR* (1923) 2, 201, by Corbett, but written in 1904 and published posthumously.

50 Geoffrey Till (ed), *The Development of British Naval Thinking* (2006), pp60–88.

51 'Thoughts on the "Unrest"', *NR* (1932) 1, 47–52, unsigned by Cdr E S Brand: and 'Thoughts on Future Policy', *NR* (1932) 4, 662–8 unsigned by Lt Cdr J Hughes-Hallett.

52 Captain Smith's reviews may be found in *NR* (1936) 2, 328–43 and *NR* (1937) 4, 717–23. Smith also reviewed Grenfell's *Sea Power in the Next War*, *NR* (1938) 4, 663. See also *The Development of British Naval Thinking*, op cit.

22 Facing the Realities of Medium Power, 1945–2001

1 James Cable, *Britain's Naval Future* (1983), p6.

2 'Let Us Take Stock', *NR* (1946) 2, 143, signed Transom; 'The Navy of the Future', *NR* (1946) 2, 147, signed Nico;

'The Post-War Fleet', *NR* (1946) 2, 150, signed Olga; 'The Shape of Things to Come', *NR* (1946) 4, 326, signed Teaboat.

3 'More Forethought', *NR* (1952) 4, 414, signed Credo ; 'The Navy We Need', *NR* (1963) 1, 48, signed Reservist.

4 'The Navy in the Missile Age', *NR* (1959) 3, 271, signed Lampray; 'Defence Policy in the Sixties', *NR* (1962) 2, 130, signed Taurus.

5 'The Importance of the Balanced View', *NR* (1951) 4, 348, by Lord Chatfield.

6 'Whither NATO?', *NR* (1958) 3, 291, signed E30. 'Regardless of cost' was the dictum of Reservist.

7 'Editorial', *NR* (1957) 2, 102; 'Musketeer', *NR* (1957) 2, 138, signed Chariot.

8 'Why Don't We Learn from History', *NR* (1958) 1, 13, by P W Gretton.

9 'The Liberation of Maraitiya', *NR* (1961) 2, 116, signed Lampray; 'Comments on the Explanatory Statement on the Navy Estimates', *NR* (1962) 2, 138, by G C Dickens.

10 'Future Commonwealth Strategy', *NR* (1947) 1, 34, by R E Griffiths; 'A Balanced Fleet for Britain', *NR* (1958) 3, 280, signed PHD; 'Some Political Aspects of National Defence', *NR* (1958) 4, 404, signed PHD.

11 'Commonwealth and Empire Defence', *NR* (1947) 2, 126, signed Cyclops; 'Policy and Strategy', *NR* (1957) 4, 377, signed GCD.

12 'Tactical Investigation', *NR* (1952) 2, 160, signed Porthole.

13 Chatfield, loc cit.

14 'The Strength of the Soviet Fleet', *NR* (1954) 2, 185, signed Typhon.

15 'Is our Policy Realistic?', *NR* (1952) 3, 278, signed Valor.

16 'Thoughts on Defence in the Sixties and Seventies', *NR* (1963) 2, 132, signed V.30; 'One Nation', *NR* (1963) 2, 159, by J H Golds; 'British Sea Power in the Next Decade', *NR* (1965) 4, 306, signed DJSW.

17 Nico, Olga, Teaboat, Gretton and Transom all agreed on this point. 'Naval Strategy: A Shifting Responsibility', *NR* (1951) 2, 161, signed WMJ.

18 'Policy and Strategy', *NR* (1957) 4, 377, signed GCD; 'The Navy and the Future', *NR* (1957) 4, 380, by Admiral Sir George Creasy.

19 'British Overseas Defence Policy in the Sixties and Seventies', *NR* (1962) 3, 247, signed Lampray; 'Crystal Gazing', *NR*

(1963) 4, 292, signed Onlooker.

20 'Balance of Power in the Nuclear Age', *NR* (1957) 4, 384, by A W Buzzard; 'Why Duplicate the Deterrent?', *NR* (1963) 2, 150, signed Moryak; 'Christian Approach to Defence and Disarmament', *NR* (1964) 4, 410, by A W Buzzard.

21 *NR* (1913) 1, unnumbered page. 'The object of the Naval Society in founding a REVIEW is to encourage thought and discussion on such subjects as strategy, tactics, naval operations, staff work, administration, organisation, command, discipline, education, naval history, and any other topic affecting the fighting efficiency of the Navy, but excluding the material aspects of the technical sciences.'

22 'Naval Necessities', *NR* (1957) 1, 23, signed Bels.

23 'Bases and the Bomb', *NR* (1947) 1, 16, signed SWR.

24 Jackson, Bill, and Dwin Bramall, *The Chiefs* (1992), p375.

25 Hill, J R, 'British Naval Planning post-1945', in N A M Rodger (ed), *Naval Power in the Twentieth Century* (1996), p20.

26 'Notes on a New Navy', *NR* (1967) 1, 11, signed ILMMcG by V Adm Sir Ian Macgeoch; 'The Most Important Task', *NR* (1968) 2, 108, signed J D; 'Concepts for British Maritime Strategy', *NR* (1979) 3, 177, signed J B Kerr.

27 'Escalation at Sea – A NATO View', *NR* (1968) 4, 316, signed JHFE; 'It Looks Like this from Here', *NR* (1969) 3, 198, signed JRH; 'The Mechanics of Deterrence', *NR* (1972) 2, 132, and 'The Mechanics of Deterrence – A Structure for the Navy', *NR* (1973) 3, 205, signed Splitcane; 'On (Conventional) War', *NR* (1981) 3, 197, by G F Liardet; 'Strategy and Maritime Capabilities', *NR* (1982) 1, 15, signed Mariner.

28 'The Offshore Tapestry', *NR* (1974) 2, 119, signed Weaver; 'The Protection of North Sea Oil and Gas Installations', *NR* (1974) 4, 349, signed TRL; 'NATO Defence of North Sea Oil', *NR* (1974) 4, 357, by Peter Heneage; 'Patrol Tasks in Expanded British Waters', *NR* (1976) 2, 130, signed RTRP ; 'Good Order at Sea', *NR* (1983) 4, 288, by C J N Morrison; 'Look to Your Moat: Defence of the Home Base', *NR* (1984) 2, 99, signed JFS; 'The Navy's Role in the Defence of our Coasts and Harbours', *NR* (1985) 1, 28, signed JFS; 'Closing the British Seas',

NR (1987) 4, 297, by James Cable.

29 'The Medium Maritime Power', *NR* (1976), 2–4 and (1977) 1, signed Marlowe.

30 'Editorial', *NR* (1985) 3, 188, pointed out that in its strategy-based introduction the 1985 Statement on the Defence Estimates used the term 'Europe' or 'European' twenty-five times, 'NATO' ten times and 'Britain' thrice.

31 'Aircraft Carriers – The Sell Out', *NR* (1966) 3, 183, signed A Junior Aviator; 'It Has Happened Again', *NR* (1966) 4, 288, signed Red Dragon; 'Time to Go Home?', *NR* (1966) 4, 296, signed Overburdened; 'D'You Hear There?', *NR* (1967) 1, 18, signed Vox non Incerta.

32 'An Admiral's Tale', *NR* (1967) 4, 286, signed Moryak; 'Limits', *NR* (1982) 2, 74, by R Hill; 'Gunboat Diplomacy – the Conventional Wisdom', *NR* (1982) 3, 174, by James Cable; 'The Long and the Short of It', *NR* (1985) 1, 13, signed Islander; 'Life After NATO – II', *NR* (1985) 2, 106, by R G Sharpe; 'The United Kingdom: International Interests and Responsibilities', *NR* (1987) 2, 107, signed Gubernator.

33 'Where do we Go from Here?', *NR* (1967) 1, 2, signed Matelot; 'Maritime Strategy in the 1970s', *NR* (1969) 1, 2, by J L Moulton; 'The Falcon Cannot Hear the Falconer', *NR* (1974) 2, 108, by W K Hutchinson; 'The UK's International Interests and Responsibilities', *NR* (1987) 4, 294, by R A G Clare.

34 'What Price Defence? Government Aims and Expenditure', *NR* (1975) 2, signed Splitcane by Adm Sir Peter Stanford.

35 'The Evolution of Soviet Naval Policy', *NR* (1975) 1, 36 & (1975) 2, 140, and 'Soviet Naval and Oceans Policy', *NR* (1977) 3, 213, by Michael MccGwire.

36 'Soviet Naval Strategy, Minus Rose-Tinted Spectacles', *NR* (1972) 3, 208, signed Lampray.

37 'The Growth of Soviet Maritime Power', *NR* (1968) 4, 308, signed JE; 'The Soviet Maritime Presence in the Mediterranean', *NR* (1969) 2, 120, by R A Smith; 'Benbow's Column', *NR* (1971) 2, 96; 'The Aims of Soviet Foreign Policy: Ideological or National?', *NR* (1972) 2, 138, by B McL Ranft; 'Soviet Defence Policies and Naval Interests', *NR* (1974) 2, 104, by John Erickson; 'The Prospect for European Defence',

NR (1975) 2, 106, signed RAE; 'The Strategy Gap', *NR* (1976) 4, 304, signed Splitcane; 'Maritime Strategy', *NR* (1977) 2, 113, signed JHFE; 'Soviet Concepts of Sea Warfare', *NR* (1978) 2, 105 and (1978) 3, 217, signed Amphion; 'The Soviet Navy Grows Up', *NR* (1979) 1, 19, signed Adison; 'The Development of the Soviet Navy Towards an Extensive Blue-Water Capability', *NR* (1985) 4, 295, by D R Clarke; 'Whither the Soviet Navy under Chernavin', *NR* (1986) 4, 285, by A G G Wolstenholme, J W Porter, and T P Tompkins; 'The Soviet Navy as an Instrument of Foreign Policy', *NR* (1986) 4, 306, by G J Wiltshire; 'A Global Strategy for the Western Alliance', *NR* (1988) 1, 3, by H Peltor.

38 S G Gorshkov, *The Sea Power of the State* (London, 1968).

39 'The Strategic Pendulum Swings East', *NR* (1973) 2, 100, signed SHD; 'Fisher Lives – OK', *NR* (1978) 2, 105, by J H F Eberle; JRH, RAE, Liardet, and Islander agreed.

40 'Defence of the Realm', *NR* (1971) 1, 12, signed RGO; 'Interdependence: A Drug of Addiction?', *NR* (1984) 1, 3, by James Cable.

41 Kerr, loc cit n26, p180.

42 'The Atlantic Alliance: the Need for a Renaissance', *NR* (1986) 4, 330, by Hugh Mulleneux; 'Concept of Maritime Operations for the Late 1990s', *NR* (1987) 2, 100, by G T Reader; Gubernator, loc cit n32.

43 'Problems Facing NATO', *NR* (1975) 1, 50, by Sir Nigel Henderson.

44 'The Utility of Navies: Concept and Propositions', *NR* (1976) 3, 202, by K Booth.

45 'Strategy and Maritime Capabilities', *NR* (1982) 1, 22, signed Mariner.

46 Watkins, Admiral James D, US Navy, *The Maritime Strategy* (1986).

47 'Have We Really Got it Right?', *NR* (1986) 4, 322, signed T E Thornton; 'Forward Maritime Strategy', *NR* (1988) 2, 128, by Matthew Allen.

48 'Maritime Strategy: National and NATO Requirements', *NR* (1986) 4, 313, by R A G Clare; 'Is the US Maritime Strategy Viable for NATO?', *NR* (1987) 1, 10, M Stanhope.

49 Pro-convoy were 'Technology and Trade Protection', *NR* (1979) 3, 185, signed AWJW; Sharpe, loc cit n32; 'Britain and NATO – II', *NR* (1986) 1, 2, by I L M McGeoch. Anti-convoy were 'The Need

for an Efficient Navy', *NR* (1971) 1, 17, signed PRC-J; 'The Royal Navy and NATO', *NR* (1973) 4, 237, by Eric J Grove. Historical background was provided by the reprints in the 1980s of D W Waters's magisterial articles on the Second World War.

50 'The Morality of War', *NR* (1983) 1, 42, by P R D Kimm; 'Faith and Fortitude', *NR* (1983) 4, 301, by W R de C M Taylor.

51 'The Impact of Arms Control', *NR* (1988) 75th anniversary issue, 7, by John Fieldhouse.

52 'The Strategy Gap: Cause and Effect', *NR* (1989) 2, 99 & 3, 218, by Steven Haines.

53 'Self-Inflicted Injury', *NR* (1966) 3, 181, signed Cecil; 'Ministerial Touchdown', *NR* (1966) 4, 288, signed Vox non Incerta.

54 'Royal Navy – Present Position and Future Course', *NR* (1979) 4, 266, by Terence Lewin.

55 Grove, loc cit n49.

56 'The Government's Defence Programme: A Politician's View', *NR* (1982) 4, 279, by Patrick Wall.

57 'Corporate 88', *NR* (1987) 4, 287, signed RVH.

58 'Interesting Times', *NR* (1989) 4, 311, by G F Liardet.

59 Freedman, Lawrence, 'Military Strategy and Operations in the 21st Century', in 'British Security 2010', the Service Defence Conference, 16–17 November 1995.

60 Cm 3999.

61 'The Gulf Revisited – Why?', *NR* (1990) 3, 196, by P McLaren; 'New Defence Perspectives in a Turbulent World', *NR* (1990) 4, 303 and (1991) 2, 100, by Michael Ranken.

62 'The Effect of Technology on the Concept and Execution of Amphibious Warfare', *NR* (1990) 2, 110, by D C Grogan; 'Options for Change – An Opportunity Missed?', *NR* (1991) 3, 196, by I R Whitehouse; 'The Fifth Pillar: The Requirement for Intervention Forces in the Wake of Options for Change', *NR* (1992) 4, 315, by R A Y Bridges; 'A Sense of Direction', *NR* (1995) 1, 3, by the First Sea Lord; 'The Royal Navy in the Future', *NR* (1996) 3, 202, by J J Blackham.

63 Whitehouse, loc cit n83; 'The Shape of the Royal Navy in the 21st Century', *NR* (1995) 3, 189, by J J Blackham; 'Letter to a Friend', *NR* (1997) 1, 9, signed Nonius; 'Oxford Strategic Studies

Group: an Address', *NR* (1998) 2, 101, by J J Blackham; 'The Right to Intervene', *NR* (2000) 3, 204, by Lord Chalfont.

64 '"Agenda for Peace" – Military Issues', *NR* (1993) 1, 5, signed JHFE; 'What Proportion of the Royal Navy's Effort should be Devoted to Preparing for Out of Area Operations?', *NR* (1993) 1, 3 & 3, 199, by B N B Williams; 'Planning the Royal Navy for the Future', *NR* (1994) 1, 3, by N R Essenhigh; 'Reviewing Defence: Establishing a Framework of Choice', *NR* (1997) 4, 297, by David J Dunn.

65 'The Royal Navy: the New Requirement, the New Structure', *NR* (1991) 3, 188, by J J Blackham; Dunn, loc cit n66.

66 'The Potential Threats to the Security and Stability of the World over the next Twenty-five Years', *NR* (1991) 2, 91, by Jeremy Larken; 'European Security and the Future of NATO', *NR* (1992) 4, 311, by Geoffrey Till; 'The State of the World in 2010', *NR* (1993) 4 and (1994) 1, 2 & 3, by Geoffrey Till.

67 'Roskill Revisited; A Maritime Strategy for the 21st Century', *NR* (1993) 2, 101, by Julian Oswald.

68 'Too Big for our Boots?', *NR* (1990) 3, 222, signed Cyclops.

69 'As It Is Now', *NR* (1994) 3, 214, by Richard Sharpe; Who Will Speak for the Navy?', *NR* (1994) 4, 336, signed OTH; 'Will the British Ever Learn?', *NR* (1994) 4, 339, by Alan Burn.

70 *Statement on the Defence Estimates 1992* (Cm 1981), p8.

71 See, for example, J R Hill in *The Oxford History of the Royal Navy* (Oxford, 1995), pp399–400.

72 'Convoy to Survive', *NR* (1990) 2, 126, by C E Stanley; 'SDE, Front Line First and National Commitments of Government', *NR* (1994) 4, 300, by Michael Ranken; Blackham, loc cit n67; 'The Problem of Resource Depletion and Increased Competition in the South Atlantic', *NR* (1995) 4, 290, by E R Hayman.

73 'The Management of Change in the Defence Environment', *NR* (1989) 4, 325, by R Grainger; 'Fleet Equilibrium and its Controlling Forces', *NR* (1990) 2, 118, by J C Kidd; 'The Environment, Green Issues and the Military', *NR* (1992) 3, 201, by T P McClement.

74 'The New Europe: a Challenge for UK Defence and Security Policies', *NR* (1992) 4, 300, by G M Davenport;

'Some Thoughts on Future European Security Systems', *NR* (1996) 2, 103, by Peter Schreier.

75 'Militarily Capable Ships, Projection of National Sovereignty and Support of National Interests Abroad', *NR* (1991) 4, 285, by Michael Ranken; 'New Bottles, Old Wine?', *NR* (1992) 2, 123, signed St Emilion; '1919/1991: The Need for a UK Grand Strategy', *NR* (1993) 4, 302, signed Trog Trog; 'As It Really Is Now', *NR* (1994) 4, 331, by N Essenhigh.

76 McClement, loc cit n75.

77 'The End of a Threat-Based Strategy', *NR* (1991) 2, 172, by Richard Hill.

78 'Wither Defence?', *NR* (1990) 3, 229, by M A Leigh; 'Terrorism – What Is It?', *NR* (1990) 4, 319, by A K Manning.

79 'Fundamentalist Islam: A Post Cold War Threat?', *NR* (1993) 4, 334; 'Tomahawks for Terrorists? A Considered Response to Fundamentalist Islamic Terrorism', *NR* (1997) 1, 23; 'Bombing Baghdad: A Just War?', *NR* (1998) 2, 118; and 'The Attack on the USS *Cole*', *NR* (2001) 1, 19, all by D G Kibble.

80 Hill, loc cit n79; 'Aspects of Soviet Thought on Deterrence', *NR* (1990) 1, 3, by W J Gardner; 'These Most Brisk and Giddy-Paced Times', *NR* (1990) 3, 216, by Michael Ranken.

81 'Asian Security in an Uncertain and Developing World', *NR* (1997) 2, 97, by James Eberle.

82 'NATO Must Go', *NR* (1991) 4, 280, by Peter Stanford.

83 Larken, loc cit n68; 'Whither NATO or NATO Withers', *NR* (1992) 2, 114, signed Gryphon; Davenport, loc cit n76; Till, loc cit n68; Schreier, loc cit n76.

84 'NATO in Evolution', *NR* (1991) 4, 321, by Nigel Goodwin; 'Current NATO Business', *NR* (2000) 2, 125, by S P Hardern.

85 'Global Security and Foreign Policy', *NR* (1998) 1, 9, by James Eberle.

86 'The UK CVSG in Joint Operations – Up-Front, Up-Tempo and Up to Date', *NR* (1997) 4, 318, by Roy Clare; Blackham, passim.

87 'Maritime Arms Control: Anathema or Fait Accompli', *NR* (1991) 4, 292, by A B Ross.

88 Ross, ibid; 'Ethics, Foreign Policy and Arms Control', *NR* (1999) 2, 114, by M C Evans; 'Confidence Building in a Naval Context', *NR* (2000) 2, 107, by Richard Hill.

89 'Lawful Occasions?', *NR* (2000) 3, 209, by Peter Kimm.

90 'The Just War in the Modern World', *NR* (1992) 3, 287, by F M Malbon; 'Humanitarian Intervention, Kosovo and International Law', *NR* (2000) 4, 318, by Steven Haines.

91 Leigh, loc cit n80.

92 'SDR and the Aircraft Carriers', *NR* (1998) 4, 307, signed MEO.

93 'Carrier 2000: A Consideration of Naval Aviation in the Millennium', *NR* (1999) 1, 3 & (1999) 2, 105, by D R James; 'The Path Towards CV(F)', *NR* (1999) 1, 9, signed DMS.

94 'Ballistic Missile Defence: A New Role for Navies?', *NR* (1997) 4, 324, by J R Stocker.

95 'Theatre Ballistic Missile Defence: Has the Lure of an Expensive New Bat Suckered the American Eye off the Ball?', *NR* (1997) 4, 330, signed Dougie the Diver.

96 'Missile Defence: the Naval Implications', *NR* (1999) 3, 198, by Neville Brown.

23 The View from Bath: A Naval Constructor's Perspective

1 See David Andrews, 'RCNC: 150 Years of Ship Design', *Transactions RINA*, vol 152, Part A1 (2010). 'Discussion and author's reply', *Transactions RINA*, vol 153, Part A1 (2011).

2 Barnaby, Kenneth, *A Centenary Review* (London: RINA, 1960).

3 Barnaby, Sir Nathaniel, 'The unmasted sea-going ships *Devastation*, *Thunderer*, *Fury*, and *Peter the Great*', *Transactions RINA*, vol 13 (1873), 1–20, including discussion.

4 White, (later Sir) William H, 'On the Designs for the New Battle-Ships', *Transactions RINA*, vol 29 (1889), 151–215, including discussion.

5 Honnor, Arthur, RCNC, and David Andrews, RCNC, 'HMS *Invincible*: The First of a New Genus of Aircraft Carrying Ships', *Transactions RINA*, vol 124 (1982), including discussion.

6 'Editorial Note', *NR* (1913) 1; the italics are mine.

7 'Letters: Speed for Battleships', *NR* (1921) 4, 678, unsigned by H W Richmond, which sparked a correspondence in subsequent editions on the speed *of* battleships.

8 'What is it that dictates the size of the fighting ship?' (1929) 3, 409–66, a ten-part article which included parts by Capt

Index of Ships

Ships have been listed alphabetically and by date of commissioning or ordering if more than one. In most cases the nationality of ships is clear from the text.

Biographies of Contributors

Professor David Andrews FREng PhD RCNC worked during his years in the Royal Corps of Naval Constructors on ship and submarine design and procurement, including the Royal Navy's replacement amphibious shipping programme (the LPD(R) and LPH) and the aviation training ship (RFA *Argus*), and now holds the chair of engineering design at University College London.

Dr Tim Benbow read philosophy, politics and economics at Brasenose College, Oxford and took an MPhil and a DPhil at St Antony's College. He also spent a year at Harvard as a Kennedy Scholar and a year at King's College London; his research and writing interests are in the changing nature of warfare and in recent British naval history.

Vice Admiral Sir Jeremy Blackham KCB commanded four ships and was Commandant of the Royal Navy Staff College, Director of Naval Plans, Director General Naval Personnel Strategy, Assistant Chief of Naval Staff, Deputy C-in-C Fleet and the Deputy Chief of Defence Staff (Capability). In 2003 he became the eighth editor of *The Naval Review*.

Dr Harry Dickinson taught at the Royal Naval Colleges at Greenwich and Dartmouth and in the History Department of the United States Naval Academy, and is now a senior lecturer in the Defence Studies Department, King's College, London. He was awarded the Julian Corbett Prize for Modern Naval History in 1996.

Rear Admiral Allan du Toit AM RAN served in the South African Navy from 1975 and transferred to the Royal Australian Navy in 1987. He wrote his first book as a schoolboy, his commands included HMAS *Tobruk* and Coalition Task Force 158 in the North Arabian Gulf in 2008, and in 2011 he was elected president of the Australian Naval Institute.

Rear Admiral James Goldrick AM CSC RAN retired in 2012 after command of HMA Ships *Cessnock* and *Sydney* (twice), the multinational maritime interception force in the Persian Gulf (2002), the Australian Defence Force Academy, Australia's Border Protection Command, and the Australian Defence College. He has been a long-time contributor to *The Naval Review*.

Professor Eric Grove wrote the standard work on post-1945 British naval policy, *Vanguard to Trident*, was a co-author of the original edition of BR1806, *The Fundamentals of British Maritime Doctrine*, and is now Professor of Naval History and Director of the Centre for International Security and War Studies at the University of Salford.

Professor Steven Haines MA PhD LLM FRSA served in the RN and RNR from 1971 to 2003, as seaman officer and as an instructor officer. He was principal author of the second edition of *British Maritime Doctrine* (1999), and has recently been appointed Professor of Public International Law at the University of Greenwich.

Professor Richard Harding FRHistS is Professor of Organisational History and head of the Department of Leadership and Development at the University of Westminster, has written widely on naval history and particularly in amphibious warfare, and was editor of the *Mariner's Mirror* (2001–2005).

Professor John B Hattendorf served in destroyers during the Vietnam War and has been the Ernest J King Professor of Maritime History at the US Naval War College since 1984. He is the author or editor of more than forty books, including the *Oxford Encyclopedia of Maritime History*, and he has been a member of *The Naval Review* for over twenty years.

Rear Admiral Richard Hill has written extensively on contemporary naval matters, including *Maritime Strategy for Medium Powers*, *The Prizes of War* and *Lewin of Greenwich*, and was awarded the Mountbatten Maritime Prize in 2000. He was the seventh editor of *The Naval Review*, from 1983 to 2002.

Commander David Hobbs MBE RN was a Fleet Air Arm pilot and his logbook records 2,300 flying hours with over 800 carrier landings, 150 of them at night. He has written eleven books, lectured in Australia,

New Zealand, the USA, France and the UK, and in 2005 was the Aerospace Journalist of the Year.

Captain Peter Hore FRHistS CMIL RN has been a member of *The Naval Review* since 1976. He is the editor or author of numerous reviews, articles and books, and associate editor of *Warships International Fleet Review*, and an obituary writer for the *Daily Telegraph*. In 2011 he was elected a fellow of the Royal Swedish Society of Naval Sciences.

Professor Greg Kennedy is based at the Joint Services Command and Staff College in Shrivenham. He received his PhD from the University of Alberta in 1998, and before coming to England in 2000 taught at the Royal Military College of Canada, in Kingston, Ontario, and has published widely.

Professor Andrew Lambert FRHistS received his first degree in law from the City of London Polytechnic, was senior lecturer in war studies at the Royal Military Academy Sandhurst 1989–91, and is now Laughton Professor of Naval History at King's College London. He has lectured worldwide and made a number of television appearances.

Rear Admiral Guy Liardet CB CBE was born in Pune, India, a sixth generation of military men with many India connections. He commanded the frigates *Aurora* and *Cleopatra* and was Flag Officer Second Flotilla; ashore he was Training Commander at Dartmouth, and Director of Public Relations. He has written RN and RM obituaries and by-lined articles for *The Times* since 1993.

James McCoy aka Seamus, plainly of Irish origins, was born in 1937 into a naval family in a naval facility in a naval port under the command of the many-named Admiral Sir Reginald Drax. He was a sixteen-year-old entry in 1954 and was absorbed into the COST scheme in 1956, and can therefore claim to be the product of two schemes of officer entry and training. He has served on exchange with the Canadian Forces and Royal Australian Navy, and commanded two ships.

Peter Padfield attended the Thames Nautical Training College, HMS *Worcester*, and subsequently served in P&O, and sailed the replica pilgrim barque, *Mayflower II*, under Alan Villiers. He has recently completed a trilogy begun with *Maritime Supremacy and the Opening* *of the Western Mind*, seeking to show the social and political effects of naval and mercantile supremacy.

Roger Plumtree was a Royal Marine (1959–68), joined the Royal Naval Supply and Transport Service in 1968, and retired in 2001 as Stores and Transport Officer (N). He has been a member and contributor to *The Naval Review* since 1980.

Cdre Ranjit B Rai IN served in the Indian Navy 1960–92, trained at HMS *Dryad* and attended the RN Staff College, and commanded the INS *Cannanore* (Ton class), *Kavaratti* (ex-Russian frigate) and *Vindhyagiri* (broad beam Leander). He was Director Naval Operations (1980), Director of Naval Intelligence (1986–88), and Defence Adviser (Southeast Asia) based in Singapore (1988–92). He wrote *A Nation and Its Navy at War*, is a broadcaster, and vice president of the Indian Maritime Foundation.

Captain Martin Reed MNI MRIN RD* RNR served thirty-nine years in P&O, and was Chief Officer RMS *Canberra* during the Falklands War 1982. He held a Royal Naval Reserve commission 1961–98, from midshipman to captain, and after the Falklands War was Senior Naval Officer for Ships Taken Up From Trade (STUFT), and chairman of The South Atlantic Medal Association.

Brigadier J M F Robbins MBE RM is the son of a naval aviator and a former WRNS officer, read zoology at University College London, and served worldwide in the Royal Marines, including Northern Ireland, NATO, USA, Kuwait, the Balkans, Iraq, Australia, and as the first chief of staff of the UK Amphibious Forces fleet battle staff.

Michael Simpson MA MLitt FRHistS was educated at Cambridge, Ohio State and Glasgow universities. Based at Swansea University, he has edited the Cunningham and Somerville papers and written on Anglo-American naval relations in the early twentieth century.

Dr David Stevens joined the Royal Australian Navy in 1974 and specialised in anti-submarine warfare. Highlights of his service included an exchange posting in the Royal Navy and seagoing staff appointments in both the 1991 Gulf War and 2003 Iraq War. He retired from full-time service in 1996 to become the Australian naval historian, and is currently the Director of Strategic and Historical Studies at the Sea Power Centre, Australia.

Captain Jeremy Stocker MA PhD RNR served as a warfare officer in the Royal Navy for twenty years, specialising in air defence, before transferring to the Royal Naval Reserve in 1996. He was a member of the directing staff at the Joint Services Command and Staff College, and was Director of the Advanced Command and Staff Course (Reserves), and now is Captain (Doctrine and Training) on the staff of the Commander Maritime Reserves.

Geoffrey Till is Emeritus Professor of Maritime Studies at King's College London, Director of the Corbett Centre for Maritime Policy Studies, and Visiting Senior Research Fellow at the Defence Studies Department at the UK Joint Services Command and Staff College. Since 2009 he has also been a Visiting Professor at the Rajaratnam School of International Studies, Singapore.

Commander Alastair Wilson RN served in the Royal Navy (1950–84): the low light of his career, while a midshipman, was to run his admiral's barge aground, together with one vice admiral, one rear admiral, one commodore and four captains, just before the Coronation Review in 1953. Thereafter things could only improve: he specialised in Torpedo and Anti-Submarine warfare, and in retirement was Secretary-Treasurer of *The Naval Review* for fourteen years.

Michael Whitby is Senior Naval Historian at the Directorate of History and Heritage, National Defence Headquarters, Ottawa, Canada, was co-author of the official operational histories on the RCN in the Second World War, and is currently preparing the official history of the RCN (1945–68), and co-authoring a history of the Canadian submarine service.

Captain Richard Woodman FRHistS FNI, Elder Brother of Trinity House went to sea as an indentured midshipman in the Blue Funnel Line and had circumnavigated the globe before being eligible to enter an English pub; in 1967 he joined the Trinity House Service. He is author of some thirty novels and many non-fiction books: his trilogy *Arctic Convoys*, *Malta Convoys* and *The Real Cruel Sea*, have been widely acclaimed, and he has written a definitive five-volume study of the British Merchant Navy from 1500 to 2010.